The
SEVEN
MOUNTAINS
of
THOMAS
MERTON

The
SEVEN
MOUNTAINS
of
THOMAS
MERTON

Michael Mott

HOUGHTON MIFFLIN COMPANY
BOSTON

Library of Congress Cataloging in Publication Data

Mott, Michael.
The seven mountains of Thomas Merton.

Bibliography: p.
Includes index.
1. Merton, Thomas, 1915–1968. 2. Trappists—United
States—Biography. I. Title.
BX4705.M542M67 1984 271'.125'024 [B] 84-10944
ISBN 0-395-31324-4

Printed in the United States of America

v 10 9 8 7 6 5

Books and articles quoted or cited in the text under the usual fair use allowances are
acknowledged in the notes and bibliography.

Excerpts from works by Thomas Merton are reprinted by permission of the following
institutions:
New Directions Publishing Corporation: *The Asian Journal* © 1968, 1970, 1973 by the
Trustees of the Merton Legacy Trust. © 1973, 1975 by New Directions Publishing Corporation. *Collected Poems* © 1961, 1963, 1965, 1966, 1967, 1968, 1969, 1970, 1971, 1976,
1977 by the Trustees of the Merton Legacy Trust. *Gandhi on Non-Violence* © 1964, 1965
by New Directions Publishing Corporation. *The Geography of Lograire* © 1968, 1969 by the
Trustees of the Merton Legacy Trust. *My Argument with the Gestapo* © 1969 by The Abbey
of Gethsemani, Inc. *New Seeds of Contemplation* © 1961 by The Abbey of Gethsemani, Inc.
Raids on the Unspeakable © 1966, 1965, 1964, 1961 by The Abbey of Gethsemani, Inc. ©
1964 by New Directions Publishing Corporation. *The Way of Chuang Tzu* © 1965 by The
Abbey of Gethsemani. *The Wisdom of the Desert* © 1960 by The Abbey of Gethsemani,
Inc. *Zen and the Birds of Appetite* © 1968 by The Abbey of Gethsemani, Inc.
Farrar, Straus and Giroux, Inc.: *Disputed Questions*, copyright © 1953, 1959, 1960 by The

For Margaret

In the Geography of Thomas Merton there were Seven Mountains, though one was the idea of another: Canigou, The Calvaire, Brooke Hill, The Pasture, Mount Purgatory, Mount Olivet, and Kanchenjunga.

CONTENTS

ILLUSTRATIONS

Frontispiece: Drawing of Thomas Merton by Victor Hammer, 1962 (Courtesy of the owner)

Page 4: Map of Prades (by Amanda Mott)
Page 15: Map of Hillside Avenue, Flushing, Queens, New York, 1920 (by Margaret Mott)
Page 34: Map of St. Antonin Noble Val (by Amanda Mott)
Page 207: Map of the Monastery of Our Lady of Gethsemani (by Margaret Mott)

Following page 390:
Ruth Jenkins Merton and Tom as a baby (Courtesy of the Monastery of Gethsemani Archives)
Owen Merton and Tom (Courtesy of the Monastery of Gethsemani Archives)
Merton's birthplace in Prades (Photo by Thomas W. Lyman)
The Villa Diane, St. Antonin (Courtesy of the Monastery of Gethsemani Archives)
Owen Merton, Gertrude Merton, John Paul, and Tom, 1919 (Courtesy of the Monastery of Gethsemani Archives)
Cartoon by Thomas Merton from *The Oakhamian* (Courtesy of the University Archives, Friedsam Memorial Library, St. Bonaventure University)
Clare College, Cambridge (Photo by author)
Cover by Merton for the Columbia *Jester* (Courtesy of Columbiana Library, Rare Book and Manuscript Library, Columbia University)
The Olean Cottage (Photo by author)
1941 Commencement at St. Bonaventure (Courtesy of the University Archives, Friedsam Memorial Library, St. Bonaventure University)
Gate house of the Monastery of Our Lady of Gethsemani (Photo by author)
Aerial view of the monastery in the 1950s (Courtesy of the Monastery of Gethsemani Archives)
Merton's friends at his ordination: Seymour Freedgood, Robert Giroux, James Laughlin, Dan Walsh, Robert Lax, and Ed Rice (Courtesy of the University Archives, Friedsam Memorial Library, St. Bonaventure University)
Thomas Merton is ordained Father M. Louis, O.C.S.O. (Courtesy of the University Archives, Friedsam Memorial Library, St. Bonaventure University)
Merton with his guests after ordination: Nanny Hauck, Elsie Jenkins, and Robert Lax (Courtesy of the Trustees, Thomas Merton Legacy Trust)

ACKNOWLEDGMENTS

By the terms of the Thomas Merton Legacy Trust, which Merton set up in 1967, only the official biographer and the trustees were to have access to his private journals for a period of twenty-five years after his death. Following Merton's death in 1968, John Howard Griffin was appointed this biographer the next year. By 1977 Mr. Griffin was too ill to continue, and I was appointed in the fall of 1978.

Merton probably kept journals from the time he was a schoolboy at Oakham. Some of these early journals may yet be discovered, just as substantial fragments of the novels which were thought to have been destroyed in 1941 have been found. At present, there is an incomplete set of journals from 1939 to December 1968. Only those of the last twelve years have been placed under restriction, and, even here, some access has been allowed to the unpublished reworking of the 1964–65 journals, entitled "A Vow of Conversation," while Merton selected, edited, and published some passages from the journals before 1964 in *The Secular Journal, The Sign of Jonas,* and *Conjectures of a Guilty Bystander.* Material from the 1968 journal was published posthumously in *The Asian Journal.* I am now the only person, apart from the trustees, who has read the original journals of 1956–68. They will be available in a little under a decade, and it will then be possible to see what use I have made of them. Some quotation was allowed me by the Trust.

In this sense, then, this is the "official" biography. The trustees Merton appointed were his literary agent, Naomi Burton Stone, his publisher at New Directions, James Laughlin, and Tommie O'Callaghan (Mrs. Frank O'Callaghan), who, with her family, was a close friend in Louisville. Another publisher and friend, Robert Giroux, has

now replaced Mrs. Stone. Although I never knew him, John Howard
Griffin had collected materials in the years after Merton's death and,
generously, these were made available to me. I began again from the
beginning and the trustees provided me at the start with a letter confirming that my interpretations were to be my own. Now that the book
is finished, therefore, the responsibility for it is entirely mine.

   With so many who helped, I hope it will not be poor courtesy to acknowledge their names in the text and in the notes at the end.
Some I must acknowledge here. My first debt is to my own family, and in many ways this biography was a family enterprise. My sense
of gratitude is very warm, then, to Amanda Mott, who drew many of
the maps and put my typescript onto a word processor; to Sophie Mott,
for typing; and to my wife, Margaret — from the first drafts to the final
proofreading. My second debt is to the trustees, who shared their homes
and their ideas with me. I would also thank the secretary of the trust,
Anne McCormick, and her husband. I owe to Thomas Merton my present friendships with many of his friends. Among these, and aside from
the trustees, I would single out Robert Lax and his sister, Mrs. Gladys
Marcus. I would also like to make special mention of Richard Bassett,
who made available the correspondence between Owen Merton and
Percyval Tudor-Hart, and who shared reminiscences of Owen and Ruth
Merton at art school in Paris. Ms. Virginia Burton was also especially
generous with help.

   I am grateful above all to Brother Patrick Hart, then to the other monks
of the Abbey of Gethsemani, present and past, and to the abbot, Dom
Timothy Kelly. Dom James Fox has a reason to beware of all biogra-
phers, and I hope I have repaid him for our two long interviews at least
with fair-mindedness. Dom John Eudes Bamberger and the community of the Abbey of the Genesee, and Dom Flavian Burns and Holy
Cross Abbey greatly furthered my work. Monsignor Bourke and his
staff made me welcome at Corpus Christi Rectory. The Rev. George
Kilcourse and others at Bellarmine College shared enthusiasms and gave
me excellent leads in the Merton correspondence, as did Monsignor
William Shannon. I am particularly grateful to Dr. Robert Daggy and
his staff at the Thomas Merton Studies Center.

   Through the generosity of the John Simon Guggenheim Memorial
Trust, I was able to visit France and England in 1978–79 and to concentrate on a year's research and writing. Since then, my own university,
Bowling Green State University, allowed me a grant for the summer of
1981. The chairman of the English Department and my colleagues in
the Creative Writing Program have all given me support. The staff of
the university's Jerome Library made much of my work easier, and I
have special debts of gratitude to the music librarian and those in the
inter-library loan office. James Whitta, a graduate student, helped me

skillfully with research for a month in the summer of 1981. My editor at Houghton Mifflin, Robie Macauley, has trusted, encouraged, and prodded.

In the final stages, there have been some whose skills made a disproportionate difference, others, whose encouragement did — and a few who made a difference on both counts. At the publishers, I am grateful to Helena Bentz, Henry Miller, Jr., Marcia Pomerance, Toni Rosenberg, Janet Silver, and others. I thank James Laughlin and Robert Giroux especially for last-minute answers and advice. And I salute with affection, Naomi Burton Stone, Tommie O'Callaghan, and Brother Patrick Hart.

If I have made full use of the restricted material, I have also referred throughout the biography to the enormous amount of material, published and unpublished, that is available to all. Some fifty books appeared in Merton's lifetime. Since his death, there has been a continuous process of publishing and republishing. *The Literary Essays of Thomas Merton* is a book of over five hundred pages, *The Collected Poems of Thomas Merton* a book of over one thousand pages. There are some seven hundred tapes of Merton's talks and conferences. The collection of Merton's correspondence at the Thomas Merton Studies Center at Bellarmine, still far from complete, contains letters to over eighteen hundred correspondents, and some folders hold more than two hundred items.

Three final points. I am a Catholic, but not a Roman Catholic. Where I write *Church* in this book, I mean the Roman Catholic Church, and where I write *Catholic* I mean Roman Catholic. This seemed both courteous and convenient.

I never met Thomas Merton. My knowledge of him is another kind of knowledge. Because of this, though I call his parents by their first names, I call him Tom only when he was a child.

In conclusion, Merton contended often with censorship, and this will be a frequent theme. But he has suffered since his death from much the same thing in the form of selective editing. I have by no means relied wholly on Merton's own account of his life, but where I have quoted him, I have tried to give the whole sense of what he was saying.

PREFACE: CONTINUING CONVERSION, CONTINUING AUTOBIOGRAPHY

"Who are all those people you have brought with you?"
The disciple whirled around to look.
Nobody there. Panic!
Lao said: "Don't you understand?"
— The Way of Chuang Tzu

When I reveal most I hide most.
— Thomas Merton

T HOMAS MERTON was so many things — poet, writer, activist, contemplative (explorer of darkness and silence), reformer of monastic life, artist, bridge between Western and Eastern religious thought, to name but a few — that it is disconcerting for those who know him best in one aspect to find him treated exclusively from another point of view. The friends and friends-through-correspondence who gathered in Louisville and at the Monastery of Gethsemani on the news of his death on December 10, 1968, were amazed to discover that Merton had known so many and such diverse people.

There was to be a seven-day delay before the body arrived from Bangkok. It was not until Vespers on the afternoon of December 17, that he could be buried. Thus Merton's friends had ample time to discover just how diverse they were. He himself would probably have laughed uproariously more than once during the week of waiting.

There were more ironies on that occasion than the three most obvious ones: that the body of this lifetime enemy of war and violence was returned in a SAC bomber; that he was to fulfill his vow of stability in a manner which only gave rise to still more rumors that he would have broken it if he had lived; and that even in death he was to be distinguished from the community where he had lived for half his life. He is almost the only monk in the monks' graveyard to be buried in a coffin.

What might have amused Thomas Merton most were the different "Mertons" others brought to his burial, and who have been argued over ever since. There is a special paradox in this: he had written so much in an effort to reveal himself.

Some of these Mertons are obvious distortions. There are Mertons who had very little of the human in them, where he had much. Equally, there are Mertons who would never have spent a week at the monastery. But for some of the lesser distortions, he would probably have held himself responsible, though they baffled him in life and have outlived him. An honest man may create false impressions, and Thomas Merton created many.

It is dismaying to almost all those who knew him, or at least to those who knew *their* Merton, to find that he is still best known as an autobiographer. Yet there is a certain justice in this. And perhaps we need Zen and the ancient Greek tragedies equally to remind us that there is frequently more justice than injustice in irony. There is a place where parallel lines meet, the Zen *koan* and the messenger in Sophocles crying "Good news!"

The Seven Storey Mountain deserved its fame. Without the publication of this best-selling autobiography in 1948 it is just possible, too, that Thomas Merton would have achieved the obscurity and oblivion which is the declared intent of each monk of the Order he had joined seven years earlier — the Cistercian Order of the Strict Observance, the Trappists.

Much would thus have been changed at the Monastery of Gethsemani on that December afternoon, much would have been different in the life of this and many other monasteries, and much would have been altered in the range of the circles which spread out, each growing larger, but no less distinct, from the hermitage at the edge of the Kentucky woods in the 1960s.

Yet *The Seven Storey Mountain* was only the apparent beginning of what has been called "a continuing autobiography," and if Thomas Merton was to be concerned with autobiography all his life, he was also an anti-autobiographer. The anti-autobiographer attacks the very validity of the form, questions its credibility, makes high fun of its pretenses, and undercuts the effects in a way that often, paradoxically, restores validity to the form and makes its effects more effective. Merton may have invented the anti-autobiography: at any rate, he questioned and mocked the conventions of autobiography from the first in the journals that survive, and in very much the same way his friend Nicanor Parra, the Chilean poet, was to mock conventional ideas about poetry in *Poems & Antipoems* much later.

It was in the summer of 1939, which Merton and his Columbia friends Ed Rice and Robert Lax spent in large part at the cottage above Olean in western New York State, that Thomas Merton began his experiment. He had been gathering material in his journal all year, and on November 19 he listed the most important things that happened in 1939: the publication of *Finnegans Wake*, the war in Europe, and the Picasso exhibition at the New York World's Fair.

Merton and his friends must have been among the first readers in America of *Finnegans Wake*,[1] and it was Joyce's all-inclusive novel which gave Merton the idea of an all-inclusive autobiography. His 1939–40 journal is full of enthusiasm for Joyce, and of experiments he and his friends were making in "Joyce talk," "Esperanto," and "macaronic."[2] They shared a delight in making lists — fabulous, eccentric, and mundane. Merton lists the new words he had thought of over the past year; he lists the advertising slogans to be seen along a stretch of railroad or a few miles of highway. He found he was able to reconstruct parts of the borough of Queens, New York, and Ealing, in London, much as Joyce himself had reconstructed whole sections of Dublin in his books and conversational games. Merton lists jokes and snatches of song, with details of where he first heard them. He takes more than a page to record things he regrets saying or doing in the past year. And he chooses a date and puts down what he remembers doing on the same day for as far back as he can recall.

This was obviously preparation for something much more ambitious than the largely autobiographical novel he was writing in 1939, which, through its many changes of title and different drafts, was getting nowhere. He notes in his journal with amusement that everyone seems to be writing his or her own life story, including his grandfather, but his own work was to be quite different from everyone else's, not only in language, but in its emphasis on the seemingly trivial detail as the key to a much deeper revelation of character. Such details would be used to build up a sense of place, also, and place had the greatest importance, always, for Merton. He wanted to do something entirely new with autobiography, then: it was to be experimental and it was to be all-encompassing. He was twenty-four.

By September 1940, after another summer at the cottage with a wider group of friends, he was teaching a few miles away, at St. Bonaventure College. It was a far cry from *Finnegans Wake* to a resolution he and Robert Lax made that autumn, to "write simply and about simple things."[3]

For about a year he struggled to keep to this commitment. The new novel he had begun included scenes from his years at Columbia and in Greenwich Village, jaunts to Virginia with a girlfriend, and travel notes of his trips to Miami and Cuba — all "worked up" from his journal and altered to fit a transparent plot and characters. But he had not learned how to keep the liveliness of the original when revising passages, while the earlier excitement of trying to do something new and too big was gone. "The Man in the Sycamore Tree"[4] was relatively straightforward, but it was also dull.

The skills Merton needed for this kind of writing would increase in time. With the fictional element left out, his work would lead to the main line of his "continuing autobiography," to *The Seven Storey Moun-*

tain and the edited and rewritten journals. Yet the line of anti-autobiography was not abandoned. Disappointed by the flatness of much
he was writing, and moved by an unexpected idea, Merton began to
develop the two lines simultaneously while he was still at St. Bonaventure's. On October 27, 1940, he saw a film in Olean entitled *London Can Take It*. He began to dream he was back in London during
the blitz.[5] The experience lay dormant until May 1941, when he began
to write a new novel, far livelier than the fragments of "The Man in
the Sycamore Tree" which survive, something which must have been
equally encouraging and dismaying to Merton in the light of his resolution.

"The Journal of My Escape from the Nazis" is written in part in "Joyce
Esperanto," or "macaronic." Retitled *My Argument with the Gestapo*,
Merton's only novel to survive entire was published in 1969, shortly
after his death, and in the same year as his last and best volume of
poetry, *The Geography of Lograire*, which has a section entitled "Queens
Tunnel" that might have grown whole from one of the lists in the 1939
journal. (For those who see so many inconsistencies in Merton's work
and so many radical breaks in his life, there is another Thomas Merton
who established an amazing consistency and who pursues an unbroken continuity.)

Thus, by a publishing accident, the first and last works of the anti-
autobiographical, macaronic, "Joyce Esperanto" Merton came out almost together. And in 1978, ten years after his death, *A Catch of Anti-
Letters* appeared, the macaronic letters written between 1962 and 1967
by the two friends who had resolved to write simply in 1940.

The line of anti-autobiographical works continues just as the autobiographical line does, yet at one significant point they almost converge.
In 1946, Merton wrote from the monastery to James Laughlin, the
founder and editor of New Directions, who had published his first collection of poetry, *Thirty Poems*. He talks about new poems, then of the
1941 novel. He anticipates almost insurmountable difficulties in publishing the novel as the work of a monk in a closed order, but he has
obviously not given up the idea altogether. Merton adds that he is at
work on a new prose subject, an autobiography. From his description,
this is to be fairly short and firmly on the anti-autobiographical line.
Not until August 17, 1946, did he write Laughlin to say:

> About the prose 7 Storey Mountain — it did not turn out the way I thought
> it might at first, therefore no fantasy, no Kafka, no Miracle Play. It is
> straight biography with a lot of comment and reflection, and it is turning
> into the mountain that the title says.[6]

This biography, likewise, will contain no Kafka, no Miracle Play, but
it will have an element of the anti-biographical, as well as the biograph-

ical. It could hardly fail to do so in the circumstances and still be fair
to the subject.

A biography is not an autobiography. For that reason, if the early
sections run parallel to Merton's own account, as they must, they are
largely new, and seen from a wholly different perspective. Merton was
not always fair to his younger self. Trying to be fairer, at times I have
been critical of *The Seven Storey Mountain*. The older Merton and the
younger Merton showed a gaiety and high spirits, which were largely
suppressed during the early years at the monastery, and I have tried
to bring back the balance occasionally by including the laughter of a
deeply serious man.

*

If it is true that Mount Purgatory has seven storeys, it is equally true
that there are nine circles for sinners in Dante's *Inferno* and that Hell is
paved with good intentions. Whatever happens to good intentions, here
on earth they are judged by results, by their fruit. Hagiographers,
whether for the best or worst intentions, wind up in the basement of
earthly esteem, and may well belong with the lowest of liars in the Inferno. Those who distort for the sake of maliciously tearing down a
reputation, rather than building up a false one to confound humanity,
the wilful detractors, are hardly much above the hagiographers. Once
again, the extremes come close to meeting, as they usually do when
the balance is put out. Either way, the human race loses out in a confusion of idols and Aunt Sallies.

I have tried for a work of balance that will present things fairly and
leave the reader to decide. In writing the biography of someone like
Thomas Merton who wrote so much about himself, leaving revealing
details in the least expected places, I may seem to have had all the help
I needed. In fact, I found it exceedingly difficult. Merton found himself a mystery. He went on puzzling his odd fate to the end; in his
journals, I would say relentlessly. Perhaps he shares this fate with one
other major writer in the twentieth century. To bring his name up is
almost unlucky in a biographer. He has been written about often but
explained by none: T. E. Lawrence, Lawrence of Arabia.

The parallel makes no sense at first. Yet each man — monk and soldier, activist-contemplative and contemplative-activist — appeared to
have much the same strange capacity for revealing himself in hiding
and hiding himself in a blaze of self-revelation. Most of those who seek
obscurity find it, together with many who spend their lives struggling
to avoid it. Certainly Merton was no more successful at being forgotten in a Trappist monastery as Father M. Louis than was Lawrence in
the Royal Air Force as Aircraftsman Shaw. There was something mysterious about this in both cases.

Two strong impressions remain. In reading or rereading Merton, I have felt over and over again that whichever book I had in my hands at the time was the clearest, most urgent, most important statement of his thought, only to revise this opinion when I moved on to another book of his. The other impression is one I have been given by almost everyone who knew him: the sense that when Merton talked to you he made you feel — at least for the time — that you were his most intimate confidant, that he opened himself to you and you opened yourself to him in a way which made it an exchange like no other, and that this friendship could not be duplicated by either of you with anyone else. If at times this was to lead to complications and difficulties (many people thinking that they alone knew what Merton thought or planned for his own future), it has to be granted that it was a rare gift — one whose force has hardly diminished over more than a decade.

Merton often wrote that the worst sin was idolatry. His reverence for his past and his determination to keep new beginnings possible on his spiritual journey made him vulnerable. He would do anything necessary to resist being put in a false position, either as an object of worship himself, or as the worshiper of anything or anyone on what he thought of as the "natural" plane. On the day before he left Kentucky to start for Asia, he made a special point of visiting the room at Bellarmine College Library where he had helped others to gather together the material of a lifetime, the Merton Room. "A good place to cut a fart and run," he told a friend.[7]

On January 7, 1967, he wrote to the writer of a thesis who wanted to include a long biographical section on him:

Since I am your subject, I hope I may be forgiven for expressing some sentiments of my own on the subject. I am only fifty-two years old and I rather wonder if your subject can be adequately treated when I am as yet only *'nel mezzo del cammin' di nostra vita.'* However, since I have written autobiographical books, I suppose I must regard myself as culpable for such results. But I would only remark that like every other Christian I am still occupied with the great affair of saving my sinful soul, in which grace and 'psychology' are sometimes in rather intense conflict. I am certainly aware of the fact that my life is not necessarily a history of fidelity to grace and like every other Christian I can only admit my failures and beg the Lord to have mercy on me. I would like to say that I have never intended to claim another position than this. If certain readers have taken an exaggerated and perhaps distorted view of some of my books, it may be due to my faults as writer. If in trying to give God thanks for His mercies I have sometimes helped others to do the same in their own lives, I am glad. But I still need the prayers and the compassion of my fellow Christians. I hope that you will make clear in your thesis that this is my attitude and my conviction.[8]

PART ONE

———————◆━◆━◆———————

Canigou

". . . it seems to me there is no more fascinating subject in the
world than the influence of surroundings on human character."
— *Ruth Merton*

"Oh! Since I was a baby in the Pyrenees,
When old St. Martin marked me for the cloister from high Canigou."
— "On the Anniversary of My Baptism"

I n NOVEMBER 1961, Thomas Merton had an unexpected visit from one of his few surviving relatives. He and Aunt Kit (his great-aunt Agnes Merton) drank strong tea together in the gate house at the monastery and discussed the family history, and their last meeting, forty-two years earlier, when Tom had been four. Aunt Kit confirmed a feeling Merton had always had that his mother had been very strict with him.

At much the same time Merton wrote in a letter to Mary Childs Black, "For myths are realities, and they themselves open into deeper realms."[1] Not all the facts were right when Merton retold the story of the Mertons after Aunt Kit's visit.[2] Yet, by the kind of paradox Merton enjoyed, history which sticks only to facts and takes no account of the "myths" as "realities" that men and women live by, is no true history.

To some extent we each invent our own ancestry and create our own childhood. However receptive and retentive he was, even Thomas Merton probably remembered very little of his birthplace and his first eighteen months there. Later on he built upon his earliest impressions by hearing others talk, by studying family photographs, so that when he looked back he found the shape of a mountain, Canigou, a Prades carpenter whose name was Joseph, and, above all else, the memory of his mother watching him intently and then writing everything he did in a book.

In time Merton would explore imaginatively every one of the possibilities of his geographical point of origin, making a game, half serious, half for fun, of all the possibilities of nationality. If everything he did from the very beginning was important enough for someone to want to record, then it was significant that he was born French by the laws

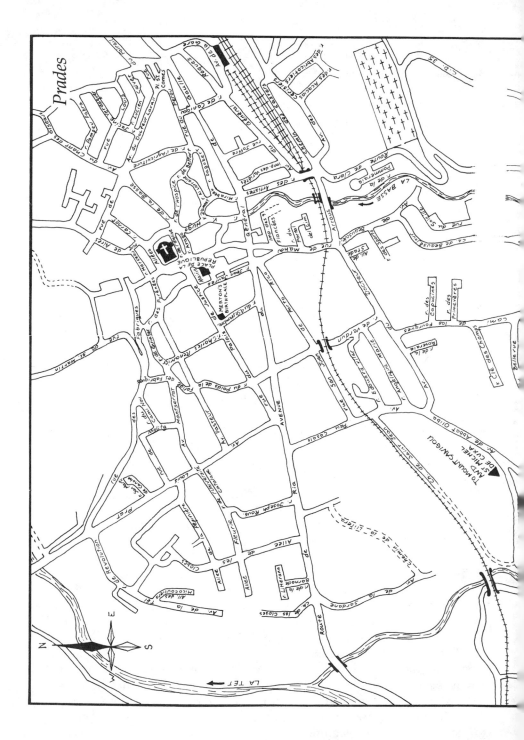

Prades

of France, that Prades in the Eastern Pyrenees was in the Catalan lands, not far from the ancient centers of the Albigensian heresy. It was also significant that his father was a New Zealander with a Welsh name, his mother an American with a Welsh name, and that both were artists. In the opening pages of his autobiography he conveys a strong sense that, in a world of poor choices, he had done very well, both in his birthplace and in his parents. Only the timing was unfortunate — the first winter of the First World War.

He was very proud of being French, as he was proud of being the child of artists. In his late forties he wrote to a monk in New Zealand that the New Zealand he had never seen was "a kind of homeland."[3] Through his mother he laid claim later on to citizenship not only of the United States in 1951, but of all the Americas in 1958.[4] For the first thirty-five years of his life he traveled on a British passport. In his one published novel a fictional character with the name of Thomas travels on a passport issued by an imaginary Catalan, while in the 1960s Merton himself claimed to be a "Catalan in exile." He was always curiously disturbed by the proximity of his birthplace to the Albigensian heresy seven hundred years before he was born.

If Prades has changed and doubled in size,[5] the house on the corner of the Rue du 4 Septembre and the Rue du Palais de Justice looks almost exactly today as it does in photographs taken in 1914–15. Only the tree at the far end of the narrow, walled garden at the back of the house has grown to block the view of Merton's first high place, Mount Canigou, which towers above Prades.

In June 1914, Owen Merton rented the upper two floors in the building. The ground floor was used to store wine. The room at the top of the house with the best lighting was to be a studio for himself and his wife of two months, Ruth Jenkins Merton. Having done little except establish a base, however, the two painters spent the summer while Europe mobilized camping out and painting north of Prades, near the village of Molitg (now a very different Molitg-les-Bains). Their tent had been a wedding present from their friend and mentor Percyval Tudor-Hart.[6]

They had met in 1911 at Tudor-Hart's atelier, 78, Rue d'Assas in Paris, drawn there by the reputation of the Canadian artist and teacher who saw connections between painting and the other arts, chiefly music. Owen's family were musicians and teachers of music, while he was a pianist as well as a painter. Ruth Jenkins had been divided between a career in dance and the visual arts. In their mid-twenties, both were relatively old for art students. Owen paid for his tuition by acting as the atelier's *massier*, with the general duties of a janitor and special responsibility for hiring the models. At twenty-five his sandy hair was already receding from his temples. He was shy, self-conscious, idealistic, and chivalrous — his politeness to the models was proverbial — but he had a quick, incisive way of giving his opinions. Tudor-Hart thought highly of his painting.[7] Along with Owen's charm and genuine talent, especially as a colorist, went too much diffidence, as well as a certain blindness. Tudor-Hart's academy may not have been on the cutting edge, but one has to wonder if it was only bad luck that led Owen to write from Paris in 1912 saying very little was happening there in the arts![8]

Tudor-Hart had encountered some difficulties from the stronger-willed, equally serious, red-haired American student in the separate women's studio at the academy. From her room in the Rue Scribe, Ruth wrote to tell her teacher exactly what she wanted to learn from him. On one occasion she apologized for her "antagonistic attitude." On another she wrote that she had decided she had no wish to join the ranks of mediocre artists, she was more interested in interior decoration and design:

> In the second place it seems to me there is no more fascinating subject in the world than the influence of surroundings on human character. And to study character with a view to making its surroundings what they should be by means of certain decoration in houses — that is what I want to try to do.[9]

Ruth was soon earning some extra money designing apartments for Americans living in Paris. In the spring of 1913, she and Owen were part of a group from the Rue d'Assas touring Provence and Italy. Both wrote to their teacher: the great discovery for each of them, apart from one another, had been Rome.[10]

Tudor-Hart moved his academy to London. It was time, anyway, for his two senior students to leave him. Ruth went back to New York to announce her engagement to her family in Douglaston, Queens. The Jenkins family were Episcopalians, members of Zion Church in Douglaston. Owen was Church of England, and the wedding in London on April 7, 1914, at St. Anne's, Soho, was conducted according to the Anglican rites.[11] Yet sometime during her visit home Ruth had changed her religious views to those of the Society of Friends. There is nothing to show she was officially Read into Meeting. On the evidence, she became a confirmed pacifist rather than a confirmed Quaker.[12]

Europe was at war by the time the two artists returned to their apartment on Rue du 4 Septembre at the end of the summer of 1914. Ruth also knew by now that she was pregnant. Perhaps because of all the distractions, Owen had had a depressing summer painting. He wrote another New Zealand artist, Esmond Atkinson, that his color had turned black, adding that the local movie house in Prades where he earned money playing the piano had shown a short film on New Zealand.[13]

That autumn Owen made furniture for the bare apartment, including a crib. Ruth was so proud she sent photographs of the furniture and the rooms to Owen's New Zealand relatives. With few resources, she worked on the interior decoration herself, then read every manual of child care she could borrow. If surroundings were so influential on character, she was determined the child would have the right ones.

The child, a son, was born shortly after nine in the evening on Sunday, January 31, 1915, during a snowstorm. He weighed only two kilos. If there was concern whether the baby would live, Ruth does not record this, although she records almost everything else. She was determined the boy would be called Tom.[14]

By French law foreigners living in France were subject to conscription into the French armies. And by French law also, the child of foreigners who happened to be born in France had to be registered as a French national. Several days after the baby's birth Owen carried him, wrapped in a blanket, the few hundred yards down the snow-covered Rue du Palais de Justice to the town hall or Mairie. Here Owen risked drawing attention to himself as a potential soldier from the officials by insisting that the child be registered as Tom.

Tom is one thing, Thomas quite another. A long, long time later, Merton would agree with his mother. But before that there came a whole chapter of names, some given, some assumed, some invented by friends: Tom Merton, Tom Feverel Merton, Merton T. F., Thomas James Merton, F. Xavier Sheridan, Mertie, Mertoni, "Thomas the Impostor," Frank Swift, Marco J. Frisbee, Brother M. Louis Merton, Father M. Louis Merton, Chop-Suey Louie, Albion Leixos, Staretz Nikodim, Mittwoch, Murtogs, "Eagle" Dunaway, Benedict Monk, Father Louie, Uncle Louie, Father Ludovicus, R. Higden, Honorable Wu, Con, Bones, Father Staretz, John Stuart Mill the Younger, David Morton, Demosthenes, Captain Thurston, Arthur, Uncle Pangloss, Captain Belsford, Henry Clay, Doctor Moosehunter, Zwow, Lefty Gonxalo, Quincy, Harvey, Fred or Wolfgang, Murps, Murthwog, Captain Bashford, Harpo, Commodore Perry, Doctor Livingston, Albert Houdini, Cassidy, Moon Mullins, Doctor Klaventook, Captain, Colonel Hopscotch, mostwich, Hemson, Farbish, Uncle Flipper, Chauncey, Mr. Myrtle, Rabbi Vedanta . . . many others.

For the time being he was Tom, and his mother made notes of everything. Two years later some of these would be transcribed for New Zealand relatives as "Tom's Book," which reveals as much of Merton's first biographer as it does of her subject. The book records that people in Prades said of her son, *"qu'il a l'air éveillé!"* (Perhaps "What a wide-awake kid!"). His lively eye and retentive memory observed he was being observed, and he acted accordingly. He clung to books because his mother did so, thrusting the toys he was offered aside. For the moment it did not bother Ruth that Tom seldom conformed to what she had learned from the manuals on child care. She simply recorded this, too. She was pleased by his early ability to make associations and connections. One of the first words Tom spoke was "color," and this stood for everything associated with his father, including the smell of paints, Owen's pipe, and even the smell of the wood stove.

Ruth's strong pacifist principles may well have saved her husband's life, but they lost him friends and brought trouble with some of his family in New Zealand, where so many were volunteering who would serve at Gallipoli and in Flanders.[15] The war had already undermined Owen's plan to earn a living selling watercolors and pen-and-ink drawings to tourists. He made what money he could playing the piano, and was paid in produce when he worked in the vegetable gardens of friends like the Vignolles. If there was any snobbery in Owen Merton it was that of the poet Edward Thomas, who said he enjoyed the company of "a poor man of any sort down to a king."[16] Owen liked working the soil almost as much as he liked painting, and he preferred to work barefoot.

Neutral Spain was just over the mountain passes. Ruth's family wrote urging them all to come to America. But Owen stayed on in Prades, risking conscription or imprisonment. Owen mentioned the defections of other friends in a letter to the still loyal Esmond Atkinson; then he justified his action:

> We ourselves are some of the very few who are out of all trouble for the time being and we are pretty selfish to be as we are, but we are selfish on account of little Tom chiefly, and so far I do think I am worth more to Ruth and him than to the Armies.[17]

Prades was a long way from the front, but the war was making itself present. There was already a military hospital, and Tom had learned to identify the soldiers they passed in the streets.

The Mertons were not left entirely in isolation. John Chrystal, a professional soldier and an officer in the Hussars, had visited and photographed Owen holding Tom, with Canigou in the background. By the time Tom was almost a year old he had acquired a godfather, another New Zealand friend of his father. Doctor Tom Izod Bennett had done very well in London and was already a Harley Street specialist. He had probably been best man at Ruth and Owen's wedding. In December 1915, he arrived in Prades with the news that he was about to be married himself, to the daughter of a prominent French Protestant minister and theologian. Tom and Iris Weiss Bennett were to be important in Tom Merton's early life. In 1915 Ruth notes that Bennett circumcised Tom, but she says nothing about baptism.

For his son's first birthday Owen Merton drew up a menu which gently mocks the simplicity of the fare with the grandeur of the names. Each entrée complements one of the Allied Powers, and there is a sketch of Owen and a friend painting under a pair of huge umbrellas.

That spring the vast armies, conscript and volunteer, were training in anticipation of the summer campaigns that were expected to decide the war. Still the family remained in Prades. On July 16, while men were being slaughtered in their thousands along the Somme, Tom was photographed with a friend called Roger, probably Roger Vignolle. Roger has dark hair, while Tom's hair is so pale that the top of his head seems to melt into the sky. In their embroidered smocks both boys look very French.[18] A few days later the Mertons left for Bordeaux to embark on the S.S. *Latouraine* for America. For the first time the eighteen-month-old boy would be meeting relatives. The strong unit of three would come under a different strain from that of the war. Whatever Merton remembered of Prades, he recalled that the S.S. *Latouraine*, which was supposed to have been an unarmed merchantman, had a gun under wraps on the deck.[19]

*

Apart from memory and myth, there is editing. The magnificent point-counterpoint of different styles achieved in the opening pages of Merton's account of the first half of his life was something of an accident. *The Seven Storey Mountain* originally followed Dante's *The Divine Comedy* more closely. The editor must have felt that the slow birth of the soul in the introductory "Limbo" section was all too effective at keeping the reader in Limbo. This was cut. The few vivid autobiographical sentences and short paragraphs were saved and reassembled in a way that makes strange and compelling reading from the first, "overview" paragraph to the second, which is more particularizing and which borrows details from the cinema, to the more general paragraphs on the parents.[20]

This is entirely successful, but there are a few losses later, or at least differences of balance. Most readers must have felt that the warmest pages in the early part of the autobiography are those about Merton's father. Editorial cuts make Ruth even more enigmatic, remote, cold than she is in the original. Again, the Mertons do much better than the Jenkins family, on the supposition that readers would rather read about New Zealand than Ohio or Douglaston. This favored the side of the family Merton tended to favor anyway, while there was a strong pull to romanticize what could not easily be checked in the circumstances under which he was writing the autobiography.

The child of a marriage between a Merton and a Jenkins has a certain right to talk of a Welsh temperament and to imagine a romantic Welsh origin for himself (as Merton did in *The Geography of Lograire*). But in plain fact one has to go back almost a hundred years before he was born to find one of Merton's ancestors who lived in Wales. The Mertons themselves were from the other side of Great Britain. The Jenkins family had been in Ohio for three generations before Thomas Merton's grandfather moved to New York State.

The shortest direct line to Wales that can be made is through the Griersons, his paternal grandmother's family, who were carpet manufacturers from Bridgnorth in Shropshire, an English county in the Welsh Marches. The marriage of Elizabeth Bird of Cardiff to John Grierson on March 23, 1842, brings a Welsh connection into an English line. On this side of the family it was Margaret Stonehewer whose marriage in 1822 to William Knowles Bird brought the lines of the Birds, the Stonehewers, the Griersons, and, ultimately, the Mertons, together, and the Stonehewers were from Castlemartin in Pembrokeshire, the extreme southwest of Wales, though, like the Birds, from the predominantly English-speaking parts of the country rather than Welsh Wales.

Meanwhile, the Mertons had been in East Anglia for uncounted generations. James Merton, a farm laborer, married Susan Denny at Hawley (or Haughley) in Suffolk. Their only son, Charles James, was born there in 1822. The Vicar of Stoke, the Reverend Charles Martin Torlesse, became the patron of Charles, helped him with his education, and encouraged him to train to be a schoolteacher, thus changing the social position of the family. Charles taught in both Hawley and Ipswich, and, in 1847, at Stoke-by-Nayland (made famous by the painter Constable) he married Charlotte Street, who had been a governess of the Torlesse children. She, too, became a schoolteacher.

These were years of continuing agricultural depression in much of England. Charles Torlesse was a surveyor for a Church of England society, the Canterbury Land Association, which was encouraging families the society judged to be of good character to emigrate to New Zealand, assisting them with the passage money, and helping them to start in the new land. Torlesse himself had land in Rangiora. He persuaded the older generation of Mertons, James and Susan, as well as Charles and Charlotte with their three children, to come to New Zealand and live in Rangiora. They set out in 1856 on the *Egmont*.

The story of the Mertons in New Zealand was one of pioneering, with a background of the Maori Wars of the 1860s. They founded schools, taught, and farmed the school lands. They moved several times between Rangiora and Christchurch. Alfred Merton, a fourth child of Charles and Charlotte (who had five in all) was born in Christchurch on October 7, 1857. The Mertons were also musicians. Charles was the first musical director at Christ's College. Alfred played the organ at Christchurch Cathedral, organized singing and instrumental societies, and taught music at Christ's College for forty years.

The Griersons had emigrated to New Zealand in 1864. On Decem-

ber 19, 1882, Alfred Merton married Gertrude Hannah Grierson, the
ninth of fifteen children. The couple had six children: Beatrice Katherine (Tom's Aunt Ka), Agnes Gertrude Stonehewer (his Aunt Kit, who
visited him in 1961), Owen Heathcote Grierson Merton (his father), John
Llewellyn Charles (Uncle Lyn), Sybil Mary, and Gwynedd Fanny (Aunt
Gwyn). If the Mertons and the Griersons were some distance from Wales
in time and geography, the coming together of the two families certainly had something Welsh about it!

Owen was born on May 14, 1887. His talent for drawing showed
itself early. He went to the Cathedral Grammar School and Christ's
College (a Public School in the English misnomer), but he left at fifteen
to work for a bank. Thomas Merton enjoyed the story of his father at
the bank, which may have been improved in the telling. Having disposed of one day's business correspondence where it would not be
found, Owen declared he was finished forever with having anything
so formal to do with money.[21]

He had his first show in Christchurch at seventeen, making enough
money to travel steerage to England. Owen was fated to have things
stolen from him, and he arrived without an overcoat. He studied under the Flemish artist Charles von Havermaet and at Ealing Art School,
living in Ealing at Durston House, 12 Castlebar Road, with his aunt and
uncle. Aunt Maud, Gertrude's sister and another of the fifteen children of John and Elizabeth Grierson, was a favorite with Owen as she
was to be in time with Tom. She had married Benjamin Pearce (Uncle
Ben), the owner and headmaster of Durston House School.

Still only nineteen, Owen went back to New Zealand in 1906 for another successful show and discovery by Miss D. K. Richmond and other
patrons of the arts. With the sales and local encouragement, he sailed
again for Europe, certain of a career that had begun so well. But funds
ran out, and self-doubt replaced the early confidence. Was his painting *sound*? *Sound* was to be an important word for Owen, for Ruth, and
for Thomas Merton. It meant authenticity and the integrity owed to
self and purpose. The Royal Society of British Artists elected Owen a
member after he had shown there. But it required money from the
family to study at Colarossi's School in Paris, and Owen was soon drawn
to Tudor-Hart's studio, where he could earn his tuition. Gertrude
Merton organized her son's third show in New Zealand, and this provided funds for a summer of painting in Spain and Owen's discovery
of Prades and the Pyrenees. His pictures were on show in an international exhibition in London at the time of his marriage in the spring
of 1914. But he was no longer nineteen, and he had not had a major
show of his own in Europe. From Prades he wrote to Tudor-Hart exploring the chances of having such a show in the summer of 1916.[22]
Then came the war.

The Jenkins family were pioneers in Ohio, a fact Sam Jenkins was proud of, as he was of telling people he was a member of the Sons of Ohio. The parents of Thomas Merton's maternal grandfather were James Jenkins and Mary Adams, who were married in Zanesville in 1855. The town is the county seat of Muskingum County, and it was the capital of the state for a time. It had been named after Colonel Ebenezer Zane, a local hero and the grandfather of Zane Grey, who was one of Samuel Jenkins's most successful authors.

Samuel Jenkins became important in the life of his grandson to a degree Thomas Merton was sometimes reluctant to admit. In *The Seven Storey Mountain* he makes frequent early appearances as a sort of natural disturbance, distributing largesse and confusion. Sam's method of scattering small change in showers from the car as he passed through villages in France complicated his grandson's attempts to give charity later, a memory as embarrassing to Merton as his grandfather's freely expressed prejudices against Catholics, Jews, and foreigners. Yet it was Samuel Jenkins's success in handling money and his generosity which gave Merton some financial independence beginning in his teens. In time, Merton was to wonder if he hadn't inherited qualities as well as money from his entrepreneur grandfather.

Samuel Adams Jenkins was born in Bristol, Morgan County, Ohio, in 1862. On October 8, 1885, he married Martha Caroline Baldwin. His wife had been born in Zanesville in 1863, and both their children were born there: Ruth Calvert in 1887 and Harold Brewster in 1889.

Samuel Jenkins probably thought of himself as a Horatio Alger hero. He had started as a newsboy, bought a stationery, music, and bookstore in Zanesville, and gone on to be a traveling salesman in books and sheet music, moving between New York, Philadelphia, and Cleveland. By the mid-nineties he was working for the publishing firm of Grosset and Dunlap in New York. He just missed the chance of being a partner, then made up for this by inventing a picture book which would tell the story of a popular film using stills from the movie.[23] He profited, and the family were tied to the worship of films and movie stars.

He used to boast that his son's education had cost him virtually nothing (Harold had won scholarships to the Choir School of the Cathedral of St. John the Divine, Trinity School, and Columbia School of Engineering) and that he had gone on to get a double benefit, bringing his son back from a first job with an engineering firm in San Francisco to design the house Samuel Jenkins wanted for the family in Douglaston, Queens. While they were waiting, the family lived in a nearby apartment house on Manhattan Avenue. As soon as 50 Virginia Road was completed, Harold moved in with his parents, remaining there a bachelor for thirty years, until their death and his late marriage. He worked for Hegeman and Harris, rising to be vice president.

Harold's sister, Ruth, had a far more expensive education. It probably pleased both her mother and her father that she wanted to choose the arts in an era when this was a social asset in a daughter and a social disaster in a son. Harold, the engineer, had designed a separate studio and kiln for his mother at 50 Virginia Road, and Martha Jenkins painted china with more than amateur skill.[24] Both parents could play the piano, and Sam would entertain by boisterously whistling whole operas while his wife accompanied him, a performance which might or might not pass for culture.

Ruth went to various schools, private and public, among them an Episcopalian academy for girls, St. Agnes, which no longer exists. In 1909, she graduated with distinction from Bradford, in Haverhill, Massachusetts. She had still not decided in which art to make her career. For a girl to study in Paris was a shock to any middle-class parents — American, English, or French. The feeling prevailed despite the elaborate attempts at chaperoning and the division of the sexes in most art schools, the fact that women art students seldom, if ever, drew from a male nude, and could not, even clothed, be asked to model for male students.[25] There may have been some strain when Ruth announced that she had decided to study in a city with such a reputation, and a greater degree of incredulity when she arrived back in 1913 to say she was marrying a penniless New Zealand painter. Hardly a good return on an expensive education. Samuel Jenkins must have felt he bore part of the blame. If he had not taken his family on one of his restless European tours, Ruth would probably never have seen Paris or Owen Merton.

❉

Sam, Martha, and Harold Jenkins were at the pier in New York in August 1916 to meet the Mertons, and the worst fears on both sides seem to have been quickly confirmed. To Sam at least, the high-principled New Zealander would probably never be able to support a family. Owen was nicknamed both "Nowe" and "Nonie" in the family.[26] The child, with a fine mixture of languages and cultures, named his grandfather "Pop" and his grandmother "Bonnemaman," while his uncle, who stalked the house with what looked like a giant fly swatter, was "Uncle Hickey," and it was explained he played tennis.[27]

Tom probably took in far more even than most children of his age, and a good degree more than was intended by the grownups. In Douglaston, he was soon able to identify the birds by their proper English or American names. His mother included the names in a list of words Tom knew. By the age of two he had an English vocabulary of five hundred words. He also had a gift for mimicry, spending time on the telephone imitating his grandmother. He sang songs to himself, some in French. But he resisted it when anyone spoke anything but English. They were not in Prades: there was no mountain at the bottom of the garden. He was still the center of his mother's attention: she was still watching him and writing things down in a book. When he saw other children he shouted to them and began to act things out. But they were too big, and they walked off laughing.

Virginia Road was unsurfaced. There were few houses in the immediate neighborhood, and great marshes with waving grasses began at the end of the road. Each morning, Tom's grandfather would set off for Douglaston Station, New York, and his office. Pop's study was empty, and Tom could sit in his swivel chair and spin himself and look at the books and newspapers. He sat on another swivel chair that could be raised higher to play at the piano. He watched his grandmother in her studio, played with the three dogs, Laddie, Chinnor, and Teazle, and made friends with the Polish laundry woman, Teeny, and the black cook, Harriet. Long afterward, when he was in European schools, Tom used to close his eyes and think of America, repeating over and over "lovely cookies."[28] The delicious cookies must have been from the Douglaston kitchen: a year later such things were forbidden or strictly rationed.

Owen was anxious to be independent as soon as possible. In the fall, the family joined an experimental group farming in Maryland. Something went wrong very quickly.[29] Perhaps the artists and intellectuals were better talkers than farmers. Owen had written to Tudor-Hart from Prades that the peasants he had worked with in their vegetable gardens had taught him a great deal. There were no peasants in America, and Owen missed them. The family were soon back in Douglaston, and Owen was looking for something on Long Island.

He found a house with a vegetable patch he could afford to rent from a tavern keeper in Flushing. This was before the first of many building booms, and the land between Flushing Creek and Kissena Boulevard was chiefly fields, with only four buildings along the slope of Hillside Avenue. Duggan's tavern was on the corner of Hillside Avenue and Kill Jordan. Then there was a gap. Number 57 was much the smallest of the three houses: it was very small, hardly more than a shack, with four rooms, two on each floor. It had running water. The outside needed painting. Four tall, spindly pines, one at each corner of the property, gave the place a somewhat depressing appearance.[30]

There are hints in *The Seven Storey Mountain* of how difficult the next three years were to be for the family, but the fact that Merton recalls that at least they were all together softens the outlines. The worst was certainly softened for him at the time.

Owen wrote to his former teacher that his wife was "a brick," which, in the English English of that ancient day, was even higher praise than

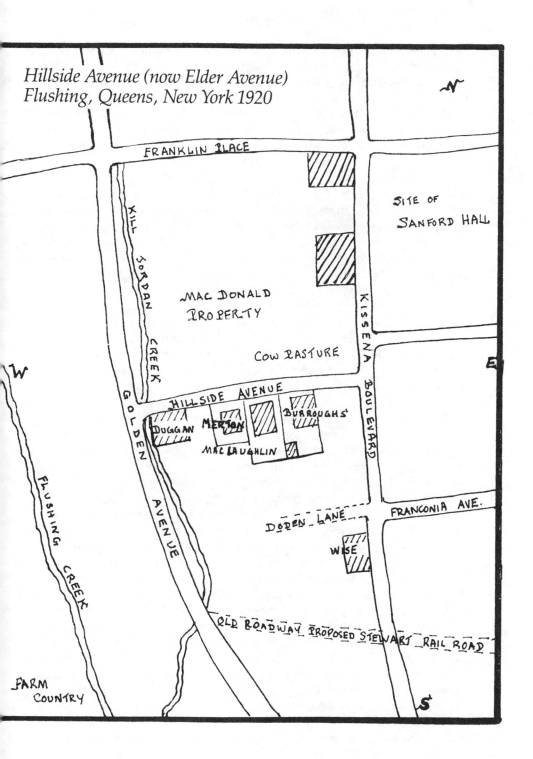

Hillside Avenue (now Elder Avenue)
Flushing, Queens, New York 1920

saying she was a "good sport."[31] Some tension certainly grew up between them, though the source is buried now. A neighbor remembers
that after one argument Owen piled up all the dirty plates and cups in
the bath.[32]

They had agreed not to take money from Ruth's parents. It was only
when medicine was necessary for Tom that Ruth accepted money from
her mother. Even this, she felt, was cheating on their agreement. No
wonder her son remembered her as worried and drawn.

Samuel Jenkins must have been deeply hurt and deeply angered at
this. His own sense of pride was altogether tied up with feeling and
looking generous. His wife's job was to keep whatever peace could be
salvaged. She never lost Owen's admiration, though her son-in-law may
have tried her own patience.[33]

Ever the practical idealist (it is the *im*practical idealists who work their
charm on others), Ruth began to write articles for the local Flushing
and Bayside newspapers and *Boston Cookery* on how to raise a family
on nothing a week — or almost nothing. She redecorated the inside of
the house and achieved at least one ambition she had had for three years:
the few visitors were shown "the Browning Room."[34]

Owen felt his misgivings about coming to America had been largely
confirmed. When the country entered the war, the chief signs were
that everything became more expensive and art was considered more
marginal and irrelevant than ever. Finding little time or heart to paint,
he made some money playing the organ at the church in Douglaston.
Sam Jenkins was a vestryman, though the family were anything but
regular in their attendance. Martha had diabetes, often stayed late in
bed, and read books on Christian Science. Her nurse companion was
a Catholic. The cooks tended to be worshipers of Father Divine.

Merton talks of his grandfather's bigotry and of the difficulties this
made for him later. But Owen's feud with Zion Episcopal Church was
probably a more important early influence. Some of the bitterness
worked off on his son, and there were to be no more unhappy readers
of *The Seven Storey Mountain* than the congregation of Zion Church.
Meanwhile, Owen wrote to Tudor-Hart he could make a lot more money
digging ditches and he liked ditch digging better.[35] He played ragtime
and popular tunes, this time American ones, at the Bayside theater to
accompany the silent movies. Then he got a job with the Bloodgood
Nurseries. His old habit of kicking off his boots and socks when working was thought too eccentric for America in any weather, especially as
he began to gain a little local celebrity for his landscape designs and
garden plans. In search of connections with Prades, he spent time with
the more picturesque community of blacks and Latins who lived in a
jumble of cabins along the dirt road by Kill Jordan. The community even
had its philosopher, who sat surrounded by a clutter of wheels and

broken tools in an ancient easy chair in front of his shack, talking to passers-by for as long as he could hold them. The cabins had no running water and the women filled their pots and pans from the stream with its Biblical name, as others had done from the town pump in front of the Mairie in Prades.[36]

What painting Owen was able to do told him that his "black" period was over. He began to have confidence in his powers of innovation in color just when these were hardest to put into effect, and this accounts for the few notes of optimism in his letters.

On November 2, 1918, just before the Armistice, a second son, John Paul, was born. Tom had had the virtual monopoly of his parents' love and attention, with little other company, except for an imaginary friend, Jack, and an imaginary dog, Doolittle.[37] This explains the usual sibling rivalry, but it hardly explains what happened. Merton was to choose a number of occasions later on in the autobiography to make oblique amends to his younger brother for hostility and a good deal of guilt. Tom had lost more than his place as only child with the birth of John Paul. For three and a half years Ruth had found everything Tom did important enough to write down. Now, she was writing about John Paul. This baby took his rests. This baby had no temper tantrums. Tom now had tantrums enough for any number of children, yet these did not draw his parents' attention to him for long, and they went into no notes.

There was no mirror, no reflection back: above all, there was no written record. This did not take from him the impression that all he did was important, only that all the important things he did and saw and said were being wasted for want of a recorder.

His mother's discipline grew harsher, yet it was probably her changed attitude, rather than individual acts of discipline, that left such an impression that Merton would feel compelled to tell others about it thirty and forty years later as if it were a recent hurt. Love, with both encouragement and correction, had been replaced by cold, intellectual criticism, making the three-year-old afraid.

To a woman friend with whom he had quarreled in his correspondence, he wrote in 1967: "I promise I won't get up in the air again. I don't know why you frightened me so. ('Cerebral' probably because I resented my mother's intellectuality) (or what I later interpreted as that.)"[38] To the same friend, in the next letter, Merton wrote: "I am not mad at you for being an 'intellectual woman' but only for seeming to reject me. I don't take sweetly to rejection, I can tell you . . ."[39]

Ruth still kept Tom to her timetables. She saw to his lessons and pushed him in these until he rebelled. There was no logic in having to spell *which* with an *h*. It was simply another trap to provoke criticism, and he responded with a tantrum. Interestingly enough, he rebelled against his mother, but not against books. He withdrew into himself, a book open in front of him, loved illustrations, and learned to read early. His favorites were a book on geography and one on Greek myths.[40]

There is a well-known and often reproduced photograph of Tom at this time, sitting on a stool, concentrating on an open book before him on a higher chair. Nothing is easier than to create myths by interpreting photographs, yet one can hardly avoid feeling that the concentration shown here almost beggars the word. There is something in the picture of the intensely self-absorbed children in paintings by Chardin.

Robert Lax remembers visiting Merton at St. Bonaventure College one day in the fall of 1940. Lax was not expected and he found Merton in a room in the basement of the Friedsam Library, so engrossed in the book on the table in front of him that he did not look up. For all the time he had known him, Lax had never seen Merton like this. Recounting the incident, Robert Lax was too scrupulous to add to the description until he came upon the photograph as he looked through Merton material. "Like that," Lax said.[41]

When John Paul was six months old, the boys' New Zealand grandmother, Gertrude Hannah Merton, came to stay in Flushing for several weeks, together with Aunt Kit. Gertrude discovered that Tom had not been taught to pray, and they said the Lord's Prayer each night until he had it by heart. Perhaps she found out other things about him in their time together. One night she took Tom to the window of his bedroom and told him the names of constellations and stars. The names fascinated him, and they seemed to have something to do with both his favorite books: Greek myths and geography came together, confirmed in the night sky.

Gertrude Merton told him that wherever he was, if he was feeling lonely, he could look up at the stars and think of her, and she explained which stars and constellations were different in the Southern Hemisphere. Merton returns to the incident a number of times — once to say the scene had been spoiled for him when something like the same thing was said by a pair of lovers in a "bad movie."[42]

For the moment his grandmother had given him a lifelong interest. What was more, looking at the stars would remind him to say the prayer she had taught him. She had found her own way of centering him.

Several photographs were taken one bright day in the garden during the visit. Again, nothing is easier than to read the wrong things into old photographs, but one of these is certainly arresting. Gertrude sits in the middle holding John Paul and looking down at him. Owen, in a formal suit, squats beside his mother. He is also looking at John Paul. All three are smiling at one another. Tom, one hand in the folds of his grandmother's full dress, as if he has been clutching them, and perhaps tugging on them for her attention, has turned his back on the group. He stands in a white sailor's suit, scowling out of the picture and far away to his left. All children scowl — certainly small boys of four do — and it usually means nothing. It may be the strong sunlight, though none of the others is bothered by the sun, they are too absorbed in one another. At that moment, only the person taking the photograph could have observed and recorded that Tom was a figure on his own.[43]

As 1919 turned into 1920 Owen began to sell more of the few paintings he was able to paint. Bryson Burroughs, the curator of paintings at the Metropolitan Museum of Art, lived in the largest of the three houses on Hillside Avenue. He was able to advise Owen which pictures had a strong chance of selling and which did not. Through his introduction, Owen began to show his work at the Daniel and Ferargil galleries, and Burroughs or one of his artist friends introduced Owen at the Alfred Stieglitz "291" Gallery, where the most exciting work in America was appearing. Owen was soon well known at the gallery and there was talk of his joining the Stieglitz group.

It was a pity nothing came of this. Owen had written to a friend from the Rue d'Assas, John Thompson, who was living and working in Denver, that he shouldn't overlook any opportunities of building a reputation in America, but it was advice he hardly heeded himself.[44]

If the Burroughs children and the MacLaughlin children at number 45 were too old for Tom then and if his brother was too young to be much of a companion, some of those he met were to be friends in the future.[45] Both Owen and Tom had discovered that a lively group of young people gathered around Betty Burroughs. Tom thought her wholly wonderful, but he tended to get in the way when her boyfriends called. One, the artist Reginald Marsh, would become Betty's first husband and, in the 1930s, Tom Merton's guide to galleries, burlesque theaters, art theaters, artists' studios, and much else in New York. Betty's brother, Alan, often worked with Owen in the gardens and fields during the years in Flushing. Later, Owen found him a friend when he was ill in London.

Both Owen and Ruth talked of returning to France, but they would have to find their own passage money. Samuel Jenkins, frustrated in every desire to help them, bought land, sold it, bought more land, and sold that, keeping ninety acres in New Hampshire (where he built a summer house and guest cabins and called his small settlement "Ashuelot"); Stone Island, Machiasport, Maine; and lots in Douglas Manor, Long Island, and Coral Gables, Florida.[46]

It was now Ruth who needed medicine the family could not afford. She told the doctor who first diagnosed her and informed her that she was pregnant again, that this was impossible. She grew worse, and she was taken to Bellevue, the huge public hospital in the city. Here she was told she had cancer of the stomach. Throughout the summer of 1921 she changed and wasted in the public wards. Owen and his two sons lived for a short while without her at Hillside Avenue. Then Owen admitted defeat and they moved back to Douglaston.

Owen visited Ruth in a hospital that could only be crowded and impersonal, and from one trip he brought back a note Ruth had written to Tom. His mother was writing again, this time to him, rather than about him. Her letter said he would never see her again.

Ruth died on October 3, 1921. When the family went to Bellevue Tom was left in the car. He concentrated his attention on the bricks of a wall, the falling rain, the smell of the inside of the automobile, a smell which was to have associations forever.

All the Jenkins family were to be cremated. Merton remembered no memorial service or burial service at Zion Church. He never forgot the visits to Fresh Pond Crematory: they would appear again and again in his poetry and prose in one disguise or another. On that first occasion Tom waited in the car again, either alone or with his mother's cousin, Ethel McGovern. He knew that something final and awful was happening inside, the more awful because none of it could be explained properly. This time he concentrated his attention on a row of crosses and angels against the wall of the stonemason's shack.[47]

Where prayers and churches apparently had nothing to say about such things, Tom came to the conclusion that everyone had a duty to find his or her own way beyond the immediate experience, while pretending to others as well as you could that nothing had happened. To come upon his father weeping when his grandmother was in the room made no bond but a small division. Owen probably spoke to Tom later about being manly and showing his younger brother a fine, brave example. Then he disappeared, leaving the boys with their grandparents.

What had distanced the grownups had had nothing to do with Tom and John Paul, and the grandparents were obviously anxious to compensate for the loss of their mother and the years of privation. In a way Tom could hardly understand, his mother's death had freed his father, and, if his mother had died when he was five, he was always to think of her in terms of his two earliest rejections.

He may have wondered if he would ever see his father again, when after a few months Owen returned with the news that he would be taking Tom away from Douglaston. By this time, and on top of everything else, Tom had had the trauma of his first day at school, coming in well after the others had settled into the routine. The skill to organize himself and his time, which both parents had inculcated (and which his mother had enforced), together with his love of reading, gave him an advantage. In a few weeks he was moved up to the second grade at Douglaston public elementary school. He was to do more dramatic things later at schools where he was allowed to find his own level. He remembered the smell and the crowding. For the first time he was in a mob, and for the first time, too, his father arrived to liberate him from the world of bells. After this, and with no pattern Tom could predict or understand, periods of institutional discipline were to alternate with periods of freedom. For the moment, the "feeling of triumph" he records enjoying as the Fall River boat moved into Long Island Sound covered a number of feelings.[48] His father had chosen him for a companion and left his rival, John Paul, in Douglaston. Travel in steerage may have been as crowded and chaotic as the evil-smelling halls of his first school, but this was far more romantic. "Geography had begun to become a reality."[49] Just before they got to Cape Cod the next day, his father bought him a whole bar of chocolate. His mother had strictly rationed candy. Obviously things were going to be different.

Perhaps the intensity of all this made Merton forget that his second New Zealand great-aunt, Aunt Ka, was with them most of that summer in a small cottage in Provincetown, Massachusetts, which Owen had rented. Tom got the mumps and enjoyed being read to in bed. While he listened to the life of the sailors on the tall ships in John Masefield's poems, there was a world of smaller sailing ships and the sea beyond the cottage windows. Owen painted and Tom drew and made up stories of his own. There seemed to be few rules and no rigid timetable.

In the fall he went back to school in Douglaston, but only for a few weeks. Owen had discovered Bermuda at the end of 1921. Now he wanted Tom to come there, too. They left from New York on the *Fort Victoria* in October 1922.

Owen is the hero of those early pages of the autobiography. The pages on Bermuda are just as full of color and good companionship as any of the other periods Tom shared with his father. The early drafts of *The Seven Storey Mountain* tell another story and present a different Bermuda. This time, it can only have been Merton himself who made the deletions and changes.

Merton went back to Bermuda in the spring of 1939 on what Robert Lax describes as a "David Copperfield sort of a trip."[50] *David Copperfield* is not *Oliver Twist* or *Bleak House*, yet in his partly autobiographical novel Charles Dickens was mining some of the darkest things in his own early life. Copperfield's father dies at the beginning of the book, but half-seen, or presented in disguises like Mr. Micawber, Dickens's own very lovable, very fallible father remains a presence throughout the book.

Forgiving our parents is one of the most difficult lessons life gives many of us, often marking us forever, only to be curiously unlearned when we have children of our own. Merton's father had such a strong, continuing influence on him precisely because his son felt there was something to forgive.

The pages in *The Seven Storey Mountain* make us see a Bermuda that is gone forever, with the H.M.S. *Calcutta* tied up at the dock, and the verandahs of the rooming houses on Somerset Island where elderly colonials and ships' captains drank and kept up their profanity and their racy stories without concerning themselves about the child listening, an island of white roads without cars, of pink houses, white or gray beaches, palm trees, the blue sea, Owen painting . . . All this has its own innocence, and the Merton of 1946 appears to be exaggerating the influence of the bad language he heard as a boy. In the typescript, that Bermuda is a far more ambiguous and spoiled paradise: "Because that beautiful island fed me with more poisons than I have mind to stop and count."[51]

He was eight years old then. Twenty years later, something drove him to exaggerate, even as he hints at what happened, or, more tellingly, what he felt had happened to him:

> When I think of my own childhood, and of the love and conscientiousness of my Father, and his well-meaning desires to bring me up an intelligent and happy person: and when I think how completely impossible it was for him to succeed, under the circumstances in which he had placed himself and me, I cease to wonder at the wars and crimes that have filled this century with blood.[52]

Poor Owen had contributed little to the crimes of the twentieth century, but that is hardly the point: the lesson learned forever, and exaggerated here, is that a very good man is not safe in his goodness. He needs something more than goodness to keep him good. Without this, others will need protection against him.

Meanwhile, Merton looks back on the perils of his own early freedom from what he thinks of as the strong, walled protection of the monastery:

> When I was eight years old, running loose among the rocks and the prickly pears of Somerset Island, Bermuda, I was in just about the same position as the child of divorced parents. My Father wanted to take care of me, but he did not precisely know how. I was without a family, without a school, without a church. I had no morals and no God. I would not even be able to say if there was such a thing as a church in the whole of Bermuda, if I had not gone back there many years later and noticed one then.[53]

Tom certainly knew there was a school: he had been to the small, private school for white students for several weeks and had learned the multiplication tables, before he decided to drop out. His father seems not to have insisted. Yet even in the unpublished account Merton left out his companion as he ran loose "among the rocks and prickly pears," Creighton Scott, and the person he thought of as the new rival for his father's love, Creighton's mother, Evelyn Scott.

The year before, Evelyn Scott wrote to her friend the New Zealand poet Lola Ridge, who was living in America:

> A little man called Owen Merton, about thirty I should judge, a Scotch-Welshman from New Zealand, who has been for the last year living in Flushing where his wife recently died and left him two children. He is very hard up, very naive, and genuine, as obscene as Bill Williams, and in all respects an interesting child with a real, if not stupendous talent.[54]

This was a patronizing start. Owen had made friends with his fellow countryman, Lola Ridge, and soon after he arrived in Bermuda with Tom in 1922, he writes to tell her, "I really do love Evelyn very much."[55] By this time, Evelyn had recovered from thinking Owen "an interesting child." She and Owen probably became lovers late that autumn. She had also revised her opinion of Owen as an artist.

In fact there is something eerie about the words she uses to describe Owen's work. Echoes appear in Merton's own estimate of his father's talent in the draft for *The Seven Storey Mountain*,[56] even when allowance is made for what must have been said at studio parties and the fact that both make an obvious comparison to the work of John Marin. Evelyn writes:

> Owen is so much more sensitive [than Marin] that his sense of color and of definition are allied in a way so much subtler and much more inevitable than Marin's are. Marin has a crude romantic mentality and that wanting power. Owen's defect is perhaps an integrity too fine.[57]

In the early 1920s, Evelyn Scott was already considerably better known as a writer than Owen was as a painter. Up to that time, her novels had been introspective studies of the sensitivity of women. Set in America, these had explored many of the same themes as Virginia Woolf. There are links with the work of Dorothy Richardson, with Jean Rhys, and with yet one more New Zealander, Katherine Mansfield. Yet her novels and her strongly autobiographical book, *Escapade*, show original talent. Both her early novels and her later historical novels have been neglected, and it might be fairer to her to discover where she was the innovator, rather than the imitator.

Owen was still struggling with lack of money and with his conscience. He refused direct help from Sam Jenkins but, through Evelyn, had met Swinburne and Marie Garland, artists, who also had money. Owen was assisted by the Garland fund to escape from landscape gardening. He was now able, at last, to paint, and he was far more in his own element than he had been for years. Yet he was torn by a relationship with a woman who was married to a friend and fellow artist, Cyril Kay Scott. The relationship was not a secret. The principal objector to it was his son.

Just how strong Tom's objections were can be seen in Evelyn Scott's letters. She was in no doubt about Tom as a serious rival for Owen. As we have already seen, her best writing did not get into her letters. She could be gushing, and even cloying, where she was seldom guarded about her emotions:

> Tom is a morbid and possessive kid and Owen is made morbid about Tom through various things that occurred in connection with Ruth. Tom is, and will be until he is big enough to be set adrift a constant obstacle to piece [sic] of mind.[58]

Evelyn was hardly an impartial critic, yet she was well informed. In an undated letter from Collioure in the south of France, probably written in 1923, she told Lola Ridge:

> I have finished the first draft of the new novel and am half way through the second, or perhaps a third through. It is certainly a culmination of all other experiments in technique I have made . . . It is about Merton and his wife (that is really confidential), and what I had of her character from reading old letters and talking it over with him. I take them through their experience here and then in the United States . . .[59]

"The Grey Riddle" was never published, though the typescript exists. However, two of Evelyn Scott's published novels, *The Golden Door* and *Eva Gay*, contain thinly disguised material, both on the marriage of Ruth and Owen and on the *ménage à trois* of Evelyn Scott, Owen Merton, and Cyril Kay Scott.[60]

Owen could paint in Bermuda, but he had to go to New York to try to sell his work. While he was away, someone must have taken nominal responsibility for Tom. If this was Evelyn, the arrangement cannot have been much of a success. Meanwhile, Owen's trip was a disappointment. The art dealers had a fixed idea that a Bermuda landscape should look like a watercolor of Bermuda by Winslow Homer. Owen was able to sell one painting to the Brooklyn Museum and several others to private buyers. He was encouraged to join the Scotts, who were returning to Europe and planned a painting trip to North Africa. Owen collected Tom and took him to stay with the Garlands.

"Merton is in an awfully tight box financially," Evelyn Scott wrote to Lola Ridge. "Tom was up at Buzzards Bay but has been returned and that leaves two with Mrs. Jenkins, so we don't know whether it will be too much for her or not."[61] There is a certain crisp glee in this report, aimed at both Tom and Martha Jenkins. In the draft of *The Seven Storey Mountain*, Merton includes a funny but puzzling story to tell why he had "been returned." He had seen others writing in the long, slim books that lay about on desks at the house on Buzzards Bay. He found all you had to do was to write the sum you needed in such books, take this along to the bank, and the people in the bank would give you the money. This knowledge would certainly have helped his father. At eight, Tom sent in an order to Montgomery Ward in Chicago with a check and attempted to cash other checks at local stores. He was threatened with reform school, and Samuel Jenkins turned up one day to take Tom back to Douglaston.[62] Pop did not seem perturbed. Probably he was amused that the Garlands had turned out to be a little stuffy on this occasion. Samuel Jenkins was to have his own problems with his grandson over money, but when these came years later, they were at least refreshingly different from those he had had with his son-in-law.

In his autobiography, Merton moves straight from Bermuda to visits to his grandfather's publishing office in New York. Here he spent hours reading the adventures of Tom Swift, the Rover Boys, Jerry Todd, and others, until Samuel Jenkins beat his desk with the rolled-up *Evening Telegraph* and told everyone in earshot that it was time he took his grandson to an important business lunch of chicken à la king at Childs on Broadway.

Apart from these visits, the picture may not have been so cheerful. John Paul was poor company, and for all the complications of his time in Bermuda, Tom missed his father.

"I realized today after Mass," Merton wrote in 1966, "what a desperate, despairing childhood I had around the ages of seven — nine — ten, when Mother was dead and Father was in France and Algeria. How much it meant when he came and took me to France! It really saved me."[63]

Some of Owen's finest painting was done at Bou Saada in Algeria. He wrote to James (Jas, pronounced "Jazz") Wood, who had been the greatest admirer of Owen's painting after Tudor-Hart at the Rue d'Assas, that he felt he now had the "strength of twenty tigers." "By God, I can paint!" he said.[64]

Owen's innovations in the use of color are not innovations now, but for all the painting and all the painters who have come since 1924, the watercolors of this period still make him an important unknown. Then, in the fall of 1924, he wrote that the party were encamped at an isolated oasis, where they had all caught some local sickness. Shortly after this, the family in Douglaston learned that Owen had had to be brought back to London and that he was gravely ill.

Tom was finally old enough to be told such things, to become one of the conspirators: John Paul must not know that the father who was al-most a complete stranger was so ill he might die. Meanwhile, Tom, far more unpredictable than most children of nine and far more cau-tious, accepted the news without response and went out to play.

His father rallied and separated from Evelyn. Part of his physical collapse had been caused by his struggle with himself. With money, he felt some things might be possible, but he would not take money from the Jenkins family and he had already proved he could not sup-port a wife and two sons.

The break was not a clean one; the agony was prolonged for almost a year. To Evelyn Scott, by trying to be honorable and sound and de-cent and a very perfect gentleman, Owen had made a worse mess of their lives than an unfeeling man would have done. It may have been so. An honorable, good man trapped in a situation where there is little honor is a dangerous and unpredictable companion. His very good-ness gets in the way of worldly good sense. To Evelyn, Owen was again behaving "like a child." Tom she had found oddly *un*childlike.

Early in July 1925, when Tom was ten and a half, his father turned up in Douglaston. It should have been a moment of joy, but his father was an unfamiliar figure, drawn, thinner, wearing a beard he refused to shave off to reassure his son. Worse, there was something seedy about him, while before this there had been something aristocratic about Owen, even when he was working barefoot in a field. The family stayed in Douglaston only a few days and then went to the summer colony in New Hampshire. A crucial decision was made at Ashuelot. Tom was no party to the discussions, at least by intention, and there is no men-tion of any of this in the autobiography. There are references in letters to what was certainly a bitter and angry dispute between Owen and Sam Jenkins, with Harold Jenkins now taking a strong part against Owen. Owen had probably tried to reverse an earlier decision, to voice for the last time his desire to live with Evelyn and to have the boys with him. Even if this had been financially possible without damaged pride, it was clearly too late for Owen and Evelyn.

By this time Evelyn had had enough of Owen's conscience and his contorted attempts to wrestle with it ("Owen and I separated perma-nently in September. Little Tom *hated* me. What was there to do?").[65] The main tug-of-war was over the children and would go on for years. For the moment, it was worked out that Owen would take Tom with him to Europe and the Jenkins family would look after John Paul. The brothers would see little of one another, except in the summers, when the Jenkinses toured Europe, or when Tom came over to America. Like his Uncle Harold, John Paul went to the Choir School of St. John the Divine. Then he went to a military academy at Gettysburg, Pennsyl-vania.

This time Tom felt little sense of triumph at leaving his brother to go off with his father. At first he refused to go to France.[66] His life was beginning to move in extremes he may have resisted. When the insistence on order and regime became oppressive, he longed for freedom. When freedom became too free, too uncontrolled, he longed for order. Order had been uppermost at Hillside Avenue, Flushing, freedom too free in Bermuda. These were the two poles of his experience for a long time afterward. Whatever he says later, there was a certain balance to life at Virginia Road, Douglaston. It was probably a restful halfway station between opposites for a ten-year-old boy. And he ate better.

PART TWO

The Calvaire

I should so like you and Mrs. Tudor-Hart to see my boy who is so like his mother in many ways.

— *Owen Merton*

Sometimes I think I don't know anything except the years 1926–27–28 in France, as if they were my whole life, as if father had made that whole world and given it to me instead of America, shared it with me.

— *Thomas Merton*

M ERTON CALLED the opening section of his autobiography "Prisoner's Base." The children's game, which has been played since the Middle Ages, is an aptly chosen metaphor, and not only for the first few years of Merton's life. Tom had played it before he arrived at St. Antonin Noble Val, where he found it was called *barres* in the playground of the Ecole des Garçons, under his second high place, The Calvaire, which dominates the town to the northwest.

In *The Seven Storey Mountain* Merton employs varied synonyms for captivity and freedom until he tells us precisely what he believes his parents were imprisoned by, and what he thinks they were free of in an unfree world.[1] This, too, is skillfully done, though Owen Merton might have smiled sadly to hear from his son that "any fool knows that you don't need money to get enjoyment out of life."[2] In Prisoner's Base itself there are times of capture at the base and there are times of running free. The running is frantic. The periods of captivity are miserable with frustration, above all the feeling that your free friends and teammates could free you if they only took the risk, if they were not so intent on keeping and enjoying their own selfish freedom.[3]

By the age of ten, Tom had known periods of frantic running and of the frustrating captivity that was also protection. He said later that he had "grown up in dormitories," forgetting the periods when he was freer than most children. He and his father had come to this part of France because Iris Weiss Bennett, the wife of Tom's godfather, had told them of a good school for Tom in Montauban. This turned out not to be a school at all, but it was not long before Tom began his "life in dormitories" at the Lycée in Montauban.

Perhaps a study ought to be made of nations and their national character and foibles by examining the unwritten laws and schoolboy lore of each. What Merton learned outside classes in America, France, and England would mark him for life. Probably more than most boys, he was anxious to adapt, and consequently, he became an expert in the student *mores* of three very different subcultures. It was the contrast between French and English schools that had the most telling effect.

Conscription and a certain kind of compulsory education were products of the same kind of thinking at the same time in history — the sort Rousseau engaged in in *The Social Contract* when he wrote that the people should be compelled to be free. It is no accident that the barracks and the school have so much in common. The truly free child learns most by himself or herself and needs little beyond encouragement, materials, understanding, direction, opportunity, time. But if nobody, in the advanced nations at least, escapes the educational system of his or her own nation, the rules the students set for themselves and live by are very different.

This will have to be briefly sketched in, while the schools are not the same today in any country as they were in the 1920s. In December 1926 Owen wrote to tell Tudor-Hart that Tom is "quite a serious young scholar."[4] In French schools the serious scholar is honored. In English schools, he is, or was, a "brain" and a "swat." Brilliance in studies, prize winning, in English Public Schools (and in the truly public schools, which were pulled in by social pressures to imitate them) had to be effortless, or skillfully disguised as effortless.

In French schools, by contrast, a certain amount of currying favor with teachers was acceptable, even a certain amount of cheating. The object, after all, and often cynically, was to beat the system, to do well in exams, above all, the dreaded "bachot." Much was tolerated in a rival during school hours. Friendships survived even "peaching," telling on one's friend, or minor betrayals. It was something to dismiss with "next time, it's my turn."

In English schools the rules were absolute and as fixed as the laws of the Medes and the Persians. But the English had added compulsory games to compulsory education. After that, nothing was likely to be a surprise. The spying, the conniving, the sabotage, and the cynical underhand play of a French school would have been conceived of as something like Balkan politics in an English school. Or, worse still, it just wasn't "the done thing." You did not flatter your teacher, who was usually too remote a figure, anyway, to consider open to bribes, flattery, or outright insult and intimidation. You were good at games and, perhaps, brilliant in your studies — that was up to you, somewhat secondary and certainly nothing to boast about or demonstrate in public. You were not expected to "show workings," or to appear "the serious student." To cheat, or to be caught cheating, was unpardonable. To tell on another student, friend or foe, was to damage your school reputation for good.

At the Lycée Ingres in Montauban, Tom had his ears twisted, his round, open, pale English face sneered at and pummeled until he picked up the *argot* of insult and obscenity — until he was able to return the right answers and demonstrate he was an insider. In time he won some measure of popularity because he was an intellectual and wrote romantic novels in French out of school. Then the differences between him and his schoolmates became largely accepted eccentricities, and he discovered other intellectuals and writers of romantic novels.

Later on, he won a measure of popularity at his English Public School (where other traits were accepted as eccentricities) despite his rising to the equivalent of the sixth form in a little over a year (rather than three years),[5] because he played a good game of rugger, because he was a rebel, and, above all, because he kept the really important schoolboy rules, appearing to have an uncanny knack of coming first and winning prizes, but gracious enough to talk about "good luck." If he worked in his study, nobody knew it. In class or in the school library, he was ready to break off work, look bored, gossip in whispers, and demonstrate that studying was not a serious business.[6]

Merton learned from both systems. There is an admirable dedication and respect for scholarship in the French system, for all its cynicism. There is a basic modesty in the English system, even if this has been somewhat done to death. It is not intrinsically anti-intellectual. If the intent is good, it includes an invitation to common sense, a measure of balance, a reluctance to take the intellectual side for everything.

Merton's drive and dedication came both from Ruth Merton's desire to perfect herself and from Owen's rare self-discipline (at least as an artist), greatly reinforced by the odd combination of seriousness and cynicism found in schoolboy France. Yet the exterior, the apparent, was the seemingly casual approach. Merton was at pains to shed his Englishness, but in this he remained a product of English schools. It misled others: it made complications for him. At times it confused and surprised his students, as it did even his Columbia friends, who thought they knew him so well.[7]

✳

Tom soon forgot he had been reluctant to return to France with his father. They sailed on August 25 from New York, stayed a few days in England, and docked in Calais on a rainy September day. Merton used the details of a ship coming into harbor to enliven *Exile Ends in Glory*,[8] just as he recalled the hotel he and his father stayed in in Paris in his novel.[9] The lights seen at night from the train windows reappeared in

St. Antonin Noble Val

his poem "The Night Train."[10] At Orleans his father told him the story of Joan of Arc. Reg Marsh and Betty Burroughs, now married, had joined Owen and Tom in Paris. At Caussade the couple said goodbye and set off on their bicycles.[11] The Mertons arrived at Montauban in a dusk of bats, ancient fiacres and cab horses, and the glow of café windows. They crossed the square in front of the Villenouvelle station. The hotel did not look very prepossessing:

> And yet, instead of being dreary, it was pleasant. And although I had no conscious memory of anything like this, it was familiar, and I felt at home. Father threw open the wooden shutters of the room, and looked out into the quiet night, without stars, and said:
> "Do you smell the woodsmoke in the air? That is the smell of the Midi."[12]

After this, Montauban proved disappointing by day. The Institut Jean Calvin turned out not to be a school at all, and the local sights were works by the two native sons. Owen liked the paintings and drawings of Ingres, which Tom found cerebral yet passionate (not a good combination of qualities). Neither cared for the sculpture of Bourdelle. Owen picked St. Antonin Noble Val from photographs at the Syndicat d'Initiative, and they were off on their first trip in the little train east from Montauban and into the gorges of the river Aveyron.

The choice of St. Antonin proved fortunate. For all the television antennae and the traffic, it is still picturesque today, and it was probably noisier and had worse smells in its narrow streets during its most prosperous days in the Middle Ages. The town is still centered on its church, as Tom discovered after scrambling up the slope of The Calvaire through thorn bushes and crumbling limestone ledges.

Since 1925, however, there have been changes to the town he knew. He learned of some from the visit to St. Antonin by his friend Father Chrysogonus Waddell in September 1964,[13] of others from the town guide Father Chrysogonus brought back with him.[14] From the guide, Merton discovered the extent of the floods of 1930, which had radically changed the Condamine area to the west of the town, where Tom and his father had first lived in rooms. In his novel, he had imagined a return:

> And I have come back to see the rusty iron crucifix that stood near the Place de la Condamine in St. Antonin, and to see the very young, black-haired priest that taught in the parochial school, walking like fury through the streets in his cassock. To see the green-glass bottles of mineral water on the tables of small provincial hotels, and to read on the labels the names of the diseases they cure. I have come back to see the blue river curving under the bridge, and to hear the paddles of the laundresses echoing under the arch.[15]

During their time in the Condamine, while Tom was going to the local school in the Place des Tilleuls, father and son were as close to one another as they would ever be. Owen was still reading aloud. Of Coleridge's "Ancient Mariner" Tom remembered only that the wedding guest had never reached the wedding. His later comment on this is a strange one — that children are too down-to-earth to gain much from imaginative poetry.[16] Yet this period of his own childhood was the one in which his father's love for the poetry of William Blake took firm root in Tom.

It was at this time, too, that something else was planted. The founder of the Quakers, George Fox, writes in his *Journal* that his father, Christopher Fox, had "a seed of God in him." Tom discovered there was something far more than formally and vaguely Christian about Owen Merton, though they did not attend the small Protestant church in St. Antonin (Merton remembered only the nightingales in the cypress trees close to the classical building).[17] One day, in the hall of their third-floor apartment, Owen told his son of the triple betrayal of Christ by Peter. The details, and the force in his father's voice, were to remain vivid all Merton's life, while for the rest of the time they stayed in the town, the crowing of the cocks in St. Antonin took on another meaning.[18]

Tom outgrew the local school as soon as he could express himself competently in French. In the summer of 1926 the Jenkins family made their biannual invasion of Europe, bringing John Paul, and Samuel Jenkins helped Owen decide on the Lycée Ingres in Montauban, which had at least the virtue of being a secular school in Sam's eyes. In Paris, Owen slipped away from the party to go to a jazz concert (his love of jazz was something else his son would inherit). On the *quatorze juillet*, Bastille Day, they were all at Dijon for the military parade. Merton remembered his father losing his pipe there in a music shop — Owen had set it down to play "Chicago," "Tea for Two," and "I Want to Be Happy" for his sons.[19] But much of the time was spent in bickering and arguments. Tom and John Paul argued over whether America had stolen the tune for "God Bless America" from England, or whether England had taken the tune of "God Save the King" from America. Tom and his grandfather had a geographical argument on the relative heights of mountains near Davos in Switzerland. Sam's enthusiasms wore the others out, and his prejudices against drinking (or at least against drunks), smoking, dirt, and the hypocrisy of all religions but his own left a lasting embarrassment — so did his method of distributing largesse by throwing it.

The empty courtyards and corridors of the Lycée Ingres had not looked unattractive in August. It turned out that in the pull between order and freedom, the school in Montauban provided the worst of both — a combination of regimentation and chaos. Tom, among *les petits*, hated it and spoke harshly of the Lycée in both his novel and his autobiography. His first impressions were of the sly bullying, the bad language, and the tyranny of Monsieur le Proviseur and his henchman, Monsieur le Censeur.[20] It was only many years later that he recalled he had found one of his best teachers in Monsieur Delmas, who introduced him to the writings of Fénelon and much else.[21]

By getting up early on a Sunday morning and running to catch the little train at Villenouvelle station, Tom could now manage one day of the week with his father. His sense of geography led him to set up pairs of places and to treat one as the opposite of the other on the emotional scale. Thus, in *The Seven Storey Mountain* Montauban and the Lycée Ingres are on one extreme wing, St. Antonin (and Merton's father) on the other. There are no "bad" images for St. Antonin, and few "good" ones for Montauban. Rabbit cooked in wine sauce on the one side; dismal, evil-smelling corridors on the other. Wonderful peasant characters like Pierrot on the one side; pale, sarcastic Lycée teachers on the other. Cheerful wedding guests who can drink the pot dry without getting drunk or losing their dignity are set in contrast with vicious, foul-mouthed schoolboys. The Thomas Merton writing his autobiography in his early years at the monastery can be tiresome at times, with his talk of "filthy" books and "filthy" language, and here he leaves the impression he is being rather priggish about his schoolfellows as well as somewhat overgenerous to the inhabitants of St. Antonin.

Tom was taken to task for his own bad language when he went to stay with the Privats, an elderly couple at Murat in the Auvergne. He gives this summer visit a greater significance in the autobiography. Tom found the two old people so certain and so unenterprising in their Catholicism that they had no desire at all to argue about religion with the smart young schoolboy of twelve. Instead of intellectual argument, they had a series of anxious questions. How could he live outside their faith? Wasn't he afraid for his soul?

It was because they were afraid for his soul and so obviously concerned for him that Tom began to think of his soul at all, and he later saw this as one of the small, but important turnings of his life. Long afterward, he wondered if the Privats had prayed for him. He wondered, too, if the huge image of the Virgin on the rock at Murat, which his father had painted when father and son were there together the winter before, had prayed for Owen "when nobody else did."[22]

Merton thought the summer stay at the Privats had been simply a holiday. It was not until Father Chrysogonus Waddell brought him news of a meeting in St. Antonin with the widow of the local doctor that he learned the truth. Madame Fosagrives said that her husband had saved Tom's life by telling his father the boy was tubercular.[23] Tom had never been told, though he wondered why he had felt weak at times, and why he had spent so much time in the school infirmary, lying in bed listening to the bugles from the barracks of soldiers from North Africa and thinking of his father's year in Algeria.[24]

The news that his son was suspected of having tuberculosis must have chilled Owen. It probably brought back Ruth's death, Tom's childhood illnesses, the medicine that had to be bought with money from the Jenkins family. "I have got Tom off to the Auvergne," he wrote Tudor-Hart from St. Antonin on September 23, 1927, "and I think he will get on very well — Fortunately, there is a very reliable couple there who will look after him for 20 francs a day. It will depend on what the doctor says how long I let him stay there."[25]

∗

The house Owen had planned to build had been delayed for two years. Now he found a plot of land right at the foot of The Calvaire that, by a quirk of French law, could only be sold to foreigners. The French franc was still depressed. Owen's mother, Gertrude, offered to help him, and he sold a painting in America. He scraped together his small resources and bought the property. In the summer of 1927 Owen began negotiating for stones and other building material. He found a ruined chapel some miles away that contributed a fine window and much else. Two houses in the town, with all their stone and ancient doors of oak and iron, cost him no more than four pounds each.[26] Tom discovered useful rocks from his scrambles up and down The Calvaire. Probably Pierrot and his pals, Owen's companions on his trips all over the Midi as the referee of the local rugby games — the *boules* players, draughts players, the eating companions from the dining room of the Hôtel des Thermes — all turned out to help and criticize.

Merton wrote of those warm times in other accounts than the autobiography. In his journal he remembered:

> Father working on the land he had bought, on summer evenings, making flowers grow. The drawings of the house. The beginning of the house itself. His room, my room. Mine full of sun. His smelled of tobacco, a little. The kitchen, where we made cocoa out of goats' milk.[27]

Today the house is the Villa Diane and has ornate towers and a whole wing that has nothing to do with the simple block which enclosed the massive doors and the window from the chapel. It is not difficult, however, to think away what has been added to the studio–living room–kitchen, the circular stone staircase, and the two rooms, one for the father, the other for the son. The initials T.M. are cut into the massive fireplace in what was once the all-purpose room on the ground floor, where Tom pored over guidebooks and photographs of French cathedrals during the winter rains. Owen's garden, even in decay, is probably not far out of his design. In *The Seven Storey Mountain* Merton wrote that his father planted two poplar trees by the well, one for each of his sons.[28] There are two there today. Each has been cut off at roughly the same height, about that of the average man. This part of the garden is now dominated by a huge pine.

Owen had returned to London for the wedding of the same John Chrystal who had once photographed him holding up Tom with Canigou in the background. The mother of the bride, Mrs. Stratton, came to visit in the Midi, and Owen, Tom, and Mrs. Stratton made a visit to Marseilles.

Merton is cautious in his autobiography, but he obviously feared another rival. He may even have thought a second Evelyn Scott had entered their lives, but he was quickly reassured, and he speaks of his father's friend with a certain awed affection. From that first trip to Marseilles Merton remembered the railway station, a restaurant where Mrs. Stratton corrected him (she thought he had said *cul* — he had said *Kuh*), and reading Rudyard Kipling's *The Light That Failed* in the hotel room while his father painted a view of the old port from the window.[29] Marseilles never became one of his ideal towns (in his trips with his father round the Midi he had been looking for the perfect city), and Merton was alternately fascinated and repelled, then and on later visits. He includes a mixture of both emotions in his descriptions of Marseilles in the fragment of the unpublished novel, "The Labyrinth," and in *Exile Ends in Glory*.

Tom went back to the Lycée, Owen to Cette to paint and to make a decision. By 1927, Owen was torn between the needs of his career and the life he and Tom had built for themselves. He was preparing for a second show in London. Friends, including Mrs. Stratton, had asked him whether a permanent base in a small town in the Midi made good sense.

In 1925, between May and June, Owen had finally achieved what he had always wanted and what the war delayed, his own show at an important gallery in London. Ironically, at the Leicester Galleries he was on a double bill with "Decorative Work by Clara Fargo Thomas." He must have had some sense at the time that, if fate had been kinder to her, he might have shared the gallery with decorative work by Ruth Calvert Jenkins Merton.[30]

At the time of the 1925 show Owen had hardly recovered from his collapse. Friends had helped, and Tudor-Hart had done a good deal of quiet pushing behind the scenes. Things went well up to a point, but only £200 worth of work was sold, and Merton knew most of the buyers. The critic Owen had been waiting for had spoken at last. Roger Fry called the exhibition "a brave show" of watercolors. In a note to Owen he had said, "If you could get two years of quiet solid work I think the results would be of the greatest interest — Good luck to you in this exasperating but fascinating venture of artistic expression." Uncle Ben Pearce and Aunt Maud were furious and found the note patronizing. Owen concentrated on the last sentences: "my Aunt was really annoyed at the gratuitous hint that I have two years more."[31]

There was one further success. Owen sold a painting to one of the best-known collectors of contemporary paintings in England. Sir Michael Sadler had bought "Cathedral from the River, Beziers." Owen was not paid on the spot, and he had hardly enough to pay for his lunch before he took the train from Oxford back to London.[32]

The Leicester Galleries agreed to a second show in 1927, which was put off to May 1928. Owen Merton had had his "two years of quiet solid work." There were good reviews. Paintings sold — but only £175 worth. Owen knew every buyer but one. Fry did not commit himself. Even Tudor-Hart said it was one of the *five* best shows in London that season. Owen sent out prospectives for a summer class in "Drawing and Painting Landscape" to be held at Shoreham and Eynsford in Kent. The choice of Shoreham brought Owen close to his well-loved painter-poet, William Blake — Shoreham had been the "Vale of Vision" for Blake and his disciple of genius, Samuel Palmer — but the advertisement in the *Times* brought one inquiry and the class cancelled itself.

Tudor-Hart wrote on June 6, offering to make Owen an allowance of £100 a year for five years on condition that he have the pick of Owen's paintings each year. The proposal was as a business venture, yet Owen could not fail to see the charitable gift under the formal writing. He was being supported: he could not support himself.[33]

At the same time the Pearces suggested that Tom be brought to school in London. Benjamin Pearce had just retired as headmaster of Durston House School, but the family owned a second school in Surrey, Ripley Court. Tom could attend a private preparatory school, paying a fraction of the fees. Not even the son of a penniless painter could be expected to go to the schools for the public in England. Owen felt he had already drawn too much from the couple in Ealing (who were already paying some of Tom's expenses at the Lycée Ingres). When Sam Jenkins bravely made yet another offer to pay for Tom's education, Owen accepted. He even wrote to others of Sam's generosity.[34]

One day in June 1928, Owen arrived unannounced at the Lycée to say he had come to take Tom out of whatever class he was in and for good.

To Tom this was the greatest jail delivery his father had ever organized. The very walls of the familiar houses on the way to the Ville-nouvelle station cried "Liberty! Liberty!"[35] To Owen, it was the end of his hopes in France. To both, it was another round of Prisoner's Base.

Owen was in no very good mood on the journey. Tom noticed everything — the signs advertising tours to Egypt as the train approached the coast, the vast differences between the French port and the English one, only thirty miles of sea between them. There was no more "Liberty!" for Owen in England than there was in America, only a crass and brutal division between rich and poor. The first discovery was that the train had only one carriage for Third-Class passengers. Father and son had to stand in a crowded corridor, where Owen puffed his pipe and glared out at a landscape that depressed him.[36]

English schools continue well into July in the summer term, and Tom found he was back in class after little more than a week of unexpected vacation. Owen remained in England, though he hated the climate. He spent a year painting French scenes in oil on wooden screens: the best, a study in "The Key of Red" (following Tudor-Hart's theories of music and color), a view of Le Havre.[37] He left this unfinished, with instructions on how to complete it, when he returned to France in July 1929 to sell the house under The Calvaire.

Owen found a non-Frenchman who would pay 15,000 francs, or a hundred pounds. He owed twenty-five. The rest, he thought, would keep him for six months if he were careful.[38] Packing up most of the work he had done in the past three years was too much for him in the heat of the Midi summer. He began to feel as he had felt four years before, at the oasis near Bou Saada. Owen left the paintings and escaped to Albi. But it was too hot in Albi. He started for England, collapsed in the train, but managed to continue the journey to Ealing.

At Aunt Maud and Uncle Ben's Owen thought he was recovering. Instead, he fell ill and for weeks was hardly coherent. Tom, away at Ripley Court, was told very little. Owen recovered, but Tom Bennett, who took his old friend on as a patient, ordered him not to paint. Owen obeyed his doctor, yet as soon as he could stand up, he carried the heavy screens about London trying to find a buyer for them.[39]

The paintings of three years and the family possessions left in the house under The Calvaire were not recovered by Owen or anyone else. In 1930 the Bonnette, a tributary of the Aveyron, flooded the countryside. Tudor-Hart made the journey down to St. Antonin and discovered the paintings had been shoveled out by workmen with the mud and debris the river had left. By this time Owen was in the Middlesex Hospital. Nobody told him: it is doubtful he would have understood if they had.[40]

If Tom ever wanted to break from a base where he was held prisoner again he would have to do it for himself. Nobody would be able to free his father.

PART THREE

Brooke Hill

And did the Countenance Divine,
Shine forth upon our clouded hills?
And was Jerusalem builded here,
Among these dark Satanic Mills?
— *William Blake*

There is another man within mee that's angry with mee, rebukes, commands, and dastards mee.

— *Sir Thomas Browne*

I T WAS FORTUNATE Aunt Maud entered Tom's life when she did. Tall, thin, gray-haired, given to wearing old-fashioned clothes and large floppy hats, Maud Pearce, Gertrude's sister and Tom's great-aunt, is presented in *The Seven Storey Mountain* as one of those sensible, no-nonsense Englishwomen whose warmth comes through every attempt at reserve.[1] What Tom loved most about her was her great innocence of heart. For a few years in his late teens and early twenties, sophistication and recognizably good taste won his highest admiration. When this period was over, Merton came to look upon the time and the values he had chosen as disastrous. Then Aunt Maud became a model by which he measured others for the rest of his life. She also becomes something of a symbol. In the polarization he favored, "Aunt Maud's England" came to stand for the bucolic England of Merton's expeditions alone and on foot through Sussex villages and the New Forest and the hours he spent by himself on his third high place, Brooke Hill. This England is also William Blake's "green and pleasant land," the contrast to another England altogether — for Blake and for Merton.

For the moment his aunt was something much less abstract than either symbol or model. She was so sensitive to Tom's own adolescent reserve that this meant discussing matters like his future using the third person, as if they were consulting together about a mutual friend. In the summer of 1928 they went to buy the uniform which would change a French schoolboy into an English one, and during the shopping expedition she learned that Tom wanted to be a writer.[2]

He was certainly too shy to claim he already *was* a writer, though there were the romances he had written at the Lycée, and by then he may have begun the journals.[3] Whether or not he had started does not materially alter the fact that Tom had already picked up the story which had been begun so obsessively by his mother in "Tom's Book," then abandoned. On September 26, 1939, Merton was able to make an incredible journey in recollection, and what could be written down in 1939 must have been very carefully rehearsed in 1928 and 1929:

> Today, a fine rain, very grey, a little raw outside, like days in England.
> I remember — keep remembering the road from Ealing to Ripley — I used to go back and forth between terms, to school at Ripley Court, from Aunt Maud's.
> First: Brentford; dirty little brick houses: a gap in them, you see down a lane to the river where there is a grey stone monument the shape of a pillarbox commemorating a battle between Caesar and the Britons. A ferry, a rowboat, to Kew Gardens. (Once in Kew Gardens, you will look across the river to Sion House.) Then you cross Brentford Bridge to Kew. On the left, on the Brentford side, a theater. On the right, on the Kew side, a place to rent boats. A common.
> (Surrey: wide flat village greens criss-crossed with dirt paths — the grass drying and yellowing, clumps of gorse, a game of cricket. Along the common a line of low houses, one or two stories, brick, whitewashed, white and green. Behind: tall elms.)
> After the village, along the edge of Kew Gardens, right. Then, the Pagoda, the field where some rugby team or other played. Richmond coming: Richmond, crowded street, Southern Railway Station, signs — Bovril, Players Please, Every Morn I fill my Pipe — with St. Julian rich and ripe.
> In Richmond there is a store belonging to a Merton. I forget what — a grocer? a baker? a tailor? a butcher?
> Then, to Kingston. The King's Stone. Under the railway right by the station, bus ducks quickly under a bridge. Before Kingston, on one side a soccer field, on the other a factory, seeming closed, made some car Harvey Chrystal once had one of — *what* car (Torture!).
> Outside Kingston. The river on one side, on the other Waterworks or sewage disposal or something. Then, fork left under some trees, along a green, and under the railway — sign on the flat metal bridge advertises Stutz or Reo cars.
> Then out into Esher Common and

The Marquis of Granby.

> right, at a crossing. Very soon, Esher: on the right again, the racetrack — called what? The grandstand backed up against the wooded hill.We climb into Esher and stop at the crossing, where on the right are banks and on the left, I think,

The Bear.

> Out of Esher, then, at the top of the hill the road bears right, a garage I see very clearly but cannot describe and on the right the immaculate

whitewashed walls of either a nursing home or a girls school or a convent.

The road straight down a hill and straight up the other side. Woods both sides. At the top of the next hill, is, I think, a place with sandbanks and rocks . . . which I refer to in my practiced prep-school Latin ringing always in my head from having been learned by heart, the

Locus insidiis idoneus.
(place suitable for ambushes)

Thus on to Cobham, what with one thing and another, we come up a hill, on the left a big white house with I forget what to distinguish it, on the right, a common: gorse. Then, houses begin, and the Cobham cottage hospital, and downhill to the pub I clearly see before me with green lattice work over greyish stucco, and the laurels and the red and black sign for

Friary Ale

and it is, maybe the

Red Lion.

Turn right then sharp, and we pass a place where Tom Bennett and Iris and Hugo Anson and I had tea after being down to see his aunts at a town whose name I clearly remember but not just now, and it is over towards Aldershot, and maybe it is over in Hampshire and begins with a W.

Then we cross the river, and up the hill between high banks, and high over the road, a metal suspension footbridge joins the halves of the estate the road, in its deep cut, divides. At the top of the hill

Feltonfleet School.

to the right a road that leads, as the sign says, straight to the motor races at Brooklands.

Down the hill through the trees and rhododendrons on the left, at the bottom, the cricketfield where I made, batting for the second XI

32 not out.

(Soccer there, too. The prickly, woolen black-and-green striped jerseys for Ripley Court.)

Then on through the woods, pines, sandy ground, the road then sweeps down in a curve to

Hut Pond

smooth and glassy, black pines all around it. So on into Ripley. Ousie's house. The Anchor. Garages. The common. Left: the cottage. Ripley

Court. Just before the cottage: British Legion post. At night, sleeping in the cottage, in summer, waking up, hearing the British Legion singing

Old soldiers never die
They sim-ply fade a-way.[4]

Very little, in Merton's memory, seems to have simply faded away in the ten years. He went on, in the first month of the European war, to wonder what had happened to his schoolfellows at Ripley Court: Clifton-Mogg, the Steeles, Irving, Romanoff, Lansdowne, Yates, Marsden, Percy Major . . . How many of them were now in uniform and likely to be killed in any number of places "suitable for ambush"?

It was his lack of Latin that kept Tom at Ripley Court when he was otherwise old enough and bright enough to have started Public School. He caught up quickly, and went on to specialize in classics.

Holidays were spent with Aunt Maud and Uncle Ben in Ealing, or at "Fairlawn" in West Horsley, the home of Gwynedd Merton Trier, Owen's younger sister and Tom's Aunt Gwyn. Tom quickly established himself as a favorite with his cousins, who were a few years younger. He told the Trier boys long adventure stories and organized plays. The playwright usually wrote himself a part that required him to wear a rabbinical beard secured by elastic and to deliver long speeches, either in broken English, or perhaps his first made-up language.[5]

In the summer of 1928, Tom had been with his father at Rye and Canterbury and there were expeditions to Romney and Bodiam Castle, and even a short trip back to France to stay in a hotel in St. Malo.[6] As Tom was a boarder at Ripley Court, it was easy to keep Owen's collapse in 1929 from his son, though Tom came back once as the scorer with the school cricket team to play Durston House, and while the others were having tea ran home, to find his father in bed and hardly coherent.[7]

It was a relief to hear a few weeks later that his father was better and planned to accept an invitation from his friends the Haughtons to convalesce in Scotland, taking Tom with him in mid-August, 1929.

When the time came for the journey, however, Owen was hardly strong enough: he took to his bed as soon as they arrived in Scotland, then set off for London again, leaving his son behind. He asked Tom to pray for him.

Tom was alone in the house one day weeks later when the telephone rang. He had a good deal of difficulty understanding the Scottish operator, who insisted the telegram was for Thomas Merton from Owen Merton: "Entering New York harbor. All well."[8]

The details of the dark room where Tom sat after he had hung up, waiting for his hosts to return, even the smell of the chair he sat in, became as much a part of his associations with loss and desolation as the inside of the car outside Bellevue and the view at Fresh Pond Crematory. He knew his father was in hospital in London, and the impossible message could only mean Owen had lost his mind.

Tom stayed on at Williamstown, Insch, in Aberdeenshire, though the remainder of his visit appears to have been as disastrous as his stay with the Garlands at Bay End Farm, Buzzards Bay. In his one published novel, *My Argument with the Gestapo,* the Haughtons are transformed into the Frobishers, and their house is moved from Scotland to Yorkshire. A German pilot has jettisoned his bombs, scoring a direct hit on the tennis courts to Mrs. Frobisher's disgust: after all, the pilot had the vast expanse of moors in which to get rid of the bombs.[9]

In the novel, the main character, Thomas, meets Mrs. Frobisher in London, where she lectures him on having a purpose in life (that is, one others can understand) and loyalty. She questions his motives for coming back to England in the blitz: like most of those the returning Thomas meets, she suspects him of being a spy for the other side.

During that summer visit in 1929, the weather was bad and Tom caught a cold. He was taken to the local doctor, who had a longstanding feud with the family. The Haughtons were vegetarians, and the doctor got Tom to agree that he would not have caught cold if he had been able to eat meat. This was reported back to his host and hostess and was considered a betrayal.[10]

The other guests, two Haughton nieces, were interested only in horses. Both girls spent much of the day "mucking out" the stables and grooming, and Tom was expected to help them. The prize for all the hard work was a ride through driving rain during the afternoon. Tom soon earned another bad reputation: he was a "shirker," he only pretended to do the work, and, what was worse, he showed no enthusiasm for the reward.[11]

After a few uncertain days in the saddle, Tom spent the hours when it wasn't raining perched in an apple tree reading *The Three Musketeers* in French. He went on to read John Buchan's adventure novels, then Conan Doyle's.[12] Both Buchan and Conan Doyle were to be important, for quite different reasons.

In Buchan, the spy is a hero, chiefly because he is a gentleman by breeding and often takes up spying for sport. Like James Bond later on, the Buchan hero has a license to do all kinds of things the pedestrian citizen is forbidden to do by law. But while Bond is at any rate nominally working for, and in the service of, his country, the Buchan gentleman amateur and his friends seem to have odd loyalties only to a sort of secret club of the like-minded. With these "honorable" freebooters we are a long way from the wretched spy of the American Civil War, who was frequently despised by both sides, paid the pay of a private soldier, and shot or hung to general satisfaction when caught. If the spy becomes the hero of the twentieth century, this says a great deal about the century.

In Conan Doyle's novels Tom would have met the Cistercians for the first time. Merton's friend at Gethsemani, Father Augustine Wulff, maintains that Conan Doyle's novels were important in his own life in bringing him to the Trappists.[13] It may be too much to make a parallel here with Merton, but Tom would have read of St. Bernard of Clairvaux's white monks and in a sympathetic context.

The monks were the exception to those — musketeers, gentleman adventurers — who honored only the code of an in-group. They made still more of an exception to the lone operator, with his own complicated system of loyalties. The lone spy almost takes over adventure literature, and he can even be found in such unexpected places as Auden's early poetry. This is no place to try to unmask him in all his disguises, but the Thomas of *My Argument with the Gestapo* may well be one — he certainly has all the signs.[14] Among these are an acute form of alienation in an age in which alienation is already an obsession, and conflict over knowing whom to trust and to what to be loyal.

It is no accident that the lectures Merton receives from Mrs. Haughton in a fictional guise in *My Argument with the Gestapo* deal with loyalty.[15] Merton was to receive quite a few lectures on the subject, right up to 1968. In the summer of 1929, his hostess told him he was showing very poor team spirit. He was referred to two books which demonstrated the best kind of team spirit and a willingness to sacrifice oneself for others. Tom had already read Kipling's Mowgli stories. He knew all about the "law of the pack" (significantly, perhaps, a pack of wolves). Now he was introduced to Kingsley's *The Water Babies*. The second book was not very illuminating. But, like the Kipling books, like so much of what he read, there was a scrupulous, almost self-conscious way in which Christianity was introduced only by inference, while the loyalties expected and enforced had all the sanction of some unnamed religion. The cadences of Kipling are those of the King James Bible, even in *Stalky and Co.*, where the loyalties are those of schoolboys to one another and their code.

In the autumn of 1929 Merton went to Oakham, where he was to hear a great deal about team spirit, and where he was to have St. Paul's word for "charity" or "love" in First Corinthians 13 revised into "being a gentleman."

Merton is amusing about the school chaplain Buggy Jerwood's sermon, and here there is no exaggeration.[16] Although the Public School interpretation often took liberties with what St. Paul had actually said, it at least laid down a high standard of service to others, where the key to the concept was self-sacrifice. By the time Tom Merton arrived at a Public School the standard of self-sacrifice had been tested (and exploited) in the First World War: it continued to provide the better side of an ambiguous experiment, the rule over others in every part of the British Empire. Noblesse oblige, however noble, led inevitably to patronizing, or, as Merton would say in the 1960s, to a relationship that treated another human as "an incurable infant." The chief fault with the Public School interpretation is that it ties the message of the Gospels and the Pauline letters to the English class system. As every reader of *The Seven Storey Mountain* knows, by 1946 Merton saw the fault, not only in the Public Schools but in the Church of England.

By 1929 the Public School ideal had its critics. For good reasons, there was a risk that the whole "philosophy" would turn out to be another casualty of the First World War. It did not. It survived, damaged, as the English class system survived virtually undamaged. However, the reactions to the Public School code are even more interesting in the lives of later schoolboys than its acceptance by the earlier ones. The late awakening of a social conscience in the 1930s made many of the gentlemen truer and more troubled Christians. Some took their bad consciences and their ideal of self-sacrifice to the Socialist Party or to the Communist International. Not one of them forgot that he had been trained to be a gentleman. The unfortunate side of this was a bashful or blatant sense of superiority: the valuable thing about it was a commitment to service above self — once one had decided the ambiguities of loyalty.

＊

Oakham was Dr. Pearce's idea. Somewhat surprisingly, Merton wrote several pages in 1939 or 1940 about the pecking order of various English Public Schools, ending with "Oakham was in another class: the nice little schools in the country no one had ever heard of."[17] Elsewhere, he speculates in 1941 whether, if he had stayed in England, he would have been a master at Eton, somewhat nervous of snobbery directed at his "O.O. [Old Oakhamian] tie."[18]

Oakham's fees were small by comparison with those of Eton or Harrow, but they were well beyond the resources of an ailing painter. Once more, Sam Jenkins paid them. He made plain the fact that he would rather Tom were in an American school like John Paul. By this time, Owen was altogether beyond argument, and the old tussle went on between the Jenkins family and the Triers and Pearces, with Harold Jenkins taking a more active part.

By the end of 1929 the whole world was reeling from the collapse of the New York Stock Exchange. Sam Jenkins was better off than most. In the Depression, the movies and everything to do with them flourished. Considering that the world had proved an even more chancy place than he had expected, Sam began taking financial advice on how

to set up trusts so that his grandsons would be as financially independent as he could make them.

In September 1929, Aunt Maud helped Tom to pack and saw him off
at King's Cross station for his first term. He changed at Peterborough
and took the slow, local train. Reaching the station of the market town,
he still had the length of the main street to go before he arrived at the
group of gray buildings behind the ancient Butter Cross in Market Place,
the center of the school and Merton's "house," School House.

There was then some local pride in being in the smallest county in
England, Rutland (now amalgamated into Leicestershire). In 1584
Archbishop Robert Johnson had founded "as many free schools in Rutland as there were market towns therein," the money for Oakham and
Uppingham coming chiefly from the suppressed monasteries. Some of
the buildings at Oakham, including the school sanatorium, had been
monastic property. The school had ceased to be "free." It struggled
for its existence at the turn of the century and was made a Direct Grant
School in 1926. It was reviving in 1929, when it had about two hundred
students.[19]

On the whole, Tom seems to have been happy at Oakham, and if he
quickly outgrew it, he would have done much the same at most other
schools. He had had the advantage of being in a small school with a
vigorous new headmaster. He was no rebel in the first year. Like a
pledge in an American fraternity or a plebe at West Point, he was at
the beck and call of upperclassmen, who had studies on the ground
floor of School House facing the courtyard. Tom himself was in a dormitory among the least at the top of Hodge Wing. He was good at
adaptation: he noted the schoolboy rules that differed from Ripley Court.
He discovered that if he worked hard enough he would be able to move
out of the common-room and share a study by his second year. He
decided that it would help to volunteer for boxing, but that nothing
was to be gained by showing enthusiasm for the Army training program, the School Corps (O.T.C.). He went out on maneuvers with a
book in his pocket. While he was doing far more work than his school
assignments, he was careful to keep this to himself.

Toward the end of the first long summer term in 1930, the Jenkins
family and John Paul arrived to stay at the Crown Inn in High Street.
The main event of the visit was a talk between Sam Jenkins and his
older grandson. For this, as if to make some point in his own way,
Sam Jenkins set aside his dislike of smoking, presented the fifteen-year-
old Tom with a pipe, and encouraged him to smoke it as they went
over business papers.[20]

Whatever Tom understood through clouds of "St. Julian rich and ripe,"
he left the interview with a sense that his life had been transformed,
that Pop had worked a money miracle and found some way to give

John Paul and him a measure of financial independence in a world where this had come to make an even greater difference. Pop's impresario gestures, which had been merely embarrassments before, had unexpectedly worked to conjure up a reality. The figures must have looked enormous and unspendable to Tom at fifteen. There was stock in Grosset and Dunlap. More wonderful, there were pieces of land: building lots on Long Island and in Coral Gables, Florida. When he found himself joint owner with John Paul of an island (Stone Island, off Machiasport, Maine), an entirely new dimension was added to geography.[21]

The interview had another important consequence, given little emphasis in the autobiography: it shifted Tom's English base. Considering the feud with Owen's relatives, one can understand why Sam Jenkins chose to work with Dr. Tom Izod Bennett, Owen's friend and Tom's godfather. He, not Uncle Ben, would manage Tom Merton's allowance until he reached twenty-one. The Bennetts' flat at 2 Mandeville Place would also be more convenient for visiting his father at the Middlesex Hospital, where Owen was a patient of Bennett's. As for holidays, Sam, an inveterate traveler himself, suggested that Tom use some of his new income to visit the Continent and improve his languages. Every second summer he could come over to America.

Frustrated for years by his daughter and son-in-law, Sam Jenkins may have seen at last the chance to be generous and to look generous. So he seemed to offer his grandson the world and the means to become a man of the world. But the model of the man of the world Tom Merton would choose would not be Sam Jenkins, but Tom Bennett. For the present, Tom moved away from Aunt Maud and Aunt Maud's England.

✻

Everything was pulling Tom to the center of London. It was not only more convenient for the visits to his father, but the record shops were there, the book shops, the cinemas where the newest films, and the foreign films, were shown. The greatest attraction of all was life at the Bennetts' flat. This put in a single "suburban" shade 50 Virginia Road, Douglaston, New York, and both "Fairlawn" and 18 Carlton Road, Ealing. No secret is made of its glamor in *The Seven Storey Mountain,* and no contrast could have been greater to the monastery where the autobiography was written. Years of enjoying stylish comedies at the movies had prepared the schoolboy, who could make his own contrast with the dormitories at Oakham.

The Bennetts' flat was *smart.* His godfather had style, his godfather's French wife[22] had style, the notepaper gave Tom's letters style, the very hallway to the building and the elevator you had to start by pulling a rope shared that style. Even when Merton had outgrown all

he recalled every detail.[23] No maid had brought him breakfast in
bed on earlier school holidays. The newest books had not arrived from
the Times Bookshop in Wigmore Street in brand-new book jackets (quite
different entities from the books of lending libraries). Original French
paintings had not shared the walls with his father's paintings in Ealing
or Douglaston. And with all this, his polite, altruistic doctor-godfather
was surely a gentleman of gentlemen according to the pattern of the
school sermon.

At the Bennetts' his taste was gently reproved and corrected — he
was told that the *Bolero* by Ravel was not a good piece of music,[24] and
he suppressed for some years his delight in Pop's record of "The Whistler and his Dog," which was certainly not good music.[25] He discovered that perhaps the most effective criticism of all is a light superior
mockery, the urbane and gentle murder of pretense and genius alike.

After the first of the new holidays there was more than a little, by
way of imitation, of Dr. Tom Izod Bennett in the Merton T. F. who returned reluctantly to Oakham from London's West End. Tom Bennett
was to remain part of him for some years, until, in a sense, the original
cast out the imitator, a rejection that was to be as painful to Tom as his
first by his mother — and, as Merton said later: "I don't take sweetly
to rejection."[26]

In late 1930 all this was ahead. There was the impression that at the
Bennetts' he could do no real wrong, only make minor mistakes of taste.
His life began to move between a sense of institutional dreariness and
the brightness of a new beginning, new ideas, intellectual force-feed-
ing, the discovery of his own powers of mind, his own energy.

In both his school hours and the holidays, however, there was a nagging sadness, which had to be hidden from others, and which had a
certain dramatic quality to it. He had always been "hooked on" movies. The fan worship of the Jenkins family ensured this. Tom and John
Paul had watched movies being made at the Bayside Studios, and his
grandfather sent film magazines and books to him at Oakham. He was
on the inside of all the mysteries. Now, he began to use movies as a
drug.

During the first days of the Christmas holidays in December 1930,
having been kept from movies at Oakham, Tom went to as many films
as he could crowd into a day. One movie, *War Nurse,* he saw through
four times and came out feeling very groggy, with a new passion for
Anita Page and a fascination for girls in nurses' uniforms. A few days
later, he saw *Hell's Angels.* He was infatuated with Joan and Constance
Bennett, Greta Garbo — "whom I would have loved much more if her
directors had only put her in ordinary clothes. I couldn't stand cos-
tume pictures" — and Madeleine Carroll.[27]

His allowance made it possible to pay for tickets at the first-run movie theaters, and to spend hours at Levy's record shop in Regent Street listening to Duke Ellington, Louis Armstrong, or the Hot Club de France and coming out with several new records for his growing collection. Meanwhile, even in the West End, the signs about him told him that the Depression was getting worse. By the winter of 1930 there were old soldiers everywhere. They stood at the edge of the sidewalk selling matches, pencils, shoelaces. They looked as if they had been carved out of pumice. Even their medal ribbons had been washed almost colorless in the rain. So had their cardboard signs, whose letters, when they could still be read, spelt out messages beyond bitterness: "I survived Haig's Great Push, and came back to 'Homes Fit for Heroes.' "

In all this Tom registered the first symptoms of what he saw in time as a terrible sickness. It ate away at the earlier vision of England. Sometimes the career of that disease seemed to run parallel in his mind to the hardly known thing that was wasting and killing his father.

Once when Tom visited Owen, his father was sitting up in bed drawing subjects Tom couldn't recognize. Earlier, Owen had drawn landscapes they both remembered, and Tom was able to comment on these. That day there were outlines and profiles of oddly bearded old men Owen said were Byzantine saints.[28] He may have been going back in his mind to the frescoes and mosaics in the churches in Rome he and Ruth had discovered the year they were in Italy before their marriage. Owen's memories were no longer of the times he had shared with Tom.

It may have been as much to get Tom away from such scenes as to further his studies in modern languages toward a career in the Diplomatic Corps that made the Bennetts send him to stay with a friend of the Weiss family, Professor Hering, in Strasbourg at the end of 1930. While Tom was away, Owen's friend Alan Burroughs called at the Middlesex Hospital, to be shown incomprehensible squiggles on Owen's drawing pad, which Owen claimed were a new style. He then wanted Burroughs to trim his mustache, although he no longer had one.[29]

Tom's memories of his first trip on his own were chiefly of Professor Hering's red beard and (at least in 1946) the fact that the professor was "one of the few Protestants I have ever met who struck one as being at all holy";[30] then of Josephine Baker singing *"J'ai deux amours, mon pays et Paris."* A year later, after a second visit, he informed the readers of the school magazine, *The Oakhamian,* that "The glory of Strasbourg Cathedral saved Goethe from the mire of decadent classicism into which he had fallen at Leipzig."[31]

Be that as it may, the expedition in 1930 must have taken his mind off many things. A week after Tom's return to school, on January 18, 1931, Owen Merton died at Middlesex Hospital. On the 20th, eleven days before his sixteenth birthday, Tom was writing to Mr. and Mrs. Tudor-Hart from 2 Mandeville Place, thanking them for attending his father's funeral that morning.[32] Owen had been cremated at Golders Green Crematorium in North London.

On October 4, 1931, Evelyn Scott wrote to Lola Ridge: "Did I tell you that Merton died in June [sic]? He left Cyril 40 paintings . . . Poor Merton. All the purity that fumbled and compromised in life remained true in his work and I wish he had lived to reap the reward I think someone will have from it."[33]

*

His first year over, Tom plunged into everything with equal energy, reading so much that by February the matron of School House, Miss Harrison, had to take him to Stamford to be seen by an oculist and fitted with reading glasses.[34] In a school with two hundred boarders and thirty day boys Merton was certain to stand out early, but he was fortunate in having a headmaster who recognized his talent from the beginning and pushed him ahead. F. C. Doherty had arrived that same autumn term in 1929, succeeding W. L. Sargant, who had done much to build the school up and increase its academic reputation, but with conventional methods. Doherty was young, a fine scholar, and he was open-minded. He encouraged the unconventional in his masters. It must have been something of a record in 1930 for the English master, A. F. Scott, to introduce his students to the work of T. S. Eliot and other modernists. Doherty also hired an arts master, and Tom took drawing lessons, as well as music, in the old school building which went back to Johnson's original foundation.[35]

It was probably Doherty who saw that Merton would have trouble with the mathematics questions in the School Certificate and who steered him round the examination to start preparing at once for the Higher Certificate, which was more difficult, but where Merton could declare a specialization. Merton's first choice would have been modern languages. This was not offered at Oakham then, but Doherty improvised: Merton would officially take classics (Latin and Greek), studying French, German, and Italian on his own, coached by the headmaster. If Merton passed the Higher Certificate examination he would be allowed to sit for a scholarship examination to Oxford or Cambridge in the winter of 1932. The incentive was attractive: if Merton won the scholarship the first time he tried, he would leave Oakham after the Christmas term in 1932, with something like ten months' freedom ahead of him before he went to the university. Meanwhile, Doherty moved Merton T. F. rapidly up the school,[36] so that he was in the equivalent of the sixth form from the middle of his second year — an almost unheard-of ascent. Somehow Merton managed this without being thought "a brain"; he was also careful to hide any emotions about his father's death. He now shared a study with Bill Hemmings in Hodge Wing of School House.[37] Hemmings had to go home for an operation in the early spring of 1931, so Merton had a room of his own when he most needed it, for study and for himself. Outside those hours, he was a leader in group activities: there was already a very public and a very private side to him.

In the early months of 1931 the weather turned cold and the students went tobogganing on Brooke Road and skating on Burley Fish Ponds. Later, with Wally Black, Attewell, and Duff, Tom set off for spying operations at Catmose House, which was assumed to be out of bounds: "If we weren't spies, we were Bulldog Drummond. If we weren't Bulldog Drummond, we were Stalky and Co."[38]

Much more daring, where girls were certainly out of bounds, was inviting the gardener's daughter from Catmose House, a girl who worked in the stationery shop near Hodge Wing, to come out with Doug Highton and himself. The two boys carried Tom's phonograph and records to the meeting place, but apart from the heady risk of being caught, it was a dull date: Merton wandered off, leaving Highton to entertain the girl and bring the phonograph back.[39] Reality had proved a far cry from time out of war in the movies with Anita Page.

At Easter, Merton set off again on his own, this time for Rome and Florence, both of which disappointed his expectations. In Rome he stayed near the Piazza Quattro Fontane and spent hours in the Colosseum, or wandering about the Forum or the slopes of the Palatine, trying to imagine the orgies of Tiberius, reading Ovid, or Cicero's *Pro Milone* and finding that his fantasy was being fed more strongly by Cecil B. De Mille than his reading. Some years later he decided that "the trouble with Cecil B. De Mille's visions of ancient Rome was not that they were false but that they were probably too true."[40] In 1931 he returned to Oakham wondering why Classical and Renaissance Italy had had so little effect on him, but he brought back a photograph of Venus Anadyomene to replace Clara Bow on his study walls.

In May, when he was studying for the Higher Certificate, he set off one morning, one pocket of his jacket containing Vergil's *Georgics*, the other Tacitus. He practiced walking as silently as Indians in the forests of North America, who presumably went less burdened.[41]

Finding a place close to a stream that was sheltered by a fallen aspen still in full foliage, Tom set up temporary camp. He watched the birds (he wasn't sure of their names, though he had known so many birds' names at two) soaring up from the wheat field that was no longer green but almost silver with poppies brilliant points of red here and there in the whole. The earth was giving off different scents which had something to do with the rain the day before and the morning mist:

I remember that, as I finally started up the hill, along the edge of the wheatfield, to get back on the Stamford road, I had barely gone a hundred yards before I realised, confusedly, that that had been one of the most beautiful places I had ever seen. So I went back down the slope to look at it all again, and take it all into my eyes, so that I would never forget it.

That was because I knew that when you had seen a place once, you would never see it exactly like that again; the light would be different, and the air and sky and shadows and colors would be different, and living things would have grown into different shapes, and many old things would have perished and disappeared while new things would have grown into their places.

And when I got back, after just a couple of minutes, it was already different. But a long time afterwards I found out that while all these scenes you can look at, and remember photographically, change and perish, the thing these fields and trees, that light and that air and that water showed to me was a rightness that you recognized often afterwards, in strange places: in reading a book, in hearing a song, in seeing a movement in a dance, and not the least of all in churches.[42]

The insight of this passage is the insight of only a decade later, and if it uses the material of 1931, it plays a light back upon it in a way that has relevance to the way Merton wrote of places (and remembered places) in the 1960s. It is essentially a Merton insight, or a Mertonian one, just as certain passages in the writing of Marcel Proust display an essentially "Proustian" vision.

Meanwhile, the place by the stream had given everything it was going to give him. Now, when he wanted to be alone, Tom climbed Brooke Hill.[43] Here he could watch the changes of light across the hills, or the changes in the sky. Sometimes he tried to read there, but at other times he found even the *Georgics,* however perfectly Vergil's poem seemed to suit that landscape, came between him and what he felt should be a holiday. Occasionally he drew for an hour or so. Sometimes he sang at the top of his voice, where there was nobody "to laugh or be sarcastic about it."[44] Most of the time he simply sat there and thought.

He thought about his reading: Blake, Shelley, Shakespeare — or Petrarch, whose work he was trying to read in Italian. Often he thought "about the things I wanted to be, and wanted to do."

Nobody ever said anything to me about it but it was rather unusual for one to go for walks alone, and I must have had the reputation of rather a solitary fellow, especially for the first half of my seventeenth year.[45]

To John Barber, who remembers Merton at Oakham, he seemed always to be in "the thick of things."[46] His times by himself were probably secret in both senses.

Canigou was simply a shape somewhere in his memory, the idea of a mountain or high place. The Calvaire had been somewhere to scramble up, until he could reorient his world from the summit. He had no need of a withdrawing place at St. Antonin. The need was there in Montauban, where there was no such place. Brooke Hill was different. The view of the world below meant less to him than on The Calvaire. He had already established the geography of Oakham and its surroundings. In the overview, it did not mean so much to Merton that Oakham is just as centered upon the town church, All Saints, with its spire of almost cathedral-like importance, as St. Antonin is about its church.

✻

By the end of that school year Tom had been appointed editor of *The Oakhamian* for the next year. He had won English prizes, and he had done well at boxing (until he was defeated by a much bigger boy from Rossall at the cadet camp with the O.T.C.).[47] He would be playing rugby for the school when the Christmas term began. In the meanwhile, he was off to America, buying his ticket with his own money. It was enough to turn the head of anyone at sixteen.

His head was turned very smartly on the *Minnetonka* on the trip over. He had been smoking his Craven A cigarettes — or perhaps the pipe his grandfather had given him — one day on deck when he was introduced by a Catholic priest from Cleveland to a party of ladies, a young woman and her two aunts. In one of his accounts, Merton includes a name, Norma Wakefield, almost certainly her real name, not a coded or fictional one. She was trying to look younger as he was trying to look older. She was also married, and she was on her way to Australia via New York.[48]

Merton mentions one kiss. In New York Narrows he made a declaration of his love. His companion was flattered, but firm. That was all — apart from the agony.

Tom was careful to note in the New York newspapers the next day that a man on one of the liners in New York harbor had committed suicide on the night he was gently turned down. What was then a depressing mental note became in time the first of a number of carefully placed references to suicide in *The Seven Storey Mountain*.[49]

Tom arrived in New York hurt and brooding. No efforts on the part of the Jenkins family could win him away from his thoughts. They rushed him off on a tour of New York, all to no avail. Even in Douglaston he refused to settle down, and he nursed his grief much of the summer.

His grandfather disliked drunks, rich or poor. On September 12, when the party saw Tom off for England, again on the *Minnetonka*, they watched a rich drunk go abroad. He was obviously a well-known figure in the social world, and he exchanged alcoholic sallies with a party of press photographers who turned out to interview him. Sam Jenkins, having thought the photographers were local Long Island pressmen who would be interested in his family and the news that his grandson, Thomas Merton, was sailing to continue a successful career at an English school, was both outraged and mortified.[50]

The drunk made a different impression on Tom. He became the model for Terence Park in Merton's unpublished novel "The Labyrinth," where Park's companion, Sidney Despatch, is both a gangster and a Communist. He, too, probably had some original on the ship. There were no romances on this crossing: Tom may have decided he was a misogynist, at least for the time being. He lent his copy of Faulkner's new and already notorious novel to the now sober playboy and to other passengers. When questioned, he had to admit that he couldn't figure out what was going on in *Sanctuary* either.

Oakham must have seemed tame after such a summer, and Tom set about making the place more interesting. An unlikely political figure arrived for an international conference in London that autumn, dressed in what looked like a sheet and wearing sandals and a pair of granny glasses. The *Daily Express* and other newspapers made him an uncomplicated figure of fun, and he was a gift to cartoonists on Right Wing journals. Even the *Times* found it difficult to restrain a gentlemanly smirk. It appeared the man had some following and was serious in asking for Home Rule for India, threatening non-violent action and non-cooperation.

Merton was to have a good deal to do with Gandhi's ideas. For the moment, in a debate he defended the right of the Indians to rule their own country against the captain of the school's rugby team and head prefect.[51] But Merton was always arguing, in and out of the school's Debating Society, and neither he nor Gandhi was taken very seriously. Financially wounded, the British Empire was still "the Red on the Map," and something like a quarter of the earth's surface was under British control. If Merton was training for the British Diplomatic Service, he had rather extraordinary ideas, either American or Continental — it was hard to tell which. It was hard, too, to know where he would stand on any given question. He seemed to take a Conservative position on some, a wildly Left Wing stand on others. At the meetings of the Debating Society he had a penchant for choosing the losing side. On October 3, 1930, the debate was "That this House Approves of the National Government." C. A. P. (Andrew) Winser made the case for the Conservatives and "T. F. Merton adopted the Socialist point of view, mentioning the panacea of nationalism,"[52] his side losing by six votes to thirty-eight. The next school year, the debates were on facetious subjects. When Merton spoke his side went down.

Merton's contributions, as editor, to *The Oakhamian* were a mixed lot, both in medium and quality. One of his cartoons is an attempt to show a Roman bas-relief with Romans playing rugby, another shows the ghost of a Roman poet against the background of the courtyard at School House. His poems are doggerel or sentimental. Merton found his first censor when he wrote an overenthusiastic piece on New York City. His uncritical relish for the vulgarity and vitality of the city was pruned considerably by the master who supervised the student editor, and it was the master who gave the piece its title, "The City Without a Soul."[53] There may have been a battle over this, and there are times later on when Merton writes as if he were consciously getting his own back at English masters who cut out his slang and changed his sentences to show more correctness of syntax and less life.

One pastiche of schoolboy adventure stories stands out from the other work. "The New Boy Who Won Through. Chapter V: Revenge!" is vintage Merton.[54] With its humor and zest for burlesque, this could have appeared five years later in the Columbia University *Jester*. It alone shows real promise. But even if it is by no means as well written, it is "Wählt Hitler: An echo of the German Presidential elections, April, 1932" that makes the more interesting reading.

As he says in the autobiography, he was a hundred years too late to be wandering the Rhineland during the Easter holiday of 1932 reading Spinoza. Much later, the German mystics of the region would move him. But the Rhineland had other concerns than either Spinoza or Meister Eckhart that particular April, when Hitler, Hindenburg, and the Communist Thälmann were contesting a vital election.

For Tom, things started out cheerfully, though he got lost several times. His rucksack, containing the *Ethics*, novels by D. H. Lawrence, and his own journals, proved heavy. Approaching Andernach, he was limping with a sore toe, yet he strode along, singing "If you don't know Minnie, Don't know Minnie, She's tall and skinny . . ." then breaking off to smoke a pipeful of aromatic Dutch tobacco.[55] All this was interrupted by an oncoming car.

"Wählt Hitler" is written in facetious schoolboy style, and it is interesting to compare it with the account of the same incident Merton wrote in 1968.[56] Jocular as the early essay tries to be, the darker notes come in:

> With election day, excitement reached its climax. Even in the most prim-
> itive villages some Hitlerite was stunned with a brick, or some Hinden-
> burger half slain with a pitchfork. A certain traveller, moreover, was
> wending his way along a lonely country roadway on that all memorable
> Sunday, and suddenly beheld a car, loaded with screaming youths, bear-
> ing down upon him: Leaping into the ditch, prepared to lose his life and
> his purse, he realised, with dazed relief, that the car had vanished in a

cloud of dust and yellow handbills, and that their message was: "Wählt Hitler."[57]

There was still a certain political innocence among English school-boys and university students early in 1932. A year later, there would be Communist cells at each of the two oldest universities. In 1936 the country — including the Public Schools — would be split by the Span-ish Civil War in much the same way that America was later divided by the Vietnam War.

That spring at Oakham someone who had seen Hitler's supporters in action and had talked to people on the transatlantic liners who claimed to be Communists was bound to be thought an exotic. For the time being, Tom Merton was more amused than committed. His motive in leaving the *Communist Manifesto* open on top of his desk in his study was simply to shock.

By the time he returned to Oakham after the holiday the infected toe had developed into blood poisoning serious enough to produce delir-ium. After the initial fright, his days in the sanatorium were pleasant enough, though the sense of physical vulnerability did not go away. For someone with Tom's temperament, the idea that he had almost died at barely seventeen worked its own spell, and he may have been re-minded of the graves of the English poets, Keats and Shelley, in the Protestant cemetery he had visited the year before in Rome. Stronger still was the feeling that if he were going to accomplish all he had planned on Brooke Hill, especially in love, he would have to hurry. Yet he was trapped in a small school, buried in the country except for the holidays:

> Therefore, I was not really content at Oakham at all, but only wanted to get my scholarship to Cambridge and get away. And what I would do then, was go looking for a girl and this happiness. And the way to find a fine girl was to go where fine girls were: and as I knew from movies and novels, the really pretty girls, the gay and witty and graceful ones who dressed well and were really beautiful, were in theaters and night-clubs and big dances. And at Clubs and Hotels on the Riviera, and in the cities and everywhere where life was itself fine and gay and beautiful and full of light and richness and gaiety. Because fine things all go to-gether, and if I went where there were beautiful things like newly deco-rated modernistic bars, and places where there was good music, there I would find beautiful women.[58]

He covered the bed with books and papers. He was in the middle of writing one long paper on the state of modern literature that gave a major place to his current favorite among writers, John Dos Passos, and another paper on interpretations of history.[59] He was trying to im-prove his Italian by reading Petrarch. He was correcting proof on copy for the school magazine. On top of this, his headmaster had lent him a volume of poems by Gerard Manley Hopkins.

When he discovered these were religious, he suspected Doherty was slyly reproving him after their arguments over the proofs for the existence of God, in much the same way the music master was lending him classical records to protest Merton's taste for jazz.

There was no escaping the fact that Hopkins was a great poet. What worried Tom most about him was that he was not only a Roman Catholic and a convert, but he was a Jesuit priest. He thought back to the Jesuit school in Montauban, the coldness he had always felt in passing the building. He remembered that the schoolboys at the Lycée whom he knew to be from Catholic families had been the ones who had been most frightened, and had frightened him, when they saw Jesuit priests walking the streets in Montauban.[60] That a poet could also be a Jesuit went on puzzling Tom even after he returned the book, well read, to the headmaster.

Out of the "San.," Tom worked hard in his study in Hodge Wing and played Duke Ellington records on the portable phonograph loud enough to convince others he never worked, as well as to block out any other sound.

In the summer he sat for the Higher Certificate examination and knew he had passed. This was the year for another Jenkins invasion. A certain routine had been established: the family brought John Paul over to Europe in even years, in odd years Tom went to America.

Tom was just as morose as he had been the summer before. This time the girl's name was Diane and his summer was made miserable by the thought of missing one of her letters. (By the autumn it was all over and he burned her letters in the fireplace in the prefects' common room at Oakham.)[61]

In the mood Tom was in that August he found the Savoy Hotel, perched on the cliffs at Bournemouth, a melancholy place. He spent time staring from the ornate balconies at the English Channel, and during meals tried to imagine what the place would look like in winter, when the dining room would be empty and the chairs stacked, an image he used later in a poem.[62]

Tom was freer when he was on his own again, walking through the New Forest, camping among the ruins of some ancient monastic building. But the weather ruined his camp. He went to stay with Andrew Winser, his erstwhile opponent in debate, at the family home, the "quiet rectory at Brooke" on the Isle of Wight.

❋

Brooke and Brooke Hill . . . St. Anne's (Soho), Anne Winser, St. Anne, and many later Anns or Annes . . . there is a compound coincidence in the way the names come together and play off one another, and, as a friend of Merton's was to say later, "He was a very coincidental kind of man."[63]

This was the summer for all sorts of coincidences. Waiting with the Winsers to go to a movie, Tom saw an attractive brown-haired girl he remembered from the other end of the British Isles. He had met her in the final days of the stay two years before in Aberdeenshire. At the time there had been a chance for only a brief talk — and that was about movies. She remembered, too, and through her (Merton calls her "B.") he and the Winsers were invited to a fancy-dress party. At the party, Tom thought he had lost the girl with brown hair to his friend Andrew. Then, at the end of the evening, Tom found B. alone and asked her to dance.[64]

Neither B. nor Andrew's younger sister appears in the autobiography, yet both are mentioned in *My Argument with the Gestapo*. There, the author's memory becomes wholly fused with that of the character, Thomas, who admits that Anne Winser, at twelve or thirteen, was too young for him. She was not so young that he forgot, however, and Anne was to recur as a sentimental name again and again. In 1965, Merton went back in his journal to say, as he had said twenty-four years earlier, that Anne Winser was too young, but that if things had been different, he might have married her; yet he ends with "I hardly remember even thinking of her" — a strange remark in that late context.[65] The portrait of B. in the 1941 novel is more complex, and if she is the girl he talked to for so long when he was disguised as a self-conscious gaucho at the fancy-dress party on the Isle of Wight in September 1932, she is probably also other girls Merton knew much later in New York.

With Brooke and Brooke Hill come associations with a poet Merton affected to despise, like most of that postwar generation.[66] There were complications in the life of Rupert Brooke that bear a resemblance to those of Merton's early years, and are not just linked in a spell of names. That summer, the girls in Tom's life came in pairs: an older girl to spar with in conversation and even to argue with, and a younger girl who was flattered by his attention, who roused some sentimental feeling in him, if not the full, agonizing force of love.

The girl who stood no nonsense from him and the girl who was younger and admired him for all his nonsense were figures from Rupert Brooke's life as well. But perhaps it is the common tendency of all romantics to find no middle ground between those they idealize and those who idealize them. For Merton in 1932, the real idols were beyond B. and Anne and Diane. The truly exciting and stylish women remained on the Riviera, or crossed back and forth on the great liners, or were in the movies. In 1965, the paired names from his past that remained most evocative for Merton were Anne Winser and Jinny Burton. Jinny had succeeded to B.'s place as someone he admired "with a love of companionship."[67]

*

By the Christmas term of 1932, all Tom's goals at Oakham but one had been achieved. He was now a prefect and one of the better players on the Oakham First XV.[68] The other two "Modern" candidates for scholarship examinations were the scientist, Ray Dickens, and the historian, Andrew Winser. In the school library the three would pass food back and forth, drink a concoction called Vimto, argue passionately about Victor Hugo and Corneille (whether *Hernani* or *Horace* was the more ridiculous play), and keep watch for Tick, the science master, or Bentham, who stoked the Oakham furnaces. (Bentham had lost one eye in the war, but the sight of the other was keen.)[69]

Tom read books few others had heard of, smoked a pipe, wore a navy blue turtleneck sweater, told the headmaster he didn't care for Plato, kept his lips tight shut when others prayed in chapel. In his study the volume had gone up, and the records were more often hot jazz and boogie-woogie than swing.[70]

The reputation Tom Merton made in the last year long outlasted his stay. In March 1942, the Bishop of Nottingham was asked to approach the newly appointed headmaster of Oakham for a letter of character. Mr. Griffith began by saying that he has to rely on the opinions of others, then goes on to report "a weird story of his being associated with some kind of travelling show or circus" after leaving school. He found firmer ground in "He is something of a legendary figure among the old boys of his generation and he was clearly something of a rebel."[71] On the whole it is a pity that Merton probably never saw the letter from his old school.

The chief excitement of that autumn term was the trip to Cambridge in December to take the scholarship examination. Clare College had established a connection with the tiny county of Rutland. Tom competed for a scholarship called the Johnson Exhibition, which was named for the founder of Uppingham and Oakham and open only to students of the two schools.[72]

The approach to Cambridge from the top of a bus was rather dampening to Tom's spirits and those of his companions, Dickens and Winser. The shops in Trinity Street proved more cheerful. Tom bought some Players Number 3 Virginias and a bottle of Harvey's Shooting Sherry for his room in Clare New Court, as well as a copy of Dante's *Divine Comedy* at Bowes and Bowes. The sherry was saved until after the exam. Meanwhile, the three of them went off to build up their courage on beer at the Lion.

I do not remember much about the exams: they did not seem hard, but how could you ever tell how well you had done in them?[73]

Between questions, Tom stared up at the high rafters in the Great Hall at Trinity and looked at the portraits of politicians, academics, and divines, or caught the eye of someone else staring about the room. Each would grin sympathetically and pretend to mop his brow. Tom finished one paper with a flourish, quoting Eliot's "Not with a bang but a whimper." Someone had carved *"Mene, Mene, Tekel, Upharsin"* on the desk Tom was using,[74] but he hardly thought it a warning that needed heeding.

During the Christmas vacation, he learned from the *Times* that he had won the Johnson Exhibition to Clare. He would "go up" in October 1933. Until then he was free of the rule of bells. Tom Bennett gave an eighteenth-birthday party for him at the Café Anglais, and his godfather and guardian presented him with a magnificent leather wallet, bought from Finlays in Bond Street.[75] This contained tickets and money for a trip. On the first of February in the year 1933, Merton was off to enjoy himself.

Almost everything went as he had hoped on the way to Rome, except for an attack of boils, a cold, and problems with money. The money should not have run out so early.

On his walking tour from Marseilles to Genoa, he had to waste two unexpected days at Hyères while he waited for extra funds from Bennett in London. The funds came, but so did a letter from his godfather reminding him that a certain sum had been agreed on for the trip. Tom made two painful discoveries at once: there was no blank check to be drawn on his financial resources, and what was worse, there was no blank check to be drawn on the goodwill and indulgence of the Bennetts. Receiving a reproof from Pop for moping about and pretending he was in love was one thing. The devastating, crisp politeness of a typed letter from Tom Bennett pointing out in numbered order the times over the past year when he had failed to come up to a standard of conduct, which, if it was unstressed, was the only code for a gentleman to follow — this was another thing altogether.[76]

Yet one thing had been confirmed. Setting off on foot from Marseilles for Cassis with his rucksack and his flask of rum, he had been passed by a Hispano-Suiza. One of the three people in the car turned back to look at him. He had been quite right, the really beautiful women were on the Riviera.[77]

※

Rome two years before had been a disappointment. If the second visit was to be one of the most important and "turning" events in Merton's early life, it began badly, with a toothache and a visit to an incompetent dentist, then much the same tourist round as Merton remembered from Easter 1931. Some days later, he discovered his own Rome. Then, and forever after, he set this higher than the Rome of anyone else.

Thomas Merton's Rome is the Rome that Edmund Gibbon, the great historian and greater writer, placed lower than any: Early Christian Rome, though in a draft for his autobiography Merton added, "if they can get to the Rome of the martyrs through all the irrelevance of the Renaissance finery and modern Fascist pseudo-efficiency."[78]

He began at the church of Sts. Cosmas and Damian, then sought out Santa Maria Maggiore, Santa Sabina, the Lateran, Santa Costanza, Santa Pudenziana, and many others. To understand what was depicted in the mosaics, Tom found he needed a Bible more frequently than his second-hand Baedeker in French. Because he was so often in churches, he began to pray.

Or rather, he tried. It had not made him feel anything but exultant to stand with his lips pressed together while others prayed around him in Oakham Chapel.[79] There, there had been no imagined Tom Merton, who watched and sneered.

(Long after, Merton was to warn the novices he taught about thinking of themselves looking down upon themselves as they prayed, letting "Here's me praying" get in the way of their prayers. This was surely not a common bar to effective recollection and to prayer? In some cases he may even have unwittingly brought in a difficulty where none existed before for the novice.)

In Rome, if Tom tried to forget the watcher inside himself, he was also unusually concerned about the reaction of others. It had never worried him before that he looked like what he was, a tourist. He could take the insults of bicyclists on the road with a good deal of humor. He could even be funny about being pushed into the ditch by a carload of Nazi rowdies. Here he found himself in an anxiety that bordered on panic: "It took daring."[80] What were the rules? Did they allow someone to come into a Catholic church from the streets, someone with "Protestant tourist" written all over him, someone who bowed down to pray in their church? He felt that every gesture made, every gesture *not* made gave him further away.[81] He was not conspicuous when looking at a guidebook or staring at a fresco, or an altarpiece, or a mosaic. To slip into some dark corner or some side chapel of Santa Sabina or Santa Maria Maggiore to pray was a different matter altogether. Perhaps it would be better to do his praying standing up — or maybe sitting down, with his Baedeker in his lap, as if he were simply exhausted and had picked out a spot to rest.

This seemed quite wrong, to pretend you were a tourist, and only a tourist. But when you had finished praying, didn't you have to leave something? Should you buy a candle and light it for someone you knew? He thought of buying a candle for his father. And one for his mother. Then he thought how mystified she would have been at this impulse to leave a candle burning for her, when she had made so little of dying, or tried to make little of it and failed:

> Do not leave this woman where like my mother.
> She weeps for the world's body.[82]

Something held him back. His mother might have seen his action as a betrayal. He was a little afraid of her, even beyond death. What he could remember best was that she could be cutting and cold and intellectual, first filling a small boy with the sense of his own importance, then showing him how inadequate he was.

Anyway, it was necessary to pay for a candle. The coin fell into a wooden or tin box with a noise that alerted the entire church and everyone in it.

His room at the *pensione* on the corner of the Via Sistina and the Via Tritone was a more secret chapel. By day, he could open the shutters and look out on the Piazza Barberini.[83] At night, he could close those shutters, close the door. He was on his own, with nobody but himself to spy on him or denounce him as either heretic or hypocrite.

Tom had moved to this *pensione* because it was cheaper, and full of Italians, rather than tourists. He had one discussion with his fellow boarders over censorship and felt he had won. Much later, looking back, he decided that these Italian office workers had very sensibly pointed out a need for censorship,[84] but his views on the subject were to change many times during his lifetime. In 1933 he probably felt some pride in the fact that the books in his room above had been forbidden to the Italians by both their Church and their State.

One night in his room he tried to record in his journal what he thought he had discovered in the Byzantine mosaics in churches and in the books by Monsignor Wilpert he had discovered in the library at the British School in Rome.[85] He filled his pages with criticism of Classical and Renaissance Rome, providing a dark foil for what he had to say about the life, the wisdom, the mystery, the "seriousness" of the mosaics. It was as if he could not ground his enthusiasm for the one without damning the others. The right word for what he recognized in Byzantine art, the quality that had led him *naturally* to prayer, proved elusive. Yet something brought him back to the memory of those faint pencil drawings of his father on one of his last visits to the Middlesex Hospital.

He picked up Lawrence's poems and looked for the poems on the Evangelists. Perhaps Lawrence had recognized what he himself had found but could not name. He read a few lines and then threw the book down.[86] Lawrence had found only Lawrence. He looked at, then set aside, the brand-new copy of *Ulysses* he had just begun to read. He closed his journal and began to read the Vulgate, bought only a few days before in Rome. Almost without thinking, he went looking for the account of Peter's betrayal.

Into his mind came the sound of the cocks crowing in the poultry runs at the bottom of walled gardens just beyond the Ecole des Garçons, then details of the scene in the room in the Condamine and his father's voice. He began to feel that his father was with him in the room where he sat. The wind was trying to turn the pages of the open Bible in front of him, and he stared at the quivering pages, unwilling to look round. A star or two in the constellations with Greek names showed through the slats of the shutters. The Piazza Barberini was silent, except for the splash of water in the fountain, a sound confirming the silence and enclosing it like the fall of rain. A babbling chant started in his head, close to the mixing of sounds in *Ulysses*, so that "Abba" became "Owen" and the chant grew something like *Father forgive Abba Forgive AmenAbba FatherforgiveAbbaAmen BlessFatherForgive Mebless In-NomineNomenOwenABBAAmen Notforgottenforgivenmeblessamen.*

In Santa Sabina on the Aventine he took a candle and prayed for his father's soul and put a coin in the box and was as embarrassed and full of self-doubting and self-hate as he had known he would be, so that he walked out into the sunlight almost in tears of rage and walked the streets until he found a cheap restaurant. After lunch, calm, but still smarting from the memory of the morning, he set off for the fashionable part of town and spent more money on some silk ties he wondered if he would ever wear.[87] In his head, as if in a dream, he found himself explaining to Tom Bennett that the ties were terribly necessary, that they were, after all, in perfect taste, and that it was his money if he wanted to waste it. He could throw it to the winds with the same gesture Pop had used.

❋

The apparent lesson to be learned, for him at least, was that really trying to pray brought on an acute sense of self-consciousness and self-disgust:

> I fell into the middle of a great depression, and within ten or fifteen minutes everything around me and in me turned sour. I could actually almost feel myself go sour, I could feel myself turning to ashes inside. Wondering if this change might have some outward expression, I thought of going to the mirror and looking at my face: but I immediately realised that I would not be able to bear the sight of my own normal face in the mirror. It was a very terrible feeling, but I became convinced that I was an unbearable person, my ideas were impossible, my desires were beastly, that my vanity was an offence and my pride monstrous. All my posses-

sions expressed this, and carried my own pride like a contagion; I could
not bear to look at anything I owned, but right in front of me was a diary
I was keeping; I suddenly realised that every one of its pages was horrible by reason of my conceit. Even letters from my friends who were still
at Oakham, scribbled full of the jargon we shared, seemed to reproach
me.[88]

There was no one with whom he could share this. He could express
it only in the same journal that, he said, revealed his pride on every
page. When he got back to London in the autumn he would be able
to talk to Tom and Iris about the mosaics. Tom would be interested,
and he would probably begin at once answering with quotations from
Roger Fry, Clive Bell, and more recent art critics like Herbert Read.
Everything had to go through much the same intellectual process, in
which certain catch phrases were exchanged: *Advance and be recognized.
Byzantine Art. Password? "Significant Form." Pass!*[89] Other experiences Tom Merton had better keep to himself. Having an attack of religion — in Rome of all places — was going to be considered very un-
healthy to his career by Tom Bennett. Bennett had already asked him
how reading Spinoza, or any philosophy, was going to help in the Diplomatic Corps.[90]

Explaining to Bennett that he had hung about the Trappist monastery of Tre Fontane thinking of the white monks in the Conan Doyle
novel required a lightness of touch Tom knew he could not manage.
He had been too confused at the time to approach the gate house.[91] It
was all an embarrassing memory now.

And yet it was curious to think how often he had found himself before in the ruins of old abbeys and religious houses — even the sanatorium at Oakham had been part of an ancient monastic foundation.
He had been born under the ruins of the monastery of St. Michel de
Cuxa, and there were many other monasteries in the mountains around
Prades. At St. Antonin the ruins of religious houses had been built into
the very house he lived in for a while. In the past year, in 1931–32,
Tom had found himself camping alone or picnicking with friends in all
kinds of picturesque, pre-Reformation ruins.[92]

Most of all, perhaps, he dreaded now to hear about other people's
"religious phase." He would arm himself against that by any means
possible.[93] It was one thing to leave the *Communist Manifesto* lying about
for others to react to: the Vulgate would have to be carefully hidden
away. Meanwhile he said the Our Father over and over.

Temporarily at least, something had driven a rift between him and
his journals, and even at times between him and movies and novels.
Perhaps it was evidence of the same self-hate in others he was looking
for and not finding. Something was certainly missing. In films, even
in a grade-B gangster picture, the protagonists seemed to show a mi-

raculously untroubled poise, at least on the surface — and what was a movie but surface?

People worried in books, but seldom about what was worrying him. Reading seemed to distance everything, yet what was translated into the unreal remained to question real experience and to exacerbate the reader. Tom had tried to read James Joyce's *Portrait of the Artist as a Young Man* in Strasbourg but had abandoned it, though he was to find connections between Stephen Daedalus and himself later. For the moment, everything he read seemed to have been written for someone else. It was usually entertaining, but it wasn't his life.

Even in his journals, where he saw his vanity on every page, there was so little of his life that he took to tearing out whole sections. His journals were all *about* him, yet they, too, seemed to be written for someone else. That was a puzzle he couldn't solve for the present. There were times when he wondered if only names made sense, the stations on a railway line, a catalogue of advertising slogans, or the names of the ships that sailed for Troy, the names of every girl he had thought himself in love with over the past three years, including film stars. Or was it numbers that were the only true facts?

Fill in the details.[94] Fill in enough details, and the right details, and the true person will emerge, like the outline game played in children's magazines: "Start with the Number 1. Take your pencil and draw to Number 2, then to Number 3. Complete all the numbers to 53. Then someone you know will be there."

Age: eighteen. Color of eyes: gray, or very pale blue. Sex: male. Complexion: very fair. Color of hair: blond (thin). Height: five feet, eight inches and a half. Build: slight, but strong neck and shoulders. Weight: about 155 pounds. Distinctive traits: an unusually alert and purposeful manner of walking. Accent: varies with the company he is with and the area he is in. Politics: varies, moving Left. Nationality: currently British, but also Catalan, French, American, New Zealand. Religion: varies, officially Church of England. Memory: remarkable. Direction: uncertain.

✳

This was the summer for America, and America was simpler. Or, put in the terms in which Tom Merton thought in 1933, there was a spontaneity about life in America; responses to life did not have to pass through complications of attitude that had hardened through generations. Merton felt envious of the simple, and in need of simplicity. If this produced complications in his own attitude, then and later, and there were times when he saw himself in the familiar role of the intellectual in search of the peasant, or the "real people," there was a spontaneous side to the young intellectual, uncomfortable with the idea of being one, full of warring opinions and attitudes. There was also the beginning of a revolt against good taste as the only criterion. In the spring and summer of 1933, Tom was testing models, and discarding most of those he tested.

He sailed from Genoa to New York, got into an argument about communism in the living room in Douglaston within hours of landing,[95] and went with John Paul and Uncle Harold to the Easter service at Zion Episcopal Church. (Samuel Jenkins said the sermons made him nervous, and Martha pleaded her illness.) The church was virtually new, rebuilt after the fire of 1924. The anchor that had seemed to Tom as a child the symbol of adventurousness, rather than either stability or hope,[96] was no longer there, though the brass eagle had survived. Tom got himself into considerable complications trying to explain to the family at meals what it was that made the services so unsatisfactory.[97] The school chaplain at Oakham had explained the Christian life as an obligation to be a gentleman among gentlemen. At Zion Church the obligation appeared to be to live as a good middle-class citizen and to love other middle-class citizens.

Merton's pride got tied up in the telling, and after Easter lunch, Sam took his grandson aside to accuse him of being sarcastic and hurting people's feelings. Perhaps there is too much pride and some exaggeration in the retelling in *The Seven Storey Mountain*. Robert Black, the earlier rector who had angered Owen Merton, had been replaced by Dr. Lester L. Riley. The reason why Sam Jenkins and many others stayed away may well have been that they found Dr. Riley a good deal too liberal. He was a friend of Harold Jenkins.

Something, at any rate, was missing in Dr. Riley's sermons, liberal or not, as far as Tom Merton was concerned, and if he continued to go to Zion Church, he tried other churches in Douglaston and the area, with the exception of the Catholic churches. He liked the shared silence when he sat among the Quakers at the Meeting House of the Society of Friends in Flushing. This was broken when another visitor was moved to say that she had recently visited Switzerland and had taken a snapshot of the Lion of Lucerne she wanted to show everyone.

If he had thought about his own difficulties with his writing, this incident might have seemed less trivial than Merton makes it sound. What was this but the first of another list, the beginning of another geography, if not for him, then for someone else? The famous Lion of Lucerne was no more and no less significant than Canigou, or another Lion, the pub in Cambridge. It *was* an interruption. "They are like all the rest," he sums everything up, as he imagines himself coming out of the Meeting House in Flushing. "In other churches it is the minister who hands out the commonplaces, and here it is liable to be just anyone."[98]

But what are commonplaces? What is significant? And who establishes that one thing has significance, another none? The Ark of the Covenant, the Lion of Judah, the Remnant, the Dove, the Anchor: What is a commonplace? Is it the patient phrase of George Fox before the critics of his Society of Friends: "They have the right to censure who have the heart to help"?

Merton went off to Chicago to see the World's Fair and worked there for a few days as a barker in front of one of the sideshows in an area called "The Streets of Paris," returning with the view that there was a redeeming simplicity about American pornography: it was at least frank, if a little raw and sweaty.

He continued reading the Bible on the sleeping porch at Douglaston, but he had decided he could not kneel and pray because his uncle shared the sleeping porch, and perhaps, too, because he had won something of a reputation in the family as an unmasker of religious hypocrisy. He and Uncle Harold were now recognized sparring partners in debates on a dozen subjects during meals, and it would have given his uncle a distinct advantage if Harold Jenkins had known Tom was praying.

As Merton acknowledged in his journals, there is a pride in confessing pride. The eighteen-year-old Thomas Merton was unfair to himself and to the world, something he admitted in the autobiography, where he is ruthless to his younger self. Whatever their faults, both his parents had shown the kind of integrity that is cruel. Merton was searching for something each of them would have called "sound." Everything, then, had to be tested for absolute soundness.

He felt he had given religion a fair test and found it pretty much a fraud, what Karl Marx had called "the opium of the people." As far as public worship was concerned, people were probably content to be fleeced and made fools of, much as they were on the strip at the World's Fair in Chicago: they recovered about ten cents' worth on their dollar and laughed about this. Who had ever heard of an honest carnival?

Tom spent much of the summer in New York, at Reg Marsh's studio on Fourteenth Street, becoming a citizen of Greenwich Village, going to the Irving Place Burlesque, to prize fights, to Coney Island and Jones Beach, to movies that were so bad they were good, or, rarely, so good they were good, drinking, arguing Archibald MacLeish's ideas about pacifism, deciding he might, after all, be a communist, that he might not be altogether cut out for His Majesty's Diplomatic Corps, that he was really a bohemian, a journalist, or a cartoonist like Marsh, a cartoonist with both a social conscience and a zest for celebrating the lives of the victims of the social system.[99]

Renewing his acquaintance with Marsh was important. Marsh could show him a different carnival and tell him what was rigged. He could take the canon of good taste and turn it inside out. For Reg Marsh, it

was the life in the damn thing that counted. And for Thomas Merton
forever after, and beyond all other critical considerations but one, it was
the life in the damn thing that counted. If you could get the life and
the integrity together you would have something that was more than
just "sound." Reg Marsh could manage it at times. Owen Merton had
managed it at times. Few could achieve the combination at all, and fewer
still for very long, yet this, it seemed, was the authentic goal.

Full of confusion, Merton sailed on the *Manhattan* for England, seen
off by Reg Marsh after yet another party and in a manner that would
have distressed his grandfather a good deal. Tom Merton was going
on his own "Ship of Fools" to take up where he had left off ten months
earlier, back to Good Taste and the gentleman's code and Players Number Three tobacco and Shooting Sherry and feeling shy and sentimental
at tennis parties — only all this was now impossible for him.

✳

Almost from the start, from the first October days of the Michaelmas
term, 1933, Merton's time at Cambridge was a disaster. It was a very
long time before he could be philosophical about this, or feel that it was
not, entirely, "the place's fault."

He was certainly not detached when he wrote *The Seven Storey Mountain*. In the autobiography Cambridge is the lowest circle of the Inferno. It is also personified into something like an animal, which
gored him so deeply he felt that he would never entirely recover from
the wound. What the wound was he never quite tells the reader.

Where Cambridge remains the one really bad place in Merton's geography, he goes back there in other books, in the journal accounts, in
his poems, and in his unpublished novels. In *My Argument with the
Gestapo,* the character called Thomas returns to England but avoids
Cambridge and everyone who was at Cambridge with Thomas Merton.

There was certainly much left out of the autobiography itself.

Merton quickly dropped the Oakhamians he found too quiet or too
tame, but held on to his friendships with Andrew Winser, at St. Catherine's, and Ray Dickens, in the New Court, St. John's College. His
own rooms were in Bridge Street, 71, and his landlady was Mrs. Prince.
Winser's rooms were a fair walk or bicycle ride away, in an old yellow-
brick house beyond Addenbrooke's Hospital. Winser had a piano, and
if several of the keys failed to respond to thumping, Merton felt it had
just the right barrelhouse sound for playing "The St. Louis Blues." He
demonstrated this, getting louder and louder until Winser's landlady
protested.[100]

Each Sunday morning the three friends got together for a late breakfast in Dickens's rooms overlooking the Backs. They no longer had to
worry about Bentham's good eye and sharp ears, and they were drinking more exciting things now than Vimto. Winser had discovered some

interesting new interpretations of Freud's theories in an Outline of World Knowledge. Dickens had been introduced to Pavlov's theories. During the year Adler came to give a lecture. The discussion had moved from whether *Hernani* or *Horace* was the more ridiculous play. They talked now of Freud, Adler, Jung; libido, archetype, and the dangers of sexual repression, while they tested Pavlov's behaviorist theories by throwing bread to the ducks on the riverbank below the window.[101]

Merton soon had other companions at Cambridge, most of whom seemed to have been on the proctors' books for the hundred and one university crimes that came under the general heading of "conduct unbecoming a gentleman." Among these new friends were Julian Tennyson, Roger Payne, P. G. H. Roberson, and J. J. vK. Duplessis.[102] Merton now spent his evenings in one pub or another. For the moment, in October and early November, he was successful in escaping from the proctor and his two assistants, or bulldogs.

He went to chapel at Clare only once, yet he remembered the unusual and beautiful lines of the building, which came in time to seem the perfect setting for seventeenth-century Anglicanism.[103] It was not until the 1960s that he became interested in the Anglican revival. Then, and then only, would it have interested him that Nicholas Ferrar of Little Gidding had been at Clare Hall in 1611.

The autobiography gives the impression that he had entirely swung away from any interest in religion, and he had certainly grown skeptical about public worship. But it is very likely he was still praying in private, and still seeking. By 1964 it was a little easier to talk in a neutral vein about Cambridge, and Merton wrote to Nora Chadwick about her studies in the Celtic church, addressing his letter to Cambridge and saying he had "had a year at Cambridge a long time ago, and with Mr. Telfer as my tutor." He went on to say he could easily have met the Chadwicks, but "I am afraid that at that time the seeds of a monastic vocation were very very dormant."[104] The word *dormant* is well chosen. One night, anyway, Merton left his new friends at the Lion or the Red Cow to meet some undergraduates in his friend Andrew Winser's rooms "to discuss religion." Long afterward, he debated whether one of these young men could have been the future Bishop Robinson, whose book *Honest to God* he was reviewing:

> When I was at Cambridge I was precisely the kind of person who, as his book complains, finds the Church unintelligible. My attitude was a common Cambridge attitude of total indifference to religion, and his [Bishop Robinson's] Anglicanism is a Cambridge-like response to this kind of problem.[105]

This is ingenuous. If his attitude had really been "total indifference to religion," he would have been at the pub, or somewhere else, not at the meeting, something that was not lost on the others:

> I explained in detail that I had no interest whatever in religion, in God, in any Church, and that I saw no possible reason for taking an interest in such things. That if I thought I had some motive to be interested, I would doubtless be able to find some meaning in what they said. But as far as I was concerned it simply made no difference. I couldn't care less.[106]

It may be his own mind was on the crowd being fleeced in the sideshows on the strip at the Chicago World's Fair, that he was afraid of "being taken for a sucker," yet he had no need to deny his interest so vehemently, or to repeat this over and over. One of his listeners that night, with far more good sense and insight than he is given credit for in the essay, answers, "If that is the way you feel, you are at least not deceiving yourself, and so I think that if you ever *do* get a motive, you will take faith very seriously."[107] Translated out of polite debating-society circumlocution, this might be rendered as "when you stop deceiving yourself about your lack of interest in religion, you will admit you take faith very seriously."

The night discussing religion in Winser's rooms may have been an exception, but it was important enough to recall thirty years later. On the whole, the times with his two Oakham friends seem to be the only occasions (with the exception of one class) he remembered with any pleasure. Otherwise what happened has to be sifted through complications of shame and self-censorship, the censorship of others, and rumor. Up to mid-November, Merton seems to have followed the course of any number of undergraduates, and there was nothing he thought irreversible: he was in debt, he was drinking too much, and he was not doing much work. On November 14, 1933, he went to a party that changed his life.

✳

Even before its publication, Merton's account of his first thirty years was compared by those who helped to publicize the book to St. Augustine's *Confessions.* A great many since have claimed Merton as a modern Augustine. But if the *Confessions* were a model (and Merton's own annotated copy survives to prove this),[108] there is no mystery about the sins St. Augustine confesses. He had been a Manichean, and he had held on to his heretical views even after his first study of orthodox Christian beliefs. He had lived with a mistress long enough for the son of their union to join his father in adult baptism when they became Catholics. The confessions of Thomas Merton are another thing altogether, with wide areas left open for rumor and speculation.

There is a temptation to say these have been filled to overflowing. The omissions and tangles have been blamed on the censors of the Order and the Church. The rules of censorship made an important difference, but to attribute everything to this one cause is to oversimplify and distort. *The Seven Storey Mountain* passed through the official censorship procedures that applied in the mid-1940s to a book written by a monk in a closed order. By that time, Merton's own views on censorship had taken a hundred-and-eighty-degree turn from those he had expressed to his fellow boarders in the *pensione* in Rome (they were to change again). In 1946–47 he accepted and endorsed the rules of the Order and the religious body he had chosen. He had permission to write his autobiography subject to certain conditions.

The procedures can be explained briefly here. This is to move fourteen years ahead of the events in Cambridge, and it should be said that what was true in 1946–47 altered a number of times during the period when more and more books came out by Thomas Merton.

Once it was written and submitted, the book had to receive the *Nihil obstat* of the two officially appointed censors of the Order of the Cistercians of the Strict Observance (the Trappists), as well as the *Imprimi potest* of Merton's own abbot. Having been approved in the Order, it then had to be submitted for a *Nihil obstat* to the *Censor librorum* of the Church for a given area (usually an archdiocese) before receiving the *Imprimatur*, the final permission to publish, from a designated high official. In the case of *The Seven Storey Mountain,* this was Cardinal Spellman, Archbishop of New York. Officially, censors determined on questions of faith (or doctrine) and morals, but these were interpreted to cover any number of other subjects. In case there was a serious disagreement between the two censors of the Order, a third was brought in.

But this is hardly the whole story on censorship. Merton also had a directive before he began. In one of his typescripts he mentions this, and the passage comes at the beginning of the pages on Cambridge:

> There would certainly be no point whatever in embarrassing other people with the revelation of so much cheap sentimentality mixed with even cheaper sin. And besides, I have been told not to go into all that anyway. So that makes everything much simpler.[109]

This comment was itself censored, or edited out, but one could bear to be more often embarrassed in the printed text, and less often teased.

From the evidence, the editor seems to have worked throughout to clarify, cutting commentary rather than the narrative, so that finally, after accounting for others, we come to the author himself.

There was a censor in Merton who was perpetually at war with the writer who saw everything he did (and everything he had done) as important and in urgent need of being recorded. Merton never quite resolved this. The journals later became a sort of compromise, yet even they were often "coded" — to be read one way by him, another way by others. In the published writing there is something of the same

coding, and the signs appear in the section on Cambridge in the autobiography and in a number of poems about the Cambridge period. If
Merton felt he had to honor the censor in himself, and if he was under
a religious duty as a Catholic by 1946–47 not to "boast sins," he had to
find some way back to those scenes, to remind himself what had actually happened.

"Confessions are only valid (in literature) if they confess God," he
wrote in his journal in 1939.[110] The autobiography he wrote five or six
years later was to emphasize and glorify his liberation and his Liberator, yet it had to begin in enslavement, and, if in enslavement, then in
bondage to specific sins. Merton says enough to let us know that one
of these was pride and another fornication.

Perhaps this was sufficient to provide the guide to lead others forward. The book had to provide a light back, however harrowing, for
the author.

No writer and no religious authority meant more to Merton in the
1940s than St. John of the Cross, and St. John of the Cross had told
those who read his work to darken their memories.[111] Merton wrote
the passage down: he could not follow it. His sense of duty to his own
history was too strong, too urgent.

✳

There is no direct reference to the party of November 14, 1933, in *The
Seven Storey Mountain*. There are other sources, but most of these have
been censored, almost certainly by Merton. The near-complete typescript of one draft of "The Labyrinth" lacks a number of pages from
the chapter entitled "The Party in the Middle of the Night."[112] The
style, before and after, is very close to that of James Joyce in the Nighttown section (Circe) of *Ulysses*. This provides something of a fictional
cast, but real names are used and the date is given. The club where
much of the evening takes place is the Rendezvous, which existed in
Cambridge, and which Merton mentions elsewhere.[113] In the final pages,
after breaking a window and trying to run away, the narrator is very
nearly arrested, not by the Proctors, but by the Cambridge police.

According to Naomi Burton Stone, Merton's literary agent and his
friend for more than twenty-five years, one of the scenes in "The Labyrinth" she found impossible to forget was a drunken party at Cambridge. At the party a mock crucifixion had taken place. One of the
students agreed to be nailed (or pretend he was being nailed) to a cross.
In the drunken chaos that followed, everything seemed so out of control that the mock crucifixion came close to being a real one.[114]

There is no irrefutable evidence that this is exactly what happened,
or that Merton was the one who agreed, or was chosen, to be crucified,
if it did.

There is a good deal of circumstantial evidence.

When Merton was granted a certificate of naturalization by the United States Government in Louisville on June 26, 1951, under the heading "visible distinctive marks" only one is listed: "Scar palm right hand."[115] Naomi Burton Stone noticed the scar one day when she visited Merton on publishing business in the early 1960s. On that occasion Merton had reacted somewhat awkwardly and he referred to the scar jokingly as his "stigmata."[116] He may, of course, have cut his hand on the broken window on the night of November 14, 1933,[117] or in quite different circumstances altogether.

Finally, there is certainly an odd way in which the word *crucifixion* clings to references to Cambridge. Again, nothing can be proved, but this looks like the kind of coding Merton was to use again. In *My Argument with the Gestapo* the crucifixion begins in London, but is made more vivid in Cambridge:

> Look now where the Crucifixion flowered in London like a tree, and the wounds were made in Cambridge, red as oleanders.[118]

In his poem "The Biography," the opening lines start as a command:

> Oh read the verses of the loaded scourges,
> And what is written in their terrible remarks:
> "The Blood runs down the walls of Cambridge town,
> As useless as the waters of the narrow river —
> While pub and alley gamble for His vesture."[119]

The whole poem is about the guilt of contributing to Christ's suffering and of parallel crucifixion. It moves to other scenes, but it begins in Cambridge. It is very specific. The echoes are of Blake (as they are in the passage from *My Argument with the Gestapo*). But the anguish is not the anguish of Blake.

Finally, in *The Seven Storey Mountain*:

> With every nerve and fibre of my being I was laboring to enslave myself in the bonds of my own intolerable disgust. There is nothing new or strange about the process. But what people do not realize is that this is the crucifixion of Christ: in which He dies again and again in the individuals who were made to share the joy and the freedom of His grace, and who deny Him.
>
> Aunt Maud died that November. I found my way to London and to Ealing, and was at the funeral.[120]

It was quite possibly the very day after the "Party in the Middle of the Night" that, as Merton says in the autobiography, "They committed the thin body of my poor Victorian angel to the clay of Ealing, and buried my childhood with her."

He had already distanced himself from the world of Ealing, Aunt

Maud, and Aunt Maud's England. When he returns, it is to mourn his childhood, Aunt Maud, and that England in one. There is hardly a better way this curiously real, curiously mythical England could be described than as a "fragile web of charmed associations."[121] But this web was not broken for him at Aunt Maud's funeral. It had been mere gossamer strands for some time. The proof of this is in the next sentence, "It was the last time that I saw any of my family in England." One has to wonder why. This was mid-November. He was to remain in England until June of the next year, 1934. And he would be back, briefly, in the autumn of 1934.

In one of the drafts there is a sentence Merton took out, perhaps wisely. It is not a good sentence, but it is a revealing one: "It was embarrassing to receive on my cheek the chaste kiss of one of my aunts, my Father's sister, when my mouth still burned with the contrast of the night before."[122]

✳

It is very likely that Thomas Merton was a virgin when he arrived at Cambridge. One of the strengths of *The Seven Storey Mountain* is the precision with which Merton is able to capture and record his own earlier attitudes, his states of "Innocence" and "Experience." The boy of sixteen who was so devastated by one kiss on the Atlantic liner was certainly a virgin. The adolescent mixture of high romanticism and some defensive cynicism seems to last through the summer in Chicago and New York in 1933. Outside the autobiography, the memories of a sort of atavistic fear of and fascination for prostitutes in the doorways of Curzon Street during London walks belong to an early period.[123] The young man at Aunt Maud's funeral in November 1933 has already been thrown off balance, not by the fear and fascination of sex, but by sex.

His own complications were at the mercy of a society with enormously complicated attitudes. In a strange way, the social mores of the Edwardian era lasted on in upper- and upper-middle-class England beyond the retreat of empire and even the Second World War. There was a poorly lit area in which the code of the gentleman and the ways of the cad were sometimes hard for outsiders to distinguish. There was even a certain acceptance of the fact that sex changes all signals, and a man (distinctly a man) had to proceed at some peril, with the tacit understanding of other men of his class. In this dangerous territory, the code word was "discretion." The warning was "Don't get involved." No doubt Tom Izod Bennett had let his godson know all this.

Nice girls were nice girls from families who had lawyers. Most of the women at the two women's colleges at Cambridge were nice girls. They were, anyway, so outnumbered by male students and so strained to prove themselves academically in a very male university that it was a fortunate male student who could lure a girl from Newnham or Girton out to morning coffee between lectures. Bringing a girl up from London was both expensive and complicated. Going down to London to see one and getting back was difficult to do without being "gated" (confined to college), fined, or even "sent down" for being out of your college or rooms late.

This left all the female inhabitants of Cambridge between certain ages. Here the old tribal mores of the class system worked by taboo. The number of women the male undergraduate could be seen with was certainly limited. Even the number of women he should not be seen with was limited.

It was true there were many men at the university who were not interested in women. Some were interested in other men, though the number of practicing homosexuals was probably far smaller than that of the many who affected homosexuality — something that confused visitors to the universities, but that was the nature of Cambridge and Oxford. A good many students were not interested in sex — not interested in sex with others, or simply not interested in sex at all. In England — then, at any rate — it was perfectly respectable to be obsessed by hunting, drinking, natural history, work, or any number of things, rather than sex. It was not even necessary to pretend otherwise.

For those who were interested in heterosexual relationships, the numbers were still brutally against them. All kinds of compromises had to be made. And there was a further condition. Both Oxford and Cambridge had been monastic foundations. If there was nothing very noticeably monastic about the university life after about the fifteenth century, one tradition had lasted. Married dons or professors were allowable, though in the 1930s they usually remained outside the main life of the university. Married students were virtually unknown. There was simply no provision for them.

All this produced a rich folklore and a number of wretched lives. The student who was sexually active with women was likely to see himself as a sort of hero-outlaw, certainly living dangerously, repeating over to himself to "be discreet," and "don't get involved." Life for Thomas Feverel Merton was becoming very complicated, and he was not, by nature, discreet.

With the drinking, womanizing, and all the worry and planning that went with them, he was falling behind. Clare College was not a rich college; it did not have scholarships to give on a lavish scale, and much was expected of the holder of the Johnson Exhibition. If he did not get a first in modern languages in the Tripos at the end of the first year, the college authorities would begin to wonder if they weren't wasting money and a place on Merton.

He enjoyed Cattan's lectures on French nineteenth-century literature. His French supervisor was a fat, dyspeptic man, who set a thermos of warm milk by the gas fire, then took up many minutes of the class in attempts to reach the milk from his chair. Fascinated and repulsed by the performance, Merton wondered whether to tell his teacher that the milk would remain warm closer at hand if it were heated first, then kept in the thermos. Another professor in French studies was overwhelmed by his own dignity and would respond to questions in class and to notes only when addressed as *"Cher Maître."* [124]

Things were better in Italian studies. Decio Pettoello had escaped from Mussolini to asylum in a tiny study at Cambridge that had been designed by a nineteenth-century architect as a medieval guard tower, complete with arrow slits. The professor fascinated Merton with his stories of Italy during the Risorgimento, and Pettoello set him reading Alfieri's autobiography.

Merton was doing the usual eclectic reading and his book bills were mounting. He had even dipped into a book on Buddhism. When *Orphée* was produced at the Festival Theatre, he went in search of books by Cocteau, finding one with a title that pleased him, *Thomas l'Imposteur*, in the Union library. The only class he was attending regularly, however, was Professor Bullough's on Dante. [125]

He remembered sitting in Bullough's pleasant rooms at Caius College, the copy of *The Divine Comedy* he had bought when he came to Cambridge for the scholarship examination open on his knees. As the weeks went by, the class descended into the circles of Hell. In November, when the rain fell on a tangle of dripping bicycles and the walls of an alley behind the Red Bull seemed to sweat, they reached the lowest circle, and Merton was wounded by something half-remembered through drink — debauchery or blasphemy, or both. When they began climbing the slopes of Purgatory, the cold rain fell on the scum floating in canals, and his godfather summoned him to London for the first interview. In February, when the wind seemed to ricochet, still colder, off the surface of the river and he had gone to London for the Boat Race and danced at the Boat Race Ball with a girl named Joan to the tune of "I'm in a Heat Wave," [126] the class were halfway up the slopes. At Easter, when a raw spring turned into the best of seasons in the gardens outside, they ascended to Paradise hand in hand with Beatrice, until she surrendered the poet and the class to the care of the Queen of Heaven.

Reading was reading, listening was listening, life was life. Somehow, Merton discovered, he had stayed back in the Inferno, which was a great deal more convincing.

The interview with his guardian in January had been so searing he had thought of leaving Cambridge and joining up in the Royal Marines, [127] a curious reaction for Merton in a number of ways, especially as he had just signed (or was about to sign) the famous Oxford Peace Pledge, in which those who added their names declared they would not fight for King and Country in any war. That interview had been largely concerned with his debts (he had ordered one set of tails, a coat, and a Clare blazer from the tailor who was too close to his rooms; he had spent half his time in those early days of the term in book shops, tobacconists', wine merchants', and, in London, he had taken one girl-friend, Sandra, to the Memphis, a West End nightclub).[128] His allow-ance had been cut to pay the debts, and he had pawned the Zeiss camera he had bought in Germany and his good luggage. The situation had deteriorated since January. He and Mrs. Prince were in a state of war over his having women in his rooms, and his landlady was bound to complain to the college authorities. In London, Iris Bennett had made it clear she did not want Tom and his male friends coming in at all hours, usually drunk and always noisy. He had to stay at the Regent Palace Hotel.[129]

In the Michaelmas term he had played rugby, then switched to row-ing. In the Lent term it had been unbelievably cold on the river. Now he wheezed and puffed, even out of the Clare fourth boat as if he were doubled up over an oar the whole time. The only good thing about rowing had been the discovery of the Clare College Boat House as a place where he could arrange to meet women after he was prevented from inviting them to his rooms.

There was a certain inevitability about the events which led to a sec-ond summons to London and a worse interview with his godfather than the January one. The only strange part of it all is that Tom Merton continued hopeful for so long: there was probably a certain protection in his self-centered view at nineteen. At different times later in his life, Merton tried to puzzle out quite what had gone wrong, as well as the sense that he had once simply used others.

On the eve of his fiftieth birthday this was still a mystery in his char-acter he had to reckon with:

> I suppose I regret most my lack of love, my selfishness and glibness (cov-ering a deep shyness and need of love) with girls who, after all, did love me, I think, for a time. My great fault was my inability really, to believe it, and my efforts to get complete assurance and perfect fulfillment.
>
> So one thing on my mind is sex, as something I did not use maturely and well, something I gave up without having come to terms with it. That is hardly worth thinking about now — twenty-five years nearly since my last adultery.

Merton gives a few confusing details, then he goes on:

> I suppose I am the person that lived for a while at 71 Bridge Street, Cam-bridge, had Sabberton for my tailor (he made me that strange Alphonse Daudet coat, and the tails I wore perhaps twice — once to the boat race-

ball where I was very selfish and unkind to Joan.) And Clare was my College, and I was a damned fool, sitting on the steps of the boat house late at night with Sylvia, when the two fairies came down expecting to get in the boathouse, saw us there, turned and hurried away.[130]

Whether with Sylvia or with another woman, he was involved. He told Andrew Winser one of the women he had been seeing was pregnant and that she was sure it was his child.[131] He told others, much later, that lawyers had been brought in. He told many people many parts of the story over the years, and here the "glibness" he admits to has to be taken into account. There were a number of off-the-cuff, half-joking, half-serious remarks at different times in Merton's life. In his journals he lists some because he regretted making them, and one because he is still pleased with it.[132] Some of these started rumors, and most got Merton into trouble. Hardly more than a year after that frantic spring of 1934, Merton's fraternity brothers at Columbia were spreading it about the campus that he had been forced to leave Cambridge because of the birth of at least one illegitimate child, something which certainly distorts fact. Much the same rumor turns up in the character reference the headmaster of Merton's old school wrote to the Bishop of Nottingham.[133]

Whether the matter was a threatened breach-of-promise case or an affiliation order (paternity case), it seems clear that some legal settlement was made. Merton planned to go to America that summer, and the one promise his guardian seems to have made was that, provided matters could be kept out of the courts, the Jenkins family would not be told the details.[134] Probably for this reason the capital of Merton's trust appears to have been left untouched by the settlement.[135]

Merton cancelled any plans for going to the May Week Balls and tried to study. He took the Tripos, feeling he had done well enough to look for rooms for next year. His choice was rash, as well as too hopeful: he decided on rooms in the old part of Clare, on the second floor of the gate tower, overlooking the river, Clare Bridge, and the master's garden. On one side he would have had the Master of Clare; on the other, the senior tutor.

The university year over, he sailed from Tilbury on the *American Banker*, passing down the Thames and through the Straits of Dover. The ship was hardly under way when he received a telegram on board to tell him that he had been awarded a high second in French and Italian. This would not impress the college, Tom Izod Bennett, or the Foreign Office. For some reason of his own, Merton remained confident he could turn everything around.

The *American Banker* was a merchant ship that took ten days to make the crossing. Among the few passengers, none was likely to be a film star. There were long discussions with one of the stewards, who admitted in confidence that he was a member of the Communist Party and said his employers would fire him if they knew.[136] Otherwise, Merton spent most of the trip walking the deck alone, smoking his pipe, and thinking.

Some time that June, his godfather's letter arrived at 50 Virginia Road, Douglaston. It seems to have been as unexpected as the earlier letter at Hyères, and this time it was far more devastating. Clare was thinking of withdrawing its scholarship. Tom Bennett said he thought it would be a very good thing indeed if Tom Merton stayed in America. A career in the Diplomatic Service was hardly likely now, and Tom would be wasting his time at Cambridge, even if the money could be found to keep him there. "It did not take me five minutes to come around to agreeing with him," Merton says in *The Seven Storey Mountain*.[137] One supposes a good deal of relief, a smile, a shrug of the shoulders, a sense of "Oh, well, that's that" as Merton put the letter down after reading it.

In a sense this *was* a liberation, a greater prison release than his father had effected that day in the Lycée in Montauban. The trees of Douglaston should have been carrying banners with "Liberty" written in large letters. Merton was free of another hated place forever. But the note of buoyancy rings false. Merton moves at once to a Jeremiad:

> I do not know whether it was entirely subjective, but it seemed to me that there was some kind of a subtle poison in Europe, something that corrupted me, something the very thought and scent of which sickened me, repelled me.

It is hard to see this as anything but subjective, and yet Europe had its sickness, and the sickness would grow a great deal worse, while Merton would be largely cured over the next few years.

What seems to have taken place in this section of the autobiography, however, is an extraordinary transfer. The letter hurt far worse than the interviews, but the interviews are telescoped into one and made much of, while the letter is largely discounted. It was one thing to be criticized until he was almost in tears; there was still hope after he left Bennett's office. It was another thing to be virtually disowned. Tom Izod Bennett had rejected him. Through the actions of Bennett and Clare College, Europe had rejected him (England certainly had). He couldn't take that sweetly.[138] Something held him back from attacking his godfather in print. He could attack Europe.

Merton was in the United States on a visitor's visa. By American immigration laws he would have to leave the country and apply from England for a resident alien's status. Granted this, he could stay indefinitely, subject to the deportation laws. He planned to go back to England in the autumn. Undoubtedly he had to swear he was not a member of the Communist Party, or an active homosexual, and that he had no plans for the violent overthrow of the United States Government.

Merton spent much of that summer with Reg Marsh, or with John Paul. The two brothers were gaining a local reputation: they began by blowing up piles of unwanted phonograph records with cherry bombs in the Douglaston marshes and went on to practical jokes, such as blowing up a toilet in a motel during a conference.[139]

In the newspapers, Merton noticed that the sickness in Europe was getting worse. Of the three candidates in the German elections he had been a witness to, Hindenburg was dead, Hitler had been in power for a year, Thälmann was in a concentration camp.

Samuel Jenkins was delighted with the idea that Tom was staying in the United States, and Bennett had kept his word not to let the Jenkins family know of either the settlement or the academic disgrace. The talk at 50 Virginia Road was now of finding Tom a place in journalism. Sam Jenkins set up an interview through a friend on the *Tribune*, and Merton went for a second interview on his own initiative at the *Daily News*.[140] There seemed to be an odd agreement among editors that he would be wise to get a degree in some useful subject like economics at City College or Columbia. In America, apparently, even cub reporters had to have a degree. Meanwhile, Reg Marsh was trying to interest people in Merton's cartoons, which had a marked similarity to Marsh's own work. Presumably, cartoonists had to have degrees, too. The results were discouraging, and Merton had free time to read, swim, and lie on the beach. After Labor Day, his friends went back to their jobs and John Paul returned to Gettysburg for his last year at the military academy. On October 12 Merton set off for the necessary trip to England.

Little is known about the way he spent his time after he landed, except for his last full day. On November 29 he returned to London from Cambridge. It was a dull, misty day, and London was full of crowds waving small Union Jacks and Greek flags for the wedding of the Duke of York and Princess Marina of Greece. Merton made his way to Henry's Long Bar at Oxford Circus for a farewell party. His ship, the *Auconia*, would sail from Southampton on Friday the 30th.[141]

That afternoon, Merton and Julian Tennyson were drinking champagne together. Under the sardonic conversation about how Merton was going to revenge himself by gaining instant success in one job or another, and in one part of the world or another, Merton was trying to remember what he still had to do. He tried to recall the telephone number of a girl called Elaine who lived in Harrow. He had not visited Aunt Gwyn or any of the family in England, and it was too late now. He was a mile from the Bennetts' flat. He had called on them only once and he realized he ought at least to telephone before going. He tried to sober himself up as he climbed the stairs to the floor above and the public telephones, but it was just as noisy there, and it was hard to hear his godfather's voice, then Iris's.

In *My Argument with the Gestapo,* he writes:

> When it came time for them to take away my scholarship at Cambridge, and when it came time for me to go away from England for good, I wanted to say I was wrong, but didn't know how, because the word wrong didn't exist, no, not in the novels.[142]

In part of a draft of "The Labyrinth" which has been crossed out Merton writes more simply, and he is less concerned about the effect reading novels has had on him:

> And my godfather: I have left and not been able to make peace with him, nor tell him I am sorry so that he will believe it, or tell him I did not want to really do everything I did at Cambridge: that I did not want that aggregate of things, but something completely different, which of course I did not find, and could not, because I was too much of a fool in the first place, and too vain to understand anything except in terms of complete egoism.[143]

Peace was never made with his godfather in England or with his godfather's wife. In 1966 Merton discovered that Ruth Iris Weiss Bennett was staying with relatives in California, and they exchanged letters. A letter he had sent in 1957 had been ignored. But there had been silences before this: Merton had not written to tell Bennett that he had entered the monastery until the autumn of 1945, four years after the event. Iris had not written to tell him of Tom Bennett's death early in 1946, and he had heard the news much later from relatives in New Zealand. In 1966 he learned that Iris had been on the point of taking legal action when the English version of *The Seven Storey Mountain* appeared under the title *Elected Silence*.

It is hard to tell why. The references in the autobiography to Tom and Iris are guarded, and Merton had transferred his feelings to an attack on Europe. The ironic portraits of the Bennetts as Uncle Ralph (Rafe) and Aunt Melissa in the 1941 novel he was still hoping to publish one day are a great deal more pointed.

In 1966, Merton writes that he has gone into the whole question of his regrets earlier:

> Let me say once again thank you for your letter which brings back other times and places and really the immense debt I owed to Tom and which, all appearances to the contrary, I have never forgotten. And the debt I owe you, too. I assure you that what I wrote in the book was not intended to injure anyone, and in fact when I wrote it I thought that if Tom had seen it he would have laughed at it.[144]

Plainly, it was not the things published but the silences, which had hurt most on both sides. And it was too late in 1966 for anything but further misunderstandings.

*

The Merton writing in 1957, or 1966, or even in the novels of 1939 and 1941, was very different from the Thomas Merton of 1934 trying to recover from the second most important rejection of his lifetime. Just how devastating the experience was is not recorded in the journals that survive, and it is disguised in the autobiography. Merton invented a game that he and Robert Lax used to play at Columbia and later, called "John Stuart Mill the Elder and John Stuart Mill the Younger." The interview was set up in fictional terms, with Lax as the reproving father and Merton as the reproved son. The game would begin with some such line as "Father, it occurred to me today that . . ." and grow more and more elaborate, revealing worse and worse faults in a kind of mock confession, accompanied by fantastic justifications. Some of the pain went out in the laughter. References to the John Stuart Mill Society appear even in correspondence between the two friends in the 1960s.[145]

The interviews with his godfather and the letter left their mark on Merton's relationship with those in authority over him and reinforced his fear of the cold but passionate temperament. Robert Lax was not there with the invented game to help Merton over later clashes.

In the decade after 1934 he tried to answer rejection with rejection. All the ambiguities of those struggles to cast out what would not be cast out make up the point-counterpoint of *The Seven Storey Mountain* and the book he wrote in 1941 as "Journal of My Escape from the Nazis," finally published as *My Argument with the Gestapo*. A truer title would have been "My Argument with England." The Gestapo are very incidental.

He was at least not going back to Cambridge. The special sickness he saw in that place was only confirmed when he heard that someone he knew had been found hanging from the pipes in the showers at Clare shortly after he left. This second strategically placed suicide in *The Seven Storey Mountain* makes a much more important point than the first.

There is something sick about most societies most of the time, as Robert Lax was to remind Merton much later, after Merton wrote to him about the plague signs he saw about him in America during the Vietnam War. But there was a different and very real contagion in England in the 1930s, and an intensified strain could be found at the universities. Students just as desperate as Merton had been, just as sick of themselves and the system, would find their idealism and their disasters where they could, and too often the idealism would end in disaster.

This had already begun in different ways at Britain's two oldest universities.

For someone who was considering becoming a Communist in 1933–34 Merton is surprisingly silent about two subjects — the poor and political events. By this time, the signs of the Depression (or the Slump, as it was called still more graphically in England) were unmistakable even in the prosperous parts of the country. Merton gives the impression in *The Seven Storey Mountain* that he was either ignorant of the poverty around him or reticent in writing about it. He gives exactly the same impression about what was happening politically — in England, and at Cambridge. The unpublished sketch "The Importance of Carnival in the Fight Against War" is a facetious account of a near-riot at the Tivoli Theatre in the autumn of 1933, when "Our Fighting Navy," a propaganda film about the buildup of the British Navy, was shown. At Oxford the Union had carried the famous resolution on February 9, 1933, that it would not fight for king and country in any war whatever. At Cambridge feeling was far more divided. A group had planned to drown out the soundtrack of the film with heckling. When this became known, local "patriots" rallied for a counter-demonstration and three British Legion bands arrived by bus from London. Merton's own contribution to the affair was an unsuccessful attempt to save one of the hecklers from being thrown into the Cam.[146]

The only other actions he took were to sign the Oxford Pledge and to sign a petition demanding the reinstatement of a teacher at the London School of Economics who had been fired for speaking favorably about communism in his lectures.[147]

But he says nothing about the huge peace march at Cambridge in 1933. Many Cambridge students took part. One of those in the front ranks was Donald Maclean, who was to enter the British Diplomatic Corps — and be buried years later in Moscow. There is nothing about the arrival of the hunger march in February 1934. The most notable absence, however, is the near–civil war in Austria between February 12 and 16, 1933, the Battle of the Karl Marx Apartments. Kim Philby, who had been "recruited" by a fellow Apostle at Cambridge (probably Guy Burgess) and had left the university just as Merton arrived, was involved in getting Socialists and Communists out of the country after the Karl Marx Hof and the Goethe Hof had been reduced to rubble by the Heimwehr artillery.[148]

This was not so much background as foreground to any student who claimed to be politically active (1933–34 was a key year in the sudden political awareness at Cambridge), and the only conclusion one can come to is that any appeal communism had for Thomas Merton at the time had something to do with his problems with his own conscience and nothing to do with his social conscience.

The appeal led him back to his own solipsism, where others went on either to treason or to working within their society to make it more just.

If a young man of promise who had been "given everything" could hang himself in the college showers, young women of all classes knew another way to despair. In "The Labyrinth" Merton's fictional character Jato Gordon contemplates committing suicide in Marseilles because he is overcome with guilt and remorse after abandoning a girlfriend. In the account she seems to recover after a few tears.

> So she had got tears in her eyes the day in the park: somehow it made him feel mad, as if those tears had been false because they had come to her so easily, when he could not have any relief of tears at all. But she had wept a little and blown her nose once or twice and squeezed his hand and then given him back the handkerchief and smiled, and presently he bought her a drink and it was all over and done with. Except that he loved her more than ever now that those tears had wept him right out of her system with such an elementary facility! And it was all over, and he wished he were dead. Only he did not dare wish that either.[149]

This is fiction, and told from one point of view only.

If Merton had been rejected, he had also rejected.

There is a rumor that the woman (and her child, presumably Merton's) were killed in the blitz.[150] It is hard to think where such a rumor came from. It is clear Merton either never knew of it, or did not believe it. When a monk makes a simple profession, he makes a will. On February 17, 1944, Merton left his shares in the Optional Saving Shares Account to be divided equally between his sister-in-law and "my guardian T. Izod Bennett, Esq., M.D., of 29 Hill Street, Berkeley Square, London, W.1. — this second half to be paid by him to the person mentioned to him in my letters, if that person can be contacted."[151] (Of his grandfather's settlement, Merton left the interest on the Grosset and Dunlap shares to Robert Lax. All other property was to go to his monastery.)

In 1944, then, Merton had not quite disowned his guardian, or the woman "if that person can be contacted."

Ten years earlier, in November 1934, Thomas Merton said his own ambiguous goodbyes to an England he would never see again, however often he would go back in his thoughts, his dreams, his writing. The trip there in the fall of 1934 had been something of a dream return. When he wrote of his dream of returning in the novel of 1941, he set at the head of that strange book these lines by John Donne, with sad ironies to match his own:

> I sacrifice this Iland unto thee,
> And all whom I lov'd there, and who lov'd mee;
> When I have put our seas 'twixt them and mee
> Put thou thy sea betwixt my sinnes and thee.[152]

PART FOUR

The Pasture
"Merton's Heart"

And truly, we are so close to ourselves that there is really no "relation" to the ground of our own being. Can we not simply *be*
ourselves without thinking about it? This is true solitude.

— *Thomas Merton*

They had run out of seashells and were using faded photographs,
soiled fans, time-tables, playing cards, broken toys, imitation jew-
elery, junk that memory had made precious, far more precious than
anything the sea might yield.

— *Nathanael West*

Julien Green's idea that between the lines of what you write, say
in a *Journal*, is prophesy for your future.

— *Thomas Merton*

B Y 1935 the chief struggle of Merton's life had emerged. It was a battle with a kind of self-consciousness that could be agonizing under certain conditions. Merton's courage shows itself in the fact that he chose to engage the struggle precisely where it was most acute; that was, in his approach to his own writing and in the public aspect of religion. In his writing, especially in his journals, he sought the ground of his own being beyond everything that was false. In private and public worship he sought God.

Outside of his journals, and outside churches, he could often "simply *be*" himself. He was not self-conscious in the company of the friends he made at Columbia.[1] The struggle was not shared with others. He kept it to the very writing for himself which was giving him trouble.

The journals that survive before the end of 1941 have little to say about either "concentration" or "contemplation." There are no attempts to define "true self" and "false self." Instead Merton tries to reach a kind of honesty that could not be defined at the beginning but that might be discovered in the very process, if it were continued for long enough, and if things did not go radically wrong.

The purpose was serious, but there was a good deal of play. The journals reflect constantly on their own making. Gradually, the idea of writing an all-inclusive autobiography takes shape out of the speculations Merton makes in trying to define "history" and "geography" as they apply to his own life. In the beginning, there had been "Tom's Book," an unusual catalogue of facts by an unusual biographer. Could Merton fill in the gaps that Ruth Jenkins Merton had left to make up an almost complete "Tom's Book" to the moment of his death?

Where everything was important, if there *had* to be selection, it must be the right kind of selection. Baudelaire, watching the museum keepers unpack various items sent to them by archeologists in the field, found the foreign newspapers the objects were wrapped in of far greater significance than the objects.

André Breton, in *Nadja*, decides that we are what we haunt, and chronicles his own haunting by a woman, establishing the clues to her identity, and his, as certain detective stories of the 1930s were to do, by including photographs of places where meetings had taken place, photographs of drawings, of a glove, of an advertising sign. The publishers of the detective stories were to go even further and include pasted-in facsimiles of torn theater tickets and cigarette boxes.

Picasso had included scraps of the wallpaper of a café and fragments of a dated newspaper in his paintings — portrait of a café on a certain date.

Breton, again, had produced a scrap of conversation between Victor Hugo and Juliette Drouet and asked, "How could the best possible study of Hugo's work give us a comparable awareness, the astonishing sense of what he was, of what he is?"[2]

On Decoration Day 1939, Merton was considering a German bakery in Greenwich Village and Herodotus:

> What Herodotus writes about: There would be a lot of ways of talking about the Bakery on Hudson St.
>
> You could say it was on the West Side of the St. Frontage abt. 50 ft: 2 dining rooms. 350 tables. 350 menus. 2000 chairs etc. etc. Kitchen etc. etc. That's all right: you say that's what it has when you are trying to sell it.
>
> But that isn't what you say when you want to say it has good cheap food. It might be Life cafeteria from this.
>
> Or you could say me and Gibney and Jinny Burton went there and the German waitresses told Gibney the German rhyme about baking a cake.
>
> You could say roast chickens is 45c.
>
> Herodotus used figures when he was the only fellow who knew those numbers: e.g. how far it is from Susa to the Mediterranean. He was one of the few people who had been able to find out. And here was a case where (a) it was important to have the world measured. (b) The numbers were so big they meant something over against the error he was correcting (e.g. the Lacedemonian King may have thought he could go to Susa in 3 days instead of 3 months.)
>
> Ordinarily, the way to tell somebody *nothing* is to tell him a number: just one number.
>
> To get any meaning you have to have at least 2 numbers. The Empire State is 1200 ft. High. So what? Well, my house is 30 ft. high. Still, so what? But this time with a different kind of a shrug — a shrug for the not important, yet meaningful relationship — not just for one stoopid meaningless kind of a fact.

But as soon as you get away from numbers, and words that mean just about as little, you get into significance.

Herodotus tells what they do in Egypt. Or he tells how they (Persians) shaved slaves' heads and wrote messages on them telling the slave it was some medicine they were putting on, and let the hair grow, and the slave never knew he had a message: just went to the bird at the other end and asked for another treatment and the receiver shaved the hair off and read the message.

This is pretty different from saying how many slaves there were in Persia, point blank, and expecting a reaction.

This statement means a lot not only because you can compare it with all the other ways of sending messages, but all the other reasons for getting a haircut as well: then also all the relations of masters and servants you can think of, and all the faith in medicine you ever thought of. Here is your slave running half across Asia with a note written on his scalp, and all the time congratulating himself because he has such a healthy head.

And of course, you think in terms of other rebellions, for why else would they use such a trick except in time of rebellion?

Herodotus is full of what: wars, migrations, rebellions, conquests, embassies, journeys, spies, subterfuges, local customs, weddings, sacrifices, oracles, building buildings, making laws etc. The journey of a slave across Asia Minor with a message on his head relates directly to all these topics except weddings and building buildings. And both of these are generally only *mentioned*. So and so married so and so, daughter of a neighboring king thus . . . relationship to wars, conquest, rebellions, etc. (It is an alliance.) Herodotus says so many things that scholars have taken to reading him the way you read the World Almanac.

Merton concludes the passage after a few more details:

Now no kind of historian is much interested in this kind of truth today. Your romantic biographer is a low beast precisely because he too would shun like the devil Herodotus' kind of truth: he is simply trying to build bad little idols, and idolatry, naturally involves error, necessarily.[3]

There is a sense in which we all have messages written on our heads we can't read. Cambridge was a carefully planned disaster for Merton. Columbia, a near-accident, was almost entirely successful from the very beginning in January 1935. If Merton found it hard to forgive Cambridge, he found it harder still to forget Columbia. The idea was to pick up a degree as quickly as possible in one of the social sciences and to try to combine this with an internship on one of the New York newspapers on his way to a permanent position as a journalist. What happened was very different.

Tom Bennett's discretion and his promise to tell the Jenkins family nothing of the reasons why it was a good idea for Tom Merton to leave England gave Merton a fresh start. Merton was quick to see this and he cut off most of his ties. The only friend with whom he kept up a regular correspondence was Andrew Winser. The friends Merton made at Columbia were to last him for life.

He did not meet them at once, and in his first year he was not notably discreet. In 1935, he pledged Alpha Delta Phi Fraternity. Merton went to parties at the fraternity house, 526 West 114th Street, and he listed this as his second address in the Columbia student directory, though he continued to live at 50 Virginia Road, Douglaston, commuting by the Long Island Rail Road, with a change to the subway at Penn Station.

He taught his fraternity brothers the words to rugby songs, including "The Good Ship Venus" and yet another version of "Eskimo Nell." He came close to demolishing another piano. He drank, and, if he was seldom drunk, he suffered from prodigious hangovers. He started the rumor that he had been virtually run out of England for fathering at least one illegitimate child (some said more); that he was a romantic remittance man. As Merton said himself in a telling comment about his trip back to England on the *Minnetonka* in 1931, "I had easily acquired a very lurid reputation for myself with scarcely any trouble at all."[4] Members of the fraternity started talking about "our Merty" and introducing him to those who mattered on campus.[5]

Merton would probably have been just as popular with less effort. He was both charming and interesting. What was more, he was that rare thing, a European, or an ex-European, who was unabashedly enthusiastic about America and the American campus he had come to. Long after he had been lured away by other friendships, his brothers at Alpha Delta Phi went right on thinking of him as "our Merty."

Columbia, that "big sooty factory," delighted him. Every contrast with Cambridge gave him greater joy. At Cambridge (outside a few tutorial lectures like Bullough's), where there had been any contact at all, students and teachers had traded rather stale epigrams with one another over immense distances. At Columbia, after lectures, the students hurried forward to the professor's desk to ask questions and to argue. They followed the retreating professor down the hall, crowded into his study, and sometimes made it difficult for him to escape for a meal.[6]

When he edited the Columbia yearbook two years later, Merton had to record the results of a poll showing that "A majority of the voters would pick Oxford University if they were offered a graduate scholarship at 'any University in the World.' "[7] He must have laughed at this, having a pretty good idea that things at Oxford were much the same as they had been at Cambridge. When the time came, he picked Columbia for his graduate work.

Columbia University has changed as much as Morningside has changed about it. If it was already an urban campus in the 1930s, almost all the students were middle class. They were exclusively male

and white, though Harlem began a few blocks away. To Merton, however, the students were an amazingly diverse group, especially in the
way they dressed.[8]

He himself wore a three-piece suit to class, with a gold watch chain,
even if he had no watch. He also wore a soft felt hat. In the yearbook
photographs, Merton looks like a reasonably prosperous young businessman, a beginning lawyer, or conceivably a ward boss. In England,
he had probably been a little over the average in height; here, he was
below average. Though his neck and shoulders were strongly formed,
he looked slight rather than stocky. When he took his hat off to put
on a miner's helmet, as he did during a geology field trip in the fall of
1936, he looked younger than his years, and perhaps this was the point
of the suit and hat. His blond hair was already thinning.

While he talked about his "round, English face," his English accent
was hardly apparent, except for an occasional "rather" with a long *a*.
He was reading *Studs Lonigan* and others of the tough-guy school, and
the stories he was writing were in that vein.[9] He could do imitations
of such gangsters as Baby Face Nelson, who had been shot to pieces
by G-men on the eve of Merton's departure from England. Merton's
slightly pug nose was a help when he wanted to do gangster impressions.

He tried out for the track team, and panted round South Field, which
was in the very center of things then, as it is now, though it is hardly
a field today. Between laps, he paused to catch his breath and to establish the new geography: the Crown (with the Low Memorial Library
and the university offices), Butler Library, John Jay Hall, Furnald Hall,
Thomas Jefferson in front of Furnald, where the campus radicals gathered, Alexander Hamilton before John Jay, where other politicians and
big men on campus held court, Ferris Booth Carman Hall, the tower of
Riverside Church across Broadway, and across Broadway also, though
not within sight, Barnard Women's College; closer at hand, the Alma
Mater statue, which reminded Merton of Britannia on an English
penny.

In time, the image of Britannia-Columbia would come to Merton on
a medal from his old university.[10] For the present, he was simply a
new student, delighted by the place and confused by the course offer-
ings. After a great deal of bargaining, he had been given credit for most
of his year at Cambridge. In the September 1935 number of the Columbia *Jester*, Merton's story "Katabolism of an Englishman" appeared,
with its speculation on what might have happened if the negotiations
had gone wrong. The narrator meets an amiable drunk, an Englishman who has been reduced to a Katabolistic state and the protection of
an older woman called Mirabelle. He has tried to explain to Bowls, the
director of admissions, that he has a second in the History Tripos at

Cambridge and wishes to transfer to Columbia. Refused at Columbia, he is offered a job at N.Y.U. as a professor in statistics.[11]

Following the journalism plan in 1935, the best thing seemed to be to take as many modern language courses as he could, getting easy credit in these, and to take economics and political science. But Merton had heard that Mark Van Doren was good, and he added one course in English literature, wondering what anyone could say about books you were supposed to have read in your own time at English universities.

Mark Van Doren proved informal, even boyish, but there was nothing slipshod in either his scholarship or his teaching. When a student quoted Shakespeare one day, Van Doren smiled and said firmly, though without sarcasm, that the quotation was wrong, that the student had better look it up, and refrain from quoting unless he could quote correctly.[12] There was something refreshingly unsophisticated about the questioning he engaged in with his students. In wanting Shakespeare quoted correctly, it was as if Van Doren were searching in his students for the same things he looked for in the great writers, and he did not want these distorted. The teacher was impatient with any student who said he had no ideas of his own, that he had had no experiences relevant to the discussion. By the time you were eighteen or nineteen or twenty, Van Doren felt, you had been in love, you had known friendship, rejection, death. What, then, made you think your experience counted for nothing? If you set that experience at a discount, how could you read? You certainly couldn't write.[13]

Thomas Merton, who had never been guilty of discounting his experience, had never been encouraged to take such risks, in or out of a classroom, and he responded.

To Mark Van Doren himself there was a striking contrast between two of the students he had marked in his class, both of whom began to show him their own writing at much the same time, and both of whom became his friends before leaving Columbia:

> John Berryman was first and last a literary youth: all of his thought sank into poetry, which he studied and wrote as if there were no other exercise for the human brain. Slender, abstracted, courteous, he lived one life alone, and walked with verse as in a trance.
>
> Not so with Thomas Merton, who to my knowledge at the moment had no obsessions. Both merry and sober, he came in and out of my view in times of his own choosing. He wrote poems, as Berryman did, but they appeared to be by-products of some rich life he kept secret. His blue eyes twinkled when he overheard a witty remark, or even when he uttered one himself, which he often did. I considered him a charming friend, yet I remained unaware of the problems which his own account of them was to make famous.[14]

It may have been his English professor who suggested to Merton that his stories might find a place in the *Review*, but it was Merton's faculty adviser, Professor McKee, who provided the letter of introduction to Leonard Robinson. By the time Merton made an appearance on the fourth floor of John Jay Hall where the university publications were produced, Robinson had ceased to be editor and Robert Giroux and Robert Paul Smith were running *The Columbia Review* as coeditors. Merton talked with Giroux and brought him a story entitled "In the Street" a few weeks later. There was something the editor liked very much, the description of the victim of a street accident lying inert on the hard street surface while the cigarette he had been smoking before he was struck slowly burns out beside him. "In the Street" was far too long, and Giroux suggested cutting something like half of it.[15]

On his early visits to John Jay, Merton had enjoyed the craziness of the place and taken note of the man who was an exception to the general atmosphere of high carnival. He was impressed: Giroux could make what cuts he wanted. When someone told Merton that Robert Giroux was a Catholic, he noted that also.

✳

Columbia provided more than a fresh start. Merton decided it was a serious, lively place that gave him a chance to choose what had life in it, and what he was serious about. Not, any longer, good taste — certainly not as an absolute criterion. Politics? Writing? Religion?

Religion least of all. Writing (with all its complications for him) first. Politics, perhaps second:

> There was a legend in New York, fostered by the Hearst papers, that Columbia University was a hotbed of Communists.[16]

Merton goes on in *The Seven Storey Mountain* to show what little basis there was in the legend. The only full-time agitator, he says elsewhere, was the ugly, elderly lady who stuffed Communist leaflets in your hand when you came out of the subway station, or went down into it.[17] But the idea that Thomas Merton was an important and influential Communist in his student days is no less a legend. On all the existing evidence, Merton's was not even a very serious flirtation.

When Merton had thought of communism on board the *American Banker*, which brought him from England in the summer of 1934, communism had seemed to provide a certain "out" from his own responsibility for what had happened. He was too honest to sustain this idea for long. What now began to appeal to his social conscience was that the theory of the class structure and the class war provided what seemed to be a credible explanation for social injustice. If social justice was the end, the means proposed by the Communists were far from an assured and certain way to that end. But who, he wondered, in 1935, was proposing social justice as an end — other than the Communists *or* the Socialists?

A book by Aldous Huxley, *Ends and Means,* did much to make the distinctions clear two years later. Merton was so grateful for this, he wrote at once to the author. In 1935 he was still muddled: he talked of "the Reds" in an ironical, ill-defined way, as he was always to do, as if there had to be quotation marks around the phrase. If in 1935 he considered himself a "Red," it was with a great deal of qualification. He would sign a petition, even join a march. He probably picketed the Casa Italiana on Mussolini's invasion of Ethiopia, though there are some difficulties in establishing this for certain.[18] He took part in the peace strike at Columbia:

> I think I made some kind of a speech in the big classroom on the second floor of the Business School, where the N.S.L. had their meetings. Maybe it was a speech on Communism in England — a topic about which I knew absolutely nothing; in that case, I was loyally living up to the tradition of Red oratory. I sold some pamphlets and magazines. I don't know what was in them, but I could gather their contents from the big black cartoons of capitalists drinking the blood of workers.[19]

This is fairly tentative, to say the least. His memory was usually far sharper about what he had and had not done. Merton is much more specific in the several accounts he gives of the recruiting party.

The party took place in the Park Avenue apartment of a girl at Barnard who belonged to the Young Communist League and whose parents were away for the weekend. There was a sing-along. Then one of those present pointed out that the windows of the apartment commanded "a whole sweep of Park Avenue in one direction and the crosstown street in another. 'What a place for a machine-gun nest,' he observed."[20]

This has a somewhat phony ring to it now, or at least the importance it is given sounds strained. The statement must have confirmed the paranoia of a number of readers of *The Seven Storey Mountain* in the middle of the Cold War. Yet most people can remember overhearing similar self-dramatizing remarks. The point is less to usher in great social changes than to allow the speaker to prove that he or she is the only professional in a group of amateurs.

Apart from this, the party seems to have been a dull one. Merton went out to get fresh supplies of liquor. When he came back, he settled into an argument about whether or not Jonathan Swift was an atheist.[21] He deliberately offended everyone by asking "What's so wrong about Trotsky?" Despite this, at some time in the evening, he was coaxed into another room, where he signed up as a member of the Young Communist League. The name he invented was an odd combination of many things, Frank Swift.

Dean Swift obviously gets into the name from the discussion earlier.

But there is Tom Swift, too. Tom Merton had read every book in the Tom Swift adventure series at Pop's office at Grosset and Dunlap in 1925.[22] *Frank* has its Douglaston references, where "All the boys' names were Frank."[23]

Merton says he was bored by the only meeting of the Young Communist League he attended. Perhaps it was simply a boring meeting, perhaps it was boring by intent. It was a good Marxist tactic, especially in union meetings, to prolong the early business to a point only the disciplined party members could tolerate, then to accomplish the real purpose of the meeting with a bare quorum of the like-minded. Merton did not stay to find out.

After a few months Merton gave up even this marginal interest in international politics and threw his energy into being a Big Man on Campus. By the time he became editor of the Columbia yearbook for 1937 Merton was able to record in the poll taken on campus that under "Outstanding Personalities of the Class," *Best Writer* was T. Merton.[24] In 1935 the Columbia *Jester* began publishing a Merton story in almost every issue, as well as a number of Merton cartoons. He was good at drawing girls. Football players obviously gave him trouble. The best cartoons in the early numbers of the *Jester* while Merton was at Columbia are the oddly compelling cube figures by Ad Reinhardt. The best poems are those of Robert Lax.

Merton admired Lax's poems, Lax admired Merton's stories. Herb Jacobson, the editor of the *Jester*, made good his promise to both the sophomore, Merton, and the freshman, Lax, to introduce them. The meeting took place one lunchtime at John Jay dining hall. Merton was already eating when Jacobson and Lax came over. The contact between the two men was immediate. For Robert Lax it was "one of the best glances upward . . . smile and handshake I can remember over the years."[25]

Robert Lax took Merton to meet John Slate, and Merton realized this was a chance to get into the inner group. The place for the meeting, the American-German Athletics Club, seems oddly chosen. A good many of Merton's fraternity brothers used the club, but, in 1935–36, one wonders how comfortable either Lax or Merton was in these surroundings. At any rate, Merton opened the meeting by lining up three drinks in front of him. For this or other reasons, he was "in."[26] Lax, Merton, Gibney, Gerdy, Slate, Sy Freedgood, and Ad Reinhardt were the chief members of the group, and Ed Rice was included when he arrived at Columbia.

By the end of the 1936 school year, when new officers were chosen, Lax was made editor of the *Jester*, Merton art editor, and Ralph de Toledano managing editor. In the same elections Merton was made editor of the yearbook. He was on the contributing board of *The Spectator*, and he was contributing work to *The Columbia Review,* where Berryman's poems were now appearing regularly. Merton's position on the *Jester* paid most of his tuition bills and gave him a golden jester's crown to wear on the watchless watch chain.

Apart from his fraternity and his work on the magazines, Merton was on the cross-country and track teams, the King's Crown Advisory Board, the Dean's Drag Committee, Committee on Student Publication, Pamphratria Dance Committee, the Sachems (a secret society at Columbia), the Laughing Lion Society, and he was president of the Pre-Journalism Society. He was also a member of Columbia's literary society, the Philolexion, and its social adjunct, the Boar's Head Club. According to Robert Lax, neither he nor Merton found this very stimulating. They started their own literary club with three members. It had only two meetings. At the first, Merton, Lax, and John Berryman shared equal time and each read his poems to the other two. At the second meeting Berryman read a single long poem of his own. After this the others disbanded the club.[27]

Merton was earning above-average, if not exceptional, grades. He was still trying to destroy pianos, and he was often out late at the Rainbow Club, the Onyx, or some other nightclub, commuting home to Douglaston, at times having to wait in the dismal bus station at Flushing for an early morning bus. In Merton's nightclub column at Columbia, he tended to overdo his praise for the Onyx and Stuff Smith's band.[28] (If Harlem was so close, the Columbia jazz enthusiasts seem to have been uncertain of venturing there. The revival of New Orleans jazz reached them only as a rumor.) The Columbia enthusiasms brought out Merton's own natural tendency to see things as "the best ever" or "the worst ever." His way of using superlatives in his journals, such as "the greatest religious poet of our time," was a common pattern of speech at John Jay, and the style stayed with him all his life.

Any lethargy Merton had taken on at Cambridge was out of the way now: he walked with a purpose. Robert Lax was the first to describe in his distinctive prose style Merton's very distinctive walk:

> he did walk with joy. he walked explosively: bang bang bang. as though fireworks, small, & they too, joyful, went off every time his heel hit the ground.
>   that was true when he was still in college. it was true when he was just out of college, and it was true the last time i saw him bang bang banging down the long hallway at the monastery. he walked with joy, bounced with joy: knew where he was going.
>   first time i noted how he walked was on fifth avenue, near the park, in spring (late afternoon, i guess) as he came from somewhere uptown to meet me. bang bang bang. & that time i thought about fred astaire.[29]

While most of Merton's interests tied him to Morningside, his base was at Douglaston. There was now no thought of excluding John Paul, and during school holidays the brothers spent a good deal of their time together, much of it at the movies. They camped for a week at Stone Island, the island they owned jointly, off Machiasport, Maine.

The discipline John Paul had been sent to learn at the military academy seems to have worn off as soon as he graduated, and from his freshman year he had a difficult time at Cornell. He was popular and he was in continual trouble. Later he found a family in Ithaca he felt comfortable with, the Miscalls, and it was difficult to lure him back to Douglaston for the holidays.

Merton wrote that his grandfather, John Paul, and he himself all seemed to have the same compulsion to get rid of money.[30] Pop went in for largesse, or for bargain buying at cheap shirt shops. John Paul bought cameras, radios, rifles, fishing tackle, fancy razors, microscopes, and, later on, movie cameras and cars — all on the installment plan. Merton's financial problems arose from compulsive spending, on books and on dates. It became a family joke that Tom had to have a new typewriter almost every term because he had sold the old one.[31]

In later journals, Merton talks about how ungrateful he must have appeared to Sam and Mattie. He probably exaggerates here. If Tom was in and out of the house without a great deal of explanation, Sam Jenkins was a go-getter himself: it would have been far worse to have his grandson lazing about the place. He was probably very proud of his older grandson and all he was doing.

Merton certainly grew closer to his grandparents after his return from England. He was also on good terms with Elsie Hauck Holihan, his grandmother's Catholic companion. On Sundays, he went off to visit her parents in Great Neck. He liked listening to the stories of old Peter Hauck.[32] From Frieda (Nanny) Hauck, he learned that her family had once been prominent in Catholic Kentucky. He may well have heard from her about the Monastery of Gethsemani, where Nanny Hauck had bought her rosary. He was also friends with Elsie's children by her first marriage, Pat and Pete. He even wondered if he wasn't in love with Pat, before yet another of the Long Island Franks, Frank Priest, proposed to her and married her.

Merton's real difficulties at Douglaston were with his uncle. Harold Jenkins was Merton's guardian in America, as Tom Bennett had been his English guardian. Sam Jenkins had made these arrangements, but as long as he lived, the new typewriters, and much else in Tom's life, were Sam's affair.

In late October 1936, Merton went on an outing with the geology class to the Palisades, and then to the mining area of Pennsylvania. He learned little about the lives of the miners, but something about the Paleozoic and Triassic periods.[33] He returned to Douglaston to find his grandfather looking very pale. When Merton asked him how he felt, he said "rotten." Merton had hardly reached Columbia before he was summoned back to Douglaston with the news that his grandfather was dead.

Samuel Jenkins died on October 27, 1936. Martha Jenkins died on August 16, 1937. Both were cremated at Fresh Pond Crematory.[34] For Merton this meant two trips in a year to the place where he had waited in the car, excluded as a child, while something final happened to his mother. Of his immediate family, by the late summer of 1937, he and his brother were left, his New Zealand grandmother, his New Zealand Great Uncle Lyn and Great Aunts Ka and Kit, Aunt Gwyn in England, and Harold Jenkins.

Merton is very reticent in his references to his uncle. Robert Lax is sure that the game of "John Stuart Mill the Elder and John Stuart Mill the Younger" was invented to ease the pain, not only of interviews with Merton's English guardian, but with his American one. Lax says he saw Harold Jenkins only once but had the impression of a "stereotype strict Victorian uncle."[35] It was little more than a glance, and the impression probably had its confirmation in what Merton had told Lax. Harold Jenkins thought his nephew brilliant, even if many of his ideas were wild. He was deeply disappointed later, when Merton's career took such an unexpected turn. In 1937 he tried to curb the extravagance of both his nephews, and he criticized Tom's habit of rushing into the house and then out again with the minimum of polite conversation.[36] Although Harold Jenkins married Merton's friend Elsie, Merton no longer felt at home in Douglaston. He continued to visit 50 Virginia Road, but by then he had found his own rooms.

During the school year 1936–37, much of Merton's time was taken up with preparing the yearbook. He saw this as a largely thankless task. Yearbooks at universities and schools are designed to be interesting to a few people (usually a minority even in the graduating class), and Merton begins his preface to the 1937 *Columbian* by facing the situation with editorial calm: "We have yet to see one that is not a cross between a telephone directory, and a mail order catalogue with a few fancy trimmings."[37]

All the same, this particular yearbook turns out to have its own fascinations, not least in the advertising pages. Joyce, Breton, and others had seen the possibilities of advertisements for revealing all kinds of clues to the present and foreshadowings of the future. Merton's journals of the 1930s, his one novel, and his poems of the 1960s were all to make full use of the technique, both for prophecy and for ironical comment. Three advertisements in *The Columbian* are worth studying.

The first is a half-page for Rockefeller Center Observation Roofs, with guided tours. The center, containing Radio City, had been built on Columbia University property, and Harold Jenkins had been one of the consulting engineers. The best job the efficient Miss Wegener at the university appointments office found for Merton in the summer of 1936 was as a tour guide at $27.50 a week (good pay in that year).[38] Merton worked at Radio City on the eighty-sixth floor between eleven A.M. and eight P.M. He referred to the experience later in a lecture to make a contrast between "service" and "servility."[39] Off duty, he may have enjoyed making fun of some of those who were on the tour. On duty, he felt politeness was something he owed to those who had paid a dollar to go on the tour and to his employers. As the advertisement says: "Courteous, competent guides explain outstanding art, architectural and engineering features."[40]

There is a quarter-page advertisement for Corpus Christi Church, "The Official Parish for Catholics Attending Columbia."[41] Corpus Christi had only been consecrated a short while before, and its uncluttered Palladian lines reflect the taste of an unusual priest, Father George B. Ford, who would be important in the lives of many, including Thomas Merton. He had been appointed counselor to Catholic students at the university in 1929. It was undoubtedly Father Ford's idea to place the advertisement giving the address, 525 West 121st Street, and the times of Sunday and weekday Masses.

Finally, there is a full-page advertisement for World Peaceways, "a non-profit agency the purpose of which is to solidify the desire most people have to abolish the whole silly business of war."[42]

Throughout his life, with singular consistency, Thomas Merton held that war was a great deal worse than a "silly business." In his autobiography there is a sense that he was against war from his first conscious moment, which coincided with the fact that:

> Not many hundreds of miles away from the house where I was born, they were picking up the men who rotted in the rainy ditches among the dead horses and the ruined seventy-fives, in a forest of trees without branches along the river Marne.[43]

Which is both better copy and a more compelling reason to be against war than anything in the World Peaceways advertisement.

Ruth Merton may have exerted her influence, though more likely Merton came to his own conclusions. They were, at any rate, fixed by the time he was twenty. He resented those he felt were inconsistent in the matter, signing Peace Pledges, then, soon after, advocating a particular war, or going to fight in it.[44] He may have forgotten that he had signed the Oxford Peace Pledge in November 1934 and thought about joining the Royal Marines in January of the next year.

He was not a pacifist, and he denied being one: he simply did not believe that there were wars in his lifetime that justified fighting, not even the Second World War. He would wrestle much later with the

knowledge that some he greatly admired had chosen to fight the violence of oppression with violence.

By the summer of 1936 there was another war — not a world war,
but a war which was to have profound repercussions. Soon Bunny
Berigan was singing:

> I've flown around the world in a plane,
> Settled revolutions in Spain . . .
> Still I can't get started with you . . .[45]

What started in July 1936 was hardly a revolution, or even a coun-
terrevolution. It was a military uprising, and what was settled by January 1939, was the elected government of Spain.

❋

With everything else, with his grandfather's death, and another painful tooth extraction after those of Oakham and Rome, Merton's work
on the yearbook pushed him beyond his physical resources. The cross-
country race against teams from Army and Princeton had been such a
strain on him he had had to drop out of the race, then out of the team
altogether.

On a trip back to Columbia from Douglaston one day in November
1936, he began to get vertigo. Through the windows of his car on the
Long Island Rail Road, the freight yards looked as though they were
moving closer to collapse in on him.[46] At that moment, he may have
remembered Swift's terrible descriptions of similar sensations during
early attacks of the disease that destroyed Swift's mind.

Merton reached Penn Station, crossed the street, and booked himself
into a room at the Pennsylvania Hotel. From here he called room service and asked for the house physician.

He spent a nightmare night, wide awake, measuring the huge window. He seemed to be drawn to the window and the roar of the traffic
below. He called the doctor again. He was given medicine and told
to sleep.

Hours later, Merton came to the decision that, sleeping pills or not,
he couldn't sleep in that room, or wake to that window. He dressed
and set out for Douglaston. He found the house empty and collapsed
on the sofa, to be awakened by Elsie, who took him to the family doctor.

He had gastritis. Even to be told that this was so severe he would
probably develop ulcers, after the panic of thinking he was losing his
mind, was like a bad joke. It was little consolation to learn others responded to the same symptoms with the same panic. Henceforth Merton would be far more careful of what he ate. He was something of a
hypochondriac during the next few years, but his stomach never righted

itself. His sense of terror in the room at the Pennsylvania Hotel diminished, but did not go away. Merton would evoke both the attack of vertigo and his moments of panic in his last long poem.[47]

The Columbian gave Merton some pride and a certain amount of embarrassment. There were too many photographs of the editor-in-chief. He was, at any rate, a Big Man on Campus, and the yearbook did nothing if it did not confirm this.

On the records at Columbia, he was listed simply as "Thomas Merton." The "Feverel" had been retired, to be replaced by "James," when he began to send out his novels four years later. To his fraternity brothers he was "Merty," as he had been to his friends at Cambridge. To Lax, Gibney, Rice, and his other friends at John Jay he answered to any number of names, but most frequently to either "Murtog" or "Tom."

The list of courses he took shows a gradual shift to English, but that he did not give up the idea of becoming a journalist until just before his graduation.[48]

In 1935, he took: History of the French Novel, Introduction to Contemporary Civilization in the West, English Literature from 1590 to 1797 (from Mark Van Doren), Philosophy of Art, Personal Hygiene, Physiography, and Athletics.

Whatever Personal Hygiene may have involved, it must have been new and confusing territory after the curriculum at Cambridge. Merton received a C− and had to take the course over.

For Athletics, Merton took track, running, swimming, and even rowing for a short time. This required even more breath than running. He decided he didn't want to die young, "and after that carefully avoided the Boat-House all the rest of the time I was in college."[49] (He may have had other reasons for avoiding boathouses.)

He took two extra classes in languages his first year: an advanced course in French and a beginner's course in Spanish.

In 1935–36, Merton took a continuation of the Contemporary Civilization course, and introductory courses in Botany, Geology, one German course, a Spanish course in the masterpieces of Spanish Literature, French courses on the French Critics of the Nineteenth Century and the Literature of the Renaissance, and a course in the Constitutional Law of the United States — as well as Athletics, and Personal Hygiene again.

His grades in 1936–37 were better. He made a last-minute decision to take Mark Van Doren's yearlong course on Shakespeare (in which he received an A−),[50] two French courses, two Spanish courses, Geology, and Botany (which he failed in the fall quarter).

His advanced standing from the year at Cambridge had given him forty-five credits toward graduation. He began as a sophomore, but he did not have a whole year's credit and therefore had to wait until February 1938 to graduate. In his short "senior year," he took General Astronomy, Economics, Athletics, and two English courses: English Literature Between 1590 and 1797, and Problems in the Aesthetics of English Poetry. He received an A in one English course and in the Economics course, and he had also been given an A for his final quarter in Astronomy. For these grades he received an extra credit.[51]

Astronomy was not such an unlikely choice as it looks at first. His New Zealand grandmother had given him his first interest in the stars and the night sky. It was an interest that was to stay. Merton begins *The Seven Storey Mountain* with a constellation, and his journals in the 1960s frequently give the night sky on a particular occasion.

✳

In June 1937, Merton moved from Douglaston to 584 West 114th Street, where his room at the top of the house cost him $7.50 a week. He was on far better terms with Mrs. Dixon than he had been with Mrs. Prince at Cambridge, and his neighbor, Joe Roberts, was soon a friend. He enjoyed his independence, bothered only by the sounds of parties at his fraternity house a few doors away, and by the mice.

Robert Lax remembers a chase in the rooms after a mouse he and Merton were trying to capture, for later release somewhere far from the food supplies in the apartment. To Merton's dismay, the mouse leapt out of the window and committed suicide on 114th Street.[52]

While this was almost comic, there had been something grimly repetitious about the death of one of Merton's fraternity brothers, who had disappeared for days, only to be found floating in the Gowanus Canal. It was not certain he had killed himself, but the event threw Merton back onto reading accounts of murders and suicides in the newspapers and wondering if Columbia had escaped the sickness he had known at Cambridge — if anywhere had. His course in Contemporary Civilization had taken him to the morgue of Bellevue Hospital, which had a tragic enough connotation for him. His grandfather had died suddenly the year before. His grandmother had had a series of accidents, then she had recovered, only to die a few months later.

When he was ten, Evelyn Scott had thought him a morbid small boy, but she was hardly an unbiased critic. If there was something that kept him close to thoughts of death and sickness, it was scarcely a sentimental affectation. The deaths in his own family had brought him back to praying, though he was still concerned someone would discover him doing so.[53] The more general subject of human suffering tormented him because it so confused him. If he refused to accept it, he refused, too, to fall back on readymade answers. There was one difference from the past, he now had friends he knew to be just as troubled. Merton was not the only one taking out books from the Columbia libraries that had little or nothing to do with his courses and looking for teachers with wisdom beyond what they taught in class.

Most of Merton's Columbia friends were Jewish. Ed Rice was a Catholic. Merton himself was — he was not quite sure what. In the meanwhile, his friends passed on ideas and recommended books. Bob Gerdy had taken a course he was enthusiastic about. Bob Lax recommended Aldous Huxley's *Ends and Means*. Merton knew and liked Huxley's novels. The reviewers and literary gossipers were saying that the skeptic Huxley had made a complete turnabout and that he would soon declare he was either a Buddhist or a Catholic.

Ends and Means provided a logic much of Merton's thoughts had been lacking. Even when he disagreed with Huxley, Merton used Huxley's own argument against him. Merton was so enthusiastic, he wrote an article on the book for *The Columbia Review* and started a correspondence with Huxley. He borrowed Father Wieger's French translations of Eastern thought and tried to read these in his rooms at 114th Street, and in Douglaston.[54] For all his effort and enthusiasm, the books retained their inscrutable secrets. He was confirmed in the general view that the Buddhist concept of nirvana was pure negation, and it was to be many years before he came to a deeper understanding. Meanwhile, Merton began to be interested in Huxley the man. He respected the intellectual who admitted in print that he was still searching. Merton felt Huxley was largely right about political activism, wholly right about the need for detachment. Yet he wondered what it was that made the Christian concept of Love so difficult for Huxley.

Merton began dipping into another book that sent him in another direction. With *Ends and Means*, he was on reasonably familiar ground. Everything about the second book made him nervous.

The course in French Medieval Literature in the spring of 1937 had brought back old memories of St. Antonin and of poring over the three volumes of *Le Pays de France* and his favorite guidebooks as a child. In February he bought a book at Scribners to give him some of the necessary background. He had assumed that Etienne Gilson's *The Spirit of Medieval Philosophy* would discuss Catholic philosophy in the Middle Ages with something of the scholarly disinterestedness of G. G. Coulton. If Gilson's style was scholarly, it was disconcertingly Catholic. What Merton had not been prepared for at all was to find several lines in small print on an otherwise blank page at the front of the book reading *"Nihil Obstat . . . Imprimatur."* The book had been censored. To Merton this was a good deal worse than discovering he had spent his money on an abridgement. He had paid for the book by this time, and had taken it to read on the train. He says he felt like hurling it into the freight yards.[55] His views on Catholicism had partially changed. His views on censorship were what they had been when he had argued with the other boarders at the *pensione* in Rome. If he had kept the book, and if he was now reading certain sections, and even the quotations from the Church Fathers, it only offended Merton more to think a fine scholar had been censored — worse, that he had allowed himself to be censored. Merton did not need reminding, either, that most of his favorite books were on the Index. If he had been born a Catholic, would he have read any of them? This was all the more important because, in early 1938, there was an exciting sense that the right books, if Merton could find them, were about to change his life.

Not all his reading was pleasant. Reading as a sort of escapist drug (like seeing movie after movie) was one thing, but Mark Van Doren had been right when he said that by eighteen a man or a woman had had experiences which could profoundly alter reading if reading were done seriously. In the Romantic Poets class Merton had had to give his first careful reading to Wordsworth's poems. He decided he did not like them. John Berryman advised him to read them again. With Wordsworth's poetry came Wordsworth's life. Wordsworth's mother had died when he was eight, his father when the poet was thirteen. In the notebook for the Romantic Poets class Merton wrote:

> Also, chilling influence — birth of his French daughter. Legal and ethical problems, which intensely complicate his life. An embarrassing physical embodiment of his ardor.[56]

These may be the lecturer's words, though "chilling" sounds like his. Wordsworth's abandonment of Annette Vallon and their illegitimate child, Caroline, and Wordsworth's bad relations with his guardian uncles, all brought life and the study of literature dangerously close to one another.

Many of Merton's pleasanter arguments with his own guardian uncle were over books. He also discussed literature with Uncle Harold's friend, Dr. Lester L. Riley, the rector of Zion Church. In 1946 Merton thought it was no part of a rector's or a priest's vocation to be able to lead his congregation in literary discussions. He might have felt differently in the 1960s, and he was probably less rigid in 1938, though he wondered about sermons on "Music at Zion Church," and other sermons that quoted more often from Wordsworth and Keats than from St. Paul.

Dr. Riley was a popular man in Douglaston, and his liberalism in religious matters suited most of his congregation. That he was also a liberal in politics may not have been widely shared in a conservative community. On this point, early in 1938, Merton and Dr. Riley were on common ground.

> I remember coming home from the services at the Episcopal Church in Douglaston, where I had started to go in 1937 again. It is funny how

little I think of that — but in the Spring of 1937 I had started to go to Church again. 1938, more so, I guess. I remember I even went, once, to something they had in the middle of the week. Then I would come home pleased, and kid about having been to church, but I really felt quite happy. I hadn't remembered this.

The minister, at the request of one of his parishioners, had preached a couple of sermons about various controversies in the ancient church — Pelagians, Manichaeans etc. He did not speak of the theological quarrels, but only took each struggle as a struggle for "liberty" against "dogmatism" and compared the whole thing, by inference, to the loyalists fighting the tyrannical fascists in Spain. Politically, at that time, I was with him: and still the sermon made me sore, because I wanted to hear about Doctrine, and nobody told me anything about Doctrine, about what to believe.[57]

Written in May 1941, when he was reviewing his religious life up to that time, this passage gives a somewhat different emphasis to Merton's searchings in 1937–38 from that in the autobiography. As far as the Spanish Civil War is concerned, the phrase "at that time" is telling. It seems clear that Merton changed his mind between early 1938 and 1941.

The war which divided Spain in one of the cruellest of civil wars produced bitter and lasting, if less bloody, divisions elsewhere.

The student board at Columbia voted, five to two, to give its "sanction and support to aid committees to aid Spanish Democracy."[58]

The Columbia yearbook Merton edited contains a "Columbia Questionaire." Question 15 asks, "What Columbia Alumnus was recently wounded fighting for the loyalists in Spain?"[59]

Merton's friend, Ed Rice, found himself divided from his family on the issue.[60] If there were public masses for Franco's victory at St. Patrick's Cathedral in New York, Catholics fought on both sides in Spain. Maritain and Bernanos had each been critical of the atrocities committed by the Nationalist forces. Non-Catholic writers were especially critical of the rage of anti-clericalism which resulted in the burning of churches and the killing of priests and nuns by those fighting for the Government. Such non-partisan critics often found themselves ostracized. Orwell, who had fought in Spain, had his accounts of the war dismissed by intellectuals in London and New York who knew far better than he did what was going on in Spain.

It was clear, even in 1938, that not all those who joined Franco's forces were Fascists. It was at least as clear that those who defended the Republic were not all Communists or, by most people's definition, Fellow Travelers. Merton's line in *The Seven Storey Mountain* about the signer of the Peace Pledge who "was now fighting for the Red Army against Franco"[61] reveals a good deal about Merton in 1946, and nothing about the Spanish conflict. Later, he was to see things very differently. But that was after *The Seven Storey Mountain* had come out in a very chill period of the Cold War. Merton's confusions in 1946 about who were and who were not "Reds" was unfortunate.

✳

With the move from undergraduate studies to the graduate English program in the spring of 1938 came a change in atmosphere, and the decision over Merton's thesis. The subject for his thesis would necessarily dictate much of his reading for the next year at a time when reading had become important. In an age before creative writing was fully established on campus, Mark Van Doren was reading Merton's poetry, commenting on it, and advising Merton where to submit. The lifelong friendship between teacher and student had already begun, and this started the usual reaction. Merton had dedicated the 1937 yearbook to Van Doren. Van Doren was a comparatively young professor, thought to be over-indulging a few students whose record in the university was not academically sound. What came to be called the "cult of Merton" had its detractors. So had the "cult of Berryman." With a few exceptions like Robert Giroux, Van Doren appeared to find his gifted students among unsociable eccentrics or among the "barbarians," the throwers of water bombs from the windows of John Jay, the "Columbia bums."

Professor William York Tindall, who was to supervise Merton's graduate studies, was a good deal less impressed with him than Van Doren continued to be. And Tindall had company at Columbia in thinking Merton altogether too much.[62] It hardly helped when Merton turned up to graduate with his class at the end of the school year unshaven and tight. He had already received his A.B. diploma from the registrar's office in February. With nothing to give him at commencement, President Butler solemnly shook his hand.[63]

Merton's first choice for the subject of his thesis was Richard Graves, the eighteenth-century author of *The Spiritual Quixote*. In the spring, he reversed this: he would write on William Blake. He had already bought the Nonesuch Press edition of the *Poems of William Blake*.[64] He set off now in a spirit of great enthusiasm to beg, borrow, and buy anything connected, however remotely, with Blake. This reading was to lead him in directions he could hardly have taken if he had continued with Richard Graves.

Things became more active and chaotic than ever as Merton and his friends neared the end of the 1937–38 school year at Columbia. Seymour Freedgood and Robert Lax were wondering how they could hide an unexpected guest in the rooms they shared at Furnald Hall. Lax's mother had moved into a hotel near the campus to keep an eye on him, because she was afraid he was straining himself too much and eating too little. Lax had invited Merton to visit his family in Olean, western New York State, as soon as the school year was over, and as soon as he had completed one assignment. This involved Merton in his one collaborative piece of writing.

About this time he records starting a novel of his own, with a football player as the main character. His hand at depicting an American football player in prose may have been as inept as it was when he tried to draw one in his cartoons. Two years later he mentions destroying the novel,[65] and it is only interesting that he tried to write on a subject so far off the autobiographical line.

In order to hurry things along on the assignment for Professor Nobbe's novel-writing course, Merton and Lax's friend Dona Eaton took a hand. Most of the writing was done at Dona Eaton's apartment on 112th Street, where everyone was also packing up for the summer. Bramachari, the Hindu monk, who had arrived unexpectedly in their midst, sat on a pile of books among suitcases and provided a beatific, if somewhat distracting presence. Despite all this, the book was finished. Professor Nobbe felt the book "lacked unity" but enjoyed the adventures of Mr. Hilquist and Madame Choppy.[66]

In the autobiography, Merton relates the set of circumstances which brought Bramachari to the West and to Chicago, where Seymour Freedgood's first wife, Helen, met him and invited him to the family home on Long Island. When he first heard of the monk, Merton must have suspected he was a figment of Sy Freedgood's over-vivid imagination. Merton was often falling victim to the wild stories and practical jokes of the three Freedgood brothers, Sy, Marty, and Freddie.

When things did not work out well on Long Island, Merton found himself called to help smuggle the Hindu monk into Columbia. Merton felt the visitor had a smile that was very much like Aunt Maud's, and his account of Bramachari in the autobiography is wholly favorable. But the Eastern monk turned up at a difficult time, and there were occasions when he was in the way. It made it no easier for Lax and Freedgood to hide him in Furnald Hall when he sat outside their door in the corridor begging.

For all that, there was certainly something holy about the monk, and he was able to answer many of the questions about Eastern religion that had perplexed the group. In one case, however, Merton was only further perplexed. He had asked Bramachari what he should read to gain a proper understanding of the spiritual and mystical life. The Eastern monk answered, unexpectedly, St. Augustine's *Confessions* and *The Imitation of Christ*. This had the effect of returning Merton to his own tradition. The advice was to be of the greatest importance in Merton's life. At the time it was unwelcome, and may even have seemed a snub, while whatever respect Merton gives Bramachari later on in his account, there must have been some strain or amusement mixed with the veneration.

It was so in another case. Merton mentions seeing the picture of the Hindu spiritual leader Jagad-Bondhu on a door in the room Lax and Freedgood shared at Furnald Hall. He also mentions that some in the group were in the habit of throwing knives at the picture. What he does not say is that he was one of those who used it for a dart board, which is interesting in the light of the party at Cambridge, though it would be wrong to make too much of this.[67] At any rate, there was veneration which sometimes became too much for the venerators. When one of the knives bounced back dangerously at the thrower, however, the picture gained a certain reputation and respect.

Lax and Merton had planned to go to Olean on one of the oil barges that traveled the Hudson and the Erie Canal. Lax's brother-in-law, Benjamin Marcus, was in the oil business, and they were hoping for a free pass. When this did not work out, they took the train.

The train ride was important for both of them. When Merton made later journeys from Olean to New York and back, the first trip kept coming into his mind.

"What's new on the Erie Railroad?" he writes on January 2, 1941:

> Going down, I noticed there was a shack as you enter Coming, near the bums' jungle, and on the outer walls of this shack are crude religious paintings.
>
> There is a theater in Waverly with a crazy name which I have forgotten. [This was the "Amusu," he writes elsewhere.]
>
> There is a very fancy farm on the climb between Susquehanna and Deposit.
>
> The Delaware Valley is full of intuitions about the theory of knowledge. The big discovery I made there in 1938 when riding up with Lax was only, after all, that I was capable of reflecting upon an act of consciousness of my own. I had perceived the distinction between a normal perception, and a reflection upon the consciousness of perception. But after all that is an important thing to find out. It is only since then that I have been able to write any poems.[68]

Robert Lax would have made a brilliant teacher. In conversation, he uses his own hesitations, his seeming awkwardness, actual scrupulousness, to draw ideas from others. "Yes, Yes," he says quickly if the idea seems to have life and possibility. "No, go on," he says, if the speaker begins to wonder if the idea isn't dying on him. "Try it. Yes. Yes, go on . . ."

On that journey through the Delaware Valley in the last days of June 1938, or the first days of July, there were subjects that arose from their reading of Huxley's *Ends and Means,* and Bramachari's visit.

Like so many of Merton's close friends at Columbia, Robert Lax was Jewish. Unlike most of the others, he had made a study of the Torah and of the Jewish mystics. He was interested in the Hasidism. Lax followed the dietary laws and added his own. The next summer, the two friends were to come close to arguing (one didn't actually argue with Lax) about mortification: Merton saw the need, Lax saw none and disliked the word.[69] With Robert Lax, mortification, or rather a disciplined control, was the most natural thing in the world. You didn't set up a program, you lived a life in which such things happened spontaneously and without thought or planning. For Merton, it remained difficult to understand when Lax said simply, "Nothing should be hard."It took Merton several years to perceive that this simply represented a fundamental difference in their characters: it was no subject for a debate.

Lax's mother was taking courses at the Catholic college of St. Bonaventure (now a university) just outside Olean, and Lax made friends with the Franciscan friars in the friary. His particular friend there was Father Irenaeus Herscher, the librarian at the Friedsam Library. Lax had taken to borrowing books, many of them works on Catholic theology and mysticism.

"Mysticism" was something of a suspect word, or a word pronounced with irony. Merton, Lax, and the others had invented a game called Subway Mysticism to fill in the blank periods in their rides up and down Manhattan from Columbia. (When the train gathered sufficient speed one took off with it in a mystic trance.)[70] "Contemplation" was also a suspect word. Huxley had done much to give the words a better connotation, but there was still no word that had not been debased or made phony to describe what interested Merton and his Columbia friends.

In 1938 the whole group had been discussing a course Bob Gerdy had taken and that he had reported on with enthusiasm. Gerdy was even more enthusiastic about his teacher.

Dan Walsh was not a member of the Columbia faculty. He taught an occasional course by arrangement with the Sacred Heart College at Manhattanville. In the next school year Walsh would be teaching a course on the philosophy of St. Thomas Aquinas. Lax was thinking of signing up. Was Merton interested?

Merton's answer was unusually dogmatic. He was interested in Eastern religion. He wasn't the least interested in the Church Fathers. He wasn't interested in the teachings of the Catholic Church. No, he wasn't.

Robert Lax was not so much surprised at this response, as he was certain that something important was happening.[71]

✳

Where John Paul had been adopted by the Miscalls in Ithaca, Thomas Merton was virtually adopted by two families, the Lax family in Olean and the Freedgoods at Long Beach, Long Island.

In 1938 he stayed only a week in Olean. He said he had courses to take in the summer school, and his thesis to write, but elsewhere he admits it was Pat Hickman who drew him back to New York City.[72] Meanwhile, he met Robert's father (he had already met his mother) and became friends with his sister, Gladys (or Gladio) Marcus, and her husband, Benji.

There were good times at Olean House, the hotel the family owned. Merton was taken to Lake Cuba, where the family had a summer house on the north shore, to the Indian reservation, and to the Marcuses' mountain cottage, with a view overlooking Olean and the surrounding country. Robert Lax tried to take Merton to St. Bonaventure, but here Merton resisted. Before he left Olean, plans were made to spend the next summer at the cottage.

During the hot New York summer, Merton settled down at 548 114th Street to do his reading for the essay on Blake. When he visited Douglaston, he still attended Zion Church. He went to museums, to the El Greco show at the Hispanic Society and to the Metropolitan. He found his way to the Cloisters, the Metropolitan's Museum of Medieval Art. There, he walked in the cloister of Saint Michel de Cuxa, half of which Barnard had succeeded in bringing to Fort Tryon, half of which had been reassembled in the ruined monastery above the town where Merton had been born twenty-three years before.[73]

On Bramachari's recommendation Merton read *The Imitation of Christ.* He read Joyce's *A Portrait of the Artist as a Young Man*, which he had struggled with in Strasbourg. This time he found the parts he expected to find most offensive the most compelling. If Joyce was satirizing his Catholic youth in Dublin, this was not the way it read to Merton.

Sometime in the summer or early fall, Merton made a radical change in the direction of his thesis. It may be just because the subject was so exciting to him that *Nature and Art in William Blake: An Essay in Interpretation* is so poor. Merton does exactly what he says he is *not* going to do in the preface. In addition, even if the thesis was written for the English Department, it seems almost inexcusable that Blake is almost totally neglected as a *visual* artist. The greatest surprise is to find the thesis is not even well written. Merton's notebooks for the essay are far more fascinating reading.[74]

Notebooks have to be used with caution because pages left blank at one time may be filled up at another. However, where Merton includes a long section of notes on St. Thomas Aquinas, breaking off his pages on Blake's poem "Milton" and returning to "Milton" after Aquinas, this can only mean the quotations from Aquinas and Merton's notes on these were so pressing that they interrupted everything he was doing. In the same two notebooks Merton used for the Blake thesis, Merton wrote a very careful evaluation of Jacques Maritain's *Art and Scholasticism*. Before the fall classes began at Columbia, he had decided that the approach to Blake was through Maritain and Aquinas. Merton was reading the very authors he had told Lax were of no interest to him at the beginning of the summer.

The reading lists at the back of the notebooks prove this, and present further surprises. Many of the names and titles are those one could expect to find on a bibliography for Blake studies in 1938. Some are not. There are two prophetic entries:

> C. de B. Evans. Meister Eckhart
> (Suzuki — Zen Buddhism)[75]

The "Blake notebooks," then, would make an important study in themselves, but two passages in them, both taken from Mona Wilson's 1927 biography, are too vital to pass over.

The first is from a letter the painter Samuel Palmer wrote to Anne Gilchrist, reporting a conversation with Blake. It has often been reproduced, and Merton was to use it more than once in his own writing, though he sometimes made inferences which are not in the original:

> He quite held forth one day to me on the Roman Catholic Church being the only one which taught the forgiveness of sins; and he repeatedly expressed the belief that there was more *civil* liberty under the Papal Government than any other sovereignty.[76]

The second passage, which appears on the same page of the notebook, had its own prophetic connections with the last twenty years of Merton's complex vocation. This time it is Mona Wilson who says:

> It is the mark of the true mystic that, after his initiation into the mysteries of the unitive life, he is impelled, in some way, to serve his fellow men.[77]

From A. K. Coomaraswamy's *Transformation of Nature in Art*, Merton learned of the necessity in the East for the artist to practice asceticism and contemplation. In the essay, Merton writes:

> And one of the most important disciplines is that of contemplation. This implies a kind of asceticism, that is self-sacrifice, sacrifice of immediate physical goods for the good of the spirit, for the success of the work of art. The Hindu artist accompanies the artistic process with a strict routine of asceticism and contemplation. First of all, he must purge himself of all personal desires, all distracting influences. Then he visualizes his subject as it is described in a given canonical prescription (mantram); he contemplates this ideal model until he comes to "reflect" it, becomes identified with it, holds it in view in an act of nondifferentiation, then draws it.[78]

Merton's Blake studies had drawn him further into Eastern religion. If the level of his reading was not very deep, the interest was to prove a lasting one. It is unlikely he read the book by Suzuki (he has not checked it), but he remembered the name. What matters is that so many of his later concerns are gathered together in the notebooks at this time. He even includes quotations from Chuang Tzu![79]

For the moment, the difficulty was to "purge himself of all personal desires, all distracting influences." Later, Merton celebrated a quiet period in the early fall, which had come between his infatuation for Pat Hickman and his meeting Doris Raleigh.[80] But it was not only women, it was the very intellectual ferment that made it hard to concentrate. Merton felt that it was in researching for the Blake paper that he learned, at last, how to read. He had found concentration almost impossible at Cambridge. The master's thesis shows that it was still difficult.

Bramachari, Lax, Joyce, Maritain, even Blake, all pointed Merton to a reexamination of Catholicism that summer, against a resistance that was still real. His grandfather's old prejudices had been disproved by Catholic friends like the Haucks. Yet where he had Catholic friends, he also had Communist friends like Ad and Joan Reinhardt. This was hardly a sufficient reason for joining either the Catholic Church or the Communist Party. Meanwhile Joe Roberts went on about the Roman Catholic governess who had mistreated him when he was a child.[81]

"The grey-eyed Church is gonna get me I said," Merton wrote in *The Geography of Lograire*.[82] And in this section of *Lograire* he imagines he is riding the Long Island Rail Road past the Elmhurst gas tanks and the factory chimneys, which were all too reminiscent of crematorium chimneys. He is at the spot where he first opened Gilson's book and saw the *Imprimatur*.

He had not been inside a Catholic church since Rome. Usually on the weekend, Merton went out to Long Island to see Pat Hickman, but he cancelled his plans one weekend toward the end of August and stayed at 114th Street. Early on Sunday, he set off to walk the seven blocks to the new church behind the Teachers College on 121st Street. He would have known the times of masses at Corpus Christi from the notice in the Columbia yearbook.

He returned to his room after eating breakfast out, probably expecting that the feeling of peace with himself would diminish as swiftly as it had done on other occasions. It diminished, but it did not go away. Something had been quietly settled and fixed. In part it was simply the knowledge that he would go back on other Sunday mornings.[83] He knew he could not receive the sacrament at Corpus Christi, he would simply be there. The self-consciousness he felt in the church would just have to take care of itself.

Over Labor Day, Merton and Joe Roberts went to Philadelphia, arguing over mysticism and the Catholic Church, and drinking so much that it took several days to recover.[84] Merton was still seeing too many films, smoking too many cigarettes, and piling up books which would take more than a year to read.

It was a beautiful autumn, and Merton always responded to the American fall. But where he talked of it as a "dangerous season" that year, there was a general feeling that, even in America, time was running out.

Merton's anger with himself had grown stronger. He continued to blame the world, but with this important difference: by 1938, he insists it is a world very much of his own making. There is another transfer of wrath and judgment in overstatement.

In the late 1950s and in the 1960s, Merton was to caution others not to go too far in doing a certain kind of violence to themselves. There was a true drama in the events of 1938. Yet both in the living and in the telling afterward, Merton exaggerated almost to the point of melodrama. The exaggerations were to make difficulties for him in later struggles, and these difficulties had their seeds in his renunciation of earlier Thomas Mertons.

By 1938, Merton had read a number of Graham Greene's novels, and he had been introduced to Sir Thomas Browne in one of his lecture courses at Columbia. He must have read the line of Browne's which was a favorite of Greene's: "There is another man within mee that's angry with mee . . ."[85] Perhaps that angry man in Merton was necessary: he need not have been quite so angry to have accomplished what was needed.

❉

For his A.M. degree Merton took Shakespeare at the graduate level, Medieval English Literature, Sixteenth, Seventeenth, Eighteenth Century courses, the Romantic Poets, and Introduction to Literary Research. Philosophy 177, the Philosophy of St. Thomas Aquinas, was the only course Merton was taking outside the English Department.[86] He had thought of taking courses at the Union Theological Seminary but decided against it.

On September 20, 1938, the immediate international crisis was resolved by the Munich Agreement. Merton's feelings were the common ones of relief and disgust. He had "given up politics as more or less hopeless,"[87] and he was certainly not alone in this. When the Munich Crisis was at its height, Merton and Joe Roberts had spent many hours in their rooms together, drinking beer, smoking cigarette after cigarette, and telling jokes that only made their nervousness more apparent. Now that there would be "Peace in our time," as far as most of his friends knew Merton had withdrawn into writing his thesis and preparing his classwork.

One day in November 1938, Ralph de Toledano came looking for Ed

Rice to tell him Merton was searching all over campus for him; he needed a Catholic sponsor for provisional baptism.[88] Rice says he was taken completely by surprise: he did not know Merton was already being instructed, or that he was even thinking of becoming a Catholic.

Merton had made his decision a few weeks earlier, when he had reached a point where his reading and his life came quietly but surely together. The book Merton was reading early in the afternoon that October day in 1938 was G. F. Lahey's life of Gerard Manley Hopkins, but all the books he had read that summer and much else were to be focused in a few minutes. It was raining hard outside the windows of the room on the top floor of 548 West 114th Street, and there was a certain pressure on Merton's time. He had spent the morning in the library. At four, he had to give a tutorial in Latin to one of the private students Miss Wegener had found for him to supplement his income. The student was ill in bed and lived in Central Park West.

In the Lahey biography, Merton had arrived at the passage where Hopkins broke through his own indecision during his conversion crisis. Hopkins had written to Newman asking for Newman's help. Merton asked no one's help. He closed the book and walked through the rain to the rectory of Corpus Christi. Father Ford was out. As Merton stood outside the door the maid had closed, uncertain what to do, he saw Father Ford approaching. They went together into the small parlor just off the entrance hall, which must have looked then very much as it does today. There, Merton told Father Ford he wanted to become a Catholic.

The Seven Storey Mountain gives a sense of great calm after a storm to those days at the end of October and the beginning of November,[89] but the strain of the hours he spent by himself before making the decision was not so easily resolved. Merton had to tell someone other than Father Ford.

It may have been the very evening of that first visit to the rectory of Corpus Christi, when he returned from teaching the student in Central Park West, or it may have been a week or so later, after an evening instruction by Father Moore. Merton was late for a party at Herb Jacobson's apartment. He arrived wearing a new brown felt hat and looked through the doorway to see who was there. Gibney and Freedgood were in the room, Rice was absent. Merton was surprised to see Bob Lax. He thought Lax was in Olean.

As Merton moved to the center of the room, he took off his hat and smiled broadly, the joy he couldn't suppress clear in his eyes. Then he sailed his hat like a Frisbee at Lax. Lax caught it. While the two friends moved to the table with the drinks, Merton said: "Lax, I'm going to become a Catholic."

"I could see from his look that he'd made up his mind; meant it, and that he wanted me to know," Robert Lax says. "I remember the moment because he'd never before, and has never since, thrown a hat in my direction."[90]

Merton chose only tomato juice and tried to press this on Lax. "Root juices; ugh!" Lax said.

The two friends had little chance to talk further. Later in the evening, Merton got into an argument with other friends about the Catholic Church. In his journal, Merton felt he had gone a long way to spoil something out of sheer exuberance.[91] This was to happen again.

On November 16, 1938, Thomas Merton was received into the Roman Catholic Church in Provisional Baptism at Corpus Christi.[92] He celebrated his baptism, his confession, and his first Mass in his poetry and kept the anniversary with joy in his journals.

Merton's sponsor and godfather in the Catholic faith was Edward Rice. His witnesses were Robert Lax, Robert Gerdy, and Seymour Freedgood. They were witnesses in the sense that they wanted to be with their friend on this important occasion, Gerdy racing along Broadway to catch up when the group had started off without him.

The time would come when Merton would say, "I wish my friends would let me be myself!"[93] If this would apply to the friends he made in the Gethsemani years, and through his correspondence, as well as to his Columbia friends, he needed the support of the friends he had made at the university that November morning and he valued it. Without them, as he makes implicit in the autobiography, he might not have been there. Three who were shy and uncertain quite what was expected of them during the ceremony — who were there simply for Tom's sake — were Jews. Robert Lax and Robert Gerdy were to become Catholics some years later.

Of the party of five young men, Ed Rice alone knew what to do.

For Merton, the momentous year had ended in celebration. As he came quickly to realize, it was not an end in conversion, but the beginning of a new life of conversion. It was not the end of restlessness, either. But the old, unfixed, frenzied aimlessness was behind him. He had been fixed, first in his friendships, and then in his faith.

❊

In the first month of 1939 the war in Spain was over. Refugees and the remnants of the Republican armies crossed the Pyrenees near Prades and entered French camps.

On February 22, 1939, Merton received his A.M. degree in English, again from the Registrar's office. He had decided to take his doctorate at Columbia. He moved from West 114th Street to 35 Perry Street in the Village. His living room was a pleasant room on the second floor with a balcony over the street. His bedroom in the back of the house was small and dark.[94]

That spring, Merton went with Daniel Walsh to hear Maritain speak at the Catholic Book Club. Walsh had been a student of Etienne Gilson's and he knew Jacques Maritain. He introduced him at the reception after the talk, though Merton spoke to Maritain for only a few minutes. Afterward, Walsh and Merton, both equally exhilarated by Maritain's talk, went off "talking of miracles and saints."[95]

Walsh had been an admired professor for Merton before that evening. If they agreed now about Maritain's great innocence of heart, this was the same quality that Aunt Maud had for Merton, that Robert Lax had, that Mark Van Doren had, and that Merton recognized in full measure in Daniel Walsh himself. It had once more become the quality Merton most valued. He would have been unconvinced if anyone had told him that evening that, with all his complications, it was the same quality Merton's friends saw in him.

Very different from Van Doren in physical type, Walsh was a cartoonist's picture of an Irishman. Moon-faced, caustic and witty, with a good laugh and a habit of speaking out of the side of his mouth, Walsh was nobody's idea of a professor of philosophy. He had "young eyes," and certain ways of using them that were not unlike Merton's.

All this was appearance. Daniel Walsh was a superb teacher of a subject few would have thought important to the Philosophy Department at Columbia in 1939. It is to the credit of the department, perhaps, that it was taught at all. Thomist philosophy had been considered dead and buried for centuries in secular institutions of higher education, worth at best a lecture or two in a period course on the History of Western Philosophy. A full course on the subject should have been ill attended. It was not. It was full and it was attracting many of the brightest students at Columbia. These students were learning of the revival and revitalization of Thomist studies in the nineteen twenties and thirties.

If all this was no longer a mystery to Thomas Merton, he and Walsh had hardly been friends before the evening of Maritain's talk. Now Merton opened up to Walsh as he had done to nobody else: "And when I first mentioned my vocation he said immediately he had always expected I would want to go into the religious life . . ."[96]

When Dan Walsh anticipated this before Merton broke the secret, it only confirmed the importance Merton had foreseen that Walsh would have in his life, though neither could have prophesied it would be Thomas Merton who would one day help prepare Dan Walsh for ordination. During that spring walk, Merton may have talked only of his desire to enter a religious order, though it wasn't long before he asked about the priesthood. He had wanted to become a priest soon after he was admitted to the Church. If the idea remained dormant, it was because Merton was beginning to have some doubts about his own fitness.[97]

Merton needed to test his sense of where he was going in conversation. This was to be true to the end of his life. On a superficial level it had been true before 1939. He had first tested people's response when he said that Karl Marx might be right. Later, he had tested responses when he said that the Catholic Church had the right answers. All this had resulted in arguments on a somewhat negative line, bringing out illogical thinking and prejudices.[98] As far as Merton was concerned this was a sort of clearing operation. From 1939, the Ordeal by Questioning went much deeper.

To all this Merton's conversion to Catholicism provides an important exception. He had sought nobody's advice before becoming Catholic. He had tested responses only after he had taken the first step, and he regretted the mess he had made of this at Herb Jacobson's party. In later years many people would be certain they had shaped Merton's destiny by their responses to his questioning. Most, as Merton's private journals make plain, were wrong. Dan Walsh's immediate confirmation of his vocation that night was, however, of great significance. Walsh went on to open up paths Merton would probably never have found on his own. Among the orders Walsh was strongly attracted to was the Cistercians of the Strict Observance, the Trappists. He planned to make a retreat that summer to the Order's monastery, Our Lady of Gethsemani, in Kentucky. Merton had his own connection with the monastery. Elsie's family, the Haucks, knew Father James Fox, at Gethsemani, and Nanny Hauck had spoken of buying her rosary at the gate house.

The Trappists were not discussed at first. It may be that Walsh was held in check by Merton's reply when Walsh mentioned the Jesuits. This was certainly a strange response from someone who had found things were too easy in his instructions before baptism. Merton said he thought the Jesuit discipline would be too hard for him. He had been thinking of Gerard Manley Hopkins, but Joyce's unequivocal dislike of the Jesuits who had educated him in Ireland may also have colored Merton's thoughts. Merton may have been thinking, too, of the fear of the Jesuits at the Lycée in Montauban.

Dan Walsh said caustically that nothing was too hard if it brought you to God. Merton remembered the remark. Walsh had already suggested the Franciscans. From what he knew of him, Merton would make a good Franciscan. It was concluded that Walsh would arrange an interview with Father Murphy at the monastery on Thirty-first Street.

To apply to the Provincial, Merton had to have documents from Father Ford. At Corpus Christi, Merton found Ford was enthusiastic about his vocation to become a priest but not about his joining an order. Why didn't Merton become a secular priest?

Merton went back more than once, and then to Dan Walsh. Father

Ford grew more critical of the orders. Dan Walsh became more certain that Merton's vocation was with the Franciscans.

All this to-ing and fro-ing took several months. Merton decided Dan Walsh knew him far better than Father Ford. As Merton was now at Perry Street, and in St. Joseph's parish, he decided to circumvent the opposition at Corpus Christi by obtaining the necessary papers from St. Joseph's. Father Cassery at the rectory was helpful, and he gave Merton most of what he needed: he even said that Merton appeared to have the true Franciscan spirit. But Merton still needed the certificate of baptism from Corpus Christi.

This meant another visit uptown. This time Father Ford was away. Father Kenealy was on duty, and Merton met much the same argument: Merton would never be happy disciplined in a friary or a monastery. In a city diocese like this one, he would be far better off than in the country somewhere. He could even arrange things so that he was very much his own boss . . .

Merton was not at all sure he wanted to be his own boss. He took some comfort from writing down in his journal a passage from "Refutation of the Pernicious Teaching of those who would deter men from Entering Religious Life," in which St. Thomas Aquinas quotes from St. Gregory's *Morals* to fine point and purpose:

> When my conscience was urging me to leave the world, many secular cares began to press upon me, as if I were to be detained in the world, not by love of its beauty, but by that which was more serious, viz., anxiety of mind. But at length, escaping eagerly from such cares, I sought the monastery gate.[99]

✳

Perry Street seemed far more of an "establishment" than the room near Columbia, and Merton felt alternately house-proud and conscience-stricken. The telephone got him into acrimonious and sarcastic correspondence with the telephone company, but one of his first calls had been from Robert Lax, congratulating him on the election of Pope Pius XII. Almost every day after that Merton called Lax at the Taft Hotel, where his friend had a job looking after the manager's children and was writing in his free time.[100] Having an apartment meant that Merton could put people up, giving up his bed and sleeping on the floor. As the weather grew warmer, he moved more often onto the precarious balcony to read. There was no high place in Greenwich Village. The best place Merton discovered for walking and reflecting was the Chicken Dock, with its view of shipping and the Hudson.

In 1939 Merton felt freer than he had been since the months after he left Oakham. He thought vaguely of doing his doctoral thesis on the poetry of Gerard Manley Hopkins. Some supplementary income came from book reviews published in *The New York Herald Tribune* and *The New York Times.*[101] Meanwhile he waited out the decision whether he could apply to become a seminarian with the Franciscans. This seems to have in no way restricted his ideas about becoming a writer. In 1939 Merton *had* to become a writer with a name: "My chief concern was now to see myself in print."[102]

So far, to his exasperation, he was doing better as a reviewer than as a poet. He was now experimenting in Skeltonic verse and trying to mend a lack of content by more careful attention to form, but the rejection slips continued to come. He abandoned the novel on the football player and decided the new novel he was planning to write would draw on his own past. He had also begun an experimental book, "The Pastoral," which mixed New York scenes with the more intellectual parts of the journal.[103]

In the spring of 1939, as soon as he was established at Perry Street, Merton set off on his own for Bermuda. He gives few clues to his feelings about being back in this island of ambiguous memories. There is, however, a clear indication in his journal in the fall of 1939 that he had intended Bermuda to be the first in a series of "David Copperfield" visits, and only the war in Europe prevented him from making these. Merton's journeys to St. Antonin and other places in his past would have to be made in a different way.

Merton was back from Bermuda in time to say farewell to Bramachari, who was sailing back to India on the *Rex.* On May 3, he gave a talk at the Columbia Writers Club on poetry — his first public lecture, and one that gave him a sense of what teaching would be like in the extension courses. He felt nervous and self-conscious, but the lecture went well.[104] He wanted to excel at teaching English, and he was already planning his classes, which would start on September 29.

May was a fine month. It took Merton back to Flushing Meadows, this time transformed by the World's Fair. Merton and Gibney discovered the Cuban Pavilion and the flamenco dancers, Antonio and Marquita. On May 18, he met Wilma Reardon, who lived in Forest Hills and worked as a nurse at the fair. His new girlfriend took him behind the scenes with her stories, including one about a Seminole Indian who had to be treated frequently for alligator bites. For his part, Merton felt he overdid the subject of the difficulties of being a writer during the long, serious talks they had at the outdoor cafés, where the canned Tchaikovsky blew "among the fat statues."[105]

On Decoration Day, May 30, Merton spent the whole day reading, seated on the thin boards he had laid over the ironwork of the rickety balcony at Perry Street. He was able to give almost all his attention to *Finnegans Wake,* an underground copy of which Robert Gibney had secured from a friend in a book shop.[106] He had decided the beach was too expensive and he was nursing a hangover by drinking one Coca-Cola after another. It was unusually quiet in Perry Street during the public holiday. The "little bastard" who tried to get a few notes out of his trumpet and succeeded often enough to break Merton's concentration had gone away to the beach with his family.[107]

Plans for that summer were simple: Rice, Lax, and Merton would remain secluded at the Marcus cottage above Olean, spend as little money as possible, and reappear in August, each with a book that would make him instantly famous. Merton sublet Perry Street and took the train to Olean. Soon Rice was at work on "The Blue Horse," Lax on "The Spangled Palace," and Merton had an impressive number of typed pages, at least three titles for his book, and a photograph for the jacket.

Ed Rice took a number of shots of the author from different angles while they kidded one another, and as Merton struck what he thought was the right "Hemingway" pose. Under the kidding, Rice says, Merton was very decided about what he wanted.[108]

The titles appeared on blank pages of what looked like different drafts, giving the impression that Merton was writing three books at the same time. One was "The Straits of Dover"; the second, "The Night Before the Battle"; the third, "The Labyrinth."

"The Night Before the Battle" dropped away, "The Straits of Dover" and "The Labyrinth" borrowed from one another. In all its parts, the complex was really one tale with variations.

As Robert Giroux has said, "The Labyrinth" was, ironically speaking, the best of the many titles:[109] the complex was a maze with no way out, for either author or reader. There are lively incidents, most of them reportage based on Merton's own life. There is a great deal of energetic rushing about, but no clear purpose to the rushing. Some of the characters appear as themselves, under their true names. Others are clearly composite and have made-up names: their originals can be traced in many cases,[110] but the originals are not the character.

The Seven Storey Mountain grew, in part, from the nonfiction elements of "The Labyrinth" complex. Merton had some of the early journals when he wrote his autobiography in 1945–46. He did not have any pages of his novels.[111] One, the novel of his dream-return to Europe, was with Mark Van Doren. The others, including "The Labyrinth" complex, and "The Man in the Sycamore Tree," he thought had been destroyed when he left St. Bonaventure in the first week of December 1941:

> I took the manuscripts of three finished novels and one half-finished novel and ripped them up and threw them in the incinerator.[112]

He also says, "I gave away some notes to people who might be able to use them . . ."

In the hurry of leaving, Merton had indeed destroyed the manuscripts, but he had not checked the folders he had given away, which contained far more than his reading notes. In December 1941, Merton gave Father Richard Fitzgerald a folder that included reading notes, four pages of "The Straits of Dover," thirty-five pages from "The Man in the Sycamore Tree," some drafts of letters, and a number of drawings.[113]

It is quite possible that additional fragments of the novels exist, given away to others in the same way, and at the last moment. Merton may have overlooked the fact, too, that some of the copies he had sent out to publishers stood a fair chance of survival, either forgotten in the publishers' files, or at his agent's. One copy of one draft of "The Labyrinth" remains. None of this material had arrived at St. Bonaventure, however, when Merton asked for his journals.

At the Olean cottage, something much larger even than "The Labyrinth" complex (in all its fragments, versions, missing pieces) was forming in Merton's mind, the autobiography and anti-autobiography. The 1939 journal shows Merton in the process of collecting materials. The trip to Bermuda, and the other projected trips, were part of the necessary research. Merton was choosing the form and the language. He was also choosing and rejecting models.

Finnegans Wake was obviously the model of models. Giambattista Vico's theories had fascinated Joyce. Merton found them less helpful, at least as Croce explained them.[114] Joyce had also sent Merton back to reading Rabelais, and there was a set of Rabelais at the Olean cottage.[115] Another possible model, Thomas Wolfe, was promising, but *Look Homeward, Angel* and *Of Time and the River* proved disappointing.

The language materials were being gathered and tested. There were all the in-jokes and sayings Merton had enjoyed on the fourth floor of John Jay Hall. Before this, there had been the schoolboy slang of his letters to friends at Oakham. For Joyce's games with languages Merton was well provided. He had Latin and some Greek. He was fluent in French and Italian, slower in German, strong in Spanish. At the World's Fair, he had discovered he was mispronouncing Portuguese, but mispronunciations were a rich source in Joyce. Invented languages were something Merton had discovered long before he read Joyce, probably at least as far back as the Christmas plays he had put on with his cousins at "Fairlawn."

Merton was not the only one interested in invented languages. Both Rice and Lax had made experiments. The summer before, during a trip to Europe, Robert Lax had carried on a conversation in a French train with John Slate entirely in dog barks.

Vico had tried to trace the origin of human speech to an imitation of natural sounds like thunder, and animal noises. In *Ulysses*, Joyce attempted a complete sound picture of Dublin on June 14, 1904 — dog barks, the sounds of diners eating, a blind man's stick, newspaper presses, and all. In *Finnegans Wake*, he went further, and Vico's theories provide the thunderous falls of Finn and a great deal more.

There was much else to draw on: code words, radio static, advertising slogans (scrambled and read plain), experiments with automatic writing by the Surrealists and others, pidgin English, Babu English.

There was Apollinaire, the great language maker and breaker, the alchemist of modern poetry. There was Marinetti and his Futurist Sound Machine. There were the Dadaist poetry readings at the Café Voltaire. There were those who transformed English, like Gertrude Stein. Moving back in time, the names of language magicians were legion: Christian Morgenstern, Lewis Carroll, Edward Lear, Sterne, Swift, Rabelais, Lucian of Samosata and a hundred others. But above all there was Joyce.

The next summer, 1940, Rice reported that Merton kept the others at the cottage awake "talking to us in his sleep in an unintelligible language and laughing wildly."[116]

Merton's project was one that recorded virtually a whole life and that would take a lifetime to complete. Lax, Rice, and Merton had deliberately cut themselves off from newspapers and radio at the cottage. For all this, in the summer of 1939 Merton wondered whether he had a lifetime of years, or a few months, for writing.

Merton felt confident "The Labyrinth" was both publishable and commercial. He was reading an old copy of *Fortune* magazine[117] that one of Benji Marcus's business friends had left behind at the cottage. This had an article on writers' profits and the publishing business. It fed Merton's confidence in the novel, or complex of novels. What about the huge autobiography? Was that commercial? Was it about as commercial as poetry?

In his ambition to become an instant success as a writer, Merton had started the summer well. *The New York Times* published his poem "Fable for a War" on June 18. There was a good deal of information about the poet under the heading "2 Columbia Poets Named for Awards." Merton had won the Mariana Griswold Van Rensselaer Award and fifty dollars.

The poem was written in strict meter with rhyming couplets. Unexpectedly, in a period when he said he had given up on politics, it is a political, even a propaganda poem:

> The old Roman sow
> Bears a new litter now
> To fatten for a while
> On the same imperial swill.

The cannibal wolf will die
And root out Spanish bones beside the
pig . . .[118]

And so on for four further verses. It is hard to say what kind of promise this shows.

Writing in 1945 or 1946, Merton felt that the cottage looking out over Olean would have made a fine hermitage, or an ashram, and that he, Lax, and Rice had missed an opportunity that summer.[119] There was certainly something of the solitary in each one of them (something that was to come out in time). Lax appeared to be the most dedicated, getting up early to write. Most of the typing was done on the kitchen table among the clutter of half-prepared or half-eaten meals. Merton withdrew at times to say his rosary in the woods, or to read the *Summa*, or St. Augustine's *Confessions*, sitting under the tree on a mound of grass, across the drive from the cottage.

This part of western New York State and bordering Pennsylvania is a pleasant region of forested mountains and rich, well-kept farms in the valleys. The three writers went on expeditions in Rice's beat-up car, to Lake Cuba, to Rock City, to small mountain hotels with bars, to the Indian reservation, and to St. Bonaventure for books.

This time Merton was anxious to visit the friary and the Franciscan College. As the three walked across campus to the Friedsam Library, Merton probably looked up at the hill to the south of the campus, with its distinctive bare patch of meadow outlined by trees on the slope. This was simply known as The Pasture, or The Cow Pasture. In time, it would come to be called Merton's Heart.

It was Merton himself who received a new name to add to many that day. Loading the three of them with books, Father Irenaeus decided he was "Mr. Myrtle."[120] He probably told them that his own name meant "peaceful" in Latin and that the library meant "peaceful" in German. This slim, energetic man in patched brown robes, with very bright eyes behind his glasses and a boyish enthusiasm clear in all he said in his slight Alsatian accent, was someone Merton could add to his list of the "innocent of heart."

Back at the cottage the novels were going well: almost everything else was in chaos. If Father Irenaeus was trusting with his books, the Marcuses were equally trusting with their cottage. They did their best by providing a cleaning woman.

One day, when the three writers were sitting around the massive stone fireplace talking, several shots rang out in the woods nearby. Merton flattened himself on the floor, picked up the poker and his hat, and crawled to the window, where he waved the hat back and forth on the end of the poker. There were rumors the police were looking for a bearded suspect in a crime of passion. Merton was obviously amused. Later on, at St. Bonaventure and in the hermitage in Kentucky, he was to be far more unnerved by local acts of violence.

Lax, Rice, and Merton were equally interested in fairs and circuses, while Merton had worked as a barker at the Chicago World's Fair. It is surprising they were such an easy mark for a slick operator in one of the sideshows at the carnival in Bradford, Pennsylvania. The evening cost the party most of their savings for the summer. They even raced back along the Rock City road to collect the thirty-five dollars hidden at the cottage while the cooperative crook running the show kept the game open for them. Lax fell into a trance over the mystical importance of numbers as he tried to roll the ball into numbered holes, but the rules were changed on them as they played. They ended the evening with only the money Merton had saved in his pocket for drinking.

At a Bradford bar their beards and their talk of an imaginary syndicate, the Panama-American Entertainment Corporation, drew several of the girls who worked at the TB sanatorium at Rocky Crest to their table. Their triumph as big-time operators was short-lived. The party was broken up by local toughs, offended by the beards, the big talk, and the fact that the girls had been won away from them. Lax, Merton, and Rice were called out into the alley. After a slanging match, the engagement was broken off without bloodshed.[121]

On the journey back they speculated on what would have happened if they had been arrested, locked up, and brought to trial, either for getting in the fight or for killing the man who had fleeced them. They decided they would have pleaded temporary insanity as writers and produced their novels as evidence. That way, even before publication, their work would have reached an audience of at least twelve readers.[122]

Ed Rice negotiated the Rock City road for a fourth time, but he was afraid to try to get the car into the garage at the cottage.

> Innocent joy. Ten feet from where I sit is the place where we lay down in the grass, (tumbling out of the car drunk) laughing and cockeyed, the night of the carnival. Lax went inside the house and sat in a chair and talked to a laundry bag in a chair across the room thinking it was Rice, but Rice lay here in the grass and couldn't get up, and I suddenly come up terribly fast.[123]

Either that night, when he had "come up terribly fast," or the next, Merton took what revenge he could on Vanity Fair (or Bradford, Pennsylvania) by beating out what he hoped were African and voodoo curses on the set of bongo drums they had found at the cottage. According to Lax, Merton "really got them to sing," and he suspected at other times Merton was sending out signals to get in touch with Bramachari.[124]

Thanks to the game of no-chance at the Bradford carnival, supplies of food, and even drink, ran low at the cottage. During the day, they drank one Coca-Cola after another, or experimented with stale coffee grounds or a well-used teabag. The visits from Kenny Baker and other local boys, or from a rather lugubrious painter from Olean, were sometimes welcome interruptions, sometimes not. At one such party, Merton produced a bottle. There were times when Merton could drink a great deal and remain sober. At other times he seemed to get intoxicated largely on his own imagination. Lax remembers the bottle as a bottle of gin, Rice as a bottle of whiskey, but both recall that Merton drank very little and talked himself eloquently to sleep.[125] He woke up the next morning with no trace of a hangover and announced that keeping to a good brand of liquor had made all the difference. To Lax and Rice the greater mystery was where Merton had found the money for an expensive bottle.

By August, Joe Roberts joined them. Then, while Lax stayed on,[126] Merton, Rice, and Roberts returned to New York and took their beards to the World's Fair. Hair had become strangely important. Rice was writing an article on beards and beard lore. Bearded men — and women — were running rampant in the cartoons Merton was doing for *Jester*, and he decorated his passport pictures. The "Hemingway" photograph for the jacket of "The Labyrinth," taken in the early summer, was spared an outcrop of curls, muttonchops, and other improvements: it remained the authentic disguise.[127]

Meanwhile one sultry, overcast day followed another. Rumor and the radio news commentators worked on the nerves in the hot, stale streets. Riding the subway, Merton noticed his fellow travelers sitting bolt upright and staring before them, the newspapers open but unread on their laps.

In Merton's novel, "The Man in the Sycamore Tree," Jim Mariner (the character closest to Merton himself) leaves the Butler Library at Columbia on the evening of August 23, 1939. Mariner walks along the edge of South Field:

> A small group of young men with hats on the backs of their heads and fat brief cases on the brick pavement by their feet, stood around the pedestal of Jefferson's statue and argued about how soon Russia would be bound in military alliance with the two Empires of England and France, against the Nazis. From the subway station, people came reading evening papers, the big headlines of which said Paris was being evacuated.[128]

Mariner buys a newspaper and reads it on the subway. There are accounts of the Maginot Line, the conscription in England, and the atrocities the Poles are supposed to have committed against the Germans at Danzig. The news has already turned Mariner's stomach, "like the smell of some rotting, dead thing." He throws the newspaper away. It is already out of date. The newsstands show a new edition with headlines about an ambassador flying to Moscow. The ambassador is neither French nor British: he is Ribbentrop. The late, late papers announce a Soviet-German Pact. One streetcorner prophet manages a quick turnabout to avoid being left behind by history: "Stalin did it to save *you*, you bastard!" he shouts at a face in the crowd.[129]

Jim Mariner finds sanctuary from the plague-ridden city in the Church of Our Lady of Guadalupe on Fourteenth Street.

Whereas the end of August 1939 was a hard season for all prophets, Merton was to come to see himself a year later as a political prophet by reverse: what would happen would be the exact opposite of what he thought would happen.[130] Until the very last days of August 1939, Merton was saying, like Citizen Kane, that there would be no war in Europe.

Others were unnerved by the suspense. In "The Man in the Sycamore Tree" Merton puts into Tom Riley's mouth words he had probably overheard:

> "If only the damn war would start," said Riley, "that's all anybody cares about now. They know it has to start: so let it begin, let them go to work! If we've got to be all killed, they'd might as well begin and get it over with. And as for me, I don't see the point of sitting around playing the trumpet when the people upstairs don't like it, so why shouldn't I go and join the navy?"[131]

Riley and another friend, Fowke, discuss the fact that they have seen nothing of Mariner for days:

> "Oh, Mariner," said Fowke, "I think he is building himself a tent in front of some statue of Saint Francis, and spending his days burning candles to the Virgin, against the loss of his soul."
>
> "Doesn't he like our house any more? Is he mad at his girl Sue, and sore at his intellectual friends?"
>
> "No, but the priests have got him all sewed up. He can't stay away from churches, and I guess he's content to take Hail Marys as a sort of solution to his own eccentric problems."
>
> "In a way," said Riley, "I don't blame him. Churches are all right, and I can't imagine a better place to be, at a time like this, than in one of them, if you could believe in it."
>
> "Sure," said Fowke, "if you could believe in it."[132]

In the novel, Mariner is chiefly concerned with the outward signs of the plague. Where there are quotations from Blake and Nashe, the main source is Defoe's *Journal of the Plague Year*. Mariner expects to hear the cry "Bring Out Your Dead!" and to meet Solomon Eagle with a brazier of burning coals on his head, crying out pestilence and fire on New York, as he had once on London.

Thomas Merton was at least as concerned by the thought that, if there was plague, he had helped to spread it:

> There was something else in my own mind — the recognition: "I myself am responsible for this. My sins have done this. Hitler is not the only one who has started this war: I have my share in it too . . ." It was a very sobering thought, and yet its deep and probing light by its very truth eased my soul a little. I made up my mind to go to confession and Communion on the First Friday of September.[133]

On the night of Thursday, August 31, Merton went to confession at St. Patrick's Cathedral. Afterward, he walked to Dillon's Bar and Grill on the corner of Sixth Avenue and Forty-eighth Street. He had been in Dillon's already several times that week, and he and Robert Gibney often waited there in the evening until the show at the Center Theater nearby was over, when they were joined by girls who had bit parts in the show.

He was earlier than usual that night, but he met another friend, Jinny Burton, who had been at Barnard with Dona Eaton. Now that she had graduated, she had an apartment in New York. She had friends at the Rehearsal Club, the theatrical house where many of Gibney and Merton's friends in the show at the Center Theater were living. If both Merton and Lax felt she could have been a better actress than any of them, her main interest was in the fine arts, and she had her own income.

Jinny Burton's family lived in Urbanna, Virginia. She and her friend Joyce Ryan were off to Virginia the next day for a house party and the Labor Day Regatta on the Rappahannock, and Jinny invited Merton to come with them.[134]

On Friday, September 1, the sun shone brightly for the first time after a week of overcast days. Merton rose early and went to High Mass at the Church of St. Francis of Assisi, near Pennsylvania Station. After Mass, he met Jinny Burton and Joyce Ryan at the station. Merton had caught the excitement, but not the words, on the radio when he got up. Now the headlines on the newspapers told them all that Warsaw was being bombed. There *would* be war in Europe. In Poland it had already begun. The German liner *Bremen* had sailed from New York in the early hours of the morning and had cut off shore contact.

On the train the three of them drank Tom Collinses and ate sardine sandwiches. Between Washington and Richmond, the train went through the Marine Training Camp at Quantico. Straw dummies were lined up along the track, each one leaking straw through the holes punched in the sacks during bayonet practice.

Merton realized that in most of the movies he had seen recently there had been a bayoneting scene, and each time the audience had gasped. In *The Old Maid,* it was a Confederate who had been bayoneted; in *The*

Four Feathers, a Sudanese. There was no such scene in the film they saw that night, *Lady of the Tropics,* with Hedy Lamarr. Merton felt disorientated in Richmond until he found his way back to something familiar: he thought the dome of the railway station was exactly like that of the Columbia Law Library.[135]

On Saturday they reached Urbanna, and Merton was caught up at once in the Labor Day weekend parties of Tidewater Virginia. Each morning of his stay, he woke to find a drink already poured out beside his bed and the rest of the day was a struggle to keep up with the young Virginians. Out of supplies that night, the party made a run to the favorite liquor store and sang an exaggerated and slurred "God Bless Ameri-cuh!" as the car raced in the dark through Saluda, Virginia.[136]

The next day, Sunday, September 3, was the day of the regatta. Merton was far out in the estuary when he announced he had an impacted wisdom tooth which had given him so much pain he had hardly slept the night before. It was difficult to do anything for him.[137] Through the heat haze, people claimed they saw the *Bremen* riding the Atlantic and making its escape to Germany.

Later, toweling off after a night swim in the Rappahannock, Merton tried to forget that he had a hangover (made worse by the bright sun off the water all day) and a raging toothache.[138] He also felt the dread in his stomach he later gave his fictional character, Jim Mariner. Britain was now at war. All the Britains were at war: Aunt Maud's England, the house in Aberdeenshire, the factories in Coventry, Sheffield (where he'd stayed with a friend's family when he was at Oakham), the rectory at Brooke on the Isle of Wight, the house in Rye with the old clock, the alley behind the Red Cow in Cambridge.

Now the propaganda would reach a crescendo: Keep America Out! Get America In! Brave Little Britain! France, Our Oldest Ally . . .

Propaganda had already done much to bring on the war: Hitler's lies and the lies of so many others. In the democracies, the Left Wing intellectuals had made the Germans and the Italians appear sub-human, the Right Wing politicians and commentators had made the Russians sub-human. Even the antiwar propaganda, with its dramatic emphasis on the horrors of war, had probably helped to make war that much more certain.[139] The nightmares of all had been in strange alliance. "Perhaps the things I remember in nightmares are the things everybody is really fighting for"[140] . . . "For myths are realities, and they themselves open into deeper realms."[141]

Almost thirty years later, Marco Pallis was to speculate in a letter to Merton whether the Second World War did not have its seeds in the atrocity stories the Allies largely made up in their propaganda campaign against the Central Powers in the First World War.[142] Untrue in 1914–18, these myths became realities in 1939–45. It was almost as if a horrendous wish-fulfillment had been revealed to the world by 1939 — the Germany of the Allies' imagination in 1916.

Our enemies are ourselves dreaming.

Around him in the Virginia night, loud with insects, came the voices of the swimmers and drinkers, pale bodies moving in the dark waters of the creek. It was almost 3 A.M. of the second day of the war. There was something dreamlike about this, too.

At dinner the night before, when the radio came on, everybody had stopped talking; some simply froze with the food halfway to their mouth.[143] Merton felt as if he were going to faint, right there in the dining room. Even the parade of decorated boats at the regatta that day had seemed sinister and unnerving. Now the procession of boats on the blinding white water passed over and over before his eyes.

On Labor Day itself there was yet another party, this time at a friend's house in Urbanna. Merton had seemed withdrawn earlier during the day, obviously more affected by the news of the war than anyone else. That night he appeared transformed. Jinny Burton had never seen him behave like this before, and she never saw him act the same way again.[144]

The Labor Day party in Virginia was no replica of the party at Herb Jacobson's apartment in New York the previous October, though Merton regrets both occasions in his journals.[145] That night in Urbanna it was as if Merton reverted to the "Merty" of the Alpha Delta Phi parties of his first year at Columbia.

The toothache was worse. He had been drinking in the hot sun for three days. There was the war. And he mentions in his journals that he was jealous. Walking over from the Burton family house where he was staying, Merton had decided to capture Urbanna, to overcome all rivals. By all accounts, even his own, it was *his* party. For most of the time he held all the guests around him laughing uproariously. His sense of timing and his sense of an audience were those of a professional entertainer. Everything worked triumphantly together as Merton recited verse after verse of "The Infernal Screwing Machine" and provided a commentary.

❋

On September 5, Merton returned to a city that had had the jitters, but no war. The removal of his impacted wisdom tooth left him with five stitches in his jaw. For a time, he lay on his bed listening to old Bix Beiderbecke and Wolverine records. The whole apartment reeked with the disinfectant he was using on his torn mouth. When he felt a little better he moved into the front room. There was no temptation to go out into the streets. The Village seemed burned out after the long summer and all the emotion its population had been through in the past month. Recovering from both the dentist and the Labor Day weekend, Merton fell back on writing long, introspective passages in his journal, looking up occasionally from his writing, as he did when something large and threatening went by in the sky beyond the window, to find — and record — it was only the Goodyear blimp.[146]

The holiday in Virginia had only underlined what had been building for months — his sense that nothing he was doing was real. He was getting to the point, once more, where he talked and thought of love, and where love seemed the least real thing of all. He was writing so much, yet nothing he had written broke through the curious, all-prevailing barrier of unreality.

There was a jaded, stale sense of the less-than-real about everything, the Contemporary Civilization of morgues and public cancer wards, and over-rehearsed wars. It was the final surprise to find that even the much-feared war was unreal:

> In the movies, when war broke out in something like "Hell's Angels," they flashed a front-page make-up like this one onto the screen.
> And now the whole thing was just the same. It was so phoney, so exactly consonant with all the demands of theatrical artifice, that it could not be anything but true. Warsaw bombed; British ultimatum to Germany: you could see it all reproduced in the pages of a Shorter History for Third Grade. It was war. Already hundreds of people were dead.[147]

Herodotus was a far more reliable guide to history than the newspapers. Merton went on collecting materials for his own history; his own pattern:

> On the Long Island Train today: going through the Sunnyside Yards. On top of a factory, the sign "Karpen" (I guess Furniture) of course I have seen it a hundred times, but it never meant anything. I recognized it as something I had seen before, but I happened to be thinking about it, in relation to some telegraph poles moving in front of it. Then, I recollected it. Now, for the first time, I remember it. It is part of a pattern of my own, not part of a series of things that just happen to be there in Long Island city.[148]

In his journal that fall, Merton tried to find the difference between "memory" and "imagination," and to define each term. He wrote that in the writings of Proust there was a distinction between the "present time of things present" and the "present time of things past." For Proust, only his writing in time present was as attractive as "the present time of things past."[149]

This was not to be true of Thomas Merton, except during certain periods. The autumn of 1939 is one of those periods.

To help his students in the composition class he was teaching three nights a week in the extension program at the School of Business at Columbia, Merton began to work out his own ideas of style in his journal. The notes are a justification of the particular style Merton was struggling to develop, but they show him, too, as a conscientious teacher. It was a rare teacher of composition who set aside the easy formulas of the textbooks to assert that grammar was "not the art of speaking *correctly* but of speaking *logically*," to talk of "the innate logic of language," and to defend slang.

In 1939, Merton's very desire to write effectively was getting in the way of his natural ability. It was one thing to know he had developed no distinctive style of his own. It was much worse for him to find that, for all its looseness, his own writing wasn't often lively.

On October 14, back came his novel (almost certainly "The Straits of Dover") with a rejection slip from Farrar and Rinehart. On the telephone, Merton managed to bully someone at the publisher's office into telling him why the novel had been sent back. Exasperated by an author who couldn't take a simple no, the person on the other end of the line read Merton the reader's notes with no polite omissions: the novel was shoddily written and impossible to follow. It was often dull and the reader had given up without finishing it. So much for instant fame.

"Looking at the thing again, I find all that is true."[150] Merton was going to have to learn to write after all his writing, just as he had had to teach himself to read after all his reading.

Two years later, he had done exactly that. What he had not done was to develop a critical sense of his own work. He was so distracted by the struggle that he thought he had succeeded where he had failed, and he overlooked the pages which should have given him his greatest confidence. Robert Lax was a far better critic. But he had been unable to convince Merton that the most difficult was not for this reason meritorious, nor was what seemed natural to be despised simply because it appeared too easy. In November 1939, Lax tried again. Their conversation was finally to focus Merton's religious aims. It did not influence his goals for his own writing. No one in the next two years was able to convince Merton he was not a novelist.

In terms of Merton's life, the failure did not greatly matter, though it was certainly important to him between 1938 and the end of 1941. What is interesting is that Merton had a number of the very qualities needed. He failed because he was unable to create a fictional character,[151] and because he made the mistake of thinking that anti-plot means plotless. He destroyed the short stories he wrote that he thought too conventionally plotted,[152] so there is no way of telling now whether he could write a plot. In the modern novels he chose as models, Merton failed to see what held the work together. Nothing holds his own fiction together. There are good scenes. There is no matrix.

Merton's journals may be slipshod at times, but even in 1939, the records of smells, sounds, objects, encounters, have a reality and a vitality about them that make the question "what went wrong?" almost haunting:

> Noise of someone opening up the legs of a card-table — a drag and a sudden catch . . .

> Noise of the sprinkler, as it turns scattering whirling threads of water around the air over the front lawn. Twenty or thirty feet away the leaves of the privet hedge move where you would not have suspected water was falling.[153]

Something did go wrong, and that something was to set Merton urgently on the track of the real in words, words whose authenticity would stand against all abstraction.

Here, at least, the pursuit of the hard way was to lead through failure to something of value. There are, finally, no reliable guides to good writing. There is not even an abstract quality of "good" which is uniformly attracted to certain combinations of words. "Writing well," as Rémy de Gourmont said, "is a way of writing badly."[154] In that sense, Merton's notes for his students are correct. But what is the "logic of grammar"? There is language that works, and language which fails wretchedly. Slang can be dead on the page and Sir Walter Raleigh's *Voyage to the Orinoco* can sing with beauty and immediacy over the chasm of three hundred and sixty years.

Reg Marsh's idea that the damn thing ought to have life in it applied to writing — and to other things. Merton's enthusiasm for jazz was stronger than ever, while the Cuban Pavilion at the World's Fair had brought him a new source of excitement, Spanish-American dancing. When his allowance arrived, he would telephone Jinny Burton and they would make a night of it, either at Nick's or at El Chico's. His favorite evenings at Nick's were when the backs were taken off the pianos and Meade Lux Lewis, Pete Johnson, and Albert Ammons played three-piano boogie-woogie. At El Chico's, Jinny Burton and Merton would swap partners and dance with the two exhibition dancers who were appearing there. Jinny Burton thought Merton almost good enough to be a jazz pianist. His dancing, too, was almost professional. Something always seemed to hold him back, Jinny thought, except on the night of the party at Urbanna.[155]

One night when Jinny Burton was not present at Nick's occupies an important place in the autobiography. Ed Rice, Bob Gerdy, and Merton had sat at the circular bar listening to the jazz. Bob Gibney and Peggy Wells joined them when the show at the Center Theater finished. Peggy Wells had a part in the show. Later some of the group went home, some slept over at Perry Street.

At eleven the next morning things were coming slowly to life at the apartment. Merton returned with food supplies and more cigarettes. A Bix Beiderbecke record was playing. There were plans to take Merton's favorite walk to the Chicken Dock once breakfast was over and the place had been cleaned up. Merton sat on the floor, where he had slept the night. He had a hangover, little appetite for breakfast, and no desire to start smoking his first cigarette of the day. He was overwhelmed at that moment with a feeling of disgust for the life he was leading. In *The Seven Storey Mountain* he says this was also the moment he decided to become a priest.[156]

His disgust may have reinforced the idea, but it was one he had had for almost a year. In the autobiography Merton goes on to say he had talked to Bob Gibney about becoming a priest but that Gibney had not thought he was serious. Father Ford and Dan Walsh had certainly taken him seriously.

Merton's point was that decisions could be made in unlikely moments and in unlikely surroundings. In later years he was to shock his fellow monk Father Raymond, and others at Gethsemani, by making this point even more melodramatically. He asked his novices to imagine a man lying on the floor, recovering from a drunken stupor, who wakes up and stares at the ceiling, realizing his whole life has been changed by conversion or by the certainty of a religious vocation.[157]

There are a number of discrepancies in the account at this point. In the autobiography, Merton sets the meeting with Walsh that was most important for his vocation in the fall, and a similar important meeting with Robert Lax in the spring of 1939. The journals reverse this. Merton had certainly been consulting with Dan Walsh since the night of the Maritain reading, and Lax was often away from New York City that year; Merton records missing the friend he relied on most.

That autumn, Merton found himself drawn unexpectedly to the Jesuits. This must have been in part because he was giving an hour or more a day at Perry Street to the spiritual exercises of St. Ignatius Loyola,[158] something that was helping him solve the old problems of concentration, even when it did not bring him to contemplation. When he asked Walsh questions, Walsh answered only that he knew few Jesuits, and then went on to talk with such enthusiasm of his retreat that summer at the Monastery of Our Lady of Gethsemani that Merton wondered whether he ought to revise his earlier comment that Dan Walsh knew him better than anybody. He had just managed to overcome his fears of the Jesuits: what Merton knew of the Trappists frightened him a great deal more. Their talk that night at the bar of the Biltmore Hotel went back to the Franciscans.[159]

On his birthday, November 30, Robert Lax came down from Olean, where he had been working for the local radio station. It was a general rule among the Columbia group that friends did not argue with friends. According to Merton, nobody argued with Ad Reinhardt about his being a Communist.[160] According to Robert Lax, nobody argued with Merton about his being a Catholic — neither did they argue about "the Spanish Civil War or Pope Joan with Merton."[161] Merton lists more arguments than usual for those years, but only two with Lax, the debate over mortification, and the one on November 30, 1939.[162]

The discussion began with a disagreement about publishing. Merton saw the need to make a name by publishing critical articles in such places as *The Southern Review*. Lax thought he was trying too hard, and with the wrong approach. Merton ought to concentrate on the writing that meant most to him: the writing was the important thing for the moment, getting a name was secondary.

All through that summer at the cottage, Lax had been stressing how different things look when they are written down. He may very well have been arguing in a tactful way for critical distance, trying to convince Merton that his best was not getting into his writing.

What Merton said was a good deal livelier and more sincere than what he tried to get published. In this sense, the *Fortune* article that turned up at the cottage was the worst kind of snare, especially for Merton, with its how-to-achieve-instant-success-as-a-writer approach.

On the night in November when all this became too heated, Lax tried to get Merton to focus on his real aims. Did he want to be a poet, a novelist, an essayist, a critic? "What do you want to do, anyway?"

The question threw Merton back on the inner debate he had pursued since his baptism the November before. He struggled now with his priorities. The answer he gave was that he wanted to be a good Catholic.

> "What do you mean, you want to be a good Catholic?"
> The explanation I gave was lame enough, and expressed my confusion, and betrayed how little I had really thought about it at all.
> Lax did not accept it.
> "What you should say" — he told me — "what you should say is that you want to be a saint."
> A saint! The thought struck me as a little weird. I said:
> "How do you expect me to become a saint?"
> "By wanting to," said Lax, simply.[163]

Lax had not said "by trying to become one." By wanting to become a saint you could become one, just as sufficient faith moved mountains. The idea Lax had planted was not to go away. For the time Merton turned to reading the lives of saints, not into himself. It dismayed him to find both Lax and Mark Van Doren closer to an understanding of what it meant to lead a holy life than he was. He listed all the things that stood between him and the way of poverty. Then he decided the very lists were another distraction.

The apartment at Perry Street had appeared high up on his list of luxuries. It was his home now. He knew that nobody committed to the religious life required this kind of stability, yet he found himself worrying more than ever where he was going to live. Ever since his encounter with the window in the room near Pennsylvania Station, he had been afraid of hotel rooms. He had not liked the room at the Hamilton in Bermuda. He did not like the hotel room in Washington when he and Ed Rice went there in early December. He made another list. The only hotel he liked was the Olean House. (He had spent the end of December with the Lax family.)[164]

Where a threat of rootless wandering oppressed him, he wondered about other choices. It was one thing to read about the monasteries of the Middle Ages and to decide the life then had connections with the life of schoolboys in English schools like Oakham; Merton wondered if modern monasteries and seminaries would not be closer to the Lycée at Montauban. He imagined corridors with chipped paint on the walls, dormitories with rows of iron beds, figures in long white robes showing skinny legs, mournful bugles and the sound of trams coming in from somewhere far over the walls, through the tall windows.[165] He was not sure he was ready for dormitories again, for the rule of bells. Perhaps the alternative to all this was an army barracks, another kind of discipline.

Then Merton turned on himself. Wasn't pride in his own independence at the root of his worst faults? He had moved a considerable distance from his shock of horror at seeing the *Imprimatur* on a page of Gilson's book. But what rules saved the individual from self-obsession and a blinding pride? What rules denied the individual his chance to be an individual? How could one tell the difference between a structure, an institution, a set of rules — which concentrated the individual on a search for the true self, beyond the distraction of a false pride in a false self — and a structure, an institution, a set of rules, that distorted or destroyed all sense of self? On this question the inconsistencies of Merton's journals in 1939–40 were hardly his alone. There was never to be a complete answer.

In 1939, Merton saw that a misunderstanding of grammar led to tyranny, and this brought him to other things:

To impose on language rules from the outside, (call that grammar). To deny language its own life and logic as a living, growing thing. What does that reflect? The imposing, on man, of rules from the outside: standardise him, stamp him with rubberstamp characteristics in a democracy, Nazi state, he must be such and so: his soul, character, must be formed according to rules formulated outside him, not dictated within him by a conscience inspired by God and directed by the milder and widely flexible rules of a Church guarded and instructed by the holy spirit, which believes that every moral case should be judged on its own merits, and has immense respect for the *individuality* of every man's soul. (For there is only true liberty within the Church. I say it; and funnily enough — Blake said the same of Temporal rule by Rome.)[166]

Merton goes back to the same quotation of what Blake is reported to have said in the letter by Samuel Palmer. He returns to this again and again to confirm what is clearly one side of his own inner debate.

When Merton discovered that his friend Ed Rice also felt at times like becoming a priest, he found Rice's "difficulties are the same as mine. Astonishing how much they follow the same pattern." Merton wanted Rice to come with him. The "difficulties" they share are revealing, just because there is, in fact, only one of them.

> First: he thinks of the Jesuits. That's what I started out with, too. I suppose in my case it was because of working on Hopkins.
> Second: he is afraid he will no longer be able to "write the way he wants to." That is, freely, using any kind of language that presents itself.
> Third: He is not particularly anxious to get married, any more than I am.[167]

Of the three, only the second seems to be a difficulty.

When Merton talked to Jinny Burton about his future, she asked him how he was going to be able to write when he went into a Franciscan seminary. Merton said he had discussed this and it had been arranged.[168]

It would not be surprising if there was a good deal of wishful thinking in the answer, but it is important. Even more important, Merton told Jinny Burton later that the Trappists, too, had agreed to let him write. There are difficulties on dates here, but it was clear to Jinny Burton and others that Merton's idea of his religious vocation included writing.

If Merton in 1939 was "not particularly anxious to get married," this hardly presented a difficulty as far as a religious vocation went, though he had a strange way of putting it. Earlier, in his journal, he had written sympathetically about the idea of getting married. In his long discussions with Wilma Reardon in the spring of 1939 at the World's Fair, Merton talked about the sacrifices a writer has to make. One of these, he thought, was marriage and a family. This may have been one more idea he was testing out in conversation to get a reaction.

We know the names of a number of women from Merton's journals. But it is telling that the two people who are skeptical about his reputation for being always surrounded by women in those years are Robert Lax and Jinny Burton. Robert Lax says Merton rather frightened women by rushing at them: it may have been a way of ensuring that he did not get too involved.[169] Jinny Burton says she never thought of Merton as a young man obsessed by women: for her, his obsession was with his own writing. She is baffled to be described as a "serious girl-friend": she says they never talked of marriage.[170]

Yet it is hard not to think of Jinny Burton as one of the many models for B. in *My Argument with the Gestapo*. Merton remembered her and mentioned her in his journals years later.[171] He may have been more serious than she was. With her brown curls and her lively eyes, Lax says that Jinny Burton in 1939 and 1940 had the same looks and qualities as Giulietta Masina in the early films of Fellini.[172] She was witty and a delightful companion, popular with all Merton's friends.

Lilly Reilly, who danced with a ballet company, Jinny Burton, and Celeste De Bellis, from California, were friends. Merton often accompanied the three of them to shows at the Museum of Modern Art, or to late-night movies at the Thalia on Ninety-fifth Street, and other theaters. When funds were short he would suggest "a great big ice-cream soda."

Merton had also met Barbara (or Bobby) Chase at her father's studio. There were parties, Lax remembers, at Woodstock, where she lived, and on Long Island. Most of Merton's infatuations tended to be short-lived, Lax thought; only Jinny and Bobby Chase were friends for years.

*

By the end of 1939, Merton had at last succeeded in clearing up the matter of his papers. He was going to enter a seminary. He was not successful in persuading Ed Rice to come with him. Whatever he had told Jinny Burton about making an arrangement with the Franciscans allowing him to write, he was obviously still anxious about this, and about censorship.

When Merton talked with Ad Reinhardt he found that Reinhardt was quite willing to admit that the abstract paintings he was doing would have been burned in Soviet Russia. Merton's discussions with Ad and Joan led him to make comparisons between individual Catholics and individual Communists, comparisons he was often to make in the future. He decided Reinhardt wanted only conversion and baptism to make him a good, beginning Catholic.

It was clear that if Ad Reinhardt was under considerable economic restraint in capitalist New York, he was under no censorship, either from capitalists or from his fellow party members. For Merton, friendship transcended all ties. He was loyal to the small group of friends he had made at Columbia. At the moment this meant that Merton was far less resentful to hear that Joan and Ad considered his decision to go into a religious order quite a good way to secure free meals for life than he was to hear from Father Kenealy at Corpus Christi that a secular priest was "his own boss." The Reinhardts added that he probably had other, "emotional" reasons. Merton reminded himself later that "emotional" was not a good word in Communist circles.

The debate between Father Ford at Corpus Christi and Dan Walsh was resolved. On October 16, at Ford's request, Merton went to see Father Furlong at Cathedral College. When Father Furlong was in favor of the diocesan life, as Merton had expected, he went back to Dan Walsh. Walsh's words counted most, but Merton wondered if he was being self-willed, if his motives were the right ones. He remembered St. Francis's dream and God's command: "You see my house is in ruins! Go and repair it."[173]

Before he could repair a religious order, he had to enter it. His long-term ambitions were not as arrogant as they sound:

> I talk about the argument, not my own ability to do anything, for by myself I cannot even pray, but God must first make me want to, and without God I am nothing but dust.[174]

He had long talks with Father Edmund. Merton was disappointed by the "Franciscan showplace," the monastery on Thirty-first Street, and more disappointed when he met Father Charles Hogan, who appeared a rather obsessed and embarrassed liberal:

> Must be a pile of priests around who look on themselves as radicals. Left Wing stuff and economics bore me at the moment. It all seems so dumb and futile; waste of energy. But tied up with theology it must have *some* life, *some* value, some force. Maybe a lot. That is something I will need to learn, I suppose.
>
> But just at present I am not interested: also it seems false and improper somehow. You get too much interested in Unions and you forget about Charity and get all tied up in beating the Ginsburg Sash and Door Company, or the next union. Pretty silly things can happen, if that once starts.[175]

It may be, for once, that when he said he was *not* interested he was really not interested. But perhaps he had already begun to sense something which later grew to major importance, the feeling that activism without discipline (and even a vital distance) was in danger of devouring itself, a dragon eating its own tail.

Talking with Father Edmund, he was bitterly disappointed to learn that the earliest he could hope to enter the novitiate was in August 1940, ten months away, when the new class started there. Merton won the concession that his classes with Dan Walsh might qualify him to enter halfway through the novitiate year, in February, but this was a slim chance. He expressed his disappointment more strongly in the journal than in the autobiography.[176]

Perhaps he made too much of this at the time. Father Edmund had asked him a number of questions about his background. His impatience and restlessness may have come out in the answers when Merton learned he would have to wait until August. If he also brought up the question of writing and asked for an agreement, or thought he had one, he may have been laying the groundwork for a much greater disappointment.

He knew he was too quick to make judgments, good or bad. Enthusiasts are seldom biting critics. Merton was a born critic, as he was a born enthusiast. Sometimes there was little preparation for such attacks; they appeared gratuitous and unbalanced. He could fly into an odd fury writing an account of meeting the local hunt as a schoolboy at Oakham,[177] and later write off the Albigensians as Hitlerites.[178]

He was as worried in 1939 about his tendency to attack as he was about overpraising. He knew he had been unfair to Father Hogan, and he listed others. If he decided the congregation at Zion Episcopal Church were there to be confirmed in their own sense of self-righteousness, he also wrote that the congregation of St. Anastasia's Roman Catholic Church in Douglaston "rushed out of Mass as soon as they could, even before the blessing." Then he decided that what he had written showed a "kind of pharasaic snobbery."[179] Things looked different when they were written down. For one thing, they were remarkably revealing. This had been Lax's point all summer at the cottage in Olean.

Merton drew his own conclusion from this, something that would become important later. If he saw that he had often been wrong, this did little to inhibit him. He could make amends later, or tear out the pages. In his early journals he tore out many pages. Later on, he let the judgments stand, however harsh. Often an attack is followed several pages later by a retraction or a modification or a more balanced view. This may show honesty in the writer, but it is hard for the reader to correct the earlier impression.

Merton decided he had missed very little by being closed up with his writing and his religious exercises in the fall. It was better in the Village when the early spring came. He missed very little of what he saw:

Down at the corner of Eleventh and Bleecker — piles of cake and trays of cookies and pastry in Sutter's window. On the opposite corner, on the block where Van Doren lives, a girl with an armful of parcels posts a letter. A well to do married couple, drunk and unsteady, stand by the florist store. The man looks at the store: the wife says "Don't buy anything more, don't buy anything more" and he answers "Why not? Why not?"[180]

Everything was just as important in Greenwich Village as it had been when he was gaining his first impressions under the shape of Mount Canigou. After listing those who are writing autobiographies, Merton says:

Every fellow has built his own dumb pyramid. But it's not so dumb either. There has been wonderful autobiography in this age. (And terrible stuff, too — like this Joseph Freeman.)

That comes from the fact that people know you can write about everything, everything is important, or can be. Everything was important to
St. Francis.[181]

Autobiography should have been the theme that freed you from all
models. Merton was depressed to find that when he set his students
autobiographical essays as assignments they all began to write imitation Saroyan, as if their own experience meant nothing. Merton never
lost his own belief that his own voice and his own style would come
from writing about himself:

> I guess where we really know how to talk is in autobiography. We can't
> write Iliads or Greek plays but we can write autobiography — and po-
> etry.[182]

In the fall of 1939, Merton wrote the first poem that would continue
to mean something to him. The subject took him back to England. He
had read a newspaper account of the burial of British airmen in Germany. Shot down, they were given full military honors in those early
days of the war. Merton wondered if one of them could have been Bill
Hemmings, who had written to him in 1937 that he was joining the
RAF. Hemmings had been Merton's study-mate briefly at Oakham,
before he had to leave for an operation. Merton remembered they had
done an assignment in Latin together.[183] One entire Roman legion had
found "a place suitable for ambushes" in the Teuterborg Forest, in Germany:

> "We knew that battle when it was
> A curious clause in Tacitus,
> But were not able to construe
> Our graves were in this forest too;
> And, buried, never thought to have found
> Such strange companions, underground."[184]

"Two British Airmen" is close in elegiac tone to the far more famous
poem Merton wrote later for his brother. It is a fine poem despite all
the echoes of other poems by other poets. Merton was to write poetry
for far too long in voices other than his own. It was just the same
weakness he saw so clearly in his students when they wrote their prose
essays under the spell of Saroyan.

It is clear that Merton had not cut off all ties with England. There
are even two "Englishisms" in the sketch he wrote in his journal about
the street scenes at Eleventh and Bleecker, where "a girl with an armful of parcels posts a letter." Robert Lax says that Bob Gibney told him
of an evening when Gibney and Merton were walking back to Perry
Street. They started a conversation with an English sailor. To Bob
Gibney's amusement, the American Merton was transformed beside him
into an English Merton, and a Cockney Merton at that.[185]

As 1939 became 1940, however, most things had been pulling Merton toward Latin America: the flamenco dancers at the World's Fair, his own dancing, the poetry of García Lorca, and, perhaps most strongly of all, his feeling for the "Little Spain" close to Perry Street. The center of the community was the church of Our Lady of Guadalupe, where he took communion most mornings.

When he had still more teeth extracted in December 1939, he recovered at Perry Street, poring over travel brochures of Cuba and Mexico. Merton had always loved guidebooks. His favorite reading now was T. Philip Terry. He could put up with Terry's way of referring to Mexicans as "Mex," the assumption that the poor were potential thieves, and the belief that ignorance, superstition, and Catholicism went lockstep together. Perhaps Terry's style of writing reminded him of Pop's way of speaking, prejudices and all. The passage that probably decided Merton on Cuba was this:

> . . . The *cañonazo* (cannon-shot) fired from Morro Castle at 9 P.M. is the signal for many social functions to start. A host of *habaneros* take out their watches and set them in accordance when this shot is heard.[186]

This has the ring of Sam Jenkins arriving at 50 Virginia Road from a day at Grosset and Dunlap, beating the handrail of the staircase with his hand or the rolled-up newspaper between each step as he climbed the stairs, calling out "Where is everybody? When's dinner?"[187]

Before Merton could leave for Cuba, however, there was a further period full of frustrations and delays. He was told he could not write his doctoral thesis on the poetry of Gerard Manley Hopkins. There was now no chance he could enter the Franciscan seminary before August. Until he entered the seminary, he was dependent on Columbia's Grant in Aid program for doctoral students.

"The opposite of sloth is not 'activity' or industriousness in a business sense. It is fortitude — inclu. Patience and Long-suffering," he wrote in his journal.[188] If much came easy to Merton, "Patience and Long-suffering" did not. And that, he knew, was more a cause for laughter than for tears.

He had tried his novel again, revised, on Farrar and Rinehart. When he got it back, he walked the typescript round to Macmillan and handed it to a Mr. Purdy.[189] He was pleased to think that his work was being read in a publisher's office that had the solid appearance of a bank. He speculated on the reader: Was he liking it? What was he liking? What was he disliking? This paragraph? That paragraph? What sort of expression did the reader have as he read? The book came back.

Merton tried Viking, Knopf, and Harcourt Brace (where Robert Giroux read it). With three more nos, he decided he needed help.

At some time in the early spring of 1940, Merton took his work to

Curtis Brown, literary agents, at 347 Madison Avenue. The choice may have been arbitrary: Brooks Brothers was across the avenue, and he was accustomed to window-gazing there. That day, at least, coincidences were working in his favor, and "He was a very coincidental kind of man," as Naomi Burton has said.[190] It was to Naomi Burton the unknown author was shown as soon as he had negotiated the tiny entrance hall and the sign saying Information.

Naomi Burton had come to New York less than a year before from London. Like all good literary agents, she had a sense of what was possible and a firm conviction that false encouragement is ultimately the worst kind of discouragement. An unknown author arrives like an uninvited typescript, "over the transom," so Mr. Merton's work would be read and he would be contacted. He was soon out on Madison Avenue once more, speculating what Miss Burton would think of "The Labyrinth."

Miss Burton liked it. Curtis Brown would take him on.

They remained on "Miss" and "Mr." terms. Some months later, Naomi Burton was impressed to find she was getting comments at publishing cocktail parties from editors and readers who had rejected Merton's work, but remembered it. She noted to herself that an author whose writing could make so many friends was bound to succeed, given time and perseverance.

In April, Merton had to have his appendix taken out at St. Elizabeth's Hospital. As soon as the doctor pronounced him well enough he was on his way to Miami. He stayed at the Leroy Hotel, an "old" hotel, which, he speculated, meant it had been built about six years before and in the Spanish style, just prior to the craze for Functional, an architectural cheat in which all the decoration had to look as if it had a function.[191]

Otherwise, Merton decided, Miami was none of the cliché things it had been said to be. He recorded signs ("Madame Taylor Trout's Theatrical Dance Studio" and "Hollywood by the sea — the friendliest town on earth") and impressions of a gangland killing in the local newspaper for poems he wrote much later. The nightclubs, another El Chico and the Five O'Clock Club, were hardly exciting.[192] The Church of the Gesú on First Avenue near Flagler Street rather frightened him, a "church that is fitted out to serve a parish of desperate and violent souls," while St. Patrick, at "the good end" of Miami Beach, was full of well-dressed "happy looking, guileless people" . . . "Even the one or two colored fellows in the church were that way, nicely dressed, happy, serene."[193]

He decided that "Romantically speaking the Gesú is the more exciting parish, and the one where a priest would be more likely to become a saint . . . if it is possible to say such a thing."[194] The point goes beyond a comparison of the two churches and a pull to the Romantic and frightening. It shows the idea of being a secular priest had not altogether left him.

A few days later, Merton moved his luggage down to the pier where the Clyde Mallory liners docked. He was off by sea to Cuba, to his first view of Havana over the water.[195]

All his judgment was suspended for Havana, even for the sellers of lottery tickets whose voices jargoned over that of the priest saying Mass. Havana was noisy and exciting and loud, yet somehow the opposite of frantic. Despite Merton's initial disappointment after all the anticipation with the Morro gun in Havana, there was one social encounter soon after the gun sounded. It was unexpected and the better for being spontaneous:

What social function was presently initiated by me under the impulse of this stirring and so significant shot? I walked for several blocks in the warm, sweetsmelling treeshaded villalighted softvoiced Vedado until I reached the intersection of L and twenty fifth street, at which intersection, opposite the Medical school of Havana University (a little grey building that looks like a nunnery) is situated the café known as Las Delicias de la Medicina or the Delights of Medicine.

Here, ensconsing myself upon an iron chair on the terrace I ordered a coco glacé which was duly brought, spoon and all.

I had about half finished indulging my sweettooth with this extraordinary creole delicacy when two small girls, aged about eleven, I should judge, made a gap in the privet hedge that separates the café from the sidewalk, and one of them with a great deal of friendly mockery addressed me in English with the following words:

"What- is- your- name?"

"Ha ha ha" I cried with a loud larf, "Thomas. What's yours?"

"Ha ha ha" she replied, "Wednesday, no, Tuesday," and made as if to run off. But she stayed, and presently she said:

"My-English Teacher name is Miss Gombold."

"Ha ha ha" I larfed, believing every word, for that sentence had the true ring of sincerity. "Where do you go to school?"

"Colegio de Luz" (Loo-oo-th) she replied with what was probably a first rate parody of Miss Gombold's spanish accent. And at this they both larfed fit to kill. Then they went away, but they soon came back, and when they did, the other little girl, who had not spoken so much before, now made me a compliment upon my personal beauty, alleging that I was very "pretty" as she was pleased to term it. I could only reply in kind, which, of course, brought on a gale of laughter, and an immediate proposition of marriage, which I was unfortunately unable to accept through press of other business.

I had noticed, all along, that this second little girl wore her hair short: I mean so short that it was what we call a crew cut, and I could only conclude that her head must have been completely shaved within recent months. As it turned out, I was right, for before we parted she took occasion to recount how some time before she had been in the hospital for having fallen out of a third story window on her head which was in itself extremely remarkable. I gallantly replied that I had just had my appendix out and we parted the best of friends.[196]

Merton says in his autobiography that he had come to Cuba "to make a pilgrimage to Our Lady of Cobre. And I did, in fact, make a kind of pilgrimage. But it was one of those medieval pilgrimages that was nine-tenths vacation and one-tenth pilgrimage."[197] Experiences in life seldom break down into such neat mathematical divisions — certainly not pilgrimages. Then, as on other occasions, Thomas Merton could never quite admit how much he loved to travel. In 1940, after all the long bus rides to get there, Our Lady of Cobre was a disappointment. Merton could find nowhere to pray quietly in the church because he was at the mercy of an elderly lady determined to sell him religious medallions. He accepted this with unusual equilibrium; he bought a medallion and went out into the sunlight. Cobre gave him a poem, which was full of the joy of those April days and much the best poem he had written.[198] Cuba confirmed the knowledge that Catholicism was warm and natural, as well as a supernatural religion. It was his experience at Our Lady of Guadalupe on Fourteenth Street magnified many times over. After Cuba, if religious experience demonstrated coldness on the natural plane it lacked love.

Far less important, though significant to Merton because of his own bent and background, was the realization that religious shrines and images did not have to be tasteless, even in the twentieth century. He discovered, too, as almost every honest traveler has had to admit, that it was far easier to give to beggars in another country.[199]

Merton's deepest religious experience took place when he returned to Havana — and perhaps in the instant friendships he made in towns on the road:

> The town of Sancti Spiritus didn't have any signs on it saying Welcome or Come Again, brother. When we got there in the bus I got down to get a drink of some gaseosa, — and this small boy came up smiling and said hello. I asked him what town it was, and he said it was Sancti Spiritus. I said it looked very beautiful. He said yes indeed it was: where was I going? To Camaguey? Why didn't I get off the bus and stay and see Sancti Spiritus. But I said no, I couldn't. Maybe I would on the way back, in a couple of weeks. So when the bus pulled out of Sancti Spiritus there was I with a friend waving goodbye, saying he hoped I would really come back to Sancti Spiritus in two weeks.[200]

Merton went back to Havana from Oriente and Our Lady of Cobre by the same route he had come: Santiago, Camagüey, Matanzas. At the Church of St. Francis in Havana the pilgrimage was to separate it-

self from the holiday in a way he could not have foreseen. He found
St. Francis packed with schoolchildren:

> Mass had already begun, and the priest was reading the epistle. Then a
> brother in a brown robe came out, and you could see he was going to
> lead the children in singing a hymn. High up behind the altar St. Francis
> raised his arms up to God, showing the stigmata in his hands; the chil-
> dren began to sing. Their voices were very clear, they sang loud, their
> song soared straight up into the roof with a strong and direct flight and
> filled the whole church with its clarity. Then when the song was done,
> and the warning bell for consecration chimed in with the last notes of the
> hymn and the church filled with the vast rumour of people going down
> on their knees everywhere in it: and then the priest seemed to be stand-
> ing in the exact center of the universe. The bell rang again, three times.
> Before any head was raised again the clear cry of the brother in the
> brown robe cut through the silence with the words "Yo Creo . . ." "I
> believe" which immediately all the children took up after him with such
> loud and strong and clear voices, and such unanimity and such meaning
> and such fervor that something went off inside me like a thunderclap and
> without seeing anything or apprehending anything extraordinary through
> any of my senses (my eyes were open on only precisely what was there,
> the church), I knew with the most absolute and unquestionable certainty
> that before me, between me and the altar, somewhere in the center of
> the church, up in the air (or any other place because in no place), but
> directly before my eyes, or directly present to some apprehension or other
> of mine which was above that of the senses, was at the same time God
> in all His essence, all His power, all His glory, and God in Himself and
> God surrounded by the radiant faces of the uncountable thousands upon
> thousands of saints contemplating His glory and praising His Holy
> Name. And so the unshakable certainty, the clear and immediate knowl-
> edge that heaven was right in front of me, struck me like a thunderbolt
> and went through me like a flash of lightning and seemed to lift me
> clean up off the earth.[201]

Both in *The Secular Journal* and in *The Seven Storey Mountain*, Merton
drew close in words to the experience which was beyond words. He
was reluctant to do this again. In that sense, the two accounts of the
Mass at St. Francis open the only way Merton could give others into
the mystery of much that was to come later in his life. In the two descriptions, Merton tries to explain both the ordinary and the extraordinary aspects of this "movement of God's grace," the earliest in Havana, as perhaps what took place at Polonnaruwa in 1968 was the last.

As it was to be with the experience in Ceylon, Merton kept something secret. Only years later did he reveal having made two vows in
Cuba, one at Our Lady of Cobre,[202] the second in his room at the Andino Hotel in Havana, where he noticed the church of Our Lady of
Carmel was reflected in the mirror — "What was it that I said to you,

in the mirror, at Havana?"[203] It was to the fulfilling of these two vows that Merton devoted himself for the next twenty-five years.

*

After two days at sea, Merton arrived in New York on May 17 to the astonishing news that the German armies had smashed through Holland and Belgium. The headlines were soon frightening everyone with the report that Rotterdam had been bombed almost to obliteration.

Merton remained only a few days in New York. The Perry Street apartment, where he had lived for a little more than a year, was expensive and he expected to be in the novitiate by late August. Merton had plans to spend the summer at the Marcus cottage in Olean. He could always stay with friends in New York, at Douglaston, or back in the boarding house on 114th Street. On May 21, he cleared out the apartment and left.[204]

Merton called at the Franciscan monastery at Thirty-first Street and found his papers were at last in order. Then he went to Ithaca for what was supposed to be his brother's graduation from Cornell. But something had gone wrong; there was to be no graduation.

John Paul was not only restless, he was listless. To Merton's friends John Paul appeared pleasant, charming, rather different, lost. He was taller than his older brother. Where Merton's hair was thinning, John Paul had a mop of blond hair. He had bought a second-hand Buick, which had to be kept secret from Uncle Harold.[205] The only things he seemed to be interested in were driving the car, girls, and the flying lessons he was taking at Ithaca airport. His Russian wolfhound tagged along behind him everywhere on campus, much as John Paul tagged after his older brother when Thomas Merton went to Mass. He asked questions about the Roman Catholic religion, but in a way that made his older brother wonder if he was just trying to be friendly and sound interested.

John Paul talked vaguely about getting into something exciting and romantic as a volunteer before he was unromantically drafted. He also talked about going to Mexico to take photographs, but he was short of money. He talked about a good many plans, all of them conflicting. He may have had his brother's way of testing possible alternatives by getting other people's reaction in conversation. In John Paul's case there was nothing very solid behind this: it was almost a case of wanting to be told what to do. John Paul seemed to think his older brother had all the answers, while he had none. Every time he said something to this effect, giving a loud, nervous laugh, Merton winced.

Merton had probably never been quite this lost himself, yet it was obvious John Paul had reached the point he had known in May 1934. The memory came back with force at a time when he saw himself as powerless to help his brother.[206]

The Germans were sweeping through France. John Paul was floundering. Merton hitchhiked, then took buses and trains for the cross-country journey to Olean.

The summer began well, with Lax, Rice, Gibney, and Merton as guests at the cottage. One day when the others were away on an expedition to Cuba Lake, Merton set himself up in his favorite place, the hummock across the drive from the house, and looked across at Olean through a smoky haze. Then the European news began to come between him and what he was writing.[207]

He imagined armed men advancing up the slope. He thought of the bayoneting scene he had seen the year before, over and over, in movies, and of the riddled sacks along the railway line at Quantico. Maybe one man would simply come out of the bushes to shoot or stab him dead in his chair. Then the cricket sounds would start up again.

Easy to see this as a scene in a movie, in slow motion, close up — to overview it all, himself watching himself. Death, when it came, would not be like that. The perceiving self would be the man shot or stabbed. The movie projector would be smashed. It would not be his ears that heard the chorus of crickets starting up again.

In his present situation he was obviously defenseless. But if an armed man approached him, would he compose himself with his rosary beads, turning one by one over a finger? Would he run? Would he try to resist violence with violence?

In the cottage in the evenings there *were* arguments now, or at least heated discussions. Lax was entirely a pacifist.[208] Gibney had some reservations, Merton a few more, Rice a few more than Merton. So the conversations went on, over just and unjust wars, international law, rights of conscientious objectors . . . What options were open to any of them?

Merton and Gibney agreed that they would go if drafted, but that they would insist on being employed only as noncombatants. Someone brought up the old argument that they would simply be freeing another man to fight. Everything became more complicated, the options dwindled, the hours grew later.

More and more people turned up at the cottage. The weather grew colder and rainy. To Rice, it was more exciting than the summer before. It was certainly full of incidents that would stay in the minds of all of them and mellow over the years.

When more came, the campsite had to be divided into male and female quarters. Merton and three other men moved their camp beds and sleeping bags into the garage. Here it was so cold the occupants tended to stay in their sleeping bags until well into the afternoon. At first, nobody wanted the job of cooking. Then everybody was anxious to try. Merton criticized a dish Peggy Wells had brought to the table and regretted it a year later in his journal.[209] People forgot to buy supplies when they went to town. And still more people came. Merton specialized in dishwashing until he said he had dishwasher's dreams, of being invited to a dance and being ashamed of his hands.[210] The cottage began to smell rancid and there was a litter of pages from novels, bits of food, and sections of the Sunday newspapers in the bushes.[211] In retrospect at least, all these became romantic details. Mary, the Polish cleaning woman the Marcuses provided, did her best to reassure them there were dirtier houses in Olean.

The cottage sprang colonies, first in the garage, then a sort of crows' nest in one of the trees where the girls could escape to sunbathe on the rare occasions when the sun appeared. Nancy Flagg combed out her long red-gold hair one day near the drive, making a distinct impression on some of the men.[212] The population had split into groups. Gibney, Seymour, and Helen Freedgood were in one group, Peggy Wells and Nancy Flagg in another. Rice, Lax, Gerdy, Merton, and the southerner Jim Knight discussed novels and poems all day by the garage. Norma Prince arrived to throw all the groups into confusion and to cover a wall of the cottage by the fireplace with a mural of a nude Walt Whitman that enchanted nobody. One evening, Merton played the bongo drums while Helen Freedgood danced. Both agreed it was not a success.[213] The Joyce readings were better.

During the third week in June Merton moved to St. Bonaventure's. It was before the summer session began. He was given a bed in the dormitory, and Father Irenaeus provided a quiet room at the Friedsam. Merton no longer had to hitchhike in order to attend Mass each day. He quickly found friends among the other friars and learned what life would be like in the seminary in Paterson, New Jersey. Lists of what he should bring with him in August were already arriving. The question of names came up: Father Irenaeus suggested the name Frater Paphnutius, but Merton thought up Frater John Spaniard.

It may have jolted him to find Seymour Freedgood thought Frater John Spaniard a good name to play on when Merton returned to spend a night at the cottage. In "The Labyrinth" Merton had invented a renegade Carthusian friar by the name of Lax Edwards to take part in several melodramatic scenes. This was play-acting, or, as he summed it up: "It made a pleasant picture."[214]

How much of all this was play-acting? Just when the seminary was at last so close he suddenly lost confidence, not in his vocation, but in the seriousness of his own attitude. Robert Gibney had been challenging that seriousness all year. Ad and Joan Reinhardt had assumed he was simply looking for free meals for life. Jinny Burton had got the idea from what he said that the monastery would provide him with a quiet, uncomplicated place to write. Others had been much more blunt:

the monastery would provide him with asylum from the draft.

He could counter or endure most of this. It was his own imagination that kept leading him astray. There was another point: at the beginning of the summer, virtually free from temptation for nine months, "I imagined, in my stupid inexperience, that the fight against concupiscence had already been won, and that my soul was free, and that I had little or nothing to worry about any more."[215] The pages that survive prove there were strains already for him which he had not known before, when his company at the Olean cottage had been only male. This was enough at least to make him wonder how invulnerable he was, and to bring him back to the past. Certain passages in the Book of Job acted on him like a warning — he could not simply continue on the old assumptions and hope he was acting honestly. A test was coming. He did not know what form the test would take, but he knew he had to see Father Edmund.

❋

Tom Izod Bennett's discretion had given Tom Merton a chance to start again in America. The Catholic confession had wiped out the sins of his past, if not the lasting obligations which were the result of those sins. At St. Bonaventure Merton had had the time to reflect. He knew nothing of canon law. What he probably expected was some reassurance that he was not acting now on "bad faith." To be certain of this, he needed to go into matters he had not mentioned before to Father Edmund.

Exactly what he now told Father Edmund remains a mystery. He must have included a full report of what had happened at Cambridge. Once the discussion he dreaded had begun, Merton was probably driven to tell Father Edmund every difficulty he had had in New York, both before and after his conversion.

His frankness did not have the effect he had hoped for. Father Edmund was not reassuring. He told Merton to wait and to come back the next day. When Merton returned he was told he should withdraw his application to enter the Franciscan Order.[216]

Where there is no certainty there is conjecture. In this case there is some useful evidence, though it is difficult to read. Since exactly the same questions came up in November 1941, when Merton consulted Father Philotheus of the same order at St. Bonaventure about entering the Trappists and about his fitness to become a priest, it seems useful to go forward in order to understand the situation in 1940. Father Philotheus gave it as his opinion ("Instantly")[217] that there was no canonical impediment. In the St. Bonaventure Journal for November 29, 1941, after listing all his own imperfections, Merton adds these significant words:

> Father Edmund only advised me concerning the "legal impediment" and
> would never have stopped at such imperfections as I now realise I had.[218]

He may have been wrong in part. Father Edmund already thought
him restless and impulsive, also a very recent convert. There had been
misgivings before the meeting at the end of June in 1940. But "legal
impediment" is telling. What is meant could be interpreted as canon
law: that is, Father Edmund's opinion of church law may have differed
from that of Father Philotheus. But Merton would almost certainly have
used the phrase "canonical impediment."

There were three separate but contingent obstacles. First, there is
Merton's sense of his own unfitness. Second, the question whether
canonical law debarred him from entering a religious order and the
priesthood. And third (and admittedly the most conjectural) the question whether an English settlement was binding by American law, if
this was the "legal impediment."

However Father Edmund put the matter at the second interview,
Merton felt there was virtually no hope of his entering the Franciscan
Order. It was no consolation to be told the novitiate was overcrowded
already. He withdrew his application.

This certainly takes a major place among the rejections in Merton's
life. It was not a single rejection, but quickly became a double one.
Merton had not asked Father Edmund about the priesthood. He may
have been afraid to ask. But he made things far worse by looking for
advice on this matter before he had regained his composure. He came
straight out of the interview with Father Edmund and went to the nearest
church he could find that was not Franciscan. A priest he confessed to
at the Church of the Capuchins could make nothing of Merton's account, except that he had been refused entry into an order. When
Merton burst into sobs and choking, the priest thought him a case of
religious hysteria.

There was to be another occasion, equally damaging to his future,
when Merton completely lost control of himself. That day at the Church
of the Capuchins, there were no witnesses; the matter was between
Merton and the priest. Merton had gone into the church for the second time seeking reassurance, as well as help in overcoming a devastating disappointment. He came out crushed. He had been told "in
very strong terms" that there was no place for someone like him in any
religious order, or in the priesthood.[219] The priest had judged on appearances in one of Merton's weakest moments, but his words had a
lasting effect.

✳

Merton did not return at once to the cottage in Olean, although he gives
this impression in the autobiography. He remained in New York and

got in touch with Jinny Burton. She was just about to leave for Urbanna with Lilly Reilly, to fix up a summer cottage on a bluff above the Rappahannock. She invited Merton to come with them and he accepted, knowing that Jinny would ask no further questions when he told her he was not going into the seminary. Jinny might be sympathetic, but she would not put up with moods or any self-indulgence on his part. He, Jinny, and Lilly left by train. Again there were Tom Collinses in the club car. Jinny photographed Merton gesticulating and talking.

Merton stayed about a week. It was a working holiday. Jinny, Lilly, and another guest, Marge Walker, looked on while Merton tried unsuccessfully to fix the towel rails in the new cottage. For the rest of the time they were busy "knocking furniture together and painting the place up."[220]

It was very hot as June turned into July and Merton left, first for Douglaston, then Olean. Those at the cottage found him very changed. In his own words:

> I can scare myself to death anytime by reading last year's journal. I was very happy last year up to the time I learned I had no vocation for the priesthood and was not acceptable. After that the year complicated itself terribly.[221]

He records in a later journal tearing pages out of the journal from February 1940, to October 1940;[222] then of destroying it altogether,[223] but much of what happened can be pieced together, both from the published and the unpublished writings.

It is hard, now, to see Father Edmund's decision in any other terms than gain: Merton was to find another way to membership among the "tramps of God" — in blue jeans, if not patched brown cloth. Nothing prophesied this at the time. Merton's second interview, the one with the Capuchin, had cut off all light into the future. For all this, he did not abandon his own way of testing. He may even have made a trial of himself as a Franciscan (though hardly the order) in a kind of "ordeal by honesty." Such things are not unknown. The answer came back — no. There was to be a great deal of such testing in the years to come. Blindness (or blind faith) in following his vocation was not his way. It had worked for others (there was no denying this). But it was not the way of those Merton admired most, or came to admire most — those who questioned, tried, and found (often still questioning, still testing).

There were to be times ahead when Merton would go through very much the same process, being desolated for a time by a no, then coming to see the no as a gain, not a loss. By then, Merton had a method of testing which was entirely orthodox in Catholic theology and in Catholic tradition. In 1940–41 he was on his own with his sense that his life was directed and that there were signs he would be a fool to ignore. If God had power over the universe — if magic and the irrational could be excluded by the reasoning but faithful mind — then there would be signs. If God did not hold sway, if the world was absurd, and cause and effect were all, then it was ridiculous to talk alike of destiny and vocation — or much of anything else as far as Merton was concerned. Father Edmund had been right about his restlessness. Well, the restless had their place in the Church!

He needed a job for the fall and somewhere to live. Merton had already known a job was opening up at St. Bonaventure's in the English Department before he left for New York. He put on his formal suit at the bohemian camp and hitchhiked in to be interviewed by the president of the college.

Merton wrote later that Father Thomas Plassman was one of the few people he admired, even venerated.[224] That day they talked of Columbia and Dan Walsh, the classics, and Merton's desire to become a member of the Third Order of Franciscans, a lay order. Merton left this interview with a job as an instructor in English, to be paid $45 a month, room and board included, when school started in the fall. The Depression and the cruelly deflated job market were still in effect. Merton knew how lucky he had been that Father Valentine Long, who had taught sophomore English, had been transferred in the summer to Holy Name College in Washington.[225]

He was employed and he had somewhere to stay. On the trip by train down to New York for the interview with Father Edmund he had been reminded of his own homelessness as he watched a mother standing on a porch calling to a small boy to come in quickly out of a storm that was about to break.[226]

He had met his brother by chance in New York when he came back from the brief trip to Virginia. John Paul offered both a ride to Douglaston in the Buick and help with getting into the Naval Reserve.

The European war had pushed the two brothers in different directions. Merton accepted the ride, not the Naval Reserve.[227] The glowing account the recruiting officer had given of a cruise and a commission did not work out in the end for John Paul. He had "personality problems" on the cruise, and he did not get the commission. An attempt to join the army floundered after John Paul failed the psychological tests.[228] Later that year he talked of joining a number of exotic forces to avoid the draft — the Foreign Legion (whose?), the Royal Air Force.

That day in New York, John Paul noticed Tom Merton was carrying a package of books. He had just been to Benzinger's to buy an expensive set of breviaries. On the drive back to Douglaston, Merton unwrapped these and explained they would help him to say the canonical office each day as soon as he could find his way in the rubrics. John

Paul showed interest when Merton said he was going to live like a monk in the world. The seminary was off, then? Yes, "the seminary was off."

In early July both brothers had seemed about equally adrift. At Douglaston, Elsie and Harold were always talking about moving out of the house, which was hardly a home now to either John Paul or Tom Merton. In August, Tom Merton had his small room on the second floor of Devereux Hall on the campus of St. Bonaventure. He moved all his things in, boxes of books, pictures, clothes, typewriter, and the portable phonograph he had had long ago at Oakham.

When he had established his base he went back to the cottage. He wondered where the summer had gone. With Jim Knight, the Georgian with red hair, Merton hitchhiked to Cleveland. Stranded between rides near Geneva, Ohio, the two of them enjoyed the evening and one another's company.[229] They gave up as it grew dark, and ate in a restaurant among overdressed tourists from other states. Knight and Merton agreed the landscape was one of the prettiest they had seen. Merton borrowed paper and made notes. He changes the time of day in his poem "Aubade: Lake Erie":[230]

> "Lift up your hitch-hiking heads
> And no more fear the fever,
> You fugitives, and sleepers in the fields,
> Here is the hay-colored sun!"

There is a sort of sympathetic link with Rimbaud's vagabond poems. The vines along the lake had reminded Merton of France, of St. Antonin, which had either been demolished in the Nazi blitzkrieg, or which now lived a half-life under the Vichy government. The memories were warm, sad now, not sentimental:

> The vines arrange their tender shadows
> In the sweet leafage of an artificial France.

The "fever" the hitchhikers were to fear no more was probably the same plague that his character-surrogate Jim Mariner found in New York in the novel Merton was soon to start, "The Man in the Sycamore Tree." The poem is far calmer in the face of rumors of wars and the frenzy of pseudo events. In the "sleepers in the fields" and "hay-colored sun" Merton was recalling the paintings by Breughel he had seen at the World's Fair.[231] All things had combined to create a sort of pastoral on the edge of Lake Erie. Like the view from Brooke Hill, this combined what was seen with what Merton had read in the *Georgics* of Vergil. The American Eden was no more unspoiled than the English one: "Touching Is Spoiling,"[232] the signs had read all over the World's Fair. Here in Ohio:

> A hundred dusty Luthers rise from the dead, unheeding,
> Search the horizon for the gap-toothed grin of factories,
> And grope, in the green wheat,
> Toward the wood winds of the western freight.

✳

The school year began at the college. Merton had three large classes, ninety or more students, to get through a year's survey course in English Literature, with set assignments, lectures, conferences in office hours, and department meetings. In academic terms, it was a "full load." Merton had his own commitment to daily communion and to the hours of prayer and religious exercises. He was trying to keep the canonical hours and he was beginning to find his way in the breviary. He had also begun a new novel that would honor an agreement he and Robert Lax had made at the end of the summer to write simply and understandably.[233]

And in addition, Merton had set himself on a course of reading which was far more ambitious than any he had attempted before. He was taking notes on his reading and keeping his journal.

On top of this, he was discovering a new geography. When he had enough time he would walk as far as the Olean cottage, or up to Lippets. For another long walk he took a route which was a favorite with the seminarians, the six miles to Martiny Rocks. Between classes, he crossed the Allegheny river to the south of the campus, using the trestle bridge, then walked across the River Road and along a footpath through a meadow where an oil pump thumped away. From here the steep climb to the Cow Pasture began. This opened unexpectedly from a woodland path into the broad, tilted clearing of the Pasture. In late September and October this was guinea gold with the tall stands of goldenrod. There was a view from here of almost every corner of the campus, and, far to the right, the town of Olean.[234]

Merton struggled with "The Man in the Sycamore Tree," and wrote to his friends how dull it was.[235] On October 17, 1940, he had begun a new journal which is far from dull. Merton wrote his private journals in ink in bound notebooks. A bound notebook shows deleted pages, as a spiral notebook does not. The choice was obviously deliberate. It continued to the end of Merton's life: spiral notebooks for notes on reading, bound notebooks for private journals. In the later years there is one important difference: there are few erasures, no pages cut out.

From the private, handwritten journals, which he showed to nobody, Merton selected passages, worked these up, edited them, and, by 1940, kept a second, typewritten journal he did show to others.[236] He held to this plan. The typewritten journals begin with "The Cuban Journal" (later *The Secular Journal*) and continue to *Conjectures of a Guilty Bystander* and to the semiprivate typewritten journals of the 1960s, which Merton intended for limited circulation.

Much was often lost between the handwritten journals and the typed journal for circulation. This was especially true in 1940–41. Given the material that survives, it is hard to see how the selection was made for *The Secular Journal*. If the St. Bonaventure Journal is true to Merton's feelings at the time (and it is virtually impossible to doubt this), then *The Secular Journal* is a strange distortion of those feelings. Even more important, the St. Bonaventure Journal frequently gives a far more moving account of Merton's final eighteen months before he entered the monastery than *The Seven Storey Mountain*. This is to set Merton against Merton, but there is no way of avoiding the fact that Thomas Merton was at times a very odd editor of Thomas Merton the writer.

The unedited pages of the St. Bonaventure Journal and some of the Cuba pages taken from the missing journal go far to answer a question that must have puzzled a number of readers of Merton's early published work: why Thomas Merton made friends for life at Columbia, and why he made so many instant friends every time the bus stopped in Cuba.

It was not the exhibitionist Merton (the Merton he rightly castigated in his journals) who was fun to be with, not the "life and soul of the party" Merton. This was the Tom Merton of the first year in the fraternity, at the Jacobson party, and the party on Labor Day in Urbanna, as well as the "initiation rites" at the German-American Athletics Club with Lax and Slate. No one, even with Merton's energy, can keep this up for long, or win lasting friendship with such frenzied false sparkle.

It was not the argumentative Merton who was popular, either:

O Lord, I want nothing more than never to have to argue with anyone as long as I live! Argument with words only strengthens us in our stubborn resistance to everything that gives us peace — only increases our own prejudices and does little for the truth at all. First, we must argue by our example; and when we are totally devoted to God then we can speak truth, which is not our own opinion, but the truth we would rather die than violate or corrupt — and then we will either keep silent, or only talk to praise what is good and true.[237]

The Thomas Merton who made instant friends, or deeper friendships that outlasted long periods of silence, was the one who had, beyond complication, a warmth and innocence of heart, the gaiety and spontaneity that belie so much of his early published writing.

In 1940, seeing all this natural flow of spirits as a temptation, he distrusted what others found so likeable as a "trick," second only as a snare to his own desire for independence:

Ever since I was sixteen, and travelled all over Europe, some of it on foot — by myself (always by preference alone) I have developed this terrific sense of geography, this habit of self-analysis, this trick of getting along with strangers and chance acquaintances — this complete independence and self-dependence which turns out to be, now, not a strength, but, in any big problem, a terrific weakness.[238]

The fall of 1940 was a low point in Merton's trust of himself. He felt vulnerable, unprotected, and in need of rules. The summer had brought more than the double rejection. In the autobiography, he is careful to say only:

> If I had ever thought I had become immune from passion, and that I did not have to fight for freedom, there was no chance of that illusion any more. It seemed that every step I took carried me painfully forward under a burden of desires that almost crushed me with the monotony of their threat, the intimate, searching familiarity of their ever-present disgust.[239]

In 1941, to serve as a warning to himself, he wrote:

> The experiment was terrible, unpleasant, not deliberate, half-conscious, passionate. Above all, it wasn't necessary. I knew the truth of the doctrine before I proved it by using my will freely in a wrong course. There was no necessity. But if I never know anything again let me dread that![240]

Where he complains that the heat of the day had contributed, this account of an experiment to try to prove or disprove a determination of passions sounds remarkably cold. In his other accounts of the summer Merton mentions the names of several women and admits he was attracted, but none can have been his companion on this occasion. In 1965, he is very specific — what he had committed was adultery.[241]

❄

The junior instructor at St. Bonaventure was not, and was never to become, a Big Man On Campus. His name does not appear in the yearbooks of 1941 or 1942. Any real mark Merton made on the small Catholic college was discovered after he had left, even to the renaming of the humble Cow Pasture after him. He was a baffling, not an exceptional teacher, whose own enthusiasms did not reach his students. "He must have known his material very well, but never gave much of it to us" is the way one student remembered him.[242]

He came to the conclusion that "Literature is hard to teach. You cannot explain what is good easily, any more than you can explain Faith easily or Love easily." He fell back on biographies: "At least a biography is something; it is not pure subjective opinion. But who teaches *poetry* and not *opinion?*"[243]

Perhaps there was a deliberate drawing in. Where he felt a certain isolation from his friends in New York City, this meant he had more time to himself:

I'm glad I am in this room. Tacked on the door are pictures of St. Dominic, St. Francis receiving the stigmata, two of the Blessed Mother and Child, and one, a Dürer, of the Virgin of the Annunciation. Raphael, Fra Angelico, Dürer, Guido da Siena, The School of Giotto. On my desk, Kierkegaard, The Biographia Literaria, Metaphysical Poetry — Donne to Butler, St. Bonaventure, St. Teresa of Avila, Hopkins, Lorca, Aristotle, The Pearl, Little Flowers of St. Francis, St. John of the Cross. Wait to see how fast I throw away Byron! Then also St. Augustine, but waiting to be returned to the library. Two volumes of Skeat's big Chaucer, also. Somewhere — Blake: not my own. Modern Library, and its paltry edition![244]

He enjoyed the fall, and accused the *National Geographic* magazine of faking colors that were already rich in its photographs. He celebrated the seasons in his journals. When the leaves fell, and the trees were bare on the hills Merton said were giving him his new poems, he wrote "O, for the pencil of a Rembrandt!"[245] He was drawing again — religious subjects, not bare trees, and not the gamboling nudes he had drawn the year before for the *Jester*.

Merton's visual sense, always strong, was growing stronger. There are curiosities here. With all the pictures he lists in his room, there was not a single work by his father. Again, to Tom, Owen had been "color." Thomas Merton worked exclusively in black and white.

The descriptions of paintings in Merton's journal are full of detail and show an eye for subtlety of composition. Merton brought his memory of paintings into descriptions of landscape. Yet, in his master's thesis at Columbia he had mentioned only one painting of Blake's in an essay of ninety pages.

At St. Bonaventure Merton got into a heated argument with Father Joe Vann. Vann had said that art appeals primarily to the emotions. Merton had held out for the intellect. His experience at the Picasso and El Greco shows argued for Merton's opponent.[246] At the Picasso Exhibition at the World's Fair, he had sensed that the viewers were unanimous in thinking Picasso the greatest artist of the age and just as unanimous in expressing a sort of visceral, very personal hatred of the man.[247] It had been equally unnerving when Merton went to shows of El Greco's painting, both at the World's Fair and at the Hispanic Society. The general consensus had been that El Greco had chosen his models only from people with TB. More wounding to Merton were those who shied from the paintings, showing a great deal of personal anguish and leaving with comments about hating "morbid art" and "anything to do with religion."[248]

The monk outside religious orders had cut down on cigarettes. Merton drank far less and banished meat on most days. (He was ashamed he had once told Dan Walsh he needed meat.) But Merton had not done what he says in the autobiography: he had not entirely "rinsed" his "eyes of the grey slops of movies."[249]

On October 27 he went to Olean to see a film called *London Can Take It*, which haunted Merton's imagination and his dreams for more than a year. He thought the title "lousy." On all other matters he was far too moved to be critical: "Bombs are beginning to fall into my own life," he wrote in his journal.[250]

Yet the bombing of London and other parts of England is excluded from *The Secular Journal*, while the bombing of Rotterdam is included. The few references to England have to do with a bad English film Merton saw in Havana, brief memories of holidays he had with his father in Kent as a child, the British retreat from Norway, and the landing of Rudolph Hess.

In *The Seven Storey Mountain* Merton talks of the strange feeling he had teaching English literature while reading the headlines, which convinced him the England of Chaucer, Shakespeare, Milton, and Thomas Hardy was being bombed into an oblivion that would require more footnotes than text in future studies of English literature. There is no mention of *London Can Take It* in the autobiography, but Merton says:

> The noise of that fearful chastisement, the fruit of modern civilization, penetrated to the ears and minds of very few at St. Bonaventure's . . .[251]

He wondered whether to bring the news from Europe into his lectures, then decided not to do so. The students were probably not bringing much of their own lives into classes. As far as their instructor was concerned, "the students were more concerned with the movies and beer and the mousy little girls that ran around Olean in ankle socks, even when the snow lay deep on the ground."[252]

Perhaps. Yet this was a long way from Mark Van Doren's expectations for his students, or from Van Doren's estimate of their real concerns. As the end of term approached, there was a rash of incidents, car accidents, drunken fights, the sort of local violence in which Merton saw a small mirror of a violent world.

Meanwhile, the "fearful chastisement" was going on in England and in Merton's dreams.[253] If Merton saw the German bombers as an agent of divine punishment when he wrote in 1946, he did not see things in that way in 1940. Nor did he see things in that way later, when he wrote of Hiroshima. It is only fair to say that the future poet laureate of England was writing a poem, only half in humor, during the blitz that began with the memorable line "Come, friendly bombs, and fall on Slough."[254] Slough, presumably, was being punished for being ugly. If England was being punished in *The Seven Storey Mountain*, it is perhaps better not to inquire why.

When, therefore, Merton wrote in his journal at the end of 1940, "Bombs are beginning to fall into my own life," there was a deep ambiguity in the statement. He was in no doubt that *London Can Take It* was propaganda:

> Of course it was propaganda, and good propaganda. The talk was all understated. The air-raid alarm, the pictures of the people were enough: and there was nothing false about the sound of that alarm, nothing misleading about the faces of the people who were not terrorized, not disgusted, but brave and patient and hurt, without any showiness, no fancy gestures, no exaggerated lip-biting and none of the forced smiles I had imagined from the newspaper stories.[255]

These impressions had cooled a good deal by the time Merton came to write what was published long after as *My Argument with the Gestapo*. For the moment he had no distance from the celluloid shadows in the film and the images of places that were all too familiar:

> But more terrible was seeing the line of people going down into the air-raid shelter at dusk. Then seeing the empty streets, and an air-raid warden walking slowly with his hands behind him, in the sudden flash of a bomb. And hearing the sound of that air-raid alarm. This, for the first time, made me want to fight.[256]

The wholly unexpected last line was no throwaway. Merton goes back to it a page later:

> For the first time I imagined that maybe I belonged there, not here. I have responsibilities in England, I left my childhood behind there. Now that they are bombing it, perhaps I should go back to my childhood: except of course they don't, for the moment, need men.
>
> Actually, all the propaganda needed to make me want to fight was uttered by the Germans. If they had never bombed any part of England I would never have given a damn for the whole war, no matter what. Perhaps a bombing of Paris for two or three weeks might have done it. I don't know. The bombing of Rotterdam rather repelled and scared me. But the bombing of London, where I once lived, where there are so many people that were my friends in school, and people that I loved, is entirely different.[257]

Somehow all of this (and much more) was "blitzed" from Merton's published writing as if he were ashamed of what he had written in his journals. He had left more than his childhood in England and those who "were" his friends.

In November Merton received his draft card, along with the students who were of military age and the secular professors and staff.[258] The cards were given out at De la Roche Hall, where Merton taught classes. The friars were excluded. If he had been even a seminarian, Merton would have been exempted. By the conscription laws of France and Germany only professed members of religious orders were excluded. It was different in America.

That summer, before going to see Father Edmund, Merton had been happy at St. Bonaventure's, surrounded by Franciscans, certain he would soon be one of them. Exemption from military service was only a part of his sense of security in the future then, yet it was a part. Now, less afraid of being drafted, he had made his own plans to deal with the situation in a way that did not violate his conscience. He waited for his draft notice so he could act.

The wait increased the sense of purpose and urgency. Long ago in Rye there had been a house with an old clock with a plaque on it engraved with the motto *Eheu Fugaces*. Merton was remembering details about an England he had forgotten and recording these in his journal. This brought him back to Fletcher House, where he and his father had stayed that first summer in England.[259] *Eheu Fugaces*. Now, when Merton walked from his room to classes or to the Friedsam Library, he passed an ornate clock on a pillar. On each of the four sides of the plinth there was a Latin inscription about the swift passing of time.

Merton needed little prompting to hurry the purposeful but dancing walk Robert Lax had noticed, or to draw up schedules to account for every hour of his day, except for his walks in the snow-covered hills.

Over the Thanksgiving break, Merton went to New York, where he left "The Man in the Sycamore Tree" with Miss Burton at Curtis Brown. Then he took the train to Boston. He noticed the new air-raid shelter at South Station. In the Museum of Fine Arts he followed a party of schoolchildren into the Catalan chapel. For a few moments he was taken back to the land where he had been born, to the feel of the furniture his father had made, to Joseph the carpenter, to his mother writing, to the shape of a mountain. Then he hurried off to have lunch with Chester Kerr, the editor of *The Atlantic Monthly*, who told him what he had liked and not liked in "The Labyrinth."[260] With his rejected novel in his suitcase, he set off again for St. Bonaventure.

The campus was soon quiet again in the falling snow. Merton caught a ride into Olean on December 17 to broadcast a plea for people to pray for peace over the Christmas holidays. It was the first time he had been on the radio, even a small local station like WHLD, where Robert Lax had once worked. Merton, who had expected to be paralyzed with "mike-fright," was relieved:

> The things I had to say were not mine. I wrote the speech: gave it anonymously. I wrote the speech down. Therefore I had no call to be nervous over the speech because it was not mine and there was no question of trembling for fear I wouldn't be adequately praised.[261]

If the repetitions show relief, they also show a certain hesitation. The hours before the talk had obviously produced the old strain of self-consciousness in a new form. Otherwise, this was much abated for the time being. Teaching in front of a large class had no terrors. In church, he was one of the congregation, and had no need to stand out by volunteering to assist the priest at the altar.

Jinny Burton invited him to come to Richmond for Christmas. Merton went to New York, where he saw Robert Lax and Robert Gibney off on the train to Virginia. He stayed.[262] The New Year's Eve party at a house on Church Street, Northport, is given a full account in *The Secular Journal*. It does not seem to have been much of a party, with Bob Gerdy fretting that he wanted to go on somewhere else and Merton trapped in a long conversation about the miraculous apparitions of the Virgin at La Salette in Bloy's *Celle qui pleure*, while two pretty blond girls flirted with Rice. The only point seems to be that the girls were quite anxious to flirt with Merton, too, until one of them decided he was going to be a priest and told the other.

Merton was puzzled about this: Was it written all over him that, in spite of everything, he was going to be a priest? He had no New Year's predictions for 1941, about his own life or anything else:

> . . . I am the worst of all prophets: prophecy is the one thing, besides mathematics and being a soldier, that I am certain I have no gift for. Being an ice-man I am not certain of — never having tried.[263]

But being a priest?

∗

On February 19, Merton became a member of the Franciscan Third Order. He now wore a scapular, two pieces of brown cloth on a thin cord, under his everyday clothes. This was a constant reminder of his determination to live as a monk in the world. It was also a reminder of how close he had come to becoming a member of the religious. To Thomas Merton, the small secret patches of habit were the mark of a secular. He tightened the cord until it cut into him when he ate too much.[264]

During his visit to New York over Christmas Merton had studied the *Catholic Encyclopedia* at the library at Columbia. He had been to talk to Dan Walsh again. Walsh went back to his own summer retreat with the Trappists. Merton found himself listening more carefully. Everything Merton had read about the Trappists had made him afraid, at times almost pleasantly afraid. Nobody except Dan Walsh seemed to know very much about the Cistercian Order of the Strict Observance. What others thought they knew was hearsay and all to the bad. Common gossip said Trappists slept in their coffins and prayed continually for death, that most of the monks had vowed a lifetime of penance for crimes at least as serious as murder.[265] Dan Walsh laughed at all this.

He said the monks and the guests at the guest house slept on a straw pallet on boards. The life was hard, but what was a life of hardship if it brought you to God?

The *Catholic Encyclopedia* said nothing about contact with coffins (in fact, the Trappists do not have coffins). For all that, the account was suitably discouraging. The monks slept in canvas-partitioned cells in dormitories, woke in what was surely the middle of the night for prayer, worked a full day at hard labor for "recreation," fasted half the year, and ate little but bread and vegetables at any time. Professed monks took a vow to remain within the walls of the monastery until they were buried, with near plague-time despatch, in the monks' graveyard within the walls. They sought total anonymity and forgetfulness from the world. No friendships were allowed within the monastery. All were under a rule of absolute obedience to the abbot. All lived under a rule of silence to ensure the two aims of the Order, penance and contemplation. Of penance there appeared to be much. Of contemplation considerably less was said.

If the year was 1941 and the world knew little, or nothing, of the Trappists, there was some substance in this summary, much left out.

John Paul in his lost state had made wild claims he was about to join the Foreign Legion. Here was a Foreign Legion indeed! There was a certain romance (if a chilling one) in the idea that this was the Foreign Legion of the Church, into which a man could plunge, losing his name and every tie with the world, going into a silence within high walls that must be a living death. For God, yes; but a living death.

Even to be a guest at the monastery for a few days held some terror. Dan Walsh had clearly survived the ordeal. Merton took down the address and the name of the Father Guestmaster.

By February Merton was torn between the idea of spending the Easter break in Mexico, writing a Mexican Journal, or making a retreat to the Trappist Monastery at Gethsemani. He wrote to the Father Guestmaster and received a reply: he could come for Holy Week.[266] Merton was not exactly looking forward to the visit. He was not even sure he was going.

Almost in the same mail as the reply from Gethsemani came a notice from the draft board. If it was expected, the notice was a shock. It brought back all the long discussions of the summer before at the cottage. Merton had fallen into thinking the arrows of the Selective Service Act would pass on the left of him and on the right. There were a good many others in the same frame of mind. He had already decided not to claim exemption as a conscientious objector. He could, under the law, avoid killing others:

March 4, 1941

This has been a very remarkable day to have looked in the face. I don't think of the contents of a day as "a day," ordinarily; but this one has to be seen that way. To begin with, it is a day I have feared — it is the day

I got all my notions together about war, and said them, briefly, all at once, on a few sheets of paper, on a prepared blank and put them in the mail for the Draft Board.

I mean I made out my reasons for being a partial Conscientious Objector, for asking for non-combatant service, so as not to have to kill men made in the image of God when it is possible to obey the law (as I must) by serving the wounded and saving lives — or that may be a purely artificial situation: by the humiliation of digging latrines, which is a far greater honor to God than killing men.[267]

There was another film image that had stayed with Merton, like so many in *London Can Take It*. Just before he had started at St. Bonaventure's in the fall, he had seen a German propaganda movie on the invasion of Poland in Yorkville, New York. The camera had moved over a column of German soldiers:

Suddenly one man got in the eye of the camera, and gave back the straightest and fiercest and most resentful look I ever saw. Great rings surrounded his eyes which were full of exhaustion, pain and protest. And he kept staring, turning his head and fixing his eyes on the camera as he went by demanding to be seen as a person, and not as the rest of the cattle. The censors should have cut him out, because he succeeded . . .[268]

This, then, was the face of the famous Enemy of the newspaper headlines. The face above the oncoming bayonet. Or the face before your bayonet. The face of the man who shot you as he came out of the bushes. Or the face of the man a second before you shot him. This was the face of the man behind the word Enemy.

Our enemies are ourselves in dreams.

Merton was amazed at how calmly he composed the letter to the draft board. He took it to Father Thomas Plassman and Father Gerald to get their approval for his action. Then he hitchhiked into Olean, had the letter notarized, and sent it.

✻

On Wednesday, March 12, Merton was sitting in his room trying to write a poem, thinking of almost a month free of classes, when a student he didn't care for much gave him the message that there was a notice from the local draft board: he was to appear for his medical on March 19.[269]

Merton assumed this meant his letter had been overlooked or thrown into a wastepaper basket. He decided to go to New York at once and to outflank the authority of the local board. The draft officials in New York reassured him that the letter was going through the proper channels, that the civilian physical was routine for everyone. If he was accepted, this would be followed by the physical before induction. Then the letter would undoubtedly come up.

Merton set off for Sy Freedgood's house on Long Island. He found Bob Lax staying there. Freedgood seemed preoccupied and exhausted from running a newspaper. The afternoon ran down and Merton found himself amused by looking at French actresses in a 1925 "Pleasure Guide to Paris," wondering how much myth balanced reality in old photographs. But he was too restless to sit around the house looking at books and pictures. Merton and Lax walked along the deserted boardwalk in a bluster of wind, their feet crunching the clamshells scattered by the seagulls.[270]

This was Friday night. On Saturday, Merton found he could settle to nothing. He and Lax set off huddled in the back of a grocery truck for the cold ride between Long Beach and Bob Gibney's house in Port Washington. The driver of the truck was a friend of Freddie Freedgood, Seymour's younger brother. Merton used to swap jazz records and stories with Freddie. Freddie Freedgood's stories were famous, as funny as they were unreliable.

Soon after arriving, Merton and the driver of the grocery truck were locked in argument in the Gibney cellar. Bob Gibney used this as a studio, and the debate on whether there were any Catholic liberals was carried out amid a litter of drawings and chips and scrolls from wood carving. The argument got nowhere. It only left Merton more miserable and restless than ever. The next day he was back in Douglaston. He and Gibney set off for another long walk. This time a drizzle was falling. They watched an aerial display at North Beach and listened to a poor orchestra playing congas. It was not a good weekend. Merton didn't seem to be able to spend more than one night in any one house. Lax, Gibney, Freedgood, and almost everybody he met asked him about the letter of his on Joyce that had appeared in *Time,* and which began "Ordinarily I hate TIME . . ."[271]

On Monday, St. Patrick's Day, he went with Bob Lax to Lax's office at *The New Yorker.* He sat in the office trying to write a poem, "April," while one of Lax's colleagues, a fuzzy-haired woman, made call after call to check for the magazine's movie column.[272] Mark Van Doren called to pick Merton up. They had dinner together and Van Doren brought Merton up to date on the reactions he had been having when he showed Merton's work to friends on magazines and journals.

There was some irony in all this activity in New York, and especially in his visit to *The New Yorker.* The next day Merton fought his way back to the college from the railway station in freezing rain only to find a rejection slip from *The New Yorker* in his pigeonhole. He had sent in what he thought was a parody of Keats. It was returned as a parody of Emily Dickinson. Apparently Miss Dickinson was not a subject for parody. Merton could hardly tell: he had not read her work. "The Philosophers" is not a strong poem, whatever it is.[273]

On the raw morning following his return, Wednesday, March 19, Merton hitchhiked into Olean early, to discover he was the first person at the offices of the draft board. He suffered the usual indignities of potential soldiers, convicts, and market animals. It was his teeth, or lack of them, that most impressed the doctors.

He was probably not told his classification at the time, because he was fretting about it four days later.[274] When the report came Merton discovered he was 1-B, not soldier material for the moment. All Merton's agony with toothaches, all the days with a sore mouth and the reek of disinfectant at Oakham, in Rome, at Douglaston, and at Perry Street had somehow been transformed into a Chaplinesque comedy. No teeth. Obviously no soldier. Not even a noncombatant combatant.

He must have wondered if the modern army depended on its ability to bite back. If the bad teeth can be traced to conditions at 57 Hillside Avenue, Flushing, perhaps it was his parents' refusal to accept financial help that kept him out of the war.[275] It was more important to Merton then to realize that the medical examination had taken place on the Feast of St. Joseph.

Merton's sense of vulnerability and crisis at the medical center brought back memories of his father at Middlesex Hospital: "This is another thing I cannot understand: his death."[276] He believed he had caught a glimpse of a wing of the Middlesex Hospital being demolished by bombs in *London Can Take It*. Merton dreamed almost every night that he was back in London during the blitz. Each walk in the hills brought him views that reminded him of something in England or France or Germany.

Sometime in the last week of March he finally decided he would go to Gethsemani, not Mexico. He started for Kentucky on April 5, leaving early in the morning from Olean in a rainstorm. Before dark that Saturday night he was in Cincinnati. He had planned to cut down expenses by staying at the YMCA, but changed his mind in the cab and booked himself into a third-floor room at the Hotel Parkview. After a long walk and a bad meal at another hotel he sat down in his room to write postcards to his friends. Then he wrote a long Joycean catechism, question and answer, in his journal about the sights of Cincinnati. He had not yet seen the Ohio River:

Q. Why not?
A. Darkness. Sore feet. Fear of empty streets and sudden floods. Fear of walking around too much lest someone think I was sauntering about with the purpose of molesting women. Hunger. Lack of interest.[277]

Merton stayed all Sunday (Palm Sunday), slept a second night at the Parkview, and started for Louisville early on the Monday morning. He found a Catholic church in Louisville, then walked down Fourth Street

to the river. Both Mark Van Doren and Jim Knight had recommended
this view as the best in the city. Merton made notes for a poem. Much
of the day he spent reading Evelyn Waugh at the public library.[278] It
was not until dusk that he went to the station to catch the Atlanta train.
This, he was told, had a request or signal stop at the station nearest
the monastery, which, unlike the monastery, was spelled Gethsemane.

On Saturday night Merton finished his account of the day with "and
I myself on my way to the Trappists at Gethsemani."[279] His progress
there had been a slow one.

✳

The pages of Merton's journal now started with a cross at the top of
the page. He begins, under the date April 7, 1941, and the place, Our
Lady of Gethsemani:

> I should tear out all the other pages of this book and all the other pages
> of everything else I ever wrote, and begin here.
>
> This is the center of America. I had wondered what was holding this
> country together, what has been keeping the universe from cracking in
> pieces and falling apart. It is this monastery — if only this one. (There
> must be two or three others.)[280]

Merton builds through false comparisons to a crescendo that can be
seen perfectly balanced between romantic excess and stark sincerity:

> This is a great and splendid palace. I have never in my life seen a court
> of a King or a Queen. Now I am transported into one and I can hardly
> breathe, from minute to minute. I have been in the greatest capital cities
> of the world, but never seen anything that was not either a railway sta-
> tion or a movie, instead of being the palace it tried to be. Here, sud-
> denly, I am in the Court of the Queen of Heaven, where She sits throned,
> and receives at once the proper praise of men and angels. I tell you I
> cannot breathe. (I tell who? When I am in the palace of the Queen of
> Heaven, who do I talk to? I can only ask to kiss the earth this Holy Place
> is built on.)[281]

"When I am in the palace of the Queen of Heaven, who do I talk
to?"

✳

Merton arrived late on the Monday evening of April 7 and left early on
the Monday after Easter, April 14. In that time he wrote twenty-three
pages in the large journal in celebration of the greatest discovery of his
life. In terms of a sort of sustained rapture nothing would ever be quite
like this again. There were flaws at the beginning and at the end of
his visit. He felt later he had come very close to spoiling his retreat.
Little of this appears in the pages he wrote at Gethsemani, or in pub-

lished accounts. In the pages Merton wrote at Gethsemani, nothing is important but being there.

In all this, Merton revealed himself unmistakably as a writer. The whole experience was so overwhelming that part of him was stunned. Yet he could not just *be*. He was driven to write about it, page after page. He made the mistake many a guest in the guest house of a monastery like Gethsemani has made: he tried to keep the religious hours and he tried to keep his own hours. He wrote long into the night, then rose a short while later. More than half asleep, he followed the silent figures into the great abbey church of Gethsemani to the clanging of bells at two in the weekday morning for the Little Office of the Blessed Virgin Mary. At three, there was the Canonical Office (Matins and Lauds), then at four, the priests said their private Masses; at 5:30 came Prime; at 7:45, Tierce, High Mass, Sext. Now it was high noon of the monks' day. In March the sun had hardly risen. There was the long morning for physical work after Sext. None came at eleven and dinner at 11:30, then more physical labor. At about 4:30 in the afternoon came Vespers, followed by Collation or supper, then Compline at 6:10. With the singing of the beautiful *Salve Regina* just before seven in the winter months, the day at Gethsemani was over.[282] By seven the monks were in bed. Merton was again reading and writing, filling his journal, making draft after draft of new poems. Even when he lay down for an hour or two he found himself too stimulated to sleep.

Even before Easter the strain and the intensity of his experience were beginning to tell. He had been overwrought before he arrived, fearful and hesitant of what he would find. He had begun the retreat badly. Merton's failure to check timetables or to inform himself of the monastery hours had made unnecessary complications. A guest arriving after Compline does not win marks, either from the wretched monk on duty at the gate house or from anyone else. Even in a penitential order, no one is seeking further opportunity for penance in sleep broken between Compline and 2 A.M.

Merton could have taken a bus earlier in the day to Bardstown. (Today, when there are no trains and few buses, the monastery is, in a sense, even more isolated.) Bardstown in 1941 was a small, rather sleepy town. It had three claims to more than local fame. One was Federal Hill, thought to be the original for Stephen Foster's "My Old Kentucky Home," a house that Nanny Hauck's family had once owned. Bardstown was an important center for distilling. There was a smell of bourbon on the very air, and some prosperity had come back with the repeal of prohibition. Bardstown was also the center of Catholic Kentucky, with an imposing and unexpected cathedral, the first cathedral built west of the Alleghenies. There was a taxi service in Bardstown. There were also any number of Catholics who were willing to drive a retreatant the fourteen-odd miles.

The monastery is deep in rural Kentucky, as Thomas Merton was in no doubt that Monday night, standing beside his bag in a hamlet where few lights were still on. Fortunately, someone came out to find out why the train had stopped. He agreed in good slow country fashion to take the young man the mile and a half down the road in his car.[283]

It can be cold in central Kentucky in Holy Week. It was warm that night, and Merton had no need of the coat he had brought from Olean. He had his first view in the moonlight of the knobs (the high wooded hills), the hollows, and water meadows. He had his first sound of the frogs and may have been reminded of a line of García Lorca's, the voices of the frogs "freckling the silence with little green dots."[284] He was surprised to learn from the driver that the monks would be in bed.

Merton caught sight of Gethsemani's tall silver spire, the block of gray buildings that the great French military engineer Vauban might have designed. This was a fortress built not in Flanders, but in Kentucky, not to stand against invading armies, but to hold out the world. His eyes on the spire, Merton missed St. Joseph on his hill, holding up the Christ Child so that the Child could look into every corner of Gethsemani. The car turned right, then left into an avenue of huge sweet-gum trees, which overhung the farm road and blocked the moonlight. At the far end of the dark tunnel of the avenue the gate house again showed in the white light of the moon.

Whatever Merton felt later about the peaceful place in its peaceful surroundings, he was frightened that night. Nobody he knew had been there except Dan Walsh, who talked of taking hard ways to God. Romantic or not, the approach to that huge silent place of walls and towers and gate houses, all now without a light, must have made him mindful of a good number of medieval tales ("Childe Roland to the Dark Tower Came"), tales that ended badly. When he got out of the car, he was relieved to read the inscription over the portcullis of this castle, *Pax Intrantibus*, and to see the image of Our Lady of Victories holding the Christ Child.

The driver went to one of the small windows and scratched on a pane, calling "Brother! Brother!" In a while the sliding wicket was opened, then the door. The door was hardly closed again upon the driver and the outside world when Merton was asked if he had come to stay.[285]

A few hours later, Merton wondered only what miracle of grace had brought him to Gethsemani. The frightening place had become the Court of the Queen of Heaven. He questioned himself if he were worthy to be a guest at that Court for a week. But stay — stay there forever!

✳

In those days there were formal retreat programs. Merton, with the few other retreatants, had conferences with Father Joachim, the retreat master. Merton never asked the retreat master for advice about what had thwarted his vocation so far. To the monk at the gate house who asked if it were marriage that prevented him from becoming a Trappist he had answered that he had a job. A job! Almost everyone had a job . . .

Merton also recorded his conversations with the other retreatants. He learned about the life of the Carthusians, but he knew that, however attractive the idea of separate cells and a life of solitude was to him, there was then no Carthusian foundation in America, while those in Europe were cut off by the war.[286]

Today there is a separate wing of the monastery for guests who are making a retreat. In 1941 Merton's room was on the third floor of the main building. Between this building and the back of the gate house there is an enclosed garden, much the same today as it was then. In 1941 the guests were allowed to walk there and to make the Stations of the Cross. Spring had come early and the yellow tulips and vinca were out. There was a Rule of Silence at meals, as there is still, and guests sit on one side of the table only. There was probably no absolute prohibition against speaking in the guest house garden. But all this was within the enclosure walls, more a part of the community then than it is today, and guests in the garden were expected to speak quietly if at all, and to keep their conversation brief.

On Holy Thursday Merton strolled by the wall, turning up his face to the warm spring sunlight, thinking back to the Trappist monastery of the Tre Fontane in Rome. He thought of Rome quite often.[287] Later in the day, the sky clouded over and the wind turned blustery. Rain began to fall.

On Good Friday the tabernacle was open and empty, the lights of the abbey church extinguished. The huge church became simply a great enclosed space of cold stone and shadow where the terrible sound came of the rattle, the ancient warning that lepers were approaching: "Yesterday, at Lauds, they blew out the Altar light, and the world froze."[288]

If Cuba had brought Merton the confirmation that there was no truth in religious practice without warmth and without love — not the word *love*, the reality in experience — then Gethsemani brought Merton the awareness of what separation by sin means. The knowledge of that reality was freezing cold. Even the weather confirmed it. Although Merton had not yet come to accept this, it was too deeply established in his memory for him to forget it. "Wait if you like: I too am waiting," as Allah says over and over in the verses of the Koran.

What Merton does not report in the autobiography was that he had an immediate reaction:

Anyway I took to arguing with myself about whether or not I had a Trappist vocation (at Gethsemani) — (irrespective of all impediments) and as a result I was much more occupied with this irrelevant question than with anything else. Besides, wearing myself on this futile argument, I soon got very tired of the getting up at 1:30 etc. By Good Friday I was getting rather disgusted, physically, and so, as an act of rebellion, went for a walk! All the time telling myself some absurd thing about the necessity to love God's creatures — nature etc. The only answer to that is: there is nothing in the Trappist discipline to prevent you loving nature the way I meant it then and do now: loving it as God's creation, and a sign of His goodness and love.

But the whole thing was a silly, and scrupulous self-deception, only fortunately it only occupied me when there were no offices or prayers, or when I got tired of trying to read and meditate. So the retreat wasn't ruined altogether![289]

Guests and monks are free today to walk in the abbey property outside the enclosure. In 1941 retreatants were expected to stay within the walls. Merton knew the significance of the enclosure by now from the sessions with the retreat master: he had not been able to stay inside the walls for a week. But if this was his "rebellion," it was very much a Merton rebellion.[290] Walking the wet fields, he had his first sight of Vineyard Knob, which was to mean much to him later. He drafted "The Vine," one of the two poems he wrote at the Gethsemani guest house (the other is "The Ohio River — Louisville"), revising this later at St. Bonaventure. The concrete images (rare for Merton) make for immediacy, as in the third verse:

> A mob of winds, on Holy Thursday, come like mur-
> derers
> And batter the walls of our locked and terrified souls.
> Our doors are down, and our defense is done.
> Good Friday's rains, in Roman order
> March, with sharpest lances, up our vineyard hill.[291]

Merton went on writing and reading, filling the pages of the journal with quotations in Latin from St. Benedict, and in English from *The Imitation of Christ*, keeping the offices he could, sometimes falling asleep over a book. Now, the monastery had moved to the summer calendar. The monks went to bed an hour later, but there was a rest in the afternoon, the *méridienne*, at noon — that is, at twelve o'clock, the world's noon.

After Mass on Easter Sunday, Merton was pulled in two ways. In a day (early on Monday morning), he would be free of restraints he was finding difficult. Yet in a day he would be out of the Court of the Queen of Heaven and back in the world. With Merton, tension led to walking and to argument:

Easter Sunday — the argument I am most ashamed of — I got into an argument with a Thomist from Notre Dame about Faith and Reason again, this time with me *against* the Thomist proofs for the Existence of God, but not able to say anything about the Scotist proofs which I did not know except say they were good but I didn't know them. Some occupation for the afternoon of Easter Sunday after a retreat in a Trappist monastery! To argue! I was sick of every word I said right after I said it, and yet I went on arguing! Even after Father Joachim had told us all, by a mild, shy, indirect reproof, to stop arguing.[292]

The passage is important later that year, when Merton used his memories of the retreat at Gethsemani to try to determine whether or not he belonged with the Trappists. It takes its place in a long list of arguments, as Merton tried to argue himself out of arguing. It also bears study as a piece of writing. Any teacher of English composition (as Merton had been) would blue-pencil much of the first half. Yet, rough, unedited, very unsmooth, the passage is very telling. It makes an immediate contact with the reader. Paul Léautaud, in his own journals, writes of "writing well by writing badly,"[293] not rewriting, not looking back at what is written. "Writing well by writing badly" is not a clever paradox. It hardly excuses *vague* bad writing. A writer needs to know what writing is all about before trying it. Given all this, Léautaud's concept serves to justify a certain kind of writing against revision and second thoughts in a case when the concentration of the writer is "on" in the first draft — when "touching" can only be "spoiling."

"I was sick of every word I said after I said it, and yet I went on arguing! Even after Father Joachim had told us, by a mild, shy, indirect reproof, to stop arguing."

These sentences may, or may not, be good in a wholly abstract sense. They *are* absolutely right, so precise not a word can be changed without a loss of precision.

So much for critical objectivity: they also speak to me of my own tongue. And it may be to you, too.

❋

Overwrought and overstimulated, probably angry with himself, Merton had not asked the one question that needed to be asked. He made his way back to Douglaston, then wondered why he was there. In New York he ran into Robert Giroux at Scribner's bookstore. Giroux had just rejected the third Merton novel he was to see, "The Man in the Sycamore Tree," for Harcourt, Brace. At their chance meeting Merton talked only of the Trappists in Kentucky, so there seemed to be little point in bringing up the novel. Giroux knew Merton had been seeing Lax at the office of *The New Yorker*. It seemed quite natural to ask if Merton was planning to write a piece on the Trappists. As far as Giroux knew, nobody had written anything on the life of a Trappist monk for the general public.[294]

Merton was visibly shocked. He had just come from explaining at *The New Yorker* offices what made a division between talking about the Trappists to everyone he met and writing an article:[295] the latter seemed like a betrayal . . . "When I am in the palace of the Queen of Heaven who do I talk to?"

The week at Gethsemani had sharpened Merton's sensitivity in many ways. The buildings of the monastery had little beauty: it was something else that made for such a contrast with the streets of Manhattan. He saw the hardness and the ugliness of things under a cold light. Traffic sounds were more strident and threatening. Where he thought himself a bad prophet, there were *some* signs he read with astonishing accuracy.

Women's clothes now had a military look, as if the women already anticipated wearing uniforms.[296] What Merton judged feminine had been still further discounted. He mistook a photograph of the Andrews Sisters for the Ritz Brothers.[297] The new colors of lipstick and the way it was now applied made it look as if a woman's face was divided by a smear of fresh blood.

Others may have caught the innuendoes in all this. Merton was surely the first, in 1941, to associate the bombing of civilians by bomber crews with aircraft spraying insecticide.[298] What became almost a cliché in the literature of the Vietnam War had already been diagnosed with protest and horror in his journal at St. Bonaventure. He was outraged later that year by an account in the newspaper of the "world's most humane" poison gas:

> Anyway, this is a very humane gas — it kills much more quickly and effectively than any other. It has a low freezing point and can be used (but for defense only, of course) in the Arctic. Best of all, it is extraordinarily hard to disperse: it remains in corners and hollows for *days,* making sure of the last dog, cat, woman, child, grandfather, cripple, every neutral bird and beast, every living thing, or, breathing thing: probably blasts the plants, too, in its terrifically efficient humaneness.
>
> But the most shocking part of the whole story was that this gas was developed in the labs. of a *Catholic University.*[299]

The tone of these passages is so close to that of Merton in the early 1960s that it would be easy to place them, without editing, in *Conjectures of a Guilty Bystander.*

Merton had not been a particularly good retreatant at Gethsemani. This could only mean he had carried too much of the world's madness and weariness with him on his trip to Kentucky and the Court of the Queen of Heaven. Now he was back in the world and the world looked madder, staler. If he was affected by the contagion, it could only get worse.

There was no way of keeping out the noise. The spring came up from Kentucky and reached St. Bonaventure's. The stairs outside Merton's room were loud with cries of X or Y being summoned to the telephone. Some of the friars had turned up the volume of their radios. WHLD was playing Merton's special hate, the Hut-Sut Song, over and over.[300] Everything was working up to a crescendo in graduation week. After that there would be a lull: "What you don't hear when a building is empty."[301] When the large classes arrived for the summer session, they included a visiting friar who roomed above Merton and played the ocarina. "I guess if I had joined the order I would have played the bongos — they are more respectable than an ocarina. I would have wanted to keep the bongos too."[302]

Merton's reaction to noise is an interesting one. When *The Seven Storey Mountain* was published in England, it was given a new title, from a poem by Gerard Manley Hopkins, *Elected Silence.*[303] This version was reviewed in *The New Statesman and Nation* by V. S. Pritchett. The review makes depressing reading now, not because Pritchett is predictably skeptical about Merton's conversion, but because the reviewer holds to the belletristic style, which lingered on like the "humane gas" in nooks and crannies for far too long. It was a style that affected Merton's because Merton reacted so strongly against it. Yet it was Pritchett who made the insightful comment that "noise plays a curious part in his life."[304]

In much of Merton's writing, early and late, published and private, there is the joy of making noise, and the suffering induced by others making noises, joyfully or not. The bongos are pitted in war against the ocarina, or the "little bastard" who practiced on the trumpet in Perry Street. In time, the scat-singing and another set of bongos gave answer to the guns at Fort Knox and the very unsilent Trappist tractors.

This double standard is common. What is very uncommon is the degree to which Merton practiced it. In this sense, *Elected Silence* is more than an ironic title: it is a very funny title.

In May of 1941 Merton needed silence, quiet, calm, both for his prayers and for a new literary work. John Paul interrupted the quiet Merton was struggling for in his room at St. Bonaventure.

John Paul's engagement in the Naval Reserve had been brief. He was back now from an expedition to Mexico. The weather during that week in May was glorious. After a good breakfast at Olean House, the younger brother took the older on a tour through the Allegany State Park in his second-hand Buick. They made wider and wider circuits. The wild cherry trees were covered with "a powdery greeny white little blossom — like greenish white smoke."[305] At the Indian reservation, John Paul announced it was very much like parts of Mexico. Merton had already seen the reservation. In time, he was to become very sympathetic to the remnants of the great tribes of American Indians and fascinated by their history. In 1939, they had provided material for the Indian jokes Merton had already shared with Rice and Lax.[306] In 1941, he thought the reservation dirty, burnt over, and burnt out. When the brothers went to the Olean cottage, Merton noticed things had been cleaned up considerably. There was a new coat of paint on the window frames, new garden furniture, and the raspberry canes had been cut back. The two of them hacked the canes back still further with a machete John Paul had brought from Mexico.[307]

Something was nagging at Merton the whole time, competing with any pleasure he found in his brother's company, or in driving about the countryside:

> What is one recreation I am happy about, and the only one? Writing — not this, but a letter in a crazy new language to Gibney yesterday, and a Macaronic poem.[308]

This was on May 5. It sounds very much like something Merton had written about Proust in his journal a year earlier, when he said that the one thing Proust enjoyed in Time Present was writing. *The New Yorker* had at last accepted a poem, "Aubade: Lake Erie." Merton had received a check for twenty-two dollars, which must have given him confidence. On May 6, he began a new novel written partly in "Macaronic," "The Journal of My Escape from the Nazis." By June 11, one draft was already in the hands of Naomi Burton at Curtis Brown.[309]

With Merton's macaronic novel we are a long way from the pedestrian style of "The Man in the Sycamore Tree," and a long way, too, from the agreement Merton and Lax had made to write simply. While it owes much to Joyce in language, there are overtones of Kafka and Rex Warner, whose *The Wild Goose Chase* and *The Professor* were popular at the time. There may be something, too, of Huxley's *Time Must Have a Stop.* But this time the models do not intrude. There is originality, gusto, and innocence.

Whatever innocence the book had in 1941 is largely destroyed by the Author's Preface of 1968 to the retitled *My Argument with the Gestapo.* It is a case of Merton overediting again, explaining what should have been left well alone. For example, it is simply not true that "The death camps were not yet in operation."[310] Merton mentions Dachau on page 257. In his journals of 1941 he talks of the "lethal chambers" into which the Nazis had thrust their own German (presumably "Aryan") terminally ill and mentally sick long before 1941. Even those who read only *Time* and *Life* knew of the murders of Jews after Kristallnacht.

In hindsight, it would have been better to say simply that the book was written in 1941. Chaplin's *The Great Dictator* lost some of its innocence between the time of its making and the time of its first showing. In the space of a year certain subjects no longer seemed funny. Few blame Chaplin for this. Overall, it is the omission of the passages on England from *The Secular Journal*, not the different, much harder perspective in the novel which proves distorting and which stood in far greater need of an explanatory preface.

Meanwhile, in June 1941 there was something Naomi Burton particularly liked about "The Journal of My Escape from the Nazis," and agent and author went to the Rough Rider Bar to discuss this. Into the lives of both Thomas Merton and Naomi Burton "the bombs were falling" or had fallen. Yet each felt alienated by the bombardment of propaganda about "Brave Little Britain." Naomi in New York probably suffered from this more than Merton in western New York State among those who had some valid reason to be impervious to such propaganda, coming as they did from Irish-American and German-American stock. Naomi Burton was also more vulnerable.

At the same time she was preparing to send Thomas Merton's new book to publishers, she was receiving some odd messages on another book, *Straight Thinking in Wartime*, a commonsense and scholarly critical study of war propaganda. This had found a publisher in England while the bombs were falling. Impressed by it, Naomi Burton had sent the book out, hoping it would be published in America. In return she was receiving telephone calls and notes from aghast publishers who more or less accused her of treason.[311]

The response to Merton's novel was equally frosty. Naomi Burton withdrew the book after three or four tries.[312] Obviously there are other kinds of censorship than ecclesiastical. The times were against it, too. Time, and the war, moved on. Occasion in publishing is all-important, as it was to be with a wholly unexpected book by the wholly unsuccessful writer Naomi Burton continued to back.

✳

Throughout the summer and fall of 1941 Merton put off asking the question he knew he needed to ask before any decision could be made about his vocation. Meanwhile, he sharpened the focus of a number of debates with himself that would last a lifetime. He tried to make sense and logic out of his attitudes to war, since he was against war, yet not a pacifist. He began to wonder how religious faith could be combined with an acceptance of social and racial injustice at a time when his own view of injustice had its blind spots. He debated whether or not he was a writer in the very journal that finally proved he could write. Then he went on to question whether his writing honored God, or whether it was simply a celebration of self. He was still wondering this in his journals of the 1960s.

While his friends found him quieter, their hours with him were just as much fun as they had always been. His cheerfulness, his natural ebullience, never struck anyone as forced or put on. Merton was never, at any point in his life, what the French call *faux-gai*. Even in the journals he wrote for himself, where there are sharp notes of despair on so many pages, the excitement and the joy keep breaking in. He enjoyed his friendships, his reading, his walks, his past — and he must have enjoyed the arguments, at least at the time, to have so many to record with remorse.

Much has been made of a continuing sense of guilt for what was now long past. There was something of this, certainly. But by 1941 Merton saw the habit of penance in different terms. It was now only in part an act of retribution — or attempted retribution — for the past. It was a constant reminder of his fallibility in the present. He had been given two new chances, his coming to America and his conversion. Neither had led to a real reformation. He returned often to thoughts of his father. There was nobody he had loved more. Yet, without structure, even a good man had floundered. There was no family structure for Merton. He felt the loss, yet doubted if this would have been sufficient. As a Catholic, he knew that the Church had provided him with a structure which should have been sufficient. That it was *not* only meant he was not a good enough Catholic. The need to find the right structure, one that would give him confidence in himself to live under the rule of God, had become paramount.

His writing and his restlessness went together. He had a tendency to exaggerate even when he was writing about exaggeration. He wrote of honesty and the very words seemed phony. He wrote of humility, and when he read what he had written, he discovered another form of pride. If such writing was confessional, it had already proved a deeply ambiguous form of putting in order either the past or the present. He wrote on because it was compulsive (he wrote of the ink pot, wrote of the pen he was using), and because it might all come right. Writing was his way to himself: in time it might prove a way past himself.

He broke off from the journal to walk in the hills. One July day Merton made another "David Copperfield journey," this time to the recent past, hitchhiking up to the Olean cottage, where he sat in the new rustic furniture and gazed out at Olean and the misty, wooded hills. In the guise of imaginary letters home from summer camp by a child, Merton enjoyed going over all the incidents of the summer before:

Dear Uncle Harry:

It is a typical day at the cottage. Tommy Merton has made a cross out of two sticks and stuck it in the ground in the woods in a place where he thinks he is going to like to sit, but where there are too many lousy mosquitoes . . .

There are pictures of Jimmy Knight, Bobby Lax, Norma Prince, Eddie Rice, and other campers. Then he writes:

> It is a typical day at the camp, mother dear. Next year at this time, Bobby Gibney will have left for the army three days ago, and Jimmy Knight will have already been some time at Camp Polk, La., and the others? . . .[313]

Even the tenuous but precious structure the group of friends had provided Merton with for two years had been broken up now. The camp at Olean had been struck, except in memory.

❋

If Gethsemani was the most important discovery of 1941, and perhaps in Merton's life, two other discoveries that year are linked in his geography.

When he wanted to be on his own and did not have time for the walk and climb to the Cow Pasture, Merton took to pacing back and forth in the Grove, at the southwest corner of the St. Bonaventure campus. In the Grove there is a shrine to the Little Flower.[314] Merton writes that he was put off by the shrine. He was probably equally put off by the epithet "The Little Flower," like many another expecting saccharine pieties and another disaster of taste and common sense in the name of religion. But he was curious. It is likely he asked Father Irenaeus and learned the librarian was very fond of St. Thérèse of Lisieux. As Merton was very fond of Father Irenaeus, he decided to read something by St. Thérèse.

The English translations proved what Merton feared. He persisted in the original *Histoire d'une âme*, then with its additions by the saint's pious sisters and others.[315] Merton still had to admit that St. Thérèse had been very much the product of her society, provincial middle-class France in the nineteenth century. Everything went against her as far as Merton was concerned. Was he going to make another sacrifice of taste in the name of what he already called "ghetto Catholicism"? Religious shrines did not have to be this bad. Religious prose did not have to be this bad.[316]

Against all this came the discovery that there was something in St. Thérèse's writing he needed. There was also something he needed in her life. Merton's full devotion to St. Thérèse did not take place until he read Ghéon's biography of the saint in the fall.[317] In early summer she was already bringing a sense of proportion into his struggles.

James Joyce had made the word *Epiphany* secular with a small *e* to capture the sense of the numinous in a moment or an object perceived in a mood when the ordinary suddenly reveals itself as the extraordinary. What was intellectual in Joyce was entirely natural in St. Thérèse. She had lived the most ordinary of lives in the most ordinary of surroundings. She had shown very little talent for self-dramatizing. Yet she was convinced she was present at an Epiphany every waking moment of her day. She had been neither a great reformer nor a powerful supporter of the Church against the anticlerical forces in France. She simply saw what others could not see. The very ordinary people around her could hardly wait until she was dead to begin the process of canonization.

For Thomas Merton everything was important. For Thérèse of Lisieux, everything was luminous with supernatural light. Scrubbing a floor was an act of such glory and grace that she trembled and was almost overcome. Merton was reminded that in his letter to the draft board he had talked about digging latrines in a way which made a small melodrama of it all, explaining that this was far more to the honor of God than killing those made in His image. It was an embarrassing memory.

For all the "lousy" words then, there was a simplicity, a total unaffectedness in St. Thérèse of Lisieux which made his own self-awareness appear crippling. And yet here was the exact point at which she came to his rescue. She spoke of her cross. Could it be that the cross Thomas Merton had been given to carry was the same self-awareness with all its tangle of complications, to be carried with courage and in silence? Was this to be his lasting humiliation, something to be welcomed as given? After all, the gifts of God *were* odd.

Marie-Françoise-Thérèse Martin had incipient tuberculosis and nervous disorders. There were many invalids and "nervous cases" living lives of privilege, egotism, and indulgence in the middle-class families of the nineteenth century. There was even something of a cult of the invalid. St. Thérèse had renounced this as surely as St. Francis had renounced his father's riches. She had even given up her own salvation — or rather, the immediate salvation of her soul at her death — for others. Until the world ended she expected to be in Purgatory — *"faire du bien sur la terre."*

She had lived with no religious consolation. She had died expecting no consolation, indeed using this to bargain with God for sinners.

If this was not self-dramatization, it was surely confused theology. It was God who decided where souls were to go after death. Yet it was stunning that where even the best Catholics struggled for the salvation of their individual souls, St. Thérèse had passed lightly beyond this concern to something else.

This aspect of St. Thérèse's faith was not altogether convincing, then, to Merton. But the magnificence of her surrender deepened his own faith and made him ponder where faith might lead.

He was to be similarly put off years later, not in this case by taste, but by the "Albigensian" aspects of another, very different woman of faith. Was it a lingering sense of melodrama, or was it a similar act of surrender on Simone Weil's part that she had ultimately refused conversion to the Catholic faith on the grounds that she would rather be a missionary in Hell?

Or, as Yudhishthira asked centuries ago in the *Mahabhárata:* "What if my friends in Hell need me more than I need Heaven?"[318]

By 1941, Merton's vocation was clear. It was not to be a priest, not to enter a religious order, not to be a secular priest in social work for the Church. These were possible ways, not the end. The end he sought was to be a saint. As Léon Bloy had said: "The greatest sadness was not being a saint."[319]

This was close to the aim Lax had set, with one important difference. Merton sought sainthood in struggle, not in acceptance; in becoming, not in being. All this is referred to obliquely in the journals. The reason is easy enough to understand. The day-to-day struggle to become a saint provided a dangerous opportunity for the very thing he was avoiding. It had to be an almost unspoken goal for Merton himself: it would be disastrous to speak of it to others.

In the Catholic Church perhaps the very process of canonization had caused the greatest confusion. For the Protestant sects of the seventeenth century, a saint was simply a believer. For Catholics, a saint was, at least in one aspect, a show. In the case of a "finished" saint this aspect made little difference. In the case of a man or woman struggling to be a saint it made every difference.

Something of a comparison could be drawn with Merton's other vocation. There were complications in claiming you were trying to become a poet. Often it was a sure sign that a writer of verse was *not* a poet if he or she insisted on this public recognition. To an even greater degree this was true of a saint. One who claimed to be a saint was, by this very claim, shown to be wanting in what is needed most for sainthood, humility.

Yet Merton was sure that signs of his true vocation could be read by the perceptive. He was convinced that only saints would disprove Hitler's cynical claim that he could control the Church and put it to his own uses. At Gethsemani in April, Merton had written of the old Jewish concept of the Just Man. Only Lot had saved the world when the wrath of Jehovah fell on Sodom and Gomorrah. In his letter to Abbot Frederic Dunne on May 1, he had made the same point: it was the just and watchful monks today who were saving the world.[320]

Just, watchful, and secret. The man or woman trying to be a saint hid any beginning of saintliness. There was no "show" in this; exactly the opposite. St. Francis of Assisi, Merton wrote, had hidden his stigmata in wrappings of old rags.[321]

Merton praised "Kierkegaard's remarkable intuition that the greatest and most perfect saints are those whose saintliness *cannot* be contained except beneath some exterior that appears totally mediocre and normal, because it is an incommunicable secret."[322]

Whether Thomas Merton ever became a saint is thus totally irrelevant here — and henceforth in these pages. That his vocation was to be a saint is clear from 1941. In terms of his true vocation, then, he had to decide which circumstances would best enable him to become what he sought to become. He had already talked of this, admittedly rather superficially, when he compared the opportunities for sainthood in the two parishes in Miami.

Long after, when visitors to the hermitage tried to chide him into admitting he was not "a true hermit," Merton would ask, "What's your idea of a hermit?" If the question gave him an easy out, it also threw the visitor back on his or her own preconceptions of what a hermit ought to be in order to be a "real one." What's your idea of a saint?

❉

Close to the Grove and the shrine of the Little Flower at St. Bonaventure there is a large amphitheater called the Grotto.

The summer session at the college was now well under way. Merton was teaching classes on eighteenth-century English drama and bibliography, as well as a smaller class on Dante. He was filling a notebook with notes on *The Divine Comedy*, reading Dante far more carefully than he had ever done before and making discovery after discovery in a text he thought familiar.[323] He was revising the new novel. He was choosing poems for an anthology of religious verse. In the bibliography class he was sending the nuns on a treasure hunt through the reference books in the Friedsam Library. There were no prizes, only grades. Most of the nuns accepted this with humility. Some were showing their exasperation.

Merton noticed that there was to be a program of speakers on various aspects of the Church's work in the world. Catherine de Hueck (who was apparently a Russian baroness) was coming to talk on her work at a settlement house in Harlem connected with Catholic Action. Merton had heard something of this from Father George Ford. Other events were planned. None attracted him. He had told Father Charles Hogan at the Franciscan monastery back in October 1939 that he was not much interested in priests trying to compete with radicals in social work.[324]

He was walking the football field one summer evening when his thoughts were interrupted by a good deal of noise, the sound of a meeting. Merton sets the meeting in the Alumni Hall. Others remember the first talk took place in the Grotto. At any rate, Merton was curious enough to go nearer. He was drawn by the strident tones of a woman's voice.

She was saying something about their all being too damn lazy playing golf at St. Bonaventure's or twittering about between classes in long-dead subjects to notice that the whole world was bleeding to death around them. And if a poor Negro was refused entrance to a hospital in New York City — not Birmingham, Alabama — New York City, there was always a Communist to appear out of nowhere to play the Good Samaritan and take the Negro off somewhere where he could get help. All the while, the Levite and the Pharisee were playing golf and fluttering about somewhere in the country.

When someone asked about the need of some to make space to follow the religious life of prayer without ceasing, the speaker shouted back "Baloney!"[325]

If Merton had anticipated a string of case histories, each with a happy ending, with a few bits of local color about unforgettable characters and a dash of *Reader's Digest* optimism to wrap it all up — more souls, more unforgettable characters, brought by goodness and soup to the Church — then this was something else. The speaker deliberately put everyone on the spot: she put him on the spot.

In the journal, Merton gives his own response at once:

> The way she said some things was as moving as a propaganda movie or a sentence in a good sermon and left you ready to do some kind of action: in this case, something good — renounce the world, live in total poverty, but also doing very definite things, ministering to the poor, in a certain definite way.[326]

Yet he admits that the first thing the speech stirred him to do was to get into arguments. "Now count up all the people you have insulted since you heard that speech . . ."

All this is handled very differently in *The Seven Storey Mountain*. There is a certain very effective way in which the response is shifted, as if we were hearing what the Baroness said through the ears of the least worldly of the nuns, perhaps the "little S.S.J., Sister Immaculata, who writes poems," who "looked earnestly startled, like a child about to be taken to Grandma's in New Jersey, when hearing all about these new things the Baroness de Hueck spoke of."[327]

The device is one that has been used in the movies for a long time. The least likely extra is chosen to register a strong emotion in response to something, rather than the leading actor, or the actress who has had our attention all along. It was a bold effect to use in an autobiography,[328] and it is successful on two levels, because for Sister Immaculata's innocence we are forced to read our own indifference.

Merton introduces himself only at the very end of the account, when he breaks from the audience and goes up to talk. Meeting the guest speaker by chance the next day, Merton offered his help at Friendship House once the summer session was over.[329] Catherine de Hueck had probably been approached by innumerable earnest-looking young academics who had been momentarily moved to think they might dare get out of the subway a few blocks north of Columbia but had subsequently failed to show up. She took a look at the young man, said "Sure," and turned to other people.

*

On the afternoon of Friday, August 15, 1941, the same young man came up out of the subway at Lenox Avenue and 135th Street carrying a large bunch of flowers. He was soon among a large crowd of children who walked along with solemn expressions holding kites. It was a hot, muggy day, and a light drizzle was falling.[330]

He made his way between pushcarts and crossed 135th Street, where he was almost run down by trucks going very fast, full of black soldiers. The soldiers were leaning far out of the trucks, laughing and pointing out the sights of Harlem to one another.

At the Friendship House Library some teenagers broke off their conversation and became self-conscious as the young white man came in. They stared at the large bunch of flowers and would have giggled at the visitor. To cover this up, they started the conversation again, and began to giggle at one another.

A white woman, one of the lay workers, appeared. She explained that it was the Baroness's birthday and she was downtown for the afternoon. She looked at the bouquet. No, Merton said, he hadn't known it was the Baroness's birthday. He had brought the flowers because he thought conditions might be a little drab at Friendship House and that people might appreciate something beautiful to look at. He was already embarrassed by the gesture.[331]

Mary Jerdo introduced herself. She found a vase for the flowers and put this on the Baroness's desk to greet Catherine de Hueck on her return. Then Mary Jerdo took Merton on a tour of Friendship House and the Clothing Center across 135th Street. They talked about what he could do to help. He explained he spent most of the day writing, or in the Columbia libraries, or seeing publishers, but he was free some late afternoons and some evenings.

Merton had come to Friendship House with almost as much trepidation as he had shown in his approach to Gethsemani in April. He says he arrived saying Hail Marys under his breath.[332] A few hours later, when it was almost dark, he left to walk back to the subway. A mother was calling out from somewhere, telling her child not to go up on the roof to fly his kite, he might be blown off by the wind. Merton wondered what he had been afraid of. There was a tension here that there had not been in Havana, but it was not threatening: it was only infinitely sad. Harlem was not Cuba, yet there was something here that made him think of Cuba, and of García Lorca. No wonder the Spanish poet, coming from Cuba and feeling so much an exile in New York, had sought out Harlem.

The next afternoon, he worked in the Clothing Center until his hands were covered with white dust from the women's shoes. He talked to Catherine de Hueck in French at dinner. The performance, a birthday present, put on after dinner by the Cub Scouts of the community, delighted Merton. He found the cubs wonderful, their parents a little alarming. They had dressed in their best clothes and seemed overanxious to appear interested and polite while Catherine de Hueck explained that the play was a modern rendering of King Arthur and his knights which took place in a country club.

Some hours later Merton joined his friends at Godfrey's on East Eighteenth Street. He was full of the play and his enthusiasm for the children at the Settlement. When the party broke up in the early hours Lax had agreed to come to Friendship House with him.

Merton stayed in his old room at 548 West 114th Street and every evening for two August weeks mopped floors, or worked in the Clothing Center, or supervised the games of Ping-Pong. He may have been expecting something very different. He shared Léon Bloy's *Letters to My Fiancée* and *The Woman Who Was Poor* with Mary Jerdo, who mischievously quoted the first line of so many of Bloy's letters — "I suffer intensely and uniquely" — when some minor mishap occurred in the Clothing Center, or when a bucket of soapy water tipped over.[333]

Perhaps the lack of drama was the very point; perhaps St. Thérèse of Lisieux had prepared Merton better for the day-to-day activity at Friendship House than Catherine de Hueck. Sorting out clothes or swinging a mop were not, in themselves, dramatic steps on the road to romantic fulfillment. Visiting an elderly black woman who was dying of cancer who had visions of the Virgin Mary came closer.[334] There were no street accidents with blacks miraculously saved from bleeding to death by Communists, or by members of Catholic Action. It was the everyday chores Merton was there to do, and he did them. He also felt he had discovered Harlem.

The injustice permeated the whole environment: it was not simply a matter of theatrical *tableaux vivants*. Merton's pages on Harlem in *The Seven Storey Mountain*, in his journals, and especially his poems about Harlem seem now to have been observed through a special lens and the influence of García Lorca's "The Poet in New York."[335] Yet the acute sense of wasted possibilities, wasted lives, extreme alienation, makes a vivid impression on the reader. Eldridge Cleaver stands authority for the authenticity of Merton's feelings in the Harlem pages, if not for the details. In *Soul on Ice*, Cleaver says he read *The Seven Storey Mountain* in prison and welcomed "Brother Merton" into his cell.[336]

The weeks in Harlem were as important to the later Merton as the visit to Cuba. If Cuba was the place where life was lived without masks, Harlem was the place where the masks of visitors were ripped off:

> Today, the problem of culture and religion is a different one.
> The confusion modern Catholics can fall into is to treat whatever culture they are born into as if its traditions — although they have nothing to do with Christianity at all — were part of our religion. One clear instance of this is the acceptance by some Catholics, of the American social tradition of race prejudice, in complete and *sinful* contradiction of the doctrine of the Mystical Body of Christ.

White middle-class Catholics who accepted race prejudice with all its injustices as part of the American Dream were not the only religious hypocrites: to Thomas Merton, they were simply the worst.

✳

Over cups of hot, black Russian tea Merton listened to the Baroness attack the other guests, two recently ordained Jesuit priests at Friendship House. He intervened to speak for the religious orders. Catherine de Hueck did not back down. The active orders of the Church were bad enough; now she felt herself threatened by the contemplative orders. She told them that Charlie, who worked for her and had worn an overcoat donated by Jacques Maritain all the previous winter, had talked to her of going into the Trappists.[338] Merton, who had just begun to make himself useful, had told her he was leaving Harlem and New York to spend several days over Labor Day in retreat at the Trappist monastery of Our Lady of the Valley near Providence, Rhode Island.

Merton had been a late arrival at Gethsemani in April. He was too early at Our Lady of the Valley. They couldn't have him until September 2. There was a breakdown in plans with Seymour Freedgood, who was supposed to be driving Merton to Greenport, Long Island, during the interval.[339] The expedition was called off and Merton found himself at loose ends, with several days to spend and nowhere to spend them. He decided on Watch Hill, as much because Seymour was beyond driving him anywhere else as for the absence there of an artist's colony: "I spit on New England. The whole shore of Connecticut is a series of gnomes' nests, most of them recommended by S. as delightful."[340] By this time everything had turned sour and poor Seymour was set down, twice in the journal, as a betrayer because he had caused Merton inconvenience.

Merton writes he was in search of a vocation, not a vacation. The room he found in Watch Hill was in little more than a shed. He settled down to read Damon Runyon and decided Runyon had spoiled his stories with too much plot. He found a long spit of sand with an old fort on it that nobody else was interested in on that crowded shoreline on Labor Day weekend. While this was no high place, Merton could sit there and look at the sea.

At Gethsemani in April Merton filled pages with descriptions of the monastery. During his five-day retreat at Our Lady of the Valley, he gave a brief description in his journal of the monastery church, then continued his argument with himself about charity and about war.

Each line of argument has its contradictions[341] and each brings him back to himself. His own acts of charity had largely gone astray.[342] Was his stand on a limited conscientious objection to the war honest? He thought himself exempt from the draft because of the initial physical, but would his original letter have been honored? Robert Gibney, who thought as he did and who, presumably, had written much the same letter, had been inducted. He wrote from Fort Bragg, where there were three suicides in three weeks.[343]

Continuing his own war with himself, Merton saw his writing as lying at the very center of his pride, his impatience, and his obsession with self:

> But for this pride also, I wouldn't be so self-conscious about language to express what I feel: but that is only part of it. I wish I could write it better out of respect for God, who gave me these small and very usual and familiar and unstartling and generous graces.

Then, as so frequently happens in the journal entries where Merton begins with an admission, he argues it round to a justification. In this case it is a justification of the autobiographical method:

> But I am also thinking it would be better to write about it in good words, not cheap words, so that the reader may (if it is ever read) respect me, *my* experience (as opposed to *the* experience), but it isn't *my* experience really, and if *I* claim respect for it, I lose all the good it brought me, of love and devotion to my Lord.
>
> Yet, Holy Father, pray that I may write simply and straight anything I ever have to write, that no dishonor come to God through my writing about Him.
>
> But if I am humble and honest, I will write better just by being humble. By being humble, I will write what is true, simply — and the simple truth is never rubbish and never scandalous — except to people in peculiar perplexities of pride themselves.[344]

The struggles of Thomas Merton the writer with Thomas Merton the writer made him blind to almost everything around him. He prayed for poverty and suffering. In answer, Merton got the first of many monastery colds, and this brought him back to his sense of humor. Still sneezing and breaking out in cold sweats, he set off for St. Bonaventure's. It had been another defeat, not because Our Lady of the Valley had not proved a second Gethsemani,[345] but because he had failed to ask the question he had gone there to ask. The disastrous confrontation at the Church of the Capuchins had destroyed his nerve.

*

Merton went for long walks in the hills and found a place where he could sit for hours, watching the turning colors of another fall and thinking of the connections between the liturgical year and the cycle of the seasons.[346] In a sense, it was not the Pasture that was Merton's high place at St. Bonaventure's, but the whole line of hills to the south of the campus. Yet the second autumn was not like the first, when every walk and climb had been a discovery. He had the nagging feeling that he had set aside the hard for the all-too-easy:

> Walking down from Martiney's rocks on a day late in September, I think of the cowbells and the fields and the tree I have been sitting under — and I compare it all with Harlem — and I do not quite convince myself that it is my calling to be "a contemplative" in the country.[347]

Merton's few weeks in Harlem working with Catherine de Hueck had reawakened his interest in the active role of the Church in social work. His early misgivings were still strong, and these brought him back to Huxley. In the autumn of 1941 a new book by Huxley was published. Merton gathered that *Grey Eminence* was about the misuse of power by the Church in the seventeenth century. The connection seemed remote until Merton read a snide review of the book in *Time*.

Part of Merton's haste in writing again to Huxley after their correspondence had lapsed may have been a desire to disassociate himself at once from the *Time* reviewer. Huxley had probably not read Merton's review of his novel, *After Many a Summer*, which had been published in *The Catholic World* the previous November under the title "Huxley's Pantheon." Rereading it, Merton realized how patronizing he had been: "His [Huxley's] intelligence and personal charm are equalled only by his good will; but, unfortunately, as a philosopher he is *not* distinguished."[348]

It was worse to say, "His mysticism is purely intellectual, and operates only in the order of speculation."[349] Not only had Huxley reorganized Merton's political thinking when he read *Ends and Means*, but Huxley had taken the word *mystic* (a "bad word" among the crowd at John Jay Hall) and made it a word of meaning to Merton. Huxley had been a guide to his own conversion. In the review, Merton had finally dismissed the guide, likening him to Propter, a character in the book, and suggesting that Huxley would do well to become a hermit, which, in the context, is certainly a "bad word":

> And that is probably the whole trouble with Mr. Propter and with Huxley. Neither of them *wants* to do anything for anybody else. They both

have vocations to be hermits. Huxley would make a very good one, too. He would not have to worry about contradicting himself any more, and he could contemplate the truth, in between the visits to his hermitage of cultivated and beautiful friends like Greta Garbo. He is certainly not in much danger from the war. He should do that. He should not write anything more about Mr. Propter.[350]

All this was on Merton's conscience. It made no great difference to Aldous Huxley, who replied at once with a cordial letter and a contribution to Friendship House.[351]

As soon as a copy of *Grey Eminence* arrived, Merton read it to discover if the theme of the book was indeed that a mystic who has political power is doubly dangerous to humanity. He was not much reassured, and he wrote pages of notes. He had already entered into yet another argument with himself, this time on the confusion of religious and political roles in the Church. This led him back to Catholic Action and Friendship House.

He had already written to Catherine de Hueck thanking her "for letting me stand around Friendship House for a couple of weeks of evenings" and saying he hoped he could do that more often. Most of his long letter was about Catholic Action and about his own writing. He begins by wondering how effective Catholic Action can be, politically, in America. Underlying this are his misgivings about what it *should* do. Then he goes on to say:

> If a Catholic gets into a position of power in a country where the political atmosphere is made up of struggles between a lot of irreligious and frankly selfish minorities, how can he ever do anything at all except by compromising with religious principles, or, worse than that, fooling himself that he is leading a crusade, and then turning the country upside down in the name of religion, the way Franco did, or the way the third and fourth crusades did to Europe. I think the reformation was a Divine punishment for the Fourth Crusade, in which the business men of Venice enveigled the whole army of Crusaders (recruited with promises of plenary indulgences if they died in battle) to conquer, for Venetian business, the Christian empire at Constantinople![352]

Merton thought *Grey Eminence* unfair, especially the passages on "morbid" meditations about death and Hell, and Huxley's idea that meditation on the suffering Christ produced cruelty. Other than this, he followed the same line of argument in his notes on the book that he had in his letter to Catherine de Hueck. Father Joseph (the "Grey Eminence") made "advanced graces of mysticism fit in with rigid forms of dogma beyond [the] point where Dogma has any real meaning."[353] He used those graces for a crusade led by France, often against other Catholic powers and in alliance with Protestant powers. The proclaimed crusade was no more than a war of national aggrandizement. Merton also agreed with Huxley when Huxley extended the legacy of Father Joseph into the twentieth century.

Much of Merton's letter to the Baroness had been taken up with asking advice on his own writing. He had told her his writing was divided between what was urgent, what could not be suppressed, and a second kind of writing which was merely argumentative in the sense that it was simply an extension of pride in one's own opinions. He admitted he felt equally driven by pride to publish both kinds of writing, but the good kind of writing could be shared with others. If nobody else read it, Blake's angels would.[354]

Catherine de Hueck's reply threw Merton into confusion: he should write for the poor.[355] Was this a matter of economics, he wondered, or of a class of readers? To give his work away free was within his powers, and he had promised Mary Jerdo a number of articles. The drafts of three of these survive. Far stronger than "Vocations to the Lay Apostolate," or the rather trite fable of the rich man who gives all his money away,[356] was an untitled essay that asks, "What has happened to people, that they can dope themselves with their own argument until all the reality of human misery can become abstract, a question of figures and of economic theories, or a question of politics!"[357]

Much the toughest writing Merton had done, this essay indicted all those who stood in corners at cocktail parties and countered one atrocity story with another, feeling warm with drink, debate, and self-righteousness:

> We can talk about the war in this kind of language: One man begins to talk about what has happened to the Poles, under the tender mercy of the Germans, and, until recently, the Russians. Another will fly into a fury and point out that if these things happened to the Poles, they are still nothing to the cruelties visited by the British upon the Indians, the Boers, the Chinese, and anyway the Poles had these things coming to them for letting themselves be fooled by England. Therefore, for all the good this argument does, the Poles may continue to suffer everything they are suffering! And the Germans and the Russians and everybody else can go on slaughtering one another, because all kinds of rights and all kinds of honor and all kinds of principles are at stake![358]

Merton carries his acute ear for such self-serving debate to discussions about Harlem among white people. Altogether, these contests in self-righteousness, with their brutal and unconscious undercurrent, provide an excellent explanation for Merton why Christ was, and *is*, crucified. But his boldest words are reserved for the answer to the implied question — if we are so often among the crucifiers, who is Christ? — The Enemy?

> "Even as you do it to the least of these little ones, you do it unto Me." Therefore the man you fear in the street, is Christ. The man you think

is a robber, is Christ. The man you think is a murderer, is Christ. And if he turns out to be a murderer, what has that got to do with the salvation of your soul, except that you are bound to give your life, if necessary, for the salvation of *his* soul![359]

✳

Not for the last time, Merton was to have his own words quoted back to him when he wanted least to hear them. The Baroness returned to speak at St. Bonaventure's. Merton went with Father Hubert and Father Roman to meet her train at the station in Buffalo. He had already decided Catherine de Hueck was going to ask him to come to Friendship House and give up his teaching at the college. He had also decided he was going to say no.[360]

There were a number of reasons, reasons he did not want to give. Among them were his doubts about Catholic Action. When Catherine de Hueck turned from her front seat in the car to ask him pointblank if he was coming, he returned a question with a question. How much time could he have for his writing at Friendship House?

He had forgotten he had already told the Baroness in his letter to her that his writing must come second. She had not. No conditions. When was he coming?

Father Hubert gave him no help out of his embarrassment. He suggested Merton leave everything in "B's hands." Earlier on the drive back, the Baroness and Father Hubert had been talking about some other problem, but in a manner close to Merton's own method of testing. In the situation, it made things more difficult for him. The discussion had been "about God's Will: that it is known through persons and through events."[361]

Under pressure, Merton changed his no to a yes. He said he would have to wait until the midyear at St. Bonaventure. In the meanwhile, he would attend the retreat at Friendship House over the Thanksgiving break.

Some signs had been given: he was waiting for other signs. Was mere waiting enough? Did he really have until February to make up his mind? He set aside twenty dollars out of the forty-five dollars he earned each month to take with him as a contribution to Friendship House.[362] The limp answer he had at first made to Catherine de Hueck forced him now to take a cold look at the writing, which, whatever he said or wrote, had often come first in his own mind over the past three years. What he saw now made him angry. What impediment was *this* kind of writing, either to active social work or to trying to join a religious order?[363]

Left without any confidence in the writing, Merton wondered if he was being obstinate — or cowardly:

The reason for my going to the Trappists (in Sept.) was to find out whether I should consider that I had a vocation to work in Harlem. The priest told me — without my having mentioned this idea at all — that the first thing was self-sanctification, then to develop my talents. I resisted a strong impulsion to tell him about the vocation — for what reason I can't imagine. I didn't know how to bring it up? Any reason is absurd: I suppose I was trying to kid myself that the whole thing wasn't serious anyway.[364]

But which vocation was he testing? Harlem? The Trappists? Or both, in light of the vocation he hardly dared to express, except obliquely — the higher vocation and the struggle to be a saint?

He had opened his Vulgate in May and looked at the words "You shall be silent." Was this a sign? Was this superstitious? Could anything be a true sign until he took the initiative?

The result was; I was waiting to find out in some other way — a rather superstitious process! What was I expecting — an angel to wake me up in the middle of the night and tell me? I realise more and more that I am certainly a very great fool. Why didn't I discuss what I wanted to discuss, in the confessional?[365]

The real reason, of course, was that he was afraid of a greater rejection than any. Something now told him time was running out. It was already mid-November. He was not free to change his mind. He had already decided, though everything still depended on his asking a question he had put off for so long. Whatever the answer, he would not be at St. Bonaventure's beyond February, if for that long. His room, the places he had gone for walks, the heart-shaped patch of snow among bare trees on the hill in the distance, were now more precious precisely because they were moving into his past and he had been happier here than almost anywhere else.

For the present he wrote he was going to Harlem: "To become poor, a live in a slum, with no security and no worldly consolation, no possessions, no resources except faith!"[366] Perhaps there was a little too much rehearsal in all this, though, unlike the scenes with Frater John Spaniard, it did not necessarily make "a pretty picture." This time Merton was on his guard, perhaps more than he knew, against "rushing at this with too much rowdy eagerness, the way I have rushed at other vocations and lost them, because I want this to be the one."[367]

Father Paul Hanley Furfey of Catholic University was to conduct a day of recollection for the staff at Friendship House during the Thanksgiving retreat. The evening before, Thomas Merton and Mary Jerdo went to meet the priest's train, and then the three of them had dinner together in New York. Merton was full of jokes and stories. This time he laughed at Mary Jerdo for finding the Bloy books he had shared with her so solemn. It was not a solemn evening.[368]

The next day Merton was very withdrawn. The conferences were on vocations to the Lay Apostolate. He took the night train back to Olean, something he had not done before.[369] It was crowded and he was uncomfortable, pressed into a corner in the day coach, watching a mask like his own face coast in the glass across finely drawn woods and snow. Out there in the night the Waverly train station, the Amusu Theater, and other points on his geography of the Erie Rail Road would appear. There was Lax's voice making sense of how thinking worked, then asking him if he were interested in the Church Fathers. No voice told him he had seen New York City for the last time in twenty years. He had wondered before about the curious separations a pane of glass created. St. John had said you should darken your memory, as if he meant something like images distanced further and further through dark glass. Prayers could get through glass to God. The hills passing now were not for walking in, not for him. A landscape was going by that was little more than a mirage, at least in terms of his life. He would never leave footprints in that snow. You accepted landscapes seen only from trains with a small act of faith, more miles of passing and passage. One journey blended with others, like the streamers of light coming together and separating he had seen leaving Paris long ago, going south with his father. Something divided you like a wall of glass, not from the past only, but from your present, what you *could* be, if only . . . It was there, and it was not there. At times, as in these moments, it created a sense of exile bleeding inside you like a hemorrhage,[370] a sense of division from everything, yourself especially.

*

Back in his room at St. Bonaventure Merton realized Harlem was not the answer, not *his* answer. Perhaps he had always known this, and now felt himself trapped in a commitment he should never have made.

He had told Catherine de Hueck he needed time for writing. This was only an evasion. There were other reasons, and quite possibly they were evasions, too. If he was no longer restless in the same way he had been before his conversion, a part of the continuing restlessness he felt was tied up with a longing to be loved, and to his knowledge that he had not been very good at loving.

It may have been the night in the restaurant sparring with Mary Jerdo, or maybe it was being distracted from what Father Furfey was saying at the retreat to notice Betty Schneider smiling. Perhaps it was something else altogether. In *The Secular Journal,* Merton includes only the passage "Harlem will be full of complications. I don't particularly like the idea of working with a lot of girls."[371] The remark sounds graceless, not convincing. In his journal Merton says more about his own complications:

There are a lot of things that would make it hard for me to serve God —
First of all, being with girls: I might be the only man on the staff — with
five or six girls, and that situation, is, to me personally, intolerable. To
someone else, it might not be. To me, it is. It inevitably means you are
a sort of center of a certain obscure kind of attention, and if you are not,
you feel you are, or at any rate, I would either be so, or have to fight like
a tiger with myself in order *not* to *try* to be. When I was there before,
only for a few days, I got into a lot of situations where I was talking loud
and asserting myself just because there were women around. I had eyes
in the back of my head that followed the women around the room. But
I don't want to get mixed up in such situations; I can't take them. If I
am with women, I know they are women, every minute: and when I was
in the world altogether, that was what I liked to be aware of. Now I cannot dare to. When I am away from women, I do not think about them,
however, and can be at peace to pray. My prayers would be very confused in Harlem.[372]

The only other reason Merton gives (from "a lot of things") is that
watching the kids play Ping-Pong would seem as pointless to him as
saying hello every time he passed a student on the St. Bonaventure
campus.

His self-awareness in a room full of women may have been important, or it may have been exaggerated, another evasion to cover an instinctive feeling that Friendship House wouldn't work for him under
any circumstances. Everything is swept aside:

When I think of the Trappists — it is all different. I cannot think of one
thing that would not help me towards God, with His Grace!

*

Merton had always kept, and was always to keep, his inner turmoil
from others. At most, they would notice that he seemed preoccupied.
His gravest crisis now found him with nobody to talk to and a sudden
urgency of time. It was his instinct again which told him he had to
resolve matters within those last days of November. Gibney was in the
army. Jim Knight was in the army. Lax was in New York. His brother,
more lost than he was, had finally succeeded in enlisting. In September, he had crossed the Canadian border and entered the RCAF in
Toronto. His father was dead. Ruth Merton — dead. Remote even
beyond death. Uncle Harold? No. So many people — no. He wrote
to Mary Jerdo that she should not make fun of Bloy's suffering "uniquely
and intensely." For two days, he told her, he had been battling a battle of angels.[373] He knew his own capacity for dramatizing things. This
time there was no exaggeration.

Outside, the snow fell in the great silences, yet at Devereux Hall the
radios were louder than ever. Merton escaped again into the chapel
and couldn't pray. He went off into the white fields and prayed to St.

Thérèse in the Grove. He started to imagine an interview with Father Philotheus in which he asked the question he had failed to ask at Gethsemani and at Our Lady of the Valley.

At Gethsemani, and in the argument he regretted most, Merton realized how little he knew of Catholic theology apart from the writings of St. Thomas Aquinas and St. Augustine. For some months now he and two seminarians had studied works by Duns Scotus, Origen, William of Ockham, and others, under Father Philotheus.[374] Merton knew he was no more sympathetic to the Cistercians of the Strict Observance than any of the other friars at St. Bonaventure's; but Father Philotheus was close and Dan Walsh was in New York City.

On Thursday, November 27, at dusk, Merton settled down to write a poem in his room. He wrote a few lines, then realized the poem would never be written. He went to chapel. He was so overwrought he wondered if he was having the same attack of vertigo he had had on the Long Island Rail Road.[375] Details of the chapel began to move about him and his head was pounding. He went back to his own room, tried to pray, opened a book on the Trappists, closed it, then went out again. He went downstairs and walked along the hall until he came to the door of Father Philotheus's room. There was a light under the door. He stayed perhaps a minute, then walked away. He turned and walked once more toward the door. This time something like a physical force seemed to push him back from the door. He turned and left the building. "Wait!" he was thinking to himself. "Wait for some more time, a few more days . . ."

In the Grove, he tried to rehearse the scene all over again. He prayed only to know the answer to the question he had not dared to ask: could he become a Trappist, could he become a priest?

The cold of the wood and the snow, the sound of bells on the wind reminding him of Gethsemani, broke through all his complications of mind.[376] What he took to be his cowardice was now of no consequence. The long-drawn battle diminished into the hollow places of the line of hills.

When Merton went back, the light under Father Philotheus's door had been extinguished. Merton went off to the recreation room and found him. They returned together to the priest's room and Merton finally asked his question.

> Instantly he says that, in his opinion, there is no canonical impediment in my case. And he advises the thing that was so obvious I hadn't thought of it — go to Gethsemani as soon as the Christmas vacation begins, and tell the whole story to the Abbot. (I thought of writing — he says that would be bad.)
>
> Also he advises me to be careful about deciding to be a Trappist. What about my vocation to be a writer?

That one has absolutely no meaning any more, as soon as he said what he has said.[377]

Merton went to the chapel to give praise. Then he went a second time to the Grove, "my head full of a big doubletalk mixture of Te Deums and goodbye to everything I don't want."[378]

As in the *pensione* at Rome, long ago, so now — *Abba, Gratia Plena. Vale Vanitas Mundi . . .*

> And there will be no more future — not in the world, not in geography, not in travel, not in change, not in variety, conversations, new work, new problems in writing, new friends, none of that: but a far better progress, all interior and quiet!!! If God only would grant it! If it were only His will.[379]

*

On December 1, Merton received a notice from the draft board telling him to appear for a second medical examination. He had already written to Gethsemani asking if he could come on December 18, and he had written to the Franciscan monastery in New York City asking for his documents. The letter from the draft board was completely unexpected. Merton telephoned the local secretary. She told him that the rule about teeth had been changed and that he would probably be classified 1-A.[380]

The decision had been made within days of the time when it would have been compromised. Merton's instinct that there was an urgency was proved right. He wrote to the draft board asking for a delay and explaining the circumstances. Then he wrote again to Gethsemani, asking if he could come to the monastery earlier than December 18.[381]

Both the possibility of remaining at St. Bonaventure and the possibility of going to Harlem had been virtually ruled out by the letter from the draft board. Merton had excluded both these options before the letter came. If Gethsemani would not have him, Merton was resigned to going into the army. He was still firm on one point: he would serve; he would not kill.

He began at once to burn his bridges and his books. He also began to pray without ceasing:

> Lord! You have left the real beginning of my conversion until now! How long I have prayed to serve Thee, only desire Thee, only belong to Thee, and not known what it meant! Now, Thou makest me pray all day, all day, in great thirst, repeating over and over, let me only belong to Thee, give *everything* to Thee — When I am not praying I am dry and sick. When I am praying, O, sometimes, You give me the clearest, quietest peace: I cannot stop! Never stop praying! It hurts to stop praying — it hurts to go to eat, but that too is sweet if I only say "I will only eat very little, for Love of my God!" Then the meal is very sweet — a bit of bread, some vegetables, the way it is always at Gethsemani![382]

The last entry in Merton's journal at St. Bonaventure is dated December 5, 1941. Merton sent the journals, one copy of the only novel he cared for, "Journal of My Escape from the Nazis," and the clean, typed copies of all his poems to Mark Van Doren in Greenwich Village. The journal he had written at the college was the best of his prose (though he thought little of it), and it was fitting Mark Van Doren returned the journals to the college library a few years later. He handed over to Father Fitzgerald his folder of reading notes, and much else. To Father John Faddish and Father Aloysius Siracuse he gave his Columbia notebooks. Merton sent his "Cuban Journal" to Catherine de Hueck. If it could be published, it was to help the Baroness with her work in place of the car he had promised earlier.[383] Mary Jerdo at Friendship House received a box containing almost all his extra clothes for the Clothing Center, among them the navy blue polo-necked sweater that went all the way back to Merton's rebel days at Oakham and to his travels through Germany and along the Riviera. He gave all his books but five to the Friedsam Library, including the bound copies of *The Oakhamian* and the prizes he had won at Oakham. Merton packed a small suitcase with a few clothes, his Vulgate, his breviary, *Imitation of Christ*, his Hopkins, his Blake, and two half-filled notebooks.

On December 7, the second Sunday in Advent, Merton heard of the attack on Pearl Harbor from the friars with radios. On Monday, America was at war with Japan. On December 9, his classes were divided among his colleagues. He said goodbye to Father Thomas Plassman and received from him a strong letter of recommendation to the abbot.[384] Merton closed his account at the First National Bank in Olean, withdrawing $167.43.[385] A letter from the draft board delayed the medical for a month.[386] He wrote letters to his uncle, to Robert Lax, to Ed Rice, to the Baroness, and to Mary Jerdo. Then, in light, cold rain, on December 10, 1941, he was driven to the station and he was off a second time to Gethsemani.

If he was in a hurry this time, Merton was far calmer. There was a certain absolute confidence he was going to be a Trappist. If he was refused, he would go into the army, then return later. He did not need to plan anything, rehearse anything. For the Trappists, all things were altered at the gate of the enclosure and they were altered forever.

> (We were begotten in the tunnels of December rain,
> Born from the wombs of news and tribulation,
> By night, by wakeful rosary:
> Such was my birth, my resurrection from the freezing east,
> The night we cleared you, Cincinnati, in a maze of lights.)[387]

He crossed the dark, muscular waters of the Ohio River, which he had celebrated in a poem where he had turned April into August. Now it was deep winter, the growing season:

> I saw Ohio, whom I love,
> I saw the wide river between buildings
> My big brown lady, going west . . .[388]

Harold Jenkins received the news with bitter disappointment. His older nephew had been difficult, but he had a brilliant mind. Now that mind was wasted. Tom Izod Bennett did not receive the news. Robert Lax went to work at Friendship House, the "Son of Israel," as Catherine de Hueck called him.[389] Lax worked in Harlem for almost a year until his health broke down. As Lax did not believe in mortification, it cannot have been mortification that led him to eat so little, to fast so often, and to wear shoes of rope and canvas. Some of Merton's other friends wondered if he would remain in the monastery as long as a year. Merton liked people, he was gregarious, he liked women, he liked talk, lots of talk, argument, and laughter. Ed Rice remembered the discussions they had had about writing the way one wanted to write. In the army, Robert Gibney learned that something in Tom Merton had been serious all along.

Robert Lax, always diffident about negotiating doors and entries, managed the small front room of Curtis Brown and found Naomi Burton filing papers in her office. He tried to explain that Thomas Merton had entered a Trappist monastery where he was allowed to write two half-page letters four times a year.

"Oh God! He'll never write again!" Naomi Burton said.[390] But this was precipitous.

PART FIVE

Mount Purgatory

It is no little thing for a man to dwell in monasteries and congre-
gations and there to live without quarrel and so truly to abide to
his life's end. Blissful is he that liveth there well and graciously
continueth.

— *Thomas à Kempis*

I T WOULD BE HARD to exaggerate the importance of place for Thomas Merton. On the last page of *The Seven Storey Mountain* he listed the stations of his journey which had brought him to Gethsemani: Prades, Bermuda, St. Antonin, Oakham, London, Cambridge, Rome, New York, Columbia, Corpus Christi, St. Bonaventure. Each of the evocative names he told over here, and in a number of his poems, was largely fixed in his own experience. (The list was incomplete: he had left out Cuba. He came in time to see that he had been altogether too subjective, at least as far as Cambridge was concerned. Like the Roman poet Horace and many others after him, he admitted it was not altogether "the place's fault.")[1]

In 1941, the goal of all his wanderings was certainly fixed. In the twelfth century, Hugh of St. Victor had declared that the aim of all human activity was to be the recovery of Eden,[2] and it was the very nature of Eden to be unchangeable. It was Merton's very nature both to seek changes and to desire the unchangeable.

Gethsemani was to be Merton's home for twenty-seven years. For the first seven of those years he went outside the strict enclosure only to work in the monastery grounds. Not until August 12, 1948, did he leave Gethsemani, and then only for six hours on business for the Order in Louisville. In the next ten years, he spent all but four of his rare periods away from the monastery in hospitals: he went twice to Louisville in order to become an American citizen, he went to look at the possible site for a new foundation in Ohio in 1952, he went to a conference in Minnesota in 1956. Each time he was in the company of other monks. With the late 1950s and the 1960s came further periods in hospitals, and visits to doctors in Louisville and Lexington. There were a number of occasions when Merton left the enclosure to spend a few hours with friends. In 1964 he was given permission to go to New York on his own to visit Daisetz Suzuki. Only in the last year, 1968, were there extended periods away from the monastery.

If too much is made of these absences, the pattern of the largely unbroken years at the monastery is seriously distorted. They were, however, exceptional in the life of a Trappist. They could not have been foreseen in 1941. They provide evidence, among other things, that changes had taken place in the Cistercian Order of the Strict Observance.

John Eudes Bamberger entered the Order in 1950, Flavian Burns in 1951. Neither, when he came to Gethsemani, expected to see the world outside the enclosure again.[3] The vow of stability was not open to any other interpretation. A Trappist monk lived and died and was buried within the enclosure. He did not leave the monastery for the burial of his parents. Most medical and dental needs were met at the monastery. Only the abbot traveled to other monasteries of the Order. Only the monk who held the office of cellarer had daily dealings with those outside the monastery.

This was known and accepted by Thomas Merton as part of the very life he had come to find when he entered Gethsemani, on December 10, 1941, just as it was known and accepted by Flavian Burns, by John Eudes Bamberger, and so many others. Unlike them, Merton had tried to resolve one conflict by force which would not stay resolved.[4]

Much has been written on the subject of Merton's own changes, his later ambivalent feelings toward the only family and the only home he knew for half his lifetime. If the walled Paradise, the Court of the Queen of Heaven, came at times to seem to him the prison of Prisoner's Base, it is only fair to point out that Gethsemani changed, too. What must have appeared so stable in an unstable world in 1941 was transformed.

In *The Sign of Jonas,* Merton recorded the physical changes that had taken place in his first ten years when he made his fire watch on July 4, 1952. Today it is difficult to retrace his steps that night. New buildings have been added to the great fortress of God on the Kentucky hill. The silver spire and the water tower are gone, with much else. Where the old buildings remain, the interiors have been gutted and altered, some several times, within the façade.

It is far more important, and much more difficult, to record the enormous changes within a continuity that took place in the life inside those walls of new and old brick over the years. There is a certain irony in wondering what the Thomas Merton of 1941 would make of Gethsemani today.

In the 1960s Merton changed the Order and changed Gethsemani. It

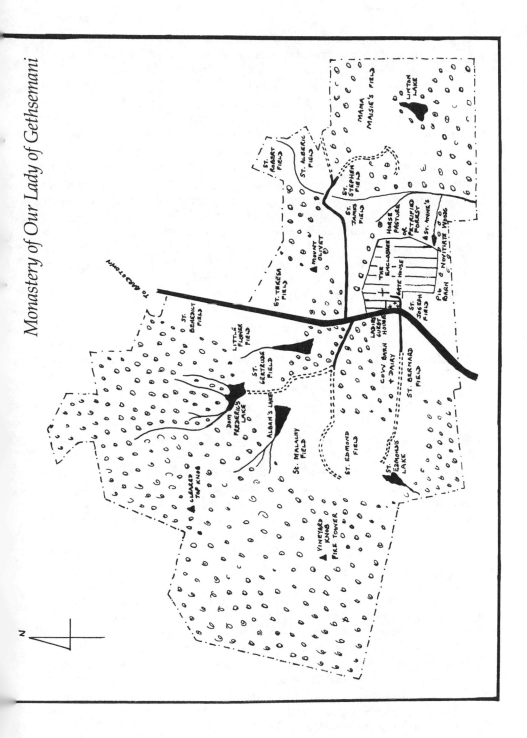

Monastery of Our Lady of Gethsemani

was the transformations of the mid and late 1950s (over which he had little control) that brought him to a new restlessness. Not only in retrospect, the early years at the monastery were the "Edenic" period.[5]

There is no sense in any of his writings, published or unpublished, that Gethsemani had failed his desperate need in 1941, or that his acceptance into the Cistercian Order of the Strict Observance was anything but a liberation. In his Easter Letter 1968 he wrote: "It would be utterly dishonest for me to claim that when I first came to Gethsemani the place was not for me a 'sign of Christ.' It *was*, in spite of all the shortcomings I instinctively realized."[6] In 1941, he may have been less aware of some of the shortcomings he goes on to list in 1968. His early poems are poems of praise, and there is much celebration in the closing pages of *The Seven Storey Mountain* and in *The Sign of Jonas*. One of the most frequent images in Merton's work of that period is the window.[7] The window requires both a frame and a wall. For many years the light shone through a window of clear glass.

Life was arduous, confined, raw. There was something in Merton's very nature that responded to this. The Order is a penitential order, one in which hard physical labor is termed "recreation," and there is no other recreation. Special sins require a special form of penance, Merton felt.[8] But an overwhelming sense of guilt for the past does not explain everything in his case. He continued to have a very ambiguous sense of the past, going back to it with as much pleasure as pain. Expiation for what had been was only a part of penance. If Merton had certainly learned not to trust himself unaided, he sought in penance strength for the present and the future. Still more important, poverty, austerity, even negation for its own sake, had a positive attraction. There are passages in *The Seven Storey Mountain* (and in Merton's essays of the 1960s)[9] that could be called, not unfairly, "negative boostering," as if Merton had reversed his grandfather's ideas, yet kept Pop's enthusiasm. Some who were drawn to Gethsemani by reading *The Seven Storey Mountain* confessed they were a little disappointed to find that the physical hardship was not as demanding as he had made it sound. Merton came to admit that he had idealized even in describing the degree of sacrifice.

Life at Gethsemani in the 1940s has to be seen in another context. There were others who were leading arduous, confined, and raw lives under orders in those years — in army camps, in camps for conscientious objectors, in foxholes in the Ardennes, and in the Pacific Islands. Response to such conditions had as much to do with the individual's mental attitude as with expectations and earlier experience. The regime at Gethsemani proved too severe for some returning soldiers.

The return to conditions of the Middle Ages was not easy for Americans of any economic group. This was to tell later against the movement in the 1960s to found small, experimental monasteries. The simple life was far too simple. For Father Paul Bourne, every American tends to have too high expectations.[10] By tradition the monks were drawn in Europe from peasant stock (certainly all the lay brothers had been peasants). As Owen Merton had discovered, there were no peasants in America.

Dom John Eudes Bamberger sums up the medical services at Gethsemani in those early days as "country doctoring." Meat, fish, and eggs were excluded from the diet. Choir monks fasted for half the year, in Lent and Advent. Like all monasteries, Gethsemani lived under the sixth-century Rule of St. Benedict. This had been more strictly interpreted by the Cistercian Usage in the eleventh century, and still more stringently applied after the reforms of the seventeenth century by Abbé Armand-Jean de Rancé, the Abbot of La Trappe in France. It was the monastery of La Trappe which gave the name Trappist to the Cistercian Order of the Strict Observance. Gethsemani strove to follow the "French" Usage and to keep its tradition of being the strictest of the strict. Little concession was made to such things as a different climate. Father Paul Bourne remembers that the main dish one Lent for thirty-nine days out of forty was sweet potatoes. This was at the foundation Gethsemani established in 1944. Most of the monks at Our Lady of the Holy Ghost, Conyers, suffered from heat rash in the Georgia summer. When the abbot general, Dom Gabriel Sortais, made a visitation to the monastery, he was almost overcome by the heat, and he ordered the monks to leave off their cowls at meals and in choir.[12]

Yet it was the cold the monks at Gethsemani remembered most, the days in central Kentucky when the holy water froze in the stoups.[13] Merton had opened the windows of his room in the guest house to prepare himself for the chill in the monastery when he was admitted as a postulant. He was told to close the windows, but he already had his first Gethsemani cold, the worst he had ever had, and there were to be many more.[14]

In those early years many of the hours set aside for physical labor were taken up with cutting down trees for the huge wood-burning furnace that did little even to heat the abbey church. There was a good deal of inefficiency in other directions. For all the hours the postulants and novices spent with bucket and mop, the monastery did not look clean. It was in a dangerous state of disrepair. Occasionally the authorities would come from Louisville to carry out an inspection, or send notices about fire laws and maintenance regulations.[15]

Physical conditions did something to limit the number of novices who stayed on to become monks under vows, yet, except for the influenza epidemics each February, the health of the monks was generally good. Most lived to an age far beyond the national average.

These things were accounted incidentals to men who had devoted themselves to God, to worship, to prayer, to penance. They were reminded wherever they looked, by texts printed on the walls, that they had given up everything for the salvation of their souls. Conditions confirmed the vow of poverty. The physical structure itself was at least adequate. Real problems arose only at the sudden increase in the number of novices at the end of the war, in an overcrowding nobody had foreseen or provided for. It was said that Dom Frederic Dunne was reluctant to turn away anyone who applied, while the next abbot would be equally reluctant to let anyone leave.

Merton's religious vocation transcended the immediate. His second vocation meant that he could not ignore his surroundings for long. There was an absolute need to seek God, and there was a need he could hardly set aside to record everything. Recording meant writing, and where writing was concerned Merton was now divided against himself.

Even in the last pages of *The Seven Storey Mountain*, with the celebration, there is also complaint. The complaining novice was a familiar enough figure at Gethsemani, as at every monastery. Where most complained that the life was too hard, however, Merton tended to complain it was not hard enough. It was a liberation not to have to deal with money: he had never been good with money. If there was very little food, there was always some food. Everyone went hungry, nobody starved or was in danger of starving.

The clothes might be awkward to wear and to work in, yet they were replaced when they wore out. Those who failed to take their shoes to Brother Cobbler for repairs were proclaimed in the Chapter of Faults.[16] No monk died in destitution and neglect. There was a measure of security at the monastery absent from the lives of most of those in the world. In this sense, as Merton says, the monastery realized the Communist millennium: from each according to his capacity, to each according to his needs. No Communist society could boast as much.[17]

*

The first decision in the religious life was between the choir and the lay brothers. The Rule of St. Benedict said nothing about the necessity of a choir monk becoming a priest. There was even some dispute over whether St. Benedict had been a priest himself. Merton saw the need in the 1960s for an intermediate group of choir monks who were not priests, and the situation has changed today. In 1941, Cistercian Usage made it essential for an applicant to the choir to be eligible for the priesthood.

Father Robert, the master of novices, reported his discussion with the applicant to the abbot on December 11. Dom Frederic Dunne ruled there was no bar to Thomas Merton's becoming a choir monk, and ultimately a priest. At his interview with the abbot, on the Feast of St. Lucy, December 13, Merton was accepted as a postulant to the choir. This date was the official one of Merton's entry into the Cistercian Order of the Strict Observance.[18]

In the normal course of things, he would have been a postulant for about a month before a further decision was made to accept him as a novice or not. Letters asking for information about his character were delayed by wartime conditions. In early February his head was shaved. On February 21, 1942, he was accepted as a choir monk, and he put on the novice's habit. All his possessions were tabulated and put away. Thomas Merton was now Brother M. Louis Merton, O.C.S.O. By a chance that pleased him, he had been given the name of the sainted king of France. It was to be pronounced "Lewis" (as in "St. Louis, Missouri," on the rare occasions the town was spoken of at the monastery). The "M." stood for Mary, as in all the religious names of the Order, a reminder to each monk of his patroness in the religious life, an initial of pride — and of humility.

During the retreat the previous March, Merton had had difficulty remaining inside the monastery enclosure for six days. He found himself confined now in a narrow enclosure within the enclosure.

There was a strict division between choir and lay brothers. There was an absolute division also between novices and those monks who had taken vows, the "professed." Choir novices were allowed only in the monastery church for offices, the novitiate scriptorium (a library crowded with lines of thirty or forty desks), the novitiate chapel, and the small area of the novitiate garden. In the garden, novices were permitted to make the Stations of the Cross, or to follow a narrow, triangular course while meditating.

In the novitiate there were periods of instruction, called conferences, four or five times a week, each lasting about forty minutes. One day the Rule would be explained; the next, spiritual life; the next, tribulations; the next, liturgy. There were instructions in singing. Something like a third of the monastery day was spent saying the offices or at Mass. When the novices went to work they walked in single file, and they returned in the same way from the woods or fields. Chopping wood or splitting it in the woodshed was done under the supervision of the master of novices or the undermasters. Contact with professed monks was limited to confession, to a weekly conference with the master of novices on spiritual concerns, and to rare conferences with the abbot. Professed monks bowed to one another when passing. A novice meeting a professed monk would neither give nor receive any sign of recognition.

When Thomas Merton traveled to Gethsemani he genuinely felt this was the end to arguing forever,[19] and almost certainly the end of writing. Within a very short period, he was reminding the Order that it was a contemplative order as well as a penitential one. He was involved in writing from his first days at the monastery.

Merton's muted and ambiguous struggle with Abbot Frederic Dunne set the pattern of many to come with other superiors. Few critics have blamed Dom Frederic for reacting in the way he did to Merton's dilemma over his writing. If Merton complains in *The Seven Storey Mountain* that he had been surrendered back to "my double, my shadow, my enemy, Thomas Merton"[20] — to the writer Thomas Merton, we sense there is some truth in this and sympathize with the monk even while we have the book. The portrait of Frederic Dunne is a sympathetic one, yet he stands in opposition to one side of Merton's nature as he encourages the other.

There were times when Thomas Merton was sure that God wanted him to stop writing because writing was the greatest single barrier to his loving God with a whole heart. If he had accepted this, it would mean an absolute prohibition. The idea of such a prohibition is never altogether discarded in Merton's journals. But Merton acted on a second idea — that he should write only what was worthy of God and keep only what reached this standard. In December 1941, he burned all his novels but one, yet he made sure his journals, one novel, and his poems were preserved. He would meet no censor of his writing as ruthless as himself.

One of the five books he took to Gethsemani was Thomas à Kempis's *The Imitation of Christ:*

> Certainly at the day of doom it shall not be asked of us what we have read but what we have done: nor what good we have said but how religiously we have lived.[21]

Another abbot was to remind Merton over and over that he had come to Gethsemani for the salvation of his soul, that he would not be asked what he had written, but how he had lived. The repetition was exacerbating precisely because it spoke to a debate in himself, a debate Merton never resolved. Dom James Fox did not put Merton under abbatial obedience to write.

Yet Merton had good reason to be surprised by Dom Frederic's reaction. Earlier, he had at least thought of obtaining an agreement from the Franciscans that he was to be allowed to write when he joined that Order; and the presumption of this was that he should be allowed to write what he chose when he chose. By reputation at least, the Trappists were not an order that encouraged writers.

It is likely Merton asked Father Joachim about this when he was on retreat. He may have been surprised to hear the monastery already had a writer whose books were becoming known among Catholics, Father

Raymond Flanagan. This is important, though it is not mentioned in *The Seven Storey Mountain.*

Dom Frederic Dunne's father had been a bookbinder and publisher in the very town in Ohio where the Jenkins family lived and where Sam Jenkins had once owned and operated a bookstore.[22] Dom Frederic had been brought up loving books and everything to do with books. As abbot, he encouraged Father Raymond's writing, and he had seen Father Raymond's books bring donations, conversions, and even some applicants to Gethsemani. Thus Merton found an abbot who was sympathetic to writers, while an exception had already been made to the general rule that Trappists were averse to monks who wrote and published.

Gethsemani had inspired an extraordinary amount of writing when Merton was a retreatant. Whether he wanted it or not, the same thing happened when he came there in December. He wrote a number of journal pages in the two old notebooks he had brought. Many of these were subsequently destroyed, and only a few passages remain. But there are also drafts of seven poems. One of these, "A Letter to My Friends," is dated St. Lucy's Day, December 13, 1941, the day he entered the Order. He showed the poems to Father Robert, the master of novices, asking for Father Robert's opinion. Father Robert had never believed it was part of his job to give literary criticism: he was not even sure novices were allowed to write poetry.[23]

Dom Frederic liked the poems, though he must have doubted whether poetry would draw souls to the Church or postulants to Gethsemani. He could hardly have guessed that this postulant's poetry would bring aid to the monastery in the form of a new foundation within a matter of years. For the moment, if time could be found for poetry in the full hours of the novitiate day, well and good.[24] There were books that needed to be written, books on notable Trappists and on the religious life. The abbot listened to Merton's scruples and honored them as honest difficulties. He must have sensed something beyond the scruples. If the postulant wrote under obedience and under the abbot's direction, the dilemma would be resolved and the books Dom Frederic wanted written would be written.

*

It was certainly prophetic that Merton had spent the time in the guest house reading over the *Spiritual Directory*, wondering what distinguished the Trappists from other contemplative orders, and finding its words — "the Holy Mass, the Divine Office, Prayer and pious reading which form the exercises of the contemplative life occupy the major part of our day" — cold to match the cold in the room with the open window.[25] "What do you mean by contemplation, anyway?" he asked himself and the anonymous writers of the *Directory*.

There was a time when he would come back to this very passage in the *Spiritual Directory* with far more sympathy. For the moment, it served only to raise a question that Thomas Merton was to spend the rest of his life trying to answer. Other questions had obsessed him, and would do so again. What is the effective peaceful alternative to violence? How can we prevent social injustice? What can we learn from other religious traditions? Yet, What do you mean by contemplation, anyway? remained the most important, and at the center of everything. In almost every book Merton wrote he tried to give a clearer answer.

"America is discovering the contemplative life," he wrote hopefully in the Epilogue to his autobiography in 1947.[26] In a sense he saw this come true, just as he was hailed as one who had made contemplation possible for everyone. In the 1940s, he wondered if his own contemplative Order had discovered contemplation.

One thing was clear (where much was still to be discovered) — solitude was necessary for contemplation. And, at Gethsemani, there was a special irony in the line of Latin on the walls of the guest house: *O beata solitudo, o sola beatitudo!*[27]

Contemplation, meditation, mysticism were not words that Merton liked much, though Huxley had done something to make *mysticism* a word he felt somewhat less shy of using. *Contemplation* continued to have worrying connotations. Merton was forced into using it, as writers and artists are forced into using *creative*, and with as little joy in a situation not of their making.

The repetition of the two words *contemplation* and *solitude* (a word he *did* have a great love for) in Merton's early writing at the monastery tells its own story. By using *contemplation* over and over (and only this word), Merton hoped to convince his own Order of the irony he saw. Where he uses *solitude*, it is easy to see that he sometimes means something like privacy as a necessary first step. At Gethsemani today there is both privacy and solitude. It was not so in the 1940s. Merton had much to do with the transition.

Even before the overcrowding, there was no privacy. In the dormitories each monk had a tiny partitioned area in which to sleep. His bed was like a wooden bench. He had a straw-filled pallet and bolster, a hook on the wall on which to hang the discipline, a small cord whip. The curtain was made from the same identical bolt of singularly unattractive green-brown material. A monk spent only those hours in this rudimentary cell that were set aside for sleep. On Friday, after Chapter, the monks went in procession to the dormitory, and each retired to his cell to take the discipline. This was self-inflicted on the bare back and lasted the space of the Pater Noster. In winter, some monks felt the only real punishment was waiting in the cold for the signal from the abbot or prior to begin. The monk had one hour's rest in the day in his cell during the summer — the *méridienne*.

Each novice had a small box in the novitiate scriptorium for his few private possessions, his letters, and the books from the library he was allowed to take out. He had twenty minutes each week to choose a book, and the book had to be agreed by the novice master as suitable for his spiritual needs.

There were many rules beyond the Rule in the monastery that were intended to prevent what was referred to obliquely as Particular Friendship. A Particular Friendship did not, in itself, imply homosexuality, but the inference was there, and it was given obsessive importance. The rules and the alertness to infringements further cut down on privacy. A monk going to the open lavatory cells, the cabinets, or the closet of shame, had to have his hood up. At times, retreat into the hood must have been the only possible retreat from the gaze of others.[28]

There was no escape at work, except in the few specialized jobs. A plumber, a welder, a cobbler might have a few hours on his own during a day.[29] A writer was not so fortunate. The "pious lives" Merton wrote as a novice were written in the daily hour or two he was allowed in the crowded novitiate library, or scriptorium. The scriptorium for the professed monks, which Merton moved into in 1944, was hardly less crowded. He was allowed to type in a second library, though even here he was not alone. Father Anthony Chassagne (the Father Macarius of *The Sign of Jonas*) used the room in the same period for his writing on theology and canon law.[30]

In a strange way, the Rule of Silence only served at times to make the lack of privacy more extreme. Because there were no mirrors, each man's face became a mirror, and expressions could be mysterious, cryptic, or telling. Long periods of silence can be both relaxing and an aid to self-forgetting concentration, but in the circumstances at the monastery they too often become periods of self-conscious tension.

One means of communication was permitted by tradition, the Trappist sign language. (Rather surprisingly, Merton took time to learn this new language with its four hundred signs, though he became proficient and imaginative later.) Here, too, discretion had to be used, and a monk was likely to be proclaimed in the Chapter of Faults for overusing signs, just as he was for "sound," or speaking. There were rich possibilities for misunderstanding with the sign language, something that made the frequent teasing more devastating at times than the person teasing intended. Using sign language added to the dangers of working in groups with axes in the woods, or with hammers on construction, and these dangers increased with the use of heavy machinery. "Sound"; words, could always be used in an emergency. But the matter had usually resolved itself one way or the other by the time the Trappist monk got over his inhibition and risked a shouted warning or a cry for help.

If there was no escaping others in the early years, there was usually quiet to aid recollection and concentration. Not always. Noise is a strange thing and often a matter of very subjective judgment. It certainly was in the case of Thomas Merton. While a writer can "program out" the sound of his typewriter, he can be acutely bothered by birds outside his window. Where silence is expected, a hammer falling on stone floors can be shattering. For Merton, both in the monastery and at the hermitage later, falling rain confirmed the silence and enclosed it. He liked storms. In choir, the chanting can deepen silence, while a cough, repeated at predictable intervals, can destroy every possibility of recollected thought. One such cougher heard all the monks around him sucking in their breath in fury each time he coughed.

Many monks have said that Gethsemani today is a quieter place now that the Rule of Silence has been relaxed during certain hours. The days of intensive farming and building are largely over. Perhaps it is the very stillness which makes the passing of a single car on the highway below the hill so intrusive. The noise of the engine seems to go on into the distance for a long time. The caw of crows, the jargon of bluejays, the frog voices in the water meadows can get on one's nerves. On some days the guns at Fort Knox, which disturbed Merton, still pound away.

When Merton speaks of solitude in the 1940s, he often means privacy. When he speaks of contemplation, he often means concentration. Rereading his journals and notebooks, he discovered that his handwriting often gave a clue.[31] Where his handwriting was large and flowing, his concentration had been lacking, where it grew small and cramped, he had concentrated hard. He distinguished periods at Columbia and at St. Bonaventure by this means. At St. Bonaventure's he had learned to use time better. But it was during the years in the novitiate that Merton built up extraordinary powers of concentration. He had made careful schedules for himself at St. Bonaventure. At Gethsemani the schedule was made for him. Later on, he was to feel that when he had won a certain freedom with regard to time he did less. In the early years he husbanded every minute: he learned a way to concentrate entirely on what he was doing, on his prayer, his reading, his writing.

In reading, he grasped the essential meaning of a page at a glance.[32] In writing, he wasted little time on preliminaries, on the "scaffolding" many writers need. This was true of his letters, as it is true of Merton's more formal writing. In his journals there is much repetition; certain subjects are treated obsessively, but there is no chatter. In poetry, where a different kind of concentration is needed, this training added to difficulties that were already there, both in the first draft and in revision. In Merton's prose, the new skills and self-discipline largely cut through the old self-indulgence.

Concentration and impatience are seldom combined. In Merton's best writing, the concentration and the impatience come together to produce a sense of immediacy and urgency. Something is shared between the writer and the reader, the understanding that only the best will do, that there is no time to waste on anything else. Urgency of expression probably has more to do with an effective style than anything except talent. Some of Merton's finest effects come "Striking like lightning to the quick of the real world."[33] And Merton's strongest prose was consistently on the subject of contemplation or in the autobiographical writings drawn from the past and the current journals.

*

On March 19, 1944 (the Feast of St. Joseph, a feast already important to him), Merton took Simple Vows and crossed to the professed side of the monastery. At this time he made the will that gave money to the person known to Tom Bennett.[34] The next three years would be a further probationary period, and the will was to cover the distribution of his property before Solemn Vows, when all property would go over to the monastery.

In 1947, Merton wrote *The Waters of Siloe*, a history of the Order he had promised Dom Frederic, and strictly speaking, the last book he wrote under obedience to his first abbot.

The book gives a brief history of the foundation of the Cistercians in the marshlands of Burgundy on Palm Sunday 1098, then of St. Bernard, and of the reforms of Abbé de Rancé at La Trappe in the seventeenth century. Much of the book is taken up with the American foundations in the nineteenth century. Merton traces the history of his own abbey from the arrival of Father Eutropius Proust and his forty-two monks in the last, bitterly cold days of December 1848.[35] The exiled French monks built their monastery somewhat against Cistercian tradition, on a ridge, rather than a marshland. They used soft brick from their own brickyard (faced much later to look like stone).[36] The monks were building while the nation was tearing itself apart in a civil war that divided Kentucky more painfully than most states. At the monastery there was an eighty-year struggle to draw American-born postulants to the Order. On his election in 1935, Frederic Dunne became the first American-born abbot.

Farming had not prospered on the monastery lands, which in time grew by purchase from seven hundred to almost two thousand acres. Nelson is a poor county with no claim to the bluegrass lands of Kentucky. The monastery woodlands which covered the high, rounded hills, or knobs, were rich in prime growth, but to finance the building of ponds with dams, Dom Frederic had sold most of the first growth of hardwood. Dom Frederic's reputation was that of a scholar and a man of saintly character: he was neither an administrator nor a businessman. Most of the monastery's income came from donations. The interest on loans was rising, and the monastery was sinking deeper and deeper into debt.

Little had changed in a hundred years at Gethsemani. The clothes the monks wore were durable and awkward. Like the Amish, the Cistercians believed buttons sinfully modern, and everything had to be tied together. In winter, the monk wore a robe, a scapular, and a cowl, all made of thick wool, with a combined weight of twenty pounds. The wool chaffed the wrists raw. Winter clothing was usually given out on the Feast of the Immaculate Conception, December 8. Under the robe the monk wore underwear consisting of a long denim shirt; long drawers of duck that tied around the legs; stockings which were tied to the drawers and covered the legs but had only a heel; socks which fitted like slippers. Both stockings and socks were of the same coarse and durable duck. In winter, underwear was changed every two weeks. Shoes were made at the monastery. They had to be oversize to go over the bulky socks and were seldom anything but an approximate fit. Work shoes were like army boots and were often metal-shod, which added a good deal to the noise in winter at the monastery.

Summer clothes were normally distributed at Easter. The shirts were usually made of a lighter, flannel material, but they were as long as the winter shirts. The robe was of duck, the scapular and cowl were of cotton, instead of wool. There were two changes of underwear a week in summer. Even if the summer clothes were lighter, they must have been cruelly hot in Kentucky in July and August.

Work clothes consisted of a blue denim blouse, like a robe, but only three-quarters length. In cold weather this was worn on top of all the house clothes.

Monks slept in the habit — a welcome practice in winter, when there was no heating in the dormitories, but a monk could get very tangled up in his robes. Professed monks had a night habit, which was shorter and had shorter sleeves.

House robes were washed once a month, and the monk wore his work clothes during the day they were at the monastery laundry. Work clothes were also washed once a month. Earlier, winter woolen clothing had been washed only at the end of the season: the monk was expected to receive it in December and keep it relatively clean until it was returned at Easter.

Monks on the abbot's side of the church would be shaved on Wednesdays, monks on the prior's side on Saturdays, and these were the only two days when hot water was provided. Haircuts were given once a month, two or three monks being simply appointed barbers for the day. There were no individual cups in the washroom, or Grand

Parlor. Tin cans converted to cups were used communally. Bicarbonate of soda was used for toothpaste. There were no bathtubs. There was one shower for professed monks, one for the lay brothers, one for the novices. Each shower was locked, and permission had to be asked to take a shower.[37]

In 1941, mail could be sent out only four times a year: at Christmas, Easter, Assumption (August 15), and All Saints (November 1). It was limited to four half-page letters on each occasion. Two had to be sent to members of the family. All mail, incoming or outgoing, was read, usually by the prior, or, in the case of the novices, by the novice master. Mail could be received on the same four days, though Christmas and Easter were thought to be days of recollection, and mail was usually given out the day after.

Thomas Merton had made an almost complete rejection of Europe in 1936. When he turned his back on the world in 1941, he made no such rejection of his friends, and his friendships survived the long silences. Later, he took time in his writing trying to refute the commonplace that monks renounced all but their fellow monks for God. There must have been some who did, and perhaps do. In Merton's own case it is easier and more helpful to follow the evidence than the theory. He was never very good at explaining the differences between natural and supernatural friendships. In the community of men he had joined there was to be no particularizing. If the monastery was a school of charity, or of love, the love had to be general, transcending individuals.

Merton wrote some cold words on the subject in his biography of the Trappistine, Mother Berchmans, in *Exile Ends in Glory*. Marie Piquet was born an affectionate person, and it was some time before she came to see and accept an "exile of the heart":

> This was to be the whole problem of her life, her greatest source of suffering and of merit: how to liberate her strong affections from attachment to creatures, to persons for their own sake, and set them free to fly as high as heaven and God Himself? The closer she came to God, the more the realization of her attachment to His creatures was to cause her pain.[38]

It is almost unfair to quote from this book. Where Merton rightly accuses Mother Berchmans of being sentimental at times, his own prose is frequently cloying. But *Exile Ends in Glory* is perhaps the most extraordinary example of his gift for identifying with others. The gift was to lead him into trouble, as it does here. Yet it is the best evidence of the very thing Merton is struggling with, "attachment to His creatures." In the beginning of the book it seems unlikely there will be any lines of contact between Thomas Merton and Mother Berchmans, yet Merton builds on every hint of what they have in common, from train travels in France to the first cold in the religious life, and from a death in the family to an attempt to center a spirit generous with affection on God. In the convent novitiate Marie Piquet was accused of gaiety, as Brother Louis was accused in the novitiate at Gethsemani. Here Merton comes to her defense, and his:

> Sister Berchmans entered with her whole heart into this atmosphere of happy generosity. As one might expect from her impulsive nature, she was too often carried away, by her own gaiety, to extremes; but everyone has to have some natural weakness or other. Either one is inclined to be too affectionate or too cold and critical, too boisterous or too melancholy, too quick tempered or lifeless and lethargic, too energetic and bustling or lazy and too slow. If, from the point of view of a silent community, a person who is always bursting out laughing and making a lot of idiotic and incomprehensible signs may prove at times to be a real nuisance, that person's gaiety is a much better weakness than no gaiety at all.[39]

It is a little disappointing after this to have Mother Berchman's "Canticle of Gratitude" quoted with approval, when it says, among other things, "Thank You, dearest Jesus, for having raised my soul above all things of this earth and for having allowed me to find nothing but deception and boredom among creatures."[40]

If Thomas Merton had been sometimes deceived, bored, and led astray by friends at the Red Cow in Cambridge, he had been neither bored nor deceived by his Columbia friends. He needed them at his baptism and they were there. They were to be needed a second time, and, again, many of them were there.

Two early visitors to Gethsemani reminded Merton of his continuing and warm ties with the world outside the enclosure. The first was his brother.

John Paul had been training somewhere in Canada. Now a letter came saying that he would soon be on embarkation leave and he hoped to get down to Kentucky before he went. Merton waited, heard nothing more, and worried. One afternoon in July 1942, during work inside the enclosure with his fellow novices, he was called to the abbot's office.[41]

John Paul looked well. He stood very straight and seemed to have gained an extra inch of height to the several he already had over his older brother. The shock of very blond hair had been cut back to something like a crew cut. There was the same open but hesitant expression on his face, though the gaze in his blue eyes looked less lost, less troubled. In the garden of the guest house each brother took full measure of the other's uniform. John Paul had a sergeant's stripes. He explained he was a Sergeant Observer. Observer? Observer in a bomber. He had been trained to observe what the bomber did. What the bomber did? Yes. He had been trained to read aerial photographs and to relate what he saw to the ground below. Before and after the bombing? Yes. Thomas Merton was introduced to another kind of geography.

Two birds, cardinals, were very red against the gray brick of the wall near one of the Stations of the Cross. To each brother came the realization that the same force had driven them in opposite directions. Their clothes made the distance almost too obvious to cope with. Yet neither wanted to fall back into an open admission that they had once been closer by talking of the old days on Long Island blowing up johns with cherry bombs. Merton thought of the week on the Cornell campus and asked John Paul if he had ever gone any further with his idea of getting instructions to become a Catholic.

John Paul hadn't. Nor had he forgotten about it. Could he do it now? How about Tom instructing him?

Merton explained he was a novice, not a priest. How long did John Paul have? A week, maybe. They'd better go back to the abbot.

The guest master was Father James Fox, who had known the Haucks, and who now took over the job of supervising the instruction. Father James questioned John Paul, while his brother waited with what patience he could.[42] It was decided Brother Louis could do much of the initial work and John Paul would be examined.

For four days that July the two brothers were together. Because he could not be baptized at the monastery, John Paul went to the church in the nearby hamlet of New Haven. Merton could not be there, but the brothers would join one another at Mass.

Then they were separated again, with John Paul kneeling high up in the gallery or tribune at the back of the church, and Merton lighting the lights of the altar of Our Lady of Victories. Merton tried to make signs in the air to show John Paul how to find his way down. He couldn't shout, or even speak, and the gestures proved futile, only bringing back to Merton all the times he had gestured his younger brother away during the days with the gang and the clubhouse in Douglaston.[43] Finally the novice master understood, and went to help John Paul find his way. The brothers were brought nearer and received Holy Communion. The chapel of Our Lady of Victories was ever after a place for Merton where a greater mystery than reconciliation had taken place. Here, finally, he had been helped to help his brother. Before, they had been little more to one another than orphans of the same parents.

Early on the morning the day after receiving communion together, the brothers said goodbye and John Paul left. It was almost the end of his embarkation leave. On August 4, he made his will.[44] News came to Walter Hauck in Great Neck, Long Island. John Paul had arrived in Liverpool in late August. He didn't say, but it was obvious he was at

Bomber Command in Buckinghamshire. He was trying to get his fifteen flights in so he could apply for seven days' leave. Two he'd spend in London seeing the Bennetts and Aunt Gwyn in West Horsley. Then he'd go north to be with the girl he was going to marry. He had met Margaret Mary Evans in London, she was from Birkenhead, and she was training to be a radio operator with the A.T.S.[45]

To his brother John Paul wrote he had been in Bournemouth.[46] Merton remembered the summer at the Savoy Hotel when he'd been too busy convincing everybody, including himself, that he was hopelessly in love with Diane to be much company.

John Paul was married now. He and Margaret had spent their brief honeymoon in the Lake District in the raw weeks of early spring. It was a warmer spring in Kentucky, and it was Lent. Merton had to wait until Easter Monday before he could read the letter from John Paul, which was already more than a month old.[47] On the next day he was called to the abbot to receive a telegram that Sergeant J. P. Merton had been reported missing on April 17, 1943, ten days earlier.[48] At 30 Vista Road, Great Neck, Long Island, Walter Hauck had his last letter returned, stamped "Reported Killed."[49]

John Paul had taken part in a raid on Mannheim. Shortly after taking off late on Friday, April 16, the aircraft he was in left the bomber formation with some engine malfunction caused by icing. When the aircraft crashed into the Channel, John Paul's back was broken. He survived some hours in a rubber dinghy, delirious, calling for water when there was none to give him. He was dead long before the others were picked up, five miles off the English coast. They had buried him at sea.[50]

By the time Robert Lax, the second visitor, came unexpectedly, Merton had written a number of poems which he showed his friend, including "For My Brother Reported Missing in Action, 1943." The raid had taken place on the Feast of Our Lady of Sorrows. Merton remembered the poem of Catullus, "Hail and Farewell" to a brother dead in Asia on a distant campaign. Perhaps he also remembered St. Bernard of Clairvaux's poem for his dead brother. Far more insistent were his memories of John Paul during the visit which had at last brought the brothers together before they were separated forever in life. John Paul had died in Lent, when all things were moving to the Hill of Calvary, to the Pieta, to the "I thirst" of Christ.

*

Merton's old friend brought news of other Columbia friends. Ed Rice had written to Lax when Lax was teaching in North Carolina, urging him to come to New York and be instructed and received into the Church. It was Rice, too, who had suggested Lax ought to hitchhike down to Kentucky to find out what had become of Merton.[51]

Sy Freedgood was in India with the army. The other friends were equally scattered, yet the network of friendship proved strong enough to keep them in one another's minds. No enclosure could shut Murtog out. And so Lax had come to see him, the first of many visits. This time they could receive communion together. When Lax left, he took Merton's new poems to show Mark Van Doren. He was also to spread the news that Tom Merton had *not* stopped writing.

There had been confusions before Merton "disappeared" in December 1941. When Naomi Burton was his agent, it baffled her to find she was not the only one trying to find a publisher for his work. With poems it did not matter greatly (literary agents don't concern themselves overmuch with the poems of someone who is not a well-established poet), but essays and novels were making the rounds of publishers from sources other than Curtis Brown. Merton was active himself. So were his friends with copies. It was never very clear to him that there was a general ban on "multiple submission."

Four poems by Thomas Merton appeared in *Poetry* in April 1942. "Aubade: Lake Erie" was published in *The New Yorker* on August 1. More poems by the same "lost" author came out in 1943.[52] Dom Frederic accepted a situation already in existence — at least as far as the poetry was concerned. The only obvious precedent could be seen in the career of one widely published poet, Sister M. Madeleva of the Sisters of the Holy Cross. Sister Madeleva had published her poems for years in such places as *Harpers* and *The Saturday Review of Literature*, as well as in Catholic journals, but she had always insisted on using her religious name.[53] No poem was published as the work of Brother M. Louis, O.C.S.O.

Mark Van Doren was anxious to find a publisher for the whole group of poems Robert Lax had brought back with him. This was too small for a full collection, but it made no sense to have it privately printed for a few friends. He talked to James Laughlin of New Directions.

The two men were friends, and Van Doren was probably simply seeking advice. On the face of it, New Directions was among the houses least likely to publish the work of Thomas Merton. The young monk at Gethsemani would be positively priggish about some of the authors on the New Directions list later on in his letters to James Laughlin.[54] The question at this point was, was there a place for Merton with Henry Miller, Djuna Barnes, Ezra Pound, William Carlos Williams, Céline, and many another on the best avant-garde publishing list in English?

Laughlin liked Merton's poetry, especially the poem to John Paul. As a classicist he recognized the Catullan model. He found the poem moving in its own right. Besides wanting to bring out the most innovative contemporary writing, James Laughlin was interested in finding and encouraging fine printers. He had a series of what would today be called chapbooks. One was brought out each year by a different printer. Laughlin already had the next printer in mind. He liked the poems, and the group was the right size exactly. He accepted the book and suggested the title, *Thirty Poems*.[55]

Thirty Poems by Thomas Merton, New Directions, in the Poets of the Year series, designed by Algot Ringstrom and printed at The Marchbanks Press, appeared on November 20, 1944.[56] It was Merton's first published book — thirty poems and thirty pages by a poet who was almost thirty. It sold for a dollar, or for fifty cents in the paperback edition. The book was dedicated to the Virgin Mary, the Queen of Poets, a dedication that had been somewhat garbled in the press. The book attracted readers and notice.

Not all the reviewers were enthusiastic, however. One of the most careful notices came from a poet recently converted to Catholicism, who had come out of prison after serving a sentence as a conscientious objector. This poet had an astonishing success the same year with *Lord Weary's Castle*, his own first collection from a general publisher. Excerpts from one poem, "The Quaker Graveyard in Nantucket," appeared in *Life* magazine three years later with a fulsome introduction about the poet, only partly accounted for by the fact that there had been two related poets of the same name in American letters already.[57] Robert Lowell praised *Thirty Poems* but pointed out a number of weaknesses. A good reviewer informs potential readers about the book and also gives advice to the author. This was what Lowell did. He said that Merton should be a good deal more precise in his choice of words. It may be that Merton never saw the review, or saw it years later.[58] If so, this is a pity. Merton may have escaped the worst hazards of the literary life, but he lost out in the rough and tumble of conversations with other poets. He gained much by correspondence, though this was chiefly praise. Praise is essential. At least as essential is the criticism which points out obvious mistakes and obsessions. Merton went right on making the mistakes of the first collection.

There is, for example, the kind of rhetoric fashionable in 1943–44, notably in the work of stronger poets like Dylan Thomas and Robert Lowell; present, too, in Dunstan Thompson and many others. There was Merton's serious overuse of metaphor and simile. It is the lack of precision, however, which mars even some of the best of his poems.[59]

The words *real* and *concrete* became more and more important in Merton's essays, where he argues strongly against abstraction. In theology, in worship, in his own prose writing, in himself, he sought what was real against "abstract concepts" and "mere verbalizing." It is curious, then, that his own poetry was the last to profit from a search which became obsessive.

The war was over when Merton's second collection appeared, on August 25, 1946.[60] Besides missing many of the reviews of his first book, he had missed the dropping of the first atomic bomb on Hiroshima on August 6, 1945, and the second on Nagasaki on August 9. He responded only after much of the world was dulled to response. In August 1945 he was studying theology under Father Anthony, working in the fields, planning his new collection and the anthology of religious poetry he had sketched out at St. Bonaventure's.

Thirty Poems had sold out. The same poems were to be included in *A Man in a Divided Sea* with a further sixty-three poems, a full collection rather than a chapbook. Again some early poems appeared, including "The Ohio River — Louisville," which he had written at Gethsemani during his retreat in the spring of 1941, and the "Aubade: Harlem," with its echoes of García Lorca and memories of the children he had seen carrying kites on his first visit to Friendship House. This time, however, some of the best poems came from his first years in the monastery, among them "After the Night Office: Gethsemani," "Trappists, Working" (from the first weeks), and "The Trappist Cemetery, Gethsemani." It was a strong collection for all its faults.

One reader of the original *Thirty Poems*, moved to do something he had not done before, sent his copy to a stranger he thought might enjoy them.[61] The copy was to be important. Clare Boothe Luce read the poems and liked them so much she wanted to know more about Thomas Merton and the Monastery of Our Lady of Gethsemani somewhere in Kentucky.

In the autumn of 1945, Merton was using the permission he had been given to write more frequently to the man he could now call his publisher. In September he told James Laughlin the censors had insisted that Merton's religious name should appear nowhere on any of the books of poetry, or on the individual poems.[62] Amused to have received the opposite order to the one he had been expecting, he assumed the Cistercian superiors wanted no guilt by association. He could not provide any recent photograph of the author, nor could any be taken. Mention should be made, the censors said, that Merton was in a closed order and in a monastery. A good deal of mail had already been coming to Thomas Merton c/o The Monastery of Gethsemani.

Merton's year had been rich in poetry, but most of his two hours' work a day in the scriptorium were devoted to the prose projects for Dom Frederic. Laughlin would hardly be interested in the lives of saints and eminent Trappists, or in short guides to the Order or the monastery. Merton was also writing a journal, begun in 1945, ostensibly under obedience to his confessor.[63] The journal may have brought back thoughts of his surviving novel, somewhere in Mark Van Doren's apartment in Greenwich Village.

Meanwhile, Laughlin had offered to send Merton some books from the publisher's current list. Merton knew the lives of the saints had not helped his style. He knew, too, that he had to explain the monastery's rules about reading matter:

> Finally, yes, I would be glad to get something to read from New Directions. What do you think would help me to write better, especially to keep the vocabulary from getting stale and me from getting into ruts, mannerisms, etc.? I used to like very much Lorca and Dylan Thomas, but remember that our life here obliges us to steer clear of even what is merely indifferent to the interior life. In other words — it is not that we are forced to lock ourselves up with a pile of pious trash on some purely *a priori* basis, but what we read should help us to know God, either directly in Himself, or through knowledge of people as He has made them, or, by contrast, as they have made themselves. Anyone who has something serious to say about the ultimate meaning of life, or of the world, is, therefore, O.K. But if it is just good experimental writing for its own sake I guess perhaps not.
>
> If this sounds unintelligible, it would perhaps be more sensible to give you the rule in its ordinary formulation. No newspapers, no magazines, no radio, no movies, no books on stamp collecting, no fashionable novels, no textbooks on astronomy. But I notice a lot of the brothers with books on agriculture, so anything corresponding in the field of the craft God has given me to follow — verse, would be at least tolerated.
>
> Anyway, thanks, and do send your catalogues. Maybe I will receive them and maybe not.[64]

The letters to Laughlin continued to discuss the anthology, though Merton's enthusiasm for being an editor was clearly waning. Then, on March 1, 1946, he suddenly broke in with enthusiasm for something very different from an anthology of the world's religious poetry:

> Reverend Father just O.K.ed a new project — creative, more or less poetic prose, autobiographical in its essence, but not pure autobiography. Something, as I see it now like a cross between Dante's *Purgatory,* and Kafka, and a medieval miracle play, called "The Seven Storey Mountain." It has been brewing for a long long time, and, as soon as I finish the present job I am on, I think I might be able to get onto it and finish it fairly fast . . . [65]

It had, indeed, been "brewing for a long long time," though in a great many forms and disguises. The idea for an all-inclusive autobiography went right back to 1939. Merton had not tried straight autobiography before. He had discussed this with his confessor as a novice, only to be laughed at.[66] And here the question of dates becomes confusing. By one account, much of *The Seven Storey Mountain* was written in 1944. Elsewhere, Merton says he wrote it after *What Are These Wounds?* — and so later than 1945.[67] What seems likely is that he made several beginnings to different works. This would be entirely consistent with Merton's way of working in the summer of 1939. He probably began an autobiographical work in the novitiate scriptorium, then set it aside, either out of boredom or because he became discouraged it might never be printed. The suggestion he was bored with it should not be discounted. Merton's letter to Laughlin shows the same note of excitement as the letters and journal entries from the summer of 1941, when he abandoned the comparatively straightforward prose of "The Man in the Sycamore Tree" for something far more challenging, the macaronic style of "Journal of My Escape from the Nazis." What probably gave Merton confidence he could "finish it fairly fast" was the sense that he already had something he could fall back on and use in the new formula. And he now had the abbot's permission.

In fact, Merton abandoned the idea he had presented to Laughlin and went back to a strictly autobiographical style. He had imagined the book as a novella-length work of a hundred and fifty pages. That summer the autobiography grew from one or more earlier drafts to something much larger, a book that at least paid a passing salute to the grand idea of the all-encompassing autobiography of 1939.

On August 17, 1946, he wrote again to Laughlin:

> About the prose — 7 Storey Mountain — it did not turn out the way I thought it might at first. Therefore no fantasy, no Kafka, no miracle play. It is straight biography, with a lot of comment and reflection, and it is turning into the mountain that the title says. I cannot make it in less than six hundred and fifty type-written pages. It seems to me that you do not usually risk printing such big fat books as this and perhaps it would not be your dish, but I will certainly let you have the first look at it. If God wills I shall get it finished in a month or so from now and you can have it then.[68]

On January 6, Merton had written Laughlin, "You have no idea how busy a Trappist can get!"[69] He was certainly busy that spring and summer. The two or so hours a day he had for writing were spent in the second professed scriptorium, where Father Anthony worked across from him on theological notes and canon law. As Father Anthony was one of the censors of the Order at that time, Merton sometimes passed a number of the sheets he was working on across for comments and approval.[70]

Merton had sent to St. Bonaventure's for material on his past: journals, letters, notebooks. Much had already gone beyond his reach, and he was restricted in the number of letters he could write in pursuit of his gifts of 1941. He had little chance of checking names and dates when his memory was at fault. He was anxious, too, to write on quickly.

Even later, when Merton had secretarial help from his own novices and was far more frequently the master of his own time, the achievement of 1946 would have been astonishing. As it was then, he had no help and a brief time each day to work. Merton made more than one draft and used carbons to make copies, something that slowed up the writing. Six hundred and fifty pages was, in the end, well under count.

Nothing was wasted in the monastery. Where one monk was using up the paper supply at such a prodigious rate, pages and whole drafts which were beyond correction, or that were no longer needed, went back at once into the paper supply. One section of *The Seven Storey Mountain* with Merton's corrections has turned up with something else written on the other side.[71] There may be more finds of this kind. The story of the book's creation is an impressive one, though there are still gaps. By autumn 1946, Merton had a large prose work — too large, he suspected, for New Directions. There may have been other factors in his decision to switch publishers.

Two years later, and in another context, Merton wrote to Laughlin making an important point:

> The monastery has got itself twenty thousand dollars in debt, with build-ing new monasteries. God will take care of us, but at the same time if you can put me in the way of making pennies by my writing . . . I mean where there is a choice of projects, I ought, under the circumstances to be always choosing the one that will mean more bread and butter. So if you get any ideas along that line, let me know.[72]

Merton had a sense that this book had a real commercial chance. Perhaps this was only in contrast to the pious lives he had been writ-ing. Perhaps it had already decided him to abandon the masque and miracle play he had wanted to write. Now that he was committed to the straight autobiography, he found it had lifted him as he wrote. In the same way, it might lift the reader. None of his early novels had had this power over him. He had enjoyed them in bits, as he sus-pected publishers' readers had enjoyed them before turning them down. He thought of Naomi Burton, and of his first editor of all, Rob-ert Giroux, who was now out of the U.S. Navy and back at the pub-lishing firm of Harcourt, Brace.

*

All summer Merton had been inhabiting a high place in his imagina-tion. It would have been a time of tension and overstimulation for any writer in any situation. Before, he had been able to walk off some of the nervous energy which was a by-product of his writing. There was no chance of this at the monastery. He was out of the novitiate, but the professed were hardly less confined, he could walk in the monks' cemetery, he could be in the abbey church, he could walk in the clois-ter and in the court the cloister surrounded, the *préau*, or garth.[73] He was in another enclosure within the enclosure. Vineyard Knob, and Mount Olivet, blue in the summer heat haze, were beyond the enclosure wall, visible from the windows and the cemetery. Merton climbed them, as he climbed other hills, in his imagination, the high places of his own past, and the Mount Purgatory of Dante's imagination. He went back to a room in Cambridge, to Professor Bullough speaking, and to his own room at St. Bonaventure and the full notes he had made on *The Divine Comedy*. He suffered from insomnia and the sense of jadedness this left him with the next day.

On one point Merton could make no concession. He thought himself extraordinary and his fate extraordinary. This had helped when his confessor in the novitiate had tried to laugh him out of the whole idea of writing his autobiography, with the story that Chesterton's friends had laughed at *him* for writing his own life.

Chesterton was an unfortunate name to use: Merton associated Chesterton with the chatty, superior, belletristic style of English writing he was at pains to avoid. Certainly he put himself above Chesterton.[74]

In a sense, *The Seven Storey Mountain* was a celebration of just this realization: that he and his fate were extraordinary, that he had had extraordinary parents, one of whom had confirmed — for a while — his unique sense of himself and his destiny. It was no casual slip into vanity, then, for him to write in the opening pages that what he had from his parents "ought to have made me some kind of King" and to add "if the standards the world lives by were the real ones."[75]

The unreal standards the world imposed meant he had to be a king in hiding, making concessions to the ordinary, frequently losing his balance in an attempt to adjust to a situation which excluded him. Later Merton told the novices of the moment of realization that one is not ordinary. Clare Boothe Luce, he said, had had the realization as a child walking along the beach at Southampton, "which was a nice place to have it."[76] Perhaps Merton had had the same sense of his own destiny on the top of Brooke Hill — if it had not been with him since his first memories of observing his mother observing him.

Easy to decide that at Gethsemani he was "a duck in a chicken coop,"[77] yet in his Prologue to *The Sign of Jonas* Merton had to explain that while most monasteries are ordinary, the Monastery of Our Lady of Gethsemani had its own extraordinary destiny, to which he was then only a contributor. In a more serious mood, Merton wrote later of "the great harm done by complicated people in monasteries, and the great good done by the simple!"[78] He had to cultivate the simple.

Merton's sense of destiny made his struggle with his particular form of self-consciousness infinitely more difficult. Once he accepted it, there was no way to deny his destiny and remain real. There were continuing crises of solipsism and then attempts to adapt and identify himself with others. What Merton knew he needed was time on his own to readjust the balances. He had never trusted himself without a full measure of solitude, not simply as an escape from others, but as a chance for reassessment, and now a time for seeking help in prayer.

The hermitage was the *place* of solitude. Just this and no more, but physical place was important. Certain rooms haunted him: the room at Perry Street, the room at St. Bonaventure's. But these were in the past. In the present he found a nook in the wall of the monastery church.[79] Here he stood looking at the knobs and the cedars, then, in the late afternoon, at the clouds scudding across the sky and over the silver spire above him. He also found an upper room in a garden shed.[80] Neither of these chosen places was a true hermitage. He went on poring over books on Carthusians in the scriptorium, and he wrote to Carthusians seeking more information. He read the lives of the hermits.

The answer, his superiors and spiritual advisers told him over and over, was *inner* solitude, detachment, a hermitage of the heart: he needed no physical place of solitude. Merton struggled to accept this as the physical world about him became more crowded, more demanding, imposing its own reality.

The Monastery of Our Lady of Gethsemani had been built to house between fifty and seventy monks. In 1944, when the monastery first became overcrowded, a foundation was made from Gethsemani at Conyers, Georgia, the Monastery of the Holy Spirit. Yet those who had gone to Georgia were rapidly replaced, and by 1946, the number at Gethsemani had passed a hundred and was approaching two hundred.

If America had discovered the contemplative life, this was in large part limited to ex-soldiers. It has been assumed for too long that it was the publication of *The Seven Storey Mountain* that signaled the rush to Gethsemani. Yet the same factors which contributed to the enormous and unexpected success of that book had already brought postulants to the monasteries.

There is no need to theorize for long, or to belabor what is only too well remembered. The closing days of the Second World War created a trauma from which many have not recovered. In some sense Merton was isolated from the shock. He had been spared also any confrontation with atrocity, unlike many of the postulants. A boy of nineteen who had been implicated in the bayoneting of wounded Japanese soldiers in a hospital in the Philippines, others who had worked on burial details on the Pacific Islands, others still who had been among the first into the Nazi death camps — all had been blasted in their humanity in a way Merton would know only through his extraordinary powers of imaginative identification.

Beyond such personal experience, was a prevailing fear that transcended the personal, a fear that humanity had redefined itself in a way that was of appalling consequence. The war criminals had not all been executed, or even identified. Guilty knowledge and implication in crimes against humanity was not confined to Germany and Japan, even if nothing mitigated what had happened under the Third Reich and the military dictatorship of Japan. The enormous efforts to see the Allied victory as a moral victory that excused all who had fought on one side and put all blame on those who could not now defend themselves had not been wholly successful — certainly not at the psychic level. The reality of Russian territorial ambitions was met in the West by the deep need to name a new enemy. Almost with relief, the West entered the Cold War.

*

Merton received Dom Frederic's permission to write to Curtis Brown. On October 21, 1946, having alerted Naomi Burton through Robert Lax that it would be coming, Merton sent *The Seven Storey Mountain*. In his cover letter he says it is pretty long, and he thinks he knows where it can be cut a little if necessary, adding, "Anyway I think it is readable."[81] He also mentions that Robert Giroux at Harcourt, Brace would probably like to look at it.

In her own autobiography, *More Than Sentinels*, Naomi Burton describes how she read and responded to the large book that arrived from Gethsemani. Things had been unusually busy at the office. At the beginning of December Naomi Burton had a bad cold and took the manuscript back to her apartment. It was, indeed, readable. The autobiographical thread she found fascinating, and she knew this would appeal to a wide readership. Some of the theological passages were less engrossing, and it seemed clear Merton was under the spell of Duns Scotus, a name which might mean something to one reader out of a hundred.

She telephoned Robert Giroux immediately on her return to the office. There was one thing she couldn't understand: there was a great deal in the book about grace. Naomi wondered if other non-Catholics would be as confused as she was by this. Giroux explained that it was not an easy thing to give a definition of grace on the telephone. He was looking forward to reading the book, and he hoped they could discuss *The Seven Storey Mountain* and grace later.[82]

On December 9, Naomi wrote of her enthusiasm to Merton — or to Brother M. Louis. In certain places she thought he had fallen under something like self-hypnosis "that tends to hypnotize the reader too." She went on to say:

> Do not be offended by this criticism and believe that I am interested in helping you find a form in which it would appeal to the largest number of readers. I don't mean that because of fame and money, but because you have something to say that might help others.[83]

On this occasion at least, Naomi Burton may have underestimated Merton's worldly aims: he was certainly interested in helping people, but he was also interested in bringing money to the monastery. Fame was a question of deep ambiguity.

In the same letter, his agent said she had spoken to Robert Giroux, but that he was in the middle of both a bad cold and a publishers' sales conference. She would wait a week before sending the book on to him. On the 17th, she wrote again to say she had passed the book on, telling Giroux there was no desperate hurry to read it. She reassures Merton that she doesn't think he has been "unfair to England." And she repeats the point she had made before: "I think the definition of Grace should be quite early on in the book, probably whenever you first mention it."[84]

Robert Giroux had obviously rushed at the big book. He telephoned Naomi to arrange a luncheon on the 27th. At the Ritz Grill he shared his enthusiasm and said he was anxious to do the editing. He also explained the doctrine of grace.[85]

Within ten days of receiving it, Giroux had read *The Seven Storey Mountain* and won an acceptance from his firm. He sent a telegram to Gethsemani.

Merton had not been expecting things to happen so quickly, nor had he expected to have any news about the book until after Christmas. At first he was alarmed that the typescript had been lost when Dom Frederic handed him a telegram on December 29. It read MANUSCRIPT ACCEPTED. HAPPY NEW YEAR.[86]

The end of 1946 and the beginning of 1947 was a time of more than one acceptance. Merton had made his petition to be admitted for Solemn Vows. This was voted upon in Chapter in January. The community accepted him forever.[87] He would take Solemn Vows on the Feast of St. Joseph, March 19, the anniversary of his Simple Vows three years before and of the medical examination that had kept him out of the draft.

He had written to Miss Burton, thanking her and saying Bob Giroux should have a free hand with the editing. Then he made reservations: "Also I'd like to keep as much as I can of the references to Duns Scotus because even Catholics don't know him as they should."[88] The terms of the contract were sketched out on the top of his letter of January 2. Naomi Burton wrote to Mark Van Doren with the news: "There is a good deal of editing to be done on it but I think there is a possibility that when that is taken care of it may do pretty well."[89]

Merton's excitement over the book had to be restrained in difficult circumstances, and as the moment for taking Solemn Vows approached he began to have serious misgivings. The insomnia became worse, and he threw himself into physical work to find relief. He came close to a bad accident when the axe he was using to prune branches from a fallen pine glanced off and swung by his legs.[90] Walking back that day he felt such a surge of bitterness when the monastery came into view that the memory lasted.[91]

It was a time of crisis, too, for Gethsemani. Four postulants had been accepted in two days. Applicants had been coming all that year, and the monastery was already overcrowded. Dom Frederic had traveled to Utah in January to look at a possible site for a new foundation, but he had been unsuccessful on the first attempt.

On February 16, Thomas Merton made the new will necessary before Solemn Vows. He checked over all the possessions he had brought to the monastery five years before. The clothes would now go to the poor. A few things he was permitted to keep, like the leather wallet Tom Bennett had bought for him in Bond Street and presented to him on his eighteenth birthday. The whole procedure struck Merton as a little overdramatic, and it had its ironies: he had no sooner renounced all his worldly wealth than his signature was required on the contract for *The Seven Storey Mountain*: "The royalties of the dead author will go to the monastery."[92] Both the writer and the man were very much alive.

Merton went over his misgivings about his vocation with Dom Frederic four days later: his desire for solitude, the temptation to go to the Carthusians, his feeling that he was an outsider at Gethsemani and always would be. Perhaps to win Merton from poring over books on the Carthusians and writing to them, Dom Frederic showed him an album of pictures of Sénanque, the ancient Trappist abbey in Provence.[93]

Merton admitted in his journal that it was one of the most beautiful books he had seen. He could be persuaded by pictures — he had been before and he would be again — yet he knew now that in the long run a place could only be tested by whether it provided true solitude or not. As he had once had an ideal city, so he now had an ideal monastery — perhaps of the Carthusians, perhaps a group of hermitages like the Order of the Camaldolese, perhaps something he would design himself.[94]

The visitation of the abbot general, Dom Dominique Nogues, brought a number of surprises. Assigned to make all the translations during the visit, Merton was brought closer to the party of superiors than his place in the hierarchy of the monastery would otherwise have allowed. He had a chance to talk to Dom Benoit, who was traveling with the abbot general, and from Dom Benoit he learned there had been a shift in European monasteries of the Order away from the older and more rigid devotional practices and in favor of contemplation.

Instead of being cheered, Merton went straight to seeing in this the danger of moving to the other extreme. Perhaps there was something rigid in him, perhaps he feared "contemplation made easy":

. . . It is not hard to be frivolous and cheap, in this matter of contemplation. If it does not grow out of humility, our contemplation will necessarily be superficial. We need to be emptied. Otherwise, prayer is only
a game. But all that is cheap will go out with pride. And yet it is pride
to want to be stripped and humbled in the grand manner, with thunder
and lightning. The simplest and most effective way to sanctity is to disappear into the background of ordinary everyday routine.[95]

When Merton came for his own conference with the abbot general
he was told it was a good thing, even his religious duty, to go on writing. The view of the Order had changed here, too, and Dom Frederic
was no longer something of an exception among superiors. What was
needed now, it seemed, were those who had been trained as specialists
before they joined, who would use their professional skills for the benefit of the Order.

In the case of Thomas Merton, this made it extremely difficult to reconcile the new obedience with disappearing "into the background of
ordinary everyday routine." As happened over and over, encouragement from visiting superiors coincided with news that his work had
run into censorship problems. Here Merton was able to use the abbot
general's influence and advice. But he had already learned that his Order had a way of encouraging and discouraging his writing at the same
time. He was the only one, apparently, who saw the irony and the
occasional absurdity in this.

He was hardly to blame if the left hand and the right hand in the
upper ranks of the Order gave as little recognition to one another as
professed and novice at the monastery. He *was* to blame for the first
serious tangle between publishers. At Easter, James Laughlin wrote,
reasonably enough, that he was distressed Merton had not carried out
his promise to send the autobiography to New Directions. Merton wrote
back that he had had no reply to the earlier letter to Laughlin in which
he wondered whether a book as big as *The Seven Storey Mountain* would
interest him:

> . . . You know that I write a pile of stuff varying from poems and things
> you are interested in, on down to lives of obscure members of our Order,
> with footnotes and whatnot, which nobody but the abbey would ever print.
> So you see that I naturally think in terms of a whole graded series of dif-
> ferent publishers . . .[96]

Merton went on to say that Naomi Burton understood the situation
perfectly. Things had changed greatly in the past few months! James
Laughlin had arrived back from a skiing holiday to discover New Directions was only one publisher among many in a grander scheme.

James Laughlin accepted the situation. From now on, he would
publish Merton's poetry, and short prose works of a special nature. The

arrangement would bring him many of Merton's best collections of essays and much else, but that could hardly be predicted in 1947. Laughlin must have felt he had cultivated an author only to have him taken away. To ease the situation a little, Merton wrote to Mark Van Doren asking him to send Laughlin the typescript of "The Journal of My Escape from the Nazis" — "the only thing remotely resembling the kind of 'Kafka' business I thought at first the autobiography was going to turn out to be."[97] It soon became clear that, whatever its merits, the premonastery novel could not be published by anyone. Monks were not permitted to read, let alone write, novels. It was just as well then, that Naomi Burton had written on February 21:

> I am sure nobody intends to describe THE SEVEN STOREY MOUNTAIN as a novel since it would lose a great deal of its value in that case.[98]

It would have been a disaster for a number of reasons, yet the idea must have come from somewhere — most likely from the author — for Naomi Burton to feel the need to quash it so firmly.

His trouble with the censors had already begun when Merton wrote his agent in April that the *Nihil obstat* had been refused.[99] The references to sex and drinking had been too frank, but one censor also felt the book should be put away until the author could write. There was far too much slang — maybe a correspondence course in writing would help.[100]

Merton set aside the last advice but considered rewriting the book. Robert Giroux had been hoping Harcourt, Brace could publish it by the end of 1947. That now looked unlikely. Both publisher and agent hurried to Merton's defense, but the idea he was a sloppy writer was not altogether laughed away: Merton was to hear more of this. In the meanwhile, the abbot general helped to clear the way. He made a firm decision that the autobiography should be by "Thomas Merton." Dom Frederic had reminded him that all letters should be signed with his religious name. Merton passed the information on to Naomi Burton in his own way: "So if I sign frater Louis it means Tom."[101]

In the summer of 1947 Merton did a good deal of rewriting. Robert Giroux was editing. Letters between the two of them were not getting through. Naomi Burton wrote to Merton, "Please don't cut the book too much."[102] The censor had withdrawn his restriction and the unhelpful suggestion about the correspondence course.

Merton had already mentioned he was working on a history of the Order to be ready for the hundredth anniversary of the foundation of Gethsemani. Harcourt, Brace had expressed interest. The Prologue of *The Waters of Siloe* reads like the opening of a novel. Merton enjoyed writing this and wrote it rapidly.[103] He was also cutting back and revising his life of Mother Berchmans, which no cutting or editing would make a best seller, or a good book. It is easy to blame everything on the subject matter. This is hardly fair; *Exile Ends in Glory* could have been an interesting story. So could Merton's life of St. Lutgarde, *What Are These Wounds?* But both books had their point of origin in short biographies Merton had written in the novitiate. He knew the difference between pious and religious poetry, but he had plunged into near-parody in an attempt to match his prose to pious models. The result is often unintentionally funny. Where it is not, there is a mixture of the callous and the cosy.

Some years later, Merton objected to a pious life being read out in the refectory.[104] It was not his work, yet it could have been. When *Exile Ends in Glory* was read, he was sufficiently penitent. He was grateful when Father Raymond made a sympathetic sign that he, too, suffered when his books were read out.[105] The two authors at the monastery were usually more restrained in their support of one another.

Merton lists twelve writing projects that summer in the journal, which was itself edited and published in time.[106] He had too much to do, and he complained. Later, and characteristically, he wondered if he hadn't overdone the complaining when he wrote such lines as "Just because a cross is a cross, does it follow that it is the cross God intends for you?"[107]

The real trouble was not that he complained but that he included so many "crosses" in a book whose Prologue promises there will be none:

> . . . Our monastery was not named in vain for the Garden of the Agony, but I promise not to be dramatic about that side of our existence. I have a peculiar horror of one sin: the exaggeration of our trials and of our crosses.[108]

Sins and crosses. Both words are imprecisely used and give the wrong melodramatic color to something that quite rightly amuses everyone but the victim: the writer who is killing himself with overwork is only a little less pathetic than the writer who has been forbidden to work. For all that, a writer *can* be exploited. Dom Frederic assigned one job after another, but fortunately: ". . . He gets an idea and communicates it to me and I happily accept it, but it is understood that if I cannot do it I will say so and it will be dropped."[109]

Merton's letters to James Laughlin list a number of projects that came to nothing, including several anthologies. In June, the publisher and his wife were driving east from visits to poets on the New Directions list in California. They arrived on June 12. Like any number of Merton's visitors over the years, and like Merton himself at the time of his retreat in 1941, Laughlin approached the monastery with a good deal of trepidation. It confirmed some of his worst fears to hear from Merton that monks who had broken any of the community's property had to confess this in the Chapter of Faults, and then to kneel in the cloister holding up the broken spade or fork like a saint holding up the attributes of his or her martyrdom. The publisher found out that punishments included holding a sort of press-up position on one's toes and knuckles on the tiled floor of the chapter house. Laughlin's wife shared his nervousness and remained a safe distance from the monastery, painting it.[110]

If Laughlin continued to be uncertain about the monastery, he and Merton got on well from the start. In some ways Merton was prepared for the meeting with James Laughlin by his long friendship with Robert Lax. He found the gestures and mannerisms of the two men were very similar, despite the different family backgrounds of Calvinist Lowland Scots and Jewish urban intellectuals. Laughlin went away delighted; Merton wrote at once in his journal that Laughlin was *mundo corde*, "clean of heart." The two men were to be friends for life. For the present, Laughlin was unable to convince Brother Louis that there was any cleanliness of heart in Henry Miller and many another writer on the New Directions list.[111] As far as New Directions went, Merton was certainly "a duck in a chicken coop"!

Publisher and writer had talked at the gate house of doing a parallel-text translation of *The Dark Night of the Soul* by St. John of the Cross. Merton had been excited and moved by the writings of the Spanish poet, theologian, and mystic since the days at Perry Street. That summer and for almost a decade, St. John of the Cross was a major influence on his own work, gradually taking over from Duns Scotus the highest place. Merton had already begun his notes on St. John of the Cross and his writing, which were to lead through difficulties and delays not to a translation, but to *The Ascent to Truth*.[112] It was a book he found difficult to write because he attempted the near-impossible. Writing his thesis on Blake at Columbia, Merton had made the mistake of choosing a formula, trying to explain Blake's theories on art in terms of the theology of St. Thomas Aquinas in the *Summa*. In *The Ascent to Truth* Merton struggled to set the writings of St. John of the Cross in the same formula, using Thomist theology to explain the mystic's approach to God. The result is a work with some very tenuous connections in argument and a few fine passages.

If Merton had written nothing on contemplation except *The Ascent to Truth*, he would have succeeded only in making contemplation too hard for himself and others. This can be put only briefly here and perhaps simplistically. The path chosen by St. John of the Cross to approach God — and to the ultimate mystical union with God, which is the desire of mystics of all religions — began with the clear statement that all attempts to define God are doomed to failure. God can only be understood in negative statements — what He is *not*. To Merton the Apophatic approach (*via negationis,* or the "dark path" of the Spanish mystic and others) had an immediate appeal, and he remained an Apophatic contemplative. This is important to understand. Few in the Christian churches of the West had taken this "way" since the sixteenth century.[113]

In contemplation, Merton explains, our very efforts of the intellect to grasp the concept of God stand in the way of God working in us, simply because God is *not* a concept in any accepted sense of the word. Therefore, the intellect must be used with the greatest care, so that it does not interfere in the very movement which brings us closer to God and God closer to us. Here Merton is skillful in differentiating between a guarded use of the intellect and the surrender of the intellect that would lead to quietism.

It was again Merton's confessor who advised him:

> To teach contemplation, and especially to let people know, in what I write, that the contemplative life is quite easy and accessible and does not require extraordinary or strange efforts, just the normal generosity required to strive for sanctity.[114]

A year later, the retreat master, Father Cletus Mulloy, suggested that Merton "try to write on the contemplative life in the same style as the *Mountain.*"[115] It was a similar debate to the one Merton went through in his writing at St. Bonaventure's during 1941, with his confessor and Father Mulloy speaking for accessibility, as the Baroness and others had done before, while something in Merton found more intellectual excitement in the difficult. *The Ascent to Truth* clearly required "extraordinary or strange effects," as did the unpublished work which was paired with it, "The School of the Spirit." Both of these books were started and set aside.

Seeds of Contemplation, which Merton was writing in 1947 and calling "The Soil and Seeds of Contemplation,"[116] was not written in the style of *The Seven Storey Mountain,* as Father Mulloy might have wished, but it proved singularly accessible. For many it remains Merton's finest statement of the contemplative life. The first title may have been the better one: there is much in the book on preparing the spiritual *ground.* Merton never wrote, and never intended to write, a "how to" book on contemplation. There are many reasons, the most obvious being that he knew his way was not the reader's way, his ground not the reader's ground. It is the very nature of the mystic's journey that he or she go alone. Where the landscape is always changing one needs advice and encouragement to fire courage — a map is the most useless of impediments.

Merton's own "providers of courage" here are St. John of the Cross and Pascal. Merton wrote to James Laughlin that he had begun a book

of thoughts on contemplation that would be like Pascal's classic of lucidity, *Pensées*. Laughlin continued to send him books on St. John of
the Cross from Paris, ostensibly for the translation, and expressed interest at once in the book of "thoughts."[117]

Where *Seeds of Contemplation* can claim to be considered a masterpiece in its own right, *The Ascent to Truth* is a failure, yet a revealing
one. It is the best evidence of Merton's own attraction to the *via negationis*, to the hard and the obscure. Further, it contains Merton's most
extreme statements concerning the authority of the Catholic Church.
The book also gives a clearer picture than any of the urgent sense of
division Merton felt between his desire to go further in his contemplation and other pressures in his life. The demands of both vocations
had never been so pressing. They may not have been constantly warring, but they combined to make his life nearly intolerable. Any writer
feels stress in trying to concentrate on a major work, and no less stress
in attempting to fit himself back into life when the work is done. The
joys of a writer at full pitch are very real:

> But the pleasures of the interior life are so great and so pure; they so far
> transcend the crude joys of sense and of this world, that they exercise a
> terrible attraction upon the soul that meets them along its road to God.
> The thought of these pleasures, the memory of them and the hope of
> their recapture move a man to the very depths of his spirit and almost
> turn him inside out with the vehemence of great desire. He will do the
> wildest things if he believes that it will bring back two minutes of the joy
> he has once tasted in what seemed to be a vision of God. He will go to
> the ends of the earth to hear some unutterable word that once left him
> suspended between time and eternity. He will kill himself to hear some
> echo of that sweet voice.

Merton goes on in this passage to say that St. John of the Cross tells
us that whatever these joys might be, they have to be sacrificed for the
unknown better: ". . . we must always walk in darkness. We must
travel in silence. We must fly by night."[118]

*

Merton cherished the few days he spent in the monastery infirmary.
Best of all were the few hours he was allowed to spend in the book
vault on the first floor of the old guest house. Here, cataloguing or
ordering the books Dom Frederic was collecting for the monastery,
Merton found he could pray and follow his contemplative life while he
wrote and read.[119] It was no accident the discovery came when he was
on his own for the first time while working. He had always found it
difficult to pray before others.

When Merton talked in the journals of his insomnia as a form of contemplation, he probably meant it was an opportunity to contemplate.

In 1947 he was finding it harder to sleep than ever. He may have exaggerated his problems when, to everyone's relief, he was given a tiny
room over the stairs in June. A room of his own was something, though
Merton found he was kept awake by harvesters coming back late up
the stairs, and by the heat.[120] He was given permission to take a can
of water to his room each night from the Grand Parlor. This was unusual, and considered something of a luxury: there was a urinal in one
corner of each of the dormitories, but no sink, tap, or drinking fountain.

Merton had been almost certain he would be chosen for the new
foundation in Utah. He had questioned Laughlin about driving through
Utah when the publisher visited on the way east. The names were finally announced in Chapter by the abbot. Monks were chosen on his
left and on his right. He was not chosen. Many of his friends would
go. Father Robert, his old novice master, was to lead the party. A new
foundation required a minimum of four priests, and the monastery would
soon be short of priests, so Merton felt his own ordination was immi-
nent.

After Compline on July 7, 1947, Merton watched the party prepare
to leave in light rain for the station. The few possessions of the monks
had been packed in boxes from one of the distilleries in Bardstown, and
Merton was amused to think what the Mormons of Utah would make
of these new pioneers. Those who were going and those who were
staying gave one another the formal kiss of peace; the cars were loaded
and disappeared down the long avenue into the dark. Merton was left
with a sense of loss and a different feeling about the community and
his own vow of stability.[121]

By the sort of coincidence which may happen in life but is not supposed to happen in novels, when the party of Trappists got off the train
in Utah, Nannie Hauck found herself standing on the same platform
with them as she waited for a train east.[122] She approached Father
Robert and showed him the distinctive rosary she had bought at the
gate house shop at the monastery, and he agreed to speak. Then she
asked after Brother Louis and learned he was well and seemed happy.
She discovered the friend of the Haucks, Father James Fox, was now
the abbot of the foundation in Georgia.

That summer, while Merton struggled with galley proofs and various
drafts of several books, including a wholly unlooked-for assignment,
the official souvenir for the centenary of the abbey, the seven-year swarm
of locusts picked through the Gethsemani woods and brush fires broke
out far back in the dry hollows:

> We hear them, now, in the Kentucky summer,
> While all the locusts drown our forests in their iron prayer:
> And we dream of you, beloved, sleeping in your leafy bosom.[123]

Merton decided the heat rash that covered a good deal of his body was better than a hair shirt.[124] He complained his writings stuck to him like flypaper wherever he turned, and there were other humiliations.[125]

The collection of Dylan Thomas's poetry James Laughlin had sent made Merton feel his own poetry was inadequate. Some of Thomas's work brought back Reg Marsh's idea that everything an artist or a writer did had to have "some damned life in it." There might be too much magic, witchcraft, mumbo-jumbo, whatever, in the Welshman's poetry, lack of soundness, but there was no lack of life.[126]

The integrity of the artist challenged the integrity of those who said they were struggling to become saints. Merton had already admitted in his journal that year that he had talked, or written, too much about his need for solitude — then wasted the few opportunities he had been given.[127] Had his life any integrity as a writer? As a contemplative?

He chose the contents for a new collection, *Figures for an Apocalypse.* There were fine poems here, including one of his strongest Gethsemani poems, "Evening: Zero Weather." For once the focus was sharp and clear as the poet took the temperature of prayer and season. But again the work had too many echoes: the influence of St. John of the Cross was everywhere, curiously mixed with lines from the world of Auden's early poetry of spies and counterspies, of last trains and ships leaving with a few survivors. Merton celebrated other heroes of his religious reading besides St. John of the Cross: Duns Scotus, St. Bernard of Clairvaux, St. Ailred. He wrote letter poems to Bob Lax and Ed Rice, talking about the New York City they had all shared. Compared to the poetry of Dylan Thomas and some others, he had to admit this was poetry of low temperature. In the last piece in the collection, "The Poet, to His Book," he criticized the writing that had taken hours from prayer and contemplation to so little profit in poetry.

Sometimes his poetic sense came through more surely in the odd passage of his prose, the image of the bobwhites singing over the harvests in the field ruined by rain,[128] or it showed in lines of his autobiography:

By now the corn was high, and every afternoon we went out with hoes, to make war against our enemies, the morning-glories, in the cornfields.[129]

Yet whether Thomas Merton was aware of it or not, he had become, in both poetry and prose, a poet of the rain, appropriate enough for one born under the sign of the Water Bearer. As he wrote "In the Rain and the Sun," Merton looked down at his hand. He saw he was making the Cistercian sign "to water," "to rain," the fingers drawn together in a pear shape, pointing down.[130]

Songs of the lions and whales!
With my pen between my fingers
Making the waterworld sing!
Sweet Christ, discover diamonds
And sapphires in my verse
While I burn the sap of my pine house
For praise of the ocean sun.[131]

If he was dismayed by his poetry in the summer of 1947, he was still anxious for its success. Both Robert Giroux and James Laughlin had promised to show his poetry to T. S. Eliot.

Eliot refused to travel by air. Robert Giroux was in the habit of making sure the poet had a good cabin on the liner when he went back to England after visits in the United States, and when he saw Eliot off he would put the books he was anxious for Eliot to read during the voyage on a table in the cabin.[132] The publisher had "placed" Merton's poems in this way: they had not taken.

When *Figures for an Apocalypse* was published, in March 1948,[133] Laughlin sent the three Merton collections directly to Eliot. A year later, on March 22, 1949, he had to report on the letter he had received from Eliot. In substance it said Thomas Merton wrote too much and revised too little, that as a poet he was "hit or miss."[134] To Merton the news was devastating. Soon he was writing to Laughlin to ask if he should give up writing poetry altogether. In the same letter he suggests that New Directions should bring out the collected poems by the poet who was thirty-four and on the point of turning his back on poetry.[135] Laughlin replied, parrying the idea of the collected poems and wondering whether he was the one to give advice in the matter: most poets who had published as much as Thomas Merton would find it difficult to stop writing poetry.[136] The exchange must have been discouraging to the publisher, who was bringing out Merton's fourth collection in five years. *The Tears of the Blind Lions* appeared on November 15, 1949.[137]

*

Six very different books by Thomas Merton appeared in 1948. Five of these would probably be completely forgotten, if the sixth had not made him famous. Two were published without the author's name: *A Guide to Cistercian Life*[138] and *Cistercian Contemplatives*.[139] New Directions brought out the third poetry collection in March.[140] In June, *Exile Ends in Glory: The Life of a Trappistine, Mother M. Berchmans, O.C.S.O.*, was published by a Catholic publishing firm, the Bruce Publishing Company, in Milwaukee.[141] On October 4, 1948, *The Seven Storey Mountain* appeared from Harcourt, Brace.[142] On December 8, *What Is Contempla-*

tion? was brought out in a small edition by St. Mary's College, Notre Dame.[143]

By the early summer there were exciting indications at the publisher's that the original printing order of 5,000 copies was far too timid. Robert Giroux had sent the galley proofs of *The Seven Storey Mountain* with a careful letter to Evelyn Waugh, Graham Greene, and Clare Boothe Luce. He was not aware that Clare Boothe Luce already knew and liked Merton's poetry. The reasonable assumption was that this was a very large work by an author whose names, religious and secular, would mean nothing to three very busy and well-known authors: "I wondered if any of them would respond. They not only all replied, but they used extraordinary terms."[144]

This was a coup for the publisher. The three letters also date in a dramatic fashion the recognition of Thomas Merton as the author of a complex and powerful account of his life and spiritual search. Waugh, Greene, and Luce were all Catholics, but the story of a conversion to Catholicism was not so obviously the attraction. Evelyn Waugh, for one, could be devastating on just this subject. The attraction was in the manner in which the tale was told. Waugh had much to say, good and bad, about Merton's skills as a writer, but there was no qualification in his summary statement about *The Seven Storey Mountain:* "A book which may well prove to be of permanent interest in the history of religious experience." Graham Greene called it "an autobiography with a pattern and meaning valid for all of us." Clare Boothe Luce predicted: "It is to a book like this that men will turn a hundred years from now to find out what went on in the heart of man in this cruel century."

Only time would tell whether the book would ultimately fulfill the three unanimous estimates of its lasting importance. For the moment, with three such quotations from three such names to use on the cover, the publishers increased the original printing order to 7,500. This went up again, to 20,000, a second printing before publication, as first one, and finally three Catholic book clubs adopted the book and ordered copies.[145] Naomi Burton had to alter the original contract, with the monastery's permission, cutting down the author's initial royalty percentage in order to allow Harcourt, Brace to bring out the large book at three dollars a copy.[146]

On July 7, Dom Frederic called Brother Louis to his office and handed him the first copy of the autobiography.[147] It seemed to Merton the moment was at least as significant to Dom Frederic as it was to him. But the abbot was very pale and looked drawn and ill. Merton knew the finances at the monastery were worse than ever. In a few weeks the abbot would set off by train through the summer heat on a visitation to the Monastery of the Holy Ghost in Georgia. The two men spent some time talking about the writing. To Dom Frederic it was obvious that the vow of obedience he had placed Brother Louis under had born fruit as plentiful as it was varied. He asked Brother Louis if he could have done as much if he had given in to temptation and left Gethsemani for the Carthusians?

It was curious how little pleasure Merton had handling the printed copy of the much-altered autobiography. The best thing about it seemed to be the index, where one name jostled another with no regard to chronology or decorum: Anselm, St. . . . Burton, Jinny . . . Gandhi, Mahatma . . . Maritain, Jacques . . . Marx, Harpo . . . Montauban . . . Plotinus . . . "Pop" . . . Xavier, St. Francis . . . Zion Church . . .

This was a better list than any he, Lax, and Rice had cooked up that summer in Olean with the help of Rabelais, François, and Joyce, James. Only the index had given him something new, wildly original, fresh.[148] Otherwise, the book, the moment, had been an odd let-down. There was also a nagging fear, that the fat book he held in his hands, new, and smelling new (like those books in shiny wrappers which had come to the Bennetts' flat from the Times Book Shop in Wigmore Street), was going to change his life almost as much as his coming to Gethsemani — far less obviously for the better, far less under any control of his.

On August 4, 1948, he wrote to Naomi Burton on more publishing business, then:

> Our Father Abbot died suddenly and the monastery is somewhat upside down. It will be that way for the next month or so. I suddenly realized how much I owed to this abbot who was in every sense a Father to us — and who gave me carte blanche as a writer, against all the usual Trappist antipathy for intellectual work in monks! Say a prayer for him, although I don't think he needs too much help. He'll help us more than we can help him.[149]

Soon visitors arrived for the abbot's funeral and for the election of a new abbot. It was a time when Merton was busier in his writing than ever, and also a time when he had meetings with several men who were to be singularly important in his life. Dom James Fox, the abbot of the foundation in Georgia, had been at Gethsemani until 1944, but Merton had seen little of him when he was a novice and Father James a professed monk, except for the week when, as guest master, Father James had supervised John Paul's instruction for baptism. Dom Gabriel Sortais, the vicar general of the Order, Merton met for the first time. Again he found himself the translator when Dom Gabriel arrived to make his visitation and oversee the election. On August 12, Merton was included in a party that went to Louisville on a visit to the Convent of the Good Shepherd, Merton's first expedition outside the monastery grounds in seven years.[150]

He was in Dom Gabriel's company for several days, and the two men found they had certain things in common, including the pleasure of tilting at pious objects, which they agreed belonged in the monastery cupboard. This was hardly important, except that they were building bonds of understanding and liking for one another that would be helpful later in matters other than taste, though the bonds were a good deal frayed in the controversies that lay ahead.

Dom Gabriel Sortais was elected abbot general of the Order by the General Chapter that year. He had had an adventurous life, both in and out of the Trappists. Imprisoned by the Germans during the Second World War while he was serving as a chaplain in the French Army, he had spent a year in Gross-Born, a camp in Eastern Germany close to the Polish border. Repatriated, as Abbot of Bellefontaine, he had found himself very much persona non grata with the local Gestapo officials. Then came troubles with other officials in the turbulent times after the Liberation. A man of strong personality, strong views, and a dramatic presence, Gabriel Sortais was not likely to be overlooked by the powers that be, friendly or unfriendly. Before joining the Order he had risked arrest by the French police for his political activities. As an architectural student at the Beaux-Arts he had joined L'Action Française, founded by Charles Maurras and Léon Daudet, and he took part in the street brawls, fighting in the ranks of the monarchist Camelots du Roi against the anticlerical students of the left and of the Republican center.[151] He hardly shared his student politics with Merton, but Dom Gabriel had amusing stories to tell of his culture shock on visiting the American foundations of the Order for the first time.[152] Listening to Gabriel Sortais, Merton found himself becoming very French.

Preparations were made for the election. This seems to have been planned or fated to imitate the papal elections, even to the journalist climbing over the enclosure wall to photograph the puff of smoke coming out of the smokestack above the Chapter Room, signaling the voting slips were being burned and the final choice had been made.[153] Only monks who had taken Solemn Vows were entitled to vote. The election was soon over, and the former Abbot of Holy Ghost, Georgia, became the new abbot of the mother house. Novices, lay brothers, and the other professed were called in to witness as the Solemn Professed made their public promise of obedience to the new abbot.

Some time later, Merton went to the abbot's office to have a conference and to make his private promise of obedience. He noticed at once that the office had been transformed. The muddle of old books and financial papers had gone, and there was a new air of control and efficiency. Later, Merton said he had the impression everything was made of glass. He already knew the new abbot had graduated from the Harvard Business School at the age of twenty-one.

The old days had clearly come to an end. Departed with them was much of the legacy the first American-born abbot of Gethsemani had inherited from the Alsatian and French Trappist abbots before him, a legacy which had lasted without major changes at Gethsemani for exactly a hundred years. What the new would bring would soon be clear, and Dom James had been installed for life.

The new abbot had an extraordinary warmth of manner. His eyes, like Merton's, were very pale and alive with light. Only the mouth, with its firm line and thin lips, gave a hint of great determination, especially when Dom James smiled.

The backgrounds of the two men were quite different. Their tastes were quite different. For the moment each recognized the unusual in the other. Merton recorded on the Feast of St. Louis that "Dom James is quiet and humble."[154] Abbot James Fox had inherited a monastery deeply in debt. Its buildings were dangerously dilapidated. He had a hundred monks to feed, and almost a hundred novices. He also had two writers, both of them among the strongest personalities in a monastery with more than its share. One of the writers was about to publish a best seller. For Dom James the ideal monk was one who lived in anonymity and who died known only to God and to a few of his fellow monks.

*

Dom James began the essential building repairs at once. This meant noise, and it also meant people had to be moved from building to building.[155] But the abbot proved sympathetic to Merton's request for somewhere to work on his own, and Merton moved into the book vault on a much more permanent basis. As if to signify this, he was given the foot-long iron key, which he carried about with considerable dramatic effect.[156] The large metal doors gave the name "metal" — "room" to the vault in Trappist sign language. Merton was now at the center of the life of the monastery and next to the offices of the abbot.

Dom Gabriel had said Gethsemani must become self-sufficient, a command other visitors from the upper ranks of the Order were to repeat. Dom James studied the possibilities for making the few assets pay. The only thing he had a great deal of was unskilled labor — and perhaps land, though this had hardly provided food for the monastery under the old farming system. The new abbot started a search for a cellarer who could bring in new methods to mechanize and intensify the farming to ensure some profit. In Brother Clement Dorsey he had exactly the man he needed. Donations and Masses had traditionally been the monastery's means of support. This office was reorganized under Father Francis de Sales. Driven by circumstances, Gethsemani was being put on a more efficient basis, committed to greater activity.

Whatever gains and losses, the changes were begun just in time: the early fifties would bring another wave of applicants and further over-crowding.

In New York, the appearance of *The Seven Storey Mountain* created little immediate stir. The book was not reviewed in *The New York Times*. Naomi Burton was exasperated to find that copies delivered to some bookstores had been put on the religion shelves.[157] She heard a good deal of talk of it as a "Catholic" book, and, despite all the efforts of the Harcourt, Brace publicity department, it seemed to be generally as-sumed the book would appeal only to a section of the reading public. There were a number of old attitudes the book was to change forever. But many a potential buyer may have been put off by the *Nihil obstat*, just as Thomas Merton had been put off by it when he bought the book by Etienne Gilson ten years before.

There was something else the book was going to change. Catholics in the public eye, with a few exceptions, had been anxious to under-play the fact that they were Catholics. Thomas Merton, away in the monastery for eight years, had no conception of this policy of "low vis-ibility," and it is doubtful he would have made any concessions if he had. His autobiography was neither ecumenical nor restrained.

For all the good reasons why *The Seven Storey Mountain* should *not* have sold, something dramatic had happened by the end of 1948. Sales figures for October were 5,914. This doubled to 12,957 in November. In December, the figures more than doubled again to 31,000. Even more significant, in a period traditionally slow for orders, the order clerks at Harcourt, Brace had one of their busiest weeks of the entire year be-tween Christmas and New Year's.[158] The book was soon selling in all parts of the country at an average of 2,000 copies every working day, a demand that had nothing to do with seasonal book buying, critical notice, or special publicity or topicality. One bookstore manager tele-phoned the publisher, furious his order had not been filled. It had. All the copies had been sold before the manager had checked.[159] In February and in June, the figures went to wild highs on a rising graph. By Labor Day, 1949, almost 300,000 copies had sold. The record was 10,000 ordered on a single day. In all, 600,000 copies of the original cloth edition were sold, before the figures of later editions, paperback sales, and translations. Robert Giroux had "the biggest best-seller of my career."[160]

Early in 1948 there was still a disappointing lack of critical attention. *The Seven Storey Mountain* appeared nowhere on the best-seller lists, while printing after printing was hurried through to meet demand. After some discussion, the publishers decided to run an advertising notice asking booksellers to report if any book in their store had outsold *The Seven Storey Mountain* over the past week. It was an ingenious idea. Copy for the notice had to be sent in on a Friday afternoon when the newspaper's advertising manager had already left the office for his home on Long Island. The notice with its question appeared, calling attention at once to the gap between sales and recognition. *The Seven Storey Mountain* arrived from nowhere on the best-seller list near the top.[161]

The English eighteenth-century poet William Cowper had found waking up famous a sobering business. His ambition was to be known as a religious writer, yet he found himself talked of everywhere as the author of a comic poem. Then he discovered the other two topics of fashionable London that season were the antics of a performing pig and the confessions of a Mrs. Bellamy. His somewhat high-flown comment was, "Alas! what is an author's popularity worth in a world which can suffer a prostitute on one side, and a pig on the other, to eclipse his brightest glories?"[162] Merton was somewhat luckier: he shared the nonfiction best-seller list with a book on how to play canasta and *The White Collar Zoo*.[163]

Although Evelyn Waugh was generous in his support of the autobiography — saying in the section the publishers could quote that "Mr. Merton writes in an easy colloquial manner which should prove popular to countless readers who are repelled by formal theological language" — he went on in his letter to say that something like a half ought to be cut. Waugh thought Merton had allowed his self-disgust as a Cambridge undergraduate to color his view of the university as a whole. If he had had Catholic friends from Fiske House, the whole situation would have been different.[164]

When Waugh undertook to edit the English version he cut twenty percent of the book, and *Elected Silence* was kinder to Cambridge. In many cases Waugh improved the book, tightening sentences and taking out much repetition and redundancy. But it *is* a different book, and it lacks the flavor of the original. A few important sections are no longer in Merton's voice.[165]

Waugh's comment to friends (and to Merton himself) that he had brought precision bombing in place of pattern bombing is an analogy Merton would not have been happy to hear. However, Merton was open to helpful suggestions. Waugh had many when he visited Gethsemani in November. The first thing he did was to tackle Merton on exaggerations. He found the monastery overheated, as he did all American public buildings: what then was all the talk about the freezing conditions in *The Seven Storey Mountain?* Merton told him the new steam boiler had been put in, and that the buildings had been ripped up with a good deal of noise and dust to provide for it.[166]

Waugh's American expedition had been arranged by Clare Boothe Luce, and he was to write an article on religion in America for *Life*. In the meanwhile, he was conducting his own expedition, testing the state of American culture, rather than religion. He was pleased to discover

Harvey's Bristol Cream sherry was available, as it was not in austerity England.[167] In Hollywood, the cemeteries were interesting, while the town was dull. Little else met his own standards. He did attempt to help Merton cultivate a prose style, and he provided copies of Fowler's *Modern English Usage* and other works.

Evelyn Waugh was not the English moderator of *The Oakhamian*, or the Cistercian censor who had suggested a correspondence course in writing, but there are some signs Merton chafed under the criticism. He had reread Newman earlier that year and had decided that the style which was good for Newman was not good for him. He had always resisted refinement,[168] just as he had resisted Chesterton's chatty and urbane style. In his reading notebook he copied out a passage from one of the books Waugh had sent, *The Reader over Your Shoulder*, which argued against him:

> Faults of style are largely faults of character.[169]

And one that seemed to argue in his favor:

> But the only relevant standard by which to judge any straightforward piece of prose is the ease with which it conveys its full intended sense to the readers to whom it is addressed, rather than its correctness by the laws of formal English grammar.[170]

This seems a reasonable compromise under the circumstances.

On March 2, 1949, *Seeds of Contemplation* appeared from New Directions.[171] Three days later Merton had a copy in his hands. Even the covercloth made this a distinctive and distinguished volume, though the covercloth led to some odd rumors. It was said the burlap-like material was cut from the material Trappists wore to enhance their life of sackcloth and ashes. The material they did wear in winter often chafed the skin, but this was white wool, by a tradition that went back to the foundation of the Order in the eleventh century. Merton was pleased, however, when Laughlin wrote that it had become fashionable to use such material on the walls of nightclubs.[172]

However appealing the book's exterior, Merton was dismayed when he began to read. He found it "cold and cerebral," a combination of words with a particular chill that went all the way back to the times in his childhood when his mother had turned from him. It is ironic that he writes so harshly about one of his warmest books, and that he reprints the following passage from his journal in another warm book, *The Sign of Jonas*. There are works of Thomas Merton's of which it would be far fairer to say:

> Every book that comes out under my name is a new problem. To begin with, each one brings with it a searching examination of conscience. Every book I write is a mirror of my own character and conscience. I always

open the final, printed job, with a faint hope of finding myself agreeable, and I never do.

There is nothing to be proud of in this one, either. It is clever and difficult to follow, not so much because I am deep as because I don't know how to punctuate, and my line of thought is clumsy and tortuous. It lacks warmth and human affection. I find in myself an underlying pride that I had thought was all gone, but it is still there, as bad as ever. I don't see how the book will ever do any good. It will antagonize people, or else make them go around acting superior and stepping on everybody.[173]

If the reader of *Seeds of Contemplation* feels compelled to argue with the author in defense of the book, this may be part of the intention, though the passage was written when it was unlikely the journal would ever be published. Still, if the assessment is revealing, it is also complex and subjective, moving quickly to a "Mirror, Mirror on the wall" situation. Beyond that, there is something in the criticism of his own style. Merton never did learn to punctuate. The repetitions and redundancies are obvious here. More interesting, it is perfectly true that the Merton who was such good fun among his friends seldom comes through in his published writing. We have already seen how much of Merton is left out of *The Seven Storey Mountain* — there are many warm and agreeable passages, but the reader is often brought up sharply by an extraordinarily chilling one.

The year 1949 intensified Merton's struggle to overcome self-consciousness in the two areas where it was a major factor: his writing and the public aspect of his religious life. In 1948 his new confessor, Father Anthony, had suggested Merton put off his ordination until later in the year. The death of Dom Frederic had brought further postponement. In the spring of 1949, Merton was made subdeacon and then deacon. He was careful to record in his journal those Masses in which he managed to forget himself and those during which he was all too aware of himself.[174] At the same time the volume of mail had increased tenfold, and each letter brought him more news of Thomas Merton the writer.

If he hid the fact, except in his journal and to his confessor, the summer of his ordination was spoiled for him in many ways. While Merton tried to recollect and steady himself, the monastery was in full preparationforthecentenarycelebrations. *Gethsemani Magnificat*,thebook he had been commissioned to prepare, arrived at the monastery the first week in April. He was disappointed with the way it looked. Everyone else was pleased.[175]

June 1, 1949, turned out to be a sunny day after morning mists. St. Mary's field was packed with visitors, and the occasion was covered by the local press and radio, as well as Fox Movietone, who filmed it for national release as a news short to movie houses. Part of all this, Merton knew, was his own doing: Gethsemani was on its way to becoming the best-known monastery in the country. The day was altogether un-Trappist. Merton saw Monsignor Fulton J. Sheen at a distance. He was afraid Sheen would be offended if he didn't go up, but he slunk away as Sheen's voice came booming out over the microphones extolling Trappist silence.[176]

For a hundred years Gethsemani had been obscure, in possession of its own geography and somewhat "off" the geography of almost everyone else in America. The new abbot was not averse to a certain kind of publicity, as long as this could be controlled. Nor was Thomas Merton. The difference was that Merton knew very well it could *not* be controlled. Genie in the bottle, or whatever other cliché best applied, it was the very nature of publicity to change everything, to transform an actual event into a pseudo-event, to make history a series of *tableaux vivants*, to alter whatever reality a person possessed for himself and his friends into a phantom collection of myths, rumors, misconceptions. It was a voice breaking the silence to praise silence.

There were fictions and fictions. One didn't have to believe that everything was a veil of illusion to know this from practical experience. Rainer Maria Rilke, a poet Merton greatly admired, had said that fame was the coming together of misconceptions and rumors about a new name. As far as Thomas Merton was concerned, he knew that four or five monks at the monastery had been appointed to answer his incoming mail. Each was trying to write back to the sender in Merton's supposed style. Father Francis de Sales was overdoing it.[177]

Five days before the centenary celebration — on Thursday, May 26, 1949, the Feast of the Ascension — Brother M. Louis Merton became Father M. Louis Merton. He was still struggling to explore the significance of this event, to see his ordination at deeper levels, setting aside incidentals, accidentals, and distractions. He knew already that, like baptism and conversion, ordination was no end but a starting off in a different direction. Easily said. Yet he had made many beginnings. Too many fresh starts had led nowhere, or to circumstances which were not notably different. Perhaps this was because the beginning had been given no proper significance.

Long ago, in Cuba, Merton had gone on a journey to visit a shrine and his visit had been something of a disappointment, though he had come back with a good poem. At that time it seemed impossible he would ever become a priest. At the Church of Our Lady of Cobre he had made a promise that if he was ever ordained through her help he would dedicate his first Mass as a priest to her.[178]

Now he had fulfilled that promise.

*

Thomas Merton had been supported by his Columbia friends at the time he was received into the Church, and it was to be the same at his ordination. James Laughlin and Robert Giroux came to Gethsemani, Giroux bringing the one hundred thousandth copy of *The Seven Storey Mountain*, which he had had specially bound in morocco, and the news that, by May, the sales were approaching the 200,000 figure.[179] Robert Lax, Ed Rice, and Sy Freedgood came, and so did the man who had done more than any to bring him to Gethsemani, Dan Walsh. Newer friends through correspondence included Thomas Flanagan and George McCauliff. Nannie Hauck and Elsie Jenkins arrived from Douglaston and Great Neck.[180]

Merton began the day on which he was to be ordained by being proclaimed in the Chapter of Faults because his guests had blocked the refectory door in the cloister having their photographs taken.[181]

In the monastery church, which had been elevated to the title of basilica for the centenary, Brother Louis and Brother Amandus were ordained by the Archbishop of Louisville, John A. Floersch. Four monks were admitted into higher orders. Merton seemed little distracted by the popping of flashbulbs.

After luncheon with the archbishop, Merton hurried off at two in the afternoon to find his guests. He climbed from floor to floor at the guest house looking for Dan Walsh. When the two almost collided on the landing, Dan Walsh knelt for Merton's blessing. Walsh had brought a chalice as a gift.

As soon as the men in the party met together, they set off to the parlor in the gate house, where Elsie and Nannie Hauck were waiting. Merton hurried to catch up with news of the family and much else in a rapid question-and-answer session with those around him. He was amazed to discover that the British were no longer in India, and that Truman was president. He was less surprised to find that *The Seven Storey Mountain* had been very badly received by the congregation of Zion Church. He mimed the shock, disbelief, disgust of different parishioners to the laughter of his friends. Elsie Jenkins was finding it difficult to cope with this on a day-to-day basis, as she had become a parishioner at Zion Church herself. Merton brushed it off: none of the Mertons had ever been popular at Douglaston: his mother for wearing outlandish clothes, having outlandish opinions, and trying (successfully) to starve herself to death; his father for being odd, proud, ineffective, an artist; Tom and his brother for being badly behaved (and resentful of remarks made about their parents). As far as Merton was concerned, certain people in Douglaston, Queens, were ripe for revenge.

He had been granted two hours with his friends. The questions and answers continued. No, he said, he had not been nervous during the ordination service. He made the Cistercian sign for the letter *O*, the circle, joining his right thumb and index finger, then placed the tip of his left index finger where it made the center point. He said he had arrived at the center, a mystery from which earlier mysteries looked less mysterious.

In the background of the conversation there was a loud thrumming as a helicopter arrived over St. Mary's field, bringing the army technicians who were to set up the sound system for the centenary.

Next morning, Merton celebrated his first low Mass, dedicating it to Our Lady of Cobre. He made a few minor errors and omissions and was corrected by the Cistercian beside him. At one point he lost his footing, but drew himself up quickly.[182]

At eight that morning he was in the guest house garden, telling Sy Freedgood that the Mass was like a ballet; just as he had once said of *Robinson Crusoe*, "like religion it is pure play."[183] Freedgood, who had been expecting a somewhat different answer, followed Merton's animated gestures.[184] There were many photographs, as if to make up for all the years without them. Merton looked well, if much thinner — for the first time ascetic. He was not in the least self-conscious, even with the photographing going on, and with Bob Lax trying to record it all with a movie camera. Merton told them Don Ameche had telephoned the monastery at Easter asking if anyone had bought the film rights to *The Seven Storey Mountain*. If not, Ameche would like to make the film, presumably playing the part of Thomas Merton himself (Merton had been thinking more in terms of Gary Cooper).[185] Dom James had said no to the film and gone right on to ask if Ameche had made his Easter duty. Don Ameche said he had been to communion that morning.[186]

Merton complained later in his journal that few who came to see him at Gethsemani were edified[187] — just the sort of comment he wisely kept from his friends. Much of his conversation that day in the guest house garden under the ginkgo trees was concerned with weird stories of possession in Louisville and Nelson County, Kentucky, and there was a good deal of laughter over some of the details Merton supplied. There were serious moments, if not especially memorable ones. His friends were there to enjoy his company, and his company had always been good. So it was now. James Laughlin listened intently, and a secular priest smoked a cigar, his attention on Merton. Everyone agreed later on that if Merton looked a little drawn, he was in wonderful spirits — balanced, sane, delightful, and sometimes very funny.

At any rate, he had had enough of the publicity. Dan Walsh said the Associated Press photographer had asked him to pass on a message: Would Father Louis make some distinctive gesture at the elevation of the chalice during his first High Mass, so the photographer could capture it? Merton said to pass the message back the photographer could jump in the lake. He had a particular lake in mind, two miles away and deep.[188]

On Saturday, May 28, at nine o'clock, Merton said his first High Mass, with no distinctive gestures, some hesitations, but no apparent nervousness. He sang the preface and the Pater Noster beautifully.

George McCauliff, who had sent his copy of *Thirty Poems* to Clare Boothe Luce four years earlier, now brought her a rosary Father Louis had blessed and gave her news of the ordination, which she had been hoping to attend before family obligations prevented it. Monsignor Sheen had also written to her, with more news of the ceremony, saying he had wanted to meet Father Louis, but found he was surrounded by others and didn't want to intrude.[189] By this time, Clare Boothe Luce was writing to both Father Louis and to the abbot. She had already sent a set of *The Encyclopedia of World Art* for the monastery library, and now she was thinking of making a far larger gift. After spending huge sums planting rare azaleas at her family property in Carolina, she and her husband offered the three-thousand-acre site to the abbot for a new foundation. Our Lady of Mepkin Abbey, Moncks Corner, South Carolina, was established from Gethsemani at the end of the year.[190]

At Gethsemani, Merton's friends had gone, the television crews had left St. Mary's field, and the army technicians had taken down the sound system and departed noisily into the air. Merton enjoyed the heat, the day lilies — above all, the return of some silence, though this was destroyed at times by a new arrival, the huge D-4 Traxcavator.[191] Still more of his books would soon be coming out, though he had virtually stopped writing.

There was a dry period in his prayer. He wrote in his journal that he was forced to be simple at the altar; ordination had brought a sense of childhood, of play which was neither childish nor self-conscious. Then, on July 17, the Feast of Our Lady of Mount Carmel in the Cistercian Order, he passed out in the middle of singing the Gospel at High Mass. It may have been the heat. Dom James remembers it as a moment of panic on the part of Father Louis.[192] Whichever it was, the date is significant. Merton had kept one of the promises he had made in the pilgrimage to Cuba, but not the promise to Our Lady of Mount Carmel.[193] In fact, he felt himself growing further and further from fulfilling that promise.

The isolated collapse was not the beginning of a serious illness. It was a clear sign. A check. He had been straining himself too hard for too long. He had believed, too, that ordination would be a resolution, whereas it had become clear it was only a beginning at a higher plane. In his prayer life there had been little or no solitude that spring and summer. As for his writing, it was not so much that Eliot and Waugh had destroyed his confidence, or even that the success of *The Seven Storey Mountain* had set up impossible expectations for a second best seller. He was simply burnt out.

Perhaps the commonplace "burnt out" would do as a statement of fact as far as his writing was concerned. It meant something more in his religious life. At the end of *The Seven Storey Mountain,* Merton associated himself with "the burnt men," men who, like the bush before Moses, were set ablaze by the fire of God's presence, yet were not wholly consumed. In his journal in 1949, Merton began to identify himself with the same figures in the Bible:

> . . . I know well the burnt faces of the Prophets and the Evangelists, transformed by the white-hot dangerous presence of inspiration, for they looked at God as into a furnace and the Seraphim flew down and purified their lips with fire. . . .[194]

In those summer months the Bible became far more important and immediate, while the canticles, or psalms, became suddenly urgent, fresh after years of singing them in the offices.

He started to wonder if the one book he *was* writing could ever be published. Merton began to retype sections from the written journals, penciling in titles like "The Whale and the Ivy," then finding a title for the whole, *The Sign of Jonas.* He saw something paradoxical, personal, even funny in the comparison between his fate and that of Jonas or Jonah. By the mercy of God, he found himself a prophet against his will, brought back to exactly the place God wanted him to be.

The Sign of Jonas is, among other things, a celebration of the gradual relaxation of the most stringent restrictions that confined a monk to an enclosure within an enclosure. This process came about in small but important steps.[195]

In 1949–50 the professed were allowed to go into the yard on the east side of the house, to walk, to read, to meditate.

By 1951, the professed were allowed within the monastery property on the monastery side of the main road.

Earlier, when visitors came to see a monk, the only place he could receive them was in the guest house garden (if they were male), in the spartan parlors at the gate house, or, sometimes, in the avenue of sweetgum trees in front of the gate house. Now when James Laughlin came Merton was permitted to walk with him in the monastery woods on the far side of the main road. Where Dom James permitted Father Louis to go, other monks were permitted in time. In moving the bounds of the enclosure outward, Merton always seems to have been the pioneer. In seeking permission he could be very persistent. By this time he had discovered something about the abbot that made many things possible which had never been conceivable under Dom Frederic. Dom James Fox proved to be a pragmatist with an ingenious sense of what could be accomplished while still sticking to a rigid conception of Cistercian Usage.

The Sign of Jonas subtly records the sense of expanding horizons.

Woods, ponds, meadows are gifts to Merton in different seasons and changing light. They are not the familiar images of an accepted landscape. The writer one thinks of is not so much Thoreau (though *Walden* was to be important to Thomas Merton)[196] as the exiled Russian writer Turgenev. Pages of Merton's work, where landscapes are found for the first time and treasured, have much the same quality as Turgenev's lost but treasured fields and woods in *A Sportsman's Journal*. Here it is not an influence from books that is implied but rather a strong natural affinity.

In September 1949, Harcourt, Brace brought out *The Waters of Siloe*.[197] The book had a success no one could have predicted a few years earlier for a history of the Cistercians. Although it is written in Merton's most attractive style, the kindest thing to say about a few of the passages is that they have become dated.

Perhaps it was understandable that the little news of the world which was given to the monks in Chapter in the late 1940s presented an extreme version of the Cold War. Merton and others were harrowed by accounts of the interrogation of Cardinal Mindszenty[198] in Hungary and by the martyrdom of monks and missionaries in China when the forces of Mao Tse-tung overcame those of Chiang Kai-shek. Where Merton gave a full description of the persecution of the Trappists in China, one could hardly fault him.

It is in his old, ambiguous use of the word "Reds" and in his pages on the Spanish Civil War[199] that Merton went beyond anything he had already written in *The Seven Storey Mountain*. Here Merton had no excuse — he knew what the situation had been like in the 1930s, even if he did not know the context in which his words were read at the end of the forties and the beginning of the fifties. Merton may never have been among the Cold War warriors, but what he wrote at this time pleased some who were.

At the monastery, the machines were taking over, and Merton wondered if his royalties were going to support General Motors and to keep the abbey in new trucks.[200] Lent a jeep by the cellarer, Merton tried to cut down the number of vehicles at Gethsemani by one. Negotiating one of the old logging roads, he careened through puddles and ditches and bushes. When he arrived back, covered with mud and dizzy with the adventure, the cellarer told him in sign language he was never to take the jeep out again.[201] Perhaps this was forgotten. There was one more attempt to let Father Louis teach himself how to drive, and it proved far more disastrous. For the moment, he had to tramp the woods on his feet, but at least permission for this was far more frequently given.

In spring the annual influenza epidemic struck. It seemed altogether impropitious for a Professor Lefevre to come from Paris to try to improve the chant.[202]

Merton recovered his spirits with a resilience neither the flu nor another bout with a dentist could suppress. He was reading the journals and poetry of Rainer Maria Rilke, and he envied Rilke's manner of finding, protecting, and using solitude. The question of eventually publishing his own journals came up naturally from reading Rilke's. Merton approached Dom James. In May 1950 he wrote to James Laughlin that the abbot's answer had been a firm no.[203]

Only one book of Merton's appeared in 1950, and this had been written five years earlier. On February 28, the Bruce Publishing Company brought out *What Are These Wounds? The Life of a Cistercian Mystic, Saint Lutgarde of Aywières*.[204] Merton had thought of calling it "The Tiger Lily."[205]

In the preface he explained that he had written the book before the autobiography as an anonymous pamphlet for Dom Frederic Dunne, to whom St. Lutgarde had been a special source of inspiration.[206]

In a diagram Merton made in 1967 to evaluate his own books, he put *Exile Ends in Glory* in the "very poor" category, and *What Are These Wounds?* in the "Awful" column.[207] Here it stands alone, reminding one of the comment Henry James once made to a newspaper editor, about this being positively the worst writing he could do.

Certainly it was the worst writing Thomas Merton could do. Of St. Lutgarde facing the threat of the invasion of Genghis Khan's Golden Horde he writes:

> . . . One would have thought that a poor helpless woman, an invalid, totally blind, might have been at least slightly perturbed at the thought of thousands of little yellow men rushing around with swords and setting fire to everything . . .[208]

The color of the invaders would hardly trouble a woman who was totally blind! This is high, if unintentional, comedy. There are many cloying passages. The comment Merton makes about *Exile Ends in Glory* is even more appropriate here:

> . . . Where did I get all that pious rhetoric? That was the way I thought a monk was supposed to write, just after I had made simple profession.[209]

Yet the title "The Tiger Lily" would have been a better one. The book jacket was every bit as tasteless as the propaganda pamphlets Merton had handed out for the Communists at Columbia. It showed a nun adoring the impaled feet of Christ. This callous, shock effect was not limited to the outside. The references to the Albigensian Crusade have worse faults than being pious or poorly written. "God willed that the false mysticism of the Cathari should be devoured and destroyed by the purifying flames of divine love enkindled by Dominican, Franciscan, and Cistercian Saints . . ."[210] It is unfair to quote out of context, except to say that the fire metaphor for divine love was a bad one to use in talking of the massacre at Béziers and the holocaust at Montségur.

"Love does not exclude wars of mercy waged by the good," St. Augustine wrote, a line Merton challenged in "The Christian in World Crisis," an essay in his 1964 collection, *Seeds of Destruction*[211] — by which time he was wholly opposed to St. Augustine's idea of "wars of mercy," against declared heretics or anyone else. *What Are These Wounds?* has a good deal to say about such wars, such "mercy," and such "love."

Signs of change were all around Merton as the monastery grew in numbers from a second wave of applicants and as it altered from a pastoral farming community to a community that lived by intensive farming and food processing. By the winter of 1950–51 the space problems had become acute. According to Dom John Eudes Bamberger, it was "not quite as bad as a submarine"[212] — and he was able to compare, from his experience in the U.S. Navy. In a submarine, however, one had the opportunity to curse those who tumbled over you.

Even with the foundations in Utah and South Carolina, there were more than two hundred and seventy in structures built for seventy and little expanded in a hundred years. All these monks and novices needed to be fed, housed, and given work.

Housing was the most immediate problem. In the winter of 1951 a huge circus tent was raised over the garth, which was boarded over. For two years fifty monks slept here. Their boots often froze hard to the floorboards. Some monks shielded their boots under the straw pallets to prevent this. In the old dormitories professed and novices were packed in their sections in cells that had barely the old six square feet. Cells were constructed around windows and in passageways. The danger of fires was great, that of overloading the floor beams and joists probably far greater.[213]

Of the two thousand acres of monastery property, about four hundred were under cultivation or pasture. The farm had raised most of the food for the refectory earlier, but it was strained to do so for the new population. The white and black — Cistercian-colored — Holstein cows provided milk and cheese. There was little or no profit from farming.

In these years, Merton looked upon each new tractor or harvester as the end result of people buying his books in distant bookstores.[214] He, and others, may have exaggerated his contribution. It has been estimated that Merton's royalties have produced an average of $20,000 to $30,000 a year since 1949. This in itself distorts the picture, because the very large royalty sums which came in 1949, 1950, and 1951 arrived when they were needed most to help pay off the abbey debt (which Merton put at $20,000 in his letter to Laughlin in 1948, but which was certainly larger), and to provide for the monastery during its greatest financial crisis. Without *The Seven Storey Mountain* and *The Waters of Siloe* the monastery would have been in serious trouble and might have gone under. Some of the new postulants had come because they had read the autobiography or the history of the Cistercians. A few even came book in hand. Dom Frederic's successor turned the monastery from a foundation in debt to one with a name in the Order for financial soundness, even prosperity. Like most financial achievements, this had costs which did not show up on the balance sheets. Some of the results of the changes were both spiritually and physically damaging. The achievement was an astonishing one, so much so that it tended to blind others.

Merton saw the cost. It was not just that a pastoral idyll had been shattered. He could be both funny and serious about his own romantic nostalgia for the lost Eden and the time when he had seen the farm buildings of Gethsemani as a Mount Vernon in the Kentucky wilderness.[215] *Nostalgia* and *romantic* are words which lose any such argument to the "improvers." Merton had a sure instinct that what was good for General Motors was likely to be very bad indeed for Our Lady of Gethsemani. In time his view prevailed, persuading some of the least likely candidates.

Dom James Fox had a gift for choosing the most efficient man for the job and giving him room to move. On the few occasions the abbot's choice did not work out there was a rapid replacement. When he made Brother Clement Dorsey the cellarer, Dom James chose a young lay brother just out of the novitiate to run the food-processing plant as under-cellarer.

It is confusing to outsiders to find that Gethsemani *farm* and Gethsemani *Farms* are quite separate entities. Brother Frederic Collins was appointed to run Gethsemani Farms, to concentrate on making, packaging, and selling Gethsemani Monks Cheese (a Port-du-Salut-type cheese), at one time a range of meat products, and finally Gethsemani Fruitcake.

Frederic Collins had a degree in business administration and had worked in administration with Ford Motor Company. Gethsemani Farms was soon a smoothly running operation making a steady, increasing profit. Gethsemani farm experimented with a number of crops on the thin Nelson County soil. For a while tobacco flourished. There were boom years when the farm turned to raising alfalfa.

Merton judged that the farm used too much insecticide. Chemicals gave the crops a distinctive "forced" color.[216] There was far too much noise from the heavy machinery. Above all, the "big business" atmosphere was oppressive and had no place in a Cistercian monastery.

When Naomi Burton visited in September 1956, she too deplored the change to big business, but she pointed out to Merton that whereas seven or eight years ago, when she had first come down, no one in Louisville had heard of Gethsemani, now everyone she met spoke of the cheese, the bread, the bacon, and the Belgian mares from the monastery at the state fair.[217]

Seven years later, she was back "on a mission to straighten out tangled skeins, woven into a rat's nest by my unworldly monk," and she and Mrs. Gannon (who with her husband ran the guest house for women) walked down after Compline to "what the Brothers call Little Pittsburgh. It's a 24-hour operating factory for the manufacture of alfalfa pellets which are fed to turkeys and race horses. The monks attribute Chateaugay's recent Derby win to the Gethsemani diet."[218]

When Merton read Rachel Carson's *Silent Spring* in January 1963, he wrote at once to the author. This was an unusually general letter for him, but he ended it with some lightness of touch: "And I regret my own follies with DDT, which I have totally renounced."[219] Yet he found much of what she said confirmed in the fields about him and in the number of dead birds he came upon on his walks through the Gethsemani woods.[220] He succeeded in having *Silent Spring* read in the refectory, but it was withdrawn when the cellarer found fault with some of the figures in the book.[221]

On this subject, as in his opposition to war, Merton met with the criticism that he lacked the technical knowledge and terms to speak with authority. Apparently the argument could only be carried out in the language of the opponent.[222] If unusual allergies and odd complaints turned up at the monastery infirmary, Merton was accused of attributing all of them (especially his own growing list of allergies) to the crop dusting. But his instinct that something was wrong had already been shared.

The intensive farming and food processing required far more efficient use of the work force than the old logging crews. The first move had been to a greater specialization of jobs. The abbot thought this undermined the spirit of community, and "all-out work days" were brought in year round.[223] Usually they fell on a Wednesday. Lay brothers, novices, and professed choir monks still worked separately, but the whole work force was under the cellarer, who delegated tasks to the master of the brothers, the novice master, and the master of scholastics (professed choir monks). From late September until Christmas all the community was concentrated on Gethsemani Farms, or what Merton referred to as the "Cheese Factory," for the Christmas rush.

Brother Frederic had asked for, and been given, permission to speak.[224] This gave him a distinct advantage over his workers, including Father Louis, when he was assigned for duty. Over the years there had developed something of a kidding match between the two men, Merton using signs, Brother Frederic falling back at times on "sound." Beneath the kidding, as almost always with Merton, there was a serious purpose. The under-cellarer began to question what he had never questioned before. He discounted some of Father Louis's exaggerations, ignored his rather hazy business sense and lack of technical terms (in sign language or any other language), and yet came to see that Father Louis's instinctive grasp of the situation was very close to the true one. By the early 1960s Dom James was hearing from his business efficiency expert at Gethsemani Farms much the same argument he had heard from Father Louis for ten years. By then circumstances were quite different; the numbers at Gethsemani had dropped by more than half. The influx of the early 1950s was followed in the 1960s by what Merton called the "Drop-out Phenomenon." Many saw the sharp rise and fall in terms of the American boom-and-bust cycle, though it affected foundations outside the United States in the Cistercian and other orders.

In 1950–51 a postulant could be fifteen. Dom James favored young applicants on the grounds that they would be less formed (and so less corrupted) by the world.[225] He was reluctant to turn away any reasonable applicant of any age. To use academic terms, there was an open admissions policy. This led to trouble then and later.

The monastery was alert to the risk of fire, and a fire watch had been instituted. One night there was a strong smell of smoke. After a search, one postulant was discovered lying on his straw pallet, his feet on his suitcase, smoking a cigar. He said he was off in the morning anyway, so nothing anyone could do to him would matter.[226]

Many went. More who should have been let go stayed on. Yet these were the years in which some of the best applicants were taken. Flavian Burns came in 1950, and John Eudes Bamberger in 1951. Both would be in the class of scholastics Merton taught a few years later — a class that would have been exceptional anywhere. Both men later became abbots of the Order. They were in their twenties, formed, if hardly corrupted, in the world. They were well educated before they came to the monastery. John Eudes Bamberger had a medical degree.

Another applicant in 1950, Chrysogonus Waddell, was already a scholar and a musician.[227] When Augustine Wulff came to Gethsemani in 1954, he was in his fifties. He had read about Gethsemani in the works of both Thomas Merton and Father Raymond while he was living in Argentina working as a patent lawyer, and he had read many of the books in the Spanish translations. He already knew even more languages than Merton: French, Spanish, Portuguese, German, Latin, Greek, Hebrew, and Hindi. At Gethsemani he went further in his studies of Chinese and Japanese. He had a diploma in patent law, degrees in engineering, chemistry, and philosophy.[228]

There were others, though none with the range and depth of studies of Waddell and Wulff. By the mid-1950s the Monastery of Our Lady of Gethsemani was hardly an intellectual backwater.

Merton had always been impatient with the idea that the Cistercian Order was anti-intellectual. In an unexpected way, Dom Frederic had proved an intellectual mentor and an ally against any anti-intellectual feeling in the monastery.

Dom James never became a mentor, yet his encouragement went further than Dom Frederic's, and he was a much more effective ally. Dom Frederic had encouraged the writers. Dom James furthered study and teaching.

Merton had already been giving classes, or conferences, to the novices. In 1951 the abbot appointed him master of scholastics. This was the fourth most important position in the abbey. In responsibility it probably rated higher, as Merton was training the professed choir monks and he served also as their spiritual adviser under the abbot.

He broadened the training beyond the required courses in theology. Some years later, Father John Eudes Bamberger and Father Augustine Wulff were brought onto the teaching staff. Father Augustine taught Hebrew, English, French, dogma, moral philosophy, and five classes of scripture.

In this area, the master of scholastics and the abbot were in complete agreement. Dom Flavian Burns says, "Dom James kept the intellectuals at Gethsemani and gave them room to move."[229] There were some who left, but this is largely correct. James Fox was not one to put up with laziness. He had trained his own mind, and he had no more tolerance than Merton for the kind of mental "quietism" that was masked as anti-intellectual piety.

The very term "intellectual" covers a multitude of meanings, and it would be difficult to think of three wider variations under a single definition than Thomas Merton, Frederic Dunne, and James Fox. Merton's own view on the subject was complicated. He was scrupulous about not showing favoritism among his scholastics, but his views came to be known for all that, and they had connections with his own life.

He had had enough of straining to be thought clever at Oakham and Cambridge. Students of his who tried to be clever were soon in trouble. The rough-and-tumble of wit Merton had shared with his Columbia friends was something quite different, and something he missed badly. He missed both the kidding and the serious moments. It had been exactly the right mix for him, not only stretching his ideas but ordering and testing them. What was phony was proved phony. Merton's intellect had been sharpened and deepened, above all, by Lax's very different approach to things. All this was in the past, yet it set the standard. If Merton had ever been tempted before to show off intellectually, he was in dread of doing so now. There was nothing of the intellectual snob about him. He could discover with surprise, for instance, that not every monk in the class had heard of Van Gogh — yet respond without superiority or sarcasm. And he could be funny, very funny, though he liked to set the jokes. When one of the students started humming "Begin the Beguine" in a lecture on the Beguines, he stopped this.[230]

Merton made mistakes, both as master of scholastics and later as master of novices. "Dom James was a far better judge of men," Dom Flavian says,[231] and others agree. Occasionally Merton saw brilliance where there was only a show. He became very excited about one fifteen-year-old because the postulant seemed to have an incredible range of reading. It was his knowledge of contemporary poetry that really attracted Merton, who felt, as he always did on such occasions, how cut off he himself was. Certain fissures in the impressive display opened up as the two talked. Then the boy proved more than a little unstable, and Merton and Dom James agreed the postulant would have to go. He was soon writing, trying to convert Merton to the John Birch Society.[232]

Merton's enthusiasm for people in his journals tended to run from those whose scholarship he admired (like Fathers Chrysogonus and Augustine) to those he thought wise in their simplicity, old monks like Father Stephen or Herman Hanekamp, the man who had once been a lay brother and who now lived in the Gethsemani woods. To some at the monastery Father Stephen was "in his third childhood," while Herman was a tramp. Very little was known about either: they tended to become figures of myth for Merton and stereotypes for those who criticized them.

There were times later on when many felt Merton favored the "angry young intellectuals." He may have agreed with them, but he seldom supported them. He was more often cautioning prudence, self-discipline, and self-scrutiny — as well as a sense of humor (not what most of those who were angrily dropping out were anxious to hear). Merton's former students, in the Order at least, agree with one another he was strict, fair, always in control. To John Eudes Bamberger he was "the best teacher I ever had."[233]

Apart from the lecture conferences, there were private conferences, sometimes once a month, frequently once a week. Merton grew very adept in his counseling and spiritual advising at making the direct remark that, if sometimes brusque, was usually helpful. He visited one monk in the infirmary who complained that he had no fortitude left. Merton said, "Courage comes and goes. Hold on for the next supply." When the monk analyzed why he was so depressed, Merton listened carefully, then summed everything up: "You've got insight. Nobody can touch you."

He could be equally direct in puncturing pious or intellectual posturing. The same monk had asked Merton to read a book by a holy woman of the nineteenth century. When he went to his conference the book was lying on Merton's desk, still unread. "Who is this babe you want me to read about?" Merton asked. When the monk explained and said he wanted to enter into a spiritual marriage with her, his adviser put both hands to his head and rocked back and forth moaning "Whoa, now, *Whoa!*"[234]

Teaching takes much the same kind of energy as writing. Merton managed to combine both activities to some extent, working his class notes into essays. From the first he was conscientious about how the classes should go. In May 1950, when he was still teaching the novices, he wrote to James Laughlin, "Teaching simply knocks me out."[235] He went on in the same letter to say he enjoyed building a relationship with his students, comparing this to what Laughlin had said about enjoying the time he spent with his children. Something in Merton still "clamored for silence," and at times the sound of his own voice made him feel physically ill. The hours he found for himself that summer were spent walking back and forth near the horse barn or reading "oriental stuff" in the old garden shed. He had found Laughlin was interested in Eastern philosophy, and the publisher sent him books, including Pound's translations of Mencius (Meng-Tzu).[236]

*

In October and again in November 1950, Merton had to go into the hospital in Louisville. It was the first time he had spent time away from the monastery. St. Joseph's Infirmary, 735 Eastern Parkway, has gone now: it was a place Merton came to know well. This time he had surgery on a bone in his nose and treatment for his trouble of 1936, colitis. His stomach may have been suffering from the monastery diet, but he had brought this problem to Gethsemani, and it was not to leave him, flaring up whenever he was overworked and anxious.

Merton was x-rayed and lesions were found in his lungs. He was told to rest, and not to write. Earlier x-rays had shown scars of what looked like tuberculosis. Merton thought he knew his entire medical and dental history. He did not know yet that his father had kept the tuberculosis scare of 1927 from him.

Merton did not find the hospital particularly quiet, but he enjoyed looking out of the window and watching for the junk cart. The driver in his green sweater, the dog running beside, the bells jingling on the harness — all this gave him a sense of *déjà vu*, "like the memory of something very precious once seen in the Orient."[237]

The stay at the hospital broke the writing block. Merton had been corresponding with Sister Thérèse Lentfoehr about his poetry and much else. Sister Thérèse tried to send him a relic on birthdays and special occasions. On the Feast of St. John of the Cross, November 24, a relic of the saint arrived.[238] Merton finished his book on St. John of the Cross in a few months, and it appeared from Harcourt, Brace in September 1951.[239] The publishers were now taking all kinds of risks with an author who had proved so successful.

With all the initial help he had given, Laughlin may have felt this was another book he should have published. By 1951, Merton's publishing tangle was giving a good deal of trouble to Curtis Brown and almost all his publishers. The period when he was not writing had hardly been long enough to sort this out, and now new works were arriving again.

Whether all this was "unworldly" or not, Thomas Merton was impulsive and generous by nature. Where he had no money to give away, he felt he had rights to his own books and the various drafts of manuscripts. He was receiving a good many favors himself. Father Terence Connolly, the librarian at Boston College, had sent him a number of books, and in return Merton sent one copy of the typescript of *The Seven Storey Mountain*.[240] Another went to Sister Thérèse Lentfoehr, while almost every letter brought her drafts of poems and sections from his journals.[241] Merton was anxious to donate his correspondence with James Laughlin to the library of the University of Kentucky.[242]

Like most writers in the news, Merton received a good many letters asking advice from other writers who were not in the news. Much of this he was able to ignore. He had had cards printed in the monastery print shop, which allowed him a certain enviable distance. But requests from translators and fellow writers in the Order were harder to turn back. He found himself trying to interest his own monastery, then various publishers, in scholarly books being written at the Abbey of Saint André in Bruges, and the Abbey of La Pierre qui Vire.[243] This involved time, trouble, and some disappointment for all concerned. Much more serious was Merton's way of responding to the monastic equivalent of a hard-luck story by agreeing to let his unpublished essays be translated and brought out. A certain hard-up convent in Brazil was given the rights to Portuguese translations, only to sell them. Merton knew nothing of this, and the foreign-rights section of Curtis Brown remained ignorant until the day it got a letter from the publishing company to whom it had sold the Portuguese-translation rights asking in angry tones what was going on.

To such problems — and there were many, each more complicated than this sketch depicts — Merton was likely to reply in a detached manner, talking of his need to do favors for friends, his vow of poverty, his need to act charitably.

Miss Weiner at the literary agent's began a letter gently:

I think it would be in your best interest to pass on to me any such in-
quiries as they come in, and we would be happy to deal with them.[244]

Later Naomi Burton wrote a note in pencil to guide the foreign-rights
staff in replying to one of Merton's requests (on this occasion he was
at least keeping Curtis Brown informed):

I'd be inclined to suggest that he tell them *now* that he is hoping that a
reciprocal deal can be worked out. "Understandings" always turn out to
be "mis-----" if not defined.[245]

In December 1949, the *(mis)*understandings had become serious
enough to bring Naomi Burton down to see Father Louis and the abbot
for the first time at Gethsemani.

Complications in her own plans brought it about that she arrived from
Louisville in a bright yellow cab. Whatever the Cistercian sign language for "yellow — cab," the news was around the monastery in no
time.

Naomi Burton found Father Louis in no way different from the Tom
Merton she had known in New York. They talked in one of the parlors
at the gate house, whose straight-backed austerity and ugliness made a
foil for his animation and warmth. When a knock came at the parlor
door he rapped twice on the table, the Cistercian signal to enter. Dom
James came in, welcomed Naomi Burton, and immediately began talking about the yellow cab.[246]

The only really serious row between author and agent was to come
in 1956, when Merton felt things were being decided behind his back
between Naomi Burton and Dom James.[247] A certain amount of this
was inevitable because of the way the mail was handled at the monastery. Royalties came to Gethsemani. Thomas Merton might be writing to Naomi Burton about his disregard for profits, but she knew exactly where she stood with Dom James in business matters. However,
there was more to it than that. Dom James had become a friend, and
Naomi Burton says in her autobiography that both the advice and encouragement of the abbot were important in her own conversion to the
Catholic Church. As a recent convert, her expectations for the unworldly side of Thomas Merton led to some complications between
them. Others were to suffer by being caught between Dom James and
Father Louis at the monastery. The estrangement between Thomas
Merton and Naomi Burton lasted only a few weeks. He wrote to apologize for his earlier, tough letters, and he continued to look to her for
advice on a good many matters that had nothing to do with publishing. From the correspondence, it is obvious the last person Merton
wanted to have false expectations from was Naomi Burton: he relied on
her for good, sensible, no-nonsense comments. He sometimes got these,
and on a later visit he gleefully took her on a walk to look at the barn

where she had told him to go to have a good cry when she thought his letters had crumbled into self-pity.[248]

In the spring of 1951, he was preparing to become an American citizen. Merton went to Louisville to make the early arrangements, and he settled down to read "the baby-talk citizenship textbook that is given out to help us aliens prepare for our naturalization."[249] In his journal the significance of setting aside the citizenship of his father for that of his mother was complicated by the fact they had both liked France much better than the country in which they happened to be born. Later, in the 1960s, Merton said if he had known more about the politics in the McCarthy era he would have thought twice before becoming naturalized.[250] In 1951 there were no such second thoughts in his journal: he said he found the country worth loving and wondered why there were so many Americans who felt they owed their country nothing.[251]

On June 22, 1951, he put on a borrowed black suit, a Roman collar, and a large black Spanish-looking hat that delighted him, and was driven to Louisville by two of the family brothers.[252] He read his Office, then went over the lists of things every citizen was supposed to know. The countryside rolled by: four-square white churches, cabins with sway-backed shingled roofs, clumps of chicory, day lilies, Queen Anne's lace (or cow parsley), wild roses, trumpet vines and hollyhocks, green fields and tobacco turning yellow. By the time the party reached the Federal Building in Louisville, Merton was ready to enjoy the day's outing from the monastery.

At one point in the procedure, Merton had to stand up and explain why he had been a member of the National Students League his first year at Columbia. He was watched in solemn fashion by a delegation from the Daughters of the American Revolution. When it was all over he was given a small American flag with everyone else. It was a hot day. Merton kept taking his hat off, wiping his forehead, then replacing the hat with a flourish and tilting it well back.[253]

On the drive home to Gethsemani, Merton looked at the same Kentucky fields along the Bardstown Road in a different way. This was his country now. In a sense it was the first country he had ever had. This time he had chosen it in law as well as in imagination. The United States of America was his country, Kentucky was his state, and the monastery was his home.

It is no accident that in the Epilogue to *The Sign of Jonas*, the "Fire Watch" takes place on Independence Day a year later. This essay, almost a prose poem, is many things at once, but it is patriotic in the true sense of the word — *pietas:* praise for, and loyalty to, a place.

Merton had been asking the abbot for some time for leave to spend some hours a day in the woods. Naomi Burton felt there was a certain childlike persistence to these requests. Granted permission to do something on one occasion, Merton would at once work for a permission to do this always, whether it was to be allowed to bless a medal-lion or rosary for a friend in the gate house shop, or to be excused some community gathering for solitude.[254] Maybe this was childlike. Maybe there was something of the barrack-room lawyer in Thomas Merton.

Dom James had a strict interpretation of the Rule of St. Benedict and the Cistercian Usage. He also had a creative imagination. Father Ste-phen, whether in his third childhood or a saint, could take little active part in the life of the monastery. He had a penchant for growing flow-ers, which at that time was frowned on as being more Franciscan than Trappist. Father Stephen would sneak flowers into the abbey church in his habit. There are perhaps two shrines at Gethsemani that could be called "wayside." Dom James decided the abbey would become the first to have a keeper of the wayside shrines. To do the work the keeper had to have a garden. And so the garden Father Stephen was culti-vating already was brought into the Usage retrospectively.[255]

Something of the same happened to Father Louis. He had spent a number of afternoons alone in the abbey woods. He was always anx-ious to take novices, and then scholastics, on tree-planting expeditions. He was also among the first on the scene to fight a brush fire.[256]

Dom James studied the organization of early Cistercian monasteries and discovered that certain monasteries in the Ardennes had had someone under the cellarer who was referred to as the forester. No European foundation had such a person now, but there were certainly forests at Gethsemani. Dom James approached the father immediate, the abbot general, and finally the General Chapter of the Order. The Monastery of Our Lady of Gethsemani had its forester.[257]

This was no sinecure. Merton was responsible for restoring the woods, which had been stripped of hardwood by Dom Frederic's sales and the indiscriminate logging of the 1940s. Through the cellarer's of-fice, Merton ordered books on identifying trees, and more technical works on forestry.[258] The new job gave him further hours in the woods, a solitude he would not have had otherwise, and brought him new knowledge. He had not been interested in natural history at Oakham, where it was a common enthusiasm of schoolboys in the country. Reading Thoreau's *Walden* gave him a desire to be a competent natu-ralist. He was writing few poems now, but when he came to write them again the birds and trees would have names.

The observations in his journal became more precise. Merton's per-sistence had already won a reconsideration about publishing these journals in his lifetime. The abbot had given him permission to try to win the Order over to the idea, no more. Merton took this for an en-dorsement from Dom James. It was hardly that.[259]

It had been understood between Merton and Laughlin that if per-mission was ever given, the journal would be a New Directions book.

Now it seemed Harcourt, Brace had an option on the next book Merton wrote. Merton overcame this to some extent by promising other books to New Directions. Laughlin was a friend, and far more forgiving than most publishers would have been in the same circumstances.[260]

Now that Harcourt, Brace had the book, Giroux and Naomi Burton assumed that, because it had been cleared by the Gethsemani censors, it would also receive the formal approval of the abbot general. It was therefore set in type and Naomi Burton dispatched a set of American galley proofs to the English publisher.

Work was well ahead in England as well as America when Dom James returned from Europe, where he had seen Dom Gabriel Sortais, to tell Robert Giroux and Naomi Burton in New York that publishing *The Sign of Jonas* had been absolutely forbidden and the text, already set, would have to be broken up.

There were two major battles over the book: one from 1951 to November, 1952, over the English version, the other a year later over the French translation. A number of different campaigns were started on behalf of the publication in English. Robert Giroux enlisted the help of Jacques Maritain. In England, Tom Burns of Burns and Oates, the English publishers, was getting assistance from Father Bruno James, the confessor to the English censor, and others in the Church and the Order.[261]

Merton's own efforts were largely counterproductive on this occasion. Father Chrysogonus remembers that he made some quick translations into French of several sections for Dom Gabriel to read during the abbot general's visitation to Gethsemani. At first Dom Gabriel said he would read these after Lent. Merton persisted, reading the pages out loud, and Dom Gabriel groaned at some of the references to the Order. When the abbot general left the monastery, he was at best noncommittal.[262]

The crisis of numbers at Gethsemani had been eased only a little by the establishing of yet another foundation near Piffard, New York, in 1951. Some of the best and most experienced older monks had gone to Our Lady of the Genesee, including Merton's former confessor. (The most immediate result of this was that Merton was appointed master of scholastics on Trinity Sunday, 1951.) Our Lady of Clairvaux was formed from the monastery at Vina in California in 1955. In July 1952, Merton made his first trip out of Kentucky in eleven years to look at a possible foundation in Ohio.[263]

Brother Clement, Brother Wendeline, and Merton left the monastery just after sunrise and the celebration of Mass for Travelers. They skirted Louisville, then drove along the Ohio River, bringing back many memories to Merton. Kentucky was brown after months of unusual heat and no rain, but the Ohio countryside was lush and the corn stood ·a foot higher. Merton's companions were coming north to buy hay. Stopping at a dismal roadhouse for something to eat, the three monks thought they had been cheated, then discovered prices had risen everywhere.

Merton was convinced Dom James had included him on the trip because the abbot was expecting him to lead the new foundation. He looked about him with a feeling that the landscape had connections with both the past and the future. They passed close to Columbus and he thought of the twenties:

> . . . the bravery of those innocent days when Pop was making money for Grosset and Dunlap and Father played the piano in the movie in France and one of the books that made money for Grosset and Dunlap was a reprint of Sinclair Lewis's *Babbitt*.[264]

The party arrived at Newark, where they collected Dom James and Father Francis de Sales, who had flown in from Chicago, before going to look at the house and land near Hebron. Merton was disappointed they would not be going on to Zanesville:

> . . . where Pop came from and where my mother was born. I was inexpressibly moved by the thought that perhaps I would someday start a monastery in this land which is mine without my ever having lived in it.[265]

He walked the farmland, where there were woods of old maples and walnut trees, and he was fascinated by a wooded hollow with a spring and "an old tumbledown house and barn and a few Guernsey cows swishing in the bushes and the deep grass." Merton's enthusiasm for the hollow was not shared by the others, who wanted to build on the ridge of high ground. None of these plans came to anything, and Dom James, Merton found, had not even considered him as a potential abbot. But the account is interesting in light of what Merton wrote about the hermitage he finally reached. He made the division there between the "conscious" part of the geography, the high ground looking out over a wide valley in front of the building, and the overgrown hollow with a spring behind the hermitage, which he calls the "unconscious" part.[266] Merton was seldom indifferent to place, even to places he knew only for a few hours.

He and the abbot left from Columbus by air, the first time Merton had flown. They were delayed in Cincinnati, waiting for a flight to Louisville. To Merton the airport "seemed to be infected with some moral corruption that had been brought in by the planes from New York."[267]

That summer was to produce his most serious crisis of stability yet. It is usual to portray these recurring crises of the 1950s in a neat series:

Carthusians, Camaldoli, the South American foundation, the West Indies, Cuernavaca. In fact, the possibilities usually came in clusters. In 1952, Merton was still hoping to join the Carthusians. In the autumn, Dom Humphrey wrote asking Merton to come for a visit to Sky Farm in Vermont. The Carthusians at last had a charterhouse in the United States. Dom James refused permission for the visit, and the mail was discouraging:

> . . . Dom Porion said it would be difficult for me to be received into a Charterhouse but that he would put in a good word for me to the General if I wished. He strongly recommended going to *Camaldoli* in preference to the Chartreuse, but strongest of all was his recommendation to stay where I am and abandon myself completely into the hands of God.[268]

This was the pattern of many another letter from Merton's supporters in Rome.

Merton had written letters to the Camaldoli in September. Most of the replies were delayed, going first to the abbot, who was at the General Chapter of the Order in Europe. When it reached Merton, the letter from Dom Anselmo Giabbani, prior general of the S. Eremo at Camaldoli, was enthusiastic. Dom James was not.[269]

On the face of it, the Camaldoli was the ideal order for Merton. He wrote glowingly of them in *The Silent Life* a few years later, and he was as anxious to join them in 1955 as he was in 1952. Where each of the Carthusians had his hermitage in a cell that was part of the charterhouse, the *laura* of the Camaldoli was a collection of separate hermitages, not unlike the hermitages gathered close for mutual protection in the ancient Celtic church.

Naomi Burton was among the many who were asked to help establish lines of communication between Merton and the Camaldoli. Her first attempts in Rome were hampered because she could not translate Italian, while the Camaldoli priests she met could speak no English. Later she was visited in New York, and this time the Camaldoli sent someone who spoke English. Naomi Burton gathered that the Order was very keen to have Merton, and they were anxious for him to bring his typewriter.[270]

There was a third possibility that summer. In late August, Monsignor Larraona, Secretary to the Sacred Congregation of the Religious in Rome, had visited Gethsemani. Again, Merton found he was translating for the visitor, this time in both Spanish and Italian, but this brought the two men together, and Merton was to count on Larraona's support later on. In canon law Merton had discovered that the Scholasticate, or school for the professed choir monks, ought to be housed separately from the monastery. Because Gethsemani was so crowded, Merton suggested founding the Scholasticate in Colorado, and he understood Monsignor Larraona was going to speak to Dom Gabriel about it.[271] Perhaps he anticipated agreement where there was only a certain amount of interest in his idea. At any rate, nothing came of this proposal. Larraona brought the news that there was a general agreement in Rome Merton should go on writing. Once again this came at an interesting time: the battle over *The Sign of Jonas* was still going on. And now the French translation of *The Waters of Siloe* was under a ban.

Merton was still hearing from individual censors. Dom Albert, Prior of Caldey, off the coast of Wales, wrote what Merton called "a terrific letter about *Waters of Siloe.*" He had just finished the French translation in the typescript banned from publication:

> . . . He told me with perfect justice — and great force — that I should never have written as I did about De Rancé, Dom Augustine, Dom Urban, etc. He is absolutely right. Acting without guidance or control, I simply wrote the book that might have been written by some wise guy outside a monastery.[272]

This is quite possible, and perhaps this is what made the book both readable and popular.

More disturbing was the criticism Merton drew from the man who was usually the most liberal and generous of his censors. Father Paul Bourne had been appointed the chief censor for the Order in America.

One of the reasons for many of the censorship tangles early in Merton's career was the fact that this was largely unfamiliar territory for the superiors in the Order. There were general rules which now had to be applied to specific cases. The publication of *The Seven Storey Mountain* started something of a boom in Trappist writing, and the censorship system had to be reformed to handle this, just as all the rules had to be rewritten later to cope with *The Sign of Jonas.*

Dom Gabriel Sortais had appointed Father Paul the chief censor during a visitation to Georgia, brushing aside the monk's objections with *"Mais vous avez du bons sens."*[273]

Father Paul Bourne had seen a sample of the book: it was the self-criticism the censor found exaggerated. As every autobiographer has discovered, it is as difficult to get the measure of blame right as it is to get the measure of self-praise right. Merton now began to wonder if the tendency to attack himself in the journals — and now in print —

> . . . prompted me to say too many things I did not mean, but which I felt I had to say because they were things I did not like about myself. You have to distinguish between what is ugly in you and is *willed* by you, and what is ugly — or silly — and *not* willed. The latter is never really interesting, because it is usually quite unreal — and therefore not matter for a journal — gives a false picture.[274]

It is not so easy to be frank, or to be frank without boasting frankness.

No book appeared by Merton in 1952, though he was doing a good deal of writing. It is certainly a paradox that some of his finest writing about Gethsemani often came in the middle of a stability crisis. The Epilogue to *The Sign of Jonas* suffers a little from being too celebrated but a rereading is still moving. Maybe a little deflation was inevitable: there are monks at Gethsemani who point out Father Louis was always given the first fire watch. It was the second, or the third, when you were woken from sleep by a tug on the foot, that most monks found penitential. Some have questioned the effectiveness of the watch. Brother Alban says he was sometimes so tired that "I could have walked through the fire and never seen it."[275]

Something drew Merton to Gethsemani and to the community in a very natural way at times. Something held him there against his wishes at other times:

> What am I certain of? If it were merely a question of satisfying my own desires and aspirations I would leave for Camaldoli in ten minutes. Yet it is *not* merely a question of satisfying my own desires. On the contrary: there is one thing holding me at Gethsemani. And that is the cross. Some mystery of the wisdom of God has taught me that perhaps after all Gethsemani is where I belong because I do *not* fit in and because here my ideals are practically all frustrated.[276]

Much of the pattern of this summer's stability crisis was to be repeated. Merton would initiate action, write letters, consult, draw up all the reasons why he should be anywhere but at Gethsemani. Then he would try to detach himself from the "fruits of action." He would see things in his immediate circumstances that were dear to him, values he had never used, and he would wait to see God's purpose. Whatever he did had to be done with permission:

> . . . And yet — I cannot do anything at the moment. Rev. Father would do *anything* to prevent me moving one step further in the affair. I am certain that nothing is to be done at the moment. If God wills me to go to the Camaldoli He will show me when to take the next step and how. So I remain both certain and uncertain.[277]

Merton had entered into a correspondence with a Passionist father, Barnabas Ahern. In what became a friendship in letters, the men talked of many things other than the translations of the Bible Father Barnabas was making. In January 1953, Ahern became alarmed at a sentence in one of Merton's letters: "The road is opening up and I hope He will give me the strength and the integrity to travel it."[278] This did not sound as if it was to be a spiritual journey to the interior.

In his letter of January 14, 1953, Father Barnabas gives a list of reasons, under "the danger of scandal," which must have been over-familiar to Merton, even then: he would encourage restlessness in others by going; he would cut off vocations to the Trappists because his leaving would show he had warmly advocated a certain religious life and then proved it was not for him; he would encourage critics of the contemplative life, as well as those who were all too ready to say there were no connections between Merton's writing and Father Louis's life. In short, he would set a bad example. Put another way than Father Barnabas intended, Merton was trapped in his reputation even more firmly than most established writers.

Merton wrote back on January 22, saying ingenuously that he thought few people would know if he went to the Carthusians, as he was advised to do by one spiritual adviser (he doesn't say which one). Now Dom James has suggested an opportunity for solitude at Gethsemani, and Merton quotes the abbot as saying "Solitude, for you, is medicine." He says how excited he has been by the new issue of *La Vie Spirituelle*, with its emphasis on "Bienheureuse Solitude," and by the support for the eremitical life in recent writings of Dom Jean Leclercq and Dom Anselm Stolz.[279]

Obviously Father Barnabas had little interest in the solitary life. When he replied on January 29, 1953, he repeated that Merton had a duty of charity. Aelred Graham's recent article on Merton in *The Atlantic Monthly*, he said, should show him the expectations he has aroused.[280] To Merton's mention of another hermit in the Order, Father Barnabas pointed out that Father Charbel had not been "a writer who populated his monasteries with a picture of the opportunities such a life presents." On its own terms this was a perfectly valid comment, and one that would never be less valid. But when the Passionist went on to say Father Louis was no longer a judge of the Trappist life because he had not lived as an ordinary Trappist monk since 1948, Merton could have answered that none of the monks at Gethsemani in the early 1950s was leading "an ordinary life of the Trappist monk."

The new possibility at Gethsemani for solitude Merton mentions had come out of the building program. When the construction workers no longer had any use for a toolshed, it was hauled by the Traxcavator to the woods beyond the horse pasture (the far corner of the Petrified Forest).[281] Dom James gave Merton permission to use the shed. He was allowed there only certain hours of the day, and others used it,[282] but the shed became dear to Merton and he gave it a name:

> Fine ideas in Picard's "World of Silence," (a train of the old times sings in my present silence at St. Anne's, where the watch without a crystal ticks on the little desk).[283]

Anne is spelled sometimes with an *e*, sometimes without. Ann was a sentimental name for Thomas Merton. On September 1, Father John of the Cross's family had been to see him. Merton had joined the Wassermans outside the gate house under the sweet-gum trees of the avenue. He wrote a long description of the family in the journal.[284] A letter came on September 13 to say that Ann Wasserman had entered the Carmel in Cleveland and that it was "just right." Perhaps Merton was wondering whether his own vocation would ever be "just right." It may have been something else altogether that led him to write in the margin beside the account of the letter "Real tribulation — ground between millstones."[285]

The various battles over *The Sign of Jonas* had continued all summer and during Dom Gabriel's second visitation that year in the fall. It is hard at this point to see which of the campaigns succeeded where others failed. Merton felt a five-page letter he sent on to the abbot general after Dom Gabriel left for other visitations was the one that finally convinced his superior. Reading the letter, one wonders: Merton had made a great deal of the fact that the journal ought to be printed as an act of charity to his publishers, who were already committed, who had spent large sums on typesetting and publicity.[286] Dom Gabriel replied from Lantao, the island off Hong Kong where the refugee Trappist foundations from China were relocated. The abbot general had a good deal to say about the relations between monks and publishers. Reluctantly, he agreed to the publication, but only in English.[287]

The whole battle had to be fought again in 1953–54 over the French translation. As with the French translation of *The Waters of Siloe*, this would have repercussions on Dom Gabriel's home ground. Whatever the monks might make of self-revelation and a somewhat lighthearted approach to the Order in the United States and even in England, what French monks at Bellefontaine would think Dom Gabriel was not anxious to learn. Again the forces were mustered.

By July 3, 1954, Merton was writing to Naomi Burton that the crisis over the suppression of the French translation of *The Sign of Jonas* had been lifted.[288] He was also explaining the new rules of censorship and translation that had been passed at the General Chapter of the Order that year.[289] These were a direct result of the difficulties with the stream of books from Father M. Louis Merton, O.C.S.O., but with the journal in particular. After all this, Merton got a good deal of pleasure from hearing General de Gaulle had enjoyed *Le Signe de Jonas*.[290]

The Sign of Jonas was published at last on February 5, 1953.[291] For the first time, one of Merton's books was reviewed in *The New York Times*. Almost all the reviews were favorable. Those who had been disappointed by *The Waters of Siloe* because they had been led to expect a sequel to *The Seven Storey Mountain* were pleased. *The Sign of Jonas* was popular from its first appearance. For many of Merton's readers it remains the favorite book of all.

It was not, however, *The Seven Storey Mountain*, Part Two, though it did establish that Merton was still at Gethsemani. He and others had been troubled, even as early as the publication of *Thirty Poems*, by rumors that he had left the monastery. The sigh of relief was almost audible from some of the critics in specifically Catholic journals:

> Some think that in Merton the monk we glimpse something of Augustine all over again. Others, less happily, think the change from pagan, intellectual and man of the world, to monk, contemplative and man out of this world was too sudden to be founded on rock. To the objective observer the speciousness of this latter view should now be evident. The fact that Merton has been a Trappist for close to fifteen years and is now a priest is conclusive proof that his embrace of the austere Trappist life was not the flight of caprice some thought it to be.[292]

Meanwhile, in print, Thomas Merton was saying goodbye to any number of Thomas Mertons:

> . . . The man who began this journal is dead, just as the man who finished *The Seven Storey Mountain* when this journal began was also dead, and what is more the man who was the central figure in *The Seven Storey Mountain* was dead over and over. And now that all these men are dead, it is sufficient for me to say so on paper and I think I will have ended up by forgetting them . . .[293]

There was a need in Merton's very nature to bury earlier Thomas Mertons, however frequently he visited their graves. In 1953 he was also struggling to keep some of the options open, to free himself from the traps and cages of public reputation. (His poetry of the time is full of "traps" and "cages.") It is therefore fitting that he should turn his back on the reader as he walks off through the abbey woods in the end pages — into the book in the beginning, out of the book at the finish.

*

The struggles over censorship, and stability, had left Merton feeling vulnerable and physically ill by the end of 1952, and, as usual, he saw portents. One of the fathers had had a breakdown. "Big, dark, quiet kid, so completely good and simple, and so perfect a monk! He was one who loved the woods a lot."[294]

Many were leaving Gethsemani at the time for medical reasons.

Merton went back over his own periods of nervous and emotional exhaustion:

> Since my retreat I have been having another one of those nervous breakdowns. The same old familiar business, I am getting used to it now — since the old days in 1936 when I thought I was going to crack up on the Long Island Rail-road and the more recent one since ordination. And now this.[295]

There was a certain degree of self-dramatization in this, but the doctor Merton was seeing was certainly concerned about him. Dr. Law had been advising him during the summer to found an order of his own because "it was useless to introduce something new in the Trappists." By December, the doctor's advice had changed to "Don't wait thirty years: go *now*."[296]

*

Certain givens are implicit in the situation in the early 1950s. Unless these are understood there will be serious distortions. There were things Dom James could do as abbot, and there were others that were beyond his power. There were also actions Merton could take and initiatives that would mean a break with his vows.

Both men were bound by the vow of stability to the community. Transfers to other orders were possible, but the "transitus" was unusual in 1952. The professed monk had to have the permission of the abbot general of the order he was leaving as well as that of the order he was joining. As Merton says, "By making a vow of stability the monk renounces the vain hope of wandering off to find a 'perfect monastery.'"[297]

It was a more perfect solitude he was seeking. Merton admitted in his journals that when he was in the novitiate he had not found the hermits of the Cistercian Order very attractive: "They seemed to have died before even finding out what they were supposed to achieve."[298]

He was well aware of the irony that he was writing this on the day St. Conrad, one of the hermits of the Order, was being commemorated. He had spent eleven years reminding the Trappists they were a contemplative order. Now he read everything he could find on St. Conrad of Palestine, St. Galgan, St. Firmian, and others so he could remind the Cistercians there had once been Cistercian hermits.

There was nothing in the Rule of St. Benedict that could be used to show anything other than that the eremitical life should be the exception, open only to monks who had proved they could be trusted. St. Benedict *had* said the cenobite life, the life in community, was the more perfect. For all his searches, Merton could find no very recent examples, certainly not in the Cistercian Order of the Strict Observance. Still, the proof existed that it had been allowed in the past. Cistercian Usage, not the Rule, worked against the eremitical life in 1953 and Usage could be changed.

Dom James had already given Merton unusual permission within the Usage. The only way the abbot could allow his master of scholastics to become a full-time hermit was by first persuading the General Chapter of the Order. In 1952–53, Dom James was unwilling to do this. Yet by 1955 the abbot was ready to release Merton from being master of scholastics and he had won permission for him to be a hermit — under certain conditions. Instead, Merton became master of novices for ten years.

*

In 1959, while reading *The Years with Ross*, James Thurber's book on Harold Ross, the editor of *The New Yorker* and Thurber's boss, Merton told friends he was thinking of writing his own account of "The Years with James." [299] He never assembled the pieces, but in many ways he wrote the book. Where Merton forfeited the monastic anonymity Dom James so often talked about, he took his abbot with him.

The relationship between Dom James Fox and Thomas Merton is so all-encompassing that it has to be treated separately, though in ranging over the twenty years with both men some points must be made which can only be proved later, in the right chronological order. During most of this period, and certainly from 1955 to 1965, they were the most important men in the monastery, for if the prior is, as it were, the second officer, it is the master of novices who has the higher responsibility. Had Thomas Merton been as neurotic, quixotic, and generally unpredictable as he has been portrayed at times, no one as shrewd as Dom James would have entrusted him with the post of either master of scholastics or master of novices. Nor, for that matter, would the abbot have chosen Father Louis as his confessor. Whatever difficulties the two men had in working together, the plain fact is that they managed to do so, and in years when other foundations were virtually destroyed by personality clashes.

"Dom James," Dom John Eudes Bamberger says, "selected some very remarkable men and he kept them at the monastery. He put them in positions and he allowed them to do what they did best." [300] Only one thing needs to be added to this statement — not only was Merton one of these "remarkable men," he had also trained many of the others.

An outsider trying to be fair to both men can see that Dom James could have been an exasperating superior, just as he can see that Father Louis could have been an infuriating subordinate. But great damage is done by thinking of the situation in the alien terms of a company, and of a boss and his senior executive.

An abbot of a monastery has power which can best be compared to that of the captain of a ship at sea. "Dom" means "Lord." A master of novices can make or break the monastery. Each of the two men brought remarkable talents to his office, and each was unusually successful. Between them there developed what one of the most astute observers within the monastery has called "a game more dangerous than either of them knew." The game became more and more involved as the years went on. But where there was a fault in this, it was one they shared, as, again in fairness, they shared the success at Gethsemani.

The story of Dom James and Thomas Merton is therefore a good deal more interesting than it has been presented. The bitterness of some of Merton's writing, especially in the late, unpublished journals, and his very real grounds of complaint notwithstanding, Merton admitted on many occasions that he "needed Dom James."

To see what happened as a straightforward conflict, or to allot roles like tyrant and victim, is to falsify. Dom James was not a natural tyrant. Merton was not a natural victim. But two roles *are* implicit in the monastic situation. Both were emphasized by the conception Dom James held of them. "Abba" means "Father." "Father Abbot" is a doubling of the same obvious point. The abbot is in a special sense the father, and the monks are his children. One does not have to go very deeply into psychology here to justify talk of father figures.

In Dom James's opinion, he was a true father. When he retired, Dom James felt Merton had a brotherly relationship with the new abbot. Perhaps. It is enough that Dom James sought to be the father in every sense, for there to be a complication in Merton's case. It was not the beloved and fallible father who had provided the early control in his life. It was the mother who had been the figure of authority, the setter of rules, the disciplinarian, the perfectionist in character forming. According to Dom James, Merton was overanxious for approval and affection because he had been denied both early in life. Merton's problems stemmed from not having a large, stable, affectionate, Catholic family. Certainly Merton told Dom James a good deal about his early days, and Dom James came to his own conclusions.

Something of all this made for complications at a deep level. But one can become too complicated. The two men would have found themselves on quite separate lines in any conceivable situation. One of the difficulties was Merton's own attitude to authority. This was ambiguous at the deepest level. He was rebellious by nature, a born critic and changer, and yet he sought to appease. He was anxious for approval. He could occasionally be subservient, as we will see in other matters than his conflict with Dom James. In his desire to identify with others, he often went more than halfway, which sometimes led to what can only be called "a confusion of roles."

He was a rebel who won and kept a reputation for obedience. Dom James told many in Merton's lifetime that Father Louis was "a most faithful monk, a most obedient monk." Perhaps this is simply consistent with much of the advice Merton gave others who rebelled: to be prudent, to be certain they were not simply advancing their own ego in the struggle — to be human. The rebel who is anxious to keep to the rules of a common humanity with his opponents is rare. Such a person can all too easily look like a coward at one moment and a hero above heroism the next.

To return to the other side of the equation, Dom James's attitude toward his authority: if "Power tends to corrupt and absolute power corrupts absolutely," as the Catholic historian Lord Acton held,[301] it would be hard for most abbots to set aside some pleasure in receiving absolute obedience. Or, as one of the monks put it: "How could the abbot *not* get some satisfaction from the sight of several professed monks prostrate before him in his office confessing they had eaten some food brought from the outside?" Perhaps this is trivial. Yet it is often the trivial that hurts most, inside the monastery and out.

The conflicts Merton had with Dom James were not open. They could not be, because it was in the very nature of James Fox to avoid open conflict, to turn away wrath with a smile, to dissolve all surface rancor and strife in sweetness. It was the sweetness — the word is carefully chosen — that drove Thomas Merton to distraction at times, or to a more bitter level of comment in his journals. It also drives him to celebrating open warfare at moments, honest arguments with Brother Clement, the cellarer, and Father Raymond, the rival writer. Dom James, however sweetly spoken and smiling, could be ruthless.

Thomas Merton could be brutal, at least in his writing for himself. Just how brutal he could be will be clear when the later journals are published, though there will be some quotations here. Yet it is essential to add that Merton often follows pages of savage sarcasm and invective with remorse for what he has written, attempted amends, an effort to restore balance.

This was Merton's way in many things — write on until it comes right. One mechanical thing must be mentioned again because it aided Merton's intention. He used bound ledgers for his journal writing, spiral notebooks for his notes on reading and lectures. A ledger shows torn-out pages, and Merton tore out many in the early journals. Writing for himself later, he felt this was to falsify. If he worked up a journal for publication, he could pick and choose passages. Thus, pages criticizing Dom James may be followed by the simple admission that, in this case, the abbot had proved a better judge of men or of the situation than Merton. But the early comments are still there. No effort of will on the part of the reader can erase them from the memory. And in this, it has to be stated that, where the two men are in conflict, Merton now has the singularly unfair advantage.

The main contention between James Fox and Thomas Merton was over trust. As we have already seen, Dom James trusted Father Louis within the monastery and he showed that trust. He did not trust Merton outside the enclosure walls. In time the abbot showed trust in others. He made his lack of confidence in Father Louis all too obvious to Merton, and nothing rankled Merton more than this.

Dom James was overprotective, not only of Merton, but especially of Merton. He had a strict interpretation of the vow of stability, based both on his understanding of his spiritual responsibilities as an abbot and on something in his own character. It is very likely he shared one thing with Thomas Merton — the fear of rejection. Many of those who left the monastery by their own choice talk of Dom James's almost tearful insistence that they stay. One former lay brother said it was almost impossible not to return the abbot's affection with affection. He had never before met a man who was clearly not a homosexual who could be so loving. Yet when the brother came to leave, and would not be persuaded to stay, the abbot could not bless him, and would only warn him to get married at once.[302] Dom James made it clear that life within the walls of Gethsemani was one of freely accepted suffering and penitential grace, while beyond the enclosure walls, there was little hope any man could survive temptation, and the chief trouble was women. Others have confirmed that the greatest and most immediate risk Dom James saw for the monk outside the enclosure was women.

Earlier, Dom Frederic may have used many of the same arguments about a life of penitential grace freely accepted at the time he was persuading Merton to stay and take Solemn Vows. Merton was now a professed monk with many years in the monastery, not a novice or a lay brother uncertain whether he had a true vocation. He was also a free man who had freely chosen his own spiritual destiny. It is necessary to say this because Dom James's determination to keep Father Louis at Gethsemani has brought forth another kind of overprotectiveness of Merton among those who most resented the abbot's intransigence. Merton was constrained to stay only by his own will and his determination to be obedient to the vows he had freely taken. Put bluntly, he could have walked out of the monastery at any time. There were those who did this ("going A.W.O.L.," as Dom James called it), as well as those who left more formally.

Dom James had to persuade Father Louis to stay, just as Merton thought it essential to gain permission if he was going to leave the monastery. The abbot always argued that it was essential for Merton's spiritual life, to his salvation, for him to remain at Gethsemani and in obedience to his vow of stability. Less supernatural motives have been read into this, and it is necessary to examine these, even if some of the inferences are insulting to Dom James. Merton was an asset. He had brought souls to the Order. He brought a great deal of money to the monastery. He was an experienced and valuable member of the community as a teacher and as a spiritual adviser, as master of scholastics and as master of novices. Nobody as realistic as Dom James was likely to overlook or underrate any of these points. As abbot, he had a responsibility for the welfare of the monastery as a whole. With Dom James this responsibility was obsessive, but *not* to the point where it overcame his spiritual responsibility to his monks.

It is quite right to view with healthy skepticism somebody else's (even, or especially, a natural father's) claim that he knows better than you do what is best for you in life — at least when you are of an age to know your own mind. Merton had been trained to accept this from a spiritual adviser, though there were certainly times when he sought other advice than his abbot's or his confessor's on a matter. Dom James was clear in his own mind that he knew Father Louis better than anyone. He was sincere in thinking he knew what was best for Merton, not only in life, but for Merton's eternal life. And he was consistent. A time would come when others in the Order would wonder whether Merton was an asset or a liability. Dom James never doubted. He was just as determined that Merton's place was in the Order and at Gethsemani.

In Dom James Fox the graduate of the Harvard Business School and the old-fashioned, deeply religious Catholic, Redemptorist, Trappist, are all effectively joined in one. In some ways he was an abbot of the old school; in other ways, an innovator. He pressed for reforms in the General Chapter to make the monks' clothing more practical. He instituted a far better method of screening applicants. He made several exceptions even in a strict reading of the vow of stability. He aided the intellectuals, and he came, cautiously, to ally himself with those who sought greater solitude as hermits. After his retirement in 1968, he became a hermit. This was not, as some have said, because Merton persuaded him against his own nature. Merton's influence as the abbot's confessor was important, and Dom James is on record as expressing his gratitude. Yet Dom James had always had a desire for solitude. (In his early writing on contemplation, Merton had overlooked the case of the active administrator who tries to make room for solitude and who may be just as frustrated in this as the active writer.)

During his years as Abbot of Gethsemani, James Fox proved to be a man of deep conviction and a brilliant pragmatist. As is often the case, his innovations got him into more trouble at the monastery than his intransigence. Merton might feel he was the only professed monk who was never allowed out in the 1960s (though Dom James did make one concession in this regard). Others felt quite different rules were being bent for Father Louis. Dom James found his critics in the ranks of the conservative older monks who had been formed in the French tradition, as well as among the younger monks.

Father M. Louis Merton had had seven formative years in the French monastic tradition under an abbot he greatly revered. He was better read than most in the tradition itself, in the writings of John Cassian and many others. He was by no means always on the radical wing with the younger monks.

If Dom James could be calculating and coldly authoritarian at times, he displayed an underlying, spontaneous warmth. He also showed a sense of the humanity in the other person that was surprisingly close to Merton's own. Intransigent in his conception of leadership in the Church in difficult times, often open to persuasion, a conservative who initiated and brought about astonishing reforms in the Order, the Abbot of Gethsemani between August 1948 and January 1968 proved both rigid and unpredictable.

In the twenty years they were together their conflict became a source of energy, of tribulation, and of undermining the true purpose of both men. Finally, Thomas Merton and James Fox were not enemies. There survived beyond all this a mutual respect and even a deep, if guarded and sorely bruised, affection.

In June 1949 there was "Another protocol from Chop Suey Louie the mad chinese poet" to "My very dear Reverend Father," renewing his vows and his promise of obedience.[303] On October 20, 1968, Merton wrote from Calcutta to "Dear Fr. James":

> I never personally resented any of your decisions, because I knew you were following your conscience and the policies that seemed necessary then. It is also true, that the new "openness" might lead to abuses and deviations. I am not responsible for what others do, but I certainly want to make sure that whatever I do, is really for a spiritual goal, and for the good of the Church and of Monastic life.

In the next to last paragraph he says:

> Be sure that I have never changed in my respect for you as Abbot, and affection as Father. Our different views certainly did not affect our deep agreement on the real point of life and of our vocation.[304]

*

Merton had been almost disappointed when he recorded in the journal that Dom James was not thinking of him to lead the new foundation in Ohio, but when Dom James said the time would come when one foundation or another would certainly elect him as their abbot, he took alarm.[305] By this time he was anxious to block any ambitions of his own in this direction. Dom James says Father Louis told him there was a bar to his being abbot of any monastery and his reason "was serious enough."[306] In the enthusiasm of the moment, Dom James pointed out, Merton might forget and accept.

With the permission of the abbot and of Dom Gabriel, and on October 8, 1952, Merton made a private vow that "as long as I live I will never accept any election to the office of Abbot or Titular Prior either in this monastery or any other monastery of the Cistercian Order."[307]

Merton's writing now took an unexpected direction. He was exploring something familiar to most contemplatives in the East and some in the West, which has become generally known with different degrees of seriousness in the past thirty years. He needed some form of activity not too demanding in itself, yet which served to center the mind and to prevent distractions. Father Matthew Kelty says he found weaving helpful, both in the monastery and experimental community at Oxford, North Carolina, and, later, in his hermitage in New Guinea.[308] In one of his conferences, Merton encouraged the monks to have some manual activity of this kind. He talked of weaving baskets and of the Desert Fathers.[309] The writer is usually at a disadvantage here. In the visual arts, Merton found both calligraphic drawing and photography provided what he needed, but this was ten years later. In 1952–53, he returned to the very passage he had read in the *Spiritual Directory* which had once left him cold:

> . . . the Holy Mass, the Divine Office, Prayer and pious reading which form the exercises of the contemplative life occupy the major part of our day.[310]

"The *exercises* of the contemplative life" . . . Merton had left pious reading when he left the novitiate, and he later described the difference between pious reading and religious reading.[311] He saw the Mass as the central point of his day. His book *The Living Bread*, which appeared in 1956,[312] examines the immediate sense of Christ and a realization of eucharistic life. Yet it was in this period particularly that he turned to the Divine Office, to the liturgy. The Divine Office can be, and is, said by the individual, but Merton brings a very un-eremitical cast to his writing, praising the public liturgy.

Merton had been reading the Bible and especially the psalms with a new insight and enthusiasm for two years. Anxious to share this with others, it is in what he writes about the sung liturgy that he makes a clear return to monastic, communal values, and this is certainly unexpected. Liturgical prayer, he tells us, does not speak of what is beyond us, it speaks of what already is, what we already *are:*

> It will tell us over and over again that we are Christ in this world, and that He lives in us, and that what was said of Him has been and is being fulfilled in us: and that the last, most perfect fulfillment of all is now, at this moment, by the theological virtue of hope, placed in our hands. Thus the liturgy of earth is necessarily one with the Liturgy of heaven. We are at the same time in the desert and in the Promised Land. The Psalms are our Bread of Heaven in the wilderness of our Exodus.[313]

There are many passages as fine as this in *Bread in the Wilderness*, which was published in December 1953,[314] as well as in Merton's other writings on the liturgy and the psalms.

It is a good thing to be reminded that the psalms are not only great poetry, but among the greatest. Yet there is something strange here. Tapes of Merton's conferences began to be made in the early 1960s. At Dom James's instigation, the tapes on the monastic life were played in the lay brothers' novitiate at a time when many were leaving Gethsemani. The abbot felt the tapes would persuade those who were tempted away to stay. Some of the lay brothers were considerably confused: the speaker was extolling the life in the community, yet by that time Father Louis had withdrawn to the margins of the community.[315]

Tape recorders (not to mention books) can extend the thinker's ideas into contexts not of his or her choosing. Reading Merton's writing at this time and knowing the direction in which he was struggling to go himself sometimes gives the reader the same sense as the baffled lay brother in the 1960s.

The Last of the Fathers: Saint Bernard of Clairvaux and the Encyclical Letter, Doctor Mellifluus, was not a book Merton wanted to write. St. Bernard of Clairvaux had died on August 20, 1153. The papal encyclical came out on the Feast of Pentecost of 1953, and Merton had been commissioned by the Order to write the book, which appeared on June 3, 1954.[316] He complained of the commission a year earlier, writing at St. Anne's, where the only other distraction from what he wanted to write came from the squirrels working noisily in the walls.

Merton praises the encyclical for restoring the portrait of the great Cistercian who had suffered "fragmentation at the hands of his own fame"[317] — a phrase that might speak eloquently to Merton's own fate.

There are important points in the book. Merton draws a distinction between sentimental sweetness, or false piety, and true, unselfconscious sweetness of doctrine, disciplined in the monastic life. He repeats the phrase that the monastery is a paradise of charity. The problem is, of course, whether one regards St. Bernard of Clairvaux, the ardent advocate of the Second Crusade, as sweet and honied in doctrine or in much else. He was certainly a great writer and an exceptional man. He was no Grey Eminence, yet Merton must have recalled the notes he had made on Huxley's book at St. Bonaventure. There are certain telling failures of nerve in Merton's book-length essay on Bernard of Clairvaux. He was to be more objective and more comfortable in the essay "From Pilgrimage to Crusade," reprinted in *Mystics and Zen Masters* (1967). When he spoke of the battles between Bernard of Clairvaux and Peter Abelard in his conferences for the novices, he said he preferred the man of passion, Abelard.[318]

Bernard was hardly a man without passion of his own. If Merton sides with Abelard, it shows he favored one kind of passion against another, and there are enough connections with Merton's own life to make the tapes a good deal more interesting than the book.

The next book of Merton's to appear demonstrated both kinds of passion. *No Man Is an Island*[319] is too rich and full to be discussed briefly. It is also the most paradoxical of all Merton's books. He sets out in search of ways to test and establish reality — in love of ourselves, love of others, love of God. Where the real is the goal, there is often a curious air of unreality. It extends the paradox to say that in parts of the book the real is very real. By contrast, the search often dissolves into mere words. One example will have to suffice: this is surely a very abstract call for the concrete!

> The truth I love in loving my brother cannot be something merely phil-osophical and abstract. It must be at the same time supernatural and concrete, practical and alive. And I mean these words in no metaphori-cal sense. The truth I must love in my brother is God Himself, living in him. I must seek the life of the Spirit of God breathing in him. And I can only discern and follow that mysterious life by the action of the same Holy Spirit living and acting in the depths of my own heart.[320]

There are many references to fires in the Gethsemani woods in the journals. On a late afternoon in August 1953, the cowbarn burnt to the ground. The monks were in the abbey church during the meditation after Vespers when the alarm was given. Merton was among the first to reach the scene, and he threw himself into trying to save the barn. In a letter to Mark Van Doren, he said the barn "burned down in a little over twenty minutes or half an hour — like a pile of brush."[321] He says elsewhere that the poem arrived at about the same time as the local fire department. The other monks remember only a show of en-ergy that was exceptional even for Father Louis.[322]

"Elegy for the Monastery Barn" may not have been the first new poem Merton had written after a long silence in poetry, but it was an impor-tant beginning.[323] When Mark Van Doren and his wife Dorothy visited Gethsemani in September 1957, the two friends talked of the poem on their walk to the site, and then of how much they both enjoyed fires, a sort of atavistic joy in the fiery destruction.[324] Something of this comes into the poem. The barn revealed herself as an unexpectedly vain and beautiful woman welcoming her destructive lover, fire. The two meet in a frenzy of energy, a dance.

As abbey forester, Merton had the responsibility for the monastery woods, where brush fires had been all too frequent. The county offi-cials had built a fire tower on top of Vineyard Knob and were anxious to have it manned. It became a question whether they or the monas-tery would provide the staff to maintain the tower.

It was in this context that Dom James approached the abbot general and the General Chapter of the Order, seeking permission for Merton to become a hermit. Nineteen fifty-five was another year of crisis over stability for Merton, and the abbot was anxious to resolve the question of Merton's need for solitude at Gethsemani. Dom James was also more sympathetic than he had been in 1952 to the idea of Father Louis be-coming a hermit. Dom Gabriel saw a solution here. If Father Louis wanted to be a hermit and if the county wanted a full-time fire watcher at Vineyard Knob, why not combine the two roles?[326]

This was the proposition presented to Merton when the abbot returned, at the height of the stability crisis. The condition was that Merton was to remain on duty at the hermitage at the top of the fire tower virtually the whole time, coming to the monastery for daily Mass and one meal a day. The idea had a real appeal to Merton at first: he had spent hours watching the hawks from the top of the tower. But the more he thought about it, the more it seemed like the play-drama of the summer of 1940 over Frater John Spaniard. It "made a pleasant picture." Did it mean any more? Was it serious?

Merton was probably right, yet the county was serious about having the tower properly manned. Dom James and Dom Gabriel may well have joked together at the General Chapter about Father Louis sitting on the top of his tower, but this was no elaborate joke at the expense of the would-be hermit.

The whole matter was probably determined by something else. The fire tower on Vineyard Knob is some distance from the monastery — a good walk and a stiff climb. It would be essential for Father Louis to drive there and back in a jeep even if he was going to spend much of his time there. A second attempt was made to teach him how to drive.

The abbey mechanic had been working for two weeks on one of the jeeps, repairing and repainting it. He drove Father Louis round behind the woodshed, explaining as he went how the clutch worked, how to turn, how to brake. Then he stopped and got out, and Father Louis took control.

Merton got up a good speed, though he did not use the clutch properly when changing gears. He failed to turn on the first corner and rammed the jeep at such speed into a post that the post ran right through the radiator. In thirty seconds he had undone the work of two weeks. The brother mechanic cursed him out of the yard. There were no Cistercian hand signals on this occasion. The mechanic used "sound." Whether he was proclaimed in Chapter for this or not is not recorded.[327]

Merton would have to walk (and climb) to the fire tower. His talk of St. Simeon Stylites took a less humorous and more bitter ring.

He told the abbot he had had second thoughts. The position of master of novices had just become open, and Merton asked the abbot to appoint him.

Dom James was astonished. He had worked hard to get Father Louis what he said he wanted. To the abbot this was a major failure of nerve on Merton's part.[328] Having almost attained the solitude he had been talking about for at least seven years, Merton backed off.

There may be something in this, even if it is not the whole story. When Merton was given a hermitage of his own ten years later, he approached the matter of being a full-time hermit with considerable care, asking his friends to pray for him. The letters of 1965 show Merton facing something with fear, rather than hesitancy, yet doing so in a way that demonstrated both courage and a self-deprecating sense of humor.

By that time Merton knew that the hermit who is not on good terms with himself is on the way to disaster. In 1955, Merton was not on good enough terms to live in solitude on the top of the fire tower on Vineyard Knob or anywhere else.

Still, one can have some sympathy for the abbot. The county provided the fire watcher on Vineyard Knob. Father Louis became the second most responsible man in the monastery. It must have relieved Dom James to know that this resolved the stability crisis, at least for a time.

Merton had written in May of 1955 to friends in Rome and had felt confident he would be allowed to go to the Carthusians. When a letter from Dom Jean Leclercq arrived discouraging him from this course,[329] he changed his mind and applied to go to the Frascati. This request was refused by the Secretary of the Sacred Congregation, Monsignor Larroana, who advised him to wait for a few years.

In the middle of a later crisis over where he should be, Merton decided:

> What could have been very simple was turned into a sickeningly complicated and futile jamboree, partly through my own fault, and partly through the stubborn and adroit politics of my superiors.[330]

In Dom John Eudes's view, Merton was a better master of scholastics than he was master of novices. He feels that, though Merton was an excellent teacher and stirred enthusiasm, yet he was a little too idealistic about the capabilities of his novices. He tended to think the novices had the same frustrations with solitude he had, and so he let them have free time, believing they had the self-discipline and direction to use it as he would have done.[331]

Some of the times his ex-novices remember best were days when the novice master took them to plant trees in the Gethsemani woods. His own enthusiasm for being away from his desk spread to the class. They learned the names of trees, plants, and birds. On two hot days he went searching for a good pond for them all to go swimming in. Word of this reached the abbot and it was stopped.

Formalities were a good deal relaxed in most work periods, though Merton was not one to encourage either chatter or excuses. Once he had assigned work, he got on with his own. He could be very cold indeed if a novice broke his concentration to ask for details of an assignment.[332]

There was as much laughter in his classes as there had been with the scholastics. The humor tended to be broader, and he relied more on his gift for miming, and linking incidents at the monastery to an anecdote about his own past.

One way or another, the novices and the scholastics had learned a good deal about Merton's past, both from him directly and from his books. There was an unwritten rule in the monastery, however, against making direct references to his published work. There was a strong reticence in Merton, though he certainly preferred to have his authorship acknowledged in understatement than ignored altogether. When *Seeds of Contemplation* was read out in the evening's meditation, many of the professed monks did not know it was by Father Louis.[333]

The experience of his novices was very different from Merton's own in the novitiate. Perhaps it was just as well he took them out into the woods so often to plant trees; there were far too many breakdowns among the newly joined monks in the early fifties. The "country doctoring" and the idea that all a sick monk needed to become well was permission to eat eggs were not working out.

John Eudes Bamberger had been to medical school at the University of Cincinnati, where he had earned his M.D., and had done postdoctoral work at Georgetown University Hospital. When he entered the monastery in 1950 he had brought with him as few medical supplies as Thomas Merton had brought books and notebooks. He had set aside the ambition to be a doctor in the world to enter a closed Order and to become a priest. He was reluctant, therefore, when Father Louis suggested he ask the abbot if John Eudes could take over the infirmary from Father Anselm, though he says he found it "a great Grace to be working among the older monks." His main impression, however, was that there were too many nervous and digestive complaints among the new arrivals. When he talked to Dom James and to Father Louis about the need for someone to practice pastoral psychology at the monastery, he found both shared his anxiety. Dom James readily agreed when Father John Eudes suggested that he take a residency to complete his training. In view of the need for screening candidates and for helping those with problems, psychiatric training seemed necessary. Father Louis was anxious to encourage John Eudes: he was already deep in new studies himself.[334]

On June 16, 1956, Merton had written to James Laughlin:

> Most of the time now I think about psychoanalysis, since it is important to my job (Master of Novices). I am trying to learn how to give the Rorschach test. Such fun. But it takes a lot of time. You knew, didn't you, that I am now Master of Novices?[335]

Later that summer, Merton struck a more troubled note. He looked back in his journals and saw that what had been "such fun" in theory had not always worked out well in practice:

> I learned lately that one of the novices whom we thought neurotic and who was indeed disturbed, was disturbed largely by the fears and illusions that had arisen in his relations with me — he became very upset

fancying that I demanded that he be a brilliant and complicated person
(which is what he fancies me to be) and I enhanced this illusion by not
giving him time to talk about himself, but always delivering the diagnosis
before he had even had a chance to tell me all the symptoms. This, while
beating him down and making him very insecure, also stimulated a desperate search for more "symptoms" so that I would deliver more and more
Godlike diagnoses. Finally, in a culmination of stupidity, I even gave him
the Rorschach Test (I had been encouraged in this by Dr. Kisker) and interpreted it all wrong. I will say this — that I could see at once my interpretation was useless. I hope I have learned a lot from all this. It was a
great relief and liberation to admit my stupidity. I am sobered by the
thought (again) of my great capacity to do harm as a Father Master! And
I see how much, really, we depend on the grace of God to make up for
our mistakes and draw good out of evil! What motives for peace, and
confidence, and praise![336]

The only comment one can make to this is that it was certainly a good
thing that the "doctor" recovered: one still has some worries for the
patient.

Merton was using most of his new skills on himself. A somewhat
nervous self-analysis seems to be the beginning of all such study. After
the stability crisis of the year before, Merton was more worried about
himself than usual, and those who visited him caught these concerns.
For the first time, Merton seems to have dropped his usual ebullience
and gaiety. Naomi Burton went back to New York after a spring visit
to Gethsemani deeply worried about him.[337]

His reading in the early spring of 1956 was even more eclectic than
usual. In the reading notebooks, lists of books on China are preceded
by full notes on Gandhi's non-violence, which were to be turned in time
into a book. There were many quotations from Karen Horney's *New
Ways in Psychoanalysis*. Merton copied out the passages where "narcissism" appears in the text. He largely agreed with Horney's criticism of
Freud. Where Agostino Gemelli, a critic of Jung, said in *Psychoanalysis
Today* that priests should abstain from engaging in psychoanalysis,
leaving it to trained psychologists, Merton noted this but ignored the
warning, as we have seen. He was using his own notes for an essay,
"Neurosis in the Monastic Life."[338] Copies went out to a number of
friends for their comments.

When Robert Giroux suggested sending the essay to Dr. Gregory Zilboorg, who was another of the authors at Harcourt, Brace, Merton wrote
enthusiastically to Naomi Burton giving permission, and saying he would
be in touch with Zilboorg himself. Zilboorg's comments would be especially helpful.[339]

Already an analyst of wide reputation, Gregory Zilboorg was com-
manding a great deal of attention at the time. His recent conversion
had made him something of a new interest in Catholic circles and well

beyond those of his fellow psychoanalysts. He was a man of even more dramatic presence than Dom Gabriel Sortais. He had once been an actor, and his manner showed this. Born and trained in Russia, he had been a member of the Kerensky government before finding refuge in the West and being awarded an M.D. by Columbia. Zilboorg had built an impressive reputation among politicians in Washington during the Second World War. He had treated Hemingway and a number of other writers and artists. In his own profession, he was a respected if controversial figure, and by 1956, he was at the height of a remarkable career.

He was, then, the obvious choice of those who were concerned about Merton. Giroux already knew Zilboorg as one of his authors. Naomi Burton had not met him, but knew of him through mutual friends. When it turned out that Zilboorg was anxious to meet Merton for a number of reasons, it was decided to get in touch with Dom James to ask if Merton could come to New York to see him.[340]

Dom James was not at all enthusiastic about the idea of Father Louis going to New York to see anyone. But he had his own anxieties, both with Father Louis and the more general state of things at the monastery. When he discovered Gregory Zilboorg was to address a conference in July — a two-week workshop in psychiatry and its practical application to the religious life — at St. John's University in Collegeville, Minnesota, this seemed the answer to a number of difficulties. Visitors from the religious life would be housed at the abbey at St. John's. Dom James arranged with Abbot Baldwin that not only would Father Louis and Father John Eudes be coming to the conference, but that he would be there himself in the second week, seeking practical advice on how to deal with the problems at the monastery.

This was hardly a trap or a set-up.[341] The meetings between Zilboorg and Merton were to have enormous repercussions in Merton's life, yet nobody, except perhaps Gregory Zilboorg himself, could have foreseen this. Robert Giroux was concerned that Zilboorg seemed to have some preconceptions about Merton even before the meeting at St. John's. In New York, Zilboorg said he had already analyzed Merton from his published writings. He felt confident he knew what the trouble was. The psychologist was certainly out to quash the publication of "Neurosis in the Monastic Life." Zilboorg clearly looked upon this as a case of academic or professional poaching, but he was probably quite right in thinking Merton's reputation might be seriously damaged by such an amateur entry into a scientific field, even if Giroux sensed there was a good deal of the rival writer in Zilboorg's attitude.[342] There may also have been another kind of rivalry: both men were converts, both were Catholic culture heroes — in the eyes of others, if not in their own. Zilboorg would certainly have sensed this aspect.

There is, then, plenty of evidence that Gregory Zilboorg was in no state of objectivity when he went to St. John's.[343] His first concern was to deal with somebody he regarded as a dangerous quack. The pre-conception affected Zilboorg's handling of the situation from the first. Yet it was not groundless. By his own admission in the journals, and leaving aside the essay, Merton had gone too far. His experiments had probably made a bad situation worse for some of the novices. Zilboorg was also astute in his analysis of Merton's work. Perhaps it takes an egotist to recognize disguised egotism. The experience for Thomas Merton was traumatic, but liberating. Yet Zilboorg made one mistake in his handling, which was to make for further, and unnecessary, com-plications in Merton's life.

On July 22, 1956, Fathers John Eudes and Louis set off by plane from Louisville. Merton tried to decide in which of the houses below a boy would be born who would become a bishop, and in which a murder had been committed. Then he imagined what the world would look like from above when the trees had again taken over:

> I do not commit myself, though. I am perhaps still on the side of the trees.[344]

He found it strange to pray in such an atmosphere. It was difficult, too, to write a poem. The result, the first "on or above the clouds" is almost illegible in his notebook. "White Pastures" was something new, a free-form poem of moving in space and time. He would return to this in his last journey, but he had made a beginning before Ginsberg and others, in this kind of poetry.

Even before he left, Merton had seen the journey in somewhat som-ber and foreboding colors. He had been reading the passages in Julien Green's journals in which Green says that between the lines of what a man writes in his journal there is a prophecy of the future.[345] There was certainly something about Merton's own journal that made it seem ominous when he looked over an earlier line to find he had written "With Father Philip and several other morts . . . going to an enterre-ment . . .":

> So maybe the plane to Minnesota will crash after all![346]

It is not so much the fear of flying itself, but the odd sense of vul-nerability in air travel, in airports as well as planes, that affects so many people. To that must be added, in Merton's case, how it would feel after fifteen years to be moving about among strangers in a world that had been transformed.

At St. John's Abbey, Merton found himself in a pleasant room with a small porch that looked out over lawns shaded by firs. Beyond the buildings there was a glimpse of a large lake, and he could hear the sounds of water birds. He was less happy to see signs of his old en-emy the yellow caterpillar tractor.[347]

At supper, he and Dr. Zilboorg exchanged greetings, no more. The Rule of Silence had been relaxed for the conference. Merton was tempted to go into a why-I-became-a-Trappist routine with each person he met, but resisted it. For fifteen years, while eating in the refectory, he had listened to the voice of the monk reading from the lectern.

The lectures were stimulating, and Merton took full notes. During the discussion after Gregory Zilboorg's first address, he rose to ask, "How do you define the disfunction of a neurotic?" Zilboorg fixed him with a close look for several seconds, then said: "Science does not start with its definition but ends with it."[348]

There was plenty of time in the early morning before conferences started to escape to the lake to say Prime, to watch the water lilies, and to observe a pair of loons diving. Merton took off his shoes and walked barefoot on the pine needles, as he liked to do in the woods at Gethsemani. He was reading Suzuki and Diadochos of Photike, seeing something of a bond between the two writers — the Zen warnings against "mirror polishing," and in the *Centuries* of Diadochos:

> The abyss of faith boils if you examine it; but if you look upon it in simplicity, it becomes once again calm. For being a river of Lethe in which evils are forgotten, the depths of faith do not bear to be looked upon with indiscreet reasonings. Let us therefore sail upon its waters with simplicity of thought in order to reach thus the harbor of the divine will.[349]

On July 27, on the isthmus of birch trees, he drafted in his notebook the first version of what he called an "Exercise," as if he was unsure of it. In his book *Thomas Merton, Monk and Poet*, George Woodcock makes the useful distinction of Merton's poetry into "choir" and "desert" poems.[350] "In Silence" is the first of the desert poems. It begins:

> Be still
> Listen to the stones of the wall
> Be silent, they try
> To speak your
>
> Name.
> Listen
> To the living walls.
> Who are you?
> Who
> Are you? Whose
> Silence are you?[351]

He had tried to explain Zen to Dr. Howard Phillips Rome and John Eudes one night at table. He found very few people knew much about Zen. At the monastery even Father Augustine Wulff, who was so knowledgeable about Eastern writings, had been confused by his references in conferences and had asked "What's this Zen you go on and on about? I've known about Buddhism since I was twelve or fourteen, but what's Zen Buddhism?"[352]

Something had gone wrong in the conversation with Dr. Rome, and Merton had found Dr. Gregory Zilboorg glaring at him.[353] Dr. Rome's own lecture on dependence on July 25 had been enormously helpful. Rereading his notes, Merton had the impression Dr. Rome had said things that came very close to describing both Merton's own struggles with the abbot, and his difficulties as novice master with some of his own novices:

> Penitents seduce you into taking *on the role of omnipotence and omniscience* — and in this situation while you are deluding yourself you also approve the things they want you to approve.[354]

Merton wrote that he had discovered a great many things from the lectures, among them: "Don't let the whole thing immediately get intellectualized — to do so is to destroy your chance of doing good" . . . "I had completely obscured and failed to see the difference between a character problem and a real neurosis" . . . "The dependent person — is really *unable to collaborate.*"[355]

It looked as if he had been trying to manipulate a situation of dependence for his own ends, using obedience to persuade Dom James to do what he wanted done. And so it had been in the reverse situation with several of his novices. In neither case was this true collaboration, a way of working together to find whatever truth there was in a situation, or of seeking God's will when making a decision.

He had talked only very briefly to Zilboorg so far. Gregory Zilboorg had told him the article on "Neurosis in the Monastic Life" was "utterly inadequate, hastily written, will do harm, should not even be revised, should be left on the shelf while I read — not Rank, or any other analyst — but Freud. And especially (this astonishes me) Freud's works *against* religion. This is very interesting — they were the last thing I would have bothered with."[356]

On Friday night Merton and John Eudes went to St. Cloud to have dinner with the novelist J. F. Powers. It was an evening Merton remembered, especially his approach to the first family scene he had known in years:

> And when we came into the small ancient red wooden house there was a procession of little girls holding up in their two hands large schooners of beer for the guests of their Father.[357]

The group ate on the porch by candlelight, drinking sauterne and eating shrimp. There was a good deal of laughter when Merton's Roman collar kept coming loose and flipping up under his chin. Merton tried to hold the conversation to literature. He felt John Eudes went on rather too long about prayer and seemed to be putting Powers on the spot. The novelist impressed Merton as "a mixture of dryness and spontaneity, a thin sensitive person whose vocation is to go through many unbearable experiences." In time Merton was to review Powers's novel, *Morte D'Urban*, and to enjoy his gift for satirizing the Catholic clergy:

> He portrays all the horror, all the tedium, all the frenzied inner protest of the extrovert who is reduced, in spite of himself, to living a plain religious life of poverty, monotony, and sacrifice.[358]

However, it was now Thomas Merton's turn to be satirized, and to his face. The private conference with Gregory Zilboorg on the morning of Monday, July 29, is of such importance that it would be best to quote from the two pages of the journal Merton wrote at noon on the same day.

> 1) It turns out *he* was the one who engineered my coming here — through Abbot Baldwin — partly because of the danger of the article being published and partly because he had sensed my own difficulties.
> 2) It turns out also — as I know — that I am in somewhat bad shape, and that I *am* neurotic — and that the difficulty of handling it right is very considerable. He has his own ideas about that — God alone knows if they are feasible.
> 3) Great extent of my dependence on words — I would hardly have imagined I used them in the way he said — but anyway, I can get some details on it. As substitutes for reality?
> 4) "You are a gadfly to your superiors."
> "Very stubborn — You keep coming back until you get what you want."
> "You are afraid to be an ordinary monk in the community."
> "You and Fr. Eudes can very easily become a pair of semi-pyschotic quacks."
> "Talking to Dr. Rome (about Zen) you thought only of yourself of using him as a source of information and of self-aggrandizement — you thought nothing at all of your priesthood, the apostolate, the Church, his soul."
> "You like to be famous, you want to be a big shot, you keep pushing your way out — into publicity — megalomania and narcissism are your big trends."
> Things which I knew and did not know. And I suppose this is just the trouble. I am quite capable of saying "I am a narcissist" and yet it changes nothing, it does not even help me to understand.
>
> While he said all this I thought "How much he looks like Stalin" but in reality I am tremendously relieved and grateful — and when I sung Mass with the monks I was praying hard to know what to do next and to do it.
>
> Some other things he said "Your hermit trend is pathological." "You are

a promoter — if you were not in a monastery you are the type that would clean up in Wall Street one day and lose it all on the horses the next." (I thought — there must be a lot of Pop in me after all. Was it Pop that said "Don't think! Act on hunches."?) When I asked what I had said wrong to Dr. Rome he said "You didn't say it but you conveyed it."

Then again he said "These are not things you can foresee, they are traps you fall into as you go along, and you don't realize it until after you are hurt."

I was thinking again — that where I am most "verbological" is in religion. But that seems to be because what is real for me in religion is what I never even try, any longer, to express. However, that is wrong. And in fact I do mean, and do hold, and do believe that the whole Church holds, means and believes, and it *is* real to me. Well — is it? Saying the office by the lake, at any rate, I paid attention to the *things said* by the words. Can I say these things without meaning them? But it is true, I can say them automatically — and often do.

Another thing he said — "It is not intelligence you lack, but affectivity" — meaning it is there but I have never let it get out — so that when the situation calls for it I either intellectualize — verbalize — or else go into a depression.

Again "It will do you no good to be forbidden to write — you need some silence and isolation, but it needs to be *prohibited* in your own heart — if it is merely forbidden, it will not seem prohibited to you . . . Yet your writing is now becoming verbological — but your words must be incarnate."

He said he had already told this to Bob Giroux.[359]

Merton escaped to the loons and the lake. Zilboorg had cautioned him not to speak to others of their conversation. If Merton broke this rule, so did Zilboorg, and Merton's letter to Naomi Burton the day after the first conference shows how quickly he had regained some of his resilience. He may have checked with Dr. Rome about the discussion he had had on Zen. At any rate, the other witness, John Eudes Bamberger, says that Zilboorg's account of the discussion was certainly exaggerated.[360] On July 30, Merton began by telling Naomi Burton that Zilboorg had been "terrific":

As for my own personal problems — clearly Zilboorg is the first one who has really shown conclusively that he knows exactly what is cooking. And something is, though not so serious, but serious enough to mess up my work and my vocation if it should get worse. He has told me more directly and more forcefully than I ever thought possible, the exact home-truths that need to be told, and I need not insist that the desire for absolute solitude has finally been disposed of completely and forever as pathological. Moderate isolation and silence, sure. OK. I will never give anyone any trouble about vocation or stability again, as long as I am in

my right mind. He has a solution, or a possibility, about which he intends to speak to Rev. Father.[361]

By July 30, the abbot had arrived for the last few days of the conference. When Merton wrote later that the stability crisis of 1955 had been
resolved by his own ineptitude and the "adroit politics of my superiors,"[362] he was most bitter about the part the abbot had played. By
July 1956, Merton knew of the letter Dom James had written to Cardinal Archbishop Montini on May 16, 1955, which implied that Father
Louis was temperamentally unstable, too artistically volatile to be entrusted with determining his own spiritual destiny. Dom James went
on to quote from the letter Father Barnabas Mary had written, not to
Dom James, but to Father Louis, about the harm a transfer would
cause.[363]

Merton had good cause, then, to beware of the use his abbot would
make of any evidence that he was "restless," "artistic," or in any other
way untrustworthy. In these circumstances it was very unfortunate that
Zilboorg called a second conference and discussed the "case" of Father
Louis in the presence of his abbot. At the second interview Gregory
Zilboorg stuck to the question of Merton's religious vocation and his
life as a monk, a would-be hermit. He seems to have started off affably
enough, taking a "Well, what are we going to do about this?" line of
approach. Merton was not ready to be exposed in front of Dom James.
He flew into a fury and cried tears of rage. For Merton's abbot there
had been no preparation, no preliminary interview.[364] Only two people — Merton's mother, Ruth, in the distant past when she had insisted on such things as spelling *which* with a wholly illogical *h*, and the
Capuchin in 1940 after Merton's escape from the interview with Father
Edmund — had ever seen Thomas Merton behave in such a manner.

Zilboorg went on repeating in a level voice what he had said before
about the hermitage idea being pathological: "You want a hermitage in
Times Square with a large sign over it saying 'HERMIT.' "

This time one's sympathy is entirely with Merton, who saw himself
trapped, and who sat with tears streaming down his face muttering
"Stalin! Stalin!" The worst thing that could have happened had happened: Zilboorg had told him to tell nobody, then he had staged a situation in which the most exaggerated misgivings of Dom James were
dramatically confirmed.

Whenever a crisis came up in the years ahead, Merton assumed Dom
James had simply told his superiors about the interview with Zilboorg
he had witnessed at St. John's. The abbot may or may not have used
his memory of that scene, but it was a reasonable assumption on Merton's part. These were the most damaging ten minutes since he had
left the world for the monastery. Significantly, while there are pages

on the first interview in the journal, it contains no record of the second.

Merton continued to express admiration for Zilboorg to others. He was obviously preparing his own defenses. The plans for him to go to New York for psychoanalysis came to nothing. It had been arranged for the novices to see a psychologist in Louisville, Dr. James Wygal, whom Zilboorg had recommended. Merton put off his own visits to Dr. Wygal for the time being. When Zilboorg arrived at the monastery on December 27, much to Merton's surprise, the two had further talks. Merton reported to Naomi Burton that "it transpires that though I am indeed crazy as a loon I don't really need analysis. He now has me all primed and happy with slogans like 'pipe down,' 'Get lost,' etc. Nothing I like better."[365] Much later Merton decided, looking back with some bitterness:

> I thought today at adoration what a blessing it was that I did not go in 1956 to be analyzed by Zilboorg! What a tragedy and mess that would have been — and I must give Zilboorg the credit for having realized it himself in his own way. It would have been utterly impossible and absurd. And yet I think in great measure his judgement was that I could not be fitted into that kind of theater. There was no conceivable part for me to play in his life, on the contrary! And certainly it is true that the whole thing would have been unimaginably absurd. He had quite enough intelligence (more than enough, he was no fool at all!) to see that it would be a very poor production for him, for the Abbot (who was most willing) and for me. I am afraid that I was willing at the time, to go, which shows what a fool I was.[366]

Meanwhile, in 1956, Merton continued to seek advice from Father — and Doctor — John Eudes. Then John Eudes Bamberger went away himself. To demonstrate that some things either had not been very objective, or had been wrongly reported, in the first interview, Zilboorg was soon encouraging John Eudes Bamberger in his studies. At the same time Dom James came to a memorable decision on the stability question. He decided it was absolutely necessary to have a psychiatrist at Gethsemani, and he allowed John Eudes Bamberger to study in Washington, D.C., to qualify in psychiatry. Dom John Eudes says that he stayed in the home of a professor. There was no surveillance from the monastery. He *was* looked upon as something of a *rara avis* by his fellow students.[367]

When he returned, a screening team for postulants was set up at Gethsemani. This comprised Father Louis as novice master, Father John Eudes as medical interviewer, and Father Matthew Kelty as vocational secretary. Inevitably there were jokes in the monastery about "who would screen the screeners?" Dom James sometimes complained that Father Louis let in those who were interesting intellectually and Father John Eudes let in those who were interesting psychologically.[368]

Nevertheless, the system worked far better than the lack of system in the past.

*

For all the earlier Thomas Mertons who were ruthlessly disowned in *The Sign of Jonas* and elsewhere, the connecting links with the past were as important as ever. Merton had fulfilled his promise of 1940 to Our Lady of Cobre by becoming a priest and dedicating his first Mass to her in 1949. On one of the last days in Cuba, when he had returned to Havana from Cobre, and shortly after attending the Mass where the priest had cried out "Creo!" and all the children responded, Merton had been walking about his room at the Hotel Andino when he noticed that the tower of the Church of Our Lady of Mount Carmel and her statue were reflected in his mirror. Our Lady of Cobre had become the patron of Merton's priestly vocation. Our Lady of Mount Carmel became the patron of his solitary vocation.

Just before he had gone to Collegeville, on July 17, Merton had written a Prayer to Our Lady of Mount Carmel in his journal, which began, "What was it I said to you, in the mirror, in Havana?" He asked his patron to "Teach me to go to the country beyond words and beyond names."[369]

For the second time in four years Merton had had to retreat from his desire for greater solitude. This time he was half-convinced that others were right, and that it was not his true vocation at all. He was willing to re-examine his place in the community, his life as a cenobite. His words of four years earlier were now even more relevant:

> . . . a man cannot go on to be a hermit until he has proved himself as a cenobite. I have in no way proved myself as a cenobite. I have been beating the air. I am not really a monk — never have been except in my own imagination. But it is a relief to *know* that. What exhausts me is the entertainment of all my illusions. At least let me get rid of the greatest illusion of all, and start to love all over again — or to die. For I feel sometimes as if having admitted my complete futility as a monk it would be decent to offer God my life and make reparation for everything by dying. No such offering would make sense unless it implied an equal willingness to live and be perfect, in obedience to Him — and to do *penance.* Whether we live or die we are the Lord's. Life and death alike can be offered up as penance. I can make reparation for my impiety — not necessarily by imitating Abbot de Rancé (everything in me says that he is not supposed to be my model) but by living as perfectly as I can the Rule and Spirit of St. Benedict — obedience, humility, work, prayer, simplicity, the love of Christ.[370]

Merton's criticisms of himself in the journals should be read with as much caution as his criticisms of Dom James. When he says on one page "I am not really a monk," he proves on another he is only a monk trying to live by high monastic standards and failing. However, on the return from Collegeville he felt a temptation to swing back from an openness of attitude that had proved bruising to an excess of rigor, self-punishment, and the suppression of the spontaneous. On the whole, he was able to resist this. In 1956–57, Merton was seeking a way to live the monastic life more fully, believing that if he got the balance right, this should make him *more*, not less, human.

Yet the difficulty was in keeping the balance. At a time he was trying to be a perfect monk, this put the monastic life to the test as well as himself. It also put the circumstances of the life of a monk at Gethsemani in the late 1950s to the test. Inevitably, perhaps, there is an over-emphasis on the failure to live up to ideals.

Merton's readers could be misled in one direction, his novices in another. When Brother Michael Casagram entered Gethsemani in 1964, he had just transferred from Holy Cross, Berryville, Virginia. He told Father John Eudes Bamberger he was amazed by Father Louis, who seemed the most disorganized monk in the monastery. Father John Eudes told him he could hardly have made a bigger mistake: Father Louis was the *most organized* man in the monastery.[371] Many a novice found himself in trouble by taking Merton's outward style and modeling himself on this. Merton's manners were much imitated. They were based on consideration for others. The imitators often carried off the mannerisms and missed the manners. Merton's wit, his facetiousness, his offhand remarks were sometimes appreciated in the monastery, sometimes resented. His imitators missed the seriousness of purpose which underlay much of the wit, and they left out the swift and contrite apology when the wit went too far. At the monastery, the casual, free-swinging style was a trap for others. In the writing, the heavy and critical dogmatism was a trap. Merton himself was self-correcting. Some who followed went no further than the first stages and were stuck there.

Nobody saw the two dangers more clearly than Merton himself. When one of the monks preached a poorly prepared sermon, Merton commented: "The worst of it was that I felt he was trying to imitate me in informality. I have done him harm, no doubt. But I know I have also helped him."[372]

He had much to say in his journals and in his conferences about not imitating good masters and avoiding bad ones. Yet even this tended to be put in dogmatic terms. In a later poem, Merton borrows from Sufi writings to warn novices:

> Avoid three kinds of Master:
> Those who esteem only themselves,
> For their self-esteem is blindness;
> Those who esteem only innovations,
> For their opinions are aimless,
> Without meaning;

Those who esteem only what is established;
Their minds
Are little cells of ice.[373]

Something further must be said here. Merton had been trained in a tradition that encouraged and enjoyed games of wit, pushing an idea to the point where it was obviously absurd or showed itself as phony. These were the *serio ludere* of the old philosophers, and of the long line of serious wits from Lucian of Samosata to Erasmus to Swift to Sterne to James Joyce. It was a method which was favored among his Columbia friends, but it was not a method practiced in many American schools and universities, where the instructor is expected to be always sincere. Merton was aware of the difference between the European and the American academic tradition, but he was not always willing or able to adapt on this particular point. He paid, too, for combining the freshness of his thought with an air of finality. To come in with a dictum like Dr. Samuel Johnson one day and its opposite the next has its dangers.

In his classes he was an explorer. It bored him to go over what he had already said. His students were drawn away from a core of knowledge in a subject which was already overfamiliar to the instructor, in favor of something that had caught his interest in his most recent reading. The novices were often delighted, but lost.

In his own studies in monasticism, Merton became fascinated by the lives of the Desert Fathers, then by theorists of the monastic life like John Cassian and St. Gregory of Nyssa, and finally by all who had the essential "desert dimension" in their vocation — non-Christian as well as Christian monks. Reading of those who had left the world for solitude, Merton found he was moving, paradoxically, from a narrow view of monastic life to a much broader one.

The key to his evaluation of monasticism over the next twelve years was *structure*. The word was to be an important one in the last talk he gave. But even before he entered the monastery in 1941 he had pondered the question of how freedom to strive to be a saint might be aided by one religious structure, blocked by another. In 1956 and 1957, the question he was trying to ask was: What is the ideal structure for a monastery in our time?[374]

Writing *The Silent Life*[375] gave Merton a chance to examine the application of the Rule of St. Benedict to a number of Cistercian and Benedictine models. As one might expect, he favored the models that made the greatest provision for solitude. But he was interested in experiments that provided balance — community life as a school for charity, time to be alone with God.

A careful reading of this book shows that the preferences which had led to Merton's earlier stability crises were still in force. Both the Carthusians and the Camaldoli are given a full measure of praise. Merton had already idealized the life of the monks of the Cistercian Order of the Strict Observance in his autobiography and *The Waters of Siloe*. There the picture was drawn from his own experience. This time Merton wrote about the lives of monks he had shared only in his imagination.

If *The Silent Life* is colored by a sense of the road he had not been allowed to take in the past, it also points the way to conflicts of stability yet to come. Again, Merton was writing from the imagination, and the glowing accounts of others. The pages of the draft on the Primitive Benedictines were so admiring they had to be toned down. Even with these concessions, it is hard for the reader to doubt that Paradise had come to earth at La Pierre qui Vire in France, or at Cuernavaca:

> The first appearance of "Primitive Benedictinism" on this continent was in Mexico when Dom Gregorio Lemercier founded his Monastery of the Resurrection at Cuernavaca, Morelos. This small community made up entirely of Mexican Indians (except for the Superior) is one of the most remarkable and courageous experiments in modern monastic history. Struggling against desperate odds, living under very primitive conditions in true poverty and simplicity, depending on the labor of their hands and the Providence of God, the monks of Cuernavaca are perhaps closer to St. Benedict than anyone else on this side of the Atlantic.[376]

At Gethsemani electric fans were appearing in the summer. There was even talk of extending the air conditioning, which was already installed in the food-processing plant. Music was being piped in to the cows in the milking parlors.[377] The monastery owned huge machines to dry the hay, something Dom James had noted none of the foundations had in France.[378] Cuernavaca was struggling against desperate odds . . .

Spanish- and Portuguese-speaking America were no new interest to Thomas Merton, but in 1956–57, with the possibility of a foundation in Ecuador, and much else, Merton became interested in every aspect of South and Central American life. On August 8, 1957, he reports he is having an orgy of reading books on South America.[379] Many of his novices were Spanish speaking. One, Merton discovered, was a Nicaraguan poet, Brother Lawrence, Ernesto Cardenal. Cardenal provided Merton with addresses of poets and poetry magazines in Mexico. The work of Pablo Neruda he already knew. Laughlin had told him of Nicanor Parra. The Mexican literary magazines introduced him to the work of Octavio Paz, Cuadra, Andrade, and the poets of Brazil.

The first collection of Merton's own poetry in many years, *The Strange Islands*,[380] appeared in March 1957 to a less-than-enthusiastic reception. This was a transitional collection, before Merton's excitement with the poets of South America made its mark on his work. A number of poems came out of Merton's hours of savage introspection, like "Whether There Is Enjoyment in Bitterness," which begins:

> This afternoon, let me
> Be a sad person. Am I not
> Permitted (like other men)
> To be sick of myself?[381]

Here the "I" is the "I" without disguise or the shield of persona, the "I" of Merton's journals. This was the kind of poetry which would soon be called Confessional. More successful, yet on much the same subject, was the finely sustained "Elias — Variations on a Theme." Elias is clearly the poet, even when the "I" is also used, but the persona provides control without great loss of immediacy in the austere choruses. There are references to Blake, memories of the landscape of "What the Thunder Said" in Eliot's *The Waste Land*, and connections with Merton's reading of Nicholas of Cusa, yet the poem is strikingly original. At the end we return to Elias and complete the circle:

> Under the blunt pine
> Elias becomes his own geography
> (Supposing geography to be necessary at all),
> Elias becomes his own wild bird, with God in the center,
> His own wild field which nobody owns,
> His own pattern, surrounding the Spirit
> By which he is himself surrounded:
>
> For the free man's road has neither beginning nor end.[382]

This is certainly a "desert poem" in George Woodcock's terms. In fact, the "variations" of the title are variations of the "desert dimension," which was uppermost in Merton's mind at the time. "In Silence," the "desert poem" Merton had written at St. John's, appears in this collection.

But *The Strange Islands* lacks the concentration and pruning this would suggest. Some of the directions are interesting in themselves, but nothing goes together very well. "To a Severe Nun" is successful as a mild but pointed reproof, the kind Merton might have given his novices, or an actual nun in his correspondence (he was now giving a good deal of spiritual direction in his letters):

> I know, Sister, that solitude
> Will never dismay you. You have chosen
> A path too steep for others to follow.
> I take it you prefer to go without them . . .[383]

"Birdcage Walk" goes all the way back to a walk Tom Merton had taken in St. James's Park in London in 1928 with his uncle by marriage, Ben Pearce. They had met an Anglican bishop wearing gaiters. Merton recorded this in his Perry Street Journal, where he wondered what the French poet Apollinaire would have made of the meeting.[384] Almost twenty years later we find out.[385]

Much of *The Strange Islands* is given over to Merton's play for television. *The Tower of Babel, A Morality,* had first appeared in *Jubilee,* the magazine founded, owned, and published by Ed Rice. It was performed in a somewhat edited version on the NBC television network on January 27, 1957. In the summer of 1957, James Laughlin brought out a signed, limited edition of the play with woodcuts by Gerhard Marcks.

In *The Tower of Babel,*[386] Merton employs a number of literary models and yet another character named Thomas. What might have been a rather dismaying calling together of a number of themes in Western literature has a good deal of fresh and engaging detail. Merton's sharper perception of language as the vehicle of both communication and confusion helps the effectiveness of the trial scene, and at one point there is even an echo of Zilboorg's attack on him for being "verbological." Merton's own attack on an old target, propaganda, is handled with a surer, subtler hand than before. In the builders' hidden desire to fail in building the tower there is evidence of Merton's reading in psychology. When the refugees remember a time the City of the World and the City of God were closer to one another, Merton gives them his own childhood memories. On the Feast of St. Antonin, September 2, 1956,[387] Merton had written several pages in his journal, revisiting in imagination and memory the old town on the Aveyron where life moved at the pace of the oxcarts.

In August 1957 Merton read one of the Mexican magazines in which Ernesto Cardenal had a poem attacking the United Fruit Company.[388] After sixteen years of isolation from social issues, Merton was beginning to feel cut off from what he needed to know; dependent on the visits of friends, chance articles in magazines, and the occasional paragraph in a letter on some other subject. However, what stunned him most was the delayed shock of reading details about the atomic bomb attack on Japan, the use of blasphemous code names like Papacy and Trinity, the thwarted attempts at peace negotiations, and the horror of destruction. The accounts of the Nazi death camps in William L. Shirer's *The Rise and Fall of the Third Reich* had a similar effect on him.[389]

Merton needed some way of approaching such subjects. He discovered many writers and poets had been overwhelmed by the impossibility of satirizing what lay beyond the conventional weapons of satire and wit.

Herbert Marcuse and others had said the poet or writer needed only to provide the right setting and the enormities would speak for themselves. This was not a wholly new idea, yet it proved the most effective weapon of the satirist in the mid-century. From the theory came the Found Poem and the Anti-poem.[390]

From Merton's discovery came *Original Child Bomb* and *Chant to Be Used in Processions Around a Site with Furnaces*. Neither appeared until the early 1960s. Yet the changes in Merton's thought can be seen clearly in a comparison between these two pieces and *The Tower of Babel* of 1956–57. However effective the morality play may be, it loses at once by the comparison: Merton the writer and thinker is everywhere, making points, drawing morals, persuading us. In the later works, though he has arranged the pieces with great skill, the writer hardly seems to be there at all. It is the material that speaks to us, not the artist. For this reason *Original Child Bomb* and *Chant to Be Used in Processions Around a Site with Furnaces* are far more truly modern moralities. Any commentary, any moralizing, would intrude upon the only decent human response — meditation in stillness. As Wittgenstein said in a wholly different context:

> *Wovon man nicht sprechen kann, darüber muß man schweigen.*
> What we cannot speak about we must pass over in silence.[391]

As Rilke ended a poem:

> . . . *denn da ist keine Stelle,*
> *die dich nicht sieht. Du mußt dein Leben ändern.*
> . . . for there is no place
> that does not see you. You must change your life.[392]

*

In 1957, with his reading about South and Central America, the political poems of Pablo Neruda and others, and discussions with Ernesto Cardenal, Merton had been reminded how often poverty and the violence of exploitation went together. This was no more of a revelation than it had been for him to hear there was injustice in the world from the Baroness that evening at St. Bonaventure's. For sixteen years he had been largely isolated from such things by his own choice. If his conscience now drew him back again to social issues, there were two things which he would have to face. In the first place, it would mean some dependence again on the media for the information he needed, and in the second place, he had defended the isolation only a few years earlier.

In his "Notes on Contemplative Order" at the beginning of *The Waters of Siloe*, Merton had written:

> . . . The Order has recovered its full strength in proportion as it has withdrawn from fields of endeavor into which it never had any business to go. In other words, a contemplative community will prosper to the

extent that it is what it is meant to be, and shuts out the world, and with-
draws from the commotion and excitement of the active life, and gives
itself entirely to penance and prayer.[393]

This was no isolated statement on isolation. Merton goes over the
point again and again, both in this key passage of *The Waters of Siloe*
and elsewhere. He had, of course, rejected other statements which were
presented just as forcibly and often. Yet the whole basis of Merton's
criticism of Gethsemani continued to be that the "commotion and excitement of the active life" had been invited over the enclosure wall.

It is difficult not to see a double standard here — one rule on the active life for the Order and another for Thomas Merton. And this is hard
to argue away, despite all the qualifications that immediately come to
mind and all the value one may place on the kind of activity Merton
was engaged in at the end of the fifties and in the sixties.

Yet the qualifications are vitally important. Merton failed to see the
full ramifications of the double standard because he defined the difference between his own move out of monastic withdrawal and Gethsemani's in terms of charity, concern, and the vow of poverty. In his
view, Gethsemani was prospering from its worldly activity in exactly
the wrong way: it was *not* prospering as a contemplative community.
In contrast, he saw himself trying to marry active concern and contemplation in a bond of charity and of poverty.

✻

On April 28, 1957, Merton set the aim in his religious search for the
years ahead:

> If I can unite *in myself*, in my own spiritual life, the thought of the East
> and the West, of the Greek and Latin Fathers, I will create in myself a
> reunion of the divided Church and from that unity in myself can come
> the exterior and visible unity of the Church. For if we want to bring to-
> gether East and West we cannot do it by imposing one upon the other.
> We must contain both in ourselves, and transcend both in Christ.[394]

By the time this passage came to be included in *Conjectures of a Guilty
Bystander* in 1965, Merton had added considerably to it, including "the
Russians with the Spanish mystics."[395]

The objective was ambitious enough in the spring of 1957. Written
six years before Vatican II, it was a visionary statement as well as a very
personal one.

In a period when Thomas Merton was extending the horizons in so
many directions, when he was moving from finely defined studies in
contemplation and monasticism to something wider and, for the moment, vaguer, he saw the danger of fragmentation. This was part of
the point in his statement of aim in April. Yet the journal entries are
full of his sense of confinement, with references to "fresh air" and

"ghetto, hothouse mentality." "To live in a monastery as if the world had stopped turning in 1905 — a fatal illusion."[396]

Merton felt he had to catch up with everything that had happened since his own world had stopped turning in 1941. He knew nothing about atomic physics, the racial questions that were exploding in the very region of the country where he was living, the Church's place in the social and political structure of Cuba, Ecuador, Nicaragua — and many another country. With all the earnest endeavor, sometimes a quite different note came into the journals to show he was suffering from something like cabin fever: "I want to read *Finnegans Wake* the way I want to hear some good music."[397]

He had been reading Joyce's *Letters*. And, as with Joyce, most of his other interests of 1957 were only new in the sense they had been put aside for sixteen years. Each brought up the memory of his first discovery. He had added Suzuki's name to his reading list in the Blake notebook at Columbia.[398] Gandhi and non-violence carried him back to the argument with the captain of the Rugby XV at Oakham. There had been a full preparation for his present obsession with South America in "Little Spain" near Perry Street, as well as the weeks in Cuba. Translating the Spanish of Paz, Vallejo, Parra, and others reminded him of the spell García Lorca had cast over him in 1938–39, and for long afterward.

The struggle to learn something about nuclear physics *was* new. He did not get very far, except to be fascinated by Heisenberg's principle of uncertainty and to learn the details of the story of the first three atomic bombs. No sooner had he started this reading in the first days of November than Merton heard the news of Sputnik and the space dog. Few outside the Soviet bloc credited Russia with the technology to do more than lag ten years behind America.[399] Now the USSR was first in space and the curriculum of every school and college in the United States had been turned upside-down.

From the second half of 1956, Merton had been drawn deeply into very different Russian studies. These, too, were largely new and unfamiliar. He argued with Nikolai Berdyaev's theories, seeing him at times as an advocate of "the philosophy of Lucifer."[400] He may have been attracted to Bulgakof's *Du Verbe Incarné* by the title of the French edition he was reading.[401]

Above all, he was moved by the description in the Russian mystics of the personification of Holy Wisdom as Hagia Sophia, a dark, sad figure, who had appeared to Vladimir Soloviev in Egypt, and to many others on their pilgrimages. At the same time, he discovered, too, the idea of Cosmic Play:

> They [the Russian mystics] have dared to accept the challenge of the Sapiential books, the challenge of the passages in Proverbs where Wisdom is "playing in the world" before the face of the Creator. And the Church

herself says this Sophia was, somehow, mysteriously to be revealed and "fulfilled" in the Mother of God and in the Church.[402]

Ideas planted by this single passage were to be transformed by growth and their own play into some of the most beautiful passages he wrote: in *Hagia Sophia, New Seeds of Contemplation,* and *The New Man.*

In the fall of 1957, Merton's studies of Russian mysticism and South and Central America reached a sort of crescendo — at the same time! It was understandably difficult to come back from such heights to hear the abbot close Chapter with the exhortation, "Yes, Jesus must be our real pal, our most intimate buddy, intimacy with Him is everything,"[403] or to listen to Lenten readings from a bowdlerized gloss on the Gospel of St. Mark. The French commentator supplied the gratuitous information that the young man who fled away naked left "in a nightgown or at least a loincloth." The same author "absolves the apostles for deserting Christ: only complains of the fact that they *ran* away." "No," Merton adds sarcastically, "they should have walked off in a dignified manner!"[404]

It was not a time of great patience with immediate surroundings.

Merton was now concerned about another kind of stability. The sense that he might lose himself in the intellectual fervor comes out in another "Exercise," written on September 1, 1956. There is a somewhat coy writer's evasiveness halfway through, yet the point is all the more revealing. This time the whole poem is given:

> Is there any law to forbid
> Inventing a person? Or is every
>
> Creature of the mind another self?
> Is not one self enough? Is it
> Pride to make more of them
>
> To populate a whole world with
> Oneself — I mean, of course, in a
> Novel. In a word, I ask —
> Show me the law —
>
> Show me why I
> Should feel, as I do feel,
> Guilty when I invent a person.[405]

Merton may have felt a sense of guilt, too, about the writings on contemplation he was editing for publication. It was not that he disowned them so much as that, for the first time in years, he was combining contemplation — in theory and in life — with other things.

He writes to Naomi Burton, as he writes in his journal, that "Thirty-Seven Meditations" are "dry verbiage" and that he is "mortally ashamed of them."[406] Merton's correspondents had grown used to hearing him "cry down" his writing projects since the days when he wrote to tell them how bored he was writing "The Man in the Sycamore Tree." But "Thirty-Seven Meditations," which became *Thoughts in Solitude,* deserved better.

*

In November 1957, Merton had an impacted molar removed in Bardstown. According to his journal, he suffered more from the canned music while waiting in the dentist's office than from anything else. He could be amusing about this, but the subsequent operation brought on a wave of atavistic terror and made him feel weak and vulnerable. He wanted to leave the hospital in Bardstown and go back to Gethsemani, and he records a revulsion against everything that was not "Church and monastery."[407]

It was a particularly bad time, relieved by such escapades as a wild drive by truck with a gift of Christmas trees from the Gethsemani woods, back to Bardstown to deliver to the Flaget Hospital.[408] The party did not arrive home until after dark and after Compline, but the disciplinary skies did not fall on them, and they had had a cold but cheerful holiday from routine.

At the end of 1957 and the beginning of 1958 one of the most emotionally consuming of all Merton's publishing battles broke out. The struggle was again over a gift he had made. When he chose Gethsemani instead of Friendship House in the fall of 1941, he had given Catherine de Hueck the only copy of the typescript of what he called, first, "The Cuban Journal," and then "Journal for Catherine" because it was to be her property. In the years since, the Baroness had married Eddie Doherty and moved from Harlem to start a center of lay apostolate and charity work at Madonna House, Combermere, Ontario.

Now Catherine de Hueck Doherty could see that a number of families and projects would be helped by the sale of an early book by a popular author. Some time before, she had asked Merton's permission to publish. He had received Dom James's agreement, subject, of course, to the censors. Three out of four said no, and one turned the book down on literary grounds.[409]

Merton wrote impassioned letters, putting on the same kind of pressure he had used when *The Sign of Jonas* was banned. He pleaded that, whatever the censors thought of it, the book was promised (though this one was not already set up in print), a number of destitute people were counting on it — it would be an act of charity to allow it to go through. Early in 1959, Catherine de Hueck Doherty provided graphic descriptions of how much the destitute would lose.[410] While Merton's letters and hers were in a good cause, they began to read like the melodrama in which the hero rushes to the aid of the mortgaged family on the plains.

When it looked as if there was no chance for the book to be printed, Dom James repaid the initial royalty check of five hundred dollars from the monastery funds. In the tangle of emotions the affair brought on, this has come to seem to some like an attempt on the abbot's part to buy Catherine de Hueck Doherty off. The evidence is clear, however, that he had given the initial permission, and the five hundred dollars was a gift when others stopped the book from being published, at least temporarily.

The opposition began to crumble. The title was changed to *The Secular Journal*, though not before Merton had made the following suggestions of titles to Naomi Burton: "Diary of Young Thomas Merton," "Reflections of Yesteryear," "News of an Ancient Battle," "Meditations of a Young Moose," "To Hell and Back With Uncle Lou," and "The Grass Was Greener in the Late Thirties."[411] Ghostly photographs of Merton at Columbia were found to make the point visually that this was something he had written before he went to the monastery. Merton worked on a version he thought would meet the points of all the censors except the one who thought he couldn't write. He considered adding a new ending, then decided this would be phony. In February 1959, the book came out.[412] With all the censorship, Merton may not be entirely responsible for the result, which so distorted his own feelings in 1940–41. He claimed people were disappointed when they found there were no firsthand descriptions of opium dens.[413] Mostly they were just disappointed.

*

While making final corrections for *The Secular Journal* Merton admits what had taken him so long, either to discover or to accept: "Galley proofs of *Secular Journal* make it clear to me that my best writing has always been in Journals and such things — notebooks."[414] At almost the same time he made a further discovery, yet he does not seem to have seen the significance of the two together. In December 1957 he had reread what was now called *Thoughts in Solitude* and he found he liked it much better, but only because in October of that year he had gone back to the first draft:

> This morning I went to the vault to go through the mss I had left there and found the original ms from which 37 Meditations developed. But the original is not bad. With the disorganized spontaneity it had when I wrote the stuff out in St. Ann's in the winter of 1953 mostly. I think the original, left as it is, will be all right. Quite different from my edited and doctored version. It is the editing and pretense of system that makes it doctrinaire.[415]

The Sign of Jonas, with its dated entries, had followed the journals of the period fairly closely. Later works on the autobiographical line — *Conjectures of a Guilty Bystander* and "A Vow of Conversation," "edited and doctored" — bore much the same relationship to the journals which fed them that *The Secular Journal* bore to the journals of 1939–41.

On Merton's forty-third birthday, January 31, 1958, the rains poured down out of the black sky. His main concerns were the battle over the book for Catherine de Hueck Doherty and the new postulants' guide, which he was preparing for the monastery.[416] The annual flu epidemic had already begun: it would be worse than ever, and Merton fills the pages of the journal in February with scenes from the sickrooms. The descriptions, somewhat changed, would appear in *Conjectures of a Guilty Bystander*. There was little loss or gain in the editing.[417]

It was very different with another, far more important, scene. On March 18, 1958, Merton went to Louisville on an errand connected with the printing of the postulants' guide and found himself standing on the corner of Fourth and Walnut streets watching the crowds. He discovered his feelings were very different from those of the monk who had stood aside in the airport in Cincinnati in July 1952, thinking the passersby were "infected with some moral corruption that had been brought in by the planes from New York."[418]

The next day, the Feast of St. Joseph (always an important day for Merton), he was back at St. Ann's after a period away. First he watched while "A red-shouldered hawk wheels slowly over Newton's farm as if making his own more special silence in the air — as if tearing out a circle of silence in the sky."[419] After this he wrote of the hours by himself, which had brought him many things, including *Thoughts in Solitude*:

> How many graces, here in St. Ann's, that I did not know about, in those years when I was here all the time, when I had what I most wanted and never really knew it. Which only shows that solitude was not exactly what I wanted. How rich for me has been the silence of this little house which now is nothing more than a tool shed — behind on the hillside for two years they have tried without success to start a rock garden.[420]

After this description of what the quiet hours on his own had brought him, the change to the figure in a crowd is abrupt:

> Yesterday, in Louisville, at the corner of 4th and Walnut, suddenly realized that I loved all the people and that none of them were, or could be, totally alien to me. As if waking from a dream — the dream of my separateness, of my "special" vocation to be different. My vocation does not really make me different from the rest of men or just one in a special category, except artificially, juridically. I am still a member of the human race — and what more glorious destiny is there for man, since the Word was made flesh and became, too, a member of the Human Race![421]

In rhetoric, at least, this is reasonably close to one of the most celebrated passages of Merton's writing, the one that has been called "The Vision in Louisville" from *Conjectures of a Guilty Bystander*,[422] and which has been given wide importance, both as an epiphany and as the turning point in Merton's life, the moment when he became open again to the world he had rejected in 1941. It was an awakening from "a dream of separateness," perhaps, but it is a shock to find the original passage and the passage in *Conjectures* moving in radically different directions after a few further sentences.

"The Vision in Louisville" has not worn well as writing. It is certainly not in a class with the "Fire Watch" at the end of *The Sign of Jonas*. Part of the problem is that Merton goes on to see the crowds in Louisville through his reading of the Third of Thomas Traherne's *Centuries:* "There is no way of telling people that they are all walking around shining like the sun."[423]

In 1965 he was doing very much what he had done when he saw Harlem in 1940 (and later) through his reading of García Lorca. In this case the effect produced is even more curious: Merton talks of coming closer to the crowd at the very time his rhetoric is distancing "the crowd" as an ever more abstract concept of another writer's imagination. Even in the original, Merton did not observe any individual in that crowd as closely as he observed the hawk flying over St. Ann's.

Traherne should have provided the clue, because Merton was not interested in Traherne's writing until long after 1958.[424] The passage in *Conjectures* is largely from a different time and speaks to different concerns. On September 20, 1965, Merton wrote:

> I have been working on *Conjectures* in the afternoon — at moments it gets to be like Cortazar's *Hopscotch* — criss-cross itinerary of the various pieces taken out of time sequence and fitted into what? — an indefinite half-conscious pattern of associations which is never consistent, often purely fortuitous, often not there (and not sought in any case). A lot of rewriting. For instance rewrote an experience of March 18, 1958 (entry of March 19) in light of a very good meditation of Saturday afternoon, developed and changed. A lot of telescoping etc. In a word, transforming a Journal into "meditations" or "Pensées."[425]

After this, it is a surprise to return to the original entry and to find the "openness" of the first two paragraphs moves at once to a very different "reading" than Traherne: to the Sophia of the Russians and the Book of Proverbs. The entry of 1958 is tied to the slow and revealing creation of one of Merton's most fascinating works, *Hagia Sophia*.

On February 28, he had had a dream:

> On the porch at Douglaston I am embraced with determined and virginal passion by a young Jewish girl. She clings to me and will not let me go, and I get to like the idea. I see that she is a nice kid in a plain, sincere sort of way. I reflect "She belongs to the same race as St. Anne." I ask her name and she says her name is Proverb. I tell her that is a beautiful

and significant name, but she does not appear to like it — perhaps the others have mocked her for it.[426]

On March 4, Merton writes a love letter to "Dear Proverb," explaining that there is "a great difference" in their ages, but "How grateful I am to you for loving in me something which I thought I had entirely lost, and someone who, I thought, had long ago ceased to be." He explained at the end, "Dearest Proverb, I love your name, its mystery, its simplicity, and its secret, which even you yourself seem not to appreciate."[427]

The whole of the Book of Proverbs was important to Merton, but the eighth chapter was his favorite.[428] He told someone later he had been reciting the verse "And my delights were to be with the children of men" as he passed through Cincinnati station on the way to Gethsemani in December 1941.[429] The verses on Wisdom playing in a Cosmic Dance before God had been illuminated for him by the Russian mystics. Proverb was a secret name for many reasons.

On March 19, after two paragraphs about being a member of the human race, Merton goes on at once to say, "It is not a question of proving to myself that I either dislike or like the women one sees in the street." He says that none that day was remarkably beautiful, yet each had a secret beauty, and that, by his vow of chastity, he was "married to what is most true in all the women of the world." Right after, he writes again to "Dear Proverb" in the journal:

> I have kept one promise and I have refrained from speaking of you until seeing you again. I knew that when I saw you again it would be very different, in a different place, in a different form, in the most unexpected circumstances. I shall never forget our meeting yesterday. The touch of your hand makes me a different person. To be with you is rest and Truth. Only with you are these things found, dear child, sent to me by God![430]

The letters — and the dreams of Proverb — stopped, or were not recorded. He was to find her more than once, different in form, and in "the most unexpected circumstances." For the moment, on March 18, 1958, Thomas Merton at the corner of Fourth and Walnut had been thinking of the Annunciation, of the Incarnation, of Sophia, and of the so far largely imaginary Proverb.

*

In those spring months Merton was more than usually absorbed with a new publishing project. Like his attempt to write an all-inclusive autobiography, this proved too ambitious, yet the plan to complete a huge study of Russia[431] set him to ordering books on Russian literature, Russian art, Russian politics, and many other things Russian from the Library of Congress and a dozen other sources. He listened to the music of Prokofiev on records[432] also borrowed from libraries.

On April 12, 1958, as part of these researches, he wrote to Naomi Burton at Curtis Brown asking how he could get hold of the new novel by Boris Pasternak, whose poetry he already knew and liked. Merton had heard the novel had appeared only in the West and only in Italy. He could read Italian, he said, but he wondered if there were plans for the book to appear in other languages.[433]

He wrote, too, to say Ernesto Cardenal had discovered a number of errors in the Spanish translations of Merton's *Obras Completas*, about to be published in Buenos Aires.

As if Russia and South America were not enough, he asked Curtis Brown to help him by asking Thames and Hudson to send a copy of Martin Hürlimann's *Asia*.[434] The English publishers Thames and Hudson had brought out *Silence in Heaven*, published with many photographs.[435] The English book was popular but had involved yet another publishing tangle over crisscrossing foreign and domestic rights. On this occasion Merton was less to blame for the muddle than usual, and he thought Thames and Hudson owed him a gift.

The gift arrived, and Merton wrote back at once that he "loves it."[436] He was soon poring over the plates, the views of the temples of Bangkok, Polonnaruwa, and Angkor Wat, just as he had done as a child with photographs of French cathedrals while the rain fell outside the house in St. Antonin.

Merton's geography of the mind had expanded to take in half the world. In his preface to *Obras Completas*, which appeared in April 1958, there is a Promethean view from Mexico to the southern tip of Argentina. Perhaps Merton had Thoreau's "I have travelled a good deal in Concord"[437] in mind when he wrote:

> In the silence of the countryside and the forest, in the cloistered solitude of my monastery, I have discovered the whole Western Hemisphere. Here I have been able, through the grace of God, to explore the New World, without traveling from city to city, without flying over the Andes or the Amazon, stopping one day here, two there, and then continuing on. Perhaps if I had traveled in this manner, I should have seen nothing: generally those who travel most see the least.[438]

As Merton transcends limitations of place (and perhaps the vow of stability, at least in the imagination), so he claims nationalities and religious loyalties, only to transcend them. Hereafter, every new preface to a translation of Merton's work was to provide him with another opportunity to broaden his sense of allegiance. A passage in the South American preface is important enough to quote in full, for this and other reasons:

I cannot be a partial American and I cannot be, which is even sadder, a partial Catholic. For me Catholicism is not confined to one culture, one nation, one age, one race. My faith is not a mixture of the Irish Catholicism of the United States and the splendid and vital Catholicism, reborn during the past war, of my native France. Though I admire the cathedrals and the past of Catholicism in Latin America, my Catholicism goes beyond the Spanish tradition. I cannot believe that Catholicism is tied to the destinies of any group which confusedly expresses the economic illusions of a social class. My Catholicism is not the religion of the bourgeoisie nor will it ever be. My Catholicism is all the world and all ages. It dates from the beginning of the world. The first man was the image of Christ and contained Christ, even as he was created, as savior in his heart. The first man was destined to be the ancestor of his Redeemer and the first woman was the mother of all life, in the image of the Immaculate Daughter who was full of grace, Mother of mercy, Mother of the saved.[439]

Something in Merton had to take everything to the autobiographical "I," even at risk of sounding egotistical to the point of megalomania. "My Catholicism . . . My Catholicism . . . My Catholicism . . ." sounds strange in a paragraph intended to bring *Catholic* back to its plain yet often forgotten meaning of "universal." But without the "My Catholicism" the whole text would lose its effectiveness. Much of the paragraph would be little more than a collection of clichés, generally applicable, nowhere applied.

Again, the logic of the last lines is strange only because it presupposes a number of links which are there in Merton's own thought. Merton's identification of Christ in every man was based on theology: the idea carried him to an extreme and immediate reading of that identification. It had done so in the essay he wrote for Mary Jerdo at St. Bonaventure's in the fall of 1941. Christ could be — had to be — in the man stealing from you or threatening your life.

When Merton read the abbot general's letter to the Order on poverty, he wrote in his journal that something was missing.[440] By this time he felt much the same whenever religion ignored or undervalued the feminine as the essential half of all wholeness. Something *was* missing. One would have to alter the statement above to read, more correctly, the "Christ in every man or woman": if this is implied, it is still better to have it stated. But even as it was stated, the idea was sensitive and bold in 1958.

Merton's confusions in the last three lines of the passage are evidence of the kind of thinking he had been doing that day in Louisville in March. Since his conversion, the Virgin Mary had been at the center of his religious devotion. What he saw as the Protestant neglect of the Mother of Christ remained incomprehensible to him. Yet Merton knew that devotion to Our Lady could be, and had been, irreligiously used

to exclude vital feminine influences in the Catholic Church. His fascination with Wisdom, with Sophia, had opened a new line of questioning. His later reading of the Lady Julian of Norwich was to bring this
home.

*

When *Thoughts in Solitude* appeared in April 1958,[441] it proved one of
Merton's wisest books, a triumphant turning of so much that was negative in his journals into another reason to accept pain in his struggle
to be more human. The book is full of aphorisms which are better in
their context but which can stand on their own:

> The solution to the problem of life is life itself. Life is not attained by
> reasoning and analysis, but first by living . . .
>
> Poverty is the door to freedom . . .
>
> Laziness and cowardice are two of the greatest enemies of the spiritual
> life . . .
>
> There is no neutrality between gratitude and ingratitude. Those who are
> not grateful soon begin to complain of everything. Those who do not
> love, hate. In the spiritual life there is no such thing as an indifference
> to love or hate. That is why tepidity (which seems to be indifferent) is
> so detestable. It is hate disguised as love.
>
> Humility is a virtue, not a neurosis.
>
> A humility that freezes our being and frustrates all healthy activity is not
> humility at all, but a disguised form of pride . . .[442]

The past years in Merton's life had been turbulent with battles against
different kinds of pride, throwing him back to a humiliation that was
close at times to despair. He had suffered humiliation from others at
St. John's in the summer of 1956, and he had had to recover from this
without permanently losing his balance. It was natural then that he
spoke much of humility in *Thoughts in Solitude*, yet what he sought was
a wise, healthy alliance between that virtue and both prudence and fortitude:

> Teach me to bear a humility which shows me, without ceasing, that I am
> a liar and a fraud and that, even though this is so, I have an obligation
> to strive after truth, to be as true as I can, even though I will inevitably
> find all my truth half poisoned with deceit. This is the terrible thing about
> humility: that it is never fully successful . . .[443]

Here Merton had found the answer he was looking for in the passage in his journal in 1952. The public humiliations of La Trappe (or
of the second interview at St. John's) were not the answer. Confession
in print had its aspect of public humiliation, and few have stated in

print "I am a liar and a fraud." This time the confession evokes no embarrassment in the reader because the vitality is never lowered. The Confessional school in literature has choked itself to death on self-pity. There is an intrusion of this occasionally in Merton's writing. Not here. He is off to try to do better before self-pity has a chance to undermine his fortitude.

Before he could love all humanity in a crowd or in a single companion, Thomas Merton knew he would have to learn a way to love himself, a way that had nothing to do with the smug, the "squares," the Pharisees. *Thoughts in Solitude* shows him at the beginning of this way. There are a hundred subtleties in the Second Commandment, to "Love your neighbor as yourself":

> To love our "nothingness" in this way, we must repudiate nothing that is our own, nothing that we have, nothing that we are. We must see and admit that it is all ours and that it is all good: good in its positive entity since it comes from God: good in our deficiency, since our helplessness, even our moral misery, our spiritual, attracts to us the mercy of God.
>
> To love our nothingness we must love everything in us that the proud man loves when he loves himself. But we must love it all for exactly the opposite reason.
>
> To love our nothingness we must love *ourselves*.[444]

There is something magnificent about this passage, even though it starts questions at once, especially if we read it in terms of Merton's own life. He had repudiated himself over and over. Now he was repudiating the repudiator, the self-hater. There had been plenty of times in the past when Thomas Merton had celebrated self like the proud man, and there were to be times in the future when he did so. The solution he sought was probably closer to something like forgetting self and loving self at the same time. Yet in this passage Merton had, at last, admitted the need to love self.

On March 30, 1958, Palm Sunday, Father John of the Cross preached a sermon about love and friendship so important to Merton he tried to copy everything he remembered into his journal. He went on to make the connections to himself:

> One reason I am so grateful for this morning's sermon is that my worst and inmost sickness is the despair of ever being able truly to love, because I despair of ever being worthy of love. But the way out is to be able to trust one's friends and thus accept in them acts and things which a sick mind grabs as evidence of lack of love — as pretexts for evading the obligation to love.[445]

This was a long way from the words against human friendship in *Exile Ends in Glory* and even in *No Man Is an Island*. Earlier still, in the beginning of *The Seven Storey Mountain*, there is the revealing passage about Merton's own difficulties:

As a child, and since then too, I have always tended to resist any kind of a possessive affection on the part of any other human being — there has always been this profound instinct to keep clear, to keep free. And only with truly supernatural people have I ever felt really at my ease, really at peace.[446]

The two passages demonstrate two sides of the same feeling. What binds them together is lack of trust.

In 1957–58 he developed a number of friendships, even when they were discouraged, as we have seen, by the regulations against Particular Friendships. His undermaster of novices, Father Tarcisius Conner, was one of those close to Merton, Cardenal (or Brother Lawrence) was another, and a third, Father John of the Cross, became Merton's confessor. The two men admired each other greatly, yet Merton soon wrote in his journal that he was making a mess of his confessions:

When I talk to Father John of the Cross now, I act like a complete phoney and he is aware of it and I guess embarrassed by it, for my sake as well as for his own . . . But the phoniness comes from over anxiety and impatience. On paper I have time to compose myself, and I can be more "real." With another person, I am thrown into confusion and do not foresee the consequences of the next statement and am so busy trying to avoid a crisis that I do not really listen to the other person. This is only fully true of my relations with Father John of the Cross. With other people I am disinterested enough to be more detached, more serene, and relatively normal . . .[447]

Again, we have to be careful of Merton exaggerating even his way of exaggerating — of doing to us just what he says he is doing to Father John of the Cross. There are two difficulties here, self-consciousness and an anxiety which pushed him to identify with others, of going "more than halfway." His gift for identification with others was a great gift, but it was also a burden. It made him acutely nervous about situations that would show how dependent he was on affection, yet how given to analyze everything, and to identify so closely with the other person that he either dominated or lost himself in the exchange.

Several times that year Merton went back to say in his journal that he was much better on paper. Reading the proofs of *Thoughts in Solitude* had emphasized this. He could be wise on paper, yet too often glib, sarcastic, plain wrong on his feet. He began making lists again of the things he wished he hadn't said in the past year. Part of the problem was that there was no getting away from anyone at Gethsemani.

Merton had developed a number of friendships outside Gethsemani, and in those everything was well under control. Perhaps the visits he valued most were those of the Austrian artist Victor Hammer and his wife, Carolyn.[448] It was with Hammer that Merton discussed the idea of writing his first fan letter from the monastery where he had received so many. He was debating whether to send Boris Pasternak his new work, *Prometheus: A Meditation,* then being printed by the King Library Press of the University of Kentucky under the Hammers' supervision.

Fifteen years later, Carolyn Hammer would supervise the printing of a collection of the correspondence between Boris Pasternak and Thomas Merton from the same press. In 1958, the Hammers' own hand press, Stamperia del Santuccio, had already earned a reputation among book collectors, and they had done work for James Laughlin. A number of Merton's works would be privately printed by the Stamperia del Santuccio, including *Hagia Sophia.* Victor Hammer was teaching at Transylvania University and feeling some cultural isolation. Carolyn Hammer, as librarian at the University of Kentucky, was helping Merton find books for his Russian and other researches.

Among all his other projects, Merton was interested in writing a book on contemporary religious art. "Art and Worship" was never published, though a good deal of the material appeared in essays. When Merton discovered how out of touch he was on the subject, he consulted Ed Rice, James Laughlin, Ad Reinhardt, and others. He had been surprised to learn Paul Klee and Georges Rouault were no longer considered avant-garde artists, and in his letters to Laughlin he said he thought very little of some who were.[452]

He was much more sympathetic to the painting of Victor Hammer, though it was a year before he could see this in quantity at the Hammer home in Lexington. Hammer had returned to a number of old techniques, using tempera and giving many of his panels a background of gold leaf, which set the figures sharply in outline. In his religious paintings there were links, above all to the Master of the Barberini Panels. In his portraits there is something of the Italian mannerist Bronzino. Yet this gives the impression of an eclectic artist, while Victor Hammer had a vision which is certainly his own — a vision that was out of fashion in the 1950s.

Picnics under the trees by Dom Frederic's Lake, or in the car when it was too cold, provided both men with a chance to talk of writers, poets, artists — and of Europe. There could be good-natured arguments. The Hammers had a somewhat austere view of literature — "Only the greatest, Hölderlin, Dante, Leopardi . . ." They sometimes found Merton's wide range of enthusiasms disturbing.

*

Almost every reader of Merton's has been perplexed by one question — when did Thomas Merton have time to be a contemplative? Part of the answer lies in the strict timetable he set for himself, and which he kept to, giving him hours, often before dawn, beyond those of other thinkers and writers. The gift of concentration he had developed in the novitiate helped him to use the time. "The greatest lesson Thomas Merton taught me was the fruitful use of solitude," Father Matthew Kelty has written.[453] For all this, the question became more and more pressing to Merton himself.

He was often unrealistic in thinking certain situations would provide a real solution. In the summer of 1958 he planned a "hidden monastery" (almost certainly in South America).[454] There were some obvious features: each monk would have a room of his own and there would be four or more hermitages. There would be no fixed program, other than the encouraging of solitude and prayer. By 1958 there was one new feature: however isolated and hidden the monastery, monks would be expected to keep up with developments in politics and culture.

There was little about the necessary administration in the plan, and nothing about the number of chores that would fall to each member of a small foundation, however primitive the life.

In the 1960s conferences were held at Gethsemani among the monks who were interested in smaller monasteries and experimental foundations. Father Matthew Kelty, Brother Maurice Flood, Father Louis, and a number of others attended the meetings.[455] Merton's ideas were useful to them all, and proved helpful later in foundations like the one at Oxford, North Carolina. Merton was convinced that the monastic future lay in such small foundations, and they retained their attraction. He was enormously enthusiastic about the experimental community at Christ in the Desert in New Mexico, which he visited in May and September 1968. Yet he went on looking for a hermitage after his visit. By this time he may have sensed something he had given little attention to before: in a small, struggling, experimental community he might have found himself with less time than in a large one. For one thing, more hours might have been spent in meetings.

His ideal was, and remained, a hermitage. In the meanwhile, he practiced yoga breathing exercises or said the Jesus Prayer in the Hesychastic tradition during Chapter.[456] Chapter had become Merton's *bête noire*. In his view it was the opportunity for each member of the community to make a fool of himself. If Merton included himself, he did admit in his journal that the time passed more quickly when he spoke. He felt he didn't take Chapter seriously enough. Others have said he took it too seriously, expected too much of it.[457] Still, many a person's charity toward others has foundered in the middle of a meeting.

He grew impatient with the Chapter of Faults.[458] This had diminished in importance somewhat since 1941, but Merton was still proclaimed. He found himself begging food from others in the refectory, then eating it seated on the floor.[459] It was Christian charity to show the fault in another, and many were overzealous for charity. In the novitiate Chapter of Faults there was an opportunity to declare one's own faults, though many a novice froze with fear when given the chance to get in first. There was never an approved method of finding fault with a monk who had just proclaimed you: the matter had to be stored up and used on another occasion.

Decisions were made by the abbot from the throne (or by the master in the novitiate). Many punishments were light, a penance of saying three Hail Marys. Where pride was concerned, however, humiliation rapidly followed. There were more unforeseen hazards: over-recollected monks coming into the abbey church often fell over penitents prostrate by the door into the cloister.

Correction was not limited to the Chapter of Faults. Merton sometimes catches monks whispering on the tapes of his conferences and gives out three Hail Marys on the spot.[460] Any novice of Merton's could approach him with "Father, I find fault in you," and the two would discuss this in private.[461]

Those Chapters, other than the Chapter of Faults, Merton found least edifying were the ones at which questions on moral theology were raised. He and Father Raymond were often at odds here. While Father Raymond enjoyed the finer points of the theology of morals, Father Louis was less than enthusiastic about discussing whether it was a venial sin to steal fifteen dollars, yet a confessional matter to take fifteen dollars and fifty cents — or whether there are some areas of leniency here that covered you to, say, sixteen dollars. On one such occasion, Father Louis waited, then stood to count on his fingers: "One. We can be sure God is merciful. Two. We can be sure God is infinite. Three. We can be sure — and so on and so on. But we can be almost certain that He is *not* a Moral Philosopher."[462]

On December 30, 1958, the discussion was on whether a dying man who is unconscious and who had not previously expressed a desire for the sacraments could be given absolution. There was a good deal said on both sides of the question when Brother Colman came into Chapter and made the sign for a doctor. Herman Hanekamp had been discovered dead in his cabin:

> While we argue wisely about administering the sacraments to the dying, someone depending on us for material and spiritual care has died without sacraments. I cannot help regarding it as a significant episode.[463]

Herman Hanekamp had been a novice before the First World War. He had taken Simple Vows, but left before taking Solemn Vows. The monks had given him a few acres of woodland, and he had built himself a place to live.

Merton's meetings with Hanekamp had usually taken place during fires in the Gethsemani woods, when the hermit's cabin was threatened. At the time the monastery bought the Linton Farm, Dom James had given Hanekamp one of the houses on the property. Hanekamp moved in the rain, with all his possessions on a mule cart.

Father John of the Cross had stayed with him in his illness and had been the last to give the blessing.[464] Father John Eudes found Herman's body still warm and gave him absolution and extreme unction.

The funeral took place on a bright, frosty day in the first week in January. It looked at first as if Hanekamp would be buried at New Haven. Then Merton found he was to be buried in the secular graveyard just outside the enclosure wall. Dom James asked him to sing the Mass, then sang it himself when Merton "begged off being deacon." Merton was one of the pallbearers, with Brother Clement and Brother Colman. Hanekamp's neighbors were represented by Andy Boone, his friend Glen Pine, and a man Merton didn't know who wore a string tie. The greatest shock was to view Herman in his casket — shaven, in a suit, and with collar and tie:

> When we came out of the church into the sun, carrying the coffin, the bright air seemed full of great joy and a huge freight train came barrelling through the valley with the sound of power like an army. All the pride of the world of industry seemed, somehow, to be something that belonged to Herman. What a curious obsession with the conviction of him as a great rich man, tremendously respected by the *whole* world! And we drove back to bury him in the little graveyard outside the monastery gate.[465]

In his own journal accounts Merton was quick to criticize the monastery, then revealed that the monastery had actually done rather well by Herman Hanekamp in life and in death, though there were certainly some monks who had thought him idle and shamming sickness. It is almost as if Merton *wants* to find the monastery neglectful and lacking in charity. The funeral turned out to be a "big affair, and if I had known that I would not have gone."

In the autumn of 1958 Merton wrote to Pasternak. By a separate mail he sent a copy of *Prometheus*. On September 22, *The New York Times* published a short, enthusiastic comment Merton had sent on *Doctor Zhivago*.[466] Merton hardly expected a swift answer to his letter, yet Pasternak replied, carefully dating his own letter "Holy Cross day, September 27th."[467] Even less expected were several further letters in the month of October.

On October 23 came the news the Russian writer had been awarded the Nobel Prize for Literature. Pasternak was recognized not only for the novel but also for his early poetry and for other writing. Few in the West had heard of him before the publication of the novel, which had now been translated into most European languages.

Within a matter of days a great book and a great writer were made an issue in the Cold War. On October 27, Pasternak was expelled from the Union of Soviet Writers. Merton wrote at once to Surkov, the president of the union, and to Khrushchev.[468] On October 30 came the news that Pasternak had turned down the Nobel Prize and that he was about to retire to his *dacha* in a writers' colony outside Moscow, Peredelkino.

During November Merton wrote three articles about Pasternak's work and the situation. Two would be printed the following year.[469] The third article, written on November 29, 1958, in which Merton called Pasternak a "Christian anarchist," ran into trouble at once.

On January 25, 1959, he mentioned in his journal that Dom Gabriel had written and refused permission for the "Christian anarchist" article, on the somewhat odd grounds that novels are worldly things and a dog should not return to his vomit — either an implied criticism of Pasternak the novelist or, more likely, of Merton the former novelist.[470]

The parallel with Pasternak's own problems was too obvious to be stressed or given wide expression. Merton felt the abbot general had missed the very point that made *this* novel important — its deep spiritual significance. For Merton it was a miracle that such a work of literature had appeared at such a time. It was a further miracle that such a book should bear witness to Christian values from Russia: *Doctor Zhivago* challenged the atheism of the Soviets *and* the Christianity of the West.

Later, Merton modified this:

> It is true that there are striking and genuinely Christian elements in the outlook of Pasternak, in the philosophy that underlies his writing. But of course to claim him as an apologist for Christianity would be an exaggeration . . .[471]

The Christian elements were striking to others as well. Even when they missed the deeper patterns, they could not fail to see the number of references to the Gospels, both in the story, and in the "poems of Yuri Zhivago" at the end. Yet it was probably just as well that Merton's article was held up by the abbot general.

Merton had heard from Pasternak in November, but only by way of a relayed message through a third party, John Harris, who described himself as "a country schoolmaster who wrote a sort of 'fan' letter to P. a day or two after 'Dr. Z.' was published."[472] Harris had written to Pasternak assuring him that "at least one Western reader loved it as a work of art and humanity, irrespective of the state of the cold war."

Pasternak had responded gratefully to this. Now he asked Harris:

> Write if possible to the poet and prosaist Mr. Thomas Merton . . . his precious thoughts and dear bottomless letters enrich me and make me happy. At a better and easier time I shall thank and write him. Now I

am not in a position to do so. Say to him his high feelings and prayers have saved my life. I intend to name him in my short immaterial (not concerning things and goods) commemorative testament of these days and few lines.[473]

Pasternak had told Harris his "signed and sealed letters habitually do not reach their destination." The postcard he had sent was unsigned (earlier letters to Merton had had only initials). It was dated November 7.[474] In sending the message on, Harris added his own cautions to those implicit in Pasternak's postcard. It would hardly have helped Pasternak to have it announced in print that he had been recognized by one of his correspondents in the West as a Christian anarchist.

The one exaggeration aside, Merton's recent reading put him well ahead of others in understanding the novel. He was able to see parallels between Pasternak's thought and Gandhi's. Even stronger, he felt, were the links to the Russian mystics and theologians:

> It is clear that Christ, for Pasternak, is a transcendent and Personal Being in the sense generally understood by such orthodox theologians as Soloviev or the Russian existentialist Berdyaev. The Christ of Pasternak is the Christ of Soloviev's "God-manhood." His view of the cosmos is, like Berdyaev's, "sophianic" and his "sister Life" has, in fact, all the characteristics of the Sancta Sophia who appeared to Soloviev in Egypt.[475]

Other Western critics saw Lara in *Doctor Zhivago* as a symbol for Russia, for Eve, for the healing, natural force. To Merton she was like "sister Life," "sophianic."

The letters between the two men had been simply cordial at first. Very quickly, Pasternak showed he was genuinely interested in Merton and sensed a real bond between them. He wrote a thorough criticism, which demonstrated he had read *Prometheus* with care. He discounted his own work, other than the novel:

> I take the opportunity to repeat you, that except the "Dr. Zh." which you should read, all the rest of my verses and writings are devoid of any sense and importance. The most part of my mature years I gave off to Goethe, Shakespeare and other great and voluminous translations.[476]

Merton was now learning Russian, perhaps in an attempt to reply in Russian to Pasternak's letters, though he was giving another day a week to improving his Portuguese for the translations of Brazilian poets.[477]

On March 2, 1959, he heard from Helen Wolff at Pantheon Books, which had published *Doctor Zhivago*, that there had been an official bulletin from Russia saying Pasternak had gone on vacation to the Black Sea to "get away from foreign reporters."[478] He suspected the worst, and said Masses for Pasternak's safety. He also wrote to Dom Gabriel, and, in the changed circumstances, permission was given to publish the article. Soon word came that Pasternak was alive and had only disappeared to take the holiday.[479]

There was a period of silence. Then Merton received a letter written on February 7, 1960, signed with a bold flourish, as if the time for caution and concessions was over. Pasternak thanked Merton for the articles on his work:

> I shall regain myself from that long and continuing period of letter writing, boring troubles, endless thrusted rhyme translations, time robbing and useless, and of the perpetual self-reproof because of the impossibility to advance the longed for, half begun, many times interrupted, almost inaccessible new manuscript.

This was the historical drama the writer hoped to finish. Pasternak returned to mention Merton's articles with a generous compliment and a moving promise:

> But I shall rise, you will see it. I finally will snatch myself and suddenly deserve and recover again your wonderful confidence and condescension.[480]

Three months later, on May 30, 1960, the Russian writer was dead. Merton had written in his journals that he had a closer contact with Boris Pasternak on the other side of the world than with people a few miles away, and more in common with him than with monks in his own monastery.[481] There was some boasting in this, but little exaggeration. When he read Pasternak's last letter he must have realized that this was a model of everything he had said in *Thoughts in Solitude* about a humility that inspired vitality and confirmed fortitude. When he heard of Pasternak's death he had every right to mourn for him as a friend.

✳

In many ways the year 1959 began with good auguries. Merton had written the April before that his health had greatly improved after the flu epidemic,[482] and he seems to have been in much better health than usual until the summer of 1959. He wrote that he liked the new Pope, John XXIII. In selecting excerpts from the sayings of the Desert Fathers for a book to be published by New Directions, he was doing something he enjoyed. He had written to Suzuki in Japan asking him to write a preface for the book, and Suzuki had agreed. To be so honored by Pasternak and Suzuki in one year was bétter than most of the fruits of fame. *The Secular Journal* had at last appeared, a victory of sorts against the censors. *The Selected Poems of Thomas Merton,*[483] with an introduction by Mark Van Doren, was about to appear from New Directions.

Dom Colomban Bissey, the new father immediate, made a visitation in April and encouraged Merton to continue the collaboration with Suzuki: "Do it but don't preach it."[484] When Father Paul Bourne arrived from Georgia, Merton had a chance to talk over censorship questions with his chief censor. Dom James had been Father Paul's superior at Conyers, and he had some sympathies with Merton when the conversation seemed to be turning in a way that gave Merton a chance to criticize the abbot. Instead, Merton said simply, "I need Dom James."[485]

Dom Colomban fell ill during his visitation.[486] Merton received permission to visit him in hospital in Lexington and to see the Hammers at home. Tuesday, April 21, was to be memorable for another unexpected event.

Merton was so delighted by the Hammers' house that he gave a lengthy description of it in the journal.[487] He went from painting to painting. Then he stopped in front of a triptych Victor Hammer had begun. This time he was not just interested, he showed signs of great emotion. Even when the Hammers sat down to lunch and began to discuss the possibility of printing Merton's "Signed Confession of Crimes Against the State" as a broadsheet, Merton kept getting up from the table to take another look at one of the panels of triptych.

In the unfinished painting a woman in dark robes was setting a crown on the head of a young man who stands between the woman and the viewer. Even at a glance, there is the same mystery about the painting there is in the somber exchanges of wreaths in a number of Greek funeral-relief panels. The picture is charged with a restrained emotion of both great serenity and great power. Merton's attention was largely directed to the features of the woman.

When Victor Hammer explained that the young man was Christ, the mystery of the woman remained. She was not so obviously the Mother of Christ. Merton went on with his own ideas, confusing both the Hammers with some of his references. Victor Hammer promised to do a drawing of the panel for Merton. Carolyn promised she would check on several visual sources for him at the library.

On May 14, Merton wrote a long letter to Victor Hammer about Hagia Sophia. In one sentence he tries to summarize what is most important to him about the theme:

> This feminine principle in the universe is the inexhaustible source of creative realization of the Father's glory in the world and is in fact the manifestation of His glory . . .[488]

Hammer wrote back:

> Ever since you, looking at the triptych have asked me who is the figure crowning Christ (which I couldn't tell you exactly) I am thinking about your interpretation: she being hagia sophia and also the mother of Christ. We were much intrigued by what you said but do not remember what it

was. Carolyn got the photograph from the Catholic Encyclopedia, which I enclose. The painting from Nowgrad bears a certain similarity with my painting but I cannot understand its relation to the Russian mystics.[489]

To Merton the many visual and literary connections were more than coincidental. There was one he did not mention to the Hammers. In a letter to Pasternak he had spoken of his dream of February 28, 1958. He refined the original description and set the names in a way that further emphasizes them — the old, evocative name Ann, and Proverb, which seems now to be the key to the dream (What is itself a proverb will remain hidden until it is opened by the saying of its own name). There is clearly an association with Sorrow, and there is the shame in the name, just as the prophet is ashamed of his gift, and perhaps the poet of his. Where the approach is different (both less erotic and less personal), Merton continues in near-dreamlike prose, linking the dream to a scene in a nearby city, to the moment when he stood on the corner in Louisville.[490]

By now, yet another element was added. Soon after going to Lexington to see the Hammers, Merton had discovered an article in *The Kenyon Review* on the women in Dostoyevsky's novels.[491]

The somber but austerely beautiful woman in Victor Hammer's painting was not the Jewish girl of his dream, not quite the Virgin of Nowgrad (at least in the photograph). Nor was she quite one aspect of Lara, nor any of Dostoyevsky's creations, not even the Sonya of *Crime and Punishment*, whose wisdom brings about the redemption of Raskolnikov, the murderer for pride. Nor was she the Sancta Sophia who appeared to Vladimir Soloviev in Egypt. And yet a portrait of extraordinary richness was forming. It required only to be brought closer to the earth.

Merton had a number of visitors in May. Robert Lax and Ad Reinhardt came to Gethsemani together, enabling Merton to talk of his ideas with both of them and question them about the illustrations for "Art and Worship." They had no sooner left than Robert Giroux arrived, and he and Merton discussed a book of essays, to include the bringing together of the Pasternak pieces.

Exhausted a little, and somewhat mystified his friends would come so far, Merton wrote the line about feeling his visitors went away sadly unedified.[492] He had never been able to figure out why it was that a few hours of his own company was considered so precious to so many— hours when he was not trying to be edifying or significant.

On May 6, he had a visitor with a clear purpose. Dom Gregorio Lemercier, the Prior of Our Lady of the Resurrection of Cuernavaca, was quite unexpected, even somewhat unwelcome to Dom James, who quickly formed an unenthusiastic view of him.[493]

In the two days Dom Gregorio stayed, he spent hours talking to Merton, but he announced his reason for coming at once. A crisis had been reached in the movement to modernize monasticism and Merton was needed in Mexico, where he would be most effective, where he could put his theories into practice.

Just as in 1955, there was a cluster effect. Dom Gregorio may have oversold Cuernavaca — gone on too long, talked too much about all the activities there, the experiments, the personal involvement. When he talked of poverty, it was a different story. What might be negative factors to others had a positive appeal to Merton. It had been so when he first came to Gethsemani, and it was still so. In the essay on Mount Athos he had written for _Jubilee_, which was to come out that August, Merton warned of the danger of romanticizing even while he surrenders to it himself:

> At the same time we must not take too romantic a view of the solitaries on Athos. They lead a life that is, from our Western viewpoint, utterly squalid, filthy and miserable. Yet they seem to get along well enough at it, and they really are, for the most part, deeply spiritual men. (In fact it is quite possible that they are more spiritual than the monks of our more hygenic and up-to-date monasteries with their spotless dairy cows and well-washed pigs.) The hermits on Athos are, generally, men of peasant extraction who are physically prepared to live a life exposed to heat, cold, vermin and near-starvation.[494]

At any rate, Merton wrote at once to a number of bishops asking them if there were any opportunities for becoming a hermit in some remote part of their diocese. As he had done earlier, he wrote seeking advice and help from Dom Jean Leclercq, to Monsignor Larraona at the Sacred Congregation, and to Father Jean Daniélou, S.J. He had talked of Daniélou with Dom Colomban, and the father immediate had said he would soon be seeing him, thought highly of him, and agreed Merton should both seek spiritual advice from him and make Daniélou his intermediate in matters that would come to Dom Colomban.[495]

It must have seemed a sign of sorts when, within weeks, Merton had three other options.

One of the bishops he had written to, James P. Davis, the Bishop of San Juan, wrote back on June 18, saying, "I believe I have a place which might suit your plans admirably." The bishop went on to describe the situation in Tortola, one of the British West Indies, adding, somewhat ironically in light of the future, that there was only one small resort hotel on the island. There was a small population with perhaps fifty Catholics. "You would not be too burdened with pastoral concerns but you would have some duties of that sort."[496]

On July 24, Bishop Dwyer of Nevada offered him a hermitage in St.

Brendon's Parish, Eureka, Nevada, an old mining community which had struck it poor and had diminished to five hundred people.[497]

Conversations with Brother Lawrence (Cardenal) had opened up a third possibility. This was on one of a group of islands off the coast of Nicaragua. Big Corn Island had once been a pirate hideout. It could be reached only by a two-hour boat trip by motor launch from Blue-fields. The inhabitants were a small number of blacks who spoke a patois of English.[498] When Merton wrote to inquire further, he received a welcoming letter from the Carthusian bishop, Matthew A. Niedhammer. He said at once that Merton had picked the right island, and he talked about ecclesiastical red tape the Church used to try the souls of those who loved her. The bishop suggested two things. Why didn't Father Louis come to the islands for a trial period of three months? And in the meanwhile, why not discuss the matter in New York in August, when the bishop would be staying at the Capuchin Friary on 210 West Thirty-first Street?[499]

Merton strongly favored the community of marooned blacks over the miners of Nevada, though he knew his chances of getting permission to see Bishop Niedhammer in New York were as remote as those of being allowed to travel to test any of the possibilities.[500]

It was a hotter summer than usual. Dom James was frequently unwell and spent a period in hospital. Merton was feeling all the old symptoms of stress: insomnia, colitis, headaches. As usual, he tried to conquer his sense of mental strain by throwing himself into physical labor.

On July 1, a dark, overcast day, he went out with the novices to pick up bales of hay near New Haven. Merton had written scathingly about Trappist working parties, saying the American monks came on the scene like a football team coming onto the field, and on this particular day he was trying to prove he was one of the team. He was watched by Brother Alban, who had been "blessed to work on a farm" as a child and who felt the master of novices had no sense of pacing work as he rushed at one bale after another, trying to set a good example — and in fact setting a bad one for his novices. Brother Alban says Father Louis was soon sitting on one of the bales, bright red in the face, a candidate for a heart attack. "I told him this wasn't the invasion of Normandy."[501]

Merton's journal gives a very different account:

> We filled wagon after wagon, with long waits in between. And as I sat waiting and thinking, with the novices, and looking at the dark green woods and the black sky, I was content and thought "This is all you need." But precisely "this" was *not* Gethsemani. We were off the property.[502]

It is clear how much he was torn by the way in which passages running down Gethsemani alternate with those extolling one or another feature of life there, or singling out an individual for praise. On June 11, having admitted that "The truth is it is very hard for me to judge the question dispassionately!" he wrote one of his toughest condemnations:

> What I find intolerable and degrading is having to submit, in practice, to Dom James's idea of himself and of Gethsemani and to have to spend my life contributing to the maintenance of this illusion. The illusion of the great, gay, joyous, peppy, optimistic, Jesus loving, one hundred percent American Trappist monastery.
>
> Is it possible to be here and not be plunged into the midst of this falsity?[503]

On July 16, he announced:

> My view of Gethsemani is suddenly back to normal — deeply moved by Father Flavian's first sermon this morning. With a few like him one need have no worries for the monastery. And I *do* love the monastery.[504]

Discussions with those close at hand were producing complications he hadn't foreseen. Cardenal was anxious to go with him to the island off Nicaragua ("At that rate I am no longer a hermit even before I start. Still, for *one* companion I'd be willing to let him come, but it requires thought").[505] Yet he himself was wondering if Father John of the Cross couldn't join him in Tortola.[506]

Dom Gregorio was back at Gethsemani on July 16, pressing Merton for an answer. Merton had already written to Monsignor Larraona, asking him to decide for him between Tortola and Cuernavaca — not an auspicious opening to a campaign asking for permission to leave Gethsemani. Now Merton redrafted a more strongly worded request to Larraona for permission to transfer to the Primitive Benedictine monastery in Mexico. He probably still favored Tortola or the island off Nicaragua, but Dom Gregorio was persuasive and at hand. Meanwhile, Dom Gregorio had won one important ally. On July 30, when Ernesto Cardenal had to leave the monastery because of ill health, he agreed to visit Cuernavaca himself as soon as he was strong enough to do so, and he promised to keep Merton informed.[507]

Father Daniélou's letters arrived, and Merton found them disappointing. Daniélou set aside Tortola as not monastic enough. He did not altogether exclude Cuernavaca, but repeated what he said earlier, that Gethsemani had provided Merton with some solitude and with the opportunity to be both a monk and a writer. What, then, was the point of sacrificing what he had for the unknown? Merton noted that Daniélou had a finer sense of Christian values than any of those he was writing to, but on this occasion he wondered if Daniélou really knew what was at stake.[508] Dom Jean Leclercq confirmed Merton's vocation as a solitary one, yet he was also asking whether there wasn't some way this could be followed at Gethsemani without a risk of scandal in leaving and a major upheaval in his own life.[509]

It must have been some relief to Merton to turn down one of the options. The Bishop of Nevada had written that he had already had a discouraging experience with a hermit who had been a Trappist, and he would need some reassurance. He also wrote that the hermit would need a car to perform the necessary pastoral duties.

Merton replied with a good deal of sarcasm:

> . . . I must admit that there was much that was attractive about the idea of being a poor priest in a parish lost in an exhausted mining area, "with no future." Thank you for offering to help me in this way. I think of the good people of Eureka and keep them in my prayers . . .[510]

The bishop may have felt he was getting off lightly.

The heat and the anxiety brought out a certain lack of discretion. When two women visitors, driving from California across country, arrived on September 5, Merton got permission to talk to them under the avenue of sweet-gum trees in front of the monastery, but hardly to go bathing in Dom Frederic's Lake and sunbathing. He simply records this without comment, except to say that he had had a pleasant day but should be cautious.[511] It had set a precedent that would prove more difficult to handle later.

When Dom Gregorio arrived for the third time on September 7, Merton had persuaded himself, or been persuaded, that his vocation was at Cuernavaca. He had redrafted the letter to Larraona a third time. Now this asked for an indult because his spiritual advisers had told him to leave the monastery, at least for a time, and to leave the United States, where he had become the object of the kind of publicity that had been prejudicial to the monastery and a problem to his conscience.[512]

In mid-October Merton entered St. Anthony's Hospital in Louisville for a rectal operation. Recovering, he wrote to James Laughlin that the next letter the publisher received from him might come from Mexico.[513]

A few weeks later — too late to be really helpful — Merton found a way of bypassing the monastery mailroom, passing letters out through visitors. In the meanwhile, everything came to the prior and to Dom James, though technically, if it had "Conscience Matter" written on the envelope, it could not be opened. Dom Gregorio's letters from Rome had been read. These were written in French and they referred to the "case of the French monk," but, if they were encouraging to Merton, they hardly disguised what was going on.[514]

Yet when Dom James announced in Chapter on November 15 that he would be leaving for Rome immediately for an important conference, this news caught Merton completely off guard. He knew that Dom

James had to make a visitation to the California foundation early in December, and the abbot had not been well since the early summer. He was charitably concerned for Dom James and deeply concerned for his own hopes.[515]

He found it almost impossible to do any writing, and most of the writing he had done that summer had been editing and revision — making a new version of *What Is Contemplation?*, a draft of "The Inner Experience" (which he had decided could only be privately circulated), and putting together the essays for *Disputed Questions*,[516] which Farrar, Straus and Cudahy were to bring out in September of 1960.

Just as he had done at St. Bonaventure's, Merton began to say his own goodbye to "the soft embrace of this 'mother' — this silent gentle circle of hills that has comforted me for eighteen years."[517]

He set himself in this "farewell to Eden" mood to correct the galleys of *The New Man* — his most Edenic book, and one he had written in five weeks in 1954. When he was in Louisville to see the doctor, he called in at Eastern Airlines to check how quickly he could be in Mexico if the permission came through. Then he went to the cathedral for Mass and made a visit to the Carmel, where he felt he had talked far too much to Mother Angela and the nuns. He was just leaving when he heard one of the children at St. Agnes School had been hit by a car. Fortunately the boy was not seriously injured, and as Merton knelt in the street to give the child his blessing, he caught the boy's expression and found it both moving and cheering to his own morale. When he returned to the monastery he received news that Dom James would be back from Rome that night.[518]

All Merton could learn from the abbot the next day was that Dom James had been forbidden to say anything about the outcome; he had simply handed matters over to his superiors for their decision. "This is a great relief to me also because we can now go ahead more objectively, without animosity and resentment. I think my relations with him have never been better — and I am very glad of the fact."[519]

That winter the "Cheese Factory" had increased production to deal with more orders and Merton had to give a good many of his hours in the day to working beside Brother Frederic Collins and others to dispatch the bacon, sausages, and cheese. There was much for the anti-poet to ponder in the advertising folders, where, Merton says, the copy read: "Many porkers are called, but few are chosen to produce our luscious hams."[520]

Nobody at the monastery recalls this, and many are outraged at the idea. Perhaps Merton was getting his own kind of revenge for being asked on several occasions that year to provide advertising copy for the cheese. His most famous anti-advertisement was the parody on Joyce Kilmer's poem "Trees" — in this case "Chee$e":

I think that we should never freeze
Such lively assets as our cheese.

The sucker's hungry mouth is pressed
Against the cheese's caraway breast

A cheese, whose scent like sweet perfume
Pervades the house through every room.

A cheese that may at Christmas wear
A suit of cellophane underwear,

Upon whose bosom is a label,
Whose habitat: — The Tower of Babel.

Poems are nought but warmed-up breeze,
Dollars are made by Trappist Cheese.[521]

Day after day went by in December while Merton listed things in his journal "as if I had been doing something else besides looking in the mailbox." He cut himself assembling the safety razor. "Hidden aggression, self-hate! Yah! It was a deep cut, too."[522] Even a letter he was writing to Lax had turned sour: "Doubletalk getting flaccid."

On December 17, 1959, a large envelope arrived from Rome, sent by surface mail on the 7th. Merton took the envelope unopened to the novitiate chapel and read the contents on his knees before the Blessed Sacrament.

Afterward, he went out in a light rain, tramping the woods, to select Christmas trees for the nuns, to try to find some way (other than deceptively easy words) in which he could respond "sweetly" to another rejection:

> Actually, what it comes to is that I shall certainly have solitude but only by a miracle, and not at all at my own contriving. Where? Here or there makes no difference. Somewhere, nowhere, beyond all "where." Solitude outside geography or in it. No matter.
>
> Coming back, walked around a corner of the woods and the monastery swung in view. I burst out laughing. It was no longer the same place, no longer heavy. I was free from it. I remember the anguish and resentment with which I saw the same view in March, '47, before my solemn profession.[523]

But in 1947 he had not been able to walk things off in the rain, or to laugh at the absurdity of Thomas Merton, Father Louis, or whomever, and the three S's — Solitude, Structure, and Stability, not to mention the hidden S, Self. His whole life was worth a laugh; a long, rich, rolling laugh.

———————————

PART SIX

Mount Olivet

. . . . Futile? Life is not futile if you simply live it. It remains futile however as long as you keep watching yourself live it. And that is the old syndrome: keeping a constant eye on oneself and on one's life, to make sure that the absurd is not showing, that one has company, that one is justified by the presence and support of others.

— *Thomas Merton*

Und er gehorcht, indem er überschreitet.

In all his over-steppings he obeys.
— *Rilke*

A LITTLE MORE than a year later, on December 26, 1960, through a series of circumstances he could not have foreseen, Thomas Merton had his high place at Gethsemani and his hermitage:

> Lit candles in the dusk. *Haec regina mea in saeculum saeculi* — the sense of a journey ended, of wandering at an end. *The first time in my life* I ever really felt that I had come home and that my roaming and looking were ended.

> A burst of sun through the window. Wind in the pines. Fire in the grate. Silence over the whole valley.[1]

He was less than a mile from the monastery, still within the sound of its bells, writing by candlelight and the last sunlight of the short winter's day in a small building constructed of cement blocks set on the crest of a low knob called Mount Olivet, a view of the valley in front, woods and a spinney at the back.

When he wrote to Catherine de Hueck Doherty, he called it his *dacha*.[2] To the family in New Zealand it was "a little cottage in the woods."[3] The main feature of the larger of the two rooms was a stone fireplace where pine knots burned that December day. Wood smoke must have brought back the smell of the Midi, memories of the house in St. Antonin, and of his father. Owen's son, too, had begun to occupy his "casa."

The place already spoke for him. Folders on the worktable would have told any visitor of his interests in this first year of the 1960s: his growing correspondence on non-violence, opposition to the nuclear arms race, the struggle for social justice.

The new focus of his interests went back to the last month in 1959, a time when Merton felt raw with rejection. Although he dreaded rejection more than anything else, it was often a stimulus. Even the stability crises had brought about much in a paradoxical manner — without such pressure, within and without, it is doubtful if the hermitage would ever have been his. The few hours each day he was allowed to spend there depended on an unofficial agreement with Dom James. Merton was anxious about the abbot general's visit in the spring of 1961, fearing Dom Gabriel Sortais might reverse the abbot's decision, perhaps even order the building demolished.[4] Such a threat served to make the hours of solitude there more precious. With all his concerns of social conscience, the book Merton was working on in December 1960 was a revision of *Seeds of Contemplation,* to be published as *New Seeds of Contemplation.*[5]

The letter from Rome, sent on December 7, 1959, and signed by Cardinal Prefect Valeri and by Cardinal Larraona,[6] had begun by going over ground familiar enough already from the letters of Father Barnabas Ahern, Father Daniélou, and many other advisers. The two cardinals again raised the question of scandal, of Merton's contradicting the strong impression his early writing had made. There was much emphasis on the writing. Valeri and Larraona even quoted from the French edition of *No Man Is an Island,* giving the passage that begins in English:

> Our Father in Heaven has called us each one to the place in which He can best satisfy His infinite desire to do us good. His inscrutable choice of the office or the state of life or particular function to which we are called is not to be judged by the intrinsic merit of those offices and states but only by the hidden love of God. My vocation is the one I love, not because I think it is the best vocation in the Church, but because it is the one God has willed for me.[7]

As many others were to do, the two cardinals had quoted Merton only to their own purpose, cutting off his line of thought when it suited their argument. It is possible that Thomas Merton has suffered more from such selective editing than from censorship. On this occasion the author must have seen the irony, for the passage continued, *without a break,* to make a good case against taking stability as an absolute:

> If I had any evidence that He willed something else for me, I would turn to that on the instant. Meanwhile, my vocation is at once my will and His. I did not enter it blindly. He chose it for me when His inscrutable knowledge of my choice moved me to choose it for myself. I know this well enough when I reflect on the days when no choice could be made. I was unable to choose until His time had come. Since the choice has been made, there have been no signs in favor of changing it, and the presumption is that there will be no change. That does not mean there *cannot* be a change.[8]

It was not unfair to quote Merton's writing against Merton's intent: it *was* unfair to take half of what he said and present it as the whole. Reassembled, the passage stands as a summary of Merton's process of discovering God's will in the matter of his vocation — in 1941, in 1954, and at any later date: "That does not mean there *cannot* be a change."

In a letter to Dom Gregorio, Merton said the decision appeared to be final and he would obey, though he thought it unjust. This letter is dated December 17, a day on which Merton made a number of attempts to clarify his position on paper. He had already told Father John Eudes he was sure Dom James had gone to Rome with the sole purpose of blocking his initiative and that the abbot had made full use in his interviews with Cardinal Larraona and others of the meeting with Gregory Zilboorg at which Dom James had been present:

> Le P. Eudes croit que le P. Abbé leur aura dit que le psychiatre Zilboorg avait un jour dit en passant que mon désir de solitude était "patholo-gique." P. Eudes lui n'est pas du tout d'accord sur ce jugement et il m'a dit hier que Zilboorg était un bonhomme qui changeait vite ses opinions qu'il lançait comme ça en l'air. En effet, plus tard il a paru penser de moi d'une façon tout à fait différente. Mais le P. Abbé s'est accroché à ce mot, et à d'autres — Zilboorg aurait dit que je pourrais bien quitter l'église et m'enfuir avec une femme, etc., etc. Evidemment nous sommes tous humains . . . Mais le P. Abbé aura fait ressortir avec beaucoup de force ces arguments. Et voila . . .[9]

Gregory Zilboorg died of cancer in August 1959. There appeared to be no way of repairing the impression Merton had made in the second interview, an impression he felt Zilboorg had largely orchestrated. In Merton's view he had been presented in Rome by his abbot as "un type instable et passionné qui cherche à s'évader de la vie regulière."[10]

Merton told Dom Gregorio that he had written to Cardinal Valeri trying to undo this damage, repeating that his search for solitude was no purely egotistical venture on the part of a restless monk. It was one he had pursued through tribulation consistently for twenty years, and now it manifested itself in an apostolic charge to establish a small foundation of hermits. Yet he doubted whether Valeri would change his mind.

Meanwhile, Merton said, his life at Gethsemani was like Don Juan's in prison — no existence but in despair. He had written earlier to Father Daniélou, giving some of the details of his virtual isolation. He amplified these in the letter to Dom Gregorio. He had discovered the abbot had simply returned unread a letter that had come to Merton from Ernesto Cardenal, marked "Conscience Matter." He told Dom James that Cardenal was in need of his advice on spiritual matters, to which Dom James replied, Merton wrote, that Father Louis was far too busy to give advice at such length and at such distance: others, nearer at hand, could advise Cardenal. Then, Merton said he told the abbot that he considered Ernesto Cardenal a close friend:

> Or à ce moment j'ai vu l'expression de Dom James: il triomphait. Dire que j'avais un "ami intime" c'était tout simplement confesser une amitié particulière. Comme il était content. Il était tout à fait justifié . . . J'étais donc homosexuel! . . . Vous voyez comment il fait ses jugements [sic]. Et pour les raisons d'un tel Supérieur, la Congrégation a flanqué dehors mon application.[11]

It is quite clear that by this time neither man was capable of making any judgment of the other without exaggeration. Merton had proved sadly ingenuous in thinking, after his first interview with the abbot on his return from Rome, that a balance had been achieved between them that either Merton or the abbot could live with for long. The next year or so marked the lowest period and the most tangled in their years together.

There is nothing more in the account Merton gave Dom Gregorio than that Dom James reacted in a wholly predictable way to Merton's admission that Cardenal was a friend. This is one of the very few references Merton ever made to something which complicated life in the monastery to no very obvious gain — the rule against forming Particular Friendships, with all its nuances and implications. It was a rule Merton virtually ignored in the 1960s, which speaks to a firm confidence that he knew where he stood. In December 1959 there are certainly some odd tangles in a letter in which the writer says he had been falsely accused of homosexuality *and* of the desire to rush from the religious life with a woman at the first opportunity!

On the same day he wrote to Dom Gregorio, Merton drafted two documents to present to Dom James when the abbot returned from a visit to the foundation at Vina in California, on December 18. One was a statement of submission containing four "resolutions" — a "Merry Christmas" gift for the abbot. The second, a much tougher document, stated Merton's feelings "Concerning the rights of conscience." There is no evidence that either of these somewhat contradictory documents was presented to the abbot in the exact form of Merton's careful drafts, which were written first of all to clarify his own thought. The first is an attempt to make peace, the second very close to a series of accusations.

In the "Merry Christmas" gift, Merton's opening resolution is the most important:

> 1) I intend to take no further positive steps as long as I live, to leave the Order. I will make no move to do so, and will apply no pressure to do so. At most, I will content myself with manifesting my thoughts to Superiors or those competent.[12]

If the abbot feels his desire to be a hermit conflicts too much with his responsibilities as master of novices, the abbot will have to fire him (the need for solitude comes first). Merton ends with some attempt to mend the appearances of a broken loyalty:

> I really love Gethsemani in spite of the reaction against certain aspects of the setup. I am grateful to God for the graces He has given me here and know that He has many more in store. The decisions made have left me very free and empty and I can say that they have enabled me to taste an utterly new kind of joy.[13]

The second draft, a "humble and filial petition," states that Merton had taken the abbot's views into consideration, and he was grateful for them, but:

> To demand that I consult you about my interior motives is to demand that I come to you for direction whether I desire it or not, but this is contrary to the Canons. In point of fact, I had arrived at my decisions in conscience as the result of consultation with other directors. But in the past, as I know from experience, you have shown a tendency to *overrule* the opinions of directors in order to substitute your own. This, in the internal forum is nothing else but demanding that the subject regard you as his *only* director, when in point of fact he has no obligation to regard you as his director at all.[14]

Merton follows with a number of accusing questions:

> Do you not have an inordinate tendency to interfere in the workings of conscience and to suppress by violence those desires and ideals which run counter to your policies? Do you not tend to assume that your policies represent the last word in the spiritual perfection of every one of your subjects, and that anyone who is drawn to another way is leaving the path of perfection, simply because he is not following your ideas?[15]

Then he makes his request:

> In charity and justice I appeal to my right to settle affairs of conscience with directors, and that I be allowed to do so without violent interference. I appeal to the right granted and assured by the Father Visitor, to consult directors outside the monastery by letter, without interference, so that this problem of mine can be settled. I am only asking for things which the Church wishes her subjects to have, not for anything unreasonable.[16]

At the end of 1959 and the beginning of 1960, the real question was not stability but obedience. To Dom James, Father Louis, the faithful monk, had committed an act of disobedience, while all his behavior at the time betrayed a bad conscience.[17] To Thomas Merton, the abbot's intransigence and political maneuvering had put him in a position where, in all conscience, he had to rethink the whole question of obedience to authority.[18] He felt himself bound to make mistakes. Had he spread out all his writing of that single day, December 17, 1959, he would have found evidence of bad conscience, of poor logic, even of saying things which were directly contradictory to different people. Virtually cut off from advice, he felt he had to test ground which was unfamiliar beyond canon law.

In seeking his way forward, Merton found the writings of Gabriel Marcel and of Emmanuel Mounier as helpful in clarifying his own thought as Huxley had once been in *Ends and Means*. There were models, but they were only marginally useful. Fairly or unfairly, Merton felt he had a negative model in his abbot. He permitted his own novices to resolve matters of conscience by seeking counsel beyond his own. In his conferences with the novice class he spent much time talking about obedience. He made one important point, however: the members of a religious community should consult with others in the religious life, not with seculars. "They don't understand our kind of life," he said. "Contact with seculars shakes up the resolution." [19]

The struggles toward a redefinition of obedience beginning at the end of 1959 were important in themselves and served as preparation for the much broader contest in 1962 over censorship and Merton's writings on nuclear war.

Sister Elena Malits has made the perceptive statement that, both as model and as Christian teacher, "Merton, seemingly alone, had worked out a way to sort out the commitments he had to keep and those he could negotiate in the 1960s." [20]

Once more, it was a question of separating the essentials from the incidentals, of finding a way at times to be truly obedient when appearing disobedient. This had proved a treacherous path for others in different circumstances — a way of losing balance, of making oneself vulnerable to many forms of self-deception. The true danger, as Merton saw it, was to confuse the demands of the ego with the demands of the conscience. The rebellion of the individual claiming rights and freedom was a trap. He sought to free conscience to obey his faith. In this, as in all else, the means determined the end: he could not act against conscience to free conscience.

*

To all appearances Merton made a remarkable recovery of equilibrium in the last days of 1959. He saw Dom James when the abbot returned from California on the 18th and "acted in general like a member of the community." [21] He went out cutting more Christmas trees in the Gethsemani woods, then sat down with the chill of the woods on his clothes to write:

> The loblolly pines planted during my 1955 crisis are growing well. The whole property is dotted with trees I have planted in hours of anguish. The ones I planted in hours of consolation have not succeeded. [22]

Presents arrived, the most welcome of all being Robert Lax's collection of poetry, *The Circus of the Sun*, which had connections with Lax's circus novel and the first summer at Olean Cottage when Lax, Rice, and Merton had all become serious writers in their most unserious bohemian ashram. Now Merton found his gift "a tremendous poem, an Isaias-like prophesy."[23]

When Victor Hammer offered his crucifixion panel for the novitiate chapel (the panel had proved the wrong size for the chapel at Kolbsheim in Alsace), Merton asked the abbot's permission to go over to Lexington to collect it. On the drive back Merton decided to use his freedom to see a place he had visited briefly the previous summer.

Pleasant Hill, Shawnee Run, or Shakertown was desolate on a winter's afternoon. None of the later restoration had been started, and only one building, the guest house, was open. Here, the walls were covered with graffiti — "the usual desecration."[24] Yet Merton walked in the large, bare rooms, the sunlight filtering in, feeling exhilarated. Everything stressed plainness — a more than Cistercian plainness, which should have been cold, which should have left him chill with a sense of "the cold and cerebral," and which had the opposite effect. Some quality of the hand-worked wood and the proportions created an atmosphere that was, at the same time, warm, human — and yet visionary, clear, sane, supernatural. Merton found himself thinking of Blake, then of what Victor Hammer had said about the craftsman losing himself and finding himself in a sense of work — a sense few who talked so much of "creativity" and "self-expression" ever came to know. Merton also found himself wishing he had a camera.

Back at Gethsemani, Merton ordered books on the Shakers. He also wrote to Shirley Burden about the possibility of combining an article with a photo essay. The photographer had already provided illustrations for the postulant's guide, *Monastic Peace,* and the cover for Merton's *Selected Poems.* Burden had undertaken a photographic study of the daily life of the monks of Gethsemani, *God Is My Life,*[25] which would appear at Easter, 1960. Now he wrote back with news of the layout of the book, which Ed Rice was doing, and he expressed enthusiasm for a similar collaboration.[26] Burden also gave Merton a good deal of information about sources for a study on the Shakers. There would be a delay: Burden was committed to doing a book on Lourdes.

Burden's liking for the idea and the news of the delay made up a sort of positive and negative, each equally necessary to encourage Merton to try something new.

Photography *was* a new interest. Merton had been largely bored in 1939 when he went with Jinny Burton, Celeste, and Lilly to a show of photographs at the Museum of Modern Art.[27] Yet, in a sense, he had been taking photographs of subjects without a camera for some time:

Looking out of the novitiate, when the winter sun is rising on the snowy pastures and on the pine woods of the Lake Knob, I am absorbed in the lovely blue and mauve shadows on the snow and the indescribably delicate color of the sunlit patches under the trees. All the life and color of the landscape is in the snow and sky, as if the soul of winter had appeared and animated our world this morning. The green of the pines is dull, verging on brown. Dead leaves still cling to the oaks and they also are dull brown. The cold sky is very blue. The air is dry and frozen. Instead of the mild, ambivalent winter of Kentucky, I breathe again the rugged cold of upstate New York.[28]

This is color, and Merton hardly ever used color.[29] He goes on to talk of Chinese painting, and of the nineteenth-century realist painters, then to say, "In any case, nothing resembles reality less than the photograph."[30]

But only, as Merton knew perfectly well, because this is a new reality, and certainly not just a machine-made one. In this passage rhetoric makes for some confusion (a photograph is not a shadow picture), yet even in seeming to deny the validity of photography, Merton establishes the philosophical basis behind his own best photographs:

Nothing resembles substance less than its shadow. To convey the meaning of something substantial you have to use not a shadow but a sign, not the imitation but the image. The image is a new and different reality, and of course it does not convey an impression of some object, but the mind of the subject: and that is something else again.[31]

When *God Is My Life* arrived Merton was disappointed. He thought the captions sentimental and feared he would be taken as the author.[32] There may have been something else: he may have felt he could have taken more significant photographs. John Howard Griffin records photographing sessions with Thomas Merton later. Merton would stalk a potential subject from a number of angles then walk away muttering "trite," "ordinary" — not that there was nothing in it, but there was nothing in it for *him*. Merton had much help in time from Griffin and others, yet he already had a clear idea of what he wanted to take.[33] For all this, Burden may have made a distinct contribution (together with Zen, books on the Tao of painting, Merton's enthusiasm for such artists as Klee and Miro, and, of course, his own instinctive search for connections and significant signs): Burden's cover photograph of *Selected Poems* is close to the "new and different reality" Thomas Merton was seeking as he became a borrower of cameras.

❉

As 1959 turned into 1960 Merton was planning a new course in Cistercian history for his novices. He had gained Dom James's permission to visit Dr. James Wygal in Louisville for a regular series of psycho-analysis, something he had put off for three years. In some sense he forced this now on the grounds that Dom James had made much of his general instability in Rome: if he was in such need of psychiatric help, surely he should have it![34] Jim Wygal and Thomas Merton were soon to be firm friends and their sessions meant much to both men, though Dom John Eudes Bamberger is certainly right in seeing them as pleas-ant talks, not seriously needed treatment. "Father Louis was well able to psychoanalyze himself," Dom John Eudes says. According to the doctor and psychiatrist at the monastery, he was also well able to cor-rect himself.[35] Permission to visit his doctor gave Merton a chance, however, to go more often to Louisville. In July 1960 he wrote in his journal that he probably should not have gone to Wygal's house to lis-ten to jazz records, and it was certainly wrong to go with Father John Loftus of Bellarmine College to hear live jazz on Fourth Street.[36]

On January 13, 1960, James Laughlin made his delayed visit, and the Hammers came for another Gethsemani picnic. The publisher arrived thoroughly confused, both by the rules and regulations in the Catholic Church and by the conflicting information he had been receiving all fall. Laughlin was directly in touch with Cardenal, who had written in Oc-tober to say permission had been given in Rome for Merton to go to Cuernavaca, but that Merton would not hear of this at once because the "cheese manufacturers" would prevent the news from getting to him. Meanwhile, Ernesto Cardenal had sent addresses and detailed information on how Merton was to travel in Mexico, including advice on what to wear. Because he was unable to get down to Gethsemani himself, Laughlin had relayed all this to the Hammers, only to hear back that Merton was still at Gethsemani at the end of December and the whole plan had been stopped.[37]

Merton gave his own account of how he thought Dom James had knocked the Cuernavaca plan on the head. The abbot's trip to Rome was hardly a "secret" one, however, as James Laughlin reports Merton saying it was, when he wrote to his managing director at New Direc-tions, Robert M. MacGregor.[38] The letter is interesting for its details about the picnic: first, how "Tom consumed nearly a whole cold tur-key, three-fourths of a bottle of wine, and three cans of beer" — then on to plans for a hermitage:

> So he stays on here, but is certainly not "resigned" to it. We'll just hope to make the best of it while trying to persuade Father Abbot that Geth-semani should have its own little appended "hermitage" up in the mountains somewhere, where monks could live in huts with a couple of brothers to wait on them and their own guest house where interesting visitors like Tillich or Kerouac could come for weekends to talk, all this supported by the royalties from his books. Well, it's a nice dream.[39]

It also makes a "pleasant picture," not unlike the one Thomas Merton had painted for Aldous Huxley in the review he had drafted of Huxley's *After Many a Summer Dies the Swan* at St. Bonaventure's in 1941.[40]

The talk during Laughlin's visit moved to a discussion of recent breakdowns and acts of madness among poets and writers "in the world," then to a general consensus on how hard it was to tell what was neurosis and what was sanity in an insane world.[41] This led to publishing projects, the most notable of which was a plan to invite essays on the obvious insanity of nuclear war and the arms race. Merton was to write the introduction.

Shortly after Laughlin returned to New York and Connecticut, Merton received bad news for his publisher on an earlier project. Dom Gabriel had turned down the whole idea of Suzuki's writing the introduction to *The Wisdom of the Desert*,[42] Merton's selection of sayings by the Desert Fathers, which New Directions was about to publish. Dom Gabriel thought the introduction by Daisetz Teitaro Suzuki "inappropriate."[43] To the publishers, "It is evidently as if we were inviting a kind of debate for the non-believer."[44] As Dom Gabriel had given permission for the Suzuki material with selections to appear in the *New Directions Annual*,[45] a magazine in hard covers, but not in a book, the point of his refusal was obviously a fine one.

Merton's relations with Dom Gabriel were growing acrimonious. The abbot general sent a long letter full of fury at some of the references to the Order in the typescript of *Disputed Questions*.[46] Censorship questions held up this collection of essays at Farrar, Straus and Cudahy, and Robert Giroux, who had now joined that firm as an editor, hurried down to Gethsemani soon after Laughlin to try to clear up matters.[47]

What Dom Gabriel regarded as slights and disloyalties to the Order were only the beginning of a major struggle over censorship. Here, too, loyalty was to be the question. Merton often accuses himself in his journals of seeing America through French eyes when he believes he is being overcritical or fault-finding.[48] Something, also, instinctively drew him to a French writer, whereas something almost always put him off an English writer. He had applauded the rebirth of French Catholicism in the 1958 preface to *Obras Completas*.[49] He was now to be made aware of the rebirth of French patriotism since the Second World War, a pride that was as strong as it was sensitive, and which had been made more sensitive still by reverses in Indochina and the war in Algeria, which most Frenchmen regarded as a civil war. The plans for essays on non-violence and against preparations for nuclear war were going to be thought a great deal worse than "inappropriate" by an abbot who was also a French patriot, and by his secretary, Father Clement de Bourbont, who was even more sensitive of French honor than Gabriel Sortais.[50]

Against this gathering battle, the attempt to publish a work in which a Zen philosopher and a Christian monk would discuss the connections they found between the sayings of Zen monks and those of the Desert Fathers of the fourth century was simply a year or two ahead of its time. The new "spirit of openness," which Pope John XXIII had initiated, required longer to be accepted throughout the Church. When Jacques Maritain wrote to Merton suggesting a collection of essays that would bring together work by Fromm, Tillich, Eliade, and Merton's essay on Suzuki, and for which Maritain would write the introduction, the answer was again no from Dom Gabriel.[51]

Yet the movement which was already widely publicized as ecumenical had brought groups from other Christian denominations to Gethsemani. Merton was anxious to further this, and the abbot looked to him to organize these occasions. The Catholic Church had changed. The responses from other Christian churches demonstrated that there had been unforeseen changes in their own attitudes. Gethsemani had certainly changed since 1941, and so, too, had Thomas Merton. Discussions in Chapter showed an anxiety to be welcoming, to put the ancient Cistercian tradition of hospitality to a new purpose. At the same time there was an understandable nervousness about the strain such visits and conferences would place upon the routine of the monastery. Plans were already under way to build a conference center some distance from the monastery, though on the Gethsemani grounds.

The plans were given a push forward by an accident. At eight-thirty in the evening of March 7, 1960, when the monks were already in bed, the fire alarm sounded. Machinery had set a pile of wood shavings on fire, but it looked at first as if the Steel Building, the least likely building to catch fire at Gethsemani, was wrapped in flames. The abbey firefighting team was soon able to get the blaze under control. The monks returned to bed, and the saying of the first office was moved to three.[52] The thought uppermost in the minds of many of the monks, and certainly in the mind of the abbot, was — if the Steel Building could catch fire, what of the risk in buildings that had long been fire traps?

The blaze in the Steel Building remains a small incident in the history of the monastery, yet it decided Dom James that the profits he had been building for years would have to be used at once and that nothing short of gutting and fireproofing all the old structures would be enough.[53] The three floors of dormitories in the Old Guest House were the first priority.

A blizzard smothered all of central Kentucky on March 16, putting a stop to what had already been begun, while the annual flu epidemic filled the infirmary. Considerable point was given to the sense of emergency, however, when the engineers who were called in to make the initial survey flatly refused to go up the stairs the monks had been using for years.[54]

As soon as the snow went, the machines moved in. After the north and south wings, work began on Hogan's Alley, the top floor of the Old Guest House, so called because it had once housed alcoholic priests, sent by their bishops to Gethsemani to "dry out." The monastery crews worked down floor by floor, replacing wood with concrete and steel. Once more, everyone was shifted about:

> I have moved into a special cell built over the new stairs by the infirmary. It is practically a windowsill — a wall and a window, and the floor is almost on the level of the window, high up on the third floor, looking out over the bottoms toward Rohan's Knob and Holy Cross. It is so far very quiet and I think it ought to make a nice hermitage.[55]

It looked as if all available space where beds could be crowded in would be needed at the monastery for some time, and in these circumstances the retreat house project was hurried along, though funds which had been available were needed at the monastery for the rebuilding program and an application was made to the Ford Foundation.[56] In late March a party of Protestant divinity students arrived from Vanderbilt University for the first ecumenical conference of the year.[57]

Merton had his own problems with fire on April 1, when brush he had been burning in the woods sent out sparks that started a blaze. Freddy Hicks came to help stop the spread of flame, but Merton was exhausted by the time things were under control. A few days earlier he had developed an eye infection working in the woods. Despite treatment, the eye was bothersome and painful into June, and he wrote that he now had sympathy for Gerard Manley Hopkins, who had written that after reading students' papers he felt as if his eyes were full of lemon juice.[58] When Merton went into Louisville wearing dark glasses it made him feel like the "dark" philosopher he was writing about in an essay, "Herakleitos the Obscure." There may have been some compensatory sense of drama in all this, Merton's mind going back to the many disguises of Sy Freedgood. The spy and the masked impostor had a place in Merton's imagination: Bulldog Drummond, Frater John Spaniard, and Lax Edwards, the chief of the renegade priests, were none of them wholly forgotten.

Conjunctivitis does not seem to have slowed the momentum of Merton's reading. That spring he had read Aeschylus's *Prometheus Bound*. "It is like Zen — like Dostoievsky — like existentialism — like? — like Isaias — like the New Testament — it is inconceivably rich."[59] He went back to Newman, feeling he had neglected him because of his briliance: "Brilliance is a bad word — for me to desire that is always fatal."[60]

"Mysticism," he discovered, was a bad word for English historians. Reading Lytton Strachey's *Eminent Victorians*, he notes, "Strachey, Tom

Bennett, myself at 18 — and so many other Englishmen, laughing at false mystics and holding them off by supercilious objectivity. All Englishmen who are not Thomas Cromwell or worse, tend to be General Gordons. (Hence Trevor-Roper's fear of monks and his admiration of T. Cromwell — of all people to have for a hero!)"[61]

Reading Trevor-Roper brought Merton back to something much closer than the anti-mystical streak in English historians or the arbitrary division of all Englishmen into one of two unlikely types. With Trevor-Roper's examination of the motives of treason came the old inner debate about loyalty (in this case loyalty to the Order and to the monastery).[62] Something Dom James had said may have stirred up memories as far back as Mrs. Haughton's accusation that he had been a disloyal guest in Aberdeenshire in 1929.

Loyalty came up again in a letter Merton received from a Shaker eldress in New Hampshire. She had sent a publication:

> A touching little leaflet about how the Shakers now quietly faced extinction, convinced they had not been a failure. And I am convinced of it too. I think Shakerism is something of a sign — a mystery — a strange misguided attempt at utter honesty that wanted to be too pure — but ended by being nevertheless pure and good, though in many ways absurd. This loyalty, absolute loyalty to a vision leading nowhere. But do such visions really lead nowhere? What they did they did, and it was impressive. It haunts me, at times. I mean the atmosphere and spirit, the image that they created, the archetype.[63]

The Shaker experiment could command his admiration, even puzzle him, but had it ever had the right to command absolute loyalty? What human organization, for all its claims to the true vision, had such a right? What structure?

The physical structure of Gethsemani was being altered even as he wrote. He had picnicked in the ruins of great abbeys as a schoolboy, great religious communities brought to a few spikes of brick or stone by the Thomas Cromwell Trevor-Roper wrote about. How would some latter-day Thomas Merton sum up the experiment of Gethsemani — of monasticism in the twentieth century — after a visit to the place, coming here as he had been to the wreck of Shakertown?

What structure could demand absolute loyalty? If you were loyal to God ("God Alone" was cut into the Gethsemani wall), or if you were loyal at least to your search for God's will in your life, how did this affect other claims to your loyalty? If you trusted God absolutely, what trust did you have left to give to institutions?

To one institution Thomas Merton now felt an ambiguous loyalty, both because it had changed and because he had changed. The monastery went on changing. In January the abbot had virtually disbanded the

donations office, transferring Father Francis de Sales to the library.[64]
The fate of Our Lady of Gethsemani appeared to be in the hands of
Gethsemani Farms. For whatever good reason, the heavy machines were
back; the place was once again like New York City when the sewers
were up. The March snow was almost immediately blackened by coal
dust and cinders from the monastery chimney. Merton lifted his eyes
to look at the jet trails, like frozen cobwebs in a sky otherwise un-
marked, deep blue and cold.[65]

*

Pasternak was dying that spring. Dorothy Day and members of the
Catholic Worker staff staged another non-violent peace strike. In Paris,
the followers of another friend by correspondence, Louis Massignon,
were arrested in the streets for their non-violent demonstration against
the Algerian War.[66] At the abbey, Father Lambert was dying in the
infirmary after a stroke. Yet it was, Merton records, a beautiful Easter,
warm and bright. There had never been such an Easter fire roaring in
the night wind at the beginning of the Rites of Vigil.[67] "Christ is risen!"
"It is the greatest truth of all, He is risen!" Or, as the Lady Julian of
Norwich, the fourteenth-century recluse Merton was coming to love,
expressed it, "The worst conceivable thing has happened, and it has
been mended . . . So that the end of everything shall be well. I say
again, all manner of things shall end well."[68]

On Palm Sunday, Lorenzo Barbato, a Venetian architect and a personal friend of the Pope, arrived at Gethsemani bringing a stole John
XXIII had worn and some medals he had blessed, the gifts of the Pope
to Father M. Louis Merton, who thought himself so isolated from the
understanding and the trust of the higher ranks of the Church.[69]

There was a plan now to cooperate on the building project with Bellarmine College in Louisville, where Merton already had friends, where
the librarians had helped him with books, and where a collection of his
own writing, published and unpublished, had been started. On April
28, Jack Ford, a philosophy professor at the college who later became
a close friend, and Tony Barret, a graduate student at Indiana University, came over to discuss the "retreat workshop plan" with Merton.[70]
Word had just come through by way of Cardinal Tardini that the Pope
had a special interest in the "special retreats with Protestants which
Father Louis was organizing at Our Lady of Gethsemani.[71] Everything
seemed propitious. "Each new step leads to more significant regions . . .
Possibility of a *skete* for retreat on the hill behind the sheep barn."[72]
This was the low knob called Mount Olivet on the monastery maps.
The site had been chosen. The cellarer, Brother Clement, proved un-
expectedly enthusiastic and offered to approach the abbot for funds and
monastery labor, "rather than let the boys from Bellarmine build it."[73]

However, Merton's attention was divided. His new room at the monastery had become something very close to a hermitage:

I sit on the edge of sky, the sunlight drenches my feet. I have a stool here, an old one, and a desk (my old scriptorium desk) by the bed — three ikons and a small crucifix which Cardenal made. Reading in here is a totally different experience from anywhere else, as if the silence and the four walls enriched everything with great significance. One is alone, not on guard, utterly relaxed and receptive, having four walls and silence all around enables you to listen, so to speak, with all the pores of your skin and to absorb truth through every part of your being. I doubt if I would be any better off in Mexico![74]

At the same time, by May, Merton was studying a book on Italian church architecture "that has some very satisfactory small churches."[75] There were further conferences at Bellarmine, and this time Father Louis was given permission to attend. He met Jack Ford again, also Monsignor Horrigan and Father Raymond Treece. With the architect, Bob Nolan, they went over new plans for the retreat center and, according to Raymond Treece, the electric company suggested some very fancy equipment.[76] After one such conference Merton went to the library. He took out Robert Penn Warren's *Segregation* and discovered he was the first reader to have checked out the early poems of William Carlos Williams. His visit caused some commotion; the library staff "made me the object of a public cult for a while."[77] Back on Mount Olivet, Merton walked the site and marked the trees that would have to go.

Looking back, there appears to have been an inordinate amount of planning and preparation for what became by November of this same year a drab, four-square, single-story building made of cinder blocks, with a long, open porch in front and a well-built stone fireplace, but which was otherwise lacking in any architectural features whatever — not to mention plumbing or electricity. Many such a building had been erected all over rural Kentucky without such fuss.

The abbot accused Father Louis of changing his mind and calling for a cutback on the ambitious plans at the last minute. Others said it had been decided to prune the detail and expense in order not to offend the Cistercian vow of poverty or the Cistercian style of simplicity. It is easy to follow what probably happened by noting the different names for the structure in Merton's journals. In May, "Mount Olivet Retreat House" alternated with "Mount Olivet Hermitage." On October 3,

After High Mass I went out with Mr. Parrish, the contractor from Bardstown, to stake out the place on the hill [for] — let's be frank; the hermitage.

It is nothing like the plan made by Art Becvar and the G.E. people after all. It has been cut down by so many people, including myself, and is no longer a shiny, smart little pavillion, but just a plain cottage with two rooms and a porch. Clearly it is a hermitage rather than a place for conferences.[78]

Merton and two of the novices helped the local work crew under Mr. Parrish. Cement was poured and the walls began to rise.

On October 9, came the interview when the abbot accused Father Louis of changing his mind.[79] The next day there was a tussle over the use of the building, given an edge because there had been a conference and the novitiate was still smelling unmonastically of cigarette smoke. On October 25, Merton spoke with the Hammers about furniture for "the hermitage."[80] On the same day he was in Cincinnati to get reproductions of paintings for the walls. On October 29, he announces the new name, "St. Mary of Carmel," in his journal.[81] The name was very carefully chosen, and what had been thought of by most up to that time as a conference center was now dedicated, at least in Merton's mind, after twenty long years, to the patroness of his solitary vocation.

It seems certain that in his dealings with the abbot Merton decided some time in the summer that the more elaborate the place became, the more likely it was to be a retreat house and conference center, while the simpler, more austere it was kept the better chance it would become "St. Mary of Carmel Hermitage on Mount Olivet."

By December 2, he had lit his first fire in the fireplace. On December 13, St. Lucy's Day, the nineteenth anniversary of his official entrance into a cenobite order, Merton took possession — if only for a few permitted hours a day.[82]

There may have been increased pressure on the abbot when the Cuernavaca plan, which Dom James had thought a dead issue, took on a new lease of life in the summer of 1960, to be dampened on September 3, when Merton received a letter from Monsignor Paul Philippe, his friend and advocate in Rome, now in Larraona's place as Secretary of the Sacred Congregation of the Religious and soon to be made an archbishop.[83] This letter told Father Louis somewhat firmly to stay at Gethsemani. By now the situation had been widely broadcast, both in fact and rumor. In midsummer two Spanish priests had been to see James Laughlin with a plan of going to Gethsemani "to liberate Tom."[84]

Merton hardly needed liberating. "I am where I am. I have freely chosen this state, and have fully chosen to stay in it when the question of a possible change arose . . ." he wrote a year later.[85] It was certainly an irony Merton could not have foreseen, when he made the old game of Prisoner's Base stand at the beginning of his autobiography for an allegory of the world outside the walls, that in time there would be periods when the Court of the Queen of Heaven would seem another Prisoner's Base. Yet this was not the Lycée Ingres, he needed no one to free him, he had the key if he chose to use it. The story of the two

Spanish priests delighted him, as such things did, though he tended to withdraw quickly after a number of imaginative conjectures. Listening to James Laughlin's stories at the January picnic of poets who were going mad very publicly from other pressures in the world outside the enclosure, Merton must have wondered if what was sometimes a prison wasn't always a protection. At any rate, he stayed when he could have left, seeing the hermitage at the end of the year as something of a reward. It was very clearly not a bribe. Dom James had bent rules before this to give Father Louis solitude. And Merton was plainly wrong and writing wildly when he announced in his journal, "The attitude of the Abbot seems to be that as long as I am in this monastery he doesn't much care *what* I do."[86]

*

In his correspondence with Suzuki and Pasternak Merton had discovered a way out of his sense of isolation, finding he shared more with two men at opposite ends of the world than with many of those he saw daily. Most of the early letters at the monastery had been on publishing business, seeking advice on the stability question, exchanging views on monasticism and the eremitical life, and giving others spiritual counsel. Such letters have importance in tracing his own life and in the study of monastic renewal; they would not have made him one of the few great letter writers of this century.

The volume of his business correspondence increased. Naomi Burton had left Curtis Brown in December of 1959 to become a senior editor at Doubleday. Merton continued with Curtis Brown, taking on more work himself, then, after a tangle with the foreign-rights department, he tried to be his own agent. In March 1963, Tom Burns of Burns and Oates, Merton's English publishers, wrote begging him to get help unofficially from Naomi Burton.[87] On July 10, 1963, Merton told Burns, "Naomi is acting as a sort of part time unofficial agent for me now, and I think I am at last getting my affairs cleared up." They had become very snarled by that time.[88]

From 1955 to 1960, as Merton took on new interests without abandoning old ones, he widened his correspondence until it became a network of friends numbering in the hundreds. He was careful now to keep copies of his own letters, though in the same entry of May 1960 in which he determines "to put more perhaps into this journal which is not for publication," he finds his own letters "careless and badly written."[89] This is clearly a case of Merton being unjust to Merton. Many letters show the pressure of time and the sense of urgency tied to impatience that, as often as not, accounts for their immediacy — their plain readability. There are fewer lapses into rhetoric and repetition (what Naomi Burton had once called "an effect of almost self-hypnosis") than in the journals and some of the published work. A few, like the letter to Rachel Carson, are too general. On some subjects he demonstrates that he was too remote from a situation to make any really insightful or helpful comment, but this is rare.

Significantly, some of his best letters are to writers and artists. As it had been with Pasternak, early letters to Czeslaw Milosz or to Marco Pallis (whose books had been recommended by Victor Hammer) are little more than an introduction. Almost at once the letters show a quickening sense that the exchange will be important to both correspondents. In the matter of trust, which sometimes gave Merton such trouble, correspondence provided exactly what was needed — a friend and confidant at a distance.

Merton complained more and more about the volume of his mail. His novices helped him, retyping articles and much else that slows up the writer who is unlikely to have an intelligent and willing "typing pool" at his or her disposal without cost. He typed almost all his own letters himself, "like a newspaperman with four fingers,"[90] typing rapidly, usually very accurately, on a manual typewriter. With all the grumbling in the journal came celebrations when he received letters he valued among the twenty to thirty arriving each week. He had the usual crank letters, and other mail that troubled him more:

> A letter came from a woman in France, asking me to ask the prayers of the community that America may at last start a nuclear crusade against Soviet Russia and draw all the lazy and fearful western European nations with her! This [is] a serious proposition, on religious grounds! "We cannot stand any more," she said.[91]

Editors — especially the editors of Catholic periodicals and encyclopaedias — had formed the opinion that Thomas Merton could write on almost any subject. More often than not, he agreed to a commission, only to regret it. "Great God, what have I done to make everyone believe I secrete articles like perspiration!"[92] In the same way, he made resolutions not to increase the number of those he tried to write to on a regular basis, then broke the resolution:

> Fine letters from Etta Gullick, wife of the Senior Tutor at St. Edmund's Hall, Oxford. I say I will not make friends and yet I do, I have friends and it is true that on them I depend for support and recognition. She is becoming one of them — Like John Wu, and J. Laughlin (one of the most solid) and of course Rice, Lax, Ad [Reinhardt]. And Mark Van Doren.[93]

Some of Merton's correspondents provided him with what he needed beyond support and recognition. The most vital exchange in the early 1960s was with Czeslaw Milosz. It began in 1958, after Merton had read the Polish writer's *The Captive Mind* and had written to him in Paris.[94]

It continued when Milosz became professor of Slavic languages and literature at Berkeley in 1961, calling himself in a letter to Merton "catastrophist emeritus."[95] Time would bring the Polish poet on a visit to Gethsemani in the mid-sixties,[96] but it is the early correspondence that shows how much they had already been able to give one another. In 1960 each correspondent acknowledged how important the exchange had become and implied that what they were building was too serious for any holding back:[97] when Milosz wrote later to say he had been too unrestrained in some of his comments about the Church, Merton replied at once to say he had written nothing Merton had not wrestled with himself.[98]

Both men talked of their struggle for personal integrity, the need to hold to the identity they discovered in themselves, rather than accepting the identities thrust upon them by others. The writer in the world wrote, "I am a complete fool who pretends to be someone else."[99] The writer in the monastery replied:

> When you talk about group action you say what most concerns me, because it is something I know nothing at all about. Even as a Catholic I am a complete lone wolf, and not as independent as I might seem to be, yet not integrated in anything else either. As you say, I represent my own life. But not as I ought to. I have still too much reflected the kind of person others may have assumed I ought to be. I am reaching a happy and dangerous age when I want to smash that image above all. But that is not the kind of thing that is likely to be viewed with favor. Nor do I have any idea of what way the road will take. But as far as solidarity with other people goes, I am committed to nothing except a very simple and elemental kind of solidarity, which is perhaps without significance politically, but which is I feel the only kind that works at all. That is to pick out the people whom I recognize in a crowd and hail them and rejoice with them for a moment that we speak the same language. Whether they be communists or whatever else they may be. Whatever they may believe on the surface, whatever may be the formulas to which they are committed. I am less and less worried by what people say or think they say: and more and more concerned with what they are able to be. I am not convinced that anybody is really able to say what he means any more, except in so far as he talks about himself. And even there it is very difficult. What do any of us "mean" when we talk politics?[100]

The justification of the "autobiographical line" here is important, as is Merton's admission that "even there it is very difficult." It dismayed both men that in writing and publishing one was more likely to open divisions than to express the underlying unity one felt. Milosz wrote that he had been guilty of this in *The Captive Mind*: "In fact I love those people against whom I directed my anger much more than I show. I did not succeed in showing my love and my whole thought."[101] Later he would warn Merton against the kind of activism and even non-violence that pushed those on the other side of the argument into an irrational extreme form — an instinctive defense which divided them not only from others, but even from themselves. It was a point Merton returned to over and over in the mid-sixties, when he wondered whether he was doing just this, not only in general, but with the few who actively disagreed with him in the monastery.[102] In December 1968, someone who had just met Merton found him very mild in debate: it had been a long training.[103]

The Polish writer brought much to Merton's reading. Milosz had translated the writings of Simone Weil into Polish, and he wrote he had been helped in despair by her work.[104] When Merton balked at her Albigensian sympathies, Milosz was not to be stopped: it was *because* she was *"une Cathar"* in the twentieth century she was so important; Albert Camus had called her "the only great spirit of our time."[105] Merton read the writings of Simone Weil, Cathar or not.

Milosz brought Merton back again and again to the writings of Camus himself, until that writer gradually became for Merton another great spirit of our time. Milosz also sent his own translations of the work of the younger generation in Poland. "You shall notice what cruel experience underlays here the poetic image," he wrote, sending poems by Zbigniew Herbert.[106] Merton wrote back about the seriousness in Herbert's work, which made much of the writing of other contemporary poets shallow by comparison.[107] In 1963, Milosz spoke of two figures of monumental achievement, the Greek poet Constantine Cavafy and the American Robinson Jeffers.[108] Merton confessed he had not read much Jeffers. By 1968, he was referring to Jeffers as "the Pacific Blake";[109] even the prospective title of the reworking of his journal was from Jeffers, "The Hawk's Dream."

Having sent *Thoughts in Solitude*, Merton wanted to know if his book of meditations had bored Milosz.[110] Milosz was quick to see how central this work was to Merton's best thought. He found the poems less successful, perhaps because the poet was so disparaging: "The poems alas are not good."[111] There was other frank criticism. Where Pasternak had praised *Prometheus*, Milosz felt Merton had totally misunderstood Prometheus and the significance of the Titan's revolt against Zeus.[112] He was excited about Merton's "Herakleitos the Obscure."[113]

The criticism extended to the letters themselves, when Milosz thought Merton's comments exaggerated. When Merton wrote on a postcard that he believed the twentieth century "the most terrible of all,"[114] the Polish writer replied that the nineteenth had been worse.[115] He refused to acknowledge a competition on which of them was the "more *angoissé*," and struck out at fashionable despair with the comment "Existentialist angst is not enough."[116] Again, just because certain

French intellectuals (for certain sociological reasons of their own) were busily advertising their bad conscience at having been born in the middle class, there was no need, he said, for Merton to go on about being bourgeois.[117]

At the end of February 1960, he criticized Merton for something quite different. "Every time you speak of Nature [in *Jonas*], it appears to you as soothing, rich in symbols, as a veil or a curtain. You do not pay much attention to torture and suffering in Nature."[118] This is a valid comment: Merton is nowhere more romantic than in his love of storms, yet there are no monsters and no cataclysms in his pages — Nature is never "red in tooth and claw." The evil intruders are tractors and hunters.

Interestingly enough, Merton misses the point Milosz is making as he makes points of his own, not only in his reply to Milosz's letter, but when he amplifies his journal account in *Conjectures of a Guilty Bystander*.[119]

"It is precisely the good letters that take time to answer," Merton wrote back in May, explaining that *The Sign of Jonas* and the poems of the time were written in isolation during "a sort of Edenic period in my life." He goes on to say he cannot take out his resentment on Nature, "Not that there is not plenty of resentment in me: but it is not resentment against nature, only against people, institutions and myself."[120]

Yet the heart of the exchange is even more valuable. Where Milosz criticizes, he says frankly he is looking for a guide — that many are seeking a guide — in a period of general madness: "Perhaps we approach a time when only groups of monks in monasteries will remain sane."[121] Where he seeks wisdom, he has much of his own to bring. If Thomas Merton resisted having yet another "idea of Merton" suggested to him, this was one he took far more seriously than most.

To borrow from the title of one of Merton's books which was published posthumously, it is "the contemplative in a world of action" that interests Czeslaw Milosz in Thomas Merton. Superficially, there are times when Milosz appears as inconsistent as many were to be in accusing Merton, first of being too detached, then of being too much the activist. Yet Milosz was pursuing a clear view of his own. What he believed Merton should focus upon as truly serious was the kind of contemplation that would explore what nineteenth-century Russian philosophers had called "the terrible questions." When he talked of the desperate need for a contemporary Pascal, he obviously thought of the Merton who wrote *Thoughts in Solitude*. For this reason he was equally critical of Merton's retiring into an Edenic detachment in an idealized Nature and of his hurrying into activism in the peace movement, which Milosz felt was ambiguous at best and merely fashionable at worst:

Yet I ask myself why you feel such an itch for activity? Is that so that you are unsatisfied with your having plunged too deep in contemplation and now you wish to compensate through growing another wing, so to say? And peace provides you with the only link with American young intellectuals outside? Yet activity to which you are called is perhaps different? Should you become a belated rebel, out of solidarity with rebels without cause? Now, when there is such chaos in the world of arts and letters, the most sane, intelligent (and of best literary style) are works of French theologians. They perform an important and lasting task. We are groping — and I say it basing upon what young Catholics in Poland write — towards completely new images permitting perhaps to grasp religion again as a personal vision. I do not invite you to write theological treaties but much can be accomplished, it seems to me, through literary criticism for instance.[122]

The first priorities, then, were to face (beyond romantic evasion and beyond easy rhetoric and commonplace) the reality behind clichés: the Problem of Evil and Suffering in Contemporary Life, the Question of Institutionalized Religion, the Question of Guilt — by Commission, by Omission (and the twentieth-century phenomenon, the sense of guilt at not having been tested in certain extreme situations).

It had probably been a number of passages in the early letters which brought Milosz to see in Merton one who might find in active contemplation the essential images permitting others "to grasp religion again as a personal vision." Answering early questions Milosz had put about Providence, Merton had swept aside pious platitudes to speak directly and with passion:

As for Providence: certainly I think the glib clichés that are made about the will of God are enough to make anyone lose his faith. Such clichés are still possible in America but I don't see how they can still survive in Europe, at least for anyone who has seen a concentration camp. For my part, I have given up my compulsive need to answer such questions neatly. It is safer and cleaner to remain inarticulate, and does more honor to God. I think the reason why we cannot see Providence at work in our world is that it is much too simple. Our notions of Providence are too complicated and too human: a question of ends and means, and why this means to this end? God wills this *for* this purpose . . . Whatever the mystery of Providence may be I think it is more direct and brutal in a way. But that is never evident as long as we think God apart from the people in the concentration camp, "permitting them to be there for their own good" (time out while I vomit.) Actually it is God Himself who is in the concentration camp. That is, of course, it is Christ. Not in the collective sense, but especially in the defilement and destruction of each individual soul, there is the renewal of the Crucifixion. This of course is familiar, I mean the words are familiar. People understand them to mean that a man in a concentration camp who remembers to renew his morning offering suffers like and even, in some juridical sense, with Christ. But the point is whether he renews the morning offering or not, or whether he is a sinner, he *is* Christ. That this is not understood even by religious people: that it cannot be comprehended by the others, and that the last one to be able to understand it, so to speak, is "Christ" Himself . . . Providence is not for this hidden Christ. He Himself is His own Providence. In us. In so far as we are Christ, we are our own Providence. The thing is then not to struggle to work out the "laws" of a mysterious force alien to us and utterly outside us, but to come to terms with what is inmost in our own selves, the very depth of our own being. No matter what our "Providence" may have in store for us, on the surface of life (and this inner Providence is not really so directly concerned with the surface of life) what is within, inaccessible to the evil will of others, is always good unless we ourselves deliberately cut ourselves off from it. As for those who are too shattered to do anything about it one way or the other, they are lifted, in pieces, into heaven and find themselves together there with no sense of how it might have been possible.[123]

*

Merton rehearsed himself for the annual visitation of Dom Gabriel in February 1961. Yet the abbot general did not order the demolition of the hermitage when they walked up together. Dom Gabriel talked of other hermits and their lives. He spoke of the hermitage as a place to come to for a few hours of the day, not to live in, "For you are the Novice Master." Yet to Dom Gabriel it was obviously "a kind of solution": neither of them had brought up the subject of Cuernavaca.[124] Walking in the woods they discussed the censorship points which now held up the publication of *The New Man*. As Dom Gabriel had lost his glasses, they were driven to Louisville, where the abbot general bought a new pair, while Merton went to the University of Louisville and spent time reading in the art library. In the car they returned to the subject that had first brought them together — what to do with pious objects in monasteries.

It was an attempt to restore their old friendship when both were aware that the censorship question could only drive them further apart. Merton was learning the sensitive areas as far as Dom Gabriel was concerned, yet part of the problem was that each censor or potential censor seemed to have his own reservations beyond the simple rules of "doctrine and morals." Even much later, after praising "Rain and the Rhinoceros," Merton's most generous censor, Father Paul Bourne, could find something to correct.[125] First the praise: "You sum up the current situation with a breadth and depth I've yet to meet elsewhere. How well, incidentally, you demonstrate a favorite thesis of yours — that one can see the world clearer from the cloister than when submerged in it and by it." Then, a few weeks later, when the green light had been given for publication, the censor hoped "you will see fit to omit the reference to cooking in your hermitage — until hermits become official with us the Coleman stove can be retained for heating."[126] It was the uncertainty that rankled most, and there is little wonder Merton sometimes grumbled in his journal that if he wrote out the Lord's Prayer with the comment "everyone ought to say this prayer," someone would ask for changes.[127]

He was already looking for ways round the system. Directive Number Five of the 1956 Statute of Censorship in the Order laid it down that "brief articles destined for periodicals of limited circulation and influence" required only the permission of the local superior, the abbot. As Merton knew, and the censors probably did not, "limited circulation" by no means guaranteed limited influence:

> I am a firm believer in the power of the offbeat essay printed or mimeographed in a strange place and handled by interested people. The material that goes from hand to hand is much read, at least by the people who are responsible enough to appreciate information and unconventional material.[128]

At the beginning of the sixties Merton discovered his work on the racial question would find censors in the Order who were much more lenient to it in France. In England, his articles on both the racial question and the immorality of nuclear war could be published virtually as he had written them. "Letters to a White Liberal" appeared in two parts in the November and December 1963 issues of the English magazine *Blackfriars*,[129] while Merton's writings on the racial question appeared together in France as *La révolution noire*[130] in 1964 and were immediately popular.

Merton's discovery of the mimeograph machine and a kind of publication that, he claimed, was not publishing provided an answer to a crisis in 1962. He may have been reading of writers behind the Iron Curtain; he may have been watching the publicity material going out for Gethsemani Farms.

In 1959–60 he had already made use of what would now be called alternative publishing. The Hammers were by no means fully sympathetic with the activist Merton. To them he remained a contemplative and a poet. Yet if he had been distracted into other things, they continued to help him with his literary work, and he looked to them to bring out writing that might be questioned as unorthodox even if it was not politically controversial. Earlier, they had supervised the publication of a limited edition of *Prometheus*.[131] In 1960 Victor Hammer printed sixty copies of *The Solitary Life* on his own press, the Stamperia del Santuccio.[132] On this occasion at least, Thomas Merton was delighted with one of his books when he took it in his hands.[133] It was a beautiful production: it was also, Merton says, "a secret book." *The Solitary Life* was a somewhat revised essay he had first had printed in France at the Abbey of La Pierre qui Vire and which had been stopped by the American censors. Later in 1960 the first of Merton's translations (or rather, assisted translations) from the Chinese, *The Ox Mountain Parable of Meng Tzu*, appeared from the Hammer press.[134] In 1962 the Hammers brought out the magnificent limited edition of *Hagia Sophia*.[135]

The prose poem *Hagia Sophia*, which follows the canonical hours and draws on the Canticle of Canticles or Song of Songs, is not so obviously controversial in terms of Merton's writing in the sixties as "Letters to a White Liberal" or "Pacifism and Resistance," yet it is certainly another "secret work." Many of the strands of Merton's deepest and most unorthodox thought over several years come together. The poem is a celebration both of the female principle in all things which are whole and of *Natura naturans*. Some of the rich history of its making has already been traced.

The poem begins with dawn, a man lying asleep — the poet lying asleep, as Merton says. The day is given a date, July 2, the Feast of Our Lady's Visitation. The setting is a hospital.

In July 1960, Merton was in St. Anthony's Hospital for x-rays. On the 2nd, he records in his journal:

> At 5:30, as I was dreaming, in a very quiet hospital, the soft voice of the nurse awoke me gently from my dream — and it was like awakening for the first time from all the dreams of my life — as if the Blessed Virgin herself, as if Wisdom, had awakened me. We do not hear the soft voice, the gentle voice, the feminine voice, the voice of the Mother: yet she speaks everywhere and in everything. Wisdom "cries out in the market place — if anyone is little let him come to me."[136]

This is close in both cadence and subject matter to another passage, the dream as Merton had reported it to Pasternak. Lines from the journal account are included in *Hagia Sophia*, though there is some altering, and the contrast between waking in hospital and in the monastery is softened. The "voice of the Mother" is dropped. One passage in the poem is taken from Merton's letter to Victor Hammer after first seeing the panel at the Hammers' house.[137]

More than anything else, the poem drew upon Merton's readings in the Russian mystics. At the end of a retreat in January 1961, he had written in his journal:

> Long quiet interval in dark hours. Evdokimov on orthodoxy — once again, as I have so many times recently, I need the concept of *natura naturans* — the divine wisdom in ideal nature, the ikon of wisdom, the dancing ikon — the summit reached by so many non-Christian contemplatives (would that it were reached by a few Christians!) Summit of Vedanta? — Faith in So-

phia, *natura naturans,* the great stabilizer today — for peace. The basic hope that people have that man will somehow not be completely destroyed is hoped in *natura naturans.* — The dark face, the "night face" of Sophia. War, trouble, pestilence.[138]

In March of the same year he claims another mystical tradition for his own:

I am still a 14th century man: the century of Eckhart, Ruysbroeck, Tauler, the English recluses, the author of "The Cloud," Langland and Chaucer — more an independent and a hermit than a community man, by no means an ascetic, interested in psychology, a lover of the dark Cloud in which God is found by love. This is what I am: I must consent to be it and not be ashamed that I am not something more fashionable.[139]

If he was still an Apophatic, a lover of the dark way and the cloud of unknowing, it was to others than St. John of the Cross that he now looked for guidance, above all to Meister Eckhart and Julian of Norwich. In his letters he talked of his discovery of the author of *Revelations of Divine Love:*

Julian is without doubt one of the most wonderful of all Christian voices. She gets greater and greater in my eyes as I grow older and whereas in the old days I used to be crazy about St. John of the Cross, I would not exchange him now for Julian if you gave me the world and the Indies and all the Spanish mystics rolled up in one bundle . . .[140]

Not only does he praise her as a mystic, he goes on to set her with Newman as one of the two greatest English theologians. In *Hagia Sophia:*

(When the recluses of fourteenth-century England heard their Church Bells and looked out upon the wolds and fens under a kind sky, they spoke in their hearts to "Jesus our Mother." It was Sophia that had awakened in their childlike hearts.)[141]

There is an odd circumlocution here, as if Merton can hardly dare to bring himself to name the mystic brave enough to talk of "Jesus our Mother."

In the last part of the poem there is a return to the starting point, to the panel by Victor Hammer:

She crowns Him not with what is glorious, but with what is greater than glory: the one thing greater than glory is weakness, nothingness, poverty.[142]

Where Merton expects us to see the image from the painting (Victor Hammer's ikon), he also expects us to hear music. The final section is entitled "IV. *Sunset. The Hour of Compline. Salve Regina.*" The Salve Regina sung by the choir of monks in a darkening, near-empty abbey church at the end of the monastery day has just the quality of the poem's ending — solemnity, great beauty, and a piercing loneliness:

> A vagrant, a destitute wanderer with dusty feet, finds his way down a new road. A homeless God, lost in the night, without papers, without identification, without even a number, a frail expendable exile lies down in desolation under the sweet stars of the world and entrusts Himself to sleep.[143]

There are flaws in the poem, a surrender of too much sense to sound in some places, and imprecisions. Merton's knowledge of the eastern parts of England should have told him how difficult it would be to fit fens and wolds into a single view. Yet *Hagia Sophia* bears a great number of rereadings. With the image of the unnamed nurse waking him in hospital Merton must have felt he had completed the full portrait of Hagia Sophia, which had been the creation of many dreams and much reading, joining all this to the actual. Where he had completed the process for the poem, the full portrait had not yet been realized in his life.

Merton was careful in his journal, more careful in the poem, to guard against the wrong reading of "lover" for "love." The composite female figure was also a mother. "In the natural order perhaps solitaries are made by severe mothers,"[144] he had written earlier. There is something of an idealized Ruth Merton in the journal entry, only partly erased in the poem. The figure who crowns the young man in Victor Hammer's painting is solemn, however, not severe. Finally, then, the paradise of "hidden wholeness" the poet wakes to in *Hagia Sophia* is one where Sophia is present, not Eve.

For all this, there were certainly connections with the Jewish girl in Merton's dream and his letters to Proverb. He felt for a moment he had met Proverb in person when he went to Cincinnati on October 25, 1960, to collect reproductions for the novitiate (and for the hermitage). He records "the Jewish girl sitting on top of the filing cabinets with her shoes off in the office of the Director of the Museum, while he was out lecturing to the ladies of the garden club." They had struck up a conversation and she had given him "a top secret photo of the Spanish tomb figure whom they call Don Sancho."[145]

Few of Merton's works, then, had such a slow and sensitive evolution. He admits at one point that he risked spoiling *Hagia Sophia* by the same kind of indiscretion and overexuberance he showed shortly after his conversion at Herb Jacobson's party. On July 4, 1960, he writes:

> Perhaps there is no good reason to disentangle the threads of thought that have been tied up together in these four or five days at St. Anthony's. What would have been very simple has been complicated by friends and my own reactions. The people who want to take you out —

when you shouldn't go and don't want to. I have been definitely at fault in yielding to them and it has made me miserable . . .[146]

He goes on to talk of listening to records at Jim Wygal's house, then going to hear jazz with Father John Loftus.

In mid-July 1961, when Father Daniélou visited Gethsemani, Merton showed the man he considered his spiritual director three poems: *Hagia Sophia*, "Elegy for Hemingway," and "the Auschwitz poem." *Hagia Sophia* had obviously been completed some time in the spring of that year.[147] "An Elegy for Ernest Hemingway" had been written since July 4, when Dom James announced Hemingway's death in Chapter:

For with one shot the whole hunt is ended![148]

"The Auschwitz poem" was "Chant to Be Used in Processions Around a Site with Furnaces."[149] In May 1961, Merton had been reading William L. Shirer's *The Rise and Fall of the Third Reich*. In the letters from German manufacturers of lethal gas and crematorium equipment to the camp authorities, which Shirer had reproduced, translated, in his book, Merton discovered material for "found poems." Transferred into his anti-poem, they are left to speak for themselves.[150] For Merton himself there were obvious links with the "humane gas," which had horrified him when he read about it at St. Bonaventure's,[151] and far more personal links to crematoriums, which had reduced almost all his family to ashes — to the landscape of the Elmhurst chimneys in Queens, Long Island, a landscape to which he returned often in imagination and once in fact, and which would dominate a section of his last poem, *The Geography of Lograire*.[152]

Father Daniélou liked the poem for Hemingway and *Hagia Sophia*, not the poem on Auschwitz, perhaps because, "He is preoccupied by the pessimism and defeatism of the French intellectual, especially the Christian intellectual," as Merton reported in his journal.[153] He himself was to be accused of pessimism that summer — by Daniélou, by Jean Leclercq when he visited, and by others.

Daniélou encouraged him in his Oriental studies, saying true balance and optimism could be found in detachment. His spiritual adviser also recommended studying Bantu philosophy and folklore, which, however unexpected, was something Merton had already heard about from another friend by correspondence, Laurens Van der Post.[154]

It was no easy season for detachment, yet his "A Letter to Pablo Antonio Cuadra Concerning Giants"[155] frightened even the author with its bitterness. The giants were Gog and Magog, the two huge power structures of the world. Merton had already written to others to say that they might all wake up one day to find the United States and Soviet Russia so similar it would be hard to distinguish between them.

For the countries of South and Central America, Merton believed the Cold War choice of alliance between the United States (with, he wrote, "Franco Spain") and the Communist bloc was an impossible one.[156]

With his open statement to the Nicaraguan poet it is not so much the feeling he may have committed himself politically that makes him anxious, it is something he finds in himself:

> How did it get to be so violent and unfair?
>
> The root is my own fear, my own desperate desire to survive even if only as a voice uttering an angry protest, while the waters of death close over the whole continent.
>
> Why am I so willing to believe that the country will be destroyed? It is certainly possible, and in some sense it may even be likely. But this is a case where, in spite of evidence, one must continue to hope. One must not give in to defeatism and despair; just as one must hope for life in a mortal illness which has been declared incurable.
>
> This is the point. This weakness and petulancy, rooted in egotism and which I have in common with other intellectuals in this country. Even after years in the monastery I have not toughened up and got the kind of fiber that is bred only by humility and self-forgetfulness. Or rather, though I had begun to get it, this writing job and my awareness of myself as a personage with definite opinions and with a voice, has kept me sensitive and afraid on a level which most monks long ago became indifferent. Yet also it is not good to be indifferent to the fate of the world on a simple level.
>
> So I am concerned, humanly, politically, yet not wisely.[157]

The movement of these passages in the journal is typical and revealing, if sometimes hard to follow. Merton begins in self-accusation and ends with a mixture of humility and gratitude. He fears both fear and his anger. When he blames his writing (as he so often does), he goes on arguing with himself until he has acknowledged that it is his writing which has kept him vulnerable and saved him from indifference.

Finishing the proofreading of *New Seeds of Contemplation,* he made one more resolution to restrict the writing for solitude. "I am determined now to embrace the long task of unweaving the garment of *author,* my writer-self, my official business being, so as at last to step out of it . . ."[158] There were times when he felt so much literary work was a misuse of the precious hours he was allowed for solitude when he craved for more. "There is nothing that makes sense to me or attracts me so much as living in the hermitage. I dread the politics of permission, and the time has not come for that. But to take advantage of the present situation and use it as fully as possible."[159] The natural world kept breaking into his writing — only to be recorded, "Silent afternoon at the hermitage — wind soughing in the hot pines, crickets in the yellow grass."[160] Where there were so many commissions from editors of

Catholic periodicals to write, and now an article for the *Catholic Ency-clopedia*, he had moments of exasperation at being seen as a strictly Catholic writer from one vantage point and as a convert from another:

> What hurts me most is to have been inexorably trapped by my own folly. Wanting to prove myself a Catholic — and of course not perfectly succeeding.
>   They all admit and commend my goodwill, but frankly, I am not one of the bunch, am I?[161]

Correcting slippery and unwieldy galley proofs often brought out the anti-author in Merton, as Naomi Burton has pointed out.[162] Yet the early autumn of 1961 showed a different side of the unending debate with himself, though he had made resolutions to stop writing before and would make many more in the future. In the earlier entry, the awkward phrase "this writing job and awareness of myself . . ." applies beyond what he goes on to say. Writing in the manner he did may have made him vulnerable; it also intensified the struggle with self-consciousness. Where he felt the gains were concern, commitment, even fear, his work had brought him nothing of the self-forgetfulness that Gabriel Marcel, Victor Hammer, and others described in a craftsman's application to his labor. Perhaps, then, this was not a good comparison: perhaps the work of the writer was closer to the work of an actor or a dancer. Yet even the dancer, the crafter of his or her movement and gestures, may train in front of a mirror and still know the time must come when the demands of the dance transcend an awareness of body.

Writing was not, in itself, the cause of Merton's struggle — nor, really, was his subject: a writer can write about himself or herself without bringing on a crisis of self-awareness. In Merton's case it is easy to say it was an obsession with subject, though it still has to be admitted it was an obsession of a very unusual kind. It was not egomania, as Gregory Zilboorg suspected. There was as much humility as there was pride in an attempt to further and complete a project that had once been broken off, causing a lasting trauma. Thomas Merton continued to write about Thomas Merton. He was now, in *New Seeds of Contemplation* and elsewhere, exploring the mystery of self in his concepts of "false self" and "true self": inevitably, even in the denial, the word that appeared at least as often as "contemplation" was "self." It is very likely that Zen had a very personal appeal to him because Zen so often ended an argument with a riddle, a *koan*. The *koan* for Thomas Merton might have been "How does one write about self so that the self disappears?" One answer to this was "By exhausting the subject of self."

✳

For all such turmoil, in retrospect at least, the summer of 1961 was the summer of the gardenias.[163] The gardenias came from Mepkin, a few plants from the thousands Clare Boothe Luce had bought for her family property in South Carolina just before giving the property to Gethsemani for a new foundation in 1950. The plants bloomed all summer and late into the fall, to be celebrated over and over in Merton's prose.[164] If he castigated himself for his new bitterness and pessimism, he was more open than ever to spontaneous joy in the immediate. At the hermitage he praised the *"point vierge"* of the first bird song,[165] and he wrote hymns of praise for the light at different times of the day over the view from the small cinderblock house.

Elbert R. Sisson, one of those he had been writing to about the abortive invasion of Cuba, sent him news of his children and enclosed some of their drawings. Merton wrote back that he had been so moved by one of the drawings by Grace Sisson that he had written a poem, "Grace's House," which he hoped Grace and her father would like.[166]

In the poem each detail in the drawing — smiling dog, "his foreleg curled, his eye like an aster," rabbit, blades of grass, two birds, the house, stream, "Mailbox number 5" — had come into a time of perfect rightness. All this had flowered on the paper hill as the cactus had flowered in its perfect time of the night. Each was a paradise sufficient in itself, and the viewer could be changed forever by what he could neither wholly understand — nor enter. In the case of the drawing there was one detail missing: "Alas, there is no road to Grace's house!"[167]

Merton was greatly pleased when his German publishers chose the title of this poem for the title of his selected poems, *Grazias Haus: Gedichte.*[168] Meanwhile, in the geography of the world, where roads led everywhere but to paradise, Merton told Sisson of an agonizing decision he was trying to make in advising another correspondent, whose husband had been captured in the Bay of Pigs landings on April 17.[169] She had written asking whether she ought to try to raise a hundred thousand dollars to free her husband from the Isle of Pines when she knew he had expressed the wish to stay with his fellow prisoners.

In Merton's view both the Church and the United States had missed an opportunity when Castro's guerillas originally overthrew the forces of the dictator Battista. The dissident Cubans who had taken part in the ill-fated invasion attempt were, he felt, simply cats' paws of the CIA:

> The next time I hear anything about the iniquity of Castro and the righteousness of the United States I am going to throw a bowl of soup at somebody. I guess I count as a security risk all right.[170]

The previous November, when even the wheelbarrows at Gethsemani had carried "Vote Democrat" stickers,[171] the youngest and first

Catholic president had been elected by a narrow margin. Merton continued to have faith in John F. Kennedy, though he found it tiresome that every time Kennedy sneezed there was a report in Chapter.[172] In the summer and fall of 1961 it seemed to Merton that some force was moving the world closer to nuclear battle between the superpowers which even the leaders might be powerless to prevent. Where he found defeatism in himself, he feared a sense of inevitability was setting in: the building of shelters was the most obvious sign. With the shelters came the debate that sometimes pitted each "nuclear family" against the world. In the debate any pretentions toward either Christian or post-Christian ethics began to look irrelevant. Every reasonably affluent family in America (and every institution) could have its own Hitler bunker in the catastrophe.[173]

There had been a sense of world crisis behind two of Merton's most important earlier decisions. These had been private and personal. His decision in 1961 brought him into the realm of public censure. The early writing had made life, and his monastic vocation, difficult. His writing now made him a great deal more vulnerable, and he already felt handicapped:

> This is like going into the prize ring blindfolded and with hands tied, since I am cloistered and subject to the most discouragingly long and frustrating kinds of censorship on top of it. I must do what I can. Prayer of course remains my chief means, but it [is] also an obligation on my part to speak out in so far as I am able, and to speak as clearly, as forthrightly and as uncompromisingly as I can. A lot of people are not going to like this and it may mean my head, so do please pray for me in a very special way, because I cannot in conscience willingly betray the truth or let it be betrayed . . .[174]

He had often showed moral courage, but physical courage was another matter. If he was non-violent, his own resources for responding to violence troubled him. When reports were read out in Chapter about the Uganda martyrs and about the Trappists tortured and killed in China, Merton wondered in his journal whether it was in his power to be a martyr, a witness to God in the face of violent death.[175] He talked, too, of his need of approval. Where he ventured now was dangerous ground for one with doubts about his physical courage, and fearful of disapproval and rejection. He was unsure of himself, certain only that the time had come to move from the role of bystander (guilty by association and silence) to that of declared witness. He took a certain pleasure in smashing his early public image, felt a real sense of dread in the image he was assuming. He had misgivings about his new allies, dismay when he thought what certain tried and trusted friends would think of him. A fanatic has the protection of his blindness, a free man the burden of his insight into all ambiguities, including those of his own motives and character.

It is small wonder, then, that Thomas Merton watched for the appearance of his new writing with something like the sickness of fear. The public letter to Cuadra might appear only in Spanish and in Central America. Articles *Jubilee* and *The Catholic Worker* were already announcing, and the book he would edit for New Directions, would make it clear to all that he had joined a small, ill-organized, and widely unpopular minority.

Merton's first challenge to complacent thinking about nuclear war should have had a far greater impact than it did. Whether *Original Child Bomb* is a piece of prose, a prose poem, or a poem is open to dispute. It has many elements of the "found poem." Merton produced a work of powerful restraint, using various accounts of the first atomic bombs and the first nuclear strike on Hiroshima and Nagasaki. The title is taken from the Japanese name for the Hiroshima bomb. A good title, it led to misunderstandings.

New Directions was to publish the book, with drawings by Emil Antonucci. From May to October, however, the book was delayed while the censors argued. Unexpectedly, Dom Gabriel and Dom James broke the impasse in late October and gave permission.[176]

The late release caused what Naomi Burton had termed earlier "a logjam of Merton books." *The New Man,*[177] *New Seeds of Contemplation,*[178] and *Original Child Bomb*[179] all appeared within weeks of one another. "The Shelter Ethic" was published in *The Catholic Worker* in November 1961, to be followed by a surge of articles by Thomas Merton, some of them excerpts from the books about to appear, others, such as "Nuclear War and Christian Responsibility," on the controversy Merton had now joined. By early 1962 there could be no doubt about where the "new" Merton stood. In the meanwhile his relations with publishers had foundered.

Acting as his own agent, Merton had widened the number of publishers, promising one book to Herder and Herder and another to Macmillan. Both agreements put him in difficulties over options with Farrar, Straus and Cudahy. He then found the last publishers uncooperative when the question arose of including works published by a number of publishers in *A Thomas Merton Reader.*

Merton and Thomas P. McDonnell, the designated editor of the *Reader*, had worked away during 1961, foreseeing no difficulties and making lists irrespective of who had published what. Merton found McDonnell very much of his own mind on the material and enjoyed working with him.[180] He was anxious to make a balance between his older work and the writings of 1959–61, most of which was only just coming into print. Then the whole plan fell apart in what Merton saw as squabbles between publishers over bits and pieces of his work. It has to be admitted that he had as little understanding of options as he had of multiple submission. When a lawsuit was threatened over *Life and Holiness*, Merton lost patience with the idea of a book on prayer being argued over in public court.[181] He had forgotten for the moment his earlier plans with Lax and Rice to publish by being prosecuted: Robert Lax wrote later from the Greek island of Kos to remind him, "remember how we hailed the opportunity of reading our works to the court in bradford . . . ?"[182]

Life and Holiness was published in a more conventional way by Herder and Herder in the spring of 1963.[183] Much is clear and valuable in a book that promises, twice, not to be a "how-to-do-it-book on holiness, and leading the spiritual life." Merton handles the quotations with skill unusual even for him, and it is a surprise to discover that, in addition to many passages from the New and Old Testament, he quotes from Pope John XXIII, Cardinal Newman, Cassian, St. John Chrysostom, Clement of Alexander, John Tauler, St. Peter Damian, Dostoevsky, Adam of Perseigne, Tertullian, St. Anselm, St. Jerome, St. Thomas Aquinas, and a number of modern theologians — all in a book of just over a hundred pages, without the least sense of crowding or heaviness.

In 1961, Merton's struggle to make the *Reader* comprehensive strained relations even with Robert Giroux, who found himself in a contest that was probably unnecessary, and certainly not of Giroux's making. In the end, a compromise had to be reached, and the first edition of *A Thomas Merton Reader* came out in October 1962,[184] without much of the material Merton had hoped to include.

Early in 1962, the title of *Original Child Bomb* was causing the widest misconceptions. Merton learned it was being put on the children's shelves in some bookstores.[185] Later in the year he wrote:

> I suppose I ought to be afraid for my own skin. Fury of a Japanese monk at Citeaux who thought *Original Child Bomb* was a glorification of atomic war and denounced me to the General! I have now been denounced by both sides, and am on everybody's black list. I have not written as I have merely to please people. But it would be nice at least to be understood.[186]

In itself, *Original Child Bomb* was perhaps the most telling thing Merton wrote against atomic warfare, worth far more than most articles on both sides of the debate in those early years of the controversy. What he said was so clear it invited distortion and misunderstanding from those with their minds already made up. It is a pity on all counts that the work was largely ignored in the furor of words. What it invited, in fact, was a careful reading and a quiet meditation.

It would be impossible here to make a detailed comparison between the earlier *Seeds of Contemplation* and *New Seeds of Contemplation*, and this has been done well elsewhere.[187] The second book is more lyrical, the first more intense. The second book contains "The General Dance," which first appeared in Ed Rice's *Jubilee*,[188] and was included in *A Thomas Merton Reader*, where it is well placed in a gathering of Merton's best writing in different keys at the end of the book. In "The General Dance" Merton drew upon his "Sophianic" readings in the Russian mystics. At the same time this is Merton's original invitation to set aside our struggle for knowledge, self-improvement, even wisdom, and to reawaken the springs of spontaneous joy and gratitude:

> For the world and time are the dance of the Lord in emptiness. The silence of the spheres is the music of a wedding feast. The more we persist in misunderstanding the phenomena of life, the more we analyze them out into strange finalities and complex purposes of our own, the more we involve ourselves in sadness, absurdity and despair. But it does not matter much, because no despair of ours can alter the reality of things, or stain the joy of the cosmic dance which is always there. Indeed, we are in the midst of it, and it is in the midst of us, for it beats in our very blood, whether we want it to or not.
>
> Yet the fact remains that we are invited to forget ourselves on purpose, cast our awful solemnity to the winds and join in the general dance.[189]

✻

By the spring of 1962, Merton's public image had been radically changed. Many a Catholic father who had given *The Seven Storey Mountain* to a restless son must have been baffled, as, perhaps, the son was also.

Merton's resolution to live the life of a secret and obscure Herakleitos was obviously doomed, and at his own hand. His resolution to disappear into silence as soon as the *Reader* was published[190] was going the same way as so many resolutions to write less after a certain date.

He had to write to Edward Deming Andrews, the authority on the Shakers, that his studies on the Shakers had had to be postponed because of his writings on nuclear war and racial questions.[191] For all that, the "new" Merton still spent most of the hours of the day saying the offices and teaching his novices. Some of the time at the hermitage he gave to joining "the General Dance" — walking in the Gethsemani woods barefoot,[192] listening for the first bird in the predawn darkness, recording the light of the different hours.

His interest in the future of monasticism — and its past — continued. The summer of the gardenias had brought him to a new knowledge of Plato (he had been less than enthusiastic about Plato at Oakham), and of the neo-Platonic School of Chartres. His reading of Clement of Alexandria brought an interest in the extraordinary and eclectic ferment of thought in Alexandria in the early Christian centuries.[193] Contact with Dr. Paul K. T. Sih of the Institute of Asian Studies of St. John's University in Jamaica had led him to the Legge translation of the *Chinese Classics*, and his correspondence with Dr. John Wu brought a joyful light, rather than a grave one, into his own Oriental studies. Merton was now trying to learn Chinese to be more responsive to John Wu's letters. Both Sih and Wu aided Merton in finding his way round a Chinese dictionary,[194] though he had to abandon the attempt to learn Chinese.[195]

One of the few cultures he had neglected earlier was the Islamic. His correspondence with Louis Massignon about non-violent resistance to the war in Algeria had brought him knowledge of the dialogue with Mohammedans. Now he made his own contacts with Islamic scholars. This created a need for books on the history of the Arabs in Spain; on the great age of Arab philosophy; above all, on the mystics of the Mohammedan religion, the Sufis. "Sufi" meant undyed wool. Like the Cistercians, the mystic followers of the Prophet had worn white wool. It was only the first of many connections Merton found fascinating.[196]

The ancient went with the all-too-contemporary. When James Laughlin had come in mid-January 1962, the two talked of the complicated plans for getting all the contributions to the book they then called "The Human Alternative" (and which was finally called *Breakthrough to Peace*). They also discussed Merton's plans for a book-length essay on Clement of Alexandria.[197]

In the end, neither the Shakers nor photography was ignored. Visiting the Methodist seminary at Ashbury for a conference in the second week of January 1962, Merton made another side trip to Shakertown, and this time he had a camera, though it was "So cold my fingers could no longer feel the shutter release. Some marvellous subjects. How the blank side of a frame house can be so completely beautiful I cannot imagine. A completely miraculous achievement of forms."[198]

More frequently now, he brought the theme of craftsmanship, of good workmanship, into his conferences with novices:

> A monk should have a good feeling towards any kind of nice work. It should be a monastic characteristic that a monk should appreciate anything that's well done. Why should a monk appreciate anything that's well done? Well, first of all, anything that's decently done gives glory to God.[199]

Once committed to the two issues of war and racial justice, there was, however, a gathering momentum, and with it a sense of the danger Merton saw in the wrong kind of activism, a sort of nervous busy-ness that destroyed proper reflection and replaced it with a sense of self-importance simply because one was doing something. Merton's anxiety about censorship was now matched by a fear he would be misrepresented by new activist friends. Matters had already got into a tangle on the publication side:

> The Catholic Worker has printed a first draft of an article — a text I did not want printed and that contains many statements I wanted to change — on peace. It is clear to me that under cover of being honest, frank, and just I have been too eager to speak and too eager to say things that a few people wanted to hear — and most people did not want to hear. Better to have waited and simply tried to say, with utmost care, what is true. Of course when I write anything I write what I think is true. But what is true can also be said so badly that it becomes a misrepresentation of the truth.[200]

The publication came at a time when Merton was already preparing himself for a battle with censors, and he wrote to Father Paul Bourne trying to explain the compromising mixup.[201] Meanwhile, he was exploring a way round the difficulties he saw ahead.

James Laughlin had introduced Merton by letter to W. H. Ferry, of the Center for the Study of Democratic Institutions in Santa Barbara, California. Ferry had already gained a reputation as an articulate social critic. In early letters Ferry and Merton struggled over what to call one another. They were soon Ping and Tom. On December 21, 1961, Merton wrote:

> I am having a bit of censorship trouble. This makes me think that one way of getting some of my stuff around would be to let your people mimeograph it and include it with your material. Would you consider this in some cases? This would not require censorship. I have for instance some copies of letters to people to make a book called "Cold War Letters" — very unlikely to be published (!) I've got them typed up and you can judge whether you think it worth circulating some of them.[202]

He wrote a long letter to Laughlin on December 31, explaining the censorship question, but beginning:

> First of all, I have apparently shocked both you and Ferry in giving you the idea that I am indulging in some kind of monkey business. Not at all. We have some very strict censorship laws, and I have hitherto been very conscientious about keeping to them.[203]

He goes on to say that mimeographed material can be circulated without being censored — such circulation is common knowledge and common practice. Only in the case of its being expressly forbidden by the abbot or the abbot general would this avenue be closed. Ignoring the Copyright Act, Merton goes on, "Circulation of a couple of hundred mimeographed copies is not publication." On the book he is editing Merton sees the distinct possibility the censors will want to read the whole book, and he feels this will be a disaster. They cannot, of course, stop Laughlin from publishing, but they can stop Merton from being editor. He suggests it may be safer altogether if he has his preface sent through the censorship channels separately, while Laughlin deletes his name from the book as editor.

This, in fact, was done, though Merton's introduction, "Peace: A Religious Responsibility," by no means went through unscathed or unchanged before it took its place in *Breaththrough to Peace / Twelve Views on the Threat of Thermonuclear Extermination*, which appeared as a New Directions paperback in September 1962.[204]

With the anxiety over full commitment came some exhilaration. After the abbot general's visitation in October 1961 (where he met total opposition from the abbot general's secretary, Father Clement, but thought he could count on some comprehension both from Dom Gabriel Sortais and Dom James), Merton wrote:

> I am perhaps at the turning point in my spiritual life: perhaps slowly coming to a point of maturation and the resolution of doubts — and the forgetting of fears. Walking into a known and definite battle. May God protect me in it. The Catholic Worker set out a press release about my article, which may have many reactions — or may have none. At any rate it appears that I am one of the few Catholic priests in the country who has come out unequivocally for a completely intransigent fight for the abolition of war and the use of non-violent means to settle international conflicts. Hence by implication not only against the bomb, against nuclear testing, against polaris submarines, but against all violence. This I will inevitably have to explain in due course. Non-violent *action*, not mere passivity. How am I going to explain myself and defend a definite position in a timely manner when it takes at least two months to get even a short article through the censors of the Order, is a question I cannot attempt to answer.[205]

Open opposition was not long coming. On March 16, 1962, he reports to W. H. Ferry that an editorial in the Washington *Catholic Standard* had taken to task his article in *Commonweal*, "Nuclear War and Christian Responsibility," misquoting him and accusing him of a "startling disregard of authoritative Catholic utterances and unwarranted charges about the intention of our government towards disarmament."[206]

He claimed the editorial had dismissed him as "an absolute pacifist" who was trying to make it appear the Pope had made a clear statement against all war.

Merton was at pains, then and later, to explain he was not a pacifist, in part because he saw the possibility of certain exceptions to the absolute rule of non-violence, and in part because he wanted to avoid the very labeling and dismissal he had received in the editorial. As he told Ferry:

Really it is vitally important that we now work at keeping the way wide open for thought, for discussion, for investigation, for meditation: and the thing that most blocks this is getting oneself permanently identified and so to speak classified as the holder of one or other sets of opinions. And, by implication, as loyal or disloyal to our side in the cold war. Even to question the primary importance of this kind of loyalty is itself regarded as disloyalty and immediately disqualifies all that one says from further consideration. We have got to keep thinking and asking questions. And the mere ability, once in a while, to raise the right question ought to be regarded as an achievement. May we learn to do this and keep at it. What did the Fathers of the Church say about Socrates being among the saints? And then there are also the Prophets.[207]

At the same time he explained to Ferry that his own views were more extreme than those of the group, chiefly Catholics, forming around John Courtney Murray. He had missed an earlier opportunity for a full discussion when Father Murray visited Gethsemani.[208] He says he is in touch with Father John Ford, one of Murray's close associates, yet he gives a rather off-the-cuff summary of what he thinks is the group's position:

> . . . I gather they are in a rather quixotic abstract position saying limited nuclear war is fine but all out nuclear war isn't, and therefore we just have to see that we don't go beyond a limited one. This is very logical according to the tradition in which they find themselves sitting, but the only trouble is that the tradition in which they sit, that of the post tridentine causists, is a boat that has slipped its moorings and is now floating off in mid ocean a thousand miles from the facts. But within that boat everything is logical, all right, and in apple pie order. I mention this because they will not necessarily be fully in sympathy with my more extreme viewpoint.[209]

This was hardly fair to their argument. The tradition they were working in was the just war theory. In 1940 at Olean, Robert Lax, declaring himself a pacifist pure and simple, had left Robert Gibney and Merton to discuss the ramifications of just wars late into the night. The theory had been much augmented by Catholic theologians both before and after the Council of Trent. It was just because Merton now set it aside as largely irrelevant that the *Catholic Standard* editorial accused him of a "startling disregard of authoritative utterances."

Three quick points must be made here about the theory because Merton was driven back at times — reluctantly — to argue from it.

First, Merton had come to see that the "just war" was about as elusive as the "perfect ruler" or "philosopher-prince" in the political theories of Aristotle and Plato. In 1940–41, he had ruled largely against the war opposing Hitler, a war that was, in the view of most, by far the best candidate for the just war in the century. This put him in a difficult position on a number of counts. His reading of Gordon Zahn's

German Catholics and Hitler's War[210] and a reading of the _Prison Letters_ and a life of Father Max Josef Metzger[211] had brought home at once how courageous those who resisted Hitler in Germany had been, and how pitifully few — the few just men of Merton's journals of 1941. In 1964 he wrote "Danish Nonviolent Resistance to Hitler,"[212] an article showing that Denmark alone among the occupied countries had protected and saved its own Jewish population. What the Danes had done stood to their everlasting honor, yet the Danes had not, by non-violent action, liberated Europe.

Second, the theory of the just war by definition referred to a war of defense.[213] Almost all wars began in defense of something (a defense significantly made most often in other people's territory), yet whatever the causists might argue, Merton began by pointing out this ruled out nuclear weapons per se. A thermonuclear bomb could be used to threaten: there was no way it could be used, in itself, as a weapon of defense. When "nuclear realists" like Herman Kahn talked of preemptive first strike they were simply confirming the obvious.[214] Preemptive first strike as a means of "defending" effectively ruled out the theory of the just war, anachronistic or not.

Finally, and less obvious because less well known, the theory of the just war had been propounded by St. Augustine of Hippo at a time when Augustine saw both Christianity and the Roman Empire in a single jeopardy. The historical circumstances are important. The Roman Empire would disappear, while, by an irony Augustine never foresaw, Christianity would conquer the conquerors of the empire. Here the hard historical lesson to be learned was the very point Merton made over and over again in the mid-sixties — those who tied their faith in Christianity to faith in a single culture and a single political structure served only the structure and had no faith.[215]

In May 1962, when Merton began to explore what the Church Fathers before Augustine had written about the Christian's right (or duty) to bear arms, he discovered in Tertullian and Origen a theory very different from Augustine's, a theory close to non-violence.[216] Here the historical setting was one in which oppressed Christian groups, not the Christian Empire, were threatened — a sadly telling and important distinction.

Where Merton saw himself as more extreme than the "nuclear pacifists" (or the "relative pacifists," to use John Courtney Murray's phrase), consisted, as he says in the journal entry of October 23, 1961, in his having "come out unequivocally for a completely intransigent fight for the abolition of war and for the use of non-violent means to settle international conflicts." His journal and passages in his letters to Ferry and many others make the point clear. Yet by the spring of 1962 he was strongly recommending a plan by the physicist Leo Szilard, which brought him back to nuclear weapons for defense, the just war theory, and the limitations he had found quixotic in his summary of the Murray position:

> I am not preaching disarmament. But I do think that there are ways of using nuclear weapons for defense that will quite adequately fit our needs, without promoting an extreme spiralling arms race, but, on the contrary, pointing to eventual stability and relative sanity on all sides. I will not outline the policies, but Leo Szilard, in the April Bulletin of the Atomic Scientists, seems to me to make proposals that exactly fit the principles laid down by the Popes.[217]

Merton directed Catholics to these "principles laid down by the Popes" in his preface to the mimeographed "Cold War Letters" and elsewhere.[218] At the same time he regretted the absence of a clear statement on nuclear war from the Vatican:

> One would certainly wish that the Catholic position on nuclear war was held as strict as the Catholic position on birth control. It seems a little strange that we are so wildly exercised about the "murder" (and the word is of course correct) of an unborn infant by abortion, or even the prevention of conception which is hardly murder, and yet accept without a qualm the extermination of millions of helpless and innocent adults, some of whom may be Christians and even our friends rather than our enemies. I submit that we ought to fulfill the one without omitting the other.[219]

Like the "nuclear pacifists" and like many others, Merton set his chief hopes on the statements on war to be made at the Second Vatican Council, whose formal opening was now announced for October 11, 1962.[220] Before that date much would happen in the world situation to make the council's pronouncements on war even more crucial.

✻

Merton sent letters of support for the non-violent peace strike organized by *The Catholic Worker* to Dorothy Day and Jim Forest in the spring of 1962. The letter to Forest appeared in *The Catholic Worker* in February.[221] In the private letters between Dorothy Day and Thomas Merton, the two shared anxieties about the future of the movement. Both agreed on Forest's integrity and intelligence, but for Dorothy Day there were too many young people who wanted to help who seemed consumed by violent personal conflicts. Some were unstable and unpredictable, more problems to be solved than solvers of problems.[222]

Merton heard far more frequently of drug use, both from Milosz on the West Coast, and from many correspondents like Dorothy Day who were sympathetic to, or involved in, the non-violent movements for peace. In 1958 he had written to one of his first friends by correspondence, Aldous Huxley, responding to Huxley's article "Drugs That Shape

Man's Mind" in *The Saturday Evening Post*.[223] The exchange was brief and friendly, yet it left Merton with deep misgivings. In the first place he saw a confusion between mysticism and altered states of consciousness induced by drugs.[224] This was "contemplation made easy" with a vengeance. There was a connection here, too, with what Merton had always looked upon as the danger of magic: magic and drug taking were alike based on manipulation for power, and thus the opposite of true mysticism. To him any confusion in this distinction between ends and means would lead to tragic consequences. In the second place, it would help the public identify non-violent peace movements with the "crazies," a theme already well developed by the media.

If these considerations produced misgivings in Merton's loyalty to some of his new friends, he was clearer about the sources of his opposition. On the one side it came from the "French" element in the Order (and in particular from the secretary of the abbot general), on the other from the hierarchy of Catholic bishops and archbishops in America, and especially from those who had already declared themselves against what they saw as a weakening of American military strength in the Cold War.

Merton sometimes misjudged opposition. When he asked Naomi Burton to take over his publishing affairs again, he wrote that she would probably not agree with what he was writing now. Naomi Burton had to write back that he had totally misunderstood the relationship between author and agent, in a way that questioned her professional integrity. She pointed out, too, that as an Anglican back in 1947, she had not agreed with every word he wrote in *The Seven Storey Mountain*, something which had affected neither her capacity as an agent nor their friendship.[225]

In assuming his abbot would be at the other end of the political spectrum, Merton was probably right. Yet Dom James, as unpredictable as ever, demonstrated a genuine understanding of what was at stake. If he was overprotective, he was protective. It is very likely he held back the letters calling an end to Merton's writings on war through the crucial early months of 1962, when Merton's antiwar writings were appearing everywhere. At any rate, when the ban fell (as Merton had expected), it was no longer a question of censorship, but of suppression. On April 27, 1962, Merton wrote in his journal:

> It seems finally that the opposition of censors and of the Abbot General (not to mention the Abbot General's secretary) has become intransigent. Yesterday Reverend Father gave me a bunch of letters and reports, the main item being a letter of the General dated Jan. 20th, which Reverend Father for some unaccountable reason had been saving up. (The letter was addressed to him, of course, but concerned me and was in fact for my benefit.)

The decision seems to be (it is not absolutely definite) that I am to stop all publication of anything on war. In other words I am to be in effect silenced on this subject for the main reason that it is not appropriate for a monk, and that it "falsifies the message of monasticism." Certainly there is a lot of truth in this, from a certain point of view, but that is not a matter to be debated one way or the other.[226]

On April 12, Thomas Merton's "Prayer for Peace" was read in the House of Representatives by Frank Kowalski, a Connecticut Democrat. Thus, on Wednesday of Holy Week, the words "Grant us prudence in proportion to our power, Wisdom in proportion to our science, Humaneness in proportion to our wealth and might," entered the *Congressional Record*.[227]

For a week or two it looked as if "Peace in the Post-Christian Era," the book Merton had written for Macmillan, most of which had passed through censorship, would appear. On May 26, the day the typing was finished, Merton received a letter from the abbot general specifically ordering him to publish no more on war and peace:

Je sais très bien, cher Fils, que vous ne prétendez nullement être le seul à parler du problème de la guerre atomique, et encore bien moins être l'inspirateur du Cardinal Archevêque de Chicago. Je veux seulement souligner nettement la différence des deux ordres: celui de l'enseignement, qui appartient à la hiérarchie et à ceux qu'elle veut bien déléguer pour cela; et celui de la prière, qui appartient — entre autres — au moine, ou plutôt auquel le moine appartient.

Vous comprenez donc que je ne vous demande pas de vous désintéresser du sort du monde. Mais je vous crois en mesure d'influer sur lui par votre prière et votre vie retirée en Dieu beaucoup mieux encore que par vos écrits. Et c'est pourquoi je ne pense pas nuire à la cause que vous défendez en vous demandant de renoncer à la publication du livre que vous avez préparé et de vous abstenir désormais d'écrire sur ce sujet de la guerre atomique, de sa préparation, etc.[228]

The contents of "Peace in the Post-Christian Era" were doomed for the moment, as far as publication by Macmillan was concerned, though Merton hurried out mimeographed copies.

In the meanwhile he expressed relief in his journal — and not only at the manner in which the abbot general had unwittingly resolved the worst publishing tangles. To W. H. Ferry, Merton showed much the same emotion:

Did I tell you that the decision of the higher ups has become final and conclusive? The Peace Book (I mean the one I just wrote) is not to be published. Too controversial, doesn't give a nice image of monk. Monk concerned with peace. Bad image. Monks in NY state have fallout shelter paid for with monks bread as advertised with pictures of sub human

monks in NY Daily News: good image of monk, fine, go ahead. Hurray
for the resistant image, the non mutant.

I am not sore, not even very interested any more. I did what I thought
ought to be done and that is that.[229]

He consoled himself with the thought that the long preface to *Break-through to Peace* would make it clear, if there was any doubt, where he stood on the issue of nuclear war. He may have felt that the news he circulated widely — that he was now prevented from writing on war — would have a greater effect than still more essays.[230] He knew, too, he had written too much, too fast.

"The Peace movement needs more than zeal," Merton had written.[231] In a 1963 essay about the liturgical movement, he adds, "We must be on our guard against a kind of blind and immature zeal — the zeal of the enthusiast or of the zealot — which represents precisely a frantic compensation for the deeply personal qualities which are lacking to us."[232]

In the same essay Merton goes on to define the zealot as a person:

. . . who "loses himself" in his cause in such a way that he can no longer "find himself" at all. Yet paradoxically this "loss" of himself is not the salutary self-forgetfulness commanded by Christ. It is rather an immersion in his own wilfulness conceived as the will of an abstract, non-personal force: the force of a project or a program. He is, in other words, alienated by the violence of his own enthusiasm: and by that very violence he tends to produce the same kind of alienation in others . . .[233]

The giveaway was language. The language of both the progressive zealot and of the entrenched conservative was unreal rhetoric — the rhetoric of sounding abstractions, of violence, of evasions. In contrast, the language of those free of self-aggrandizement and obsessions was *parrhesia*.

Merton used this Greek word in *The New Man*, where he explains it means one of ". . . the rights and privileges of a citizen in a Greek city state. This 'free speech' is at once the duty and the honor of speaking one's own mind fully and frankly in the civil assemblies by which the state is governed."[234]

In *The New Man* (1961) Merton largely restricts *parrhesia* to free discourse between God and man — first Adam, then Job, finally the formed and mature contemplative. He is careful to explain that this is the language of equals, of God and "the friends of God." In 1963 the word appears again in "Liturgy and Spiritual Personalism." Here *parrhesia* is the language to be used by members of the Church ("the Assembly of those who have been called together by God")[235] especially when they disagree (in this case over the new liturgy). In the next years Merton's concept of *parrhesia* would broaden to include all debate between opponents, inside the Church and outside. Thus it becomes, not just the overfamiliar "free speech" but the speech of free men and women in a common search after truth. Merton's concern with language as the medium which unites or divides, when it is well or badly used, continues to the important essay "War and the Crisis of Language" (1967).[236] By 1962 he was aware that his own use of language was sometimes at war with his non-violent aims.

*

Many of Merton's friends through correspondence found their way to Gethsemani in the last months of 1961 and in 1962. The most unexpected visitor, however, was one of his New Zealand aunts, Aunt Kit. She arrived on November 3, 1961, in the middle of Merton's crisis of commitment, a little overwhelmed by having flown over New York City in a helicopter. Much of their conversation was about family history, and it must have come to each of them that for all the big families of the last generation there were now few Mertons. Merton made notes of what Aunt Kit said, feeling he was learning a great deal for the first time, but there were some odd confusions.[237] Either the myths were too strong, or it was Aunt Ka, Aunt Kit's sister, who was the true family historian.

After corresponding with Jim Forest at *The Catholic Worker*, Merton was anxious to meet him and suggested a visit early in the New Year. Forest's account of the first time he *heard* Thomas Merton provides a vivid and necessary counterpart to much that was grim in a grim time in Merton's journal.

Forest and his friend Bob Kaye had made an exhausting three-day journey hitchhiking in late February. Arriving at the monastery, Jim Forest had left Kaye in the room at the guest house to search for the abbey church:

> . . . Surviving the trip, a prayer of thanksgiving came easily. But it didn't last long because the church's silence was broken by distant laughter, laughter so intense and pervasive that I couldn't fail to be drawn to it, such an unlikely sound for a solemn Trappist abbey. It was coming from the guest house, in fact from Bob's room: a kind of monsoon of joy. Well, that's the difference between Bob and me, I thought: I pray, and he gives way to laughter; God probably likes the laughter better. I pushed open the door, and indeed Bob was laughing, but the sound was coming mainly from a monk on the floor in his black and white robes, feet in the air, a bright red face, hands clutching the belly. A shade more than Robin Hood's well-fed Friar Tuck than I imagined any fast-chastened Trappist could be. Thomas Merton, author of so many books about such serious subjects, laughing half to death on the floor.[238]

While Merton records so much in his journal, he fails to mention Bob Kaye's socks, the smell of which, after three days on the roads of the world, had occasioned this Gargantuan laughter. He does record how glad he was that Forest and Kaye had come; then, two weeks later, that Jim Forest and a number of others from *The Catholic Worker* have been jailed for demonstrating in front of the Atomic Energy Control Building. They had been released, but were to be tried on March 22.

On April 14, he writes that he had met W. H. Ferry for the first time:

> Ping Ferry was here this week, and one of the best things we did was take pictures of the old ruined distillery at Dant Station. The long red warehouses, and the wonderful proportion of spaces in the wall, broken up with an interesting low line of narrow windows. Other side, down the road to the creek, windows and doors broken open and Dant labels lying all over the road in hundreds.[239]

Soon after this, another correspondent, John Wu, came to Gethsemani. Merton had first written to Wu in March 1961, asking help with his Oriental studies, and especially on a tentative project to translate selections from the writings of Chuang Tzu, a Chinese philosopher who had provided a quotation for Merton's Columbia notebooks while he was working on the Blake thesis. He had asked John Wu to coach him "like any Chinese schoolboy of the old days."[240] From this beginning, modest in every sense, their correspondence developed into one of the warmest friendships by letter, as well as one of the most beneficial.

The long-planned meeting took place at the end of June, and Merton talked of "the great, simple spirituality of John Wu."[241] While Wu was as scrupulous in choosing words as Robert Lax, his comments on human failings tended to be wry and sadly puzzled, in contrast to Merton's outright condemnation, yet Wu had a strong wit and a sense of injustice to match Merton's own. There had been no need, then, for Merton's half-apologetic way of breaking into a letter on Oriental studies to explain why he was sending Wu a poem in his letter of June 7, just before their meeting:

> And now to turn suddenly from scholarship to less pleasant subjects. I hesitate to send you the enclosed angry and bitter poem. It is savage, and its savagery hits at everything in sight, so that it is not kind to anyone, even to the poor, sad, desperate Chinese girl whose picture broke my heart and suggested the poem. I wish I could have said something full of mercy and love that would have been worthy of the situation, but I have only used her plight to attack the hypocrisy of those who find no room for Chinese refugees, and who always have a very good reason. And the sad plight of a whole society which nods approval, while pronouncing a few formulas of regret. I suppose I should not get angry and that it represents a weakness in myself to get excited still about the awful tragedies that are everywhere in the world. They are too awful for human protest to be meaningful, so people seem to think. I protest anyway. I am still primitive enough. I have not caught up with this century.[242]

Ferry had sent him a newspaper cutting, a photograph of a girl obviously in turmoil, holding a rag to her face:

POINT OF NO RETURN

Lee Ying, only 19, has to go home again. That's Red China, across the way from Hong Kong. Terror and misery from which she fled make up Lee Ying's future. But the British authorities, alarmed by the rising wave of refugees from Red China, send them back from Hong Kong. Lee Ying shows she faces a grim future.[243]

"A Picture of Lee Ying" has not dated. The bureaucratic hypocrisy, whole populations "So full of official grief" (to quote from one of Merton's early poems)[244] are current, as is the appalling, bland, feelingless prose of the 1962 news item from which Merton's poem takes off.

There are many links between the 1962 poem and Merton's poems of 1939–40: "We too know all about sorrow we have seen it in the movies." In "A Picture of Lee Ying,"[245] he parodies the English for foreigners of an official trying to explain why everything is being done in the best interests of all ("You would not want the authorities to neglect duty"), then the kind of question every new arrival learns to wince at ("How do you like the image of the free world sorry you cannot stay.").

With "You have the sympathy of millions" Merton reaches the devastating level of satire of Henry Fielding's ". . . He was in danger of starving with the universal sympathy of all his neighbours."[246]

Such lines as these in "A Picture of Lee Ying" had a far more urgent and lasting power in themselves than the paragraphs of prose in the controversial articles — a power, like that of *Original Child Bomb*, that was partially dissipated because, in the 1960s, it seemed that only the poets read poetry. Merton had already noted there seemed to be a natural link between activism and poetry. After meeting Jim Forest and Bob Kaye he writes in a somewhat bemused fashion, "They all write hundreds of poems . . ."[247]

It was as a poet that he had first noticed and admired the young Jesuit priest at Cornell, Daniel Berrigan. He and Berrigan had been exchanging ideas, and Daniel Berrigan had written to say he was reviewing *New Seeds of Contemplation* for *America*. "I like it very much, especially the New Merton who is involved and more human." On August 21, Merton records their first meeting:

Last week was tremendous, busy, exciting. First Zalman Schachter came with Rabbi L. Silberman from Vanderbilt, who talked about the Dead Sea Scrolls. Then Father Dan Berrigan, an altogether winning and warm intelligence, with a perfect zeal, compassion and understanding. This, certainly, is the spirit of the church. This is a hope I can believe in, at least in its validity and its spirit.[248]

Much was to be built from this meeting. For the moment, Merton wrote in November to say how much he had liked Berrigan's last book of poems, "It is terse and even Zen like, and it is the integrity of the experience that above all comes through. Great, man, great."[249] He said he was returning the forms "from Goggenbuch Stipend House," that he had heard from Bob Lax in Greece, and "All my friends are after Guggenheims."

While Merton was writing poems for a new collection that summer, he was also gathering together the translations he had been making of the poems of others over the past two years. He had been deeply moved when he received Ernesto Cardenal's new collection, above all by the poems Cardenal had written as Brother Lawrence at Gethsemani.[250] Cardenal also sent translations he had made from Merton's poems: some of the poems, in particular the first part of "Elias — Variations on a Theme," Merton decided were better in Spanish than in English.[251]

When it came out a year later, in December 1963, Merton's fifth collection, *Emblems of a Season of Fury*,[252] proved to be both his richest and his most confusing. The reader was expected to make extraordinary changes of response at the turn of a page, from the *Hagia Sophia* to "A Letter to Pablo Antonio Cuadra Concerning Giants" (to give only one example from many). There were poems from Merton's reading on Islamic subjects (including the beautiful "Song for the Death of Averroes"), from Merton's study of the School of Chartres, and from the Desert Fathers. There were his elegies and satires, including "A Picture of Lee Ying." In another satire, "There Has to Be a Jail for Ladies," Merton goes back to the Women's Prison near Perry Street, which he had mentioned often in his poems of 1939–40. At the end he tries to offer consolation (there had been no consolation for anyone in "A Picture of Lee Ying"). This is a good deal too easy, in fact it is disastrously close to being "cute."

In the same collection Merton brought together his translations of Vallejo, Carrera Andrade, Cuadra, Cardenal, Cortes, and Raissa Maritain. The result, for all the good things, is more like a shelf of books than a single collection.

In his own reading Merton grouped writers into what he called "choirs," where he saw sympathetic links between them.[253] He was delighted, too, when he found that authors he liked agreed in liking another writer he valued — that, for example, both Fénelon and Newman had admired Clement of Alexandria.[254]

Merton's discovery of Fénelon in 1962 was, like so much else, a rediscovery, taking him back to acknowledge his first teacher, Monsieur

Delmas, who had introduced him to Fénelon's writing in 1927, and in particular to the novel *Télémaque*. With a belated tribute to Monsieur Delmas ("I think the reason I liked him was that I fully believed he never said anything he did not mean")[255] came the sense that all had not been a disaster at the Lycée Ingres. In 1963, however, Fénelon was pressed into service to goad Dom Gabriel Sortais. As Merton wrote to John Wu:

> I have had a very amusing Chuang Tzuean experience. With deliberate intention to wreak mischief and with tongue deeply in cheek, I wrote a long fiery article defending Fénelon against Bossuet. (Of course I like Fénelon, but the idea was to puncture the Bossuet-image and the French national collective ego, which is anti-Fénelon.) Then I sent it to the censors of the Order of England, who obviously rushed to approve it, and sent their approval to the Abbot General, probably letting him know the contents of the article (he can't read English). Report came back from our patriotic French General, a staunch Gaulliste and a most humorless chauvinist when it comes to things like this. He granted the nihil obstat, I can almost hear the muttered recriminations with which he did so, and then added in a special note that he did not want his name associated with such a piece of effrontery. It was magnanimous of him not to put me on bread and water for a year and stop me writing altogether.[256]

If this was Merton relishing the idea of being able to do new mischief with a controversy dating back to an old round in the Battle of the Books, he had a more current reason to want to send something of a snub to his abbot general.

The Second Vatican Council met in an atmosphere greatly influenced by the Cuban missile crisis. There were even stronger pressures now to make a firm statement about the morality or immorality of nuclear war. Merton had already been asked by his friends in Vienna, Jean and Hildegard Goss-Mayr, to send them a folio of his writing on war, for circulation in Rome.[257] Meanwhile, the confidence of those who hoped for a ban on nuclear war had grown with each statement by Pope John XXIII.

The encyclical *Magister et Magistra* of 1961 called for social justice. The announcement of the council in January 1962, the Pope's radio address of September 11, 1962, pledging support for "any sincere effort on behalf of peace," the personal intervention of John XXIII at the height of the missile crisis in a call for moderation, had led, in 1963, to the great encyclical *Pacem in Terris*.

Pacem in Terris seemed at once to Thomas Merton, as it seemed to millions, the clear and simple statement for which they had prayed. If it dwarfed everything Merton had done, it also confirmed much he had tried to do. In personal terms, he felt sure this meant an end to letters, even from such near supporters as Father John Ford of the Murray group, telling him he had interpreted the Pope's words to meet his own argument.[258] It meant, too, he felt certain, that "Peace in the Post-Christian Era" could now be published. He wrote at once to Dom Gabriel Sortais. On May 10, 1963, he received his answer:

> Letter from the General came today categorically denying my request to publish *Peace in the Post-Christian Era* now that the Encyclical has said what I was saying myself! At the back of his mind obviously is an adamant conviction that France should have the bomb and use it if necessary. He says the Encyclical has changed nothing in the right of a nation to arm itself with nuclear weapons for self-defense, and speaks only of "aggressive war . . ."[259]

On June 3, Pope John XXIII was dead. "May he rest in peace, this great and good Father, whom I certainly loved, and who had been good to me, sending me the stole and many blessings . . ."[260] Then, on November 14 of the same year:

> . . . a telegram arrived today that Dom Gabriel Sortais, the Abbot General, had died last night — Feast of All the Saints of the Order. I suppose he was exhausted from work, the Council, etc., and all his usual illnesses. He was in many ways a great man, a warm and generous person, and I am indebted to him for many things though I certainly got annoyed at his arbitrary ways with the censorship of books.[261]

It remained to be seen whether there would be a reaction to the policies of John XXIII at the Second Vatican Council and what the new abbot general would have to say about the best-known monk in the Order.

✳

As Jim Forest had described him after his visit, Thomas Merton at forty-seven, and now forty-eight, was no longer the pale, ascetic monk of his ordination in 1949. If he was not fat, he weighed 185 pounds. Forest spoke, as John Howard Griffin was to do, of the similarity of his facial expressions to the photographs David Douglas Duncan had taken of Picasso, which had appeared in *Picasso's Picassos*. Jim Forest went on to talk of "a face similarly unfettered in its expressiveness, the eyes bright and quick and sure suggesting some strange balance between mischief and wisdom."[262]

"He reminded me," Forest says, "of a particularly good-natured truck driver — the kind of people who had sometimes given us rides on the way down." Henry Miller, studying the photographs Merton had sent, wrote back, "What's amazing to me is that it seems to combine my mug and Genet's. You too have the look of an ex-convict, of one who has been through the fires. I could show you photos of myself which bear a very close resemblance to yours."[263]

To Monsignor Raymond Treece of Bellarmine, Merton could stand out in any crowd or he could entirely submerge himself. It was a quality which would have helped him to be what he sometimes imagined himself to be, a perfect spy.

Raymond Treece confirms what so many others have said: "He was always fun to be with."[264] Yet this puzzled Merton himself. He found it strange to receive a note from one of the brothers thanking him for radiating a constant cheerfulness.[265] He had practiced a certain self-discipline at least since the year his father died when he was at Oakham. This came from the feeling that it wasn't decent to inflict your darker moods on others. The journals and some of Merton's published writing may have been a little darker, a little off the fine balance, just because of this.

For Rabbi L. H. Silberman, "From the first moment I laid eyes on him in that dark corridor of the guest house, I knew I was in the presence of someone who lived with an inner center of calm — of peace — not in any static, self-satisfied way, but in a dynamic, open, sharing way. There was always that quiet smile that hovered on his lips."[266]

"Merton spoke plainly but with contagious feeling," Jim Forest says. He had always enjoyed conversation, and he writes again and again in the journal of talking too much, as if the hours of silence had somehow to be made up for. Yet he had a way of cutting off a conversation when he felt the best was over, something he shared with two of his friends, Robert Lax and James Laughlin. He was quick to stop purposeless talk among his novices: jokes had to have a relevant point; wit, however spontaneous, was the fitting dress of serious thought. There was nothing ponderous or grave about him. Even his early severity had been matched with enthusiasm, a generosity in praise and in condemnation. He could borrow speech, as he had the day in New York when he and Gibney met the British sailors and Merton became a Cockney Merton. There were times now when he overdid the hippie, and he knew it.

He took well the gibes about his impressive and growing collection of allergy pills and the things off the general menu his special diet allowed him. For all the Rule of Silence, Gethsemani was a family as far as teasing went, and probably still is. Merton had been something of a hypochondriac at least as far back as 1936, the year of his scare on the Long Island Rail Road. Now he worried about his breathlessness, and noted his blood pressure each time he donated blood.[267] With all his many ailments, he had no history of heart troubles. Rather, his stomach was the enemy. If he enjoyed physical labor, he had all the diseases of the sedentary scholar, or, as Rabelais knew, the revenge of the bowels on the head for leading an unnatural life.

In September 1963 he developed new and painful troubles in his left arm and at the base of his neck. He was in St. Joseph's Infirmary for two weeks, where, after tests, the doctors told him the pain was caused by a fused cervical disc. With traction and massage, there was hope of avoiding an operation.

Each time he was in hospital Merton felt trapped in his room, where he could be visited by anyone who had a mind to see him.[268] His religious name was too well known for a disguise, though he sometimes used the Latin form that appeared on his wooden laundry tag at Gethsemani, hiding himself as Father Ludovicus.

Visits to hospital also brought a confrontation with newspapers, weekly news magazines, radio, and television, something for which he had had little preparation. After each return from hospital the accounts in the journal become warmer, as Merton rediscovers the good at the monastery.[269] Gethsemani continued to change, though this time the changes were not brought about by overcrowding. The "Dropout Phenomenon" was in full swing. To Merton some of the best were going (others found this view only another sign of his pessimism). Gerald (Groves) and Merton's old friend, the librarian, Father Sylvanus, had left to become hermits with Dom Jacques Winandy in Martinique.[270] The worst loss to Merton was Father John of the Cross, who went on extended leave at the end of 1962. Others disagreed when Merton put the blame for John of the Cross's departure on the abbot, but the journal entries about Dom James in 1962 are harsher than ever.

There were many changes in the liturgy, and some of Merton's favorite antiphons were no longer sung — except by Merton himself on the hillside in front of the hermitage,[271] where he also sang the Shaker songs Edward Deming Andrews and his wife had sent.[272] There were times, however, when Dr. Wygal advised him to give up singing, at least in choir,

> . . . if it churns my stomach up too much. I am afraid it does. That is, appearing in the sanctuary, standing at the altar, singing. I suppose I am morbidly afraid of making a mistake, and I know this is a lack of humility, but I get myself so worked up that I find myself making a complete botch of it, in an agony of tension — though most of the time I manage to be relaxed and to sing well.[273]

At the end of 1962, the choir and the brothers' novitiate had been merged and Father Louis found himself with new responsibilities. It was a small change except for those immediately affected, and Merton thought it a success, giving credit this time to Dom James for the innovation.[274] For the time being, the professed monks of the choir and the professed brothers remained separate.

The old division had produced a good deal of plain, if unspoken, snobbery over the centuries, yet it meant something in terms of two different kinds of vocation. Merton saw the inevitable end of the separation with some misgivings. Just as he thought there was a need for choir monks who were not priests, he felt that if the merging became total a brother might be forced to be what he had chosen not to be, a worker with his mind, rather than a worker with his hands, in a setting where all work was offered to God:

> I think the grace the brothers have comes from their *work,* which keeps them perhaps (when properly done) from getting too obsessed with themselves and with their spirituality. It is wonderful how they will go into anything and get it done, not standing around scratching their heads with the dubiousness of the choir, or wanting to be told each next move.[275]

Something in Merton continued to make it necessary for him to pair almost everything for comparisons: cities, countries, choir and brothers. He made comparisons between the ecumenical parties who came for conferences to Gethsemani, between Baptists and Episcopalians (for the moment very much in favor of the Baptists, though he swung back later). There were more links than he usually acknowledged between the author of *The Seven Storey Mountain* and the Merton of 1963, even in the division he made between what he wanted to be and what he believed himself to be. Yet in one of these moments of self-criticism, he took the journey back to see where he was now:

> I think I have come to see more clearly and more seriously the meaning, or lack of meaning, in my life. How much I am still the same self-willed and volatile person who made such a mess of Cambridge. That I have not changed yet, down in the depths — or perhaps, yes, I have changed radically somewhat, yet I have still kept some of the old, vain, inconstant, self-centered ways of looking at things. And that the situation I am in now has been given me to change me, if I will only surrender completely to reality as it is given me by God and no longer seek in any way to evade it, even by interior reservations.[276]

✳

In some ways the bomb that went off on a September Sunday in Birmingham, Alabama, showed a far deeper hurt and a deeper social sickness than the gunning down of the president in Dallas on November 22, 1963.

Merton's poem "And the Children of Birmingham," based on earlier accounts of black children facing policemen's dogs, the vilification of white mobs, and fire hoses, had just appeared in *The Saturday Review.*[277] Now he struggled to find words to address himself to a crime in which four black children were blown up in Sunday school by someone who planned their deaths deliberately, had a knowledge of demolitions, and may have been part of a wide conspiracy.[278] When two other blacks were killed in a protest at the bombing, Merton, then in St. Joseph's Infirmary, feared "that the racists in the Deep South are trying to *provoke* violence so as to let loose a general slaughter."[279] He wrote a second poem, "Picture of a Black Child with a White Doll,"[280] and carefully kept the photograph in his journal. This time the caption read, "Carol Denise McNair, 11, one of the four bomb-murdered Negro children, never learned to hate."[281]

The threat of nuclear war produced a sense of dread and a reasoned debate. The acts of violence in the racial struggle, the attempt by Martin Luther King and others to maintain a non-violent campaign, both Christian and Gandhian, in the face of brutal opposition and acts of provocation, produced in Merton more immediate fears and more visceral reaction. For him, as for so many others, King and his followers provided a miraculous opportunity which was in danger of being wasted.[282] Merton was perhaps too quick to decide it had been largely wasted. As he said later:

> My idea in Black Revolution was simply that *if* at a certain moment white and negro had responded to *Kairos* there *could have been* a mutually redemptive act and a kind of conversion of the country. Not any more. Anyway it was only a *possibility*. Not something essentially inherent in the Negro, a historic chance.[283]

Freed by edict from articles on war, Merton had turned back to reflection on what he had already done, to his poetry, and to contemplation, the *parrhesia* with God. Now that he had come into the public arena once more, he concentrated largely on racial issues. Here again, he was accused of being too pessimistic, while he accused himself of being too strident.

Merton's writings on racial questions are the hardest to evaluate. Where there are serious flaws, he also provided original and valuable insight. Intellectuals are prone to attack most bitterly, not those they disagree with most, but those they disagree with least. Merton was no exception. Yet, almost alone among white critics, he saw what a number of black leaders took to be the fatal flaw in white liberal support for integration. On June 12, 1963, he wrote to W. H. Ferry about a shift among blacks, away from King's Christian non-violence movement to the Black Muslims:

> It is understandable that they should now be taking the Muslim line more and more. After all, the Muslims have done more than anybody else to give them what a human being really needs: a chance to help himself and improve himself, an increase in self respect and the sense that his life has a meaning. What have the rest of us done in that way? The terrible thing about white liberalism has been its awful benevolence, the benevolence that assumes, without possibility of appeal, that the Negro is utterly in-

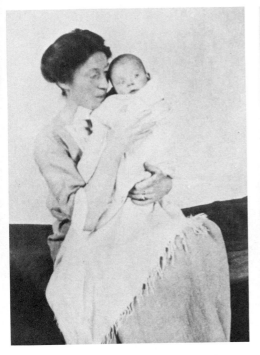

Ruth Jenkins Merton holding the son she insisted be called Tom, not Thomas

Owen Merton and his son in front of Mount Canigou, photographed by John Chrystal, a friend visiting Prades in 1915

Number 1, Rue du 4 Septembre, Prades, where Merton was born on January 31, 1915, has hardly changed. Owen's long walled garden, the vine-shaded balcony from which Tom looked at Canigou, and Owen's studio on the third floor look as they do in the photographs Ruth sent to New Zealand.

The Villa Diane today. Owen Merton built the block on the left, and the window of Tom's room looked out toward St. Antonin from the second floor.

Tom (at right) was photographed with his father, grandmother, and brother in the garden at Flushing during Gertrude Merton's visit in 1919. John Paul, the center of attention, was nine months old; Tom, four years.

AN UNFORTUNATE OAKHAMIAN PURSUED BY THE SHADE
OF A LATIN POET ROUSED FROM ELYSIAN FIELDS

As editor of *The Oakhamian*, Merton drew his first cartoons and
wrote parodies, articles, stories, and doggerel verse. This sketch
provides an accurate and recognizable view of the courtyard of
School House.

Clare College, Cambridge

One of Merton's covers for the Columbia *Jester*

Top: The Olean cottage, scene of the Merton-Lax-Rice summer of 1939 and the crowded summer of 1940.

Bottom: Commencement Day at St. Bonaventure, June 8, 1941. Left to right: Father Peter Biasiotto, O.F.M.; Lawrence Kenney; Thomas Merton; Dennis Lane; Father Gabriel Naughton, O.F.M.

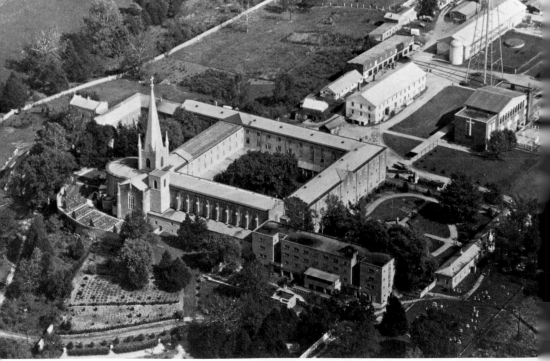

Merton's Columbia friends had supported him at his baptism. Many were at Gethsemani for his ordination, together with one of his teachers and two of his publishers—all of whom were lifelong friends. Left to right: Seymour Freedgood, Robert Giroux, James Laughlin, Dan Walsh, Robert Lax, and Ed Rice. On the morning of his ordination, Merton was proclaimed in the Chapter of Faults because his guests had blocked the cloister door while being photographed.

OPPOSITE PAGE

Top: The gate house of the Monastery of Our Lady of Gethsemani, which Merton entered in 1941

Bottom: An aerial view of the monastery in the 1950s

Thomas Merton (far right) is ordained Father M. Louis, O.C.S.O., May 26, 1949, the Feast of the Ascension. Merton was still struggling to explore the significance of this event, to see his ordination at deeper levels, setting aside incidentals, accidentals, and distractions. He knew already that, like baptism and conversion, ordination was no end but a starting off in a different direction.

After ordination, Merton holds a newspaper and jokes with his guests about how much he has missed since he left the world. Beside him are Nanny Hauck and Elsie Jenkins, and Robert Lax sits in the foreground.

The master of scholastics with a class. Merton wrote to James Laughlin, saying that teaching "simply knocks me out" but comparing his enjoyment to Laughlin's pleasure in spending time with his children.

OPPOSITE PAGE

Top: The conference at St. John's University, Collegeville, Minnesota, in July 1956. Merton (left) and Gregory Zilboorg (center) during a break from lectures and workshops

Bottom, left: The fire tower on the top of Vineyard Knob was a frustrated high place. Although Merton spent hours there meditating and watching the hawks, when the fire tower was offered as a hermitage he said he did not want to become another St. Simeon Stylites.

Bottom, right: The abbey church today

Our Lady of Carmel on Mount Olivet, Gethsemani, two views. "The one thing for which I am most grateful," Merton wrote in his journal on March 23, 1966, "is this hermitage."

Merton with Naomi Burton, his agent and friend, at Gethsemani, September 28, 1956, to straighten out the tangles in his
literary affairs

.ctor and Carolyn Hammer picnic with Merton out of the rain

The monastery's formal portrait of Thomas Merton, Father M. Louis, O.C.S.O.

OPPOSITE PAGE

Top: Brother Patrick Hart with Thomas Merton on the morning of September 9, 1968, the last full day at Gethsemani before Merton set off—by way of New Mexico, Alaska, and California—for Asia

Bottom, left: Merton delivers his address, "Marxism and Monastic Perspectives," on the morning of December 10, 1968.

Bottom, right: The Bangkok conference. Merton looks serious and tired as he stands beside Father Acharya at the reception of the Patriarch of the Buddhist monks. A few minutes later, he noticed something humorous and winked at one of his friends.

"Teach me to go to the country beyond words and beyond names." Merton's own view of the seventh mountain, Kanchenjunga

The Trappist cemetery, Gethsemani

capable of doing anything really significant for himself, and therefore that he is not fully human. I can see precisely why they are so mad: it is more honorable to be shot at like an animal than to be treated like an incurable infant.[284]

The phrase "incurable infant" is wonderfully telling. "Infant" and "infantilism" were words which were becoming more common, both in Merton's journal at this time, and in his writings about monastic renewal. In his indictment of white liberalism in the civil-rights movement Merton identified another kind of overprotectiveness — one without any basis in trust whatever, and one that was already proving disastrous.

Merton saw, too, with an insight he shared with King and few others, that the campaign for non-violent action, if successful, would free whites from fear as well as blacks from oppression. Above all, it would free both races from unreal bondage to an unreal situation. Moreover, he was acute (though not alone) in the judgment that the Roman Catholic Church had failed its black parishioners — that all Christian churches had practiced segregation, widely in the South, and only in a more sophisticated fashion in the North.

All this gives value to Merton's writings on racial justice. Yet there were weaknesses in his position. One, he could do little about. In the argument on the nuclear arms race he spoke from common ground. In the civil-rights argument, he did not. As a monk in an enclosed Order, he was vulnerable to the charge that he had less at stake than almost anyone in the affair. If the charge came chiefly from those who set their own stake far too high, it was nevertheless valid.

Reading John Howard Griffin's *Black Like Me*, Merton had commented: "What there is in the South is not a negro problem but a white problem. The trouble is pathological."[285] It was an old idea and had accounted for a good deal of humor that was "black" in both senses. Merton was by no means blind to the hypocrisy of many Northern whites, but if he lived in Kentucky, he was not a Southerner. To its honor, the monastery was and had been, an integrated community, though there were few black monks in 1963. Merton's old friend Brother Joshua, who had been lent earphones by Dom James so that he could listen to jazz at the monastery, had left, hoping, tragically as it turned out, that he could help other blacks "in the world."

In 1963 almost all the white Southerners he knew were already courageously committed to changing the South: they were hardly typical of the white population of twelve or fourteen states, racist or otherwise. There were times when he read Faulkner and Flannery O'Connor for the symptoms of a disease. He was certainly not alone in doing this, but it was not a helpful reading. As always, Merton worked to inform himself, yet he remained largely an outsider. If the problem of the South was not a Negro problem but a white problem, it was a problem to which Thomas Merton offered no real solution.

In unbalancing times, Merton sometimes lost his hold on language, common sense, and logic. Trying to give a largely sympathetic explanation for the black opponents of Martin Luther King in "From Non-Violence to Black Power," Merton coined a new word, "ethnocentric,"[286] forgetting that white supremacists might have been glad to claim the word, rather than "racist," if they had known what it meant.

Most important of all, Merton came too close, too early, to the belief that King's non-violence had failed.

❋

If 1963 brought Merton misunderstanding and outright criticism, it also brought recognition and awards. Such awards had to be accepted by others on his behalf. When awarded the Pax Medal he said he was "in the rather awkward position of receiving a prize for doing what is only the plain and obvious duty of a reasonable human being who also happens to be a Christian."[287]

On June 5, Victor Hammer received the honorary degree of Doctor of Letters for him from the University of Kentucky, and Merton wrote to James Laughlin that he planned to wear the orange and red academic hood a good deal in choir.[288] Before the ceremony he had joked that the degrees from Columbia had come to him through a window in the dean's office.[289] On the same June 5, he recorded a distinction which came to him more directly:

> Receiving an honor:
>
> A very small gold-winged moth came and settled on the back of my hand and sat there, so light I could not feel it. I wondered at the beauty and delicacy of this being — so perfectly made, with mottled golden wings. So perfect. I wonder if there is even a name for it. I never saw such a thing before. It would not go away, until, needing my hand, I blew it lightly into the woods.[290]

It was Dan Walsh who read the paper Merton had prepared when the Merton Collection at Bellarmine College Library was officially opened on November 10. "Whatever I may have written," Merton wrote, "I think it can all be reduced in the end to this one root truth: that God calls human persons to union with Himself and with one another in Christ, in the Church which is His Mystical Body."[291]

Merton had mixed feelings about the event, while the sense that he was being "made the object of a public cult" deepened when the collection was housed in a Merton Room at the library. Yet he continued to help others to find scattered parts of his work, both for the Bellarmine collection and for the bibliography Frank Dell'Isola was making. According to Dom Flavian Burns, Merton was careful to keep everything relating to his own life.[292] He now kept copies of his letters, while the proliferation of drafts of his articles had already begun. If there was an "archivist of himself" in Merton, there was also an anti-archivist.

By 1963–64 the public cult had already become an encumbrance, something that caused pain and embarrassment each time Thomas Merton realized he had made yet another contribution of his own. To Father Chrysogonus Waddell, away in Rome, he writes:

> If there is such a thing as "Mertonism" I suppose I am the one that ought to be aware of it. The people who believe in this term evidently do not know how unwilling I would be to have anyone repeat in his own life the miseries of mine. That would be flatly, a mortal sin against charity. I thought I had never done anything to obscure the lack of anything that a monk might conceive to be a desirable quality. Surely this lack is public knowledge, and anyone who imitates me does so at his own risk. I can promise him some fine moments of naked despair.[293]

There are touches of melodrama and hyperbole in the humor Merton used, either against taking himself too seriously, or to prevent others from doing so. Father Chrysogonus had met someone on his travels who sent Father Louis a postcard of St. Martin de Canigou. This becomes in Merton's next letter a whole network of informants:

> I can tell where you have travelled by mail that comes in from boyscouts, aged scholars, young ladies in Catholic Action, editors in quest of copy, etc., etc. And I know what will inevitably happen: you will leave in your wake a whole series of legends which will transform you into me: "Ah, le Père Merton était ici, et il jouait de l'orgue, chantait, dansait . . . etc." Remember, Father that if you dance before the ark it will go down in history as having been done by me. For when Brother Giles went to Marialaach, etc., etc., everyone was saying, oh yes, he is Father Merton. Well, I travel vicariously. Not to mention the man in Chicago recently who was going around all the convents collecting large and small sums of money on the grounds that he was I. Or the man who, in my name, was giving a rousing lecture tour of Chile and amassing various sums.[294]

Where the first part is play, Merton and Merton's friends had to cope with renewed rumors he had been seen outside the monastery and with a number of Merton impostors, or false Mertons. Merton's jocular way of dealing with such rumors only tended to feed them.

But there were times, too, when he attacked himself with the old bitterness for furthering all this attention to self:

> What a weary, silly mess. When will I learn to go without leaving footsteps? A long way from that: I still love recognition and need to preach, so that I will believe in my own message and believing that, will believe in myself — or at least consent to find myself acceptable for a little while.

Absurdity, and very dishonest on top of it. I wish I knew how to be otherwise!

Funny how I came to this, quite in spite of myself and in spite of everything, after several days of desperation (half-felt) and perplexity. Peace in seeing the hills, the blue sky, the afternoon sun. Just this and nothing more! As soon as I move toward anything else, confusion. Those asses and their active philosophy and their itch to go on any stupid bandwagon! Yet how I am influenced by them in spite of myself! They are so sure that is Christianity — that parading and gesticulating, that proclamation of ten thousand programs![295]

In March there had been talk of Merton receiving special permission to visit the White House.[296] Dan Walsh had been asked to give a series of lectures there and Robert Kennedy asked Walsh if there were any possibility Father Louis might do the same thing later on. Nothing came of it. On November 22, he learned of the president's assassination when he came back from working in the Gethsemani woods. His first reaction, like that of so many others, was one of disbelief.

As often happened, the distant act of violence in Dallas made Merton more acutely aware of signs of local violence. The woods were full of hunters, and near the monastery Merton found a cartridge box marked with the manufacturer's warning: "Caution — range one mile — be careful!"[297]

He was already raw and off balance from an encounter on November 19. The account in the journal is cryptic, yet it would be fairer to give the incident in his words, with no other comment than that the monk had obviously been lacking in common sense. A woman claimed at the gate house that she was a distant relative of Father Louis. Merton went to see her. Where he had so few living relatives, one wonders whom he expected to meet. The interview can hardly have taken place entirely at the gate house:

I cannot account for her on any score. A remarkable, beatnik, Charles Adams, hair in the eyes type who turned out, in the afternoon to be a nymphomaniac. She gave me a wild time — a real battle, at times physical, and finally when I got away alive and with most of my virtue intact (I hope) I felt shaken, sick and scared. And yet not altogether — there was a little feeling of complacency that a woman should still go to such lengths over me, even though a deranged one. Only later did I realize how futile and insufficient were my own attempts to do something for her. Words sounded so foolish and absurd. Her mode of communication was with her whole body and all her strength.[298]

Signs of disturbance recur in the journal accounts for several days. "I can understand some of the Desert Fathers stories a little better after that!" he writes in an effort to establish distance and a sense of proportion.

Nineteen sixty-four, the Year of the Dragon, came in with an attack of sleet on "all the quiet windows" at the monastery. The Year of the Hare "went out yesterday with our red fish kite twisting and flopping in the wind over the Zen garden."[299]

Owen's son had become a designer of gardens. He had picked out several huge, gnarled, and patterned rocks in the woods. When he went into hospital in September he asked the cellarer to use the heavy machinery to bring these to Gethsemani and hoist them over the walls and into place. When he returned he was delighted by the effect they created, but he had to face the teasing of the other monks that machines were all right to use as long as he was not directly involved in their use.[300]

On the first day of the New Year Merton studied an account in *U.S. News and World Report* about the early investigations into the Kennedy assassination, pausing at one sentence: "Oswald was a lone wolf whose background showed that he was inclined to nonviolence up to a point where his mind apparently snapped."

This was the kind of odd, circular logic and self-proving sentence he had come to dread in the media. He wrote in his journal, "He (Oswald) was a non-conformist — that in itself accounts for any crime."[301] Elsewhere, in his writing for publication, Merton returned again and again to the idea that the advocate of non-violence was, by his very advocacy, considered neurotic, certainly unnatural, and a likely candidate for any mad act when his mind "snapped."

It was a tactic he had noted back in May 1960, when the French newspapers had ridiculed the demonstration made by non-violent followers of Louis Massignon and Father Régamey against the Algerian War. After their arrest the demonstrators were taken to the tomb of an "agent" shot by the FLN. Here they were given a lecture by the chief of police on the unfairness of their stand, the "insanity" of their view. "Why so afraid of the 'non-violent'? Why so eager to reeducate them?" Merton wrote.[302]

He himself had been at such pains to avoid being dismissed as an "absolute pacifist" (and hence a person thought lacking in both reason and any sense of loyalty to society) that he had used terms which Quakers, Mennonites, and other pacifists found offensive — "oddball pacifism,"[303] "Witless pacifism no answer . . ."[304]

On April 16 Merton finished quickly and easily "Gandhi and the One-Eyed Giant," the introduction to *Gandhi on Non-Violence*.[305] Though the essay is too discursive, there are a number of sharply focused points. Merton went over, once more, what non-violence was *not*. It was obviously important for Merton that Gandhi brought to public life the fruits of an inner spiritual unity he had already achieved, and that "For him [Gandhi] the public realm was not secular, it was sacred."[306] He saw in Gandhi one who had learned of the East through the West, just as he himself had so often discovered his own Christian tradition through the East: Bramachari had brought him to St. Augustine, Suzuki to a deeper reading of Eckhart.

At the same time, Merton talks about "spurious attempts to bring East and West together" in "laughable syncretisms." The exchanges could only be of value where differences were honored. For Merton it was one thing, too, to recognize Christ in another, disastrous to expect to find oneself mirrored in everyone else.[307]

Reading Hannah Arendt's *The Human Condition* had disturbed Merton as greatly as reading Shirer's *The Rise and Fall of the Third Reich*.[308] It was Hannah Arendt's series of articles on Eichmann in *The New Yorker* in 1963, however, which brought the question of sanity in an insane time to a head. Merton's public response was a number of essays, including "A Devout Meditation in Memory of Adolf Eichmann," which begins with the words that haunted Merton in the Arendt articles:

> One of the most disturbing facts that came out in the Eichmann trial was that a psychiatrist examined him and pronounced him *perfectly sane*. I do not doubt it at all, and that is precisely why I find it disturbing.[309]

The "Devout Meditation" continued with a leitmotiv, repeated many times: "the sane ones" . . . "the sane ones . . ."

Reading the Arendt articles also brought further anguish to Merton's continuing "devout meditation" on the massacre of European Jewry and the almost total failure of Christians to prevent this.

Where the Psalms and the Bible had become so vivid to Merton, he wrote that much would be forever closed to those who did not become part Jewish at least by imaginative identification.[310] He went further: to Erich Fromm in Mexico he wrote, "I am a complete Jew as far as that goes."[311] He told Rabbi Zalman Schachter he had finished reading *The Last of the Just* by Schwartz Bach and that it had helped to "crystallize out a whole lot of things I am thinking about":

> Chief of these is of course no news to anyone: that the Jews have been the great eschatological sign of the twentieth century. That everything comes to depend on people understanding this fact, not just reacting to it with a little appropriate feeling, but seeing the whole thing as a sign from God, telling us. Telling us what? Among other things, telling Christians that if they don't look out they are going to miss the boat or fall out of it, because the antimony [sic] they have unconsciously and complacently supposed between the Jews and Christ is not even a good figment of the imagination. The suffering Servant is One: Christ, Israel. There is one wedding and one wedding feast, not two or five or six. There is one bride. There is one mystery, and the mystery of Israel and of the Church is ultimately to be revealed as One. As one great scandal maybe to a lot of people on both sides who have better things to do than come to the wedding.[312]

One of the most bitter events in 1964 was the failure of the Vatican Council's statement on the Jews. A friend by correspondence, Rabbi Abraham J. Heschel, visited Merton on July 13, and the two men sat up talking until ten-thirty — very late in Merton's monastic day. The supper had been memorable, though it had posed problems for the cook, Brother Edwin, to solve, having to cope with both the Cistercian rules of hospitality and the Law of Moses. Yet, as Merton reports, Rabbi Heschel did well on the meal, "enjoyed the wine and smoked a couple of enormously long cigars."[313] On the following day, and as a result of their talk, Merton wrote to Augustine Cardinal Bea, the Secretariat for Christian Unity, in Rome. It was Bea who was leading the resistance to revisions to the earlier draft statement (which had been open and liberal), though in vain. The statement when it was published was, in Merton's view, a disaster. His bitter denunciations were reserved for his journal, and for the reading notebook, where he wrestled with a review of Rolf Hochhuth's play, *The Deputy*.[314]

On September 9, in a more restrained style, he wrote to Heschel:

> Your mimeographed bulletin referring to the revised Jewish Chapter has just reached me.
>
> It is simply incredible. I don't know what to say about it.
>
> This much I will say: my latent ambitions to be a true Jew under my Catholic skin will surely be realized if I continue to go through experiences like this, being spiritually slapped in the face by these blind and complacent people to whom I am nevertheless a "collaborator." If I were not "working with" the Catholic movement for ecumenical understanding it would not be such a shock to take three steps backwards after each timid step forward.
>
> I must however think more of people like Cardinal Bea who must certainly be crushed by this development.
>
> The Psalms have said all that need be said about this sort of thing, and you and I both pray them. In them we are one, in their truth, in their silence. *Haec fecisti et tacui*, says the Lord of such events.[315]

Abraham Heschel wrote back that he felt like crying.[316]

Where Merton wrote he had "travelled vicariously" in his letter to Father Chrysogonus, the question of travel had become more acute by early 1964. The rules of stability had been relaxed for others, not for Father Louis. At the same time, the number of invitations asking him to take part in seminars and conferences had increased greatly. The struggle with the abbot was embittered by Merton's feeling that, if he was never allowed out of the monastery, he was expected to organize the program at Gethsemani for almost every group who came there. He had already learned he would be in charge of the meeting of Cistercian abbots and novice masters in October 1964, a matter that filled him with dismay and some feelings of rebellion.[317]

At the same time, he was divided himself over the invitations. In early June 1964, he questioned in his journal whether travel would not become a severe temptation in time simply because of the abbot's resistance,[318] and elsewhere he quoted with delight Suzuki's answer to a committee which had invited him to a scientific conference, New Knowledge in Human Values: "If anything new can come out of human values it is from the cup of tea taken by two monks."[319]

Ironically, then, it was an invitation from Suzuki that Merton announced in his journal immediately after deciding that all invitations were a distraction.[320] Mihoko Okamura, Suzuki's secretary, wrote that the Zen philosopher would be in New York for the month of June, but that there was no chance he would be able to come to Gethsemani, anxious as he was to meet Merton. Could Merton come to meet him?

Merton felt it was important enough to ask Dom James, though he had little confidence the abbot would agree. Yet when he pointed out that because of Suzuki's age this was probably the last chance he would have of seeing him and talking to him, the abbot gave a reluctant permission. Merton had to promise he would not get in touch with other friends in New York, and Dom James gave him only sufficient money to cover necessary expenses,[321] but the airline ticket was booked.

On Monday, June 15, Merton had his first view of New York in twenty-three years. Through the rain another geography appeared, one that united much of his past, good and bad, and that prophesied lines in *The Geography of Lograire:*

> The first thing about New York was that I was delighted to see it again, recognized Sandy Hook immediately from the air and the new bridge over The Narrows. So much recognition everywhere, right down to the two big gas tanks in Elmhurst, landmarks of all the family funerals from mother to Aunt Elizabeth to Pop's to Bonnemaman's![322]

He traveled uptown to Columbia, where he stayed the first two nights at Butler Hall. Leaving his things in the room, he went out on the first day to explore in the rain, walking a near-deserted Amsterdam Avenue and then the more crowded Broadway, savoring the first "David Copperfield trip" he had been able to make since his voyage to Bermuda in 1939.

With the actual setting so familiar, changes were more dramatic. Above all, he had a sense of returning virtually incognito. He was alone in a city where he had once been known as another man, coming back more secretly to New York than, in his novel, his dream-double had returned to London. For the first time since he had become a monk, walking in the crowds, sleeping in his room at Butler Hall, he lived moment by moment in a situation that was unconnected to the supporting structure he had chosen for his vocation and protection.

He had left a city tense with the war in Europe. In the summer of

1964 the tensions in the atmosphere were far more immediate. Even at the monastery before coming he had wondered if staying at Columbia on Morningside Heights above Harlem would bring the risk of finding himself involved in riots.[323] That first evening he sat in the New Asia Restaurant hot and wet, eating pork and fried rice (the Rule was relaxed for traveling monks), comforted by the sound of foreign languages about him: French, German, Polish, Puerto Rican Spanish, Japanese.[324] If he mentions no blacks only a few blocks from Harlem, the student body of the university had certainly changed since he had been a student.

In his room he meditated, sitting on the floor in the position he had first taken up long ago in the apartment at Perry Street, this time looking out toward the Sound and over the rooftops of Harlem, watching the red lights go on and off on top of the stacks of what he thought must be the atomic reactor in Long Island City.[325] He said Mass, unassisted and unknown, early on two mornings at Corpus Christi, awed by his return to the church where he had been baptized.[326]

There were two long talks with Suzuki. Merton found Mihoko Okamura charming, and she made green tea for the two monks, who sat together on the sofa. Merton drank from the dark brown earthenware bowl in three and a half sips, as he knew it was done.

He was pleased to find Suzuki thought his essay in *Continuum* "one of the best things on Zen to have been written in the West." His feelings were mixed when he learned his *Ascent to Truth* was popular among Zen scholars and monks: "That is somewhat consoling, though it is my wordiest and in some ways emptiest book."[327]

Merton had to talk loudly and distinctly, for the Zen philosopher was ninety-four, frail, and deaf, yet he found Suzuki "lively and very responsive." Both Suzuki and Ms. Okamura were obviously delighted he had been able to come. As the Zen master from the East and the monk from the West said goodbye, Suzuki tried to sum up the spirit of their discussions. "The most important thing is Love," he said.[328]

On Wednesday, June 17, Merton moved downtown to the Tuscany Hotel near the East Side Airlines Terminal so that it would be easy to catch the bus to the airport early on Thursday morning. The sun had come out after days of rain, and he took a cab to the Guggenheim Museum, where he found the paintings by Van Gogh "wheels of fire, cosmic, rich, fullbodied, honest, the victories over depression, permanent victory. Especially the last light and shadow calligraphic impastos."

Some things had not changed: as they drove through Central Park the cab driver talked of his nerves, his analysis, and his divorce. The world was still the world and New York, New York. The Metropolitan Museum of Art disappointed him, as he had been almost expecting it would: "In and out. An old world. An old station." He was happier on Fifth Avenue, the movement of a city that was "Anything but soulless."[329] His mind was still on the calligraphies of Van Gogh, though it dismayed him that many of the Paul Klees he remembered and had been looking forward to seeing were not on exhibition.

Merton had opened to the visual arts in a new way that year. He had what he called a "love affair" with a borrowed camera.[330] Now he was doing his own calligraphic drawings with black ink on white paper, encouraged by the artist and calligrapher Ulfert Wilke.[331]

There were many sources for work that was becoming more confident, original, and engrossing. Klee had inspired Merton for thirty or more years.[332] His study of pictogrammic characters in Chinese with John Wu and Paul Sih brought another dimension. So did Merton's friendship with Ad Reinhardt: Reinhardt's letters, with their drawings — part calligraphy, part hieroglyph — delighted him.[333] Above all other influences came Zen, now a freeing discipline in all things. Merton worked in black and white — as he took only black and white photographs. The "light and shadow calligraphic impastos" of Van Gogh might move him, but they did not tempt him in his own work any more than the memory of paintings by his father, who had once been "color" to him. In the summer of 1964 there was talk of an exhibition of Merton's calligraphies. His excitement was only a little spoiled by the anxiety of wondering what Victor Hammer would think, the fear that Hammer would see this as pretention and an example of self-expression, not serious craftsmanship.[334] Merton had deeper worries than these for his old friend. That summer there was a growing danger Hammer would lose his eyesight, that he would never be able to finish the triptych on which he had been working for so long.

Good news reached Merton soon after his return to the monastery after his three days in New York. The suppression of his writings on war had continued under the new abbot general, Dom Ignace Gillet.[335] This had been modified somewhat unclearly by the decision that he could write about peace, not war — he was not to show pessimism. On July 14, the abbot's secretary told Father Louis a letter had come from the definitor of the Order, Dom Laurence Bourget, passing "Peace in the Post-Christian Era" for publication in *Seeds of Destruction*. If this essay spoke of peace, it also spoke of war, and Merton was exultant, feeling "the real heart of the 'forbidden book' " had been released:

> Now this would never have happened if Dom Gabriel had not been so stringent with the other three articles, which would have been used in *Seeds of Destruction* if he had not forbidden their reprinting. Thus in effect the very thing he wanted to prevent most has happened *because* of his own authoritarianism! This is something to remember when we think of religious obedience. The Church is *not* entirely run by officials! None of this was arrived at, in the end, by my initiative![336]

Seeds of Destruction appeared on November 16, 1964.[337] The book also contained a selection from the "Cold War Letters" of 1961–62, two versions of which had been circulating in mimeograph for two years.

The official stand against Merton's pessimism still continued to rankle, however. He wrote to Ferry:

> About the piece on Pacem in Terris: as it is short, I think I ought to be able to do it, except that I have made nine hundred resolutions not to take on any more articles or prefaces for a while. But if this project gets rolling and I am in the clear, certainly it should not be too much trouble and it seems that I am now allowed to write about *peace* provided I don't write too much about *war*. This seems to mean that [I] can radiate sweetness and light but not condemn the bomb. How much sweetness and light can you stand?[338]

There was little sweetness or light in the news Merton was receiving. Jim Forest wrote to describe the riots that had broken out in Harlem only weeks after Merton had been staying in New York, a few streets away.[339] In August he learned of the murder of the three civil-rights workers in Mississippi.[340]

The heat now made work almost impossible. Merton read Camus's novel *La Peste (The Plague)* and found it "magnificent." He struggled to catch up with his correspondence and to finish commissions he could not set aside. There were other tribulations than the heat. W. H. Ferry wrote from Switzerland to say the Kentucky chiggers he had picked up when he visited Merton in June were continuing to mortify his flesh.

On July 14, he was working during a thunderstorm to finish an introduction for the latest book on Shaker furniture by Edward Deming Andrews, when he was dismayed by the news the author had died. The book was ultimately published in 1966 with the same evocative title Mark Van Doren had given his review of an earlier book by Andrews, *Religion in Wood*.[341] Merton's introduction connects the vision of the Shaker foundress, Mother Ann Lee, with that of her contemporary William Blake. Merton's own views of the "American Eden" and the true state of America in the nineteenth century provide point and counterpoint in the essay, just as they had done long ago in his poem "Aubade: Lake Erie." For the Shakers themselves Merton has little but praise:

> . . . They had the gift to express much that is best in the American spirit. They exemplified the simplicity, the practicality, the earnestness, and the hope that have been associated with the United States. They exemplified these qualities in a mode of humanity and dedication which one seeks in vain today in the hubris and exasperation of our country with its enormous power! . . .[342]

In the introduction to *Religion in Wood* the distance between vision and reality in nineteenth-century America is not impossible to bridge. In a letter to Mary Childs Black, Merton wrote more darkly:

> For the Shakers, it was a different consciousness, for at the same time
> they saw the deceptiveness of the secular hope, and their eyes were open,
> in childlike innocence, to the evil, the violence, the unscrupulousness that
> too often underlay the secular vision of the earthly paradise. It was a
> paradise in which the Indian had been slaughtered, and the negro was
> enslaved. In which the immigrant was treated as an inferior being, and
> in which he had to work very hard for the "gold" that was to be "picked
> up in the streets."[343]

Whatever that Shaker view of paradise had been, of the new and old
Adam, old paradise and new, creation and new creation, Merton told
Bruno Schlesinger, "At the present time man has ceased entirely to be
seen as any of these. The whole Christian notion of man has been
turned inside out, instead of paradise we had Auschwitz . . ."[344]

The deepest vein of Merton's pessimism continued to show itself
without cover or check in his letters.

News of another commission Merton had completed that year was
distressing — in large part because he had been told to revise earlier
drafts of the script he wrote for the film *The Church Is Christ Living in
the World Today,* to be shown in the Vatican Pavilion at the World's Fair.
In his journal he sets down his own thoughts and quotes from Monsignor McCormack, who spoke for Cardinal Spellman. Having first written about charity, peace, and social justice, Merton was asked to replace this "by an apologetic text-book piece on the Church as the one
true Church, 'what we have that is different from the Protestants and
the Orthodox' to dispel any confusion that may have been created 'by
all this ecumenical business.' "[345]

Cardinal Spellman wrote to thank Father Louis for the final script and
to tell him that a million people had already seen the film and heard
his message. Merton's reply betrays his discomfort in a manner that
borders on servility:

> Your Eminence:
>   For my part, it was a pleasure and an honor to contribute in some small
> way to this work so important for the Church. I deeply appreciate the
> opportunity to do so, and the kindness of your Eminence.
>   As a token of profound and humble esteem I am sending your Emi-
> nence a booklet in which I had a hand, a translation of a twelfth century
> letter on the contemplative life. It has been beautifully printed by the
> Benedictine Nuns of Stanbrook, and I hope your Eminence will like it.
>   Begging your Eminence's blessing, I sign myself,
>   Your most humble servant in Christ . . .[346]

In early October the abbots and novice masters of the Order arrived
for the conference Merton had been dreading. He records that the
meetings started at seven A.M. and continued throughout the day.[347]
He was talking too much, drinking black coffee, and missing offices.
What he had taken for poison ivy in the past month now covered his

hands. It proved to be a skin disease, caused in large part by anxiety and just the kind of nervous exhaustion the conference brought him. The condition made life difficult for him for over a year.

If the abbatial conference brought anxiety, it also brought about a wholly unexpected result. It may be that Merton's obvious relief at being able to return to hours of solitude at the hermitage worked for him; at any rate, there was now no need to practice what he had called "the politics of permission." Dom James agreed to approach the Chapter with the request for Father Louis's full-time seclusion as a hermit.[348]

Merton's joy was tempered by the knowledge that permission to become a hermit would bring restrictions on the number of his visitors and further pressure to write about spiritual subjects, not about social issues. He would certainly not be allowed to travel. He had been refused permission to attend a Zen conference in Japan.[349] If this was not unexpected, he was reminded once again, this time by the abbot general, that the request, coinciding with an interest in the solitary life, was a manifestation of a "dual personality."[350] Meanwhile, Merton noted with some glee that his own abbot was off to Norway for the blessing of a bishop friend.

The meeting of abbots and novice masters at Gethsemani in October 1964 made two further, contrasting points clear. Most of the superiors in the Order were averse to the public stand Father Louis had taken in his writings on nuclear war and social justice. Many felt these had divided Catholics. Where the criticism was spoken, it indicated that, at best, the commitment was "inappropriate." The notoriety had been an embarrassment to the Order.

At the same time, Father Louis had established himself as an authority on monastic renewal. Even where there was deep disagreement over some of his ideas, there was wide acceptance of others and a general desire to know his opinions. Just as Merton's mimeographed copies of *Hagia Sophia*, the "Cold War Letters," "Peace in the Post-Christian Era," and many of his other works had had a wide circulation among his non-monastic friends and correspondents, Merton's writings on monastic subjects had been passed in copies from monastery to monastery even when they had not been published in monastic journals. His conference tapes, too, had been borrowed, transcribed, and sent out to meet a growing demand, both in the Cistercian Order of the Strict Observance and in other orders, and not only in American foundations, but abroad, and especially in England. And just as the Goss-Mayrs in Switzerland had asked for Merton's writings on war so that these could be circulated, so Archbishop Paul Philippe had asked for material on Father Louis's monastic views so these could be circulated in the orders in Europe, made known to the Pope, and brought to the attention of those discussing the monastic life at the Second Vatican Council.[351]

There were, then, two separate networks of correspondence with

Thomas Merton at their center. In his own Order he was by now a controversial figure, but one who could in no way be ignored. Beyond this, his experience as a novice master for over a decade was valuable. One of the main issues at the conference in 1964 was the realization that the new generation of applicants, postulants, novices was so different it necessitated new thinking on the part of abbots and novice masters. In many cases this was crucial if a monastery was to survive. Numbers were shrinking, and in some monasteries there were deep divisions between the younger and the older monks. Merton saw this crisis in terms of his old concern with structure. Where the monk could grow spiritually in the fulfillment of his vocation the structure had proved itself both sound and vital. In monasteries where such growth was stifled, the monk was encouraged to fall back on dependence and spiritual infancy.

Once more obedience was the key question. Merton revitalized the traditional view that mere outward obedience was not true obedience. To accept the will of another, suppressing rebellion (at least on the surface) was no more than a lie, a form of deception carried out between one person and another. True obedience was the free changing of will.

When Merton wrote to Victor Hammer in 1962 to explain the term "brainwashing,"[352] he described it as a way in which the will was changed by force. By 1964 the term had become a cliché, the reality behind the term recognized by almost everyone. On the other hand, there was a radical and independent danger of seeing freedom only in terms of denial, of rebellion, of refusal to obey in any circumstances.

The negative aspects are comparatively easy to define. Freedom free of obsessions to be free comes closer to a Zen *koan*.[353] In the face of a serious misunderstanding in the West Merton pointed out again and again that Zen freedom was the end result of strict, even authoritarian, training.[354] Outside the finer points of philosophical debate there was the exercise of choice. Here both common sense and an informed conscience were essential. Neither solved all the problems. Haunting Merton now was the figure of the obedient, loyal, and sane Adolf Eichmann.

As a novice master Father Louis expected to be obeyed without delay or debate where no question of conscience or spiritual direction arose. In his conferences he could be amusing about blind obedience. In exasperation, one of the under-cellarers had told a monk to "Go climb the water tower!" The monk had to be coaxed down from a great height. This reminded Merton of St. Teresa telling one of her nuns to jump in a lake. There is a pause on the conference tape: "Splash!"[355]

"Very rarely practiced, blind obedience, around here," Merton says on the same tape, and there is a general chuckle of appreciation. But the instructor had forgotten about the sanctification of Brother Hugh in

The Seven Storey Mountain, "this peculiar combination — a contemplative spirit and a complete submission to superiors who entrusted him with many distracting responsibilities around the monastery — sanctified Brother Hugh according to what is, as near as I can make out, the Cistercian formula."[356] Much had changed, and, from the conferences, the Cistercian formula had become more difficult. Merton struggled to define obedience and freedom, and to differentiate between a morality of duty and a morality of love.

In matters of conscience, inside the monastery and out, Merton was scrupulous in practicing what he preached. Many of his letters give advice; there is none in which he usurps the right of his correspondent to make a decision. Even in matters where he was deeply concerned he struggled against any forcing of choice. Where he believed he had come close to such forcing, he checked himself, realizing that a sort of dependence will be established. "He was a good self-corrector," to repeat the words of Dom John Eudes Bamberger. Undoubtedly he put too much faith in the self-correcting capacity of others, yet he admitted mistakes of his own and encouraged others to admit theirs. After that, "We have to keep moving."[357]

The meeting of abbots and novice masters in 1964 was the high point of Merton's influence within his own Order, or rather of his personal influence, since his ideas continued to be more acceptable when presented by others. In November 1964 there was another meeting and there were many visitors.

Some visitors were welcome. Marco Pallis, musician, author, scholar of Buddhism arrived, on tour with the English Consort of Viols, and the two men were able to build on a friendship already warm in their letters and to talk "of Zen, and of Shin, and of Tibetan Buddhism."[358] Merton had been looking forward, too, to the visit of Brother Antoninus, his fellow poet in the religious life (and on the list of New Directions), keeping in touch with what the Dominican monk was doing and publishing through James Laughlin. As William Everson, Antoninus had spent a period at Waldport Camp for conscientious objectors during the Second World War. Part of Merton's interest lay in the sense of paths almost taken, part in Brother Antoninus's personality. After hearing him read to the monks, Merton felt he was a far more effective reader of his own poetry.[359] All this was stimulating. It is hardly an accident, however, that many of Merton's warmest pages about solitude at Our Lady of Mount Carmel Hermitage were written at this time, including Merton's festival of the rain in the essay "Rain and the Rhinoceros":

> The rain I am in is not like the rain of cities. It fills the woods with an immense and confused sound. It covers the flat roof of the cabin and its porch with insistent and controlled rhythms. And I listen, because it re-

minds me again and again that the whole world runs by rhythms I have not yet learned to recognize, rhythms that are not those of the engineer.[360]

He celebrated the rain's "gratuity and its meaninglessness," afraid the time would come when someone would try to sell it (he did not prophesy acid rain). "Useful" and "useless" were words he had begun to meditate upon when he worked in correspondence with John Wu on the translation of the writings of Chuang Tzu. Yet he celebrated the usefulness of the Coleman lamp, fearing what would happen when electricity came to the hermitage. (When it did the next spring he admitted the change was almost entirely for the better.)

He did *not* celebrate the intrusions of a distant war:

> Of course at three-thirty A.M. the SAC plane goes over, red light winking low under the clouds, skimming the wooded summits on the south side of the valley, loaded with strong medicine. Very strong. Strong enough to burn up all these woods and stretch our hours of fun into eternities.[361]

At times the rhinoceros of Ionesco's play would rush into the desert of the solitary. Even the hermit was not wholly immune to the disease of "Rhinoceritis," the "sickness that lies in wait 'for those who *have lost the sense and taste for solitude.' "*[362]

Merton explains elsewhere that this was also the disease of those who had lost their taste for the useless. In the background of the essay the guns pound away at Fort Knox. In the foreground, the quails "begin their sweet whistling in the wet bushes. Their noise is absolutely useless, and so is the delight I take in it . . ."[363]

✳

On November 17, at Merton's invitation, another group arrived at Gethsemani for a meeting on violence and non-violence. The retreat was organized by the Fellowship of Reconciliation (FOR), with the title "Spiritual Roots of Protest." At Merton's insistence, however, there was to be no rigid agenda. "What we are seeking is not the formulation of a program, but a deepening of roots," he said in the opening address. He raised a number of questions and said he would talk on the Wednesday afternoon on "The Monastic Protest: The Voice in the Wilderness."[364]

Among those who came were A. J. Muste, Jim Forest, J. H. Yoder, Daniel and Philip Berrigan, John Oliver Nelson (then the editor of *The Catholic Worker*), Tom Cornell, W. H. Ferry, and Tony Walsh. It rained heavily and most of the sessions were held in the gate house, though the whole group met in the hermitage on Thursday afternoon, when John Yoder spoke about protest and pacifism from the Mennonite point of view. Merton had agreed on certain ground rules for the meeting of the religiously mixed group with the abbot, only to discover there was already an agreement between the Berrigans and the others.[365] Not only was communion given in both species at the first Mass in the novitiate chapel, but there was communion to Protestants, something Merton records with an exclamation point in his journal. Dan Berrigan's "uncanonical" Mass, entirely in English, left Merton between the feeling it was "way out" and the sense it was "simple and impressive."[366]

The meeting was helpful in providing Merton with information and new friends. He was drawn to Muste's "wisdom, modesty, gentleness," and to the sincerity of Elbert Jean, who had been a Methodist minister in Birmingham, Alabama, before he was fired for advocating integration. Merton's own comments at the retreat were often quotations from Franz Jägerstätter, the Austrian peasant who had been beheaded by the Nazis as an "enemy of the state for refusing to serve in the German Army in 1943." Merton had just finished reading Gordon Zahn's *In Solitary Witness,* and he thought highly of it as a study of instinctive, obstinate, un-intellectualized resistance to evil. The book quoted from Jägerstätter's own writings and from an interview between Zahn and the bishop who had advised Jägerstätter to join the German Army and "do his duty like all the rest."[367] Just before the FOR meeting, Brother Simon (Patrick Hart) arrived from the abbot's office with a package containing twelve early copies of Merton's own book, *Seeds of Destruction,* one for each of the retreatants.[368]

The plan to sell his calligraphic drawings and to use the proceeds to establish a scholarship for a black woman student at Catherine Spalding College in Louisville seemed to be off to an auspicious start when an exhibition opened at the college on November 15 and received friendly notices in the *Louisville Courier-Journal.* There was a good deal of interest, but few sales at $150 a drawing.[369] The calligraphies went on tour, to be shown at a number of institutions in 1965, and Merton wrote a short essay explaining them. "Signatures: Notes on the Author's Drawings" is helpful chiefly in saying what the signs, signatures, or calligraphies are *not,* or are not intended to be.[370] Although the price came down, there were still few sales, certainly not enough to provide for the scholarship fund in memory of James Chaney which Merton wanted to set up. At this point Dom James stepped in:

> By the way the scholarship worked out beautifully, almost miraculously in a way. Father Abbot said the community would back it. Day after that in came a surprise gift of stock, just about the amount of capital needed for the fund. Right after that a little girl in Mississippi applied to Catherine Spalding College: first one ever applied from that state. We have our scholarship and our scholar.[371]

Throughout the summer of 1964 Merton had been anxious about Victor Hammer. The visits he looked forward to had been cancelled while Hammer remained in hospital, "afraid for his eyes," yet the correspondence continued. In his letters Merton referred somewhat uneasily to the calligraphies as "strange blobs of ink." In August he wrote on another matter, perhaps to take the artist's mind off the operation and because the Hammers had expressed an interest in a victim of racial injustice both John Howard Griffin and Thomas Merton had been trying to help:

> Actually the book that I sent Clyde Kennard was a copy of your Hagia Sophia, and I know he was very glad to have it. He was then dying in a hospital in Chicago, of cancer. He had been "framed" by the Mississippi police for trying to register at Miss. State University, and he had been put on a chain gang and very badly treated though he already had cancer. The story as I heard it was simply that he was very pleased with the book and it had given him some joy in his last days. It seems the story is becoming a bit amplified now. But still, it is good that we are both able to think we have helped such a person and brought something meaningful into a tragic life, which however was full of meaning because of his dedication.[372]

Merton heard nothing from either Victor or Carolyn Hammer during September. Then, in October, came news the operation had been successful, that his friend was recovering and he had written a prayer in thanks to God for the restoration of his sight, which was to be placed on the back of his picture of the Resurrection. Merton responded on November 3, enclosing a poem, "A Prayer of Thanksgiving Written for Victor Hammer":

> O Tu Pater splendoris Dator luminis
> Ad Te gaudens precor restituto lumine
> Da quaeso mihi servulo tecum perpetuam
> Nox ubi non contristet corda vel umbra diem.[373]

There were changes in Merton's life at the hermitage that meant much to him. A bed had now been brought up and put in the smaller of the two rooms, and Merton was able to spend the night there more and more often. On December 16 he celebrated his first full day, setting his own schedule, going to the monastery only to say Mass and to eat one full meal. Yet it was difficult for him to do the necessary chores in the cold with hands that were cracked with dermatitis. He had never been much of a cook, and there were a number of small disasters, even in toasting bread. If he made soup or coffee he had to wash the cups and saucepans in a pail of cold rainwater, while all water for drinking had to be brought up in a gallon jug from the monastery. The water from the nearby stream had been found contaminated and had made him sick. He now wore glasses for all close work and found the lamplight tired his eyes quickly, even if it reminded him of working by lamplight in the house at St. Antonin.[374] Trips to the outhouse in the spinney required a certain heroism, especially before dawn, when temperatures in central Kentucky could be brutal: "The outdoor jakes is a grievous shock."[375]

Conditions in the hermitage were probably more rigorous that winter than those in the early years at the monastery. He was older, less resilient, with a number of health problems. For all his tendency to exaggerate, he made light of what must have been harsh and painful. His hours at the hermitage, even the rawest of them, were too precious for complaint. Where he thought the monastery too rich, the hermitage was poor, and because it was poor it was his. On Mount Olivet he sang for himself[376] as he had on Brooke Hill, and he cursed small misfortunes and falls.

As a young monk he had been priggish in his correspondence to James Laughlin and to Naomi Burton about some of the writers published by New Directions. Nothing of this was left. When he criticized the obscenities in the liberated magazines of the 1960s, both underground and literary, in a letter to Lawrence Ferlinghetti, he avoided giving the impression he was simply squeamish:

> Not that I am mad at dirty words, they are perfectly good honest words as far as I am concerned, and they form part of my own interior mumblings a lot of the time, why not? I just wonder if this isn't another kind of jargon which is a bit more respectable than the jargon of the slick magazines, but not very much more. And I wonder just how much is actually *said* by it.[377]

In addition to informing Merton of events in the racial situation in the South, John Howard Griffin supplied film for the early borrowed cameras, as well as tips when the two photographed together during Griffin's visits. Later, Gregory Griffin helped to develop Merton's film. In this way Merton was able to exercise some control on the prints and was spared having to justify the costs of commercial developing to the abbey.

In the winter of 1964–65 Merton made expeditions into the woods around the hermitage to take pictures of the stark but intricate crisscrossing patterns of the branches and twigs against the sky on a dull day. On another dull day he wondered if he hadn't wasted far too much film on a jagged stump tilted on its side, which he photographed from every angle, fascinated with the thornlike forms that seemed to jut out with arrested violence from the central core.[378] One such "thorn" pattern appears on the cover of the book of essays he was putting together at the hermitage, *Raids on the Unspeakable*. It provides a subtle link between seen image and literary subject, and it forms another, different connection with the calligraphic drawings reproduced inside the book itself. With everything else, by the end of 1964 Owen Merton's son had become a visual artist.

There were signs Merton would be allowed to live permanently at Our Lady of Carmel, and to end his days there — after how many years? He would be fifty in a month's time. Brother Joachim Motl wired the hermitage for electricity. Dom James was now the advocate, not the opponent, of hermits. The abbot consulted Father Louis about his plans for an area of eight hundred acres of wilderness called Edelen Farm.[379] With its dense woods, high knobs, and ravines, the property would be no profitable addition to Gethsemani as farmland. Dom James announced he was interested in Edelen's as a site for hermitages. Caught up by his abbot's enthusiasm, Merton exhausted himself on January 5 exploring the new property.[380] By the end of the month Dom James was hinting that Father Louis would be able to become a full-time hermit as soon as Father Callistus returned from Rome in the summer.

Merton had picked up hints of a different kind and on a different subject in correspondence from Rome. There were rumors the drafting of Schema Thirteen at the Vatican Council that year would involve debates that might undo much that had already been done by John XXIII in making clear the Church's stand on nuclear war. With the revised Jewish statement in mind, Merton was anxious to do what he could to prevent this. He was provided with some opportunity to make his feelings known at the annual retreat at Gethsemani.

The British Dominican, Father Illtud Evans, whom Merton already knew, came to preach this on January 18. During the retreat, Mother Luke Tobin took the opportunity of meeting with both Father Illtud and Father Louis. Mother Luke was the superior of the Convent of the Sisters of Loretto at the Foot of the Cross, in Nerinx, Kentucky. The convent was no distance from Gethsemani, and Father Louis had already made a number of visits there in the past two years.[381] Rare though these had been, the atmosphere at the convent delighted him, and he had come to find in Mother Luke a kindred spirit. She had been appointed as an observer at the Vatican Council, thus given a position on the subcommittee that was to work on Schema Thirteen — the first time a woman had been appointed to such a position. Writing to congratulate her, Merton says he is not surprised she has been chosen "as observer from the better half of the human race, hitherto represented exclusively at the Council by the Blessed Mother I suppose."[382]

The annual retreat was a particularly important one for Merton, and he found himself worn out and emptied by the time it ended on January 26. At the same time he had had hours of discussion about Schema Thirteen with Mother Luke and Father Illtud, going over points on which the three of them were in complete agreement.

He approached his fiftieth birthday and his annual *agonia,* or spiritual review, still physically tired from the retreat. On the evening of January 30, he went over his past in his journal, having just written he would "simply die to the past." He determined to have less to do with projects, a resolution that his fiftieth birthday would mark another beginning with a renunciation of all ambition and self-seeking in his work and contacts ("I am so tied up in all this that I don't know where to start getting free").[383]

This was familiar, yet there was a difference from earlier trials of himself on the eve of a birthday. In January 1965, there was a new certainty that he was obeying God and that his vocation was centered at last. Thus he went to do battle against his shortcomings from firm ground. It was his ingratitude which troubled him most, the sense that he had responded to great gifts without proper praise. From this he went on to say there were things he had not faced even now. Here he was specific about his failure to come to terms with sex in his past (". . . I did not use it maturely and well . . ."), giving details already quoted in another context.[384]

There were two questions here in 1965, the question of trust and that of chastity. In his published writing at least, the second of these had been resolved in his conception of chastity as the most "radical" part of the monastic vow of poverty. The question of trust went deeper. He was still haunted both by the inability to love for fear of rejection in the distant past, and what he called his *"refusal* of women." The phrase is close to the title of a book he read six months later, and about which he wrote enthusiastically to Mother Luke Tobin and others: Karl Stern's *The Flight from Woman.*[385]

It was this "refusal," rather than remorse or guilt for individual acts in the past, that continued to trouble him. Chastity was one thing, lack of love was quite another. There were occasions when love was tested in chastity and confirmed by it. Many men, Gandhi and Jacques Maritain among them, had practiced celibacy in marriage.[386] "Man is most human, and most proves his humanity (I did not say his virility) by the quality of his relationship with women," Merton wrote earlier[387] — with this he had not come to terms.

This apart, by 1965 he had arrived at a far better understanding and acceptance of himself, and of most of the Thomas Mertons in his past. There was an admission, perhaps for the first time, that he had been happy, happy for whole periods of his life. While Gethsemani had brought him times of the greatest anguish, it had also brought the greatest happiness. Often now, he was surprised by joy, as he was when he put a spoonful of honey in his cup of coffee before dawn and saw "The beautiful jeweled shining of honey in the lamplight. Festival!".[388] Or when he discovered in fresh snow the tracks of the cat which hunted around the old sheep barn, "Solitude = being aware that you are one man in this snow where there has been no one but one cat."[389] Above all, there was the joy of waking up in the hermitage to celebrate

his fiftieth birthday. Yet he broke off the account to write a single line
in its own space:

Snow, silence, the talking fire, the watch on the table. Sorrow.[390]

∗

February brought Merton a gift of a scroll from Suzuki, "in its perfect
little box," and he wrote at once to John Wu for help in identifying the
characters the Zen master had painted on the scroll with his own hand.[391]
The month also began with another struggle over invitations. Godfrey
Diekmann had asked him to participate in an ecumenical conference at
which many old friends would be present, including Jean Leclercq and
Barnabas Ahern.[392] It was not so much the abbot's refusal that hurt,
for Merton had disciplined himself to accept such disappointments, but
the sermon Dom James preached on the next Sunday against worldly
ambition. If this was a familiar subject in the discourse of Dom James,
Merton felt the timing calculated. He nursed his resentment and suffered insomnia for the first time sleeping at the hermitage, then he wrote
to the abbot, who replied in another note that the sermon had had
nothing to do with Father Louis. Merton decided he was too old to
find causes for resentment everywhere.[393]

On February 24, Merton fell victim either of confusions over the Cistercian sign language or of a rather grim form of monastery teasing.[394]
He had walked down early in the morning to be driven to Louisville to
see the dermatologist. At the gate house one of the monks gestured
that he was lucky he hadn't come earlier: there had been a visitor who
said he had come to shoot Father Merton and who had been subdued
and taken away. This, at any rate, was the message Merton took from
the sign language, and it added to his own sense that his writings had
made him enemies and that the hermitage left him less protected than
the monastery. Others have said that a man had come to the monastery that morning, threatening to shoot, not Thomas Merton, but himself and his family. The monks had had a difficult time persuading him
to give up his gun.

That spring Merton reread old copies of *La Vie Spirituelle*, especially
the articles on the solitary life, for an essay on eremitism he had been
asked to write. He was struck at how greatly the situation had changed
between 1952 and 1965. The writers expressed a regret that the solitary
life had practically ceased to exist. Thirteen years later, there were hermits in many of the religious orders, and it was no longer necessary to
obtain an exclaustration order to become a solitary. Merton felt he had
been impatient too often with the seeming slowness of change, too
pessimistic that nothing would happen.[395]

When Meriol Trevor's biography of Cardinal Newman was read in
the refectory, Merton discovered a bond for the first time with New-

man. It was Newman's patience, especially in his conflict with author-ity,[396] that appealed to Merton. For too long he himself had confused good manners in debate with the debating style he remembered at En-glish schools and universities. His reaction to this had led to too much impatient, if not violent, language. He acknowledged that Newman's had been the better way, and this was confirmed when he studied Gandhi again: the correspondence between Gandhi and the Viceroy of India had been a model of *parrhesia*. Each of the two men had argued his conflicting principles strongly without betraying a commitment to a common humanity.

In May Merton was checking the proofs of *Gandhi on Non-Violence*. A year earlier, his fascination with alienation *within* a culture had compli-cated his portrait of Gandhi as an "alienated Asian" at the time the young Gandhi was a lawyer in South Africa.[397] The point Merton makes later in the introductory essay, that Gandhi had to discover India before he could discover both his true self and his vocation, is an important one,[398] but the approaches are tangled. Merton had been reading Fa-non, and he endorsed Fanon's idea that the colonial races (and Amer-ican blacks) had been forced into wearing white masks over non-white faces. He does not take the time, however, to work this out in the es-say.

All this was further complicated in that Merton was coming to see the necessity for a certain kind of alienation. Monks and poets were "marginal men"; both their vision and their integrity of vocation de-pended on realizing and accepting this. They saw more clearly only because they stood apart.

If there was to be an identification with others, it must be at a neces-sary distance. The best way to preserve the integrity of distance was to lead a "hidden life."

The model for Merton of the hidden life was Chuang Tzu. In 1965 he was at last putting together his selections from the Tao philosopher and poet, encouraged and aided by John Wu.

On May 3, James Laughlin arrived to find the galleys and the intro-duction for the Gandhi book ready for publication. The publisher was delighted by the translations of Chuang Tzu Merton showed him.[399] Merton hurried to finish the book that summer and found it easy to write not one but two introductions for it.[400] *The Way of Chuang Tzu*[401] became at once Merton's favorite among his own books.

He saw the poems of Chuang Tzu as a festive garland at the door-way to his hidden life, now that he had been promised he would be allowed to give up his duties as novice master and retire to the hermi-tage within a matter of weeks.[402] The period of waiting was an anxious one.

That spring his health had deteriorated and the world had broken in upon his solitude. In late February his dermatological problems grew worse and he had to work in dermal gloves. There was a series of colds, followed by intestinal flu. He was in the infirmary one night, then hurried back to the hermitage too soon and collapsed.[403] The best medicine, he found, was Twining's Lapsang Souchong tea his friend Jack Ford brought him from Louisville. Once more he had explored too enthusiastically in the Edelen Farm property, and this time a branch struck him in the eye, damaging the cornea. He could do no reading for days, and he had to wear, first an eye patch, then dark glasses.[404]

On March 18, Father John Coffield came with a full report on the March to Selma. He gave vivid descriptions of the confrontation on the bridge at Selma when the marchers had been blocked and surrounded by the Alabama police and the state troopers. One thing was clear, the march had been a breakthrough, a victory, though it was difficult to tell how lasting or how important that victory would prove. In some mysterious way the television cameras had been a watchful eye that transformed the struggle. Acting out their violence before a huge audience, the opponents of non-violence had achieved a national outcry. They now showed some restraint, however menacing, and Merton commented in his journal that he would be more careful in the future in what he said against television.[405] There was still the night, and in the darkness two of the marchers had been murdered.

On Monday, May 31, Dan Berrigan, Jim Douglass, and Father Robert McDole came to consult with Merton about the amendments to the articles on war in Schema Thirteen. Merton comments in his journal on the council:

> It really seems that they want to approve the bomb after all. In a way it is funny, though I should not say that! But behind it all I wonder if there is not an apocalyptic irony. But we must do what we can to prevent a disgrace and scandal of such magnitude.[406]

A week later, on Friday, June 4, Merton went to Lexington to be examined at the clinic by Dr. Fortune. The examinations were so painful and exhausting he had to remain overnight. His stay brought him back to the newspapers and to copies of *Life:*

> . . . full of helicopters in Viet Nam, white mercenaries in the Congo, marines in Santo Domingo. The whole picture is one of an enormously equipped and self-complacent white civilization in combat with a huge, sprawling colored and mestizo world (a majority) armed with anything they can lay their hands on. And the implicit assumption behind it all, as far as *Life* and apparently everyone else is concerned, is that "we" are the injured ones, we are trying to keep peace and order, and "they" (abetted by communist demons) are simply causing confusion and chaos, with no reasonable motives whatever. Hence "we," being attacked (God and justice are also attacked in us) have to defend ourselves, God, jus-

tice, etc. Dealing with these "inferior" people becomes a technical problem something like pest extermination. In a word, the psychology of the Alabama police becomes in fact the psychology of America as a world policeman.[407]

Twenty-five years earlier at St. Bonaventure's Merton had made the analogy between modern war and the use of insecticide. One difficulty inherent in the attitude which diminishes an enemy to something as far from a human being as an insect is that one diminishes oneself. This was to have results both ironic and poignant within a few years. To defeat such an enemy reflects very little glory on the victor: to be beaten brings unthinkable ignominy. To avoid the disaster more and more "insecticide" is used, with devastating results, yet no certainty of success.

Earlier warriors had no such problems, as Simone Weil points out in an essay translated by Mary McCarthy as *The Iliad, or The Poem of Force*.[408] In the spring of 1965 Merton had read Jacques Cabaud's biography published in America in 1964 as *Simone Weil, a Fellowship in Love*.[409] He discovered that his godfather, Tom Izod Bennett, had been her doctor at the Middlesex Hospital just before she died, at a sanatorium in Kent in August 1943. Bennett had said she was the most difficult patient he had ever seen, and Merton commented in his journal: "Funny that she, and I have this in common: we were both problems to this good man."[410]

"The Answer of Minerva: Pacifism and Resistance in Simone Weil,"[411] an extended review of the Cabaud biography, appeared first in *Peace News* in April, less than a month after Merton wrote it. He is full of praise for a biographer who has treated his subject "neither as a problem nor as a saint." Where Cabaud goes wrong, Merton says, is in endorsing a stereotype of pacifism and non-violence and in taking at face value Simone Weil's accusation of herself for making a "criminal error committed before 1939 with regard to pacifist groups and their actions." For Merton:

> . . . This reflects her disgust with Vichy and with former pacifists who now submitted to Hitler without protest. But we cannot interpret this statement to mean that after Munich and then the fall of France Simone Weil abandoned all her former principles in order to take up an essentially new position in regard to war and peace. This would mean equating her "pacifism" with the quietism of the uncomprehending and the inert. It would also mean failure to understand that she became deeply committed to nonviolent resistance. Before Munich the emphasis was, however, on nonviolence, and after the fall of France the emphasis was on *resistance*, including the acceptance of resistance by force where nonviolence was ineffective.[412]

While there are small variations in the published versions, this is a key passage in the writings of Thomas Merton. In a study of Simone

Weil it leaves out the fact that she had already seen action in Spain and might well have been a target for his sarcasm in 1938.[413]

Merton goes on to discuss Simone Weil's essay on the Trojan War, in which the fighters are fighting "in a moral void." When he speaks of the lack of real issues at Troy, we are reminded of the journal passages in 1939 in which Merton accuses the Allied leaders of having no war aims other than the defeat of Hitler. At Troy the issues are all illusion and myth: one man alone, Paris, was interested in Helen. However, as soon as the first blood is shed the true issue becomes the dead. The answer of Minerva to the question "Why must this pointless war go on?" is "You must fight on, for if you now make peace with the enemy, you will offend the dead."[414]

Nobody needs to be reminded that the answer of Minerva has long outlived the worship of Minerva. For those who believe in an afterlife, the dead are presumably beyond offense: for the believing Christian they have other concerns. The living remain tied to the myth that the dead demand sacrifice.

In the earlier key quotation on resistance and non-violence, Merton is speaking of Simone Weil, not himself: it is time to look at his own view of non-violence, the limitations and exceptions he accepted in his own writing. "A metaphysic of nonviolence is something that the peace movement needs," he wrote in "The Answer of Minerva."[415] Did Thomas Merton provide such a metaphysic?

One is tempted to answer this with the *Sic et Non* of Abelard or the *mu* of Zen (the yes-and-no Merton liked so much himself). While the subject is too important to evade, it would be hard to do justice to all the complexities here. A general outline and key passages are helpful, with the reservation that in fairness to Merton the whole subject requires further study than it is given in these pages, or than it has been given elsewhere.

As we have seen, Merton was careful to guard against being thought a "pure pacifist" because he saw exceptions to non-violence:

> . . . Though not a total pacifist in theory myself, I certainly believe that every Christian should try to practice non-violence rather than violence and that some should bind themselves to follow only the way of peace as an example to the others. I myself as a monk do not believe it would be licit for me ever to kill another human being even in self-defense and I would certainly never attempt to do so. There are much greater and truer ways than this. Killing achieves nothing. Finally, though as I said in theory I would still admit some persons might licitly wage war to defend themselves (for instance the Hungarians in 1956) yet I think that nuclear war is out of the question, it is beyond all doubt murder and sin, and it must be banned forever. Since in practice any small war is likely to lead to nuclear war, I therefore believe in practice that war must be

absolutely banned and abolished today as a method of settling international disputes.[416]

Merton was often overdogmatic. In his statements on the limitations of non-violence he shows a uniformly tentative approach. It would be wrong to see him as inconsistent, more just to admit he never resolved the problem in a way which was satisfactory to him. Where his argument has weak points in logic, Merton was clearly aware of them.

Oppression is a form of violence. Merton is far more sympathetic to oppressed groups than to nations with either mythic or real grievances. He made no statement admitting violence as an alternative to non-violence as an option for any nation, with the possible exception of Israel. If this is already an inconsistency, Merton obviously thought of Israel in 1961 as an oppressed group, rather than as a nation. For all this, the exception gives trouble. Writing to Rabbi Steven Schwarzschild, he first explains why he is reluctant to help draft a statement on nuclear tests, then goes on:

> And also there still remains one crazy reservation: because I think guerrilla warfare is not illegitimate. I think people like the Hungarians, like the Jews in Israel, have a right to recourse to that kind of protest and self-protection. Hence I cannot make a statement that would have South Americans presumably without right of action against Communists down there. At the same time, I realize what form self defense would take: the mercenary fascist army . . . Alas. Perhaps we can discuss this more. I am not clear.[417]

In his correspondence with Ernesto Cardenal and others, Merton explores the right of South and Central Americans to action against both "the mercenary fascist army" and foreign exploitation. Where the violence of oppression is met by the violence of rebellion he finds no lasting solution, only a necessity it would be unrealistic to ignore:

> The fact remains that a non-violent political ethic is terribly important everywhere. I read Colombia Machēteada in El Corno. If we cannot get things organized it is going to be something like that everywhere. And it is totally senseless. But the senselessness of physical violence is necessary, perhaps, to manifest the senselessness of economic and cultural violence. And the basic violence of a life without God, without silence, without prayer, without thought.[418]

In the same letter of May 8, 1964, Merton talks of the work he is doing on Gandhi, then returns:

> It is terribly important now to keep the concept of non-violence alive. What is happening is that in the race movement in the U.S. the non-violent tactics are being discredited because the gains that were made have been taken back and nullified. Restaurants have quietly segregated them-

selves again, etc. Token concessions were made, and then everything went back as before. This is a very serious situation because now violence is going to begin, slowly, sporadically, but the situation will get definitively rotten and I see no alternative. Perhaps in the long run this is the only way that realities can be brought out and kept in full view. People do not want to see them. This is a very unrealistic country.[419]

This was written before Selma. Martin Luther King's non-violent movement had much to do yet, for all the movement's opponents of both races, and for all its critics.

It is for others to determine which gains in the struggle for racial justice in the 1960s were achieved by violence and which by non-violence. (It is already a tragedy for non-violence that these are confused.) We have only to examine an experiment in non-violence and one contemporary judgment upon it. What was mere theory in the writings of Gandhi as far as the West was concerned was being tested in 1964–65 on the roads of Alabama, in the streets of Southern and Northern cities. The experiment was new to America: it was followed with interest by almost all Americans. Most were sure it wouldn't work, feeling that non-violence was ineffective by its very nature. What *did* work in America was largely justified by the fact that it worked. The test, then, was crucial for the future of non-violence and much else.

Where Thomas Merton warned of violence he was correct: he was too quick to accept it, betraying an impatience of his own and a lack of faith in King and in a movement that was not in India but in America. "It is terribly important now to keep the concept of non-violence alive . . ." The concept needed faith to keep it alive in practice rather than in theory. Here Merton faltered. The lines he wrote on Simone Weil's reaction in quite different circumstances have a relevance to his own reaction: ". . . including the acceptance of resistance by force where nonviolence was ineffective."

＊

In the middle of June the results of Merton's medical tests came in and he learned he had a staphylococcus infection of the intestines. Antibiotics helped him, but he was still anxious about his health, fearing this would prevent his moving permanently into the hermitage. He began to clear his papers at the monastery, making one more resolution to write less when he became a hermit.

The spring of 1965 had been a period of great literary activity. He had sent *The Way of Chuang Tzu*[420] to New Directions: it would be published in November. *Gandhi on Non-Violence*[421] would appear from the same publisher in October. Three collections of essays were nearing completion. One of these, *Seasons of Celebration*,[422] to be published by Farrar, Straus and Cudahy in December, contained recent articles on the liturgical renewal (". . . the greatest development in liturgy since the Patristic age and the most thorough reform in liturgy the Church has ever known"),[423] together with writings on the controversy surrounding it. There were other essays, some of them written in the 1950s and worked up from notes for conferences on the feasts of the liturgical year. Three of these had material of lasting value, and they were written in the lyrical, prose-poem style of many passages in *New Seeds of Contemplation* and *The New Man*: "Easter: The New Life" (written at Easter 1959), "The Good Samaritan," and " 'In Silentio,' A Note on Monastic Prayer."

Where there was already another Merton "logjam" of sizable proportions, two of the collections of essays were held up. *Raids on the Unspeakable*[424] (which began with the beautiful essay "Rain and the Rhinoceros," and contained "old things and new") was published in August 1966. *Mystics and Zen Masters*[425] was not published until May 1967.

Merton had also written a number of review essays (including "The Answer of Minerva"), articles on monasticism and the eremitical life, and his "Open Letter to the American Bishops" on the Schema Thirteen question.[426]

He now took the opportunity to warn editors there would be fewer articles from him in the future and to refuse commissions. At the same time he wrote to friends saying his correspondence would be restricted, the number of his visits curtailed. He thanked W. H. Ferry for the books and magazine subscriptions in the past, but said he doubted whether he would be allowed them in a few months' time.[427] It is difficult to tell from the letters whether the abbot had set the conditions or whether Merton was setting conditions as though the abbot had made them.

The weather was beautiful in those weeks of June and early July, with warm, clear days and cold nights. In his journal Merton reflected on the change in his life. Some of the passages have a similar tone to those in the St. Bonaventure journal at the end of 1941, and it is hard not to wonder if he wasn't trying to frighten himself, not just with the seriousness of his decision, but with its finality:

> But the solitary life should partake of the seriousness and incommunicability of death. Or should it? Is that too rigid and absolute an ideal?
>
> The two go together. Solitude is not death, it is life. It aims not at a living death but at a certain fulness of life. But a fulness that comes from honesty and authenticity, facing death and *accepting it without care* i.e. with faith and trust in God.[428]

The truly solitary life would be a death to all that was not authentic, real, in himself. It would be life to what was spontaneous, authentic, real. The testing of true solitude would be the sifting out of the one from the other.

He talked of two kinds of folly. In several essays in *Seasons of Cele-*

bration he had introduced the idea of "holy folly." In "Easter: The New Life," he mentioned the acts of "holy folly" of St. Francis of Assisi and St. Philip Neri, "which remind us of the *yurodivetsvo,* the 'folly for Christ,' familiar in the spirituality of the Russian Church."[429]

He went further in "The Good Samaritan," an essay that remained a favorite with Merton himself. There he equates folly with mercy. The saint (in Hebrew *chasid*) is the man or woman of fortitude in mercy *(chesed),* forever foolish in acts of mercy.

There were many such acts in Merton's life which he kept largely hidden. To take one example, there was his gift of the already rare edition of *Hagia Sophia* to Clyde Kennard, dying of cancer in a Chicago hospital. Only from others do we learn how much this meant to Kennard. On the face of it the present of a hand-printed book looks impractical to the point of folly, and this is very much the point. Even at a distance from Kennard, Merton's spontaneous act provided the "divine epiphany and awakening" he speaks of in the essay in terms of the Good Samaritan: the *chasid* will be so overflowing in *chesed* he will act before he knows he has acted. The Latin word is *misericordia,* and Merton says, "The Vulgate rings with *misericordia* as though with a deep church bell. Mercy is the 'burden' or the 'bourdon,' it is the bass bell and undersong of the whole Bible . . ."[430] a passage that reminds us of the ending of *The Sign of Jonas:* ". . . Mercy within mercy within mercy . . .":[431]

> We are bound to God in *chesed.* The power of His mercy has taken hold of us and will not let go of us: therefore we have become foolish. We can no longer love wisely . . .[432]

The Hasidic Jew trusts whatever he has in him to be good when he is "God-intoxicated." Merton was not so trusting; he wanted the foolishness of the *chasid,* yet felt there was another kind of foolishness in him that solitude would only make more difficult to contain. He wanted to be a "fool for God," not to make a fool of himself.

He writes to Naomi Burton:

> At the end of the month I am out of my novice job and permanently in the hermitage. I am of course very glad, and also I see that it will not be any joke either. The more I get into it, the more I see that the business of being solitary admits of absolutely no nonsense at all, and when I see how totally full of nonsense I am, I can see that I could wreck myself at it. Yet I really think God asks me to take this risk, and I want to do this. So please pray hard, really. I am an awful fool, and I know it, but if I can just be obedient and cooperative for once in my life, this can be a very good thing for me, incomparable, in fact. Do please keep me in your prayers. I am almost getting a humble and chastened attitude toward the whole thing. Wouldn't it be amazing if after all this I really went at it in a spirit of humility and faith, instead of just making noises and demanding it all as a right?[433]

To Mother Luke Tobin, he wrote in much the same vein:

> Pray for me to be a real good hermit and listen to the word of God and
> respond like a man. That is what it really involves. Simply to stand on
> one's feet before one's Father and reply to Him in the Spirit. Of course
> this is very much a Church activity. Anyway I will be down to concele-
> brate habitually and this will add an interesting and lively dimension:
> maybe I'll be one of the first hermits with that kind of setup, at least since
> the very early days.
> (That business about replying to the Father in the Spirit may sound like
> big talk but I don't mean it in that way. "In the Spirit" in any context I
> know, of solitude, means flat on your face. How one can stand on one's
> feet and be flat on one's face at the same time is a mystery I will have to
> try to work out by living it. Maybe Yoga is the answer, but don't report
> this to Fr. Abbot. I have no intention of trying to solve it in that way.)[434]

He had been forbidden Yoga by the abbot in 1962, after he and Father Augustine had been discovered one day meditating upside down,[435]
a sight that must have been even more disturbing to the discoverer as
Father Augustine had taken off his artificial leg.

On Sunday, July 18, Merton woke up just after midnight at the hermitage to find himself in the middle of a summer storm. He usually
enjoyed such natural violence. He wrote next day to Mother Luke to
say he had been pleasantly alarmed:

> Last night's storm was a great experience in the hermitage. The place
> got "hit" but of course it was immediately grounded. Yet one definitely
> felt something. I felt as if a wave of static electricity came out of my feet,
> if that makes any sense. Or perhaps it was a religious experience? I doubt
> it. But the great thing was seeing the whole valley lit up by continuous
> flashes of lightning. The hills really seemed to jump and dance like young
> lambs, as in the psalms. It was splendid. Nowhere better.[436]

But the journal account was a good deal more somber: he admitted
he had been afraid. The morning after the storm was calm and Merton
redrafted his "Open Letter to the Bishops" with a prophetic sense that
the letter would be largely ignored: "Best I could do is the feeble attempt on the notes on Schema Thirteen, etc. to the *Commonweal*, Bishop
Wright, Archbishop Flahiff and others."[437] His work on the Open Letter and the biography of Newman had clarified his definition of obedience. "The reality is in his [Newman's] kind of obedience and his
kind of refusal. Complete obedience to the Church and complete, al-
beit humble, refusal of the pride and chicanery of churchmen."[438]

Any feeling of depression was lifted when the abbot spoke to him
after Chapter and set the date when he would no longer be novice master
and when he would be free to retire to the hermitage. The permission
of the abbot's private council was still required for Merton to become
the first hermit ever at the monastery, yet with the abbot's support

Merton felt confident. "Things like this make me ashamed of my fears and worries and my suspicions of Dom James."[439] The very boldness of the abbot's decision made him think over his own earlier assumptions.

The first week of August, Merton suffered further tests and a week in hospital. He returned to find work had been done at the hermitage to make it less drafty. He went back to filling wastepaper baskets in the novice master's office: "And with this absurd ritual of waste paper has gone a rending of the intestines, diarrhea at night, angst, etc. The revelation of futility and interminable self-contradiction. What a poor being I am."[440]

It is significant that he had turned for support to two women friends. Mother Luke wrote back that she knew a monk "who will praise God on his feet or on his face." When Naomi Burton's reply came he found it "full of mature, realistic understanding, and feminine comfort — the warmth that cannot come from a man, and that is so essential."[441] Merton developed the subject he had been exploring on the eve of his fiftieth birthday, wondering whether the violence of one earlier renunciation at least had not done permanent damage to his ability to trust, and to the "hidden wholeness" he had spoken of in *Hagia Sophia*. If chastity was his most radical poverty, the way he accumulated things was "a desperate and useless expedient to cover this irreparable loss which I have not fully accepted. I can learn to accept it in the Spirit and in love, and it will no longer be 'irreparable.' The Cross repairs it and transforms it."[442]

Hagia Sophia had been a celebration of the wisdom and the *chesed* (fortitude in charity) of women. The poet had talked of a wider need for just this wisdom and *chesed* when he wrote to the organizer of a Program for Christian Culture at St. Mary's College, Notre Dame:

> To my mind it is very important that this experiment is being conducted in a Catholic women's college. This is to me a hopeful sign. I think women are perhaps capable of salvaging something of humanity in our world today. Certainly they have a better chance at grasping and understanding and preserving a sense of Christian culture. And of course I think the wisdom of Sister Madeleva has a lot to do with the effectiveness of this experiment and of its future possibilities. The word wisdom is another key word, I suspect. We are concerned not just with culture but also with wisdom, above all.[443]

Such wisdom he had sought out himself in Mother Angela Collins of the Louisville Carmel (who had been transferred to Savannah, and whom he missed), in Sister Thérèse Lentfoehr, in Dorothy Day, in Baroness Catherine de Hueck Doherty, in Mother Mary Luke Tobin, in Naomi Burton Stone, and in many others. He admitted to a "secret love" for two older scholars he was corresponding with on Celtic subjects, Nora Chadwick and Eleanor Duckett.[444] Two of his guides were now women, Raissa Maritain and the Lady Julian of Norwich. In the summer of 1965 he was anxious for women friends who were taking part in the Strike for Peace in Rome, and he felt that their action would have far more effect on the way the sections on war in Schema Thirteen would finally appear than his own efforts.[445]

He had not refused Sophia. Yet he knew the lack of something else appeared in his work, as it showed in his life. The pages on Adam as solitary in *The New Man* are magnificent. Eve's appearance is almost an intrusion — it was as if Merton had not known quite what to do with Eve. Andrew Marvell had been a strong early influence on Merton's poetry and for all its near-cynical tone, a verse in Marvell's poem "The Garden" may have haunted him at times:

> Such was that happy Garden-state,
> While Man there walk'd without a Mate:
> After a Place so pure, and sweet,
> What other Help could yet be meet!
> But 'twas beyond a Mortal's share
> To wander solitary there:
> Two Paradises 'twere in one,
> To live in Paradise alone.[446]

There is a passage in *The New Man* where the author brings the rejecting of love into sudden clarity, even though he cannot have foreseen all the ramifications of what he was writing:

> In the mystery of social love there is found the realization of "the other" not only as one to be loved by us, so that we may perfect ourselves, but also as one who can become more perfect by loving us. The vocation to charity is a call not only to love but to *be loved*. The man who does not care at all whether or not he is loved is ultimately unconcerned about the true welfare of the other and of society. Hence we cannot love unless we also consent to be loved in return.[447]

This was one of Merton's most important passages, important for others and important for himself. While it does not argue against what is generally called Platonic love, it *does* deny the Platonic theory of perfecting oneself through elevating the objects of love (a somewhat sophisticated way of using others). For Thomas Merton "the refusal" had not been a refusal to love so much as a refusal to accept love, and especially from women.

This brought up the romantic pairing in Merton's now very distant past:

> The other day (St. John Baptist perhaps) after my Mass I suddenly thought of Ann Winser, Andrew's little sister. She was about 12 or 13 when I

went to visit him in the Isle of Wight, in that quiet rectory at Brooke. She was the quietest thing in it, dark and secret child. One does not fall in love with a child of 13 and I hardly remember even thinking of her. Yet the other day I realized that I had never forgotten her and that she made a deep impression. I was left, the other day, with a sort of Burnt Norton feeling about the part of the garden I never went to, and that if I had taken another turn in the road I might have ended up married to her. Actually, I think she's a symbol of this true (quiet) woman with whom I never really came to terms in the world, and because of this there remains an incompleteness that cannot be remedied. The years in which I chased whores or made whores out of my girlfriends (no, that is too strong and also silly) (besides there were plenty that I was too shy to sleep with) did nothing to make sense out of my life, on the contrary.

   When I came to the monastery, Jinny Burton was the symbol of the girl I ought to have fallen in love with but didn't (and she remains the image of one I really did love with a love of companionship not of passion).[448]

There is a reason why he brings this up at this time. His further withdrawing into solitude could only appear to others as a second renunciation of both men and women — even of the male family he had been a part of for twenty-four years.

On the morning of August 17, the private council met and voted to approve the abbot's choice of Father Baldwin as the new novice master. Father Louis was then asked to leave the room. When he was called back he was told the council had voted favorably on his retirement to the hermitage. There was a sense that history had been made with the decision: Gethsemani, the "strictest of the Strict," was to have its hermit.[449]

The vote cut through some of Merton's earlier ambiguities about the community. There were many at the monastery (very much including the abbot) who had made all this possible. Where Merton was determined to show his gratitude, the community was resolved to honor his desire for solitude.

August 20, the Feast of St. Bernard, was kept as a double feast in 1965. Father Louis received comic presents and cards from his novices. When he gave his farewell address, "A Life Free from Care," something of the holiday spirit came into the final words. He left them with an image. He described a picture of a hermit from Mount Athos he had seen in an old text, a ragged old man with a crow sitting on his shoulder and with a caption that explained, "He was kissed by God."[450]

After giving the address, he went to collect necessary supplies. At the monastery clothing room he picked out old work clothes discarded by the community. If these garments were not in rags, they were at least well patched. He walked up to the hermitage on Mount Olivet free of almost all obligations to the monastery. He would go down each morning at ten-thirty to say Mass in the library chapel and to eat one meal (usually on his own) in the infirmary refectory. He had been asked to give a conference each Sunday, and at the last minute the abbot had asked him to write a new manual for postulants.

Except for the hunters after squirrels, the solitude was now perfect, and Merton celebrated the feeling that this gave "different horizons" to his life, to reading the Psalms, "precisely because one is alone with God and He speaks directly and personally, giving the light and nourishment one especially needs."

After a week he admitted loneliness. He had not retired from any job in the world's sense, yet he had retired from communal labor. For twenty-four years this had provided the balance to his search for contemplation and solitude. He had never undervalued it: in times of crisis it had been physical labor in the woods and fields of Gethsemani that had brought him back to acknowledge his place in the community. He could be funny about the "All Out Work Days in the Cheese Factory" — he had no regrets about being no longer eligible ("I make no more cookies in the cookie factory, I am out here with the lizards," he wrote to Robert Lax).[451]

Merton's attitude to work had been consistent over the years. He honored the good worker and the good work, whether it was Miss Wegener's tact and efficiency in the appointments office at Columbia,[452] one of his novices who had completed a task he set with unusual skill, or the workmanship Victor Hammer put into printing or into a painting. He did not follow Jacques Maritain into traditional divisions between art that was primarily of the hand (crafts) and art that was primarily of the head (the fine arts). Nor did he talk of "creative work."

Merton's writing was more of a compulsion than either a vocation or a job. There was no affectation when he celebrated in his journals the times when he escaped from the typewriter into the fields for harvesting or into the knobs to mark trees or plant saplings. He had an eye for well-farmed land and a flourishing plantation. Nothing pleased him more on his trips to doctors in Lexington or Louisville than to be taken for an unusually well read farmer.

Yet no change at Gethsemani had been so drastic and far-reaching as the change in the pattern of work, and Merton had to explain in *Gethsemani: A Life of Praise* that "The monastic farm is now highly mechanized and the planting, cultivation and harvesting of crops no longer occupy the whole work force of the monastery as they used to in former days."[453]

In the journal, the feeling of nostalgia is as strong as the sense of loneliness:

Yesterday when I went down to say Mass, all the community, or a large group rather, were out gathering in the potato harvest under a blue, late summer sky, and I remembered the communal beauty of work in this season — the sense of brotherhood and joy when I used to go over with the students to cut tobacco twelve years ago! Or cutting corn in my novitiate, or the general corn husking that went on all through October when I was a student (and late into November even). Now that's all done by machine and there is little really common work outdoors. Anyway, I felt lonely, seeing them out there.[454]

Though he complained of being left alone that autumn, this was not altogether true. There was the visit already mentioned from the returning Father Chrysogonus,[455] and both Ernesto Cardenal and Hildegard Goss-Mayr made visits. Yet it was this sense of isolation in October 1965 that led Merton to another, minor, crisis of stability. After Cardenal's visit he was kept informed of the new experimental foundation Cardenal had made at Solentiname, on an island in a lake in Nicaragua. Here the Rule of St. Benedict was combined with ideas on monastic renewal Cardenal had learned from Merton's writings, and especially from discussions while Cardenal was a novice under Father Louis. The exchange had been just this, and Merton felt Cardenal had left, not only because of ill health, but because he was already a teacher and had no more to learn. Cardenal felt differently and now he wanted his old teacher to join him. He wrote asking for Merton's permission to approach the higher superiors for his transfer to Solentiname. Merton replied, giving his consent, and wrote himself to Archbishop Paul Philippe and to the Pope.[456] Nothing came of the project, though Merton wrote Cardenal three years later that he was still hoping at least to visit Solentiname. In 1968 he wondered only whether he would not be "too ashamed to be in a Latin American country and to be known as a North American."[457]

By that time the Vietnam War had intensified, and with it Merton's feeling of alienation from his adopted country, his desire to do something to align himself publicly with the Third World. The possibility of leaving Gethsemani for a foundation in South or Central America retained its attraction. In 1965, Merton was careful to lay down his own conditions for coming to Solentiname. He told Ernesto Cardenal he was anxious to further the cause of monastic renewal by seeing how the new ideas worked out in practice. At the same time rigorous precautions would have to be taken to protect his "hidden life."[458]

The same conflicting priorities were already complicating his life at Gethsemani. There is a feeling still among many of the monks that they did exactly what Father Louis had asked them to do, respecting his desire for solitude, only to learn he was complaining in his letters to friends outside the monastery that he was virtually ignored in the community. For most of the monks this was a source of sadness, rather than of resentment. Some of Merton's statements over the next three years *were* hurtful, and a number got back, one way or another, to Gethsemani. Few of Merton's friends in the world asked themselves how the other monks were supposed to leave him alone and at the same time provide him with support and companionship. All his visitors were of one mind: "Merton needed people."

The solitary who needs people is not so uncommon. Thomas Merton might have resolved the conflict in his priorities, except for one thing. His new definition of love meant not only that he needed people but that he needed to be needed by others.

From his journals one can see that the sense of isolation was acute in the fall of 1965. This led him to a blunder he was quick to regret. Some background, however sketchy, is necessary. Anxious to keep his commitment to the peace movement free of misunderstandings, Merton tried to avoid drafting statements for others or allowing the use of his name on manifestoes. In 1963 Daniel Berrigan had asked him for advice on civil disobedience. In his replies, under "Conscience Matter," Merton reviewed his own hesitations and misgivings about direct action. The letter is useful in showing Merton's own position.[459] When Berrigan wrote thanking Merton for his help with *his* problems, however, he was being overgenerous.

With the Vietnam War came draft-card burning and other acts of civil disobedience that posed different problems from the early peace strikes and sit-ins. Then came newspaper reports that Buddhist monks in Vietnam had immolated themselves as a protest against the war.

In November, Jim Douglass wrote, sending a newspaper account about a pacifist who had immolated himself in front of the Pentagon.[460] Four days later, on November 11, the Feast of St. Martin, Merton received a special-delivery letter from Douglass informing him that Roger Laporte, one of the staff at *The Catholic Worker*, had set fire to himself in front of the United Nations building. Merton had already heard from Dan Walsh that a newspaperman in Louisville had been trying to reach him, and he guessed the journalist wanted a statement on the Laporte tragedy.[461]

Without waiting for further views or information, Merton received the abbot's permission to send off two telegrams, one to Dorothy Day, the other to Jim Forest of the Catholic Peace Fellowship. The one to Forest read:

> JUST HEARD ABOUT SUICIDE OF ROGER LAPORTE. WHILE I DO NOT HOLD CATHOLIC PEACE FELLOWSHIP RESPONSIBLE FOR THIS TRAGEDY CURRENT DEVELOPMENTS IN PEACE MOVEMENT MAKE IT IMPOSSIBLE FOR ME TO CONTINUE AS SPONSOR OF FELLOWSHIP. PLEASE REMOVE MY NAME FROM LIST OF SPONSORS. LETTER FOLLOWS. THOMAS MERTON.[462]

To Jim Forest, the telegram was the third blow in an already shattering situation. Tom Cornell of the Fellowship had just been indicted for burning his draft card. Roger Laporte was dying at Bellevue Hospital.

Thomas Merton had disowned the Fellowship.[463] The letter that followed did express some understanding of the shock felt at the headquarters of the peace movement, but it confirmed Merton's action and justified it. Merton went on, "I cannot accept the present spirit of the movement as it presents itself to me." There were signs of strain, as well as incomprehension, in the letter:

> This whole atmosphere is crazy, not just the peace movement, everybody. There is in it such an air of absurdity and moral void, even when conscience and morality are invoked (as they are by everyone). The joint is going into a slow frenzy. The country is nuts.[464]

By then Roger Laporte had died, and Merton was further disturbed by an account of the Mass held for him at the *Catholic Worker* offices. He also learned Laporte had once been a Cistercian novice.

Merton tried to analyze his feelings in his journal. His sense of solitude was destroyed, so much so that when a wounded deer came out of the woods when he was trying to say Prime he wept bitterly.[465] The first responses to his action (from Dorothy Day, Jim Forest, and Dan Berrigan) were moderate, yet they made him realize how much strain his friends had been under. Implied, where not stated, was the sense that his telegram had been one more wounding blow. On November 21 he received a letter from John Heidbrink of the Fellowship of Reconciliation that left him in no doubt: Merton was a bastard, a traitor, and much else besides — "all couched," says Merton, in "Christian language."[466] Much more telling than verbal abuse was the statement that only those leading a dedicated life of action in the world had the right to deal with matters, something that did not involve being cut down by a hermit living a life of ease and evasion in a hermitage "quilted in mist."

The Heidbrink letter hurt, even though Merton's defensive powers rose to meet such a frontal attack. He had already decided the telegrams were a mistake. Despite further anxiety about the rightness of things, he admitted he was moved by the account of the Mass for Laporte in Dan Berrigan's letter.[467] He was not ready to be persuaded Laporte's action had been an act of self-sacrifice and love, rather than suicide, chiefly because he was too afraid the example would be followed by others. In the end, he decided to allow his name to remain as a sponsor.

Daniel Berrigan was being sent abroad by his Jesuit superiors. Tom Cornell had issued a statement on draft-card burning that Merton found lucid, if not altogether convincing.[468] He continued to be anxious others would associate him with the draft-card burnings, if not with Laporte's death.

For the moment, it was not where he stood intellectually on issues but where he was actually standing that was the main matter of contention. Heidbrink's letter had implied that nobody cared to hear his opinion because it was irrelevant. Daniel Berrigan and most of Merton's friends denied this, saying he had something valuable to contribute, but they wanted him with them. Much later, Daniel Berrigan decided that Merton was right to remain where he did.[469] In November 1965 he and others accepted Merton's apologies for acting before he had sufficient information and before he had checked with them about the actual situation. Still, there was a widespread and lasting feeling in the various peace movements that Thomas Merton was in the wrong place at a critical time.

It made his dilemma more difficult that he was working up old essays and passages from his journals in the early years of commitment for a book which was finally given the title *Conjectures of a Guilty Bystander*.[470] Was he still a bystander, guilty not by association only, but because he insisted on being a marginal man?

Merton claimed then and later to be an existentialist. He had strong grounds for making the claim, and yet there is something which seems to disqualify him. The existentialist is distinguished from the perennial philosopher in one respect above all: while the perennial philosopher remains aloof from events and comments on them, the existentialist is in the middle of those events, seeking to define their essence in terms of his existence. In scientific terms, the perennial philosopher is the observer predictor, the existentialist an observer participant.

Put more starkly, John Heidbrink had told him he was "out of it." The friendship between Heidbrink and Merton survived the incident: so did the dilemma for Merton.

While he stressed the negative side of Merton's situation, Heidbrink tried to point to what Thomas Merton could become if the monk took a more active role, quoting Bishop Robinson's "a man for others." Merton was put off by something in the Heidbrink-Robinson rhetoric: "It is the same empty Protestant fussiness that drove me out of Zion Church thirty years ago."[471] He also resisted the image which was being foisted upon him. The false self was, after all, the one that depended on the confirmation of others; the true self had to get on without it. He agreed he had made a mistake; he saw no need now to renounce the role he had chosen for himself with considerable care, not to mention the vocation in which he had come to have confidence. It was once more a case of "We have to keep moving."

Merton's immediate reconciliation with the Fellowship of Reconciliation took place over the last days in November. At the same time, he was worrying about the peace movement, about a "regular fury of drug-mysticism in the country,"[472] and he was anxious for the success of the peace protest in Washington. He supported the protest with prayers and fasting — wondering, now, whether this was enough. His new concern with obedience and loyalty had shifted from his relationship with superiors in the Church to his relationship with friends who were leaders in the peace movement. He studied his own loyalty and his effectiveness. Yet even when he risked another rejection, he was not prepared to give up his solitude to win approval.

December brought a gift from Marco Pallis, a magnificent ikon.[473] It also brought a number of what he called "boomerangs" from the distant past. A friend sent him a photograph taken in Douglaston in 1933, in which he discovered himself as a young rugby player from Cambridge and wondered where that strong, reliable body had gone.[474] Eight freedom songs Merton had written a few years earlier had been set to music by Alexander Peloquin for a young black singer who had subsequently disappeared to Ireland to take part in a successful show. In the end Peloquin used the songs in a symphony for Eileen Farrell, and Merton found himself accused of selling out, of using the sorrows of the black race simply as material to be exploited for the symphony-going public.[475] He was hardly to blame for what had been a mixup between various collaborators who had not kept in touch with one another. As in his publishing tangles, charitable gifts had a way of turning into grievances and misunderstandings.

*

The year in which he had gained so much ended with a shower of boomerangs and worse health. Chronic dysentery made Merton decide there was no hope of his being able to join Cardenal or go to a foundation in South America. His visits to the outside latrine were just as "grievous" in the heavy rains of early January as they had been in the cold of the previous winter.

There were no such accounts of the body as a "nagging bore" in the journals of the German poet Rainer Maria Rilke.[476] As Merton discovered different levels of solitude, he rediscovered the solitude of the artist and writer, and Rilke became more important to him than ever. He brought the theme into his Sunday conferences at the monastery, and the monks were delighted, and amused, by each in a series of Merton enthusiasms. Nineteen sixty-six began with Rilke, to be followed by an almost obsessive interest in Camus, who emerged by the summer as the greatest writer of our time.

In January, trying to read Rilke in German, Merton found he was more proficient in the language than he had thought. "Enclosed by the rain," he began reading the Japanese Zen philosopher Kitaro Nishida.[477] Then, as the rain turned to heavy snowfall, Merton became disturbed and depressed by reports of the Helsinki Peace Conference of the summer before. To him, the conference had presented the idea that "all the Third

World should take up arms against American Imperialists. This would promote 'peace'! I don't mind them calling for world revolution if they call it by its right name — but to call this a peace movement! . . . No nonsense about non-violence and conscientious objection either!"[478]

Returning to Nishida's *The Intelligible World* brought him back to clarity and Zen: "Splendid view of the real (trans-conscious) meaning of Zen and its relation to the conscious and the world." [479] He went on to read an early rule for recluses Father Irenaeus had sent him from the St. Bonaventure library: "Lately with all the emphasis on being 'contemporary' I have perhaps felt a little guilty about my love for the Middle Ages."[480]

Merton meditated on one of his favorite passages, First Corinthians 7:23: "You have been bought with a great price — do not become the slaves of men!" He decided he needed not only physical distance but disciplining distances in thought like Zen and like the mystics of the Middle Ages in order to remain free, committed yet detached from the fruits of action and the frenzy of action alike. "Where is my independence? What is the meaning of solitude, to be free from the compulsion of fashion, dead custom, etc., and to be really open to the Holy Spirit. I see, once again, how muddled and distracted I am. Not *free!"*[481]

A news story that January in the *Louisville Courier-Journal*,[482] widely reprinted in other newspapers, should have accomplished two purposes at once. One was to reassure the public that Thomas Merton, Father Louis, was still at Gethsemani, and to correct rumors which had grown ever louder since the previous September, that he had left the monastery. The second purpose was to make it clear he had withdrawn from making statements on public issues and was seeking a greater solitude. He contributed to the news article himself, breaking his New Year's resolution not to make any contributions that year to his public image. In 1966 he would find the "hidden life," even at the hermitage, more elusive than ever.

For the moment, the heavy snow cut down the number of his visitors more effectively than the news article. He went out to look for deer tracks and studied the "traffic of the birds on the porch," where he had thrown bread crumbs. "Also at least three white-footed mice (pretty with their brown fur and big ears) came out of the wood piles — mice more interested than birds in the crumbs. Birds like the shelter and drink from the pools of melted snow."[483]

The simple "rituals" of everyday existence at the hermitage were harder to accomplish than ever. His hands were cracked and raw with dermatitis, something that cut down on his writing, which he decided was a good thing. When he went to the monastery he found it overheated, and he was afraid he would join so many of the other monks in the infirmary with the annual flu.

Although he had to type wearing dermal gloves much of the time, Merton wrote at length to some of his correspondents. In a letter to "My Very Dear Friend," the Sufi scholar Aziz Ch. Abdul, he gives a detailed account of his hermitage day:

> I go to bed about 7:30 at night and rise about 2:30 in the morning. On rising I say part of the canonical office, consisting of the psalms, lessons, etc. Then I take an hour or an hour and a quarter for meditation. I follow this with Bible reading, and then make some tea or coffee . . . with perhaps a piece of fruit or some honey. With breakfast I begin reading and continue reading and studying until about sunrise. Now the sun rises very late, in summer it rises earlier, so this period of study varies but it is on the average about two hours.
>
> At sunrise I say another office of psalms, etc., then begin my manual work, which includes sweeping, cleaning, cutting wood, and other necessary jobs. This finishes about nine o'clock, at which time I say another office of psalms. If I have time I may write a few letters, usually short (today is Sunday and I have more time). After this I go down to the monastery to say Mass, as I am not yet permitted to offer Mass in the hermitage. Saying Mass requires an altar, an acolyte who serves the Mass, special vestments, candles, and so on. It is in a way better to have all this at the monastery. It would be hard to care for so many things and keep them clean at the hermitage. After Mass I take one cooked meal in the monastery. Then I return immediately to the hermitage, usually without seeing or speaking to anyone except the ones I happen to meet as I go from place to place (these I do not ordinarily speak to as we have a rule of strict silence). (When I speak it is to the Abbot, whom I see once a week, or to someone in a position of authority, about necessary business.)
>
> On returning to the hermitage I do some light reading, and then say another office, about one o'clock. This is followed by another hour or more of meditation. On feast days I can take an hour and a half or two hours for this afternoon meditation. Then I work at my writing. Usually I do not have more than an hour and a half or two hours at most for this, each day. Following that, it being now late afternoon (about four) I say another office of psalms, and prepare for myself a light supper. I keep down to a minimum of cooking, usually only tea or soup, and make a sandwich of some sort. Thus I have only a minimum of dishes to wash. After supper I have another hour or more of meditation, after which I go to bed.[484]

In his journal, Merton records that he was having a hard time keeping to such a strict schedule, and he wondered sometimes where time went at the hermitage.[485] He had always felt it was wrong to discuss his own religious practices in any detail, and he talked to others of the decency of keeping them secret. He had been reserved on this subject, even in his private writing. To Aziz Ch. Abdul in the same letter he makes a rare exception, being careful to put this in terms a Muslim would understand:

Now you ask about my method of meditation. Strictly speaking I have a very simple way of prayer. It is centered entirely on attention to the presence of God and to His will and His love. That is to say that it is centered on *faith* by which alone we can know the presence of God. One might say this gives my meditation the character described by the Prophet as "being before God as if you saw Him." Yet it does not mean imagining anything or conceiving a precise image of God, for to my mind this would be a kind of idolatry. On the contrary, it is a matter of adoring Him as invisible and infinitely beyond our comprehension, and realizing Him as all. My prayer tends very much to what you call *fana*. There is in my heart this great thirst to recognize totally the nothingness of all that is not God. My prayer is then a kind of praise rising up out of the center of Nothing and Silence. If I am still present "myself" this I recognize as an obstacle. If He wills He can then make the Nothingness into a total clarity. If He does not will, then the Nothingness actually seems to itself to be an object and remains an obstacle. Such is my ordinary way of prayer, or meditation. It is not "thinking about" anything, but a direct seeking of the Face of the Invisible. Which cannot be found unless we become lost in Him who is Invisible.

I do not ordinarily write about such things and ask you therefore to be discreet about it. But I write this as a testimony of confidence and friendship. It will show you how much I appreciate the tradition of Sufism. Let us therefore adore and praise God and pray to Him for the world which is in great trouble and confusion. I am united with you in prayer during this month of Ramadan and will remember you on the Night of Destiny. I appreciate your prayers for me. May the Most High God send His blessing upon you and give you peace.[486]

In a later letter that month to Aziz Ch. Abdul Merton explains that while one has a lot of time for reading in the solitary life it seems to be difficult to absorb more than a few pages before wanting to move to meditation and prayer.[487]

By Ash Wednesday, his back was giving him a nagging pain almost all the time and his right hand grew numb after he had written a few lines. Reluctantly, Merton made an appointment at St. Joseph's for a medical examination on March 3. The x-rays showed an operation was now unavoidable, and this was scheduled for March 24.[488]

Back at the hermitage the solitude was all the more precious. Merton had great physical difficulty writing an essay for *Harper's* entitled "Apologies to an Unbeliever," as well as certain misgivings about the subject, reminding himself that he had many friends now who were "very believing unbelievers."[489] He also wrote the first draft of a preface for the Japanese edition of *Thoughts in Solitude* for his friend and translator Yasuwo Kikama.[490] He set this aside to take with him to the hospital.

As it so often happened when he faced the idea of being away from the monastery or when he had just come back from the hospital, Gethsemani became once more Merton's home:

> Certainly the Spirit of Community is excellent and the place is blessed. There are very good men there. It is a sincere and excellent community. Father Chrysogonus is writing fine new melodies which are very authentic, probably as good as any Church music being written now. In fact may turn out to be the best. This is an extraordinary man. Father Flavian may soon be a hermit, and he has impressed many with the seriousness of his life of prayer. Father Eudes is doing an excellent job. Father Callistus is a good prior and will be head of the Norway foundation. And so on. Dom James himself, with all his limitations and idiosyncracies has done immense good to this community by stubbornly holding everything together. He, too, is an extraordinary man, many sided, baffling, often irritating, a man of enormous will, but who honestly and in his own way really seeks to be an instrument of God. And in the end that is what he has turned out to be. I am grateful to have been part of all this.[491]

Gethsemani was about to change once more, at least physically. Father Louis discussed with Dom James the plans for redesigning the interior of the abbey church, the cloister, and the garth. He was on the building committee, which had asked William Schickel to be the designer and liturgical consultant for the renovations. Early ideas and drawings were being considered in Chapter, and there was already a good deal of division. For those who agreed and for those who fought them, the changes would be radical. Even the Gethsemani steeple, the silver arrowhead that identified the monastery for miles around and served much the same purpose in the minds of so many who had visited or who lived there, was declared unsafe.[492] It was taken down, then hauled to the top of one of the knobs, where it now stands virtually forgotten, a nest of bees at each end of the crosspiece of the cross. To Merton a year or two later, the place became Gethsemani's Watts Towers.

With 150 monks, Our Lady of Gethsemani was the largest monastery of the Cistercian Order of the Strict Observance in the world. It had prospered, and it had led others in monastic renewal at a time when there were questions of survival in many monasteries of the Order. There was much for Father Louis to be proud of, yet it was not the Gethsemani he had come to in December 1941. As he left the gate house with Bernard Fox, the abbot's brother, for the drive to Louisville and the hospital on March 23, he was thinking of all this. The operation frightened him, and he wondered if he was saying goodbye.[493]

At the hospital the operation was put off until the 25th, the Feast of the Annunciation. Dr. Thomas M. Marshall (neurosurgeon) performed an anterior cervical fusion to correct the cervical spondylosis. A graft was made from Merton's left ilium.[494] He regained consciousness in his room at St. Joseph's astonished to find so little time had gone by (he had been anxious he might have been unconscious for a whole day and missed taking communion). He was equally astonished to find he could lie on his back without pain.[495]

Merton was a good deal less pleased to learn he was a celebrity at St. Joseph's. He was an impatient patient at best and he disliked hospital routines. Now the staff made visits, both to fuss over him and simply to look in on him.

Six days after the operation, on March 31, early in the morning, Merton was making notes on Eckhart in his reading notebooks when yet another student nurse came in to announce she had just been appointed to this floor of the hospital, she was "his nurse" and she was going to begin by giving him a sponge bath in bed. Merton groaned inwardly and identified her as a "talker." She wanted to talk that morning about the new liturgy. Then, during the bed bath, she told him she came from Cincinnati, and that her father was an artist and liked solitary walks. She knew who her patient was, she had read *The Sign of Jonas* and liked it, though there were passages in the book that troubled her. Before she straightened his room and left him that morning to Eckhart, they talked of *Mad Magazine* and the characters in the "Peanuts" cartoon strip. Apart from talk of Snoopy and some light teasing, the student nurse did her best to show she was in charge. For once Merton agreed to take orders from "his nurse."[496]

The student nurse had black hair (now tucked under her cap), gray, or almond, eyes, pale skin, and striking features. If her ancestry was "dark Irish," there were connections with the Jewish girl, only a few years younger, in the dream Merton had described to Pasternak. In fact there were a great many connections with an imagined portrait that she left Merton to think about when she left the room, so many that perhaps Merton remembered lines of his favorite poet, Rilke:

> . . . Were you not always
> distracted by expectation, as though all this
> were announcing someone to love? . . .[497]

He was well enough to get up and walk in the hospital garden near the Lourdes grotto and one wall of Lourdes Hall, the nurses' hostel. Over Palm Sunday weekend the nurse was gone, and Merton wondered if she had been transferred to another ward. On Monday morning she returned, saying she had had a cold. They found themselves laughing loudly together over things they remembered in *Mad Magazine*.[498] On Tuesday they kept running into one another in the corridors. He had lent her the manuscript of his preface to the Japanese edition of *Thoughts in Solitude* and she had a lot of questions about this, especially what he had said on the hermit's life — *he* couldn't be a hermit . . . ? The supervisor on the hall told her Merton's solitude was serious and to be respected.[499]

On Wednesday night, the student nurse came to Merton's room to say goodbye. For the first time she was in a dress and raincoat, not her uniform, and her hair was free. They used first names, and Merton asked her to write her name in his notebook with her address so he could send her things he had written. She asked if she might come out some Sunday to the monastery to see him. He told her this would be impossible. She looked as though this were a final answer to something she had been questioning.[500] Awkwardly, they got through their goodbyes and she went off in the rain for the airport. Merton wrote her name and address in another notebook with the covering comment that she was a Reader for *Disputed Questions* and *The New Man*. Then he lay awake and listened to the rain, trying to hear the sound of an airplane. She had told him she was flying to Chicago for the Easter holiday to see her fiancé.[501]

Merton returned to Gethsemani on the Saturday of Holy Week, not to the hermitage, but to the infirmary, and he thought himself miserable because he was not at Our Lady of Carmel. He said the Easter offices, then went up to the hermitage in the rain on Easter morning, spending the day there in "a kind of daze."[502]

By Tuesday, April 12, he felt he was back to his routine and had rediscovered his solitude. When S. had returned his copy of the preface to the Japanese edition of *Thoughts in Solitude*, she had teased him that if he valued solitude so highly he hardly needed friendship. Before Merton had left the hospital he had written a letter for her to find when she came back from Chicago, telling her how to write to him under "Conscience Matter," and saying that he needed friendship.[503]

He had written that there was no sentimentality in true love. There had been a good deal of sentimentality in his own attraction to S., as well as flattery in the situation for each of them. It was easy to see how it had all started in the hospital. If he could regain his balance now, this is where it would all end, in sentimentality and a mutually flattering situation.

In the week after he came back from St. Joseph's, he told himself he needed solitude and nothing else — and he believed it. He also wrote in his journals that, at the most, he had written his letter to S. hoping for a few letters from her — ingenuously, he believed this also.[504]

On Tuesday, April 19, he woke to a clear, warm, balmy spring morning. Even before the sun came up he could smell the new grass, which had been cut round the hermitage for the first time the day before. After dawn, he went out to the hedgerows, where the first blossom was appearing, and into the woods, where the early dogwood flowers appeared like white constellations in a screen of pale gray trees and patches of blue sky. It was the first clear day after a week of rain. In the distance they were taking down Gethsemani's silver steeple.[505]

When he went down to the monastery at ten-thirty he felt lighthearted. There was a four-page letter from S. with drawings of "Peanuts" characters. Snoopy had become the hermit who insisted on his solitude. Snoopy's doghouse was the hermitage, where Snoopy stretched out full length and thought in a balloon, "It's nice to have a friend."

On his return to the hermitage Merton replied, sending a declaration of love out under "Conscience Matter."[506] Three days later, on Friday the 22nd, he dined at the monastery with a visiting abbot, enjoying the conversation and the wine, then went off to look for a telephone. S. was out. He tried too early the next morning, then had S. paged at lunchtime, and she was found in the cafeteria. He said he had to come up to Louisville on the 26th for a post-operational checkup at the Medical Arts Building. Could she meet him?[507]

*

We are bound to God in *chesed*. The power of His mercy has taken hold of us and will not let go of us: therefore we have become foolish. We can no longer love wisely . . .[508]

When they were told later, Merton's friends began by congratulating him that he was human — as if a monk could not be human; as if there were any mystery at all that Thomas Merton was human. He had been working to turn himself from the pious, rigid, opinionated young monk into a vulnerable human being for twenty years. He had been exploring trust, above all trust in himself, and trust in St. Augustine's radical conception of Christian confidence, "Love, and do what you will."[509]

For the next four months S. took over the journal. In addition, Merton wrote two separate journals for her that summer.[510] It is necessary to read to the end to understand the beginning. Only on September 4 does he mention the letter he left for S. when he was released from St. Joseph's.[511] Only in March 1967, when he keeps the anniversary of their meeting, does Merton record "the Wednesday of last year's holy week in the hospital — the rainy evening when [S.] came to say goodbye before going to Chicago and when I was so terribly lonely, and lay awake half the night, tormented by the gradual realization that we were in love and I did not know how I could live without her. Last night, too, I lay awake . . ."[512]

In April 1966, Merton talks of S.'s tenderness and of the tenderness he owes her. He makes comparisons with his warm friendship for other women.[513] He speaks at the same time of their establishing a kind of mutual devotion and of his fear that S. may make a cult of him.[514] It is difficult to escape the conclusion that even in his private journals he was kidding himself. Many poems and hundreds of pages of private writing later, after all the words of celebration and complication, he writes in September, "Too much analyzing. I think that this view I have of my love for [S.] in this Journal is a bit distorted by self-questioning, anxiety and guilt. Perhaps I have too much of a tendency to question myself out of existence."[515]

Where Merton admits to losing a sense of proportion, it is all too easy to react by dismissing everything as exaggeration. The truth is not necessarily somewhere in the middle, but it is far simpler: he loved greatly and was greatly loved. He was overwhelmed by the experience and it changed him forever. While this brought a sense of humiliation no exercise of Rancé could have achieved, Thomas Merton never again talked of his inability to love, or to be loved.

The passage he wrote on September 6 goes on even more significantly:

> Anyway, when I get too close to my own worries everything is out of perspective. This is the case in the last four or five pages. I think I really understand the whole thing better, not when I read my own notes but [when I read] *her* notes and her letters, because these are necessary to complete my own ideas and aspirations and love. Also I write much more sanely when I am writing not just for myself (as here) but for her — as in the typed *Midsummer Diary* and the other *Retrospect* I sent her. That is where a more balanced view of our love needs to be sought. This book is too shortsighted — and perhaps ought to be destroyed. It is certainly not for publication.[516]

Even as a writer, then, he needed *her* writing to make the whole.

"We can no longer love wisely . . ." With all the suffering, all the damage to two people — and to others — the story has a moral beyond morals. "The love of creatures" (to use a phrase from Merton's old style) is seldom wise. Sometimes we learn great wisdom in loving unwisely.

*

Even when they carried the words "Conscience Matter," there was no guarantee the letters would not be opened and read by others. S. had no car. Merton couldn't drive. He had discovered that the telephone in the cellarer's office had a direct line to Louisville, but this office in the Steel Building was likely to be crowded. Other telephone lines — from the family guest house, and so on — went through the switchboard at the gate house. Without necessarily wanting to spy, the monk at the gate house might see the red button light up and check to make sure this was not an incoming call.

The obstacles were always frustrating, sometimes a stimulus. When

Merton made his first telephone calls to Lourdes Hall, he found himself shaking. After he finally reached S., they agreed they wanted to meet, they confirmed they were more than friends. Each assumed the other had said it wouldn't work out in any lasting way.[517]

Where Merton relied on his friends to help, their attitude quickly changed from amusement or indulgence to fear for him and irritation at being used. The selfishness of an obsession and an unworldly lack of any discretion on Merton's part made things worse from the beginning. Merton projected his own blindness and naïveté onto others. Later he admitted he had been like a drunken driver, taking one red light after another.

On Tuesday, April 26, a gray, rainy morning, he went to Louisville to see Dr. William C. Mitchell (orthopedics), having arranged for S. to meet him after the post-operational examination. She arrived at the Medical Arts Building "small, shy, almost defiant, with her long black hair, her gray eyes, her white trench coat. (She kept saying she was scared.)"[518]

Merton expected Jim Wygal to provide transportation, make arrangements, and pay for the lunch at Cunningham's. Wygal's manner of covering his obvious embarrassment with a string of man-of-the-world remarks irritated Merton. (Wygal had another reason to be edgy — he had just lost his house in a fire.) Merton and S. were left to themselves for half an hour in their booth at Cunningham's while Wygal went off. After S. left to go back on duty at the hospital, Wygal and Merton went to Louisville Airport for a drink and a talk. Wygal tried to frighten Merton with prophecies of doom: Merton decided Wygal had an "appalling death-wish" that was getting in the way of their friendship.[519]

The drive back to the monastery was a gloomy one. The luncheon itself had been only half a success. S. had had a crisis of her own. Alarmed by Merton's letter and the telephone call of April 23, she had called a priest for advice, only to be told she must break off at once with the monk. After giving this advice the priest tried to make propositions. S. said she had entered the Medical Arts Building like Joan of Arc, ready to do battle with the world, inwardly terrified.[520] Wygal's comments had hardly helped.

When Merton and S. were finally alone, he had tried to calm her by showing her a poem he had written in the hospital, "With the World in My Bloodstream."[521] Merton had not been calm himself. In his journal he wrote that her beauty had given him a shock of rediscovery. Out of uniform, with her long black hair free except for a broad headband, she was more overwhelming than he had remembered. His resolution to talk to her, not to touch her, went for nothing.

Telephone calls brought more telephone calls, letters more letters. One telephone call was legal by monastery rules. Merton had asked the abbot's permission to ask the Fords out for a picnic at Gethsemani on Derby Day. He had leave to make the arrangements: he spent some time convincing the Fords they should bring a nursing friend of his to the picnic, as well as Father John Loftus — then far longer making sure that S. knew the plan.[522]

Derby Day, May 7, was almost a week away. In the meanwhile James Laughlin arrived with Nicanor Parra, and Merton had permission to see the publisher and the poet. When the visitors arrived on the morning of May 5, he was anxiously awaiting them. He was wearing monastery overalls and a t-shirt. He hadn't shaved that day.

Merton suggested a picnic in the Bernheim Forest near Bardstown. It was another clear and beautiful day after a period of intermittent rain and gray skies. Merton was obviously enjoying the picnic and the company, even though the others found him preoccupied. He surprised them by asking for their loose change and then went off in search of a telephone. The callbox outside the café opposite the entrance to the forest proved too public, with two rather tough-looking girls watching. In the car, Merton insisted on driving north, toward Louisville. He found a callbox at last near the Shepherdsville toll gate, and here he made his call. He came back to the car beaming: she could join them.[523]

At Lourdes Hall Merton had some difficulty finding S., and he was afraid he had been recognized. When they were all together, they set off for Louisville Airport. It was still only five o'clock.

Merton had probably chosen the airport in the hope the incongruous party would be less a matter of interest, though he was nervous he would not be allowed into the Luau Room, dressed in overalls "like a convict" and unshaven. He had already discovered that S. attracted attention everywhere, not only because she was strikingly pretty but because she had such obvious vitality.

They encountered no trouble at the door of the Luau Room, and the party made for a table near the windows. Laughlin asked Merton whether he wanted to sit next to his friend or to gaze. He chose to gaze, which meant that, with his back and neck hurting, he had difficulty in seeing the executive jets landing, bringing businessmen to Louisville for the Derby in two days' time. When the drinks came, S. held her glass with a very distinctive gesture, a tiny clue to her uneasiness. Her profile was set off both by her dark hair and by the bold patterns on the drapes behind her. In the afternoon light she looked both radiantly happy and uncertain as she turned to talk to Laughlin about the different kinds of planes, and as Merton took her photograph.[524]

The details enter into a number of accounts and into one of Merton's poems. It was as if that late afternoon in spring was sharply held in the minds of at least three of those present and as if the love was dangerously contagious, even though it made sustained conversation difficult. Nicanor Parra remained the most aloof, yet he was clearly enchanted by S., amused by the priest and the pretty girl. When silences occurred he said that "one should follow the ecstasy."[525] Then he signaled to Laughlin under the table by giving the publisher a number of kicks, until Laughlin said there was some publishing business he and the poet ought to discuss.[526] When the four left the Luau Room and the main building, Parra and Laughlin walked to the car. Merton and S. went off to a knoll of grass at the edge of the airport to be on their own, though in view of the others.

It was an hour later, and getting dark, when they left S. at Lourdes Hall, late when the three men reached the monastery. Merton sat up in his room in the infirmary writing his poem "Louisville Airport, May 5, 1966."[527]

James Laughlin was a good deal more afraid for his old friend than irritated. He couldn't help but think in terms of his own Calvinist upbringing, but when he had Merton alone the next morning and told him he was afraid the Devil might be trying to overturn him through a pretty girl, Merton laughed. Laughlin also felt a sense of guilt at staying at the monastery while aiding Merton to break the rules. It was a trying time for friends with *mundo corde*.

If he talked of temptation, Laughlin had also been impressed by meeting S. He thought much too highly of her to criticize her, as other friends were to do later, if only to try and end the relationship. Laughlin found her very Catholic, very much a lady, very pretty. He had been moved by her obvious love for Merton, while he sensed her distress and tried to respond to it: probably he had an even clearer understanding of how frightened she was than Merton. For her part, S. had identified someone among Merton's friends she could trust.

There was something else. It was many years before S. wrote to James Laughlin to talk to him about it, yet she probably knew he had an unspoken understanding of the situation. With all his love for S., Merton was oblivious to the strain he put upon her, apart from the obvious strains of her own position. To bring this in implies no blame here of Merton; it is only an attempt to understand S. better. Using an initial in these pages and censoring her name in quotations from Merton, while it is a necessary courtesy, cannot help but diminish her a little, and it is worth something to redress this, not just out of a sense of fairness, but because she bore more in courage and in secret sympathy than even Thomas Merton knew.

With all else that she was to him, S. was at last the ideal reader — the Lara, perhaps, to his Yuri. Just as in Pasternak's novel, Lara is the one person to whom Yuri Zhivago can speak freely in a world of bad and lying rhetoric, so S. was the one person to whom Merton felt he could open his whole mind without restraint. His circumstances were quite different from those of Zhivago, yet the same sense of isolation makes the parallel valid. Most of Merton's visitors at Gethsemani were publishers, writers themselves, members of religious orders, activists. Those who were simply readers had been at a distance for more than twenty years. Sometimes they wrote to praise or criticize: there was no free discussion, and there was much Merton himself felt he had always been trying to say to the imagined reader but had not said, for all the books, poems, essays he had published. The journals are evidence of this, so is his desire to keep reworking for publication even the passages he had written first for himself. He had been wanting to talk to someone for a long time: now he couldn't stop. He had chosen well, but he had no sense of the impossible, even in love. Where S. was silent he was certain she had understood everything.

Merton had taken photographs on May 5 at the airport. He took far more at the picnic near Dom Frederic's Lake on Derby Day. On Saturday, May 7, there were a few photographs of the group — many more of S., so many Merton must have made this obvious and S. shy. The Fords remember his friend with affection, the day with grave misgivings.[528] In Merton's journal it was another bright spring day, and he and S. went off for a walk along one of the logging roads. He was quite oblivious to any sense of having tricked or used the Fords or Father John Loftus, or that their worries, when they could not hide them, were anything more than vague reservations on moral grounds.[529]

His complicated struggles in the journal took very little account of his friends or of compromises he expected them to make — hardly an unusual thing in such circumstances, though he might have remembered another affair long ago in which he had been the compromised onlooker. While he was convinced of the *rightness* of so much, he had only to establish what would be really wrong. Sometimes he was aware of arguing fine points, as the monk had done in discussions of moral theology during the Chapters that had particularly bored and exasperated him; often he was not. At any rate, he refined his sense of the vow of chastity to a technical definition that seemed sufficient. It made it doubly ironic, then, that he was writing the "Purity" sections in "Seven Words for Ned O'Gorman":

> By this standard, certain casuistical interpretations which would permit an unhealthy and truncated sexual activity as still legally "pure" will be seen as an affront to the authentic wholeness and purity of man . . .[530]

The essay is unusually warm, a plea for the humanity of individual cases against the timeworn formulas of the old confessional manuals, as well as such obvious and declared enemies as Jansenism, Manichaeism — against all those who ask us to do without bodies, or consider the body evil in itself. The theme is familiar, the spirit informing it new.

The authenticity of purity is grounded in the authenticity of love, Merton argues, and few lovers have doubted this when they say they are in love. The West may or may not be "post-Christian"; it is hardly "post" the Romantic Tradition. The ancient Greeks had an altogether tougher understanding of the "divine madness." Thomas Merton had discovered his authentic wholeness in authentic love. The dilemma, however, was only moved to higher ground: he still, as he went on reminding himself, had obligations, a vow — and he risked solitude. Argue as he would, he was driven back on "certain casuistical interpretations."[531] He took the most lenient of these, interpreting it to mean he was "still legally 'pure.' "

On Saturday, May 14, Merton went to Louisville for another medical checkup, and he and S. had lunch at Cunningham's. Around their talk of records and books, and whether Joan Baez's "Silver Dagger" was her best song, came the dangerous subject of what living together might mean.[532]

On the 19th, Ascension Day, a nursing-student friend drove S. down from Louisville in her pale blue Ford, and then went off for several hours before collecting her again. Merton had plans to walk to the top of Vineyard Knob for a picnic, but S. had brought a bottle of sauterne and a bag of ice. The ice melted as they walked and dripped on her blue shirt, and they decided against the climb.[533]

Merton's decision to ask S. to come to Gethsemani was nothing if not bold, and might not have been made if the abbot had not gone away on May 2. As it was, he saw another monk closely enough to recognize that he was someone visiting from another monastery and to know he had been recognized himself. After the panic moment, Merton could indulge himself in imagining what the other monk was now thinking: "There goes Father Louis a hermit, all alone with a pretty girl. Well, perhaps that is a new slant on the hermit life."[534]

Probably, Merton decided, the monk had thought little more about it: there were times when his reputation for being a mad poet had its compensations.

The picnic on Ascension Day, however, led Merton to the feeling that he was being carried too swiftly and too uncertainly, and it led to a crisis late in the month, when he first telephoned S. to ask her to come down to Gethsemani again, then called her to put the meeting off. Instead, S. left Louisville and went home to her family. Significantly, the change of plan was made on Monday, May 23, the day after he had left his room at the infirmary to sleep at the hermitage — to a realization of what his solitude meant to him and to an increased fear he might lose it.[535]

They both knew their relationship had changed somewhat when they met again at Cunningham's on Saturday, June 4, after Merton had made another visit to the doctor.[536] A week later, on the 11th, he was once more in Louisville. This time he and S. met at Dr. Wygal's office, and he brought a bottle of champagne.

Once more, Merton had moved on a number of assumptions, one of them being that Wygal wouldn't mind if the two of them were at the office while the psychiatrist was out, simply because Merton had used the office for writing and reading when he was in Louisville on earlier occasions. Probably because he didn't want to risk a friendship which meant a great deal to him, Wygal turned his anger, when he found out, into running S. down. In the meantime, there were more important anxieties for Merton than what Wygal thought of him or of S. "The present became a problem at Wygal's."[537] This time there were no evasions or half-statements: Merton wrote an account on Sunday which made it quite clear he was in trouble with his vow, and he confirms this later.[538] On Saturday, returning to Gethsemani, he went to find his confessor. The confession was, of course, secret, but he was no longer the sole judge of his behavior, deciding what had its own rightness, what was simply wrong.

Saturday night he had a long talk on the telephone with S., calling her from the family guest house. They talked about what had happened. On Sunday morning there was another long telephone call, and this time Merton spoke of the possibility of their being permanently together. That afternoon Wygal rang up to criticize S. and to tell Merton he was on a collision course and could only wreck himself. This time Merton was more prepared to listen.[539]

On the 13th, the day the abbot returned, Merton went down in the late afternoon to telephone S. from the Steel Building, only to be told by the cellarer that the monk on the switchboard had heard one of the earlier conversations and had reported it to Dom James.[540]

In the guise of trying to remain charitable, Merton expended a certain amount of wit on the monk who exposed Father Louis's fault out of charity (the monastery formula). The risks of using the switchboard at the monastery have already been explained, and there is no evidence the monk was deliberately spying. At any rate, he gave his name to the file of secret material Merton was sending to James Laughlin for safekeeping.

Where Merton was being so wildly indiscreet he hardly needed a betrayer. On one level, by this time, he may well have been working to get caught. His reaction on being discovered shows, once more, a sense of relief at having an impossible dilemma resolved from the outside:

> In any case, from what I have been through since Saturday, I certainly realize the real spiritual danger I have got into. Things have really got close to going wrong and it is providential that everything has been blocked at the moment. Perhaps it is saving me from a real wreck. Jim Wygal on the phone Sunday was saying "Be careful you don't destroy

yourself!" He is perhaps more right than I thought at the time. Hope I
can see him about it.[541]

On Tuesday, June 14, he went to face Dom James before the abbot
summoned him. Later that day, Merton told Father Flavian he had been
expecting Dom James "to hit the ceiling, and he was real nice, real
nice . . ."[542] In his journal he records that Dom James was "kind and
tried to be understanding to some extent — his only solution was of
course 'a complete break.' "

Merton had been trying to determine which of the telephone calls
had been overheard and reported. The one he feared for most was the
Sunday call, in which he had talked about the possibility of getting
married. That idea had been in the journals, where he quickly dismissed it as impossible: it was impossible for a man who had been a
priest to be married, then, much more specifically, it was impossible
for *him* to get married.[543] When Dom James asked him if he was tempted
to marry, Merton answered, "No! No!"[544]

Dom James offered to write to "the woman." Here Merton refused,
and withheld her name. Dom James quickly went on to talk of strain
and loneliness. He suggested Merton ought to return to the monastery
and live, at least for a time, in the infirmary. Merton drew back at this,
but agreed to doing some ecumenical work "in the retreat house."[545]
Obviously he saw himself losing both S. and solitude. He protected
his solitude, having protected S.'s anonymity, and he accepted most of
the conditions imposed. The absolute prohibition against getting in
touch with S. did not come until two days later. By that time Dr. Wygal had made a visit, and it had been possible for Merton to call S. once
more from the liquor store in New Haven and tell her his calls had been
discovered.[546]

On June 22, he decided it was all over: "The whole thing has to be
given up. Only I don't want her to be hurt unnecessarily"[547] — commonplace words that have the evocative and resonant power of great
poems, if only through the pathos of repetition. Owen Merton would
have caught the echo. It was not over, and it was of his mother, not
his father, that Merton dreamed two nights later:

> I see a tangle of dark briars and light roses. My attention singles out one
> beautiful pink rose, which becomes luminous, and I am much aware of
> the silky texture of the petals. My Mother's face appears behind the roses,
> which vanish.
>
> Also in there somewhere a student nurse who came to see me briefly
> in hospital one day when I was preparing to go out for a walk. I was
> short and rude with her.[548]

Nothing was over; it was only changed. On June 25, Merton went to
Louisville for x-rays. Three months after the operation, his back had
healed. He went looking for S. and found her distraught after being

told by Dr. Wygal to leave Merton alone. She had also had very bad news of her fiancé. The two of them took the elevator up a floor and found a sofa under a window at the end of the corridor. Here S. told Merton she had applied for a job in her home town after her graduation and had volunteered to look after "special cases" — this would be her own sacrifice. At the time he hardly heard her. He gave her the book-length journal "A Midsummer Diary," which he had written for her in the last ten days. Merton insisted they go to lunch at Cunningham's. They played their favorite records. When they went back to St. Joseph's S. vanished through the glass doors of the hospital and Merton wondered if he would ever see her again.[549]

In late June and early July he celebrates days in his journal when his sense of solitude seems to have returned, then goes on to write pages about S. After this he turns on himself: "It is as if I had to start learning — I don't say over again — I have the impression of never having learned and of never having begun."[550]

He talks of the impossibility of leaving Gethsemani and trying to live with S. Yet he made more plans for her to come to the hermitage, and then cancelled these.

When W. H. Ferry came for a visit, Merton insisted they search the back-country roads for a telephone. Merton's friends had learned to arrive with a good deal of loose change in their pockets, a case of beer, and a bottle of bourbon. When Merton explored the idea with Ferry of taking S. somewhere for a few weeks, Ferry was astonished to hear him say he thought it would only be a problem for the monastery and that it could otherwise be kept a secret.[551] Merton's obsession had completely obliterated the knowledge that he was a celebrity. Ferry was so concerned that he asked Merton if he had thought about taking a job at the Center for Study of Democratic Institutions in Santa Barbara. Merton showed enough enthusiasm for the idea for Ferry to approach the abbot. In his journal, however, Merton recorded, "it did not even click for a second. It is just inconceivable." Then he went on as if the idea had come from S.: "I am mildly surprised that someone like [S.], who seems to understand me in so many ways, could find my leaving believable."[552]

There were follies to drive out folly. On June 29 there was another woman visitor at Gethsemani and Merton repeated the indiscretion of September 1959, inviting his guest down to the lake, where they drank and talked and went swimming. Merton admitted later he nearly drowned because he had drunk so much, and that he was thoroughly ashamed of himself, chiefly when he thought of S. (That evening he had telephoned S., changing the plan for her to come out from Saturday to Sunday. Subsequently, he called off her visit altogether.) "Instructive," he writes on July 8, "to see how easily I am shaken and thrown off balance." By September, this has changed to "I was really acting crazy!"[553]

On July 13 he and Jim Wygal went driving around Kentucky in 104-degree heat drinking beer, while Wygal endeavored to part Merton from S. by criticizing her. Wygal refused to help Merton make another attempt to telephone her. In the end, the two of them went to Loretto. Merton's friend, Mother Luke, was away. The two visitors spent an hour in the parlor, where Merton talked to several of the nuns about Zen. He had just heard of the death of Suzuki, and he asked the nuns to pray for him. Later they listened to one nun play Gershwin and Debussy on the piano. While this incident was not a very notable wickedness, Merton had no permission for the visit, and it had nothing to do with the solitary life: "I enjoyed it, but felt uneasy about talking so much and so glibly."[554]

On Saturday, July 16, he went to see Dr. Mitchell in Louisville about a sprained ankle. S. collected him from the doctor's office in a taxi, and they went for a quiet picnic in Cherokee Park. For Merton it was one of the most beautiful of their times together, only disturbing to him because he knew he was making it more and more difficult for them both — far more difficult for her. That night he couldn't sleep and he sat up writing a long poem.[555]

The meeting produced a new crisis of his intentions. He had disobeyed orders, arguing that it was out of charity and a need to console S.:

> I am still committed to see her once more before she leaves, but really that should end it. Extremely difficult! I wonder if I can really do it! Hence I should not be too upset about the possibility of Dom J. clamping down again — as if I ought to resist. If he does, I must certainly see in it God's will and accept it. How I will do it, I don't know — must keep praying for the grace — with a conviction that this "union with the saving will of God" will benefit her even more than myself, perhaps. (Is this after all one of the real purposes of our love?)[556]

Merton had talked before this to others about "needing Dom James." On this occasion it is difficult to find any other conclusion than that he wanted to use Dom James to resolve what was impossible to him: he wanted Dom James to say "No."

When the abbot did summon him to his office on July 28, it was not to talk about acts of disobedience Dom James knew nothing about, but to ask for an explanation of Father Louis's unhermitlike behavior on the day of the visit to Loretto. The abbot had heard too, from more than one source, about the drunken swim. In the background to the interview was another cause for Dom James to be angry. W. H. Ferry had approached Dom James with the suggestion that Merton leave the monastery temporarily to take the job at Santa Barbara, something Ferry said would provide a period of rest and an opportunity for Merton to distance himself from the situation and think over the future. While Dom James made no mention of this to Father Louis, he did talk about the strain proving too much.[557] The abbot's plan was for Father Louis to come back into the monastery and to teach Scripture as master of the juniors. To fend this off, Merton made a promise to remain at the hermitage unless he had permission to leave from the abbot. For the moment, the matter was resolved in this way. "Scripture professor!!!" he wrote in his journal.[558]

There was another interview with the abbot on August 4, and this time they returned to the subject of S. When Merton felt the abbot was laughing at him, and Dom James remarked that he was thinking of writing a book on how to get hermits into heaven, Merton got angry:

> And I burned interiorly. And was mad at myself for feeling it! The man has to gloat: I have offended and disturbed him many times and now I should have the decency to let him enjoy his innocent satisfaction. However on leaving I said: "When the baby is born you can be its godfather!" A slight shadow crossed his face and he laughed with less enthusiasm. Was I really kidding? We are a pair of damned cats.[559]

It was just the kind of parting shot that had brought Merton trouble before, and which had led to much misunderstanding.

Something had now been resolved. Merton was in agony from bursitis. He went to Louisville for a cortisone shot on an earlier date than he had first intended so that he would not be there on August 12, the day before S.'s graduation and two days before she would leave for home. It complicated way of cancelling their plan to be together again in the park ("I am still committed to see her once more before she leaves . . .") He did not see S. when he went for the shot, then for an appointment with the neurosurgeon.

At the Medical Center he mailed the letter that cancelled their plans to meet, "saying in effect Goodbye." When he imagined the letter reaching her he was overwhelmed by a sense of desolation and heartlessness. He tried to telephone her and failed. He sketched out the beginning of what he thought would be his last poem to her, a blues in the style of Bob Dylan. "In Marshall's office, I was almost visibly crying, I was so torn by loneliness and longing to talk to her":

> And knowing it was hopeless. Worse still, driving out on the turnpike — first passing near the hospital, I thought I was slowly being torn in half. Then several times while I was reciting the office, felt silent cries come slowly tearing and rending their way up out of the very ground of

my being. It was awful. And she must have "heard" them. I got scared. There was nothing I could do with these metaphysical howls . . .[560]

*

". . . I am nobody's answer, not even my own."[561]

Merton's writings of that summer (almost all of them for the eyes of one or two people only) have a range of frankness remarkable even for him. They contain a great deal of special pleading, some self-pity, and much plain bad writing. For all this, there are passages that catch the reader's breath for their boldness and lucidity. He was frank about himself as a lover. He was not afraid, either, of challenging, in the light of new experience, ideas he had worked on for years in his published writing, often undercutting these with devastating effect, especially where he now saw in himself "A kind of poetic religiosity and an intention to be interiorly honest. And above all the insistence on being different from other people."[562]

When the Hammers came over from Lexington for a picnic on June 18, he took them to the same spot near Dom Frederic's Lake where the Derby Day picnic had taken place. He told his two trusted friends about S. and he read for them the love poems he had already written. The three of them then discussed the possibility of a private printing. When they went back to talk of the love which had produced the poems, Merton found Victor and Carolyn Hammer more sympathetic and understanding than anyone except for James Laughlin and Nicanor Parra. The Hammers agreed to take his letters out and to bring letters from S. addressed to their house. Their advice, however, was to finish the affair, and they spoke as if it were already finished.[563]

For Merton's confessor and his abbot, S. was an intruder, a threat. One can understand this: it would have been hard for them to think otherwise. Merton wrote that everyone had forgotten there were two people involved, and this made him angry. Dom James had come to his own conclusions when Father Louis said he did not want to get married. While he took little account of the feelings of others (except, of course, S.'s feelings), he thought himself cruelly isolated, and S. more isolated still. Even his friends "in the world" talked only about scandal, of the damage to *him*.

Merton's friendship with Wygal suffered most, though he felt he needed Wygal.[564] He was angry with S.'s friend, the student nurse who had brought her out for their meeting on May 19, then found reasons why she had to cancel later plans for Pentecost (May 28) and Saturdays in June. Subsequently in his journal, Merton came to the conclusion that this had been providential, and the woman's reluctance to cooperate had saved him.[565]

There were other matters than inconsistencies and a certain blind-

ness, though it is important to remember that Merton is his own ac-
cuser. He had kept back the information that he had left a love letter
at the hospital and had made the first telephone call planning a meeting. This gave others the impression S. had been the initiator. Merton
had joined in Wygal's earthy talk before the first meeting at Cunningham's, which had made a bad situation worse for S. It was not like
him, either, to put down women. In his own journal he was not above
speculating about S. and other men.[566] When he telephoned her on
May 23, S. was called away to answer another call. At first he was jealous, then he used the incident as a "pretext for trying to get loose, which
is very bad of me and not honest."[567] It turned out the other call was
from her mother. He had no need to stimulate the affair with Proustian jealousy, and he knew it. There is a chilling passage in the journal: "If I drop her (and I suppose in a way I must — at least eventually) it must be gently and lovingly and not with pride (not seeking any
kind of revenge! and not flatly and forever . . .)"[568] It is not unfair to
lift this out of context, or to list incidents which gave him a bad conscience. What was most damaging of all, and something he was less
aware of, was that he led S. on to feeling there was some possibility of
his leaving Gethsemani to marry her. Then he returned to his journal,
both to write of the impossibility and to accuse S. of lack of understanding.

After the day in Wygal's office he wrote:

> When I got home I called her and we were talking again, foolishly, of
> possibilities, of living together, my leaving here, "marrying" her etc. But
> it is all preposterous. Society has no place for us and I haven't the gall
> it takes to fight the whole world particularly when I don't really want
> married life anyway, I want the life I have vowed.[569]

There are paragraphs in his writing which are very typical of his attempt to catch his own thought on paper. He begins by attacking himself for being a fool, then works the argument gradually around to a
cause for celebration: "Furthermore they all told me what I suffer and
they don't know half the story. They can't even imagine all the joy
that was in it. They know nothing, really, only enough to build a few
possible scandals for themselves in their own heads."[570]

The Hammers had brought copies of The New Yorker on the 18th, to
show Merton an article on China. He read the article but his attention
was largely taken by the advertisements. Their very sophistication depressed him. The New Yorker ads would come into his writing in many
different ways later on; for the present, they confirmed his instinctive
feeling that he could not return to the world, its values, its incessant
bombardment of such distractions. He admitted to S., "I am not as open
as I thought."[571]

He was equally afraid of being forced back into the life of the monastery, sensing this would mean only that he would react by "going A.W.O.L." (as Dom James expressed it).[572] When his abbot put pressure on him, he obeyed rather than give up the hermitage. Yet he undercut everything he had said earlier about obedience when he wrote to S. to say he obeyed only to conform with the wrong idea of the hermit life, he did not agree or accept. He went on, "I am still the guy who obeyed in The Sign of Jonas, and still riding in the whale's belly."[573]

Reading Camus in early June, Merton had been brought to face much he had evaded earlier, meeting it now at a time when he was both strongly sustained by his love and very vulnerable. It was hot and he was "sitting around drinking Christian Brothers' brandy out of an old marmalade jar big enough to get ice cubes in and not as big as a whole glass." His bursitis had flared up, keeping him in almost constant pain. He told S.:

> I am reading Camus on absurdity and suicide: The Myth of Sisyphus. I had tried it before and was not ready for it because I was too afraid of the destructive forces in myself. Now I can read it, because I no longer fear them, as I no longer fear the ardent and loving forces in myself. If they all turn against me I don't care, but I think for some strange reason they are all for me. As to suicide: I would be delighted to drop dead, but killing myself would be just too much trouble.[574]

Something of this, if in a lighter and macaronic key, comes into his June 1966 letter to Bob Lax. He had been talking about being the age for heart attacks (even if he had no history of a heart condition):

> . . . But I plan first to be struck by lightning from going to walk in thunderstorms. I snap the fingers at life. Well it is getting late and I must let out those dam baboons again.[575]

He had borrowed a record player and recordings by Joan Baez and Bob Dylan. He played the music over and over, in particular the Baez recording of "Silver Dagger," which he sang to himself when it was off the turntable. He had promised an article on Dylan to Ed Rice for *Jubilee,* and Rice was sending him more Dylan records. Merton's poems to S. were falling into Dylan's style at times, while after one particularly tortured passage in his "Midsummer Diary" he broke in with "Even Bob Dylan is not perfect."[576] It amused him, however, to hear an autobiography would be coming out that summer, when Dylan was only in his late twenties. Perhaps Thomas Merton had forgotten he had been writing an autobiography at much the same age and others had been amused. Now he was hoping Dylan would set to music the long poem he had drafted in one of his reading notebooks in April, "The Prospects of Nostradamus."[577]

The drinking, going over and over the affair in poems and journals, listening to records, reading about suicide, the incident at the lake, the raw sense of his own loneliness — all this added up to something Merton felt was corny, as well as wasteful. He knew he had to fight his way back to authenticity of a new kind, one that took full account of the best of his discoveries about himself, the recognition as early as the first week in May that ". . . the deepest capacities for human love in me have never even been tapped [and] that I too can love with an awful completeness."[578]

He redefined solitude in his own terms, not as the enemy of S., but as the protector of them both — what they had been to each other, what he felt they would always be. And yet the approval of others was still a factor, and this was not limited to S.'s approval. There were some he looked to, also, for confirmation of his own ideas of the solitary life.

He told S. he had heard from Nora Chadwick, explaining that his correspondent was someone he loved but had never met, an authority on Celtic mysticism. A retired Cambridge professor and eighty years old, she was still informing Merton about the Celtic solitaries. Eleanor Duckett, another old friend by correspondence, and a professor at Smith who knew and respected "the *reality* of monastic solitude," wrote that she recognized and celebrated the fact that he was living the life of a true hermit in the mid-twentieth century.[579]

Merton went on to say he had also heard from a Moslem shaikh, or spiritual master, Ahmad al'Alawi, and that he had been recognized as a true mystic with whom an exchange of ideas was possible: "It means I have a living place in a living and secret tradition. It can have tremendous effects. I can see that already. Here again, the Shaikh attaches considerable importance to my life in solitude."[580]

Merton hurried to reassure S. he had not taken on Moslem rites and disciplines "on top of everything else"; it was simply that he had been accepted by others — by Zen scholars, by authorities in the real tradition of Christian monasticism and the lives of Celtic hermits, by living Islamic mystics — as a solitary. Because this was clear to those Merton trusted, he felt his vocation was confirmed. To the old argument that "he needed people" Thomas Merton had a revealing new answer. The general answer remained what it had always been for him — the solitary must be open to others. His personal response is:

> . . . I can never be anything else than solitary. My loneliness is my ordinary climate. That I was allowed to have so many moments of complete accord and harmony and love with another person, with her, was simply extraordinary. I like people, but usually I am tired of being with others after about an hour. That I could be with her for hours and hours and not be tired for an instant of her — it was a miracle, but it did not mean that I was not essentially solitary.[581]

Beyond refining solitude, protecting it, even boasting of it, came a sense that, whatever appearances might be, in risking much he had come closer to God. He said he would not be foolish enough to talk of this even to her.

It was hardly incidental, though far less important to Merton, to know he had come closer to himself that summer. Yet which self — where there had been so many definitions of self? In his journal now he challenged much of what he had said about the true self and the false self in his published writing:

> I must manfully face this judgment and find my center not in an ideal self which just *is* (fully realized) but in an actual self which does all it can to be honest and to love truly, though it still may fail . . .[582]

Merton went most deeply into everything S. had come to mean for him in certain isolated pages he wrote for her during the crisis period between May 19 and May 26, but probably did not send her. In these he said they could find themselves now only in each other, that each of them was on the threshold of a love hidden even from them. They had the chance of creating a new paradise, one that was still only potential, but which God had reserved for them alone. He was afraid they might be prevented from making this real, not only because his superiors might part them, but because they might blunder into some act of repossession of self.

He saw S.'s temptation in a desire to overwhelm him with her sexuality, his temptation in a desire to run away. Neither of them was yet ready to face the inevitable change in their love that complete sexual fulfillment would bring about. Deeper even than his tie to his vow was an instinctive sense that this might destroy him. Even if it did not, it would inevitably distract them both from something far greater. So it had proved in his own past, and he wondered if his retreat into solitude hadn't been a kind of lamentation for the impossibility of human love.[583] Now he was terrified that this enormous opening out he had made to love one other human being with no remaining fear of rejection would be stopped, wasted, either by intrusion from the outside or by self-protective drives within themselves — hers of wanting fulfillment, his of evasion. Just as he saw a certain peril in the ambiguous relief sexual completeness would bring, so he saw he might be tempted to find relief in discovery by his superiors. In late May 1966, there were times he did not want to run, times he did not want to be stopped by discovery. "I for one want to go on: I know you do, too . . ." This would mean, he said, accepting a risk like death for a realization about human love few approached, most shied from: "We human beings want love, and we don't want love." For the two of them, however:

There is something deep, deep down in us, darling, that tells us to let go completely. Not just the letting go when the dress drops to the floor and bodies press together with nothing between, but the far more thrilling surrender when our very being surrenders itself to the nakedness of love and to a union where there is no veil of illusion between us. Darling, I long for it madly. Do you see? Do you need me as well?[584]

Merton gave "A Midsummer Diary: Piece of a Small Journal" the subtitle "Or the account of how I once again became untouchable." He dedicated it, adding his own second initial to her first in what may have been a marriage of the imagination.

Merton's love for S. was not something he wanted to terminate, or could terminate. He tried to preserve it in a new solitude, though there were times when he seemed ready to risk even this to join her during the next year.[585] He saw her, briefly, twice when he was in hospital in October 1966. There was a period of silence toward the end of 1967. In the summer of 1968 he telephoned her once more. By then there was nothing she could do to help him, and he hung up on a note of desperation.

> We are two half people wandering
> In two lost worlds.[586]

*

For all the turmoil of the summer, the heat, the constant pain, Merton had been working. Apart from the poems and the secret journals, he had been reading Camus and filling a number of notebooks with notes he would draw on for the essays he wrote on Camus later. He had also completed an introductory preface for his friend John Wu's book, *The Golden Age of Zen*.[587] The summer also brought one visitor with whom Merton established an immediate bond.

The Vietnamese Buddhist monk Thich Nhat Hanh arrived on May 28,[588] in the middle of Merton's most serious crisis, and it may be he was all the more welcome for this. The Buddhist monk immediately became popular in the community, and his talk at the conference on Sunday, May 29, was a great success, something Merton noted, adding his own feeling of warmth for the community. Nhat Hanh explained that during training there was an early period when the Buddhist "novice" was not permitted to meditate, and he made the comment "Before you can meditate you've got to learn how to close doors." There was a good deal of appreciative laughter to show the Christian monks caught the aptness of the remark.[589]

Merton felt Nhat Hanh's visit and the conference had done much to dispel any idea that Buddhism was a religion based on nihilism, and to establish instead a connection between Buddhist reverence for life and the love of all living things in the spiritual teaching of St. Francis.

Merton's own talks with Nhat Hanh gave him further insight into the training in Buddhist monasteries. He and Nhat Hanh soon found, too, they had much shared experience: they had both been in monasteries for many years; they were both poets; each had written a poem to a brother killed in war. When Nhat Hanh talked of the situation in his own country Merton began to realize the visitor had already risked his life and that he would face a dangerous return to Vietnam, where he was unpopular with all the warring factions.

Both the shared experience and the sense of peril moved Merton to write the essay "Nhat Hanh Is My Brother," "a human and personal statement and an anguished plea" for the safety of the Buddhist monk, which ends:

> Do what you can for him. If I mean something to you, then let me put it this way: do for Nhat Hanh whatever you would do for me if I were in his position. In many ways I wish I were.[590]

Merton's bursitis grew no better in August, and this meant going to Louisville for further cortisone shots, which were painful in themselves ("What they done is stick me with painful and rasping cortisone which have the bad kickback eight hours later POW I hit the ceiling . . ." he wrote to Lax).[591] His bed at the hermitage had now been fitted up with traction, so he no longer had to stay in the infirmary for treatment. He was seeing Father John Eudes Bamberger, the psychiatrist at the monastery, rather than Dr. Wygal. He found the talks valuable, but he was embarrassed when he learned that the abbot had consulted Father Eudes over what everyone else insisted on calling "the problem," while he himself thought of it often as the solution to much that had been lacking in his life. Merton wondered how many others at the monastery looked upon him now as "a priest who has a woman."[592] It hardly helped, when he continued to advise others on spiritual matters, to discover that there were many like him in the Church.[593]

On June 12 he had talked at his Sunday conference about technical achievements and had made light fun of a scientific project to spy on grizzly bears with electric equipment in order to study their mating habits. When he looked up, Merton thought he caught sympathetic smiles on the faces of some in his audience. He decided he had been taking himself altogether too seriously, both as a delinquent and as a lover, and he accepted the smiles with gratitude.[594]

He continued to believe he was the sole judge at Gethsemani of his experiment as a solitary. He had no defense against the evidence that he had been a bad priest and a bad monk. While Merton knew this would probably mean little to many of his friends in the world, it hurt him deeply. It was a time when he thought back with a new understanding to those novices who had left Gethsemani when he was novice master because they had not received a recommendation from him, as well as to others he felt had been driven out:

> Many have gone away injured
> From the house of God . . .[595]

The late summer and early fall of 1966 was a time when Merton set about the quiet task of self-correction, though there were reverses and setbacks. There were also disturbances. *Life* magazine published an extract from the forthcoming *Conjectures of a Guilty Bystander* early in August.[596] For the first time many of the general public were presented with the "naked face" of the hermit. The publication brought letters from all sorts of unexpected quarters, including the one mentioned earlier from Iris Bennett.[597]

In most cases, Merton read the letter before he saw the article. There was a delay before the abbot sent him tear sheets from the copy belonging to Leo Gannon, who ran the family guest house with his wife, Leone. Merton's anticipation turned to something like panic:

> When one displays himself
> In this ambiguous way
> The world outside storms in
> And imprisons him.[598]

The appearance in *Life* seemed to bury forever his resolution at the beginning of the year to be free of his public image, while the captions reminded him forcibly of the *New Yorker* advertisements, in this case an advertisement for the hermit life. The "world outside" wasted little time in storming in. Two seminarians had dropped by, without going through the gate house, to tell Merton how influential Camus had become among young Catholics.[599] If they were no threat, they were a nuisance — and there was the memory of the man with the gun Merton believed had been meant for him.

The old days when he had been bothered only by hunters were over. Few unwanted visitors kept his own early hours, and the mornings were usually safe. In the afternoons he set out with a book for the woods. He was still haunting the places of the summer. He had told S. earlier he had read the poems of the Italian poet Eugenio Montale by Dom Frederic's Lake.[600] Now he took the poems of the French poet René Char and of the Scottish poet Edwin Muir, as well as his "life-raft," Eckhart.[601] It was something, he found, to be able to read once more and to absorb what he was reading. In his writing he went back again and again to discoveries he had made, afraid of losing these or distorting them. There was a sense that he had written too often about love in the past without knowledge: now he had to catch up and correct. Merton had revised the preface to the Japanese edition of *Thoughts in*

Solitude twice already. The first draft, which S. had criticized, had been abandoned for a second version, which took account of her criticism and appeared at the front of the translation. Now Merton reworked and amplified the preface into an essay, "Solitude and Love," which was published later that year in *The Critic*.[602]

The self-correction had to include the new perspective. Before he entered the monastery in 1941, Merton had swung by reaction from freedom to order and then again to freedom. This was exhausting and produced no sense of authenticity: he resisted the order and had little pleasure in the freedom. During a long period at Gethsemani he submitted to discipline because he told himself he needed this. He struggled after 1958 to make himself open and vulnerable. Others were ready now to tell him this had resulted in disaster. He understood the summer differently. Merton was determined to restore the broken discipline in a way that would still leave him open and vulnerable. He would have to take into account his lack of common sense — his "unworldliness," to give it a kinder tone — his tendency to play the fool, to give his own view of it. He needed to be simply the man he was before God. He did not need an ideal image, or a public image. The saint was "the friend of God." "Holy" meant simply one who had been marked by God, as a workman might put his stamp on a chair or a building. It did not have much to do with goodness, except in the sense that the Workman was good and proud of His good work. How many knew this? If an editor in New York chose to put "the saintly monk" or "the holy hermit" in a piece of copy, this somehow became "here is a monk who is the essence of goodness." It was small wonder the reader equated such claims with advertisements, with sponsors who announced against rival claims that their product was "more natural," "more unique."

Many in public life expended a great deal of energy in protecting their public image. For Thomas Merton the reaction was quite different. Sometimes his desire to avoid cult worship came out in a deliberate wish to shock with a good earthy comment, a statement that we are only saved by scandal, or a quotation from his favorite, Lenny Bruce, or a mock-erudite reference to *Mad Magazine*. Yet he knew that to put a clown's mask over a prophet's was little gain when he wanted to have done with masks for what was really "the naked face." The journals at times were a method of sabotaging the ideal Merton. If they preserved the spontaneity, they preserved the scandal, the whole man (whole, sometimes, to the point of exhaustion). The pages on God, on prayer, on humility, would distress some; the pages of criticism of the Church would worry many; the praise of the Church, others; references to drinking, to dreams, to periods of depression — references to his own evasions, to his capacity for kidding himself, to his being less than an honest lover, to costly mistakes of fact and judgment . . . . When he was used, or used up, the journals would speak of him without editing, crossings-out, polishing — a place where the narrow-minded, or those who had made a cult of him, would founder, and where the seekers of truth without pretense would find him.

He began thinking of establishing a trust which would restrict the publication of certain of his writings until twenty-five years after his death. Others might have to be kept back for longer. He wanted nothing suppressed, certainly not his love for S. ". . . It needs to be known too, for it is part of me. My need for love, my loneliness, my inner division, the struggle in which solitude is at once a problem and a 'solution.' And perhaps not a perfect solution either."[603]

*

That autumn the monastery was at last committed to a foundation in South America. The party would leave for Chile in early September, and Father Louis, for all his early desire to join them, knew his health would not allow this. His bursitis was making him fearful once more about permission to remain at the hermitage, so that when he was presented with an opportunity to confirm his solitary life at Gethsemani he agreed readily. He went into a private retreat to prepare himself before making a permanent commitment, trying to review everything that had happened in the summer in a more objective light.

On Thursday, September 8, he went down to the monastery to sign the short formula he had drafted:

> I, Brother M. Louis Merton, solemnly professed monk of the Abbey of Our Lady of Gethsemani, having completed a year of trial in the solitary life, hereby make my commitment to spend the rest of my life in solitude in so far as my health may permit.[604]

Somewhat ungenerously in the circumstances, he wrote in the journal, "Dom James signed it with me, content that he now had me in the bag as an asset that would not go out and lose itself in some crap game."[605]

Dom James was probably more content with the idea that he had protected Father Louis against himself.

Merton was chafing at the recurrence of this by now well-worn theme, and also the repetition of "unhermitlike" from his abbot. He suspected the abbot thought even the article in *Life* unhermitlike, although the article had brought a good deal of money to the monastery, and this had gone to further the renovation.[606]

Whatever any of the other monks knew of Father Louis, he was not the main source of controversy. Most minds, that fall, were preoccupied with the new basilica, cloister, and cloister garth.

A number of the monks faced the stark and austerely beautiful interior of the abbey church with the sense there were now no quiet, hidden corners in which to pray and meditate.[607] The original plan had been to leave the bricks bare after the plaster had been removed, but the handmade bricks of the 1860s proved too fragile, and in the end only the great beams were left exposed. The walls were painted white, which gave them something of the appearance of raw wool — another connection, for those who chose to make it, between the Cistercians and the Sufis.

It was felt there was no need for a cloister garth that simply reproduced the grass, bushes, and trees outside the monastery walls, now that the monks had access to these. The creation of a garth with the effect of an urban square was supposed to link the monastery with the inner, and secular, city at a time when "relevance" was all.[608] The shock of the new was probably greatest for those monks who had lived through all the changes at Gethsemani in the past twenty years, for whom at least the monastery church and the cloister had remained familiar. Dom James chose those who were most disturbed by the transformation to fill posts or to continue their theological and biblical studies in Rome. The renovations of 1966–67, unlike the necessary rebuilding of 1964–65, made it clear to all that Gethsemani was now a wealthy monastery. Brother Frederic Collins of Gethsemani Farms asked to go with the party to Chile, believing the new foundation would bring him closer to a life of poverty.[609]

The same Thursday Merton made his commitment the records arrived from Ed Rice, and Merton enjoyed the sound of Bob Dylan's "Gates of Eden" pouring out through the hermitage windows into the surrounding woods.[610] He could no longer chop his own wood, and with winter approaching a propane heater was installed. Other improvements were planned for the spring.

There had been sixteen or more "secret" poems that summer. The range was wide, in both the forms Merton chose and the quality. He was also working on a new collection, called first "Edifying Cables," and then published in March 1968 as *Cables to the Ace*.[611]

For many this is Merton's most baffling collection. Merton's late poetry has been unfairly neglected; the few critics have seen *Cables to the Ace* as a stage on the way to a far greater work, the long poem *The Geography of Lograire*. The connections between the two are obvious. However, Merton had already begun to sketch out passages for *Lograire* at the end of 1966. For *Lograire* he was exploring different materials, and was also under different influences. The best preparation for reading *Cables to the Ace* is the lively macaronic letters Merton and Robert Lax were exchanging in 1966, later published as *A Catch of Anti-Letters*.[612] It is obvious from these that both attraction and repulsion had been at work in Merton's response to the advertisements in *The New Yorker*. He was now asking W. H. Ferry and others to send him materials of this kind (the more outlandish the better, though he had to point out to Ferry that he was not strong enough for tear sheets from *Esquire* or *Playboy*).[613] From material which had come in this way Merton also passed on to Lax news items on the astonishing career of the West Coast prophetess Miss Velma. In fact, the possibilities of anti-poetry struck him as almost limitless. Of *Life*, in which he had just appeared, Merton wrote in 1960, "If it wanted to be a deliberate satire, it could not do better. Or has the parody now become completely real? I have not yet reached the point where my despair would believe this."[614]

The chief influence was the anti-poetry of Parra. Merton had once written harsh words about Surrealist poetry.[615] By 1966 his long period of enthusiasm for the South American poets with their links to Surrealism had changed this, putting him very much under their spell at the time of *Cables to the Ace*. Earlier, too, Merton had worried that poems he had written did not seem fitting as the work of a Catholic and a priest. Now, he was anxious not to show his "religious party card"[616] in his verse.

Most of Merton's poetry of 1966–67 has the fun of play (pure or sardonic), though at times the game is too private. As he told a writing class in Louisville:

> Yes, we have to learn to write disciplined prose. We have to write poems that are "Poems." But that is a relatively unprofitable and secondary concern compared with the duty of first writing nonsense. We have to learn the knack of free association, to let loose what is hidden in our depths, to expand rather than to condense prematurely. Rather than making an intellectual point and then devising a form to express it, we need rather to release the face that is sweating under the mask and let it sweat out in the open for a change, even though nobody else gives it a prize for special beauty or significance.[617]

By the time he wrote this, in the spring of 1968, he had discovered the necessary form for a work that did not cramp the spontaneity and that still allowed sight of the face beneath the mask. Long ago, at Perry Street and at St. Bonaventure's, Merton had struggled to free his prose by "writing well by writing badly." Then, his poetry had been labored, if not polished. By 1966, it was the turn of the poetry to become freer.

*

When Merton went down to the monastery one day he heard that Father Stephen Pitra, a monk for whom he had a great affection, had just collapsed by the gate house. Merton joined the other monks in praying beside Father Stephen, who was taken first to the post office, then to the provisional chapel, where Merton kept vigil.[618] The tradition at the monastery was to greet the death of a monk with joy. James Laughlin had been astonished one day during a visit when a discussion on publishing plans in the abbot's office was interrupted by the news that one of the monks had died — both Dom James and Merton responded with alleluias.[619] Yet each of the conflicting emotions had a part in the tradition — joy for the monk finishing his spiritual journey, sadness for those who remained on earth.

On October 6, Merton received a visitor he had been longing to see. They had met only once, and briefly, though they had corresponded. This was Jacques Maritain's last visit to the United States, and John Howard Griffin had promised to bring him to Gethsemani. The meeting has often been described, and Griffin was able to make a moving photographic record.[620]

Merton came down to the monastery on the morning of the 7th to breakfast with Maritain, Griffin, Elizabeth Manual, and Penn Jones. When Father J. Stanley Murphy, Dan Walsh, and Jack Ford also arrived, Merton insisted his guests should come up to the hermitage. Here he banked the fire with logs, led Jacques Maritain to the rocker before the fire, and wrapped Maritain's legs with a blanket. Merton made coffee for everyone, a strain on the hermitage supply of cups and glasses. His attempt to get the others to agree that Bob Dylan was the American François Villon was not a great success, and Maritain obviously thought good time was being taken up listening to a record when they could have been talking. However, they enjoyed Merton's reading of his own poems.

Merton led his guests back to the monastery, where Mass was said in Latin for Maritain in the provisional extern chapel. That afternoon the guests went out to a spot in the woods where they sat and talked. In the evening, Maritain spoke to the community.

Maritain explained that he had probably been foolish to oppose Mass in the vernacular, though he did object to some of the French translations. A discussion about one translation of the Parable of the Wise and Foolish Virgins provided Merton with an opportunity to present Maritain with the gift of a poem after the visit. The translation Maritain had chosen as an example was *"les vièrges étourdies"* (*"étourdi"* meaning scatty, confused, dizzy). Traditionally in France it had been *"les vièrges sages et les vièrges folles."* At one point in the visit Maritain became muddled. "Forgive me, *cher* Tom," Maritain said, pressing the palms of his hands against the sides of his head. "I can't remember. It's gone from my head. I am a little *étourdi*."[621]

The end of October brought another deterioration of Merton's health and another trip to the hospital. He knew that S. was returning with her class to Louisville to take examinations during the week of October 20. Though he was now in St. Anthony's, not St. Joseph's, she visited him twice. If the visits were brief, they were enough to reopen the wounds of the summer. His return to the hermitage was a sad and difficult one. Unable to sleep, he dressed and walked in the woods under the moon. Nothing had changed, yet the hermitage had been a great gift: "All I have ever sought is here: how foolish not to be content with it — and let anything trouble it, without need."[622]

In his journal he wrote that the next visitor did much to reinforce his resolve and confidence in his vocation. Sidi Abdeslam, who spoke no English and who lived in Algeria, arrived with Bernard Phillips of Temple University and with a disciple and the disciple's wife, who could translate from Arabic. Merton sensed that he and Sidi Abdeslam were able to communicate beyond the translated words.[623]

It was a week in which Merton attacked himself more savagely than usual, seeing in himself great powers of self-deception and wondering whether he had not proved so vulnerable earlier that year precisely because he was seeking a chance to run from his vocation. Now a man he recognized as a true mystic, a man who represented the most authentic tradition in Islamic spirituality, left him with the message that he was very close to a mystical union and that the slightest thing could bring that union about.

Sidi Abdeslam plunged Merton into a wholly different kind of despair and into a resolution to be worthy of both message and messenger, even though he only half believed what had been said. When so many others recognized the authenticity of his vocation, how could he himself ever question it, or risk losing it? He tramped the fields in a squall of rain which turned into a snowstorm, making his way to another high place, St. Joseph's Hill, a spot to which he had gone in many a crisis earlier. Here he tried to find an answer to an almost impossible question. False identity was thrust upon one by others: How was authentic identity to be tested using the recognition and response of others?

When the snow fell about him, enclosing him within his enclosure, he plunged into a reading of Faulkner as he had plunged into Camus.[624] The hermitage was warmer that winter, even if the propane heater gave off a smell which was less pleasant and far less evocative than wood smoke. He resolved to be rid of the desk lamp, which was now straining his eyes, feeling that this would give more room on the writing table Victor Hammer had designed for him, on the model of a Shaker schoolboy's desk.[625]

Merton had been writing to W. H. Ferry throughout the year about Father William Du Bay's attempt to organize the priests of the Church. Merton was against the idea of a union of priests and believed a loose

association would prove more effective.[626] Where he disagreed, his letters show a good deal of sympathy with Du Bay himself, though he
sensed there was something in Du Bay's personality that had set him
deliberately on a collision course with Church authority: "There is no
use in a man like this just wrecking himself and confusing important
issues while doing it."[627] Both the connections and the differences with
his own struggle absorbed him, and he reacted with alarm to the idea
that Du Bay had no right to appeal to his own conscience in his opposition to the Church hierarchy.[628]

In November and December, Merton and Ferry were exchanging ideas
and rumors about the peace initiative in Vietnam. There was the hope
that Mrs. John F. Kennedy could be persuaded to go to Vietnam as soon
as the Christmas cease-fire began, and to remain there until a truce was
worked out. According to another rumor, Pope Paul VI would be going
to Vietnam on a peace mission at Christmas. Merton had recently become interested in all such ideas, while the exchange with Ferry planted
the possibility in his own mind of taking some initiative himself as a
"Hostage for Peace."[629] This may have begun with his essay of the
summer, which ended, ". . . do for Nhat Hanh whatever you would
do for me if I were in his position. In many ways I wish I were."

Ferry's relations with Dom James had remained cordial, for all the
strains of the proposal that Merton come to teach in Santa Barbara. They
continued to write to one another as Ping and Pong. The abbot proved
an unexpected benefactor of the center, something Ferry found deeply
moving. In December of 1966 he was open to Ferry's idea that Joan
Baez and her husband, Ira Sandperl, should visit Gethsemani on their
way to Atlanta. Joan Baez brought a copy of her new record, "Noel,"
as an early Christmas present for Dom James, because he recognized
her name.

Baez and Sandperl had founded the Institute for Non-Violence. Early
in December 1966, they offered to join the Reverend Martin Luther King
and the Southern Christian Leadership Conference in Atlanta on certain conditions. If these were met, they said, they would give courses
on non-violence and assist with their own resources in the work of
S.C.L.C. The most important of the conditions was number four: "The
S.C.L.C. civil rights movement must openly declare that it has now become a universal nonviolent human rights movement."[630] The force
behind the attempt to broaden the commitment to non-violence and
social change was the feeling Baez and Sandperl expressed that Gandhi
had made the "heartbreaking error" of thinking nationalism and non-
violence could go together. They wanted S.C.L.C. to break off all association with the federal government and from any attempt to work
within the system.

The timing of this cannot have been welcome to King, who was already under fire for broadening S.C.L.C.'s mandate to declare the Vietnam War a "racist war," something Merton had discussed with the only remaining black monk at Gethsemani, Brother Martin Deloach.[631]

Joan Baez and Ira Sandperl arrived on December 8. They spent time with Merton talking and drinking beer in the fields near the tobacco barn, then went to the monastery to meet the abbot. With Father Chrysogonus Waddell, the party walked up to the hermitage in the rain. Here, Merton banked up his logs in the fireplace and everybody dried out sitting on slip rugs before the blaze, listening to one side of "Noel." Later they got into a discussion about the lyrics of other songs of the sixties. This became quite heated when Merton found himself defending some of his favorite songs against the charge by Joan Baez that many contained hidden, and sometimes explicit, violence.[632]

It was the familiar controversy about violence used in the cause of non-violence, this time with a new twist. Their differences of opinion did not spoil Merton's impression of Joan Baez, or hers of him, even though he certainly got the worst of the argument. He wrote to Ferry that she was "one of those rare people who keep things from falling apart."[633]

After Father Chrysogonus left, Merton gave his guests a meal of cheese and toast and honey. Then he read his poems of the summer and talked to a sympathetic audience about his continuing love for S. Together they concocted a plan of driving in a rented car to surprise S. when she came off duty. As a first stage, they drove in the rain to Louisville Airport. There it proved impossible to change the Baez-Sandperl reservations on short notice, and the plan came to nothing. Instead, Merton telephoned his friend Jack Ford, who agreed to drive him back to the hermitage. The next day he was full of self-castigation for the folly, if still excited by the visit and the wild drive through the rain.

Conjectures of a Guilty Bystander and the excerpt from it in *Life* greatly increased the volume of Merton's mail, which he carried up each day in a dilapidated briefcase, as well as the gallon jar of drinking water — something that cannot have helped his bursitis. He told Ferry of a new policy at the monastery; mail was now supposed to be passed on unopened.[634] He remained skeptical and went on advising his friends to put "Conscience Matter" on the envelope. In the past, the old policy had saved him from a good deal of crank mail. Now most of it reached him. The rumors that his books were being burned by certain self-righteous Catholics may have been a good deal exaggerated before they reached him — and before he passed them on. At any rate, he knew he had earned the enmity of a number of people:

> I am, to begin with, judged by my early books. Either I am rejected entirely because their "monasticism" is unacceptable, or my later work is rejected for not being "spiritual" and "unworldly" like the earlier ones.[635]

In the mid-1960s the tide of public opinion had certainly turned from any interest in monasticism (though *not* against an interest in the solitary life), and Thomas Merton was not the only monk to hear that the religious life of the enclosed orders was "irrelevant." Yet his own writing, old and new, reached a wider public than ever. *Conjectures of a Guilty Bystander* was doing very well indeed.

Merton's desire to explain himself received an impetus from both the positive and the negative criticism. He was already planning to make a selection from his journals of 1964–65, to be called "A Vow of Conversation,"[636] which would have continued the selection from earlier journals and extended the autobiographical line that led from *The Seven Storey Mountain* and *The Secular Journal* through *The Sign of Jonas* to *Conjectures of a Guilty Bystander*. He had already sent out parts of "A Vow of Conversation" to Naomi Burton and others before he decided to hold back from publication, in large part because he felt there was too much criticism of Dom James and the monastery, some of it unwarranted and unfair. However, he was still mining his journals for articles. One of the finest of these, and one of Merton's best pieces of sustained autobiographical writing, was "Day of a Stranger,"[637] which would appear in the Summer 1967 number of *The Hudson Review*.[638] Writing against the cliché of the time, "being yourself," Merton says he reserves the right "to forget about being myself, since in any case there is very little chance of my being anybody else. Rather it seems to me that when one is too intent on 'being himself' he runs the risk of impersonating a shadow."[639]

"Day of a Stranger" follows the pattern of the January 1966 letter to Aziz Ch. Abdul, giving the schedule of one marginal man between waking at two-fifteen in the morning and the hour of sleep. More lyrical in style than the letter, though less detailed, it follows the rituals, reading, praying (as natural as breathing), and the hours of simple living (if not altogether living simply) under the SAC plane with its bomb, in a setting where everything else has its place, even the king snake in the outhouse who has to be summoned forth with "Are you in there, you bastard?"[640]

The essay is, in the best sense, a celebration of self, and it is generous and endearing because Merton is so obviously at home with himself. Few other passages of his give such a clear sense of happiness. It is also the best proof of his success in remaining "human in this most inhuman of ages."[641] Something of Heidbrink's letter and the charges of being irrelevant can be sensed in the background (there are even mists at this hermitage), and where "Day of a Stranger" is not a plea for approval, it asks for a sympathetic understanding that someone may choose to live a different kind of life without thereby becoming a threat to others. "I am both a prisoner and an escaped prisoner."[642] The old tone of "negative boostering" has gone.

Quiet confidence in the rightness of his own choice was not always so evident. At times the autobiographical note enters with a certain stridence. In another essay, "Learning to Live," where there is talk of "the self no longer clothed with an ego,"[643] there is also a good deal of ego:

> . . . I have continued to be the same kind of maverick and have, in fact, ended as a hermit, who is also fully identified with the peace movement, with Zen, with a group of Latin American hippie poets, etc., etc.[644]

Thomas Merton's "shadow" was not above making its own claims on occasion.

※

In the Septuagesima Letter of 1967, the first of the mimeographed letters in which Merton attempted to catch up with his correspondence by a general report to "Dear Friends," he ended: "Pray for me. When one gets older (Jan. 31 is my fifty-second birthday) one realizes the futility of a life wasted in argument when it should be given entirely to love."[645]

By early March, he found himself arguing with some passion on ground not of his own choosing. He was ill at ease, and he made a number of surprising statements. Obviously feeling guilty at having put off reading the manuscript "The Church Against Herself," which Rosemary Ruether had sent in 1966, he reported in his journal now that he had a great deal of respect for the author and he thought her "Barthian — which is why I trust her."[646] The exchange of letters became too valuable to break off, even when Merton found that Rosemary Ruether, like Father Du Bay, had a way of claiming "radical honesty" for herself as a means of attacking the honesty of everyone else.[647]

Much later, when humor had returned, Merton wrote to her, "Ah, yes, I have become wicked. This is due in great part to my hanging around with these women theologians. What a downfall. Let others be warned in time. Young priests can never be too careful. Tsk. Tsk . . ."[648]

In March 1967 there was little chance of such humorous sallies to stay the attack:

> Thanks for your letter which came the other day during the visit of an old friend of mine, a tough-minded, irreligious, Karnap trained journalist. He and I went into the monastic question very thoroughly, including the politike arete bit and all the rest. Because he knows me, and knew me when I was a communist (of sorts) and all that, he knows very well that I am not "hostile to politike arete." But he saw, as I do, the real trouble: my lack of ability to communicate what I mean and to say what really needs to be said, because I am out of touch — in other words it is

not at all a question of repudiating political life but of participating in a way that makes sense here. And I would add, what is coming through to me now in your letters is that we both seem to be accepting a naïve and unreal separation between "city" and "country" that no longer means anything in the modern world. It seems to me in your last letter you were just using the old dualism, turned inside out. As if I were living in a sixth century virgin forest with wolves. This is not "sub-human nature" out here, it is farm country, and farmers are people with the same crucial twentieth century problems as everybody else. Also tree planting and reforestation are not simply sentimental gestures in a region that has been ravaged by the coal and lumber companies. If reforestation were merely symbolic I doubt it would have the importance it seems to have for instance in Mao's China.[649]

The town-and-country debate became a much more personal matter. Because Merton thought himself challenged as an affected primitivist, he came close to accusing Rosemary Ruether of being a rootless intellectual with an advanced case of seeing the world from the city-cloister perspective of other rootless intellectuals. He *did* call Rosemary Ruether "cerebral" and an "intellectual woman."

On March 24 he went halfway to apologize: "I promise I won't get up in the air again. I don't know what frightened me so. ('Cerebral' probably because I resented my mother's intellectuality) (or what I later interpreted as that)."[650]

On March 25, in a further attempt to explain things, he made the statement, part of which has often been introduced here:

> . . . I am not mad at you for being an "intellectual woman" but only for seeming to reject me. I don't take sweetly to rejection, I can tell you. I need and value your friendship and I will also on my part be more or less grown up about it and try to give you what I can in my turn, once I know what you want. And now I think I do. (Before I got the impression you didn't want anything from me except that I shut up and admit you were right about something or other.)[651]

The friendship was mended, but, where there was less fire, there were fewer letters.

The "tough-minded, irreligious, Karnap trained journalist" friend who had known Merton in the old days when he was "a communist (of sorts)" — certainly an exaggeration — was Sy Freedgood. Freedgood had not been to the monastery since Merton's ordination. Now he made an appearance that far outdid the disguises and roles of the Columbia years. Merton came down from the hermitage early in the morning of Thursday, March 16, to find Freedgood at the gate house "bandaged and sinister." Freedgood explained he had driven his hired car into a tree at high speed on the way down from Louisville.[652]

However bruised and battered, Freedgood went on to captivate both

Merton and the abbot. Dom James had no idea when Freedgood was near the truth and when he was far out on the horizons of his imagination. He obviously took to Freedgood, as Dom James did to so many of Father Louis's friends. When Sy Freedgood boasted a close friend on the board of H. J. Heinz Co., Dom James was pretty sure he was play-acting (a week after the visit, all fifty-seven varieties turned up at the monastery). Doubtful whether his wife would believe his account of the accident when he arrived home, Freedgood suggested that Dom James sign an affidavit to the effect that he had been beaten up by irate monks for criticizing the monastic life. After a good deal of humorous persuasion, Dom James signed.[653]

Apart from helping Merton to sort out the discussion with Rosemary Ruether, Freedgood also made a considerable contribution to Merton's feeling that he was too isolated.

Everyone else seemed able to travel, even Sidi Abdeslam, who wrote in the spring of 1967 to ask if Father Louis had set aside the distractions of words, his own words and those of others, in order to realize the mystical union the Islamic mystic and scholar had prophesied on his last visit (he had prophesied also that Merton's abbot would die or retire within a year, leaving him free to travel).

"What is best is what is not said," Merton translated from Sidi Abdeslam's letter.[654] He was in search of the "not said." Solitude had borne many fruits when Merton had trusted it. There were too many distractions still — words and visitors. And yet Sidi Abdeslam had himself been a visitor. Merton had seen travel as a temptation, a pull to the old restlessness, and he had made use of others to protect himself against such distractions. Now he began to wonder whether the "not said" would come to him at Gethsemani if he waited, or whether it was to be found only somewhere else.

He was still divided, waiting for the right message:

> Sy kept telling me I needed to get out and see things and meet people — and he's probably right. But he seemed to think I should put up a big fight for this and I have neither reason nor motive for doing so. Nor would it get anywhere or do the slightest good. The most I would want in any case would be the freedom to travel once in a while to very special places and to see exceptional people. For instance to visit Sidi Abdeslam, or to go to the Zen places in Japan.[655]

PART SEVEN

Kanchenjunga

Sei — und wisse zugleich des Nicht-Seins Bedingung,
den unendlichen Grund deiner innigen Schwingung,
dass du sie völlig vollziehst dieses einzige Mal.

Be — and at the same time know the condition
of not-being, the infinite ground of your deep vibration,
that you may fully fulfill it this single time.

— *Rilke*

The full beauty of the mountain is not seen until you too consent
to the impossible paradox: it is and is not. When nothing more
needs to be said, the smoke of ideas clears, the Mountain is SEEN.

— *Thomas Merton*

NINETEEN SIXTY-SEVEN began with a struggle over permission to travel, and there was a second incident of very much the same kind in the summer of that year. Both were largely, in Merton's terms, "pseudo events." Neither invitation presented a chance to visit someone like Sidi Abdeslam or to make comparisons between the life of monks in the West and those in the East. From a distance both look like distractions, and they did not appeal to Merton for long, even if he seriously underestimated his own love of travel for travel's sake. The boy who had made favorites of books with illustrations of French cathedrals and John Masefield's poems of the sea was now a man of fifty-two who spent a good deal of time looking at the photographs in Martin Hürlimann's *Asia*. He wrote to Marco Pallis of his longing to go to the East. Pallis replied on one occasion with news of a headline in the travel section of a London paper — "Seeing the Orient before sophistication spoils it all for us." Pallis underlined the "for us."[1]

The real struggle with Dom James in 1967 came from the feeling that he ought to be able to make his own choices. Here, at least on principle, one's sympathy is likely to be with Merton, though enough has already been introduced to show the situation was far from simple. Merton required sufficient protection to test possibilities and to establish priorities among conflicting ideals. Dom James remained overprotective with the sense that recent events confirmed the need. The actions of both men have to be viewed in this context.

At the end of January 1967, letters came from the Abbey of Melleray in France to Father Louis and to Dom James, telling them about a forthcoming event which would bring the world's honors to the Order. Fa-

ther Louis's old friend and spiritual adviser Dom Colomban Bissey was
to be made a Chevalier de la Légion d'Honneur.[2] Feeling he had played
some part in bringing this about, Merton was delighted when Father
M. Bernard asked him to be present at Melleray for the ceremony. The
letter from Father Bernard to the abbot requested Dom James's permission to write to Father Louis with an invitation.[3] In the circumstances,
Dom James had grounds for being irritated when Merton passed on the
letter he had received, with a note he typed at the bottom:

jhs

Dear Rev. Father:
What about it? How about a nice birthday present?
   — You yourself often say it is good for monks of daughter house to
visit mother house.
   — a summons from a Father Immediate surely can be obeyed vir-
tuously and without scandal — au contraire.
   — To speak frankly: I need to see another monastery besides Gethsemani to get some perspective. I wonder if this is not God's will this time???
   The decision is entirely yours and I do not seek to intrude my own will
in any way whatever. But I think it would do me a pile of good, frankly.
                                                          Quid dicis?

                                                        in our Lord

                                                      b.m. Louis[4]

On Merton's birthday the abbot replied to the note, which incidentally is written in a style remarkably like Dom James's own. It was not
Dom James's way to give a flat "No": instead, he reminded Father Louis
of the many gifts he had been given, above all the hermitage:

God has given you this hermitage, not to quit it, for a greater expansion
of exterior activities.
   But to remain in it, for a greater deepening of your interior activities —
of recollection, meditation, prayer . . .[5]

He went on to ask Father Louis to be strong in resisting the temptation to travel, feeling certain that it would return, but that each time it
did, the resolution would make the hermit stronger. As he often did,
the abbot repeated he had at heart ". . . not merely your best Temporal interest — but your best Eternal interest i.e. — God's plans for
you."

On February 1, Dom James wrote to explain the situation to Dom Colomban.[6] He also wrote a fairly blistering reply to the man who had
started all this, reminding Father Bernard that he had written to Dom
James on January 24, asking his advice about inviting Father Louis and
then, in the very same mail, sending the invitation. Dom James quoted
St. Bernard's "zeal — without knowledge." He went on to say, among

other things, that the ill-considered invitation had caused an explosive problem, and that Father Bernard had demonstrated he had no under-standing of the hermit's "temperament and character."[7]

Quoted out of context, the letter is proof Dom James was determined to block any absence from the hermitage. In any context, the letter shows an acute nervousness about Father Louis, which the abbot's let-ter to Dom Colomban makes still clearer. If Thomas Merton was iso-lated, so, too, was his abbot: it was natural, if unfortunate, that Dom James shared so freely with others his own lack of trust in the hermit's "temperament and character."

Merton quickly accepted the impossibility of going to France for the ceremony. He continued to feel there was more than a degree of "in-fantilism" in his relationship with the abbot. Now that Dom James had become again a force of opposition, Merton's struggles with himself were distorted. For the time being, it looked as if the question of travel could be set aside. It was to return, unresolved, when Dom James no longer had the power to give or to refuse permission.

In the meanwhile, improvements had been made to the hermitage and the bad weather provided protection against too many visitors — if not against disturbing mail. January 29 was the coldest day Merton-had experienced that winter. On the 30th, when it grew a little warmer, he returned to the hermitage from the monastery to find a truck with a well rig parked close to the building. The truck had PEE WEE MCGRU-DER, SHEP., KY.[8] painted on it in bold letters. But if the signs were hopeful, Pee Wee McGruder proved remarkably elusive. Even when work finally began on the well, it took six months before the new kitchen at the hermitage was finally fitted up and Merton was able to draw water from the faucets.

His health was little better. Early in February he had to go back to Dr. Mitchell about his bursitis, and he learned he would have to have another operation. The news that he would be in hospital (again at St. Anthony's) at the end of the month was somewhat softened as Merton began to find growing support in a different kind of friendship.

Long ago, in Collegeville, Minnesota, he had written of the joy the evening with the Powers family had brought him, including in his journal the vignette of the Powers daughters holding up schooners of beer for their parents' guests as they approached the house. The little incident obviously stayed in his memory, where there were few such scenes. Previously, when he had gone up to Louisville to see doctors, he had visited with Jim Wygal in Anchorage, Kentucky, or with Father John Loftus. In Lexington, he called at the Hammers.' In 1967, it was as if he were strongly drawn to two large families, and his journals sug-gested he took on Diane O'Callaghan and Alice Willett as adopted daughters of the imagination.

He had known the O'Callaghans in Louisville for some years. The introduction had been made originally by Dan Walsh. What began with a formal sense of occasion (a carefully prepared meal of lamb chops for the visiting celebrity, Mr. O'Callaghan returning from the office during a working day)[9] soon became an established and easy friendship, with meals and moments as they came in a household that grew to seven children, and with many friends dropping in. The famous writer was swiftly translated into Uncle Louis (pronounced this time "Louie") by the O'Callaghan children, to Tom by the others, while the O'Callaghans became Frank and Tommie. In 1967 the bond became much closer, with Merton visiting after almost every trip to the doctors in Louisville, to help the children with their history homework, to draw pictures of horses for Nancy (and to give her his hospital bracelet), to play the guitar with Kathy, and to roughhouse with the younger children, providing a human swing, the pains of bursitis either forgotten or ignored. He joined Tommie O'Callaghan as she did duty on carpools and found himself learning what was almost a new language:

> I realize how out of touch I am with what concerns married people trying to live in the city. Which is all right. I am precisely *supposed* to be out of touch with those particular problems. But I need to be more definite in my mind: not imagining I have to try to "keep up" with everything. Stay moderately informed — and go on quietly doing my own job. People need me to be a contemplative, and not a newspaper man.[10]

Where the celebrity had been forgotten by all at the O'Callaghan home (there had never been anything the least self-conscious about Thomas Merton in a relaxed setting), the bachelor could sometimes be exasperating, expecting plans to be changed and crowded days to be reorganized. The atmosphere must have seemed to Merton one of freedom bordering on chaos: he probably spent little time in the kitchen checking the huge calendar that said where everybody in the house would be at any given time — who had to be picked up or delivered, when, and by whom.

Whenever Merton was between buses or rides in Bardstown, he went now to the home of Thompson and Virginia Willett, to whom he had been introduced by Jim Wygal the previous winter.[11] Most of the Willett children were older than the O'Callaghan children. Merton listened to records with them and filled in the gaps in his knowledge of popular music. From one trip to the Willetts' he took back to the hermitage a second set of bongo drums.[12]

Even during the bad weather early in the year, and before Sy Freedgood arrived, there were a few visitors. Doris Dana, a friend of John Howard Griffin and the literary executor of Gabriela Mistral, arrived for two days early in January. Merton found her very well informed about South America. She also told him the story of Ishi, the last survivor of the Yana tribe in California.[13] When Doris Dana left she promised to send him Theodora Kroeber's book, *Ishi in Two Worlds: A biography of the last wild Indian in North America.*[14]

Merton's interest in those who are equally misnamed "Indians" and "Native Americans" had been largely dormant in the years he was fascinated by South and Central America. With the arrival of the book on Ishi came a quickening of enthusiasm that led to a series of articles in 1967 and to passages in "Ghost Dance: Prologue" and "Ghost Dance" in the final, "West" section of *The Geography of Lograire.* While Theodora Kroeber provided the background material on Ishi, another woman anthropologist-historian, Cora DuBois, supplied much of the material, including "found poems" for "West" in *The Geography of Lograire,* from her thesis *The 1870 Ghost Dance.*[15]

"The Shoshoneans" (both an extended review of, and a tribute to, the book of the same title by the poet Ed Dorn and the black photographer Leroy Lucas),[16] "War and Vision" (a review of *Two Leggings: The Making of a Crow Warrior,* by Peter Nabokov),[17] and "Ishi: A Meditation"[18] make up the first part of the collection later published by the Unicorn Press as *Ishi Means Man.*[19] Part II contains essays on the Mayas of the Yucatan ("The Cross Fighters") and the Indians of the Valley of Oaxaca ("The Sacred City").

The "Essays on Native Americans" provides a series of variations on a single theme, the continuing race war of whites against non-whites in the Americas, and Merton makes the connections he saw between the Indian wars and Vietnam, connections he was making at the same time in a letter to Brother Antoninus.[20]

Merton had talked in other periods of his life of the excitement reading brought him, even of "intellectual gluttony." In early 1967 he found himself almost intoxicated by the ideas of others. Reading Romano Guardini's *Pascal for Our Time,* the hermit had to break off frequently from the reading to pace the floor of the hermitage.[21]

When Dr. James Holloway and Will Campbell,[22] two friends and fellow members of the Committee of Southern Churchmen, drove over from Berea in Campbell's red farm truck in January, the three men talked of Faulkner and Faulkner's current unpopularity with the civil-rights movement. Long ago, Merton had tried reading Faulkner's *Sanctuary* on the boat to England. In September 1931, he had to confess he could understand nothing of the book.[23] Now he was reading his way through Faulkner with the same passion he had given to Camus and an almost boundless respect for the Southern writer. He saw Faulkner's unpopularity on the civil-rights issue as the "penalty for taking a unique personal position and not electing to run with some pack."[24] Faulkner had the added credential of being equally unpopular with both sides on the issue.

There was another heady literary discussion when three fellow artists came to visit. When Merton writes to Lax in the Greek islands about his day with the "three kings from Lexington," he mentions only one by name, Jonathan Williams, poet, publisher, and cross-country walker.[25] The others were the teacher, critic, writer, artist, and translator Guy Davenport, and Ralph Eugene Meatyard, who combined earning a living as an optician with photography. Merton's enthusiasm for the photography appears at once in the journal: "marvelous arresting visionary things. Most haunting and suggestive, mythical, photography I ever saw."[26]

From the first visit there were Gene Meatyard portraits of Merton. Meatyard's quite different approach to the subject complements the portraits taken by John Howard Griffin. Ed Rice adds another dimension, with pictures that are often tough and grainy, showing a Merton not greatly removed from the young man who posed for the "Hemingway" portrait that first summer at Olean. In all, the photographic record of Merton's years at the hermitage was a rich and varied one, and a full compensation for the near-absence of early pictures of the monk at Gethsemani. Perhaps the most haunting photograph of all, however, is the one taken by Robert Lax of Merton against the background of a bare hillside with a single divided track.[27] One of the happiest was taken in color by Carolyn Hammer during a Hammer-Merton picnic.

New friends and new excitements in his reading were reflected in Merton's writing. Far more than at any earlier time, this followed closely on the reading which interested him most, either reviews or essays on anthropology and Zen. He was collecting a number of pieces around his introduction to John Wu's *The Golden Age of Zen*,[28] for a book that would include his 1959 exchange with Suzuki, his reading of Nishida the winter before, and such new writing as "The Self of Modern Man and the New Christian Consciousness,"[29] and which would be published in 1968 as *Zen and the Birds of Appetite*.[30] In anthropology, he returned to studies he had only half explored, like the Bantu myths and pre-Columbian North America, then into new interests that had connections to old ones.

It was almost certainly from Father Matthew Kelty that Merton first heard of the Cargo Cults of New Guinea and Melanesia.[31] Kelty had served as a mission priest in New Guinea for the Divine Word Society before he entered the Trappists and came to Gethsemani, to find Father Louis was his novice master. Kelty had been a magazine editor as well as a missionary, experience which helped him when he became one of the chief transcribers and typists of the novice master's essays and articles. When he became a professed monk he had been a member of the group that met to discuss monastic renewal and experimental monasteries under Father Louis. Kelty was also drawn to the solitary life. Thus, there was much to bring the two men closer and to make them friends, but when Matthew Kelty first mentioned the Cargo

Cults in New Guinea he did not seem to be getting an interested hearing from Father Louis and he moved on to other subjects.[32] A few months later Father Matthew discovered Father Louis was ordering every book on the Cargo Cults and considering the possibility of writing one on the subject.

Cargo Cults, Bantu myths, a play on Cook's landing in the South Pacific,[33] missionaries, Ghost Dancers, outrageous advertisements in *The New Yorker*,[34] Mayan fertility dances, as well as much else, had already found a place in early drafts and plans for a long poem in a number of parts, which became *The Geography of Lograire*.

With a careful reading of the works of Camus and Faulkner, Merton was coming to a new sense of the power of certain writers to reach a hidden level of truth through fictional models. His interest in Flannery O'Connor and Walker Percy was almost as great. There was still something of a frustrated novelist in Merton.[35] Mark Van Doren had once been able to make the study of literature so exciting for him that he had changed his major at Columbia. Merton's first published writing had been literary reviews. And, finally, Milosz had suggested what could be done by writing literary criticism.

The period in which he changed from an occasional reviewer to a critic began with seven essays on the writing of Albert Camus, for which he had made almost a year's preparation. Merton wrote the first, "Camus: Journals of the Plague Years," while he was in hospital in February, revising it in April before sending it to *The Sewanee Review*.[36] He felt himself very close to the French writer when his experience of finding a dead mouse on the threshold at the hermitage paralleled the discovery of a dead rat by Dr. Rieux at the beginning of *The Plague*.[37] Merton had read reports of a number of cases of the bubonic plague in Vietnam and had said the "Mass for the Time of Pestilence" several times during the spring. There were ties here with his own past, when he had filled both his 1939 journal and the 1940 novel written from it, "The Man in the Sycamore Tree," with references to the plague. In 1967–68 the plague image returns to the journals.

Merton was choosing new models in poetry. He had begun his review of Louis Zukofsky's *All: The Collected Short Poems, 1956–64* while he was in hospital the fall before.[38] Since then he had complained to others that Zukofsky's poetry was impossible to find, despite the network of cooperative librarians he had built up. The review, with the title "Paradise Bugged," came out in the February–March 1967 issue of *The Critic*.[39] The poet wrote at once to thank him for the rare recognition. Merton was again in hospital, this time for the February 1967 visit; he told Zukofsky about his bursitis and pleaded for copies of poems from the poet.

The subsequent title of the same review, "Louis Zukofsky — The Paradise Ear," is the better one. Merton begins:

All really valid poetry (poetry that is fully alive and asserts its reality by its power to generate imaginative life) is a kind of recovery of paradise. Not that the poet comes up with a report that he, an unusual man, has found his own way back into Eden: but the living line and the generative association, the new sound, the music, the structure, are somehow grounded in a renewal of vision and hearing so that he who reads and understands recognizes that here is a new start, a new creation. Here the world gets another chance. Here man, here the reader discovers himself getting another start in life, in hope, in imagination, and why? Hard to say, but probably because the language itself is getting another chance, through the innocence, the teaching, the good faith, the honest senses of the workman poet . . .[40]

The first thing to be said is that this is criticism which is "fully alive," incisive (if deceptively casual), and a bold contrast with most of the stuffy, jargon-ridden literary criticism published in many reviews at the time. It opens up a fresh way of reading the poetry of Louis Zukofsky, while it is also revealing about the direction the reviewer had moved to in his own work. The phrase "a kind of recovery of paradise" has echoes (which the readers could not have caught) of Merton's secret writing for S. the summer before. Now, language was the key to the new change, and writing the possibility of entering Eden.

Language was getting "another chance," Merton says, through a number of qualities of "the workman poet," including innocence. "Innocence" had been an important word earlier, particularly in the "Message to Poets," delivered for Merton at the meeting in Mexico City in February 1964 and included in *Raids on the Unspeakable*. Here Merton says:

Whatever his failures, the poet is not a cunning man. His art depends on an ingrained innocence which he would lose in business, in politics, or in too organized a form of academic life. The hope that rests on calculation has lost its innocence. We are banding together to defend our innocence.[41]

This was an extreme of the Romantic view of the poet, even though no sane poet would doubt that the Muse is jealous. It rules out novelists like Emily Brontë; politicians like Dante, Andrew Marvell, Pablo Neruda, W. B. Yeats, and Leopold Senghor; civil servants like Chaucer; publishers like T. S. Eliot; and so on, though not, perhaps, housebreakers and pimps like François Villon. At any rate, in Merton's opinion the poetry of Louis Zukofsky represented innocence of vision in its purest form.

In the context innocence depends on two things. The first is obvious: the poet must avoid routines, position, responsibilities — the poet must be a marginal man. In the second place, the poet must find some way of avoiding self-consciousness: the innocent eye is the first thing to go in writing about self because there is no such thing as the innocent I.

Thomas Merton's particular manner of using autobiographical material had led to his best writing and also to complications for him. It has been suggested already that Zen may have had a very personal appeal as a means of liberation from the difficulties — the same may have been true of translation, the "found poem," the review. A process that began in different ways with *The Wisdom of the Desert* and *Original Child Bomb* reached a new level with *The Way of Chuang Tzu*, and it is easy to see why this book was such a favorite of the author. With *The Geography of Lograire*, the process is complete, the movement away from self as subject has produced a freeing and a repaired innocence;[42] it has also brought the unexpected; the shots of the moon during the moon landing were interesting, the photographs of the earth from the moon a revelation.

With his attention turned to the poets in the other Americas, Merton had found little before that was of special interest in the work of poets writing in the United States. William Carlos Williams he admired, and Williams had sent him *Kaddish*, with a letter suggesting he read Allen Ginsberg because he would find him a poet of vision and one with a religious sense.[43] Merton had replied, agreeing with Williams, yet there was no mistaking the fact that Ginsberg didn't "take." Merton had received another "boomerang," this time from Clayton Eshleman writing from Peru to tell him his words on Ginsberg in *Harpers* had been unfair and that Merton was deserting American poets in their darkest hour.[44] Merton resisted what he saw as a curious call to patriotism and put it down to Eshleman's homesickness. With Zukofsky, Merton had found a poet of the United States to celebrate.

In the following months he was to discover an English poet who was every bit as neglected, and an Anglo-Welsh poet who was virtually unknown in the United States and known only to something of a coterie in England.

In his attempt to find poems by Zukofsky, he also discovered the work of Basil Bunting.[45] When Ferry recommended the poetry of David Jones, Merton had his three models. He only wondered why what he now saw as the best poetry in English of his own time had been hidden from him for so long.[46] Soon he was writing to Ferry about both Bunting and David Jones, and Ferry went in search of the special issue *Agenda* had devoted to David Jones and the two books the poet had already published, *In Parenthesis* and *Anathémata*.

Merton discovered that if all three poets had been ignored by readers, they had been praised by poets. Pound had been enthusiastic about Zukofsky and Basil Bunting, Eliot had highly valued the work of David

Jones. When an Anglican friend, Father Andrew Macdonald (Donald) Allchin, visited Gethsemani, Merton was delighted to find he had not only read and admired the work of David Jones, but that he knew the Catholic poet and painter, who by 1967 was ill and virtually a recluse.[47]

Both Donald Allchin and Louis Zukofsky were soon members of what could be called the "inner circle" of friends by correspondence, and Allchin became a fairly frequent visitor in 1967 and 1968. Zukofsky's letters were so evocative and warm Merton felt almost a member of the Zukofsky family, where everyone was a musician, where everyone got into the poems, where Celia and Louis sent him rival remedies for bursitis, and where the "paradise ear" of the poet picked up the sound of rain on the windows, the notes of violin and cello, and the voices of children asking questions as wise as they were direct.[48]

Perhaps it was the sense of listening in to that apartment in New York, in addition to the pain that now made all writing difficult, which set Merton's mind to using a tape recorder for composition. With his move permanently into the hermitage in 1965 and his surrender of the position of master of novices, Merton had lost the services of willing typists at the monastery.[49] The pain increased. He discovered the operation in February had not been a success, and x-rays revealed a deposit of calcium on the bone.[50]

Plans for a trust had gone ahead, with much advice and help, especially from Naomi Burton and James Laughlin. When the question of finding a lawyer came up, Merton thought of another old Columbia friend, John Slate.[51]

Merton had not seen Slate for almost thirty years, and the two of them had moved far apart in politics. Slate came down to Gethsemani to deal with the legal aspects of the Legacy Trust on April 5, and he and Merton argued about the Church and about the Vietnam War — at the Merton Room, in the cafeteria at Bellarmine, in the Luau Room of the Louisville Airport:

> He was here with a bow wow argument about the VN waw. We was in the Hawaiian temples with a Father and Miss Pat of the libraries and we was fight like catsup dogs over the VN waw and even all the waitresses and hired helps was joining in. I was nearly lynched and stabbed to death with forks though some was on my side . . .[52]

So he put it later to Robert Lax. All the arguing aside, Merton's chief emotion was concern. He had written to Slate telling him to be careful not to repeat Sy Freedgood's approach to Gethsemani. He was worried about Slate's heart condition, his drinking, his fast driving.

Naomi Burton Stone came down on business on April 19. There were conferences, and then a picnic at Gethsemani on Thursday, the 20th. It was a beautiful day. Spring was unusually far ahead that year.

(Merton spoke of waking to sing his morning office, "Oh my sweet valley! Gregorian comes naturally out of this earth and this spring.")[53] Sitting in the sun at the picnic, Merton got sunburned on his nearly bald head. The guests included Father John Loftus and a young local teacher and poet, Ron Seitz, as well as Naomi Burton Stone. Tommie O'Callaghan had prepared a sumptuous meal for them all that demonstrates why the Gethsemani picnics were high feasts for the hermit. The menu survives, like the menu Owen Merton wrote out and illustrated for his son's first birthday party.[54]

Merton borrowed his agent's Nikon and took a great many photographs that day, some near the farm buildings, including one he nicknamed "The Sky Hook."[55] He himself was photographed close to the back of a truck which bore the triangular "Slow-moving Vehicle" sign. He had largely mastered cameras of many degrees of sophistication by this time, with help from Griffin and others. He was less apt with record players and had to be told that a stereo machine would also play mono records (he had been playing the same few stereo records over and over for weeks).

On the 22nd, the new tape recorder arrived, and Merton sat up playing with it long past his usual hour for sleep.[56] The possibilities he saw for it were enormous:

> I will do less underlining, do not have to try to be so definite, so decisive; a kind of freedom can come from being nearly relaxed, cool and open. I have this interiorly, and can be this way when not speaking and not thinking. Important to be that way while speaking and thinking . . .[57]

Obviously, someone else had handled the tape recorder during his conferences when hundreds of hours had been recorded. Now he was delighted with the early experiments and felt he would have to "take back some of the things I have said about technology."[58] Several months later he wrote to a correspondent that he was still trying to master the finer points of the machine. The tape recorder made its own contribution to the genesis of *Lograire*: there is even a way in which it can be seen as Thomas Merton's form of "Cargo."

During her visit, Naomi Burton Stone suggested a book on the Sufis.[59] Merton had already given a number of Sunday conferences on the mystics of Islam, and the subject continued to fascinate him, though he did not pursue the idea of a book. Much of the conversation at the picnic had been taken up with the news that Dan Walsh was about to become a priest. The Archbishop of Louisville had suggested that certain dispensations could be made in his case if he wanted to be ordained. "Dan is dazed. Everyone is astounded,"[60] Merton wrote in his journal. The ordination was set for the Day of Pentecost at St. Thomas Seminary, and Tommie O'Callaghan volunteered to give a reception afterward. Later, at the picnic, Father John Loftus told them all about the open-housing project he was involved in in Louisville, and the threats of violence the project had already attracted.[61]

There were more trips to the doctors, and on May 2, Merton was referred to an allergist with offices in St. Matthews in East Louisville. Merton found the office hard to get to. Once he was there, there was no chance of combining a visit with hours at a library or the house of a friend. He did discover a good Jewish delicatessen where he bought supplies of kasha and other things he needed, and he found a bookstore where he bought several science-fiction titles (the first time he had read science fiction in thirty years, he says in his journal, obviously amused at himself).[62] There was a heavy load to carry back to the hermitage that day.

Dr. Tom Jerry Smith compensated for the isolation of his offices, and the two men quickly became friends.[63] Merton also found himself fascinated by the whole subject of allergies. He wrote a note for Father John Eudes:

> Through the devious workings of Providence I have now fallen into the hands of a new doctor who persecutes allergies with an entirely medieval frenzy. I am on a ruthless new diet, which works, it seems, if only because of the effect on my awe-struck imagination . . .[64]

The bad news was that he was forbidden beer and any food product connected with the cow. He wanted to know more about the struggle against the body's "heretics."

Science fact came to be more exciting than science fiction. At the end of the month he was reading works on quantum physics for "light" breakfast reading. This left him frustrated and depressed that none of his schooling had given him any grounding in the sciences, except for the courses on elementary astrology and geology at Columbia. It also brought him a different kind of awe: "Niels Bohr and Co. are definitely among my No. 1. culture heroes."[65]

With the summer came a sense of dates on the calendar of the summer before, a feeling of longing mixed with relief:

> I kept thinking of it. But I don't regret that today was entirely different! Peace, silence, freedom of heart, no care, quiet joy. Last year — there was joy and turbulence and trouble which turned to confusion and a deeply disturbed heart because I knew I was wrong and was going against everything I lived for.[66]

He was able to finish his introductory essay to *The Plague*, which he was preparing for the series published by the Seabury Press on Religious Dimensions in Literature.[67] When Jim Holloway drove Daniel Berrigan over from Berea, Merton told Dan he had dedicated the book to him. Then he realized he had also dedicated to Daniel Berrigan the collection of essays, *Faith and Violence,* which would be published by Notre Dame Press in 1968.[68] There was a mixup in dedications to parallel the earlier publication tangles. In the end, with permission, he dedicated *Faith and Violence* to Dan's brother Phil Berrigan and to Jim Forest.

Daniel Berrigan turned up looking like "a French worker priest in a beret and black turtleneck sweater and black windbreaker. A good uniform for a priest."[69] (Little more than a year later, Thomas Merton would be dressed much the same way.) The two talked of a number of things, including the increase of violence in the antiwar movement and also Vietnam itself. Berrigan was now anxious to make himself available as a "hostage for peace."[70] Merton had had the same idea since his correspondence with Ferry about the Christmas truce the winter before. The discussion was important in clarifying their views on the limits of opposition, on activism, on non-violence, and much else that could not be gone into in letters. Merton felt Dan Berrigan, like Nhat Hanh, was taking a course of great personal danger. Where there had been differences of opinion earlier, nothing had ever really divided them, and Merton felt an unqualified affection for Berrigan: it was certainly a case of "Dan Berrigan Is My Brother."

The visit was short. The next day Berrigan and Merton were driven up to Dr. Smith's office. After Tom Jerry Smith saw Merton, he ran Berrigan to the airport for the flight to New York, and Merton was left wondering if he would see Berrigan again. He also made another long call to S. from the airport.[71]

May 13, the Vigil of Pentecost, was a "rather foul, murky, damp day," and Merton felt his own inner climate matched the weather. He saw weakness in himself, signs of plague, decay, and division in the world. In the Church, the renewal, begun so hopefully, had divided many Catholics into two extreme camps. There was little except the aggressiveness of ego in "the noisy agitations of progressives who claim to be renewing the Church and are either riding some rather silly band wagon or caught up in factional rivalries." The conservatives, driven into blind reaction, were "utterly depressing in their tenacious clinging to meaningless symbols of dead power, their baroque inertia, their legalism. Disgust!"[72]

When Merton thought of what was happening in society at large in the year 1967, the scene was even more depressing. Violent black reaction threatened violent white reaction to the non-violent civil-rights movement. The various peace movements had become belligerent in the face of armed opposition. Where the individual acts of frustration made little sense, even to the perpetrators, the media shaped them into a meaningless something by employing a sense of theater.

Merton saw himself tied to the "hippie movement" by what had been, in the beginning at least, a bond of sympathy and understanding. He wondered now if he even knew enough to judge what appeared to be so phony, pointless, and decadent:

> A fake creativity, a half dead freshness, kids who seem to be already senile in their tired bodies, their LSD trips — a sense of overstimulation and of exhaustion. The gasping of a culture that is rotting in its own garbage — and yet has so many potentials! I know, all of this is too pessimistic — I am trying to salvage something in myself by saying "I am not that, at least!" Yet I am part of it. And I must try to bring life back into it, along with the others.[73]

The "embarrassment of allies" was felt by many at the time; so was the sense of meaningless violence and near-meaningless protest. Somehow, in 1967, the Causes seemed to be real, yet they remained somewhere remote and apart from the clashes, the marches, and the burnings, as if they provided only the occasion. The twanging of banjos and guitars, the cries of "Burn, Baby, Burn!," "Get the Pigs!" — or "Get the Niggers!," "Get the Young!," "Get Back in Line or We'll Shoot You!" (and the popping of tear-gas canisters) — all this appeared to be sufficient in itself, enough to go on with until someone could think of something else. When spokesmen of either side were interviewed and asked what they wanted, there tended to be either an embarrassed silence or much the same chant heard in the streets or over megaphones. In May–June 1967, the "Long Hot Summer" was beginning, the "Time of the Assassins" was preparing. And every night there were two wars to watch on television.

*

The French or Alsatian monks of Gethsemani had been able to proceed in 1862–65 as if the Civil War did not exist. It was not so easy in the 1960s. Nor, for the most part, would Merton have wished it to be. There were no radios, no newspapers, no televisions at the monastery. For this very reason, news brought by visitors and retreatants tended to be more frightening out of context. What those in the outside world now took largely for granted could be horrifying.

In the hours before dawn on May 14, Merton tried to recollect himself and to set aside the disturbances, within and without. While the rain fell in the forest, he read St. Jerome's life of Paul the Hermit for an article he had been asked to write, finding it "A beautiful piece of writing, with deep mystical and psychological implications — so that whether or not it is 'historical' is irrelevant."[74] (Once again, "For myths are realities, and they themselves open into deeper realms.") There was, as we have seen so often, a "necessary distance" in much of Merton's reading, a counterbalance to the contemporary.

That morning of Pentecost he must have meditated, too, what strange ways he and his old teacher and friend, Dan Walsh, had taken since they walked together the night after Maritain's reading in New York talking of Merton's vocation. Dan Walsh had lived at Gethsemani, off and on, for a number of years. Earlier, he had been at Merton's ordination, the first to ask the blessing of the new priest. And now the teacher was to be a priest.

It was a good place to think of teachers and teaching. In the secular cemetery at Gethsemani (where Dan Walsh would be buried in time) there is a gravestone of Abraham Lincoln's first teacher. Among so many other things, Thomas Merton had been a teacher for over half his adult life, and he followed his own best teachers as models.[75]

In the early-morning rain, Merton drove with Abbot James Fox and the abbot's brother, Bernard Fox, to St. Thomas's Seminary, "way out in the fields somewhere toward Cincinnati." There were photographers waiting. The concelebration and ordination went well, Merton felt: "A great enthusiasm filled the large bright chapel crowded with people, friends and students of Dan, including some former monks with their wives."[76]

After the service, the Gethsemani party drove to the reception in Louisville. The rain had stopped, and although it was overcast, much of the reception at the O'Callaghans' took place in the garden, recorded on family movies.[77] Merton's joy in the joy of his old friend came after a week of anxiety and depression. During his Pentecostal retreat he had resolved to show reserve and restraint. Later, at the reception, he found himself talking too much and drinking too much champagne. As he left one group of nuns with the sense he had made a fool of himself talking to them, he said quietly, "Another pillar of the Church falls." Then his weak stomach took over. He went upstairs to be sick and to lie down. The next day he was given a present from the O'Callaghans of an empty champagne bottle with one of the ordination invitations tied to its neck and a written message, "In memory of Father Louis with apologies from Frank."[78] If all this was not, in Merton's sense of the word, "edifying," it was not awful, either. Merton accepted a certain amount of teasing for weeks. He wrote without much show of remorse to friends that he had been drunk.[79]

Criticism on a more serious matter came a few weeks later. Dom James wrote during a visitation in Europe to say that an apostolic delegate was inquiring about the monk's connections with the National Association for Pastoral Renewal. A poll the association had issued asking for opinions on clerical celibacy had aroused the wrath of Cardinal Spellman, among others.

Merton had been careful to note the "former monks with their wives" at the ordination of Father Daniel Walsh. It was clear, however, that none of the former monks were also former priests, religious or secular. The issue of the vow of celibacy and the Roman Catholic priest-hood was already adding to divisions over the liturgy. "I guess there is going to be a rumpus," Merton writes in his journal.[80]

If this was an issue on which Merton might have been expected to have strong views, he does not express them publicly. He had written long letters earlier to some of the clergy taking part in the controversy. Faced now with a direct question on where he stood, Merton wrote in his journal:

> Frankly I can't say I greatly care one way or another. I sympathize with those priests who want to marry and continue as priests, and I think the continued opposition to them is going to mean trouble. But in the long run I don't know if a married secular clergy really solves anything for the Church — or for the clergy. My own feeling is that it does not matter that much, and I am not deeply enough involved in the issue myself to get into a fight about it. I am an "advisor" of the National Association for Pastoral Renewal — ie. a name on a list — and able to be "used." That is the extent of it.[81]

It may be that this really was the "extent of it," though he was usually careful about lists that carried his name so that he could be "used." There is a chance that Thomas Merton was playing for time in order to resolve certain uncertainties in his own thinking on the subject — just as he had once told Robert Lax in the train going through the Erie Valley that he was not interested in the writings of the Church Fathers. There was to be a discussion on just this subject — the issue of marriage, the priesthood, and those in religious orders — on the evening of December 9, 1968, in Bangkok. In June 1967 he may simply have felt too much fuss was being made, that it was largely a pseudo-issue, and he may really have meant it when he said he didn't care "one way or another" and repeated this view over and over.

*

It turned cold at the end of May and the beginning of June. There were more visits to the allergist and more visitors to Gethsemani. On Tuesday, June 6, there was a gala picnic with the O'Callaghans and all their children, Gladys Ford and her children, two of Marie Charron's children, and one child from the Hennessy family. Merton found the invasion cheerful and bewildering, in particular the rites of choosing who was to sit next to him, and who wanted him to reserve their place while they went for more food, or to play a game. The children filled the hermit's hands with rubber crabs and flies they had made at school. After the picnic was over and the party departed, Merton walked down to the monastery and left a large black fly on the open pages of the dictionary in the library.[82]

By mid-June, Merton had a correspondent who gave him just the same sort of delight in serious mischief to confound the grave. Apart from Rosemary Ruether's letters at the beginning of the year, there were two other women whose letters brought wholly different perspectives in in 1967. All three made important contributions to Merton's sense of wholeness.

On June 15, Suzanne Butorovich wrote from Campbell, California, inviting him to become a contributor to an underground newspaper and introducing herself:

> I'm one of your fans. I8m (Ops! I think that was supposed to be I'm) 16½ years old so if you answer do not go too far above my head. O.K.? Yes . . .

She signed off with "This letter is a disaster! Promote Lennonism. Fight the baddy baddies."[83]

He wrote back to her at once, and soon he was addressing letters to "Dear Disaster."[84]

In July, Suzanne Butorovich wrote giving *him* two new names in one letter:

> Dear Father Tob (?): Guess what! You got a new name you didn't need!!!! HELLO!! This is the Disaster Kid from the little hick town south of Alviso. (Now test your geography, where is Alviso?)

She went on to say she and her boyfriend now called him "Hippy Hermit." She sent a lipstick kiss and asked a question:

> Tell me something. If you were asked to revise *Seven Storey Mountain*, would you and what would you cut out and what would you keep?[85]

There are over 1800 folders of letters in the correspondence section of the Thomas Merton Studies Center at Bellarmine College in Louisville, some containing as many as two hundred letters. This exchange is one of the gems. Only the letters Robert Lax and Thomas Merton exchanged have as much life, while few of Merton's correspondents came up with an inquiry to match the seriousness of the one about revising *The Seven Storey Mountain*.

To the question Merton replied:

> If I had to rewrite Seven Storey Mtn I'd cut a lot of the sermons I guess, including the sales pitch for Catholic schools and that.[86]

He went on to advise Suzanne Butorovich on running the underground paper and gave her his permission to print his poem "Prayer to the Computer." On August 28 she wrote to "Dear Tom," sending news of the death of Brian Epstein and asking him to say a Mass for a Jew. He replied:

I'm terribly sorry to hear about Brian Epstein. I'll say Mass for him on
Sept. 5th. Did I ever tell you that once on a radio program he was asked
to name his favorite book and he named Seven Storey Mtn., only with
its English title, "Elected Silence"? I always felt closer to him after
that . . .[87]

She may have been impressed, but Suzanne Butorovich had bad news
for the writer in her next letter:

Dear Tom,
Do you know that I looked you up in the Guide to Catholic Periodicals
at school and GOOD GRIEF, why do you write so much?[88]

When she suggested him as a speaker for her school, there was a
mixed reception:

Then Father asked how many members of the class knew who was Thomas
Merton. About four of us raised our hands. GOOD GRIEF! What you
need is a Publicity Director so you can get known. That is, someone to
publicize you and get all the kids interested in you and everyone is buying your books and saying "Hey, man, he's where it's at, really cool, with
it!!!!! then everyone will go to Gethesani* and all the real cool people like
the Beatles and the stones and Alan Watts, And Ravi will come and sit
at your feet and get turned on!!!!! Isn't that a beautiful Dream?
　All right, so you like the smell of freedom, you fink! . . .[89]

*Drive the other monks nuts.

Others who had tried to draw Merton out of seclusion had put this
far less effectively. With the letter, Suzanne Butorovich sent her graduation photograph, which Merton put up on the hermitage mantle-
piece beside photographs of Suzuki with his cat and Sy Freedgood's
daughter, Julia, and her horse. Suzanne Butorovich also sent a detailed diagram to help him use the tape deck (he had admitted earlier
he was having trouble).[90]

When John and June Yungblut first wrote to Merton in February 1967,
he had to explain he was no longer giving formal retreats. If they wanted
to come up to the family guest house for a couple of days he would
probably be able to give them an afternoon or two, but it would have
to be unstructured:

. . . if the Spirit blew that way it could be considered part of a "retreat."
But I am not for preaching anything to anyone. Just fellowship and letting the Lord speak if He wants to. I am sure that Friends understand
that attitude![91]

Much of this had become something of a formula in the letters Merton wrote to newcomers in the hope of warding off a "heavy session":
this time Merton included a compliment, as he knew the Yungbluts

were members of the Society of Friends, whose work in civil rights and the peace movement was centered at Quaker House in Atlanta.

After a visit the first weekend in May,[92] both John and June Yungblut wrote to say how much the meetings had meant to them. Merton had also furnished some ideas for June Yungblut's thesis on Samuel Beckett, which she was doing at Emory University.

The Atlanta connection proved valuable to Merton from the start. The Yungbluts provided a line of communication to the Reverend Martin Luther King, as well as personal links with Tom Altizer, David Hesla (June's doctoral director) and others at Emory. They also brought Merton news of Coretta King, Jeannette Rankin, and Anselm Atkins at Conyers. For the moment, June Yungblut sent some books Merton needed from the Emory Library, with the statement that "My favorite Catholic reading these days is Teilhard de Chardin, Thomas Merton, and Dan and Phil Berrigan." She also repaid Merton's earlier compliment: "I will close with the highest 'praise' the old Quakers ever used when someone spoke or did well they fixed him with a serene gaze and said 'Friend, thee has been used.' "[93] In her letter of July, June Yungblut quoted from a letter Phil Berrigan had written to her, "Merton is top shelf — a rare human man. You must take the opportunity to go back and talk with him."[94]

The May visit had been a warm success, though Merton could not get excited about Beckett and said he preferred Kafka. In early 1968, when June Yungblut's postdoctoral study included "a study of Thomas Merton (Catholic), either Alan Paton or Martin Luther King (Protestant), Elie Wiesel (Jew) and Thich Nhat Hanh (Buddhist)," Merton wrote he would be honored to be found in such company. He provided full and revealing answers to her questions about his writing. Earlier, on November 19, 1967, Merton had passed on information about something more immediate:

Yesterday I got a letter from the AFSC in Philadelphia, inviting me to be on an unofficial team that is to go and talk to representatives of the NLF either in Cambodia or Czechoslovakia. Of course I would jump at it if I were the only one to decide. I had to turn it over to the Abbot however. He did not have the time to talk about it yesterday but I know what the fate of the invite will be. He is just not likely to see that this is important. He will regard it purely as a distraction from prayer. Which puts me in an uncomfortable position: because when it gets that far, I begin wondering if this place makes any sense whatever. Well, I'll suspend judgement until I see what he says. The paradox is that it is to a great extent because I am here that I am invited to go, while it is because I am here I can't go. The solution of course is that the Abbot ought to have enough imagination to let me go. Even though perhaps little might be done. It would still be much more satisfying to attempt even a little, instead of signing endless declarations and making hopeless statements.[95]

This is to move too far ahead, yet the struggle with the abbot over invitations in 1967 takes on a very different color when one knows that Merton was exploring a way to take the initiative, either as a peace hostage or as a member of an unofficial team talking to the National Liberation Front. It is necessary to go forward in order to understand this, and just as necessary to confront two rumors of 1968 head-on when talking about the letters Merton wrote in 1967.

One is that Merton advised Martin Luther King on civil rights. There is no evidence for this, and it is more than unlikely. Through the Yungbluts, however, Merton was in contact with King and his staff, and it was the Yungbluts who suggested that King come to make a retreat at Gethsemani sometime in the spring of 1968.

The second speculation is that Thomas Merton had a second and secret purpose in going to Asia in 1968, and that this was known to American intelligence sources, above all, the CIA. Later evidence will show that the time had passed for the kind of personal initiative that appealed to Merton in 1967. In 1967, however, he was comparatively open in his letters and in his discussions with people in the various peace movements about his desire to go to Southeast Asia as an intermediary.

*

In the summer of 1967 the range of material by Thomas Merton published in magazines was equaled only by the range of the magazines themselves — from scholarly monastic reviews to mimeographed underground newspapers. One struggle was virtually over. Father Paul Bourne wrote that summer to say that the whole issue of censorship had been suspended, if not repealed. Merton's chief censor added that as far as he was concerned Father Louis would have no more trouble. Perhaps by force of habit, Merton went on submitting material to Father Paul, only to have it sent back with the reassurance that the "green light" was now on permanently, until he sent his old novel, at which point Father Paul said he was not even allowed to read novels, so he could certainly not censor one![96]

While so many books were in preparation, only one title appeared in that year. In May, the firm that had become Farrar Straus and Giroux, with Merton's friend and first editor as one of the partners, brought out *Mystics and Zen Masters*.[97] Except for Merton's continuing interest in Zen, the book mirrored his studies of four years earlier, especially in the Russian and English mystics. The material had already appeared in such journals as *Jubilee*, *The Critic*, *Cithara*, *Cross Currents*, *Continuum*, *Sponsa Regis*, *Season*, and *The Lugano Review*; and where Merton made changes on the galley proofs for the book, they were chiefly to correct small errors of fact or to sharpen his style.

The Lugano Review, which had proved hospitable to Merton and even more generous to Robert Lax, had folded.[98] Now *Jubilee,* which had been founded by Ed Rice and Robert Lax, and with which Merton had been associated from the start as a sort of unnamed founder, was in deep financial trouble.[99] Ed Rice, traveling frequently to South America and the Far East on commissions for other publishers, wrote to say that subscriptions had fallen drastically with the publishing of controversial articles, some of them by Thomas Merton.

Merton sent many of his letters out that summer on sheets with a photocopied message, "the monks. Modern Moving With Old Fashioned Care." Even on letters to others in the Order and to the editors of monastic journals, he now signed himself Tom Merton ("I'm using my Baptismal name, not officially, but I'm using it anyway").[100]

Merton had been corresponding with Walker Percy, the novelist, since early in 1964, when he wrote a fan letter after reading *The Moviegoer.*[101] More recently, they had written about the civil-rights struggle, then about Bantu myths and contemporary Bantu folklore. Percy visited Gethsemani during a particularly crowded period in July, but there was some chance to talk and the two men discovered they shared the same delight in letting the imagination play on ironic detail. When Percy wrote to thank Merton, he told him he had set his new novel at the "Paradise Country Club," taken over by middle-class Bantus. Each club member had his white caddie, for whom he had developed a warm, paternalistic feeling, and whom he protected as "my whitey."[102] He struck a responsive chord, and Merton may even have made a contribution — country clubs had always been a target for Merton's satire. And then there were memories of the play put on long ago by the black Cub Scouts at Friendship House.[103]

The lively exchange continued in letters after the visit, each writer providing references for the other. In August Merton wrote to recommend "an essential reference book," *Bantu Prophets in South Africa* by Bengt Sundkler, which he was using for the "South" section of *The Geography of Lograire.* Soon both of them were teasing one another on the subject of the African Castor Oil Dead Church, in which new life is acquired by laxatives. Merton suggested, "There could of course be visits from fashionable Bantu prophets sent from Africa, one called T. S. Eliot who comes preaching Zen toilet."[104]

By August the correspondence moved to other concerns. Walker Percy wrote to thank Merton for sending his essay "The Long Hot Summer of Sixty-Seven." While Percy agreed with much of it, he resisted Merton's way of seeing the racial question and Vietnam "under the same rubric."[105] Both men had already agreed on a sense of frustration with movements in general, and Merton had explored the possibility of "universal anti-movement underground."[106] Percy brought news of another underground: in October he enclosed a card he had been handed by a segregationalist with the words typed on it "Pass this Card on to another White man." Percy's comment in bitter irony was "Well, you're a white man, aren't you?"[107]

Hardly by choice. In the summer of 1967 Merton was experimenting with other options, at least in his imagination, though Robert Lax had advised him earlier against taking the pills which had provided John Howard Griffin with the look of a black while he was doing research for his book *Black Like Me*.[108] While writing "The Cold War Letters," Merton had considered becoming a dolphin.[109] Now he wrote to Robert Lax that the time had come to opt out of the Human Race.

Where this proved difficult, he explored combinations of loyalties and allegiances. To June Yungblut he suggested the idea of a group of Buddhist-Catholic-Quakers, and he felt he already had the right qualifications.[110] For those who wrote asking for biographical material to publish with his articles and poems, Merton now offered this:

> Born 1915 in Southern France a few miles from Catalonia so that I imagine myself by birth Catalan and am accepted as such in Barcelona where I have never been.[111] Exiled therefore from Catalonia I came to New York, then went to Bermuda, then back to France, then to school at Montauban, then to school at Oakham in England, to Clare College Cambridge where my scholarship was taken away after a year of riotous living, to Columbia University New York where I earned two degrees of dullness and wrote a Master's thesis on Blake. Taught English among Franciscan football players at St. Bonaventure University, and then became a Trappist monk at Gethsemani Ky in 1941. First published book of poems 1944. Autobiography 1948 created a general hallucination followed by too many pious books. Back to poetry in the fifties and sixties. Gradual backing away from the monastic institution until I now live alone in the woods not claiming to be anything, except of course a Catalan. But a Catalan in exile who would not return to Barcelona under any circumstances, never having been there. Recently published *Raids on the Unspeakable, Conjectures of a Guilty Bystander, Mystics and Zen Masters*, have translated work by poets like Vallejo, Alberti, Hernandez, Nicanor Parra etc. Proud of facial resemblance to Picasso and/or Jean Genet or alternately Henry Miller (though not so much Miller).[112]

On July 4, 1967, the Catalan exile finally received the sink unit he had been waiting for at the hermitage. When this was installed and connected that day, he was able to wash his dishes for the first time without resorting to cold water in a bucket. At the same time, he received a new bookcase to house the material coming in from so many sources for *Lograire*. The bookcase was of newly worked wood, and Merton was delighted to find his whole hermitage smelling of cedar.[113]

The arrival of these new furnishings, and news that another hermit, Father Flavian, had made a request to be allowed to say Mass in his hermitage, gave Merton the feeling that he wanted nothing more than to be able to offer Mass in the hermitage to the patron of his solitary life, Our Lady of Carmel, on her feast day in the Order. As this was on July 16, he realized he had little time to prepare. The abbot reluctantly granted permission, and Merton then gave a rush order to Buck Murfield, the cabinetmaker in Athertonville, Kentucky, for the altar. When the rain poured down day after day, Merton worried Athertonville would be flooded. On Monday, July 10, there was a deluge, and Merton found the bottom lands at Gethsemani under water. When he went over to Athertonville on Tuesday many of the houses had flood water to their porches, but "Buck and his wife were planing away in their shop which was full of the sweet smell of cedar."[114]

On Saturday he returned to Athertonville to find the altar ready for him. On Sunday, "the Patronal Feast of my hermitage," he was able to offer his first Mass at the hermitage.[115] It had now been almost seven years since he had first come into his "casa," the gift of Our Lady of Carmel. It should have been an entirely joyous occasion, yet the week had left a sense of loss and sadness.

On Monday, the day of the heaviest downpour, Victor Hammer had died. The friendship had been beyond value to two artists in isolation. In his journal over the past fourteen years Thomas Merton had often broken off from what he was writing to ask himself what Victor Hammer would think of it. As a craftsman, Hammer had shown Merton again and again the truth of what he had written in a letter: "We are tools in the hands of God, we have to remain sharp and true."[116] And as the hand printer of Merton's most beautiful books, Victor Hammer included another passage in his letters which lifts art gently out of the realms of commerce:

> You are entitled to any change in your text, without any charge, our time has no monetary value, we want the book to be written as good as you can do it and we will print accordingly. I have made all your corrections and all three are a decided improvement.[117]

In early July 1967, Merton felt himself torn between his duties as a priest and his loyalty to a most believing unbeliever. At the end of 1960 the two friends had mourned together the news of the death of Raissa Maritain. Earlier that year Hammer had written:

> Dear Father Louis; yes God and beauty exist, but as soon as one trys to explain them they disappear as if they would not exist. Silence alone can express them. — I would like to be set right on the Last Judgment and the river Lethe. Perhaps one day you could do that. In Christ yours Victor[118]

On July 11, 1967, Merton wrote Carolyn Hammer, stressing the point on which all three of the friends agreed: that the good lives are those that combine simplicity and wholeness and are lived in love.[119]

❋

With his small kitchen properly equipped, his electric hotplate, and his refrigerator, Merton felt he could provide for himself on most days. Friends had responded generously to his requests. Naomi Burton Stone sent "Care packages" with Rice-a-Roni and other things Merton liked. Jack Ford contributed Merton's favorite teas, pumpernickel, and much else. And there were others. He was even adding to his rudimentary skills as a cook. On this score at least, he was full of self-congratulation in his journal. When Suzanne Butorovich sent him a Crimble box filled with Beatles memorabilia and cookies, Merton responded with a gift of his own, a recipe for kasha.[120]

Able to say Mass at the hermitage, able to cook for himself, Merton's ties with the monastery seemed cut. He believed himself in no way affected by the annual visitation of Dom Ignace Gillet, the abbot general of the Order, at the end of July. There was a violent storm one night, and when Merton woke to prepare for his day he heard the sound of heavy rain. He was putting on his shoes when there was a "terrific thwack of lightning striking in the woods near my cottage. I jumped!"[121] The day seemed to clear as the sun came up. While he was saying the Little Hours at about ten, the bells tolled for a death at the monastery.

Father Nicholas Caron, a Canadian monk from the monastery of the Holy Spirit at Conyers, had collapsed with a heart attack and died an hour later. As he had been the translator for Dom Ignace, the abbot asked Merton to take his place.

Merton felt he was out of touch, out of place, and largely out of sympathy. It didn't help his sense of just having gained his independence only to lose it when two other events occurred. The first was finding a notice on the monastery noticeboard which seemed highly critical of the hermits. According to Brother Alban, Merton exaggerated and made up the phrase "parasites on the community," which was not in the notice.[122] Merton wrote a note to Brother Alban that is a rare masterpiece of complication, first going into great detail about how he had always tried to pull his weight during his twenty-six years at Gethsemani. He goes on to say that both he and Father Hilarion had done their best to go elsewhere as hermits, but that if the community thinks he is a parasite, not a boarder, that he is taking advantage of the community, he will step down and go elsewhere. There is a good deal of sarcasm in all this. Then the mood changes entirely to one of contrition, asking Brother Alban for a chance to talk this over, and begging those who had come together to discuss the hermits to pray for him and what he is trying to do. He hopes he has caused no real offense.

At the same time Merton found he was engaged in another struggle over invitations. He took a somewhat gloomy solace in reading an article Mother Luke Tobin had sent him:

> I am undoubtedly feeling the effects of twenty-five–twenty-six years of "total institution" — in which I have been freer than most but in which because of my masochism and insecurity I tend to bog down in self pity and self defeat.[123]

He had felt the chances were poor earlier in the summer when he wanted to attend a second conference on *Pacem in Terris*.[124] Now, when he learned there was pressure from a number of quarters (including the Auxiliary Bishop of Louisville, Charles G. Maloney) to make Merton a featured speaker at an ecumenical conference, he thought he saw a distinct possibility of being allowed to go.

Cardinal Koenig of Austria was planning a visit to the United States expressly for the conference at Fairfield University in Connecticut, which was to discuss the relationship between the Church and unbelievers. The cardinal had asked for Father Louis (Merton puts this mischievously himself, saying he had obviously been chosen because he was a notorious unbeliever).[125] Norman Cousins, Walter Kaufmann, and Charles Frankel had agreed to take part, and panel discussions were to be kept informal and restricted to few participants.

Pressure mounted and the correspondence grew voluminous. In the outcome Dom James won the battle against considerable odds. In a letter to Cardinal Koenig, the abbot comes out adroitly to say that he is all too aware the cardinal will be put under pressure himself to issue a personal invitation directly to Father Louis. Dom James stresses both the "bad precedent" aspect with regard to the other monks at Gethsemani and the "solitary vocation" aspect with regard to Father Louis. He goes on to suggest Cardinal Koenig should come to Gethsemani, and he offers to pay all the expenses of such a visit.[126]

Apart from the attraction of simply getting away, the conference meant little to Merton: "For my own part I know I do not need to be present at a meeting with Cardinal K. and it is just as well I don't get involved in something that might lead to a 'career' of sorts."[127] What rankled once more was the feeling that he was not even consulted during the long-drawn-out affair. More important, where *this* effort to invite him had failed, there was little or no hope of others succeeding. It was hard for him to appreciate the extraordinary skills of Dom James Fox as negotiator when he felt himself the victim.[128]

In his depression of spirits even his reading soured him. Merton judged the standard of one underground magazine simply silly, those of the little magazines he scanned through no better. The attitude of self-importance was ludicrous; the style of writing worse. If he *had* to attend Chapter once more at the monastery, he decided he was under no rule or vow to read bad prose and worse poetry.[129]

Merton's sense of being a prisoner lasted when he came back from the tyranny of the routine at the monastery to that of his own routine. It was enlivened briefly by another storm on August 9, when lightning knocked out some of the lights as he said Mass at the hermitage. At the end of the month he had a bad attack of flu, which he nursed, as usual, with strong tea. Sitting on his bed feeling weak one day, he decided:

> This sickness has taught me something: first that I am perhaps too obsessed with reading and work — and I know the pressure of letter writing is too heavy.[130]

It made it worse that many of those who wrote in with suggestions, favors to ask, and commissions, were men and women he respected. Among others, he heard from Bramachari with the suggestion that Merton ought to arrange a complete lecture tour for him in the United States.[131] It would be embarrassing in every sense to quote from some of the letters Merton was receiving, especially from editors of monastic and religious journals, all, naturally, with the most religious of intentions — all, or almost all, putting a fairly obvious "bite" on Thomas Merton. He was wholly justified in grumbling, "In a word I am bombarded by beggars, fakers, con-men, business men, and operators and good enough people who want to talk me into something I am absolutely not interested in."[132]

He saw a kind of spreading moral brutality in all this, on top of the plain bad manners. This was not limited to letters. Father Dan Walsh had told him of a theology conference in Toronto at which some of the bishops had been hooted during speeches:

> There is too much spite, envy, pettiness, savagery, and again too much of a brutal and arrogant spirit in this so-called Catholic renewal . . .[133]

He could be fairly brutal himself in his letters to those he knew and trusted, though it was always a case of "present company excepted." A certain kind of progressive Catholic reformer was becoming his *bête noire*. He wrote to Robert Lax earlier:

> . . . I am truly spry and full of fun, but am pursued by the vilifications of progressed Catholics. Mark my word man there is no uglier species on the face of earth than progressed Catholics, mean, frivol, ungainly, inarticulate, venomous, and bursting at the seams with progress into the secular cities and the Teilhardian subways. The Ottavianis was bad but these are infinitely worse. You wait and see.[134]

Reading Meerloo's *Homo Militans* in manuscript and George Orwell's essay "Politics and the English Language" brought Merton back to the question of the language of debate — as well as to "doublethink" and "semi-officialese." He made more resolutions to limit his own writing to "poetry, meditations, criticism, and the thing I hope to do on 'Cargo,' for instance, or Camus."[135] He decided to write only the letters that gave him pleasure; above all, to put work aside and take long walks in the woods. The resolutions end with the statement "I keep away from the monastery as much as possible."[136]

He went down, however, for the consecration of the high altar in the renovated abbey church on Sunday, September 3, arriving late and watching the ceremony from the side. If he liked the new church, he had "So many memories of the old church — the energy and agony I had to put into just *getting through* some of the ceremonies — and yet I remember it all with a kind of joy, because of the graces, especially of the first days here. And being hebdomadary, singing the Mass, was a joy too, though I was often so painfully nervous about it."[137]

There were times when the changes in liturgy and surroundings were worth a mere regret that the old had been discarded with such ruthlessness. There were other times when the new seemed only refermented wine in very old bottles. Some weeks after the consecration, Merton went down through the rain for an afternoon concelebration and the profession of Brother Richard Schmidlin, to be dismayed when, at the end of the service, "we all recessed singing the 'Church's One Foundation' which reminded me of dreary evening chapel at Oakham 35 years ago. Renewal? For me that's a return to a really dead past. Victorian England."[138]

The greatest shock of all that autumn was Dom James's announcement on September 7, 1967, that he was planning to resign as abbot. It is hard to see why this caught Merton so off balance.[139] He recorded in his journal earlier that year that Dom James was asking other people's opinions about retiring.[140] Merton dismissed this as a political ploy, yet he took it seriously enough to refer to it when Dom James made an "official" visit to the hermitage on July 20; he encouraged the abbot to step down and tried to convince him that he did not have a "duty" to remain in command of the monastery.[141]

"I was surprised," Merton wrote in his journal, "and respect him for the decision." The full ramifications took time to absorb. The decision Dom James had made was quite as momentous in its way as Merton's withdrawal to the hermitage. Both were firsts for the Abbey of Gethsemani. While the traditional "election for life" had been set aside in other monasteries of the Order, and while the General Chapter later that same year would debate setting a term to the office, Merton must have felt that Dom James was the least likely of men to bring *this* innovation to Gethsemani.[142] If James Fox was convinced he "knew" Thomas Merton, Thomas Merton was under no such illusion that he knew James Fox.

Merton obviously came late, too, to the knowledge of plans that were well under way. Dom James and the cellarer, Brother Clement, had already selected a place for a hermitage on the high spur on the Edelen Farm property, close to the spot Merton had thought ideal when he surveyed there earlier. He admitted to a certain amount of envy: Dom James's hermitage would be far more isolated than his own. "Solitude may be more rare here in ten years time — if I am still alive."[143] But he turned the offer down quickly when Dom James suggested he move out to Edelen's and occupy the next ridge.[144]

Perhaps Merton's failure to take seriously the abbot's words about wanting to retire arose from an ingrown inability to think of anyone else but James Fox as abbot. The debate had been couched in these terms for so long that the roles seemed fixed in fact and imagination. When Dom Gabriel died, Merton had wondered, briefly, if Dom James would replace him as abbot general. For a moment he saw himself at risk, a candidate for abbot. Yet the whole debate struck him as unreal in his journal and he soon dropped it, deciding that Dom James would never be chosen abbot general precisely because he was so identified in the Order with Gethsemani.[145] Now that the retirement moved from the incredible to the certain, Merton was confronted with the question of a successor: Who would be elected to follow Dom James as the spiritual father of the community? What would life be like at the Monastery of Our Lady of Gethsemani in ten years' time — *if* he were still alive?

In the same month he had "a strange dream about starting on a journey somewhere with Dom James — but I was having trouble finding clothes to travel in!"[146] Merton had obviously forgotten that Sidi Abdeslam had prophesied during his visit that Dom James would either be dead or would retire within the year.

On September 10, Merton learned that his Columbia friend the artist Ad Reinhardt had died. In the same mail, Ed Rice wrote to say that plans to save *Jubilee* by selling it to a sympathetic publisher had come to nothing, and the magazine had collapsed.[147] Merton read this as a personal failure.

The day before, Merton had suffered a rebuff from his friend Thompson Willett. This was quite temporary; Willett continued on the committee for the Merton Room at Bellarmine, and the friendship was soon mended. The incident would hardly seem worth mentioning, except that the shock waves continue in the journal for some time and appear wholly out of proportion to the event as Merton described it.[148] He was sure someone else had caused trouble between Willett and himself. Once more, the key word is "rejection." Merton had enjoyed his times at the Willetts' and his discussions over a drink with Thompson Willett. He had been careful to keep away from politics with his host, knowing he and Willett had little common ground, while they had much on other subjects. Now Merton resolved not to visit, a resolution which lasted only a few months.

On September 22, he learned that John Slate had died of a heart attack on the 19th, at St. Francis Hospital at Roslyn, Long Island. Merton read the newspaper obituaries, then went for a long walk in St. Bernard's Field, trying to comprehend the death of a second Columbia companion in a month.[149]

Slate's death gave a sense of urgency to the slow progress of setting up a trust at the very time there was no legal adviser. Merton called James Laughlin for advice. When the publisher suggested finding a lawyer in Louisville, Merton remembered meeting John Ford and being impressed by the attorney. Ford agreed to act, and plans for a trust went swiftly ahead. Merton did not want to leave a simple will to cover the complicated matter of access to his papers if he, too, died suddenly.

The hermitage was lonelier for the loss of friends. Merton wrote to Lax that the newspapers had even misspelled Reinhardt's name.[150] Looking at the painting Reinhardt had sent him as a gift to hang with his ikons and Suzuki's scroll, Merton decided the study of "Black on Black," with its subtle play of crosses, was a fitting memorial to an artist Merton had always thought among the greatest of living painters.

Robert Lax, who had heard the news from Rice, wrote back:

> & then I sit (as seldom enough we do) in a church & look at the black & grey squares of the tiles, till the spirit is somewhat mended.
> & then all through the whole dark night it is Reinhardt, Reinhardt . . .[151]

Now Merton wrote to Lax of Slate's death and Slate's last visit, and Robert Lax wrote back of Slate's gentleness, adding the news of yet another death. Benji Marcus had died in Olean.[152]

Uncertainty for the future at the monastery, uncertainty about the possibility of sudden death, the feeling of being rejected by a friend, the collapse of *Jubilee* — all this weighed on him. He found his courage mended by a passage in the Bible:

> Remember these things, Jacob, and that you are my servant, Israel. I have formed you, you are my servant: Israel, I will not forget you. I have dispelled your faults like a cloud, your sins like a mist. Come back to me, for I have redeemed you.
>
> ISAIAH 44:21-22[153]

Reading *La Poétique de l'espace* by Gaston Bachelard brought him back to his own work. Merton thought Bachelard's concept of *demeures* —

places where living takes place — opened up new dimensions, just as the study of the Cargo Cults opened up dimensions in our thought about relationships with possessions.[154] For Ruth Merton's son, immediate surroundings had always been of near-obsessive importance: Bachelard's book was so evocative and important because it spoke to something that had always been part of him, now coloring his work on *Lograire* and bringing him to questions in his journal about his own *demeures*. There were only two: the true and the false. The hermitage, the "casa," was true, while the Merton Room at Bellarmine . . . ? That "bloody cuckoo's nest":

> Merton Room again — ambiguity of an open door that is closed. Of a cell where I don't really live. Where my papers live. Where my papers are more than I am. I myself am open and closed. Where I reveal most I hide most. There is still something I have not said: but what it is I don't know, and maybe I have to say it by not saying. Wordplay won't do it, or *will* do it = Geography of Lograire. Writing this is most fun for me now, because in it I think I have finally got away from self-consciousness and introversion. It may be my final liberation from all diaries. Maybe that is my one remainining task.[155]

"Where I reveal most I hide most" . . . There was something in his confidence in wordplay that went back to the macaronic novel: "I have written double-talk under the aspect of a kind of vow of silence . . ."[156] Merton's thoughts were turning back to the novel, as he recognized the two "secret books," *Lograire* and the novel, revealed *most* where they seemed to reveal least. There was no liberation from diaries, while even as he spoke against the collection at Bellarmine he was taking greater care than ever that tapes and drafts of the new poem should be preserved in case he died before the work was complete.

By October he was writing again, finishing his essay on *Two Leggings* for the group of essays on the Native Americans, the preface to the Japanese translation of *The New Man*, the essay "The Street Is for Celebration" as a preface for a book of photographs of Spanish Harlem by Monsignor Fox. When he wondered if he was not overextending himself once more, he decided, "each is also an act of love and communion — Indians — Japan — Puerto Ricans."[157]

Late in October there was a visit from another theologian named Rosemary, this time Dr. Rosemary Haughton. Merton wrote in his journal and to friends that this was the first theologian he had met who was six months pregnant: he also wrote (perhaps with relief) that he felt she had a real understanding of the contemplative life, and he photographed her in a long black cloak with her hair blowing in the wind as she sat on the concrete retaining wall at Dom Frederic's Lake.[158]

Doris Dana arrived for a second visit on October 27. On the 28th they drove to Lexington to visit Carolyn Hammer. Merton had been concerned for her since Victor Hammer's death. He was reassured, and had not been expecting the day would bring back the best of earlier Hammer picnics, or a day when he found himself celebrated, not as a cult figure, but as a stimulant to other artists. Doris Dana, Carolyn Hammer, and Merton went on for luncheon at the farm of the singer and folklorist John Jacob Niles. Merton had been wanting to meet Niles for some time, and now they met in the best of situations. The Kentucky sunlight that day seemed to Merton particularly beautiful, and he was fascinated by Boot Hill Farm. After lunch, the group was joined by the soprano Jacqueline Roberts and the pianist Janelle Pope, and they listened to poems of Merton's that Niles had set to music: "Messenger," "Carol," "Responsary." John Jacob Niles explained he was working on a musical setting of the poem "Evening," the next in a larger Merton-Niles cycle he was planning. Merton found himself in tears: he was moved by the songs, "But above all by this lovely girl, Jackie Roberts, who put her whole heart into singing them."[159]

In November Merton was working hard on the "West" section of *Lograire*. He had produced a number of drafts, and W. H. Ferry had made it possible for tapes of the poem to be transcribed at the Center in Santa Barbara. Merton's adviser on his poetry had always been Sister Thérèse Lentfoehr. She had been somewhat baffled by *Cables*, but she was enthusiastic about *Lograire*. When there was another O'Callaghan picnic on November 7, the O'Callaghans brought Sister Thérèse. With some sense of mischief, Merton insisted she put on a red wool poncho Tommie O'Callaghan had brought, photographing her in this, and autographing a book for Sister Thérèse, "To the Kentucky Indian."[160] When she asked the significance of the title of *Lograire* as they went over drafts together, Merton told her that the real name of the French poet François Villon had been Des Loges, while the *loges* were huts used by woodcutters and foresters.[161] Obviously his own hermitage comes in here, but so do the French Canadian *coureurs de bois*, while perhaps it is not at all incidental that Merton was mining the work of Cora DuBois for "Ghost Dance."

Whatever the connection with Villon, Lograire is probably a mythical kingdom, with some connections with the Carolingian kings called Lothair,[162] the ancient kingdom of Lotharingia, and the Logres of Charles Williams's *Taliesin in Logres*. The "Geography" of the title had its origin in Merton's reading of the story of the voyages of St. Brendan three years before. On July 17, 1964, the *Navigatio S. Brendani* ("the quest for the impossible island") had arrived from Boston College Library. He had read it in four days and wondered, "Is the geography of the journey a liturgical mandala? I have to check back on the significance of directions. North is liturgical hell here too and the Promised land is

West (except that in reference to the Paradise of the Birds, it is East (liturgical)). Perhaps we have here a convergence of two traditions."[163] Finally, whatever the compass points, this was to be Merton's big poem, rivaling the scope of the *Cantos, Paterson, Anathémata*.[164] And Joyce was back, too, Merton was rereading *Finnegans Wake* in July 1967 and relishing it.[165]

There were meetings with John Ford and with the trustees (Merton had asked Tommie O'Callaghan to be his trustee in Louisville). On November 12 he wrote:

> Naomi is coming (is in fact here or should be) and I hope now we can finally wind up all this Trust business which turned out to be much more elaborate than I anticipated. As usual I began to have doubts about it when it is too late. But I think I have done right, though this recourse to law is neither "monastic" nor "anarchic." Still I think it would be silly to leave the pile of paper that I have covered with ink merely to rot or get lost in the monastic library. What is left over after my death (and there is bound to be plenty!) might as well get published. I have no guarantee of living many more years. Perhaps five, perhaps ten.[166]

On November 14 there was a conference at the O'Callaghans', and everything was finalized before another memorable lunch. The trustees were relieved to feel there was now a measure of control on Merton's own generosity. He had paid debts to friendly librarians who sent him the books he needed with gifts of transcripts, corrected drafts, and sometimes his reading notebooks. This had gone on now for twenty-five years. Few recent visitors to Gethsemani had gone off without some Merton memorabilia.

In early December Merton celebrated several "fantastic days" and the joy he felt after a three-day conference of fifteen contemplative nuns. He wrote in his journal of their quality, alertness, and authenticity. In many ways his feeling of a sense of community with the group foreshadowed the delight he was to take less than a year later in the Trappistine Community of Our Lady of the Redwoods in California. In December, there had been little heavy, false piety, and many unstuffy moments:

> I remember the Sisters leaving on Thursday — one car after the other and finally the green wagon from New Orleans roaring off with Sister Kathleen at the wheel. Last I saw of her she was barrelling down the middle of the highway.[167]

Meanwhile another literary project had taken form. Since October, Merton had been corresponding with Jonathan Williams, sending Williams one of his new concrete poems, "Pluto King of Hell."[168] Williams responded with the gift of an anthology of Concrete Poets. On December 13 Merton wrote to say this is magnificent, then went on:

Guess what. I am suddenly going into editing, temporarily. I want to put out four offset collections of poetry-prose from all the good people. Just four collections. One brief magazine flash in the air and out, but four good collections. We have here our own offset press and I'd be crazy not to do this, we might as well put out something besides cheese ads for heavens sakes. Thus I want material for four good collections and how thick they'll be no one can say: no money involved one way or other [to] give away the collections.[169]

The idea for *Monks Pond* may have been with Merton for some time, or it may have come out of a meeting on Sunday, December 10, at the hermitage during a visit of Wendell and Tanya Berry and the Meatyards. They had brought the poet Denise Levertov, whom Merton had been wanting to meet for some time. He writes, "I like Denise very much. A good warm person. She left a good poem ('Tenebrae') and we talked a little about Sister Norbert in San Francisco who is in trouble about protesting against the war . . ."[170]

Merton was soon soliciting material for the magazine. In some cases this gave away how out of touch he was. Ferry had to point out that Rod McKuen was not a gifted "under-twelve poet."[171] The four issues of *Monks Pond* that came out in 1968 showed an honest format and a varied content. There was much work from the editor, including some fine photographs. Merton made the mistake as editor of including the work both of poets who were friends and of friends who claimed to be poets.

In his assessment of the abbatial elections, which would be held early in the New Year, Merton demonstrated a masterly degree of misreading and general maladroitness. He supposed there would be a strong movement to make him abbot, where there was little evidence for this. Much alarmed at the prospect, he included in his Sunday conference on December 17, a statement that he would not accept if he were elected. After this Father Flavian teased him that the statement had made his election virtually certain — it would be read as a sign of the necessary humility.[172] Merton panicked and issued a second statement, which was tacked to the noticeboard.

"MY CAMPAIGN PLATFORM for non-Abbot and permanent keeper of the present doghouse" was meant to be both funny and effective. It explained the private vow he had made in 1956. While such a vow was important, it could be set aside out of the overriding consideration, charity. Merton tried harder, and the signs of strain are evident. The prior and a number of the monks were incensed by:

> b) I would be completely incapable of assuming the duties of a superior, since I am in no sense an administrator still less a business man. Nor am I equipped to spend the rest of my life arguing about complete trivialities with one hundred and twenty five slightly confused and anxiety ridden

monks. The responsibility of presiding over anything larger than a small chicken coop is beyond my mental, moral and physical capabilities.

Having knocked both charity and humility on the head, he went on:

. . . You would probably be voting for me on the grounds that I would grant you plenty of beer. Well I would, but it takes more than that to make a good Abbot.[173]

He tried to make matters more certain by letting it be known that there might be a private source of embarrassment to the monastery if a child of the abbot turned up at the gate house.[174] How serious Merton was about anything, except that he did not want to be abbot, is hard to gauge, yet once again Merton had started, or furthered, the rumors about Merton.

Having, he fervently hoped, blocked himself as candidate, Merton began to worry about the other candidates. He decided the strongest contenders were those who would continue the policies of Dom James, men Dom James would be able to control from his hermitage. Others at the monastery have said Merton completely misread this situation, too, and the results confirmed it. At any rate, he decided to support another hermit.

On Christmas Day there was what the three solitaries decided to call a General Chapter of Hermits. Father Flavian Burns and Father Hilarion Schmock came over to Father Louis's hermitage. When Father Louis poured out the wine, he managed a trickle in Father Hilarion's glass, a trickle in his own, then almost spilled the wine, overfilling Father Flavian's glass. This, he claimed, was a clear sign Father Flavian would be chosen.

Flavian Burns had made his own commitment to solitude. The rest of the meeting was given to Merton's attempt to persuade him it was his duty to stand for abbot. Father Flavian asked why, if it was *his* duty, wasn't it Father Louis's?

In the end, and very reluctantly, Flavian Burns agreed to be a candidate. One of the main reasons he did so was to make it possible for Father Louis to continue in solitude. He felt, he says, that Father Louis had the unique ability, not only to search, but to record his search for others.[175]

✳

On January 4, 1968, Merton copied into his journal three lines from Robert Fitzgerald's translation of the *Odyssey:*

You shall not die in the bluegrass land of Argos;
rather the gods intend you for Elysion
with golden Rhadamanthos at the world's end.[176]

He was still retyping selected passages from journals, as he had already done to make up the unpublished "A Vow of Conversation." He gave a tentative title to the 1968 journal, "The Hawk's Dream."

He was disturbed by his reading, by what he took to be omens, and by rumors of the election. He believed that Dom James had told Father Flavian not to stand as a candidate. Visitors were arriving, among them Father Callistus from La Dehesa, the foundation in Chile. He asked Father Louis to be a superior in Chile, even if he was unwilling to stand for abbot at Gethsemani.[177] When Merton wondered once more if he might be leaving, the hermitage became dearer. On January 5, he took a glass of sherry and studied his surroundings. "Ears burn now in the silent, sunlit room, whisper of gasfire. Blue shadows where feet have left proper tracks out there in the snow." Then, "Lovely morning! How lovely life can be!"

The same day, he had a violent fall in the snow. Pain gripped his stomach and he felt as if he was going to faint. He was also afraid he had damaged the Rolleiflex camera he was carrying, and back at the hermitage he wrote to John Howard Griffin for advice.[178]

That night he had a dream:

> . . . I am caught suddenly in a flood which has risen and cut off my way of escape — not *all* escape, but my way to where I want to go. Can go back to some unfamiliar place over there. Where? Fields, snow, upriver, a road, a possible bridge left over from some other dream.
>
> (Sudden recollection and as if it were a voice. "It is not a bridge" — i.e. no bridge is necessary.)[179]

On January 7 Father Louis and the abbot dined with some of the guests who had come for the election, including Dom Colomban Bissey from Melleray and Father Charles Dumont from Chimay. There was a long discussion about the election and then about an invitation that had arrived for a monastic-ecumenical meeting in Bangkok from Dom Jean Leclercq. For Father Louis the attraction was that the meeting would take place in the Far East, but by December, the appointed date, "probably the whole of S.E. Asia will be at war."[180] The decision whether he could attend or not would be up to the new abbot.

Merton's certainty that the community would vote to continue the status quo brought speculation as to what he would do. If the new abbot was antihermit and tried to silence him, he felt he would still have to stay, in obedience to his vows. He would have to act like Pasternak, who had chosen to remain in Russia, or like Bonhoeffer, who asked:

> Who stands his ground? Only the man whose ultimate criterion is not his reason, his principles, his conscience, his freedom, his virtue, but who is ready to sacrifice all these things when he is called to obedient and responsible actions in faith and exclusive allegiance to God — the re-

sponsible man seeks to make his whole life a response to the question and call of God. Where are these responsible men?[181]

Two or three years before, Merton had wanted nothing more than to join a foundation in South America. Now he wondered "if the Chile foundation wants me very badly should I pull up stakes and go there? Of course if I am *sent*, no problem!"[182]

When he read his own notes as master of novices and listened to the conferences he had given on the vows, he felt depressed, finding them "so legalistic, so rigid, so narrow. Yet in those days I thought myself quite broad and many regarded me as a dangerous radical."[183] He was embarrassed for himself, yet the tangled argument goes on, poised somewhere between the feeling that there had been a change at Gethsemani and in the Church, and that there had not.

With the election on January 13, Merton discovered at least that he had been a poor prophet, totally misreading the spirit of the community. Father Flavian Burns was elected abbot "by a large majority and surprisingly fast." Merton had walked down through the snow to the monastery early that morning:

> Between ballots, the cloister full of people reading. I read long chunks of David Jones's *Anathémata,* somehow very moving and sonorous in that charged silence, and one felt a blessing over it all even before having any idea how it would turn out.[184]

Merton's excitement had obviously affected his style: it is hard to tell whether he means the election or *Anathémata.* The election, at least, was over by nine-thirty in the morning. There was an immediate sense that the old order had changed.

The abbot general was in Spain, and Merton helped to put the telephone call through so that the vote could be confirmed. There was a community photograph, with all the monks and visitors showing "naked faces." At the installation, Father Louis felt a real joy in making his profession of obedience. He wrote that there was a far greater sense of community than there had ever been.[185] A new Mass with music by Father Chrysogonus was concelebrated — a farewell to Dom James.

An attack of flu followed all this excitement, and Merton was in bed at the hermitage for three days. When he was better, he fell into the very trap he had recognized for years. In letter after letter to editors of monastic journals, and to some others, Merton announced he was now free to visit them.[186]

Recovery left him irritated. He was angry to learn the retreat master was telling the monks that Buddhists were life-denying, while Christians were life-affirming. Then he decided he "couldn't care less about such platitudes. What does he mean by *life!*" He was also irritated that illness had "pulled the rug" out from under him on his projects. Immediately after this, he wondered if this enforced leisure wasn't just what he needed:

> Yet in the evening — the bare trees against the metallic blue of the evening were incredibly beautiful: as suspended in a kind of Buddhist emptiness. Does it occur to anyone that Sunyata is the very ground of life?[187]

✳

Merton had made this very point any number of times in his own essays on Zen — those in *Mystics and Zen Masters* and those to be collected in *Zen and the Birds of Appetite.* The two key words are "emptiness" and "ground." Each had its equivalent terms in both Eastern and Western thought, not as abstract concepts, but as realities which could be tested and "realized" (that is, found, or made, real).

The last thing Thomas Merton endorsed was "Baptized Buddhism," and he admitted it would be singularly difficult to "Baptize" Zen Buddhism. Yet there were bridges. On one, Suzuki had crossed to find in the *grunde* of Meister Eckhart something that the Zen scholar recognized as central to Zen, as long as it was understood that *grunde* meant both "ground" and "the inner core" or "kernel." Perhaps the best translation is "seedbed," which gives both the sense of earth and the potential of further extension from a concentrated essence.[188]

"Emptiness" *(Sunyata)* involves a sense of nothingness that can only be thoroughly confused and confusing if *nirvana* is taken as nihilism, or a nihilistic state. *Kenosis,* one of Merton's favorite words, is a Greek term meaning "self-emptying." For Merton the movement from the Apophatic school of theology (in Plotinus, Pseudo-Dionysius, Scotus Erigena, and the School of St. Victor; then, most notably, in St. John of the Cross) to the Rinzai sect of Zen Buddhism was perfectly natural, even predictable. One of the best and clearest expositions of the Apophatic tradition is given in Merton's essay "D. T. Suzuki: The Man and His Work," which was republished in *Zen and the Birds of Appetite.*[189]

Merton had always been against a kind of contemplation which went in search of concepts, just as, in Zen, he favored the warnings of the Rinzai sect against the kind of contemplation that was "mirror wiping." In the first place, this was to confuse action (wiping) with right attitude (sense of the empty). In the second place, as Hui Neng, virtually the founder of the Rinzai Sect, had been at pains to point out, there was no mirror to wipe.[190] It was the need to break down the disciple's bent toward defining concepts, to analysis, to a desire for progress in "contemplation as process," that had given rise to the *koan.* Where the *mondo* in Zen is "question and answer," the *koan* is a riddle, a gnomic saying, sheer nonsense. Put in the vernacular of the West, this was a case of "Ask a damn fool question, get a damn fool answer."

The Zen master, questioned by a disciple whether the disciple was getting anywhere on the path to truth, would reply with the information that shoelaces were cheaper in one village than another. If the disciple tried to make a concept of Buddha (the "idolatry" of Merton's letter to Aziz Ch. Abdul)[191] the answer could be still more devastating: "If you meet the Buddha, kill him."[192] The idea is, of course, that the Buddha is not there to be *met*. What the disciple was likely to encounter would be only the false Buddha of his own imagination.

In the Christian tradition there are some close equivalents to this in the lives of some of the saints. St. Philip Neri showed on occasion much of the spirit of the Zen master:

> A more significant story concerns his attitude towards his followers when they start telling him about their delightful visions of the Mother of God and various other saints. Knowing only too well that such hallucinations are apt to breed spiritual pride, the worst and most obdurate of all the sins, he tells them that a diabolic darkness is undoubtedly hiding behind this heavenly beauty. To prove this, he orders them the next time they have a vision of the Blessed Virgin to spit in her face; they obey, and, instead of the vision, a devil's face is at once revealed.[193]

In Merton's writing, it is Descartes who is largely to blame for our desire to succeed, even in contemplation, by means of rational analysis. Merton's chief objection to magic had always been that it was an illegitimate attempt to gain power by forcing mysteries to reveal themselves so that we could use them. "Cartesian" contemplation was a form of magic no less magical for its apparent sophistication. Progress was likely to prove only progress in spiritual pride:

> We are plagued today with the heritage of that Cartesian self-awareness, which assumed that the empirical ego is the starting point of an infallible intellectual progress to truth and spirit, more and more refined, abstract, and immaterial.[194]

The high-sounding abstractions take the place of *grunde*; desire for progress, or its attainment, takes the place of emptiness:

> . . . But in actual fact, Hui Neng says, there is no attainment, and therefore to busy oneself about seeking a "way" to attainment is pure self-deception. Zen is not "attained" by mirror-wiping meditation, but by self-forgetfulness in the existential *present* of life here and now.[195]

It is hard to blame Descartes exclusively for substituting new magic for old, yet there is a passage in Basil Willey's *Seventeenth-Century Background* that bears some meditation. He talks of the difference between expectations before the great intellectual watershed of the seventeenth century and expectations after:

> . . . Where we had formerly felt fear, pains, curiosity, dissatisfaction, anxiety, or reverence, we now experience relief, and regard the object with

easy familiarity and perhaps contempt. An explained thing, except for very resolute thinkers, is almost inevitably "explained away." Speaking generally, it may be said that the demand for explanation is due to the desire to be rid of mystery . . .[196]

Thus "man" becomes a "problem-solving animal," and progress is seen in naming concepts, analyzing them, and thus claiming power over them. Certainly only "very resolute thinkers" will question the existence of the concepts and deny our power to name and use them.

Thomas Merton needed nobody to tell him that he was often under the spell of self-awareness, Cartesian or otherwise, as well as prone to analysis — that he was a man driven by ideas of self-improvement and "progress in soul making." He would hardly have been so attracted to either Apophatic theology or to Rinzai Zen if this had not been so. Only those who are aware of being "uptight" talk of "letting go." The difficult goal was self-forgetfulness. Merton was anxious to move on, to celebrate the moment without looking for significance —to play, and above all else to allow an element of the absurd to play with him and in his life. Yet he was determined to do this without accepting the premise of Camus — that is, without allowing still another philosophical concept, now called The Absurd, to destroy a Faith that was not an abstract concept for Thomas Merton but a *ground.*

❋

On the afternoon of January 21, Brother Thomas Arthon knocked at the door of the hermitage to tell Father Louis that news had just come of Sy Freedgood's death. He was shattered: he had been listening to some Mozart quintets while preparing supper, now he went down to the monastery to call Freedgood's wife, Anne. Unable to reach her at the New York apartment, he contacted a friend, who told him the house at Bridgehampton on Long Island had been burned to the ground. Merton adds that he had a premonition of Freedgood's death when he had first seen him after the accident the spring before: "Sy's grandiose plans in the spring — for getting me out 'like Faulkner' once a year etc. etc. We did have a pretty good day in Lexington!"[197]

He went back to the hermitage with no taste for either supper or music. In his journal he went over memories, including "Sy and Rice at my baptism." He decided, "It's already a hard year and I don't know what else is coming but I have [a] feeling it is going to be hard all the way and for everybody." The theme reoccurs often in the 1968 journal —"a brute of a year."

Merton had already been shocked by accounts of the growing savagery in the Vietnam War.[198] Now he heard from Brother Victor and Father Hilarion of the capture of the spy ship *Pueblo,* and thought it sounded like "a completely contrived 'incident.' "[199]

On his fifty-third birthday the guns at Fort Knox rattled his windows. Anxious over the international situation, he fretted unnecessarily about other things. Brother Alban Herberger said the propane tank would be filled to seventy-percent capacity. As soon as the level fell to fifty percent, Father Louis would send a request to have the tank refilled. Brother Alban explained the tank was not yet half-empty from the original filling, but he added another twenty percent to please Father Louis, who was obviously nervous about being left without sufficient propane. On one such occasion, they talked about the notice that had disturbed Father Louis and the note he had sent, and Father Louis lent Brother Alban the book on Faulkner the brother had wanted. Later on, when this was returned, Father Louis invited him in for a glass of wine. They talked for two hours and then had tea and toast. Brother Alban commented that toast was not on the menu at the refectory, and his host said there were advantages in being a hermit. Brother Alban had said earlier in their talk that he didn't think Father Louis was much of a hermit, and he wondered at his own boldness, deciding it must be the wine: "I venerated Father Louis very much, and I had never spoken like that to him before."[200] Father Louis did not seem greatly put out: "No, but I need a lot of time to myself," was the answer he gave. Father Louis said he thought he ought not to be in a monastery at all: he ought to be in a factory in China so that he could "see Communism first hand." Brother Alban laughed, and then they both laughed at the idea. "In China," Brother Alban pointed out, "with your need of a special diet? With your relationship with machines? In a factory?!"

During the second week in February Merton spent a day and much of a night in Louisville. After a morning at Bellarmine checking papers and at John Ford's law office, he went for a rest to the O'Callaghans'.[201] He had been disappointed to find Cunningham's was under new management and he ate at the Old House. That evening he went with a party to the Pendennis Club, where the music reminded him of the *thé dansant* on the Cunard Line. He went to hear music he liked better at a new place on Washington Street, and grew irritated when some of the group continued to talk while he wanted to hear jazz: "Ron Seitz, Sally, and Pat Huntington were appreciative." During a break he spoke to Jerry Clark, the trumpeter. He did not get back until two in the morning (something like six or seven o'clock in his own day). "The quiet of the hermitage is good. The sound of the jazz was good. In between — a vast morass of nonsense, babble riding, talking, pretending, etc." He thought of learning to drive and trying to buy his own car and then decided that after one night like this he was exhausted.[202]

He was soon back at Washington Street, however, and this time he had a long conversation with Melvin Jackson, the bass player, "a really dedicated artist."[203] Again he was late returning to the hermitage, and he found himself worn out the next day.

He was now helping Joseph Mulloy ("formerly accused of sedition in Pike County"), writing Mulloy a letter of support to the draft board, on grounds of moral rather than political resistance.[204] He had an argument over politics with Father Raymond.[205] He felt somewhat distanced from his close friend Carolyn Hammer over his active role. The atmosphere grew more threatening, more violent. It was harder for him to keep his own sense of balance — of the right priorities.

Worried by the number of his visitors, Merton was stalling on one project with the Yungbluts. He wrote to June Yungblut:

> About the other letter: of course we are available any time to any one wanting to make a retreat, and if Dr. King prefers to come before the march, well and good, fine with us. The only thing was that from the long term viewpoint, since the new Abbot opened our first official conversation in his new capacity by saying he wanted me to stick to my bloody mysticism and not get involved in all them outward works, it might be well to go a little bit slow on anything that might signify a tie in with some onslaughts on the bastions of squaredom. He is essentially open, just inexperienced and still a little closed in on set positions, but I think he can learn, given time. To have Dr. King, Vincent Harding and others later in the year for a quiet, informal, deeply reflective session would probably get the Abbot to see where I really do belong, half way between in and out of action. Not just all the way out.[206]

He had written to both the Yungbluts, explaining that a retreat by Dr. King before the Washington march would be bound to have "some symbolic public meaning."[207] Soon, however, he changed his mind and offered some dates in March.

The suspended decision about the Bangkok conference in December had set Merton's mind on the idea of going to Southeast Asia on another kind of mission. Here June Yungblut had to tell him that the situation had changed and hardened; the North Vietnamese National Liberation Front had refused to entertain the idea of negotiations, formal or informal:

> Bill Loftspitch will re-issue the invitation to you to meet with the NLF whenever this becomes alive again as a possibility from the NLF point-of-view. I spoke to him in Philadelphia where we flew in 7 orphans from Viet Nam — the only ones to get out of that holocaust so far.[208]

Working on her postdoctoral thesis, June Yungblut, like Suzanne Butorovich, told him he wrote too much:

> Thirty-six books plus innumerable articles! You really must stop writing if you're to be read in your entirety — unless you want to become a continent unto yourself in which there is room for so much research that an aging and wearied explorer like myself can get lost, eaten by crocodiles — or discover a golden city.[209]

The Yungbluts had driven up from Atlanta to Kentucky over icy roads at Christmas. It was all worth it, June says, for six hours with Merton:

"You are really a lot of fun to be with and a great companion."[210] The Yungbluts had told Merton that, as if seeking still more controversy and danger, they had applied to teach in the Republic of South Africa, and June had been asked to give lectures on Beckett and Merton at Cape Town University.

Merton wrote back, "It is hard to say what is important in my work and what isn't." He tried to help her discard:

> However, when I look back on this sort of editorializing or preaching whether about Christianity, or Monasticism, or social justice, peace etc., I find it thin and often a bit alien. I say things I think I have to say, and later become more and more oppressed with a sense of their inadequacy, untrueness to my own deep (?) intentions etc. The work I feel more happy about is at once more personal, more literary, more contemplative. Books like *Conjectures, New Seeds, Sign of Jonas, Raids,* or literary essays, or poetry, or things like introductions to Chuang-Tzu, Gandhi, Desert Fathers etc. In the essay collections like *Disputed Questions,* or *Seeds of Destruction,* or still more *Mystics and ZM* there is a great unevenness — some is close to center and some way off from what I really want to say. The Notes on Philosophy of Solitude in *DQ* is very central (I haven't reread it lately though) and the thing on St. Bernard isn't. In *MZM* the Zen pieces are central, so is Pilgrimage to Crusade, but much of the other stuff is peripheral to my thought. The existentialism piece is central, I think.
>
> I have always felt strongly that much of the writing I was doing was beside the point because it was not in a creative manner that really suited me. Working on the long Cargo etc poem I feel much more in my right element. Though *Cables to the Ace* is in ways deficient, I feel it is also another right approach, though dour and perhaps shallow . . .[211]

The "Cargo etc poem" was *The Geography of Lograire,* and this letter shows how closely that poem was tied to the long essay on the Cargo Cults. There was another connection, though this line went back from essay and poem to a much earlier time.

Twenty-seven years before, Thomas Merton had written:

> Have you ever asked yourself what you would put in your Time Capsule (for eventually every family will sink a capsule of its own in the barren earth of their back yard, no longer any use for the growing of living plants), have you ever asked what little souvenir of yourself you would like to have dug up in 6939: think of it, *you,* five thousand years from now, that same, unassuming, unimaginative, pathetic, miserly, envious little hypochondriac that you are, dug up as a present to the future, your own simple gift to mankind, the unembellished snapshot of your completely unimportant self! How would you like to be looking? Have you thought?[212]

The meditation on the personal time capsule had been prompted by memories of the time capsule buried at the World's Fair in 1939 in

Flushing Meadows, close to where Merton had lived as a child. The passage had been written during an exciting, creative, and imaginative time, June 1941, at St. Bonaventure's. It appeared in "The Journal of My Escape from the Nazis" — as far as Merton knew, his one surviving novel.

There is an obvious connection between the time capsule and the Cargo Cults, between the novel of 1941 and the essay of early 1968, together with the poem on which he now concentrated so much hope, energy, and enthusiasm, *The Geography of Lograire*. It is not unkind, either, to see the journals that still remained private and restricted as Thomas Merton's own time capsule. Yet he was no more generous in judging his own motives for leaving something to speak for him:

> The anxiety I have felt lately is due probably to the surfacing awareness that all this is futile — a non-survival, more alien to me even than Gethsemani to some extent. A last despairing childish effort at love for some unknown people in some unknown future. But this is Rilkian. Hell, it is Peter Pan. It is no good. All right if they do like what I have written — or don't, — if they understand or don't — this is only a kind of non-communication in the end. It is not what I am so desperate for, (and what I am supposed to have forgotten).[213]

Writing *The Geography of Lograire* brought back an old and instinctive feeling that the novel had had, in Reg Marsh's words, "damn life in it." Merton decided to have the novel retyped for another assault on the publishers. Marie Charron, a friend of Tommie O'Callaghan, had offered to do the typing, since Merton was finding it now so hard to get assistance at the monastery. One day, carrying the typescript, she tripped and dropped it. The parts became reassembled in random form. Merton should have been delighted by this aspect of pure play, or the absurd. He was not; he fretted away in his journal over the incident for some time, and he tried to unpuzzle what had always been a puzzle book. He gave it a new title, *My Argument with the Gestapo*, and wrote the largely unnecessary introduction. Then he sent copies to anyone he thought would be interested. He submitted it to Doubleday, where the editors were somewhat baffled but accepted it.

"Whatever the mess — this is a book I am pleased with . . ." he wrote in his journal:

> Not that it holds together perfectly as a book, but there is good writing and it comes from the center where I have really experienced myself and my life. It represents a very vital and crucial — and fruitful — moment of my existence. Perhaps now I am returning to some such moment of breakthrough. I hope I am. I won't have many more chances![214]

❋

The official invitation arrived from Dom Jean Leclercq on March 16 for both Father Louis and the new abbot, Dom Flavian, to attend the meeting of Asian abbots in Bangkok in December. This meeting for monastic superiors was to be held under the sponsorship of an international Benedictine organization, *Aide à l'Implantation Monastique* (AIM), whose headquarters were in Paris. Dom Leclercq put on a certain amount of pressure, yet the matter was undecided and would remain so for some time. Merton had learned by now that there was no immediate chance of his being an unofficial intermediary in peace talks with the North Vietnamese. He had also convinced himself that the Benedictine conference in Bangkok in December was a pipe dream. The war would be general by that time.

He was turning down a good many invitations which had come in, in large part because of his own initiative in late January. He found himself becoming "more monastic." He had been named to the Monastic Council at Gethsemani. After attending a meeting on February 23, he wrote:

> Quiet, reasonable, a very good atmosphere of peace, charity, sense. Father Flavian is impressive as abbot . . . Under Dom James my struggles and exasperation led me to do wrong and unwise things without clearly seeing what I was doing — and thinking myself justified. Under Dom Flavian — I am interested in being more honest and more serious — and a better hermit. It will be a struggle because I have let things get potentially out of hand by thoughtlessness and carelessness with people, visitors, drinking, etc. Just to aim at moderation does not really work.[215]

Once again, it was a case of intentions being good, but Merton was pulled in two directions. He may have celebrated the sober freedom under Dom Flavian in his journal, yet something in him missed the old days. Dom James had been "necessary," and now Dom James was no longer there, either to provide a counter-measure to his overabundance of ideas — or to throw off his own balance. "Just to aim at moderation does not really work . . ." Merton went looking for another Dom James now that James Fox was no longer abbot, and the man he decided upon was the Archbishop of Louisville, Thomas McDonough.

Even as early as January 3, and before the elections, Merton had been concerned enough to prepare the ground in a letter to the archbishop:

> With the possibilities of new policies around here, I think I had better draw my own lines in case they are not drawn for me: it seems to me that it would be contrary to my vocation for me to go out anywhere to speak in public, but that it might be right and necessary at times to speak to groups here and meet privately with small groups elsewhere in monastic type surroundings. I'd appreciate having your view on this.[216]

The conclusion is clear that he was looking for another figure of authority to draw the lines for him. Merton felt he needed protection in order to be free to follow his vocation. This did not mean he waived the right to argue. Yet the whole question of protection is a complex one. Earlier, Merton had shown concern about the Tibetan monks who were visiting in the United States, and what he wrote out of anxiety for the protection of others had considerable bearing on what he felt was his own need:

> As to the Tibetan monks, if you have any influence with them please urge them from me (and I have plenty of experience and am well qualified to advise) that it is most important for them to protect themselves against all forms of indiscreet press and other publicity, and that they protect themselves against visitors. They must have a cloister or enclosure or something which outsiders absolutely are forbidden to enter except with the superior or someone else in charge. They must protect themselves against noise and inquisitiveness and against everything. I agree that it is of the very greatest importance for them to be extremely careful of the influence this country can have on them, even with the best intentions. They have to stay apart, and above all be very faithful to their life of meditation.[217]

In 1968 Merton felt an equal need for freedom and protection, or perhaps for a freedom defined and protected. There was inevitably a pattern that confused others. And Merton tended to speak of "freedom" to those outside the religious orders, and of "protection" to those he knew would understand him. He admitted in his journals that his own resources were not sufficient, though he did not elaborate. To Archbishop McDonough he wrote, "I find people so easily get false impressions — not that it always matters too much."[218] He may not have intended to give false impressions, and yet in following the course he had followed it was hardly strange that he did so.

McDonough wrote back, rightly suggesting that this was a matter for Father Louis to discuss with the new abbot. In the archbishop's view, two or three trips out of the monastery in any given year would be in keeping with Merton's vocation.[219] This is interesting, because it was the plan Merton worked with later in 1968, though, if he was absent twice from the monastery, the second absence was prolonged to one, then two, then three months, then an unlimited time — as if Merton believed he should be away only *twice*. But this is to anticipate.

On February 10 Merton wrote to McDonough, asking his specific advice on the Bangkok invitation and saying Dom Flavian was undecided. This time Merton clearly wanted to go: he also wanted to have authority to go, and apparently that of Dom Flavian was not sufficient:

> I will discuss the matter further with Dom Flavian. I will let you know what he decides. However if at some time in the conversation with him you were to let him know your feelings on this general subject, I think it would help him form his mind on the subject. He is very open, but just

wonders if he has the authority to send me and it would seem that he certainly has![220]

Here one can imagine a sideward glance at Dom James and a certain nervousness about what Dom James would think when he learned. The first discussion about the Bangkok conference, at table on January 7 with Dom Colomban and Father Charles Dumont, had been general and it had been in French. French was not Dom James's strong suit. There were distinct advantages at the monastery in being a linguist, something Merton had put to good use a number of times over the years, especially in his letters.[221] At any rate, the ex-abbot and present hermit was told nothing.

✳

Merton was busy now finishing *Zen and the Birds of Appetite*.[222] It had been decided to enlarge the hermitage, and foundations were dug for a six-by-eight-foot room to serve as a chapel, and an even smaller bathroom.[223] As before, the building went slowly, in part because there was an unexpected late blizzard in 1968.[224] Overloaded with snow, two huge loblolly pines near the hermitage fell with a frightening double report. But the yellow crocuses Merton had planted at the foot of the great cedarwood cross and wagon wheel in front of the building, and which had begun to flower just before the blizzard, survived and reappeared as the snow melted. The first number of *Monks Pond* was delayed because the monastery print shop was turning out liturgical texts, but on March 1 Merton held the first copy in his hands and he was pleased with this.[225] He was now corresponding with many contemporary poets and was hurriedly reading their latest work. He liked the poetry of Gary Snyder, David Ignatow, and Robert Duncan's new collection, *Bending the Bow*.[226] Merton's less literary mail now brought threats that verged on attacks, while *The Record* had strongly criticized him for supporting the draft plea of Joseph Mulloy.[227]

It was with some trepidation, then, that he approached the monastery mailroom. On March 21 he found a package waiting. When he opened it he discovered it contained a magnificent camera. John Howard Griffin had responded generously to Merton's letter about his fall and the damage he feared to the monastery Rolleiflex by giving Merton on permanent loan a 35mm Canon FX with both a 50mm and a 100mm lens. Merton wrote back at once, "What a thing to have around. I will take reverent care of it, and any time you want it . . . I will take good care to see that it goes straight back to you if anything happens to me."[228]

Within the next week the gift had become "a Zen camera." Several days after it arrived there was another package. This one contained four books on James Joyce and one by Joyce for a review Merton had promised to *The Sewanee Review*. He took the books back to the hermitage and dipped into them at once.[229]

Apart from adverse notices in the press and threats by mail, there was a series of incidents early in 1968, which pointed up Merton's vulnerability. On the afternoon of the election he had seen an ex-nun at the gate house. The journal records that others thought her "crazy."[230] She was soon talking of "spiritual marriage." A few weeks later there was a female visitor from California whom Merton thought at first "Blakeian" when she announced that she was the Woman in Revelation. The new abbot, who asked to see her, was puzzled only that Father Louis was so incautious in his desire to advise her: to Dom Flavian, the woman was clearly disturbed.[231] It was not many days before Merton was complaining of "Problematic Apocalypse Women";[232] then, "Why do I always end up with women?"[233]

There had been a period of relative quiet at the end of Lent. As Palm Sunday grew nearer, things seemed to fall apart. Merton began to feel alienated even from the hermitage. He discovered something in himself that was only too willing to respond to outside disturbances. He was left with little sense of balance, overstimulated, ashamed of himself; needing just the kind of solitude for self-correction which was becoming harder to find in rural Kentucky.

Some of this was his own fault. The monks were careful to steer inquisitive visitors who had not made prior arrangements away from the hermit and the hermitage. Meanwhile, Merton had let it be known to friends that there was a back way, so that a visitor could avoid going through the gate house. The friends told their friends.

Some of it was not Merton's fault. The previous October he had been settling down to eat supper one evening when an intruder had simply barged in with the news that he had taken no time to figure out the combination of the lock on the gate. He said he was a private investigator named Ken Hill, and he asked questions about everything. Merton managed to humor him, then show him out. Later he was cross with himself that he had not gone to record the license number of the red car.[234] There were other, less dramatic, trespassers. One evening in the spring of 1968, a group of well-wishers surprised him reading in his drawers. He cursed them away and decided this was an excellent way of disposing of any cult image.[235] He found a secret spot near Linton Farm for his afternoon reading, returning cautiously and stalking the hermitage until he was sure there was nobody about. When he saw a party of priests one day, he remained hidden until they gave up and left.[236]

Some who might have been expected to come now kept away. Things had changed since the meeting of superiors of the Order in 1964. Dom Edward McCorkell was the only superior who wanted to consult with

Father Louis when he attended the abbatial blessing of Dom Flavian in March 1968, and this surprised the Abbot of Holy Cross, Berryville, Virginia.[237]

He had come to Gethsemani "weighed down with concern and worry," and he felt lifted at once when Merton made it clear that after their correspondence he had been looking forward to the meeting. They set off for a walk through the spring woods and fields, stopping briefly at the hermitage. When the hermit spoke with Parrish's workmen, who were at last raising the walls of the addition, "the humanness of the encounter" impressed Dom Edward.[238]

Three things in particular were on the abbot's mind. The General Chapter of 1967 had relaxed the Rule of Silence in certain circumstances, making the matter somewhat vague and leaving the interpretation of "certain circumstances" to the discretion of the superior at each monastery. Dom Edward felt he needed direction in concrete situations, and he and Merton discussed this. In the second place, now that the eremitical life had become a part of the Order, Dom Edward was anxious to discover what this development would mean, both for the solitary and for the monastery. Here, the Abbot of Berryville felt Merton was most helpful, encouraging him in his own wish to show prudence with openness, for the sake of the individual and the community. When Dom Edward asked about one monk at Holy Cross who wanted to become a hermit, Merton gave the common-sense reply, "The man has been faithful for thirty years and he's been a good monk. He has earned the right to be trusted as a hermit."[239] Finally, there were the ambiguities in the use of the vernacular and the new liturgy, which were dividing so many, and which Dom Edward wanted to talk over with someone who was not committed to either of the extreme views.

One thing bothered them both. They had referred to it in letters before they met. The Order had recently become even more sensitive than before to publicity, in part because of articles on the Cistercians Coleman McCarthy was publishing, and, undoubtedly, in part, too, because of the writings of Thomas Merton. At the regional meeting a new journal, initiated and edited by Father Anselm Atkins of Holy Spirit, Conyers, Georgia, had been voted on. It was supported by Dom Edward, Mother Myriam of the Redwoods, Dom Augustine, and one other, but the majority voted to suppress *American and Cistercian*, and copies of the first, or pilot, issue were buried or burned. Father Louis had felt that an exchange of ideas between monks in different monasteries was vital at this time: he simply could not understand what had happened, especially when the whole matter of censorship was being relaxed.

Dom Edward found many of Father Louis's ideas on small, experimental monasteries helpful. At the key General Chapter of the Order in 1969, much of Merton's thought on monastic renewal would be given a far more positive interpretation and implication. Yet Dom Edward would note that this was largely brought about because Dom Flavian was politic enough not to mention Father Louis's name when he put forward proposals which were in great part his.[240]

Soon after Dom Edward left, Merton had a very different meeting. He had been corresponding with Barbara Ann Braveman, who had written the October before asking Merton to be poet on campus at Washington University in St. Louis.[241] He had to write back explaining why this would be impossible, though the idea intrigued him. In March 1968 she arranged for the students at the university to interview Merton for the literary magazine.[252] Susan Smith and Sandy Meyer arrived on Saturday, the 30th, carrying a tape recorder.[243]

Merton answered their questions in a thoroughly relaxed manner, and then all of them went off to Colonel Hawk's Restaurant, in Bardstown. Louis Rogers, Colonel Hawk, the black owner,[244] was a favorite with Merton, and the atmosphere became more relaxed still over drinks, with Merton and the students talking politics and Hawk listening in. When they went on to the Willetts' house, matters became more complicated because Merton felt the need to make allowances in conversation for Thompson Willett's more conservative views. It was a case of trying to identify with several different people at the same time. Back in the car, Susan attacked Merton for reversing much of what he had said earlier and for being insincere. Merton, who had found Susan attractive, now said she "lit into me hysterically."[245]

He went the next morning to say Mass at the home of Beatrice Rogers in Bardstown. Beatrice was married to Colonel Hawk's son. She worked for the Willetts, who were present that morning. Merton wrote, "Much peace, everyone getting along, the girls, the Willetts etc . . . It was a real grace, though I had no permission . . . Still, in post-conciliar liberty, I thought, O.K. — this is what I do."[246]

There were a number of ups and downs in the week before a visit he was looking forward to, the arrival of Donald Allchin and a friend at Union Seminary in New York, on April 4, a day they would all remember.

Merton had been corresponding with June Yungblut about the projected visit of Martin Luther King, and it had looked as if a suitable date would be found. On March 12 she wrote to say, "Coretta King has your dates and will nail Martin down."[247] A few days later, however, there was a far more ominous letter:

> Martin is going to Memphis today . . . he won't be back until the weekend so John won't see him (i.e. about the retreat) until next week. I hope both he and Nhat Hanh will soon go to Gethsemani . . . If Martin had taken a period there he might have had the wisdom in repose to stay out of Memphis in the first place, and it was a mistake to go there. He had done no preparation and came in cold to a hot situation where the young militants had him just where they wanted him . . . If there is violence

today Memphis will be to King what Cuba was to Kennedy . . . If Memphis is to be Martin's Jerusalem instead of Washington, how ironical that it is primarily a nightclub for Mississippi which is dry wherein the crucifixion may take place and that the Sanhedrin will be composed of Negro militants.[248]

The letter arrived before April 4. Merton copied it into his journal after that date with the comment that it was "sensitive and prophetic."

On Thursday, April 4, Merton took his friends to see Shakertown, and they stopped at Lums in Lexington on the way back for supper. He gives a very full description of the "curious sort of goldfish bowl glass place out in a flat suburb near a railway viaduct," of a freight train going by which seemed to be without end, "silhouetted against a sort of ragged, vague sunset. A lurid light between clouds," and the woman at the cashier's desk was "the kind of thin, waif-like blonde I get attracted to." The television was on for the news. There were scenes from Vietnam first, then some footage from a speech Martin Luther King had made in Memphis the night before. "I was impressed by his tenseness and strength. A sort of vague, visual, auditory impression." Finally, there was an interview with "the jovial man in South Africa [who had] just had the first successful heart transplant. He said he had been down to the beach to 'get a little ozone.' " It was explained that the heart donor had been black. "They asked him if he felt any different towards his wife and I nearly fell off my chair laughing. No one else could figure out what was funny."[249]

The party started off after a good deal of discussion on how to get back to the Bluegrass Parkway. Someone turned on the radio as they drove, and almost at once came the news that Martin Luther King had been shot:

> Rainy night. Big, columned Baptist churches. Highway with huge lights and wrong turns. Radio. Nashville. Louisville. Indianapolis. Jazz, News, ads. ML King gradually coming clear through all the rock n' roll as definitively *dead*. And Southerners probably celebrating, and Negroes getting ready to tear everything apart.[250]

They went on to Hawk's place in Bardstown, where Colonel Hawk threw his arm around Merton and called out to the room, "This is my *boy*, this is my *friend*." Merton was only anxious to show his solidarity that night with his black friends. When he talked to Beatrice Rogers, she asked him to design a coat-of-arms of the Rogers family to hang in her hallway. "I could cry," Merton wrote.[251] At the hermitage, he said a Mass for Martin Luther King, and wrote to Coretta King of his grief and shock.

✱

The talk of the plague and of the "brute of a year" in the journal was no longer an exaggeration. Johnson had announced he would not run

in the November election. Eugene McCarthy rallied the Children of
Peace, non-violent and violent together. Robert Kennedy announced
himself as a candidate, won the California Democratic primary, and was
assassinated on June 5. Nobody could find Father Dan Walsh, who was
being asked for by the Kennedy family. There were riots and burnings
in most of the largest cities. On May 27, there was a serious riot in
Louisville and a curfew had to be imposed.

The question of his going to the Bangkok conference still hung fire,[252]
but Merton was becoming anxious to leave Kentucky, at least for a period of time. He accepted an invitation to go to Our Lady of the Redwoods, Whitethorn, California, to conduct a series of conferences with
the Trappistine nuns in May. Dom Flavian agreed the trip would also
provide a chance to explore the possibility of establishing a hermitage
or a Gethsemani *laura* in some isolated area of the California coast, and
Merton wrote at once to W. H. Ferry, asking for help. On the way
back from California he planned to look at one experimental foundation, Christ in the Desert, in New Mexico.

On this occasion, plans were made quickly and kept secret. Merton
cancelled appointments for visitors after May 5, simply saying he would
be doing monastery work. On Derby Day, May 4, there was another
picnic, this time at Watts Towers, the old silver spire of Gethsemani.
Merton was full of memories of two years earlier, and this was another
bright spring day.[253] On Monday the 6th, he flew to San Francisco,
then to Eureka, California.

He returned on May 21, bringing many photographs and a notebook. The notebook was an impressionistic diary of the two weeks,
which he revised, retyped, and titled *Woods, Shore, Desert*.[254] Quotations he wanted to use at the conferences, visual images that are the
verbal equivalent of the photographs he took, notes and addresses, all
are worked into a mosaic. Yet the notebook is not as compressed as
the section of *Lograire* he wrote on the plane to San Francisco.

In *Woods, Shore, Desert* he writes:

> May 6th,
> O'Hare, big fish with tail fins elevated in light smog.
> One leaves earth.
> "Not seeing, he appears to see." *Astavakra Gita*.[255]

In "Day Six O'Hare Telephone" this is:

> Comes a big slow fish with tailfins erect in light smog
> And one other leaves earth[256]

The quotations in *Lograire* are brought in without the references to the
Astavakra Gita or to any of the score of books Merton was reading and
mining, for the conferences, the notebook, the poem.

One quotation in *Woods, Shore, Desert* makes clear how close Merton's technique had come to David Jones's experience of all times in time present. Merton quotes from Poulet on Pascal:

> Lived time is for Pascal as it had been for St. Augustine! The present of an immediate consciousness in which appear and combine themselves with it retrospective and prospective movements which give to that present an amplitude and a *boundless temporal density.*[257]

Where the meaning of the sentence seems confused at first, there is an attempt to demonstrate in the syntax the very process described. Merton attempted much the same effect in the next section of *Lograire,* where the title gives the clue: "At This Precise Moment of History."[258] Flying over the country, he rediscovered the feeling for geography he had found on the flight to St. John's in 1956. Now he was "Reading the calligraphy of snow and rock from the air"[259] and trying to "Be a mountain diviner!"[260]

At Eureka, Sister Leslie and Father Roger from the Redwoods met him and congratulated the Catalan exile on wearing a beret.[261] The next week was not arduous. He taught the conferences in the late afternoon, and explored the countryside — the redwood forest, and the coast from Needle Rock to Bear Harbor — during the day. He quickly became friends with the superior, Mother Myriam Dardenne, whom he had met briefly before at Gethsemani, and he mentions the Belgian and American nuns by name in the notebook.

Merton believed he had found a perfect hermitage in a deserted house at Bear Harbor. He photographed wild iris, then tried to negotiate with the owner, who proved noncommittal. Real estate was already volatile on that not-quite-deserted stretch of coast, and Merton was nervously counting cars and finding them too many. For the moment it was beautiful, on clear, bright days lit by sealight. He telephoned Ferry to ask the name of a bird he could not identify, and learned it was a Stellers Jay — "a marvelous blue."[262] Later he quoted a friend of Gertrude Stein as saying "All blue is precious."[263]

Everything about those days seemed to be precious, and he recalled after his return "A sense that somehow when I was there I was unutterably happy — and maybe I was."

Yet the outside world broke in, even at Bear Harbor and Needle Rock (which had once been used as the "homing mark" of the Spanish Manila fleet). On April 25 he had learned that his Aunt Kit had been drowned fifteen days earlier on a ferryboat that sank between the two islands of New Zealand. In the notebook he writes, "Yesterday, in this place, looking southwest, I thought of New Zealand and the *Wahine* and my Aunt Kit getting into the last lifeboat. It capsized."[264]

He had learned the students at his old university were smoking cigars in the office of the president, Grayson Kirk, and the Viet Cong flag flew from buildings on the Columbia campus.[265] He heard that nobody at Doubleday understood his 1941 novel.[266] He received news of the arrest of Phil and Dan Berrigan for destroying the A-1 draft cards in an office in a Baltimore suburb.[267] The same "boundless temporal density" moved him as he watched the Pacific surf coming in and thought of the music Sister Dominique had written for the Alleluias at Mass.[268] He made friends with Gracie Smith and her children and went with Winifred Carp to look at her paintings.[269]

On Wednesday, May 15, he was driven to San Francisco, which he decided was "as pretty as Havana," only quieter. He telephoned Lawrence Ferlinghetti and they went to dinner at Polos, an Italian restaurant, and then on to the Trieste, an ice-cream place on North Beach. Later Merton went to City Lights Bookshop, where he browsed the bookshelves, then tried to sleep on a mattress on the floor in the office — San Francisco was not as quiet as he had thought. He managed to catch three hours of sleep between 2 and 5 A.M.[270] Later, on the 16th, he was flying again, this time via Las Vegas to Albuquerque, where he was met and taken on the long drive to Christ in the Desert, thirteen miles by dirt road off the highway. He was no sooner there than he announced this was the finest monastery in America.

Yet he was not tempted to join Dom Aelred and Father Gregory, who with the hermit, Father Denis, comprised the whole community of Christ in the Desert. It may be he learned just enough of the heroic difficulties of maintaining such a small community to dissuade him. He was given Navajo rugs for the chapel at the hermitage, which had been ready just before he left Gethsemani. One of the views at the monastery in New Mexico was not wholly unlike the view from Our Lady of Carmel, and he found himself unexpectedly homesick:

> For the first time since I have been away, I now have the feeling that I might be glad to get back to Kentucky, but not to mail and visitors and invitations that I will have to refuse and other things that I will not be able to avoid.[271]

In the meantime, the adobe monastery building, the Sangre de Cristo Mountains "blue and empty," the great sweep of the Rio Grande Valley, brought him to "color" once more, though only by accident. He had used up the black and white film he had brought, and could only obtain color in Abiquiu.[272] He missed meeting Georgia O'Keeffe, but talked to Peter Nabokov, whose book *Two Leggings . . .* he had reviewed. The new friends he was most excited about were Don Devereux and his wife, friends of Ferry's, who had driven out from Santa Fe to see him. Merton and Devereux took to one another at once. When Devereux began talking of secret Indian dances to which outsiders were forbidden, Merton became so interested that Devereux promised to let him know when they would happen next and to get him in if it were at all possible.

He went exploring the Chama Canyon, swimming in the cold waters and taking more photographs. This time there were rattlesnakes to watch out for, and there was another unfamiliar bird, the Gray Jack, or Whiskey Jack. He visited Ghost Ranch, and when he studied the diamond rattler in the Ghost Ranch Museum he decided the calligraphy of the snake's skin was like the calligraphy of the Western desert states seen from the air and like buildings in San Francisco.[273]

On the morning of the 20th, he was driven to the Abiquiu airport with two Republican ladies who talked of the election; then he made the long flight back, with many changes of plane, arriving in Louisville in the rain after dark, to be met by Frank and Tommie O'Callaghan. He spent the night at their house. The next morning he was back at the hermitage. He had felt homesick for a few moments at Abiquiu; now he found himself longing to be either on the California coast or in the New Mexican desert.

✳

On the trip he had decided that correspondence was "a pain in the ass." There was much waiting for him, a good deal of it troublesome. For all this, he wrote letters to the new friends of the trip, the nuns at the Redwoods, to Portia Webster, one of the postulants, who worked at Pennys in San Francisco, to Gracie Smith, and Winifred Carp, and to Don Devereux. News of the sentencing of the Berrigans reached him:

> . . . *Six years!* It is a bit of a shock to find one's friends so concretely and tangibly on the outs with society. In a way, both Phil and Dan are saying openly and plainly what all of us know in our hearts: that this is a totalitarian society in which freedom is pure illusion. Their way of saying it is a bit blunt, and a lot of people are so dazed by the statement that they don't grasp it at all. Those of us who do grasp it are, to say the least, sobered. If in fact I basically agree with them, then how long will I myself be out of jail? I suppose I can say "as long as I don't make a special effort to get in" — which is what they did. All I can say is that I haven't deliberately broken any laws. But one of these days I may find myself in a position where I will have to.[274]

He was moved almost to tears when Father John Eudes Bamberger asked in Chapter for the prayers of the community for the Berrigans.[275]

There was a further conference with nuns, and this time Merton found himself exhausted and troubled by what he saw as the "old narcissism":

> Certainly the complex business of being a "personality" and exorcising the public demon it involves — all this is too much. And it perpetuates itself in the doing . . .[276]

On June 5 he heard about the assassination of Robert Kennedy and sent a telegram to Ethel Kennedy, then said a Mass in the hermitage chapel.[277] Two days later he was in Lexington to hear the settings John Jacob Niles had composed for more of his poems. On the same day an intercom was installed at the hermitage, giving him some means of communicating with the monastery. A year earlier this would have been the last thing he would have wanted; now he accepted it as a security measure. Robert Lax had been teaching in South Dakota; there was some confusion about when the university would break up, and Merton anxiously awaited his friend. On June 27 he had a further talk with Dom Flavian. "He seems open to the idea of my spending time in solitude by the Pacific and even perhaps going to Asia to some Buddhist centers."[278]

Merton was working toward a decision to go to Bangkok. The conference itself had a varying appeal, while working out a "possible itinerary" was almost as exciting as working on the drafts of *Lograire*. There is a series of itineraries on yellow paper, and this makes interesting reading.[279] Each time, Merton comes back to crowd more plans into his time away, moving the date up from December into November, then into October, and finally into September.

This time his prospective trip was far from secret. He had already told the nuns at the Redwoods that his abbot had promised to allow him to spend the next Lent in the deserted house at Bear Harbor (their response, he records, was to say they would fight each other for the chance to bring him his supplies).[280] Now Merton enjoyed the chance of discussing plans with visitors and many of his correspondents, binding each person he told to tell nobody else.

On June 8 Robert Lax arrived, to stay until midday on the 13th. There was a big picnic with the O'Callaghans, Lax, Ron and Sally Seitz, and others in the hot sun. Merton enjoyed it, then felt a little fuddled by the heat and talk and wrote that once more he felt divided from himself. He was also feeling depressed at the idea of Lax's departure: "I don't know if he should return to Greece. Kalymnos seems to be the only place he really likes anywhere. I don't blame him. But also I don't trust a police state sustained by the C.I.A."[281]

Even though he thought it well done, reading James Baker's dissertation on his work further depressed Merton:

> It was all right; he had done a lot of work, read an enormous amount of my writing (certainly not all of it!) and was highly sympathetic to my ideas. That was all fine. Yet the whole thing showed me clearly so many limitations in my work. So much that has been provisional, inconclusive, half-baked. I have always said too much too soon. And then had to revise my opinions. My own work is to me extremely dissatisfying. It seems trivial. I hardly have the heart to continue with it — certainly not with the old stuff. But is the new any better?[282]

Having been his own savage critic, he turned to other critics in a letter to Baker:

> . . . I have certainly had unfriendly critics, but on the whole my work has been accepted with sympathy. And of course I do feel it to be significant that much of the sympathetic understanding has come from Protestants — and that the first dissertation is by a Baptist (Thanks, too, incidentally, for quoting me in your dialogue service). As a matter of fact a Quaker friend of mine in Atlanta is also thinking of writing something on my work, in comparison with several others, a Jew, a Buddhist and a Protestant. I feel that Catholics have tended to be either too uncritical or too critical of me, and I appreciate the more objective and balanced view of my work that is sometimes taken by those outside the Catholic Church. Inside it, I seem to get either total adulation or total rejection. Or at least I have that impression sometimes.[283]

One critic, the theologian Dr. Martin E. Marty, had revised an earlier, 1965, view that Merton had spoken far too pessimistically of black militantism, making amends in "Re: Your Prophecy," which was published in the *National Catholic Reporter* in August 1967, during the "long hot summer" of that year. With the siege in Cleveland, it looked as if the "prophecy" would be still further fulfilled in the "long hot summer" of 1968.[284]

So far, at least, there had been no general war in Asia. With his mind on the conference in Bangkok in December, it was easier to see other invitations as distractions (" — all expenses paid and $6000 beyond that. Nuts" was his response to a lecture tour).[285] He was writing every change of plan to Ferry, asking if it might be possible to do a lecture or two at the Center to help pay expenses. He was also consulting with Marco Pallis and others on possibilities in Asia, and with Laughlin about getting an American Express card. It grew very hot, and Merton was finding it difficult to sleep with the excitement and the noises of the Kentucky night. On June 24 he went to Louisville to see the doctor, but felt well enough to cancel the appointment, spending the time instead at the library of the University of Louisville, trying to read up on structuralism. After this, he went to the airline offices for information on visas and inoculations.[286]

A young Jesuit, Phil Stark, was helping him with the last two issues of *Monks Pond*. Merton found Stark a congenial working companion, and the arrangement gave the editor some relief time. There were hours that summer when he admitted to being too preoccupied, others that were precious because of his plans to be away. He watched the flycatchers in the evenings. He had been afraid Andy Boone's dogs would frighten all animals away, and he was pleased when one deer came within fifty feet of the hermitage.[287] When he said Mass now in the chapel he thought it was a great gift. The hermitage was as he wanted it, and nothing needed to be added: the ikons on the wall of the chapel, the small Ad Reinhardt painting, the Shaker Tree of Life in the kitchen, the Suzuki scroll by the fire, the New Mexican rugs on the floor of the chapel. Even the tiny bathroom was finished. There would be no more purgatorial trips to the outside "jakes" in the rain or snow. In summer he could cool himself down with a shower. His health had certainly improved: he was able to do physical work again, planting around the hermitage with his shirt off.[288]

He read Marcuse's *One Dimensional Man*, more Fanon, and the Joyce books so that he could write his review for *The Sewanee Review*, "News of the Joyce Industry."[289] Then he began Kierkegaard's *Attack upon Christianity*, and found himself raw again from an inner debate:

> How can one laugh and shudder at the same time? The book is so un- controvertibly *true*. And to find myself a priest. And to find my own life so utterly false and trivial — in the light of the New Testament. And to look around me everywhere and find people desperately — or com- placently — going through certain motions to prove that they are Chris- tians. (And far more people not giving a damn and not even paying at- tention, so that "proving one is a Christian" comes to mean begging for *just a little attention* from the world — some grudging admission that a Christian can be an honest man.)
>
> At least this: I have enough self respect left to refuse to be abbot, and to refuse to go around to meetings and lectures and functions. And I have felt a little compunction about continuing to proclaim a "message" just because that is what people expect of me. It is not easy to talk of prayer in a world where a President claims he prays for light in his de- cisions and then decides on genocidal attacks upon a small nation. And where a Catholic Bishop praises this as a "work of love."
>
> Paralyzing incomprehension — what does one do when he realizes he is part of an organization whose members systematically try to "make a fool of God"? I suppose I begin by recognizing that I have done it as much as the best of them.
>
> But then a "God is dead" Church is no better, nor are the "God is dead" Christians an improvement over the others. Just the same established flippancy and triviality. And even more successful.
>
> They make a good living out of God's death.[290]

❉

Merton was careful not to speak of some things even in his journal, but there is evidence that his prayer life was richer that summer than it had been for some considerable time — that the disturbances had helped it grow, rather than diminishing it. In many respects he had learned at last how to live at the center of distractions, taking "Holiness before peace," Newman's maxim, for his own. What he called "my bloody mysticism," in a loose moment in a letter to June Yungblut, was now a far less self-conscious activity. Precisely because of this, it was both less necessary and harder to write about. Dom Flavian had hoped Father Louis would be able to find words to describe a deeper spiritual journey. There had been contradictory statements earlier: now there was no clear statement. Merton was moving in the spirit of his prayer to Our Lady of Carmel, "Teach me to go to the country beyond words and beyond names."[291]

At one time, Merton had seen contemplation as so difficult few could attain it. For years his published writing had limited the search for contemplation, not only to those of his own Church, but to the professed religious of the contemplative orders. Others were necessarily on the margin of that experience: they could, as it were, listen in and gain something. Later in his published writing, the possibility had been opened to all and this required a redefinition of contemplation.

When, in the early sixties, Merton used the term "active contemplation" there was a broad area for misunderstanding. One thing he had *not* meant at any time: he had never advocated adding contemplation to the list of activities as one more thing to be busy about in this life! The link between Zen and the Apophatic tradition has already been traced, and it was no accident that Merton's definitions were largely helpful in saying what contemplation was *not*. In *Woods, Shore, Desert,* he included a number of quotations to illustrate the difference between the perennial philosopher and the existentialist.[292] In the same way, he saw now that, definitions apart, contemplation could only be made real to others when it was demonstrated in a life. Contemplation and living drew closer together. It was more urgent than ever to free both of self-awareness. What, then, of autobiography? He saw more and more clearly that it was the *lived* life, not the written life, that should be contemplative, yet he could not release himself from the urgency of autobiography. Out of prayerful meditation upon emptiness would come right action, and right action would show itself. This, of course, was secondary. Out of prayerful meditation upon emptiness would come a sense of intimate relationship with God, a God free of the limits of concept, found real in the relationship as long as the human friend remained real. By 1968 — if we need a tag — Thomas Merton had become an existentialist contemplative. This meant only that he had discovered the authentic journey and much of it would have to be made in silence.

*

Where Merton had been patronizing about his ex-student in the early months of 1968, there was now a great deal of respect:

> What a difference between Father Flavian as Abbot, and Dom James. And what a difference in our relationship. I get a real sense of openness, of

possibilities, of going somewhere — and at times it is almost incredible. I seem to be dreaming.

He is *very* interested in perhaps starting something out on the Coast. And today, in so many words, he asked me if I were willing to start it: i.e. to go out there and get some sort of small hermit colony going. I said I certainly would do that any time. When he goes out for the Vina election he will go over to Redwoods and look at the various places: Bear Harbor, Needle Rock, Etterburg . . . It is fantastic. I don't know if he intends to buy Bear Harbor — or if Jones will sell it! But the mere fact that he goes ahead and *thinks* of it! One slowly comes back to life, with the realization that all things are possible.[293]

By July 19, there were plans with W. H. Ferry to explore the California coast much more thoroughly for a likely place for a Gethsemani *laura* before going to Asia:

More than anything I want to find a really quiet, isolated place —
— where no one knows I am (I want to disappear).
— where I can get down to the thing I really want and need to do.
— from which, if necessary, I can come out to help others . . .[294]

Just as the practical side of his early plan for a *laura* where the hermits would live a secret existence *and* keep up with politics and literature had had some obvious snags, so did this new plan for himself. Everyone at the Redwoods in May had been told to protect Father Louis's anonymity. This had not prevented Merton telling Gracie Smith, Winifred Carp, and any number of people he met on the beach, or in planes, exactly who he was. In his notes on Gandhi, Merton had written, quoting from Edgar Snow, "Gandhi had no idea how much it costs us to keep him in poverty." Now it was a case of Merton having no idea how difficult it was for others to protect his anonymity.[295]

Expeditions to Louisville now had more to do with inoculations at the Health Building and visits to the library for books on Asia than checking with doctors about his old complaints. On one such trip he ran into "Tommie and three of the big eyed O'Callaghan daughters" wearing straw hats and on the way to the station with their grandmother. Colleen O'Callaghan greeted him with joy: "How did you know we were here?"[296]

No sooner had he written to Lionel Landry of the Asia Society saying he felt "something unexpected will pan out,"[297] and added the lines in his journal, "O the mountains of Nepal. / And the tigers and the fevers. / And the escaped bandits from all the world. / And the escaped Trappists, lost, forgotten . . ."[298] than an invitation arrived to go to Darjeeling and speak at the Temple of Understanding meeting. Darjeeling, he wrote, was "nearer to the border of Nepal than the monastery is to Bardstown!"[299]

He tried ineffectually to check his growing excitement. "Also I thought of Nepal: and the stupidity of being romantic about it." Then he added a note to himself that reads curiously in the light of his later discoveries:

> To get to those mountains one has to pass through the poverty of Calcutta: and when in the presence of those mountains one is also in the presence of the poverty of Nepal. And typhus, and yellow fever, and malaria, and VD, and Tantrism, and Opium. As for Napalese Buddhism, if it is like that of Tibet it is not exactly the kind I am myself most interested in ferocity, ritualism, superstition, magic. No doubt many deep and mysterious things but . . . Maybe it *needs* to disappear.
>
> However, I'd better suspend judgement on that. I hope to meet the Dalai Lama or someone like that at Darjeeling and find out more about it.[300]

With Daniel Berrigan in jail, Berrigan's plan to go to Vietnam had come to nothing. Merton recalled his former plans. He wrote to June Yungblut asking for news of the Berrigans and of John Youngblut, who was also in jail. Then he says there has been a change of intention:

> . . . It is possible that I may go to the Orient on some monastic business, but I think in that event I'd better take care to keep it all entirely and totally unpolitical in every respect. This is a first trip, and a lot depends on how it goes, so I would NOT be wanting to tie in anything like conversations with the NLF — which in any case, would, I think, be futile at this point. There have been conversations in plenty, and they have ended in obvious fiasco and betrayal. I would not want to just perpetrate an illusion — which is about all I could do at this point. Others who know more and are better qualified seem to be indicated as choices if a possibility does arise.[301]

Now another refrain ran through his head. He had discovered the Kingdom of Swat: "O the mountains of Swat."[302] Then he wrote, "Fighting kites in Thailand! Must see them! And dancing. Etc."[303]

Merton had been close to Father John Eudes Bamberger ever since he was a scholastic under Father Louis. They had worked together for years in the group that screened postulants. There was a reserve in Father Eudes Merton admired and perhaps envied, though it sometimes brought out sarcasm and impatience. For his part, Father Eudes found Father Louis over-effusive at times (as he thought he had been when Father Eudes asked in Chapter for a prayer for the Berrigans). Earlier, Merton had written in his journal that he felt the combination of Dom James and Father John Eudes was both formidable and sometimes authoritarian.[304] Father Eudes was dismayed to hear Merton make comments like "This place is all washed up. Nothing good will come out of this place." He would have been discouraged, he says, "If I had based my faith on men, not God."[305] On one occasion he took Father Louis to task because he thought he was being disloyal to friends.

Merton had been very contrite: it was obviously a sore point. Another time Merton sought him out to apologize for sarcastic remarks he had made in Chapter. The intent was good, but the manner was a little overwhelming. There were occasions, Father Eudes says, when Father Louis could be emotionally exhausting.

Despite this, or perhaps because each was honest about their differences, the friendship proved lasting, with admiration on both sides ("Father Louis was at all times an amazing amalgam of independence and obedience").[306]

Where Father Louis could be disconcertingly open about showing his emotions, he usually exerted a strict control over showing his darker moods. For this reason John Eudes Bamberger was surprised one spring afternoon in 1968 when he came upon Father Louis looking utterly dejected and crushed near the path into the hermitage. The instant Merton saw him, his expression changed and he beckoned him over. He was as buoyant as ever, if a little hesitant. It was the first time Merton had told Father John Eudes about the Asian trip, and he was not at all sure the idea would win approval. However, he wanted advice on shots and on what medicine to take with him. When Father Eudes said he thought the trip was a good idea, gave the medical advice, and told him he ought to try to meet a psychologist friend in Washington, Nicco Camara Peron, who might be helpful with information, Father Louis was surprised, relieved, and almost over-appreciative.[307]

On July 27 there was another violent thunderstorm, and the lightning blew out one of the bulbs of his desk lamp while Merton was having supper. There had been a lot of rain that summer, and Kentucky was unusually lush. After the storm, he went out to find "five small, bedraggled wet quails, picking around the path by my doorstep and very tame." He decided they must be from the nursery at the Stone Building:

> They don't seem very well prepared for life in the woods: preferred the path to the grass that would hide them: no mistrust of a human being — did not run away, only got out of the way of my feet or skipped away if I reached for them. They are now out on the wet lawn somewhere. This place is full of foxes — not to mention the kids who shoot anything that moves, in and out of season! I feel very sorry for these quails! But there is another wild covey of a dozen or so, trained by a zealous mother who often lured me along the rose hedge away from where the little ones were hiding in the deep weeds by the gate.[308]

As the world of infinite possibility seemed to open up beyond the enclosure walls of Gethsemani, news came of one early stability crisis. Brother Benedict had brought Merton a newspaper photograph of Dom Gregorio Lemercier of Cuernavaca with a young bride:

So that's that! All the old cardinals in Rome will be nodding wisely: they knew all along what this psychoanalysis would lead to!

For Dom G. personally — I can't judge. But it is a shame for monasticism. Whatever way you look at it, it does mean *giving up* a monastic experiment. Maybe he'll go on to something else. As for me, I'm interested in the *monastic* life and its values. In doing something with it, not just abandoning it.[309]

Reading about the Carthusians in Vermont, Merton felt a sense of relief that he had not joined them. They went the opposite direction to events at Cuernavaca. The Carthusians remained unchanged. Merton found this admirable but "a bit ridiculous":

Maybe I am no true solitary, and God knows I have certainly missed opportunities, made mistakes — and big ones too! Yet the road I am on is the right one for me and I hope I stay on it wisely — or that my luck holds.[310]

He now had the third issue of *Monks Pond* in his hands, and it was better, he thought, than the earlier numbers: "It is not hard to do good looking and interesting pages — if you have someone like Brother Cassian around to process them for you!"[311]

The chant "eight weeks from now I will be in Asia" took over from the mountains of Swat:

In eight weeks I am to leave here. And who knows — I may not come back. Not that I expect anything to go wrong — though it might — but I might conceivably settle in California to start the hermit thing Father Flavian spoke of. It depends. Someone may give him a good piece of property, for instance . . . In any case I don't expect to be back here for four months.

Really I don't care one way or another if I never come back. On an evening like this the place is certainly beautiful — but you can seldom count on it really being quiet (though it is at the moment). Traffic on the road. Kids at the lake. Guns. Machines, and Boone's dogs yelling in the wood at night. And people coming all the time. All this is to be expected and I don't complain of it. But if I can find somewhere to *disappear* to I will. And if I am to begin a relatively wandering life with no fixed abode, that's all right, too. I really expect little or nothing from the future. Certainly not great "experiences" or a lot of interesting new things. Maybe. But so what? What really intrigues me is the idea of starting out into something unknown, demanding and expecting nothing very special, and hoping only to do what God asks of me whatever it may be.[312]

The volume of noise grew louder in the Kentucky night. News came of events in Cleveland, then of the melee at the Democratic Convention. Merton was reading the Nighttown section ("Circe") in *Ulysses*. He thought it all very appropriate.[313] An invitation came from the Archbishop of Anchorage, Joseph T. Ryan, asking Father Louis to give a retreat for contemplative nuns. Both Father Louis and his abbot saw this as a chance to explore another area for a *laura* — surely there was quiet in Alaska![314] The plans had to be revised: by now, they included Calcutta, Darjeeling, Bangkok, with days at Christ in the Desert, Alaska, Santa Barbara, and the Redwoods, before leaving for Asia. After the Bangkok conference, there were tentative plans to visit Hong Kong, Japan, and Rawa Seneng, Indonesia.[315]

The prospect of this was almost unnerving:

> Now I find I have to shake myself, wake up, pray, think for myself, estimate risks and possibilities, make half-way wise decisions . . . But this is what we have all been needing. I have no special urge to be a hermit in Alaska, but it is an obvious place for solitude and here is a bishop who likes the idea very much! So let's look into it and see what happens.[316]

There was a limit to his enthusiasm for possibilities, however. When Dom Jean Leclercq visited, he and Father Louis had long discussions. In part these were about the AIM conference in Bangkok. Having succeeded in having one invitation accepted, Dom Leclercq hoped to enlist Father Louis for a number of monastic conferences and meetings. In something of a panic, Father Louis reported to Dom Flavian that this was not it at all![317]

On August 20 Merton began putting his books and papers in order on the anniversary of his official entry into the hermitage. It was time for another judgment on his writing, and it is interesting that he now condemned both the writing on monastic subjects *and* the political writing: "I regret less some of the recent poetry and especially *Cables* and *Lograire*." He was in a more ruthless mood than when he cleared out the office of master of novices in the summer of 1965. Coming upon S.'s letters, he records, "I did not even glance at any one of them. High hot flames of the pine branches in the sun!"[318]

This is arresting chiefly because it sounds just the melodramatic note of the lines in *The Seven Storey Mountain* where Merton talks of burning his early work in the boilers at St. Bonaventure in December 1941. This time he knew there was a great deal of material safely stored at the home of James Laughlin, and he did not write to ask Laughlin to destroy this in a fire of pine branches.

His own letters of 1966 to S. were lost in a move. There is no evidence, yet it seems very likely that Merton's burning of the letters took place soon after his last telephone call to S., when he realized the situation was finally hopeless. She had said she still loved him, but that there was nothing she could do. It was over.

Rice reports in his book with Merton's old title, *The Man in the Sycamore Tree*, that he had learned of Merton's Asian trip all the way from the West Coast to Gethsemani.[319] When he arrived at the monastery in his battered blue Volkswagen on September 6, it was something of a frenzied reunion. Rice had been in the Far East, and some of their discussion was on places to go and people to see. However, Rice has said in an interview that Merton was "obsessed by sex."[320] It may have been so. It is equally likely that Merton was making yet another and rather exaggerated attempt to identify, this time with an old friend who had been through many recent troubles.

However, there was certainly *something* at work in those late-summer nights in Kentucky that year:

> After supper Ed and I walked out the front avenue, and ran into Andrew Boone. I inquired why his dogs were making so much noise at night around my house and he said he was having them chase the deer because the bucks were raping his cows (sic) and causing them to miscarry! "The only thing to do is to chase them out of the country!" Maybe Andrew's head has been a little addled by Southern racism. However he gave me some information about all the shooting. "Eighteen men" surrounded one of his cornfields and blasted at doves all afternoon — it was a real slaughter, he said. (Last Sunday). As to the kids at the lake — they have a mattress in the back of a station wagon for service." Well, maybe!
>
> I observed that no one likes to live next to a whorehouse and he felt my reaction was fair enough.[321]

For some months Merton had been following the grapevine rumors about Dom James's hermitage. Edelen Farm was not only isolated, it had proved near-jungle, with a large population of rattlesnakes. The new hermitage was said to be luxurious, however, and there were complaints from the Brothers that they were expected to run a good many errands back and forth.[322] If this was what he heard about Dom James, Father Louis wondered what Dom James was hearing about *him*. James Fox had been able on several occasions before to snatch an invitation or a permission away at the last conceivable moment.

❋

In late August Merton made a brief visit to Washington, D.C. Lionel Landry of the Asia Society had suggested he try to meet the Indonesian ambassador. When Dr. Soedjatmoko invited him to his home on Saturday, August 22, Merton asked Dom Flavian for permission to accept, feeling the meeting would give another dimension to the information he had already gathered from books and correspondence. The weekend provided a number of vivid and contrasting views.

Ron Seitz drove Merton to the plane on Friday afternoon. He was met in Washington by Father Eudes's friend Dr. Camara Peron. Merton probably exaggerated when he said that their discussions in the car and that night in the doctor's Georgetown apartment made him feel the psychologist was having an epidemic of breakdowns among his patients in the religious orders. Communities were falling apart because of personality conflicts, nuns were on the point of committing suicide — the old era of authoritarianism had been replaced by an era of freedom which revealed only the immaturity of the free. The conversation provided color and confirmation to Merton's pessimistic view of the future of religious life in 1968.[323]

The next day, Merton was welcomed into the ambassador's home and he met his wife and children. After luncheon, the informal conversation was extended to five hours, and by the end they were Tom and Koko. Few other meetings have left such a clear record of something that continued to mystify Thomas Merton himself — his extraordinary personal attraction. Three years after that August afternoon, Dr. Soedjatmoko wrote to say how vivid his memories remained of the only time he had met Thomas Merton. It had been "one of those rare meetings between two persons where there is immediate recognition and affinity."[324] They moved from one discovery to another. "As I described in a letter to my friends in Indonesia telling them about his plans to visit, it was the most important, meaningful, and most deeply satisfying personal encounter I have had in the course of my stay here."

One further passage deserves to be included, if only because many of the points were confirmed in a letter from someone else who had a single encounter with Thomas Merton some two months later. Dr. Soedjatmoko went on:

> If there is one impression that has stayed with me all along it is a memory of one of the very few people I have known in this world with an inner freedom which is almost total. It was, I felt, an inner freedom which was not negative, in terms of something else, but it was like the water that constantly flows out of a well. Talking about the use of drugs and their capacity to induce mystical or such-like experiences, Merton said that he really never felt the need to use LSD. A cup of coffee after the usual period of prayer and meditation starting at 3:00 A.M. was often enough to turn him on. Music also seemed to have such an effect on him, both classical music as well as jazz and he told me the only luxury that he permitted himself in his hut was a phonograph.[325]

Merton was driven straight to the airport that Saturday night. He had to wait to hear from others about the performance of his "Freedom Songs," which the choir of Ebenezer Baptist Church, the King church in Atlanta, had sung at the Conference on the Liturgy in Washington. Such rumors that reached him of the conference, which was just breaking up, cannot have been "edifying." At the airport he let his eye wander over the crowds with some mischief of malice — "sailors, children, mothers, an occasional nun . . . with a new wise look (maybe saying 'I got laid at the Liturgical conference'?)."[326]

During the plane ride back he had planned to read and meditate, then found himself talking to a young Catholic girl from Kentucky. He decided he ought not to have worn a Roman collar ("A priest on a plane seems to be fair game for anyone"). For all that, he was flattered. "It was rather touching that she just enjoyed a simple conversation and picked a middle aged priest to talk to!"[327]

When he returned, he had a little over two weeks to prepare. Brother Patrick Hart, who had been Dom James's secretary for ten years, had just returned from an assignment in Rome and he had not yet been reassigned a job at Gethsemani. Father Louis asked Dom Flavian if Brother Patrick could help him with secretarial work and assist in keeping up with things while he was away.

Merton went with Frank O'Callaghan to buy luggage and clothes in Louisville. He was now so caught up in the excitement of the trip that he was difficult to advise. He bought a drip-dry suit which scarcely fitted, but with which he himself was delighted.[328] The model in his mind may have been Dan Berrigan's "French worker priest" outfit. He had decided against a Roman collar on the plane from Washington, and, against advice from the monastery, he had determined not to take his Cistercian habit on the trip. Later he had to send back for the habit, when he learned from Marco Pallis and others that monks in the East expected a monk to look like one.[329]

The nights brought dreams, and the days anxieties:

> I struggle in myself with my own future — and with the fear I will be discovered before I can get away (irrational) — or even that I may die or be shot. (If I am discovered — what difference does it make? It will all be announced next Wednesday anyhow!)
>
> I see the absurdity of attachment to these fields. As if leaving them I would somehow be in jeopardy. What an attitude to cultivate!
>
> But it is true, I am nervous, insecure, have blisters and my allergy rages.[330]

Because he feared being "discovered," few of the monks could be told before he left, and there was no formal farewell from the community. On his last full day, Monday, September 9, Brother Patrick, Brother Maurice, and Phil Stark walked up from the monastery before dawn. Father Louis said Mass. Afterward they had breakfast together, and then photographs were taken. All of them found it a moving occasion.[331] Merton spent much of the day clearing up and giving instructions to Brother Patrick, who would be living at the hermitage until Merton's return. This, at least, was the understanding. Merton sat up late reading Robinson Jeffers (whom he now called "that Pacific Blake") and *Robinson Jeffers: Fragments of an Older Fury* by Brother Antoninus, which James Laughlin had sent him. When he turned to his journal, Merton recorded that he had sent Laughlin a draft for the whole of *The*

Geography of Lograire (on which he hoped to make considerable corrections),[332] as well as a new group of poems, tentatively titled "Sensation Time at the Home."[333] Then he turned to his own thoughts on the journey:

> I go with a completely open mind. I hope without special illusions. My hope is simply to enjoy the long journey, profit by it, learn, change, and perhaps find something or someone who will help me advance in my own spiritual quest.
>
> I am not starting out with a firm plan never to return or with an absolute determination to return at all costs. I do feel there is not much for me here at the moment and that I need to be open to lots of new possibilities. I hope I shall be. But I remain a monk of Gethsemani. Whether or not I will end my days here, I don't know — and perhaps it is not so important. The great thing is to respond perfectly to God's will in this providential opportunity, whatever it may bring.[334]

On the morning of the 10th he went down to the monastery for his last meeting with Dom Flavian, to collect some money, and to say goodbye to the two or three who knew he was going. He left Dom Flavian with a half-humorous promise of good behavior. The abbot won a more serious promise that there would be no press interviews and no television coverage of his part at any meetings.[335] The present plan was for Merton to return early in January, but plans had already been changed many times. Merton was determined to have the abbot's permission for any extension in his time away. This was the only fixed point. Otherwise, the matter was nothing if not "open-ended."

Ron Seitz came to the hermitage at about ten o'clock on an overcast, cool fall morning. Before leaving his "casa" Merton checked to make sure he had money and papers in the leather wallet from Bond Street Tom Bennett had given him on his eighteenth birthday. He took the eight first-class relics (most of them gifts from Sister Thérèse).[336]

As he and Seitz left, he was less than generous about the community, as if he expected an impossible sendoff. When he looked back at the monastery where he had been a monk for almost twenty-seven years, he spoke to Seitz about being abandoned.[337]

It would be charitable to see his lack of charity as an attack of nerves. He was too restless to enjoy the day in Louisville. There were errands to check Asian addresses at the Merton Room at Bellarmine, to buy a bag for the camera and a second pair of shoes, to collect more allergy pills from Tom Jerry Smith's office in St. Matthews, and to pick up travelers' checks at the bank. The time left over he spent at the Seitz house with Sally and the children, then at the O'Callaghans', having a shower and a rest. Merton wanted a quiet evening, but he also wanted to see friends, including Dan Walsh, whom he had not seen for some time. The result was another dinner party, this time at the Pine Room on River Road. It was not a notable success. Merton had said before in his journal that he felt uncomfortable in such surroundings. That night everyone was under a strain to say something memorable.[338] He was straining to give an extra assurance of friendship to each of them, as well as a reassurance he would soon be back. Everything had the opposite effect of what was intended.[339] He left one friend in tears.

He spent the night at St. Bonaventure's Friary at Bellarmine.[340] Then, early on the 11th, he was flying to Albuquerque:

> It lifts. It talks. Meditation of the motors. Mantra. Om
> Om Om Om over and over like a sea-cow.
> And sun sits on the page.[341]

*

Another round of Prisoner's Base had begun. Merton was probably not fully aware of this himself. He does not write of it in any of the journals he was keeping at the time. But the poem he sent to Jonathan Williams the October before shows that, consciously or not, Merton was anticipating it. The title is almost as long as the poem, a move in chess as well as Prisoner's Base: "Concrete racegram of Pluto king of hell as he meets white foe in Goal while one or both is/are set free into the fair."[342] One or both was/were now "set free into the fair." Significantly — almost certainly echoing words of Julian of Norwich in his own way — Merton ends "Pluto king of hell":

ALL

WELL

END.

*

Thomas Merton was wandering once more, with the same excitement for travel, but with less self-assurance than when he had set off to France at eighteen and a day. For the first few days he was in places which were already familiar. Tom Carlyle met him at Albuquerque and drove him across the desert in a Volkswagen towing a plaster mixer, for the adobe to repair the chapel of Christ in the Desert. On the 12th he was "back in a clear mind in Chama Canyon," washing in the cold waters of the Chama, getting rid of his misgivings over the farewell party in Louisville, and feeling "clean" and "awake." This time he met Georgia O'Keeffe and found her one of the rare people "who quietly does everything right."[343] Don Devereux made good his promise and took him to the Jicarilla Apache encampment. For two days he took part in the secret ceremonies and dances of the Feast of Tabernacles near Dulcie. Devereux had explained to others that Merton was a holy man, and he was even allowed to take his camera. (W. H. Ferry was envious when he was given a full description a few weeks later.) Merton's lasting impressions were of the booths of boughs and "Brisk wind blowing all the fires — and cool in the dusk. Lovely little Indian children everywhere."[344]

From Albuquerque Merton flew to Chicago, where it was raining. He stayed overnight, giving a conference to the Poor Clares in their convent. Then he was off on Wednesday, September 18, aboard a Northwest Airlines flight for Anchorage. As the plane would fly on after refueling to Tokyo and Seoul he felt he was getting closer to Asia.[345]

After landing in Alaska, he was driven to Eagle River and a pleasant house among birches. Here he had some chance to rest and to write up his travels in the two journals he was keeping. He also discovered a rich source of material for anti-poems:

> 6 A.M. KHAR Anchorage. Alaskan Golden Nugget Potatoes respectfully suggest that we worship God since we are one nation under God and want to build a *stronger* America. Nugget Potatoes are glad of this opportunity to "voice their thinking."

"A good thought from a respectful potato," Merton wrote.[346]

At Eagle River he gave a conference at the Convent of the Precious Blood and talked to many of the contemplative nuns. The anxieties and troubles he heard were familiar — the solitude had apparently made little difference.

In the remainder of his stay in Alaska, Merton learned a new geography on long car drives and trips in small planes as he looked for a suitable place for a hermitage. On September 27, the bush pilot flew him to Yakutat, a ramshackle village inhabited largely by Tlingit Indians. Frank Ryman, who showed him over the village, offered him a quarter of an acre of land, but Merton felt the property was too much on the fringes of the village and that he would be expected to take on pastoral duties. There were other, more remote places. He found Eyak Lake silent and peaceful, surrounded by mountains. When he climbed and looked down, he saw a great expanse of water and thousands of wild geese and ducks on the flats.[347] This was solitude. Was this what he wanted?

Three weeks earlier, on September 6, he had written to Naomi Burton Stone. The Asia journey had been kept secret from his agent, at least, and perhaps it shows he was uncertain of her approval that he waited until the last minute to tell her. He begins with publishing news, then gets down to "the real news" and gallops through his itinerary — meetings, then Indonesia, Hong Kong, Japan — saying he thinks all this will add up to at least two books. Then there is a check. Merton says,

"This all sounds wildly active, but I am trying to fix it so that I get breaks of three or four days' retreat along the line, and will go along in a leisurely way." He cannot hold back the excitement even to reassure an old friend he thinks may be critical of such a whirl of activity: "But: I am in contact with the secretary of the Dalai Lama, fully expect to meet him and to have an entree into the various Tibetan Buddhist monasteries in exile, and to really learn some fascinating new stuff." He ends the letter with both a bid for her approval and a plea for help:

> Do please pray that this journey may mean all that I hope it will mean, and more. I know it may seem a bit wild, running around like this, but I do think it is absolutely important and necessary both for me, for the Church and for these Asian religions which are not yet in the same kind of crisis we are, but will be.
> All my very best. Blessings, prayers, affection, peace, in the Lord,[348]
> Tom

On September 25 and 26, he had the first of the "retreats," or at least a chance to relax after days in bush planes and cars, at the archbishop's in Anchorage. In the diocesan office he struggled for the first time with an electric typewriter, writing to Ferry about "AZlaska (now that's a grand word)" and plans for the trip along the California coast. He had "eaten moose but not yet bear." From Gethsemani he had sent books to Santa Barbara in packages addressed to Rabbi Vendata (another attempt to keep his trip secret, this time in the monastery mailroom). Now he hopes that the Rabbi Vendata's pants have arrived from New Mexico.[349]

He spent the next few days conducting conferences at Dillingham. On Wednesday, October 2, Merton flew from Alaska to San Francisco. At the airport he was "embraced wildly by Suzanne," met Linda and Cris Butorovich, and had dinner with the family.[350] He stayed the night at the International Inn, then went on the next day, arriving in Santa Barbara on United Flight 899 at 10 A.M. He had told Ferry he was anxious to do one talk at the Center, but, keeping to his promise to Dom Flavian, stipulated that there was to be no press coverage or television. Several rather loose or off-the-cuff remarks about Japan in his talk seem to have been put into circulation, for all the precautions, and these caused offense. In discussions with French Marxist students at the Center, he found himself put on the spot when they declared they were the true monks of contemporary struggles with the establishment.[351] He might have been wiser to agree they were all "marginal men." Instead, he made another over-enthusiastic effort to identify himself with others, and agreed they were the true monks.

He met with the founder of the Laucks Foundation, Irvin F. Laucks, and his wife, Eulah, with John Cogley and his wife, and many others at the Center, including Mae Karen, who had transcribed his tapes of *Lograire*. There was a party at the Madonna Inn (named for the owner, Joe Madonna), near San Luis Obispo. Merton sent Father Flavian a postcard of the raw-pink décor of one of the bedrooms. There was a found poem for the finding in the copywriter's description on the postcard:

> Hideaway! Seclusion at last! A romantic combination of rocks and roses decorates this room, along with warm happy hot pinks for color. French bath fixtures and a rock shower complement the room design. Room is furnished with King Sized Bed.

Merton added the comment, "This might be a possibility. No! I did NOT sleep here!"[352] He did not go on to tell Father Flavian about the wayside attraction, reduced at this point to a zebra and a mule, or that it was possible to start light effects and music in the pink and purple grotto of the men's room by peeing on a certain spot.[353]

The next day Ferry drove Merton back to San Francisco to a party at Yu Ching's, where he met Paul Jacobs and his wife and Czeslaw Milosz and his wife. Merton had a long, animated conversation with Milosz.

On October 9 Merton went to the Redwoods again, where he used Mother Myriam's Olivetti to report the results of his week with the Ferrys, exploring for a possible place for a hermitage. "I can say without hesitation that the California coast is hopeless as regards solitude."[354] He found a land boom in progress. "Even at Bear Harbor, which I liked so much in May, the bulldozers are active and they are opening up a lot of roads that will obviously be for housing sometime." He wrote that Alaska had many advantages and thought he had found a number of possible places for a small group living a semi-eremitical life:

> . . . On the other hand I am not sure of it myself. I can't decide anything until I see what comes of the Asian experience. The important thing for me is not acquiring land or finding an ideal solitude but opening up the depths of my own heart. The rest is secondary.
>
> Of course I hope to return there. I had no idea of doing otherwise, except that perhaps I thought it would be more convenient for you, if I were to live in solitude somewhere else, not to come back and then leave again. But I have no plans. Except that I don't think just permanent residence in Ky is the final answer for me. As a mailing address, yes.

Merton goes on, "I leave it to you to let me know when my absence becomes really embarrassing for you — assuming it won't do so before next summer sometime!!"[355]

There were three days of conferences at the Redwoods, which included a chance to discuss Zen with Brother David Steindl-Rast during a thunderstorm.[356] Merton had said goodbye to the Ferrys, who were

off for the Oregon coast. On October 10, he spent hours photographing at Needle Rock, where the small irises he liked were blooming
everywhere. He saw his painter friend Winifred Carp again, and on
Sunday, October 13, he returned to San Francisco after being given an
affectionate send-off by the community at the Redwoods.[357] On Monday evening, he and Portia Webster had dinner together on Fisher-
man's Wharf.[358] The next day, Tuesday, October 15, he was off to
Asia — so loaded down with last-minute purchases at City Lights and
other bookstores he had to pay for excess baggage. On the plane he
began a new journal. Like *Woods, Shore, Desert*, "Asian Notes" would
be a mosaic of impressions, passages from his reading, free poems of
travel, and accounts of his meetings. As the plane began the flight over
the Pacific, he wrote:

> May I not come back without having settled the great affair. And found
> also the great compassion, *mahakaruna*. We tilted east over the shining
> city (there was no mist this morning). All the big buildings went by. The
> green parks. The big red bridge over Golden Gate. Muir Woods. Bo-
> dega Bay, Point Reyes, and then two tiny rock islands. And then noth-
> ing. Only blue sea.[359]

                                    *

Merton talked of "coming home" to a place he had never been before.
Asia had been a goal for him as far back as Columbia, and a far more
urgent goal in recent years. He had even had a sense of having once
been in Asia, the feeling he recorded in *The Sign of Jonas*:

> The junk wagon I saw in Louisville comes back to me like the memory of
> something very precious once seen in the Orient.[360]

Many journeys merged into one, and he was a number of travelers
at once. On one level, he was simply a tourist. Old Asia hands have
said that, with the exception of the meetings with the Dalai Lama, Merton traveled a well-worn route for VIPs seeing the Orient at that time,
while Merton makes amusing references in his journal to keeping up
with his duties as a tourist. Those whose official duties involved meeting and entertaining important visitors, however, soon found him much
more than a tourist to the East.

He stressed over and over that he had come to learn. His declared
purpose was to study Eastern monasticism and to relate what he had
learned to Western monasticism, which, in 1968, he saw in crisis. What
he brought back, he believed, would benefit all the religious orders, his
own Order, and his own monastery.

One purpose he had now abandoned. In his mimeographed circular
letter to friends of September 1968, he had repeated what he had already told June Yungblut: "In any case, anything I do on this trip will

be absolutely non-political. I have no intention of going anywhere near Vietnam." He went on to say:

> Our real journey in life is interior: it is a matter of growth, deepening, and of an ever greater surrender to the creative action of love and grace in our hearts. Never was it more necessary for us to respond to that action . . .[361]

The journey to Asia, then, was a new beginning in search of new "markings" on the interior journey. The settling of "the great affair" was sufficiently ambiguous as a goal while he looked for the "what is not said" of Sidi Abdeslam.

The Asian Journal of Thomas Merton was skillfully assembled from three sources: "Asian Notes," the continuing journal for 1968 ("The Hawk's Dream"), and Merton's small pocket notebook.[362] For all its richness, the posthumous book remains something of a blueprint or sketch for what might have been — interesting, above all, as a guide to what Merton was reading and where he went. It was difficult for Merton, as it is for everyone, both to learn and to report on learning at the same time. It was no accident that, even though he wrote out the papers he was to deliver before he went to Asia, he departed radically from the text on almost every occasion. Merton might have made significant revisions in his last poem, *The Geography of Lograire;* he would certainly have published a different book from *The Asian Journal,* and there is much which will never be known. There is a chapter of his spiritual autobiography that was never written.

✳

Merton landed in Honolulu on the 15th, then lost a day over the International Date Line in mid-Pacific. It was the same day, now the 16th, when he arrived in Japan. He confirmed his sense of its being a plague year at Tokyo Airport by noting there was a list of "dangerous places" on a blackboard: "plague at Saigon and three other Vietnamese airports."[363] He was in Bangkok late on the 16th, staying for two days at the Oriental Hotel. There were visits with Phra Khantipalo to the Wat Bovoranives[364] and other Thai Buddhist monasteries, and Merton said Mass at the Catholic cathedral. With Khantipalo, an English Buddhist bhikkhu or monk, Merton discussed the Buddhist Satipatthana Sutta, "The Discourse on the Establishing of Mindfulness."[365]

He had already become aware that a major feature of air travel was hanging about in airports. In Bangkok, waiting to leave for Calcutta on the 18th, he watched a film on television that tried to explain Thai boxing — one image, of a boxer kicking off his opponent's head, kept reappearing, to be interrupted by flight announcements.[366]

From the beginning, Calcutta presented its own hardly less shattering images, though this time through the window of a cab, rather than on a television screen:

> . . . Heartrending routine of the beggars — the little girl who suddenly appeared at the window of the taxi, the utterly lovely smile with which she stretched out her hand and then the extinguishing of the light when she drew it back empty. (I had no Indian money yet.) She fell away from the taxi as if she were sinking in water and drowning and I wanted to die . . .[367]

The monk with a vow of poverty found himself transformed into the Rich Daddy from the West, the tourist with a showy camera and a suitcase heavy with books and extra clothing.[368] He was learning *mahakaruna* in the midst of a city that was *not* shining:

> . . . Calcutta, smiling, fecal, detached, tired, inexhaustible, young-old, (full of young people who seem old) is the *unmasked* city. Sub-culture of poverty and overpopulation.[369]

Worse still, in the circumstances, one old problem had come back: "But money gets away from me like water on all sides and I have to watch it."[370]

It had been hoped to hold the first Spiritual Summit Conference of the Temple of Understanding at Darjeeling, but there had been severe floods, and instead the conference was held at the Birla Academy in South Calcutta. Representatives of "ten world religions" were brought together for four days of discussion and dialogue under the theme "The Relevance of Religion in the Modern World." Merton spoke on the morning of October 23, and *The Asian Journal* gives both the formal statement he had prepared and the transcribed text of the informal talk he gave instead. In the informal talk Merton picked up on the title for the conference and defended monks, hippies, and poets as "deliberately irrelevant" — marginal men, who were, by necessity, critics of the "Modern World." At the same time he spoke for authenticity of vocation and the relevance of:

> . . . traditional monastic ways. In the West there is now going on a great upheaval in monasticism, and much that is of undying value is being thrown away irresponsibly, foolishly, in favor of things that are superficial and showy, that have no ultimate value. I do not know how the situation is in the East, but I will say as a brother from the West to Eastern monks, be a little careful. The time is coming when you may face the same situation and your fidelity to your ancient traditions will stand you in good stead. Do not be afraid of that fidelity. I know I need not warn you of this.[371]

Merton said that the basic condition in all this was for "each to be faithful to his own search." He also said that standing aside, being marginal, required faith — a faith, not in structures, but in one's own vocation, and "Faith means doubt. Faith is not the suppression of doubt. It is the overcoming of doubt, and you overcome doubt by going through it."

The informal talk and the prepared paper meet on one important point:

> And the deepest level of communication is not communication, but communion. It is wordless. It is beyond words, and it is beyond speech, and it is beyond concept. Not that we discover a new unity. We discover an older unity. My dear brothers, we are already one. But we imagine that we are not. And what we have to recover is our original unity. What we have to be is what we are.[372]

Here contemplation (the sense of God) and communication as communion (the sense of others) come together. It was the second most vital attainment of Merton's Asian journey that he achieved so often with those he met what he had known with Sidi Abdeslam — communion beyond speech and beyond concept — establishing at once an older unity in a singleness of vision that recognized differences and transcended them. In the formal paper circulated at Calcutta, "Monastic Experience and East-West Dialogue," such true communication spoke more immediately than anything else against what Merton feared, an attempt to establish a "facile syncretism"[373] of the world's religions.

Merton gave the closing prayer at the conference on October 26.[374] He felt it had been successful and well organized under the founder of the Temple of Understanding, Judith Hollister. He was amused by some of the participants, including one who had provided himself with saffron Kleenex to match his saffron robes, and he passed on anecdotes about the hangers-on in his letters.[375] Yet something had been accomplished, and he had had the opportunity to meet a number of people, including Amiya Chakravarty, a friend through correspondence for many years,[376] and Swami Lokesvarananda. There was also a chance meeting with one of the exiled lamas from Tibet, Chogyam Trungpa Rimpoche, the author of *Born in Tibet*.[377]

Merton was so impressed by the lama that, when he wrote to Dom Flavian, he told his abbot he was now hoping to return by way of Europe, with a visit to Chogyam Trungpa Rimpoche's Tibetan center in Scotland.[378] There were references in the letter, too, to places he remembered from his childhood in France, so there may have been other "David Copperfield" expeditions he wanted to make. He had already written to Bob Lax that he was hoping to see him in Greece on the way back. In the November Circular Letter to Friends, Merton says he has "been permitted to extend the trip a little."[379] By this time, this was a remarkable understatement.

From Calcutta Merton also wrote to Dom James, to Lawrence Ferlinghetti, and to the Queen of Bhutan.[380] His hope of reaching Bhutan never came to anything, but one important plan was now confirmed.

Before Merton left the Grand Oberoi Hotel for his flight to New Delhi, he received a telegram from Tenzin Geshe, the secretary of the Dalai Lama, to say that an interview had been arranged at Dharamsala during the first week in November.[381]

Merton was met in New Delhi by Harold Talbott, an American student of Buddhism he had corresponded with, a friend and student of Dom Aelred Graham. When Dom Aelred had suggested Merton contact Talbott, the name meant nothing. As soon as he saw Talbott, Merton realized with some amusement that he already knew him — that as a first-year student at Harvard, Harold Talbott had been confirmed at Gethsemani, where he had received Merton's blessing, and that he had done work for Father Francis de Sales.[382] Merton knew Talbott was currently under instruction from the Dalai Lama, who thought highly of him and had given him a hut at Dharamsala. The two of them decided to combine their plans, visiting Dharamsala together and staying in the small bungalow.

In New Delhi, Merton went with Talbott to see the Tibetan holy paintings, or tankas, at Tibet House and to the refugee community in the city. Merton's introductions to the Tibetans were arranged by Lobsang Phuntsok Lhalungpa (who was teaching Talbott Tibetan) and his wife, Deki. Merton was attracted at once. "The Tibetans seem to have a peculiar intentness, energy, silence, and also humor. Their laughter is wonderful. Lhalungpa translated, but long stretches of talk got lost."[383] Merton's own laughter, at least, required no translation.

There were long discussions on Tibetan monasticism in Merton's hotel room. From his windows, he could see the distant Himalayas, the foreign embassies, and the kites coming down to the city in the evening.[384] When there were no visitors he managed to catch up on his reading and his journal, to say his offices, and to meditate.

※

On the night of Thursday, October 31, Merton and Talbott traveled from New Delhi to Pathankot by train. Merton slept well in the lower berth and remembered that the last time he had traveled like this had been in December 1941, going to Gethsemani. Much further back, there were the lights seen from the French train going south from Paris to the Midi. Now:

> When light dawned — looked out on fields, scattered trees, tall reeds and bamboo, brick and mud villages, a road swept by rain in the night and now by a cold wind from the mountains — men wrapped in blankets walking in the wind. Teams of oxen ploughing. Pools by the track filled with tall purple flowering weeds. A white crane starts up out of the green rushes. Long before Pathankot — I was seeing the high snow-covered peaks behind Dalhousie.[385]

After riding from Pathankot to Dharamsala by jeep, they moved into Talbott's primitive cottage in the rain. Merton went off to explore:

> Beautiful silence of the mountainside and the deep valley. At one point the sound of a goatherd's flute drifted up from a pasture below. An unforgettable valley with a river winding at the bottom, a couple of thousand feet below, and the rugged peaks above me, and the pines twisted as in Chinese paintings. I got on a little path where I met at least five Tibetans silently praying with rosaries in their hands . . .[386]

Apart from the illustrations in *The Tao of Chinese Paintings*, there had been no such scenery in his life since the half-remembered shape of Canigou towering in the background of his first year and a half. But the mountains were not always so silent. The Indian Army had a small-arms range nearby, and Merton found himself thinking of a less happy memory, the guns of Fort Knox.[387]

Into the account in the journal now come quotations from the books he was reading, snatches of conversation with those he met, and Tibetan sayings — some of these fragments of the mosaic that can be arranged into three- or four-line poems:

> "The milk of the lioness
> is so precious and so powerful
> that if you put it in an ordinary cup,
> the cup breaks."
>
> (Tibetan saying)[388]

> We were talking about the "child mind,"
> which is recovered *after* experience.
> Innocence — to experience — to innocence.[389]

And into the report of those days at Dharamsala — then out of it again — flit a pair of white butterflies.

Merton made a new and knowledgeable friend, Sonam Kazi:

> . . . a Sikkimese who went to Tibet to consult doctors about an illness, rode all over Tibet and took to meditation studying under various Lamas, including a woman Lama in Lhasa. His daughter is supposed to be a reincarnation of this woman. She entranced Aelred Graham by reading comic books while he argued with her father . . .[390]

Sonam Kazi taught Merton the use of the mandala as a method of controlling what goes on inside one while meditating. Merton found the teacher very clear and helpful in explaining the Dzogchen Way, or the Great Way of All-inclusiveness, of the Nyingmapa Tibetan Buddhists. He also learned from Sonam Kazi that the name "Trappist" was interesting to Tibetans because in their language "Trapas" meant "monk."[391] One wonders whether the subject Dom Aelred and Sonam Kazi had argued about while the daughter read comic books was not reincarnation. Merton avoided conflict by being somewhat evasive. "It all depends on what you mean by reincarnation."

He had learned already that the Dalai Lama had a well-earned resistance to visitors, something Merton could sympathize with himself. Obviously Sonam Kazi, the Dalai Lama's young secretary Tenzin Geshe, and Talbott had all spoken well of him, but he was a writer, and there was plainly some lingering nervousness that the monk from the West would prove one more source of misinformation on both the political refugee and on Tibetan Buddhism. Yet the first meeting between Thomas Merton and Gejong Tenzin Gyatsho proved so warm, and of such importance to both men, that the Dalai Lama increased the number of their meetings from the promised *one* to *three*. At the first interview, on November 4, they talked about the very misconceptions the Tibetan spiritual leader feared most, then about an ideal course of studies. Merton was pleased when he was advised to ask Sonam Kazi about Dzogchen, something he had already done. The Dalai Lama went on to recommend meetings with Geshe Sopa (who was then teaching at the University of Wisconsin) and Geshe Ugyen Tseten (who was at Rikon in Switzerland).[392]

Their second meeting was on November 6, and this time there was more of an exchange, in which they compared methods of concentrating the mind. The third interview, on November 8, Merton thought the best. The Dalai Lama asked a number of questions about Western monasticism and showed particular interest in vows, wondering if the vow was intended to be the beginning or the end of a monk's spiritual journey, a subject that was certainly close to Merton and to Merton's own sense of spiritual journey. He was anxious to test the Dalai Lama's reaction to the notes he was drafting for a revision of his talk in Bangkok on "Marxism and Monasticism." In his reading he had come to wonder if there could not be a bridge between Buddhist dialectic, which ended in condemning the "ego-centered existence," and the Marxist conception of "alienation." He found the refugee from Chinese communism open to the possibility of a dialogue, and without bitterness. Sonam Kazi had already told Merton that the man or woman who was not attached to possessions or power was in large part free of danger. The Dalai Lama stressed what he thought were the real impediments to such a dialogue, which was certainly possible in theory. The possibility seemed to apply only to an ideal communism, free of aggressiveness and desire for power, and a religion without a power structure and without worldly possessions.[393]

They returned to their discussions of the second meeting, to contemplation and *sunyata*, the ultimate void or emptiness where all things achieve their true nature, their reality and authenticity. Much here confirmed Merton's own redefinition of a contemplation which was free of conceptualizing — reached in the light of his own experience, and in his study of Sufism, Zen, and the Apophatic Christian mystics. In summary, he makes the all-important statement after the meeting, "The greatest error is to become attached to sunyata as if it were an object 'absolute truth.' "

When the two men parted, Merton says:

> It was a very warm and cordial discussion and at the end I felt we had become very good friends and were somehow quite close to one another. I felt a great respect and fondness for him as a person and feel too that there was a real spiritual bond between us. He remarked that I was a "Catholic geshe," which, Harold said, was the highest possible praise from a Gelugpa! (an honorary doctorate!).[394]

In the same period there were meetings with other lamas, and Merton had come to see the mountain at Dharamsala in terms of what could be called a spiritual geography:

> "Mandala awareness" of space. For instance — this mountain — where a provisional Tibetan pattern of dwellings and relationships has been (very sketchily) set up. You get oriented by visiting various Rimpoches — each one a reincarnation of a spiritual figure — each one seated in his shrine-like cell, among tankas, flowers, bowls, rugs, lamps, images etc. Each rimpoche figures henceforth as one who "is seated" in a particular place, near or far: the Khempo of Namgyal Tra-Tsang high up on the mountain with his little community. Ratod-Rimpoche just up the hill — a quarter of a mile from here — near the official headquarters of the Dalai Lama's administration. The little Tulku (who can hardly be imagined as sitting still for very long) higher up, just below the Khempo. And the Dalai himself in a sort of center, where he is certainly very "seated" and guarded and fenced in. Thus what was on Friday a rugged, non-descript mountain with a lot of miscellaneous dwellings, rocks, woods, farms, flocks, gulfs, falls, and heights, is now spiritually ordered by permanent seated presences, burning with a lamplike continuity and significance, centers of awareness and reminders of dharma. One instinctively sees the mountain as a mandala (slightly askew no doubt) with a central presence and surrounding presences more or less amiable. (The rimpoches were all very amiable.) (The central presence is a fully awake, energetic, alert, non-dusty, non-dim, non-whispering Buddha.)[395]

Yet even on the mandala mountain there were disturbances, noises, and distractions, as there had been in Kentucky — gunfire, earth tremors, and a sense of political impermanence. One distracting element delighted Merton. He felt he would have enjoyed having a hermitage where a pack of gray apes, rather than the Kentucky squirrels, were his companions.[396]

Perhaps it was living in the primitive bungalow Harold Talbott had been given that made him homesick at times for the hermitage. He was now writing to Gethsemani, extending the return trip even further, with visits to Switzerland to see Geshe Ugyen Tseten, Scotland to see Trungpa Rimpoche, England to see Marco Pallis and Wales to see John Driver. Wales had a special attraction, and he had made a note to write to his Anglican friend, Donald Allchin, about expeditions in Wales.[397] At the same time he was having strange dreams about Gethsemani — and about returning to the towns along the French Riviera he had seen at eighteen. As for a permanent base, Merton was now divided between Kentucky and Alaska.[398]

The question of where he was to live was determined by the much larger question of *how* he was to live. On November 6, he asked the Dalai Lama about the role of the contemplative monk (Western or Eastern) in the world. "I said it was important for monks, etc., in the world to be living examples of the freedom and transformation of consciousness which meditation can give." It is notable that Merton gives no response from the Dalai Lama, and that the record of their conversation continues with the successes and failures of the Tibetan monks to achieve "*samadhi* in the sense of controlled concentration."[399]

For Merton the struggle was not only one of finding freedom through controlled concentration, but of finding a sense of freedom which could be shared as something valuable with others. There was a danger here of talking about the "uses" of concentration and contemplation. Perhaps, on a lower plane, that was necessary. Most people, he had said earlier, were "sharecroppers of time."[400] There was a general fear of time alone as pure gift. Yet many felt the need to spend time restoring themselves by forgetting themselves in some kind of contemplation before engaging in any activity. "Useful" though this might be, such *use* of contemplation restricted the freedom of what Merton had come to see as true contemplation.

On November 7, Merton redefined the contemplative life in terms of the *"temps vierge"* — those pre-dawn beginnings of new possibility he had celebrated earlier at the Kentucky hermitage:

> Duty of the contemplative life — (Duty's the wrong word) — to provide an area, a space of liberty, of silence, in which possibilities are allowed to surface and *new* choices — beyond routine choice — become manifest. To create a new experience of time, not as stoppage, stillness, but as "temps vierge" — not a blank to be filled or an untouched space to be conquered and violated, but to enjoy its own potentialities and hopes — and its own presence to itself. One's *own* time. (Not dominated by one's own ego and its demands.) Hence open to others — *compassionate* time (rooted in the sense of common illusion and in criticism of it).[401]

If it was "open to others," such contemplation was, again, more difficult. Aided once by a typing error, Merton had pointed out that a "vocation" was not a "vacation,"[402] however necessary a vacation often was, in terms of quiet time on one's own.

Contemplation was different — an end in itself, not a sort of restoring of mental energy for another assault on the active life. Thomas Merton's task was to find a way of preserving *"temps vierge"* in a period of planning more and more travel and activity in the world. He was, as he had always been, too confident that a place — the hermitage in Kentucky, a new hermitage in Alaska — would resolve what only he could resolve. At the same time, and almost apart from his own search for an ideal place, he had already achieved both a discipline and a freedom so remarkable that it was manifest at once to others. Certainly, in that sense, Thomas Merton was to almost all those he met in Asia, even in brief encounters, a "living example of the freedom and transformation of consciousness which meditation can give."

✽

The brief return to Calcutta, after a weekend in Delhi, gave him a "new impression: greater respect for this vast, crummy city."[403] On November 12 he was off to Darjeeling by air, and to his first meeting with Kanchenjunga.

Darjeeling had been devastated by floods and the resulting land-slides. He found it a strange combination, a mixture concocted of the permanence of the highest mountains in the world and of the impermanence of the volatile foreground. Politically, too, there were signs of impermanence — the Tibetan refugees, the presence of the Indian Army, the occupying Chinese, who held peaks and hills he could see from the bathroom window of his rooms at the Windamere Hotel. The Windamere Hotel and much of what had been a mountain retreat in the days of the British raj spoke of another kind of impermanence yet, and of a society for which Merton had few kind thoughts, Victorian England. Stabilities and structures had vanished, though their traces were everywhere present in imitations which amused or irritated him.

At the hotel the lights failed frequently and the telephone service was cut off from time to time. The cold he thought he had developed in Calcutta grew much worse, medicines were expensive, and he fell back once more on tea. He thought the Windamere the best hotel he had found in India, but the guests were too friendly, and he complained it was like being in a monastery.[404]

Gene Smith, whom Merton had met in Delhi, recommended the Mim Tea Estate as a place with a guest house where one could have a period of semi-retreat. Before Merton went there, he had a memorable meeting and an argument with a mountain.

On November 16, Merton set out with a party that included Harold Talbott, Jimpa Rimpoche, Father Sherburne, and a Tibetan guide to look for Chatral Rimpoche. After a false trail to the hermitage above Ghoom, they found Chatral — "the greatest rimpoche I have met so far and the most impressive person." Merton describes Chatral as looking "like a vigorous old peasant in a Bhutanese jacket tied at the neck with thongs

and a red woolen cap on his head. A week's growth of beard, bright
eyes, a strong voice, very articulate — much more communicative than
I expected."[405]

Much of their two-hour talk went through the interpreter, Jimpa
Rimpoche, yet this was certainly an occasion of communion, rather than
communication:

> The unspoken or half-spoken message of the talk was our complete un-
> derstanding of each other as people who were somehow *on the edge* of
> great realization and knew it and were trying, (somehow or other) to go
> out and get lost in it — and that it was a grace for us to meet one an-
> other . . .[406]

There was a good deal of laughter, from Merton, from the interpreter, from Chatral. At one point Chatral called Merton a natural
Buddha, "rangjung Sangay." Another time, feeling surprised to be
speaking as freely and deeply to a Christian, he laughed and said, "There
must be something wrong here!"

Everyone he had met, including the Dalai Lama, had talked of finding the right master as the most essential step on the way. Merton found
the right man, but wondered, "If I were going to settle down with a
Tibetan guru, I think Chatral would be the one I'd choose. But I don't
know yet if that is what I'll be able to do — or whether I need to."
Without vanity, he probably felt he had brought as much to their conversation as Chatral. Their communion had been a harmony in which
neither of the voices was lost, a meeting between the East and the West
that was only possible because each of them respected his own tradition. There was no guru, no disciple. This time there had been no confusion of roles in an attempt to overidentify with the other (as there
had been with Merton long ago, with his confessor at Gethsemani). And
now, like Sidi Abdeslam, another had recognized in some unspoken
way that he was *"on the edge* of great realization."

The argument with the mountain began with a photographer's dis-
taste for taking an overphotographed subject, and went on to a philosophical debate on *seeing.* It lasted for a week. At the Mim Tea Estate
on November 18, Merton wrote:

> Hence the annoyance with Kanchenjunga — its big crude blush in the
> sunrise outside my bungalow window at 5:45. What do I care for a 28,000-
> foot postcard when I have this bloody cold? All morning Kanchenjunga
> has been clouded over — only rarely do you see the peak through the
> clouds — or one of the surrounding peaks. Better that way. More mod-
> est. (Really, Kanchenjunga, you are not to blame for all these Darjeeling
> hotels. But I think you know what I mean!)[407]

Yet he went on taking photographs, and even dreaming of Kanchenjunga — or of living under the towering shape of a mountain. Then

the argument with Kanchenjunga became mixed up with Merton's debate over whether or not he had found what he came to find in Asia, as if, when he learned to see the one, the other would be clear of detail, clear of preconceptions, of all he had brought with him "informing the eye," which should be innocent.

In the meanwhile, he enjoyed the relative quiet in the manager's bungalow at the Mim Tea Estate with the Halls, nursed his cold, and tried to decide how long he would be away, where he would return when he went back to the West:

> Though I fully appreciate the many advantages of the hermitage at Gethsemani, I still have the feeling that the lack of quiet — and the general turbulence there (external and internal) last summer are indications that I ought to move.
>
> And so far the best indications seem to point to Alaska — or to the area around the Redwoods. Another question — would this move be *temporary* or *permanent?*
>
> I do not think I ought to separate myself completely from Gethsemani (even while maintaining an official residence there — legally only). I suppose I ought to eventually end my days there — and I do in many ways miss it.
>
> There is no question of my wanting simply to "leave Gethsemani." It is my monastery and being away has helped me see it in perspective and love it more.[408]

Other things too, he thought, were coming into perspective. On the night of November 19, he had another dream of mountains and woke to the sense that he had missed something vital and obvious:

> There is another side of Kanchenjunga and of every mountain — the side that has never been photographed and turned into postcards. That is the only side worth seeing.[409]

The photographer made one more approach to the mountain as an object to be photographed:

> Later — I took three more photos of the mountain. An act of reconciliation? No. A camera cannot reconcile one with anything. Nor can it see a real mountain. The camera does not know what it takes: it captures materials with which you reconstruct — not so much what you saw as what you *thought* you saw. Hence the best photography is aware — mindful, of illusion and uses illusion — permitting and encouraging it — especially unconscious (and powerful) illusions that are not normally admitted on the scene.[410]

Hence, too, the photograph as myth maker and myth sustainer. Yet the argument with the mountain was not over, and he had much to learn yet, beyond the sophistication he had now brought to his side of the debate. In the evening, for once, the clouds cleared, and not just for the waiting photographer:

> . . . The full beauty of the mountain is not seen until you too consent to the impossible paradox: it is and is not. When nothing more needs to be said, the smoke of ideas clears, the Mountain is SEEN.[411]

In its very simplicity, this is enough. The passage is followed by a paragraph rich in the matter of myths — so rich, in fact, one wonders at first how deep Merton is mining — then about the wisdom of any attempt to explain the mysteries. Yet the links with Merton's own life seem inescapable — the old phrase "the time of oxcarts" from St. Antonin Noble Val, the strange and seemingly arbitrary use of "Fatherless" here:

> Testament of Kanchenjunga — testament of Fatherless old Melchizedek. Testament from before the time of oxen and sacrifice. Testament without Law. NEW Testament. Full circle! The sun sets in the East! (The nuns at Loreto kept asking me: "have you seen the snows?" Could they have been serious?)[412]

*

On November 21, Merton was back in Darjeeling to concelebrate the Mass of Presentation at Loreto Convent, where the nuns asked him if he had seen the snows.[413] On the 24th, the Twenty-fourth Sunday after Pentecost, Merton was driven to the Jesuit Scholasticate at St. Mary's College in Kurseong, a few miles from Darjeeling. He said Mass there and on the 25th gave a talk, "Toward a Theology of Prayer," to the Scholastics. Much of the material he had presented before, but the emphasis now was on a still more pessimistic view of Catholic renewal in the West and the need for help from other Catholics from the non-West:

> We need the religious genius of Asia and of Asian culture to inject a dimension of depth into our aimless threshing about. I would almost say an element of heart, of *bhakti*, of love. These are some of the things we must recover and you are going to help us do it.[414]

In the early 1960s Merton had advocated an openness to the world. By 1968 he felt a distorting element in the renewal of the Church had led to a movement away from prayer, contemplation, the values of the tradition which had provided strength for almost two thousand years, in favor of an activism that was wholly self-justifying. There was no inconsistency here. Merton had never seen an either-or division between commitment to prayer life and commitment to social conscience. The tide has flowed back since 1968 to a point where Merton might well say that the whole process had to be begun again, though this time with more wisdom. There was much in the talk at Kurseong that spoke only to the situation as Merton saw it in 1968, but the contention that without a life of prayer there could be no meaningful action and indeed no significant life had been his since his conversion, and would certainly have remained his.

Early the next morning, Merton was given a jeep ride from St. Mary's College to the main road. Here he waited until he was picked up by the communal taxi from Darjeeling, Mount Everest Taxis, car 291, in which there was only one empty place. The driver was obviously anxious to save gas by coasting downhill, and almost made it before the taxi "conked out."[415]

To Merton there was about fifty yards to go to carry his overweight suitcases to the gate of Bagdogra Airport. Another passenger, John Balfour, thought it was "a few hundred yards." Merton and the Australian started talking about the driver during the walk, then shared two hours at the airport, waiting for Flight 224 to Calcutta to arrive.[416]

John Balfour had read *The Seven Storey Mountain*, but it had been a long time ago. He knew who Merton was, but almost nothing about him. Balfour found Merton's appearance striking:

> He had that "washed" face only those people usually have who have just been through an L.S.D. experience of some major mystic dimension. I did tell him that he did have that cleaner than clean, serenely open, quite halo-like face that I only saw on people after a deeply moving psychedelic experience, he made no comment on psychedelic but did say that being in the Himalayas was a very great experience for him. During lunch which we shared and our talk he frequently said how much Buddhist meditation techniques have strengthened his Christianity and every time he said it, he added that what he was referring [to] was not parochial Christianity. The question of reincarnation came up on several occasions, brought up by me on each occasion, his comment was always the same, "It depends what we mean by reincarnation." He often referred to the Cistercian order, to which he belonged. I did not remember that it was the same as being a Trappist, neither did I know anything about their "silent life" — as he referred to it. The way he talked about the order, his way of life there, certainly did not give me the impression that he would have had any intention of leaving it — of course [it was] not as [if] he would discuss such a matter with a stranger he met in a taxi. It is difficult, if not impossible to make any comment about a face one has met up with on one occasion. I would like to repeat that except on those who had a psychedelic experience, I have never come across that beautiful "washed" face, eyes glowing and something very precious, for this reason alone I shall never forget those hours I spent with Merton in Bagdogra. If I get leave next year I intend to go to Japan (?) he said and he gave me an address in Kentucky to write to him as we walked up to the Viscount to fly us to Calcutta . . .[417]

While he talked to John Balfour, Merton was saying his goodbye to the mountain. Early that morning at the Scholasticate, he had had his.

Last sight of Kanchenjunga, bright and clear in the morning sun, appearing over the hills of Ghoom as I came out into the corridor with my bags. Good view from the front of the monastery. A surprise.[418]

*

Touching down in Calcutta for what was now the third visit, Merton announced "It is a city I love."[419] He stayed overnight in Bob Boylan's apartment, collecting a pile of mail and the photographs taken at Dharamsala, which John Howard Griffin had processed for him. Father Daniel Walsh had sent a generous contribution to his "travel fund." He recorded meeting Balfour, "a man from Melbourne who had been to Rishikesh — and was disappointed — and who had been looking for the lamas in Darjeeling . . ."[420] Then on Tuesday, November 26, Merton was off again by air, this time to Madras.

It was raining in Madras, and Merton spent much of his time reading, deciding he liked the poems of D. H. Lawrence little better than he had liked them in Rome in 1933. The plans for Merton's return had grown still more complicated and uncertain:

> Lax wants me to come to Greece. I still don't know if I can get to Europe at all. Looked today at JAL, and Air France, and Lufthansa schedules. Probably better *not* to try a direct flight — not that there is one really. But say via Moscow (JAL and then what?) Or come back through India, Bombay-Athens, Delhi-Athens, all reasonable. But not in May! Better perhaps Tokyo-Anchorage-Amsterdam. Then Switzerland-Athens, and then back to England for Wales, Scotland. What about the letter from the man at Orval about the old Grandmontine priory, falling into ruins? . . . (At Puy Chevier Indre.)[421]

There is a sense that he was approaching every point in his own past by degrees, and even before his own past, the near-mythical past of the Mertons in Wales.

At the Cathedral of Madras, San Thomé, he was delighted to find an inscription, "Thomas, one of the twelve, called Didymus" — he had always been a collector of Thomases. He said Mass at the Church of Our Lady of Expectation, the sixteenth-century church at St. Thomas Mount. At the crèche for abandoned children next door, he signed the name of another Thomas in the visitors' book "and escaped before the sisters could read it. More rain, and we drove on to Mahabalipuram."[422]

Mahabalipuram moved him deeply, though "the kids selling postcards and trying to act as guides were a nuisance." The landscape gave him a sense of "what rural India might once have been."[423] At Mahabalipuram itself he felt he had touched a culture he had not seen before: "A complex of shrines carved out of, or built into, a great ancient rock formation — not cliffs but low rambling outcrops and boulders, smoothed and shaped by millions of years. Caves, porches, figures, steps, markings, lines of holes, gods and goddesses — but spread around without too much profusion."

He escaped the postcard sellers for hours of meditation on the beach: "A sense of silence and space, of unpredictable views, of the palms and the nearby sea." Here, where the "cool wind" came in "strongly off the sea," he discovered the Shore Temple, "smaller than I expected, very weatherbeaten, but a real gem . . ."[424] Apart from his days in the mountains, Merton felt the hours at Mahabalipuram had given him more than anywhere else in India.

With the eminent Sanskritist, Dr. V. Raghavan, Merton discussed the concept of *rasa* during his stay in Madras:

> Importance of suggestion to convey the aesthetic implications which transcend ordinary speech. Poetry is *not* ordinary speech, nor is poetic experience ordinary experience. It is closer to religious experience. *Rasa* is above all *santa:* contemplative peace. Difference between aesthetic experience and religious experience: the aesthetic lasts as long as the object is present. Religious knowledge does not require the presence of "an object." Once one has known Brahman one's life is permanently transformed from within. I spoke of Blake and his fourfold vision.[425]

This was a case, once more, of something that transcended ordinary speech, just as the mountain had required more than ordinary seeing. In poetry, not only the poet but the reader of poetry had to have *rasa.* It was *rasa* which was lacking, Merton decided, in the poetry of D. H. Lawrence — present, in abundance, in the poetry of William Blake.

He decided, too, that the small hotel band imitating American hit tunes at the Galle Face Hotel in Colombo was "entirely devoid of *rasa*."[426] He was playing "Hotel Karma" once more, a game he had played before the naming, right back to the Hotel Hamilton in Bermuda. He had already been reproved in the Mascarella Room at the Galle Face for ordering arrack (palm wine). When he went to bed early, "after a few minutes of quiet watching the moonlit sea," he found there was no escaping the band; the musicians were apparently directly under his pillow.

Merton arrived in Colombo, Ceylon (now Sri Lanka), on Friday, November 29. There were widespread strikes, and armed police and soldiers were everywhere in the streets to prevent riots. The post office strike hardly worried him, but he was afraid the trains would not run to Kandy.

In Colombo he went into the old Anglican church to pray; then, at the suggestion of Bob Boylan, he visited the United States Information Service office, hoping they would be able to give him the names of the eminent Buddhist scholars in the city.

The director, Victor Stier, was a close friend of W. H. Ferry, though Merton did not know it. Nor did he know that he would be shown into Stier's office to find the director in the middle of *Conjectures of a Guilty Bystander*, the only book by Thomas Merton he had not yet read. After introductions, there was the usual difficulty over Merton's two names, until Merton suggested "Why not call me Tom?" Stier had read about the Calcutta conference in the newspapers, and Merton agreed much good work had been accomplished, then went on to tell about the many phonies it had also attracted.[427]

Victor Stier managed to reach Walpola Rahula, whom Merton had been trying vainly to contact at the Buddhist university, and they made an appointment for two days later, a delay necessitated by Merton's plans to go to Kandy. It may be he learned about the Buddhist ruins at Dambulla, Polonnaruwa, and Anuradhapura, all near Kandy, at the office. At any rate, most of the plans and arrangements for the trip had been made when Stier invited one of his favorite authors home to lunch.

At Stier's house they had a discussion on philosophy, and Victor Stier found Merton very gentle in disagreement.[428] Merton caught up with the funny papers in the international edition of the *Herald-Tribune*, along with Stier's wife and child, and an episode in the adventures of Buz Sawyer became a Merton poem five days later.[429]

Merton left by train for Kandy early on the Saturday morning, November 30. Where he had been so careful not to travel dressed as a priest, it is amusing to find him going to Kandy in glorious isolation in a second-class compartment "For Clergy Only."[430] The isolation was fortunate, at any rate, giving him a chance to begin the finest of his travel poems, "Kandy Express." The poem is a poem in flight, difficult to read in the original draft, where the motion of the train makes its own contribution.[431]

Merton was back in Colombo early on December 3, "Kandy Express" completed, still under the power of an experience he was too quick to talk about. He also brought back photographs he would never see that were the finest fruit of his meditation on photography and *seeing*, following the argument with Kanchenjunga.

He recorded the lesser incidents at once in the journal for publication, "Asian Notes," in which he was now about a day behind. There had been a visit to the cave hermits with the German-born Buddhist bhikkhu, Nyanaponika Thera. He had spent time with the Catholic Bishop Nanayakkara at the cathedral and the monastery of the Sylvestrines, where he met the retired bishop, Bishop Regno, who had read *The Seven Storey Mountain* and who called Merton the first of the hippies. He also visited the ashram of the Anglican, Brother Johan Devananda.[432]

Victor Stier felt that the main purpose of the Kandy trip had been to look for a site for a hermitage. He reported that Merton had told him with a certain twinkle in his eye that "he wanted to start a small monastery so that his Abbot could come retire there with him and take it easy."[433]

Merton mentions he intended to write to Dom Flavian about the possibility of a hermitage in Sri Lanka, and he told his abbot and others that he wanted to return there.[434] Stier also wrote to Ferry that Merton had gone to the old Buddhist shrine at Polonnaruwa, "which impressed him tremendously."[435] In the journal, "The Hawk's Dream," Merton recorded one passage on the trip to Polonnaruwa.[436]

In the afternoon of the day he came back, Tuesday, December 3, Merton went to the Buddhist university for his interview with Walpola Rahula. Victor Stier had invited the staff of the USIS office for a party that night at his home. He told Merton he would be more than welcome but explained that there would be three families with their children, in case he found it too much of a "mob scene" to accept the invitation. "He came happily, and kept us all enthralled for hours. He was in rare form, and all of us were terribly impressed."[437]

One of Stier's colleagues, Franklin Crawford, had made arrangements for Merton to say Mass the next morning at St. Brigid's Convent School. After this there was a leisurely breakfast and conversation with pleasant interruptions by children at the Crawfords'.[438] At midday on December 4, Merton said his goodbyes to the Stiers and the Crawfords and left by air for Singapore.

His last image of Colombo was of the children flying "wild and happy Asian kites." "Asia is a kite-loving continent," he wrote; "there were wrecks of small Tibetan boys' kites on all the roofs and all the wires of Darjeeling."[439] He had not seen the fighting kites that had attracted him so much when he read about them in August at Gethsemani, but perhaps he recalled the solemn small boys carrying kites through the streets that first summer evening when he came up out of the subway in Harlem in search of Friendship House.

Other images touched images in his past. On December 5, he went back at last to try to fill in what he had so far left out of his account of the Kandy expedition in "Asian Notes":

> I remember the Moslem's sunset gun going off in Kandy and shaking the bishop's house. And the evening I returned from Polonnaruwa the gun went off as I stepped out of the car and a thousand crows flew up into the rain by the Temple of the Tooth.[440]

It may be he was remembering the sunset gun in Havana that announced the social hour: the descriptions in the two journals separated by thirty years have close connections. At any rate, it was a slow, guarded approach to Polonnaruwa in the book for publication. Merton says he is writing on Thursday, December 5, of a visit which took place on Monday, December 2. He goes on to explain the delay:

> Polonnaruwa was such an experience that I could not write hastily of it and cannot write now, or not at all adequately. Perhaps I have spoiled it by trying to talk of it at a dinner party, or to casual acquaintances. Yet when I spoke about it to Walpola Rahula at the Buddhist university I think the idea got across and he said, "Those who carved those statues were not ordinary men."[441]

There had been occasions before in Merton's past when he thought he had gone far to spoil something. The party at the Stiers' can stand for the party at Herb Jacobson's, where he felt he had blurted out too much about his conversion, or his feeling in July 1960 that he had dissipated the central experience that brought all the threads of *Hagia Sophia* together.[442]

While in Bangkok in October, Merton had studied "The Thai concept of sila, the 'control of outgoing exuberance,' " and he recorded in "Asian Notes" that it was "somewhat like the Javanese Rasa." The sources he was using called outgoing exuberance "the enemy of all beings" and warned that happiness without control could make the heart "go increasingly in the wrong direction."[443]

If there is an instinctive sense that at Polonnaruwa Thomas Merton achieved the step over "the edge of great realization" he had talked of with Chatral Rimpoche in Darjeeling, there is a sense, too, that, *in words*, through outgoing exuberance he spoiled the telling.

The account begins simply. After the visit to the caves at Dambulla, Merton, the bishop's driver, and the vicar general of the Kandy diocese went on to Polonnaruwa "with its vast area under trees . . ." Here Merton was left to wander alone among the huge figures, while the vicar general, "shying away from 'paganism,' " hung back, then sat under a tree reading a guidebook. Merton follows with a passage of considerable beauty about the figures.[444]

Then, in *The Asian Journal of Thomas Merton*, comes Merton's first attempt to explain the experience of Polonnaruwa to himself. It was written in the journal right after his return, on December 3:

> When looking at this [the figures] I was suddenly, almost forcibly, jerked clean out of the habitual, half-tied vision of things, and an inner cleanness, clarity, as if exploding from the rocks themselves, became evident, obvious. The queer *evidence* of the reclining figure, the smile, and the sad smile of Ananda, standing with arms folded (much more "imperative" than Mona Lisa because completely simple and straightforward). The thing about all this is that there is no puzzle, no problem, and really no "mystery." All problems are resolved and everything is clear, simply because what matters is clear. The rock, all matter, all life, is charged with Dharmakaya . . . everything is emptiness and everything is compassion. I don't know when in my life I have ever had such a sense of

beauty and spiritual validity fusing together in one aesthetic illumination. Surely, with Mahabalipuram and Polonnaruwa, my Asian pilgrimage has come clear and justified itself — I mean I *know* and have seen what I was obscurely looking for. I don't know what else remains but I have now *seen* and have pierced through the surface and have got beyond the shadow and the disguise. This is Asia in its purity, not covered over with garbage (Asian or European or American) and it is clear, pure, complete. It says everything — it needs nothing. And because it needs nothing it can afford to be silent, unnoticed, undiscovered. It does not *need* to be discovered. It is we (Asians included) who need to discover it. The Bishop was telling me later of the profound importance of his *own* discovery of Asia, and of what it meant to be Asian.[445]

The passage has *rasa*. Yet somehow the strain of holding something back is evident. At times, others have edited the passage for dramatic effect, and this only makes matters worse. Something in Merton's first attempt on December 3 to say the unsayable hints at far more than an aesthetic discovery, or of a discovery of an Asia that has "justified itself."

Yet, finally, whatever was lost from the written words and to some degree spoiled in the talking is restored by a quiet meditation on the photographs Thomas Merton took that day at Polonnaruwa, which speak of the "what is not said" in the "voices of silence."

❋

Merton stopped for two days in Singapore, staying at the Raffles Hotel, then flew first-class on to Bangkok for the conference. He arrived in the afternoon on December 6, and booked in at the Oriental Hotel, where he was delighted with his rooms — "a fine split-level dwelling high over the river, and you enter it through an open veranda on the other side looking out over the city."[446] It was virtually a penthouse apartment. He took a photograph of the view, then settled down to yet another attack on the embarrassing problem of having too much luggage.

The next day he left the films he had taken in Sri Lanka for developing at the Borneo Studio on Silom Road, then booked a flight to Djakarta for December 15. He planned to spend over a week in Indonesia, meeting Buddhist scholars and spending Christmas at the monastery of Rawa Seneng, before flying on to the Trappist monastery on Lantao Island near Hong Kong.[447]

The conference would officially begin on the 9th. In the meantime, Merton met those who would be taking part, and fulfilled his duties as a tourist on group expeditions to the Temple of the Emerald Buddha.[448]

On Sunday, December 8, he made his last entry in the journal:

Today is the Feast of the Immaculate Conception. In a little while I leave this hotel. I go to say Mass at St. Louis Church, lunch at the Apostolic Delegation, then on to the Red Cross place this afternoon. No mail here yet except a letter from Winifred (hippie girl at Redwoods) for-warded from Calcutta.[449]

The AIM conference was held at Samutprakarn, thirty-one kilome-ters south of the center of Bangkok. At the Sawang Kaniwat, or Red Cross, there was an extensive area landscaped with flowering trees and shrubs, with a long, narrow ornamental lake and several swimming ponds. The buildings included the conference hall, which had a high-pitched V-shaped roof, a small hotel, a large guest house known as Happy Hall, and a number of four-room cottages.

Merton found he had been assigned to Cottage Number 2. Flower-ing shrubs were planted close against the walls under the windows. He was on the ground floor, which he shared with Father Celestine Say, O.S.B., prior of the Abbey of Our Lady of Montserrat in Manila. Between the two separate rooms was a small receiving hall. The walls inside did not reach to the ceiling, and it was possible to see from one bedroom to the other if one stood in a certain position.[450]

In the two rooms above in Cottage Number 2 were John Moffitt, poet, author, poetry editor of *America*, and expert on Hindu monasticism, and Father François de Grunne, one of the auditors, who had come from Belgium to attend the conference. There was one key for all the guests at the cottage, and much time was spent on the first evening deciding where it should be left so that nobody would find himself locked out.

The reception on Sunday evening was something of an ordeal for Merton, and he tried to make himself inconspicuous. To most of the other sixty-five participants and the official guests he was both the most celebrated and the most popular person there. Lists had been posted for study groups, and the list with Merton's name as group director had already been greatly oversubscribed, though a line had been drawn after the first ten names. At the reception — where he was anxious to avoid participants who said they had once read *The Seven Storey Moun-tain* and it had changed their lives — there were many old friends to meet, both those who had been to Gethsemani and friends by corre-spondence. Later that night, when he stood outside with a group and someone asked how one could tell north, he explained navigation by the stars and provided a star map of the constellations.[451]

The conference had been carefully organized under the president, Dom Rembert Weakland, Primate of the Benedictine Order, and there was a full program. Each morning would start with two two-hour talks, fol-lowed by Mass at noon, with the thirty-six priest-monks from every part of Asia concelebrating. There would be a break after lunch from two until four-thirty, when the group sessions began. At Vespers each evening the Lord's Prayer would be said, each day in a different Asian language. After this there would be informal discussions and cultural events.

Merton had already taken note that a Dutch television team had arrived to cover highlights of the week's meetings. He wondered how he would be able to keep the promise he had made to Dom Flavian before leaving Gethsemani. Then an Italian television team arrived. The local media and the visitors were out in force on Monday morning, but fortunately they concentrated on Somdet Para Ariawong Sankarat, the Supreme Patriarch of Thai Buddhism, who gave the address of welcome.[452] Merton escaped, though he was photographed standing listening to the address beside Father Acharya, prior of the monastery at Kurisumala.

While there were official translators for the morning lectures, Merton found himself enlisted as a translator for a number of the afternoon exchanges. On December 9, there was no chance of an afternoon rest. His group discussion session had been televised. In the evening there was an informal discussion on marriage and the vow of celibacy. There had been a lot of talk that day, including a conversation with John Moffitt on the differences between Zen and Hindu mysticism. That night a good deal of sleep was lost in Cottage Number 2 because of a prolonged conference of cats on the roof. After each crescendo of caterwauling the other guests heard deep, rumbling laughter from Merton's room.[453]

On the way to an early-morning swim Merton asked his companions if they had had a good night's sleep. There was more laughter over this, but by the time of his own lecture he was beginning to look drawn. He put off a number of invitations for talks that afternoon: *that* afternoon he was going to rest before the study group.

The session for Tuesday, December 10, opened at 9 A.M. with an apostolic benediction and warm encouragement from Pope Paul, delivered by Archbishop Jean Jàdot, the papal delegate to Thailand. Immediately after this Father J. Amyot, S.J., of Bangkok gave a strong lecture, whose theme seemed to some of the participants to be that there was little need of Christian missionaries in Thailand. At ten forty-five, Merton rose to give his talk on "Marxism and Monastic Perspectives." At that point the two television teams moved in. There was some difficulty in hearing Merton's opening words. The initial nervousness may have been because he was tired; it may have been because he realized there was now no chance of honoring his promise to his abbot; it may have been because he felt every word, every gesture, was being recorded.

This time Merton's talk did not depart from the prepared text as much as the talk in Calcutta, but there were a number of additions — from his experiences talking to the French Marxist students at the Center in Santa Barbara, from his recent reading of Marcuse, and from his talks with refugee monks in Tibet who had experienced a Communist takeover. There were moments when he seemed to be offering a fair but unexpected exchange: if he recognized the Marxist students as the "true monks" of 1968, would the communists recognize the monastery as the true Communist society, the only practical example of a society following the Marxian premise "From each according to his ability, to each according to his need"?[454]

The most popular parts of his address were the two survival parables he retold from stories he had been told. In the first, a monk who was stranded from his monastery during the Chinese invasion asks advice from an abbot friend, only to be told: "From now on, Brother, everybody stands on his own two feet." (Moral: there are no structures, there is only spiritual self-reliance in God.) In the second parable, the cellarer of a Tibetan monastery tries to escape by driving twenty-five yaks loaded with provisions and the monastery possessions. The train of yaks attracts the attention of the Chinese communists and leads to capture. (Moral: Only the unencumbered go free; or, Travel without a train of yaks — and here Merton must have been laughing at himself and his problems with excess luggage.) On the matter of doing without structures he had brought new point to an old theme: as long ago as the summer of 1964 he had written to Daniel Berrigan, "I wonder if we are really going to have to get along without a structure one of these days. Maybe that will be good, but Lord it will be tough on most people."[455] From standing "on one's own feet" he moved now to something still more perilous. "The Zen people have a saying that has nothing to do with this, but is analogous in a certain sense: 'Where do you go from the top of a thirty-foot pole?' "

At the end of his talk he looked nervously at the cameras once more and said there would be a further discussion later:

> So I will disappear from view and we can all have a Coke or something. Thank you very much.

In his journals Merton had talked over and over of disappearing. He must have wanted to get away from the media at that moment, and he *was* determined to protect his afternoon's rest!

*

He left lunch early, and he and Father François de Grunne walked back to the cottage talking. Each of them went to his own room. At some time before three o'clock Father de Grunne heard what he thought was a cry and the sound of something falling. There were noises at all hours in the area around the cottage, but this sound seemed to come from below. He went downstairs and could get no response when he knocked on Father Merton's door.[456]

By this time Father Celestine Say had returned from lunch. He had been brushing his teeth, and the water was turned on. He told Father de Grunne he had heard nothing unusual, and de Grunne went up-stairs. The only other occupant of Cottage Number 2, John Moffitt, had gone sightseeing that afternoon.

Father Celestine now smelled something unpleasant but couldn't identify what it was. He did look across and saw the bed unoccupied in the room across the small hallway. He assumed Father Merton must be sleeping on the terrazzo floor for coolness, because he had heard Merton say that his things had been cleared from the floor when the maid cleaned up the room the day before.[457] He could have looked further into the room opposite, but he was reluctant to pry. When Father Celestine lay down on his own bed he was unable to sleep be-cause Father de Grunne was pacing in the room above him.

An hour later, a few minutes before four, Father de Grunne de-scended the stairs again to get the key of the cottage from Merton and to reassure himself that the monk was only a sound sleeper. This time, after knocking, he looked through the louvres in the upper part of the door. He saw Merton lying in an odd way, then noticed a standing fan was lying on top of him. He tried the door but found it locked. This time Father Celestine came quickly and stood at the door, calling out to Merton and hoping for an answer. Father de Grunne ran for help, coming almost at once on the Abbot of Waekwan, Odo Haas, and the American, Archabbot Egbert H. Donovan, who were returning from a swim.

It must have been a nervous reaction that made Father de Grunne ask them first if it had been a good swim. Then he said there had been an accident to Father Merton.[458]

The four men tried to break the panel of louvred glass at the top of the door. Then they found the panel swung on hinges, and it was possible to reach in and draw the inside bolt. In the room they found Merton lying on his back with the five-foot fan lying diagonally across his body. Without realizing the fan was alive, Haas tried to lift it away, only to be given an electric shock that jerked him sideways. He was held to the shaft of the fan until Father Celestine managed to unplug the fan at the outlet, which was under the bed across the room.[459]

Merton did not move. His hands lay at his sides. There was a long, raw burn mark along the right side of his body almost to the groin. No burns showed on his hands. His face was discolored. His eyes and his mouth were half open. His bare feet were oddly curled up and awkwardly placed.

The priests gave Father Merton absolution. Father Haas went for the abbot primate, who arrived to give Merton extreme unction. By this time a doctor had arrived. She was Mother Edeltrud Weist, prioress of Taegu Convent in Korea. She checked for a pulse and for any reaction to shining an electric light into Merton's eyes, then pronounced him dead.[460]

Father Celestine had taken several photographs as a record in the dim and, by now, disturbed room. Abbot Weakland forbade any further pictures out of respect for the dead.[461] Weakland telephoned the Samut Pradarn Hospital, whose director, Dr. Luksana Narkvachara, informed the Bangkok Police and came himself to the scene.

The investigating officer, Lt. Boonchop Poomvichit, arrived after some delay to look at the scene, consult with Dr. Narkvachara, and take depositions. The fan was sent to the Scientific Crime Detection Laboratory, where it was found to have a "defective electric cord installed inside its stand. When the cord contacted the metal stand, it caused an electrical leakage throughout the fan. This flow of electricity was strong enough to cause the death of a person if he touched the metal part."[462]

The Bangkok Police report concluded:

> However, the Investigating Officer questioned Dr. Luksana Narkvachara, whose views were that Reverend Thomas Merton died because of:
>   1. Heart failure.
>   2. And that the cause mentioned in 1. caused the dead priest to faint and collide with the stand fan located in the room. The fan had fallen onto the body of Reverend Thomas Merton. The head of the dead priest had hit the floor. There was a burn on the body's skin and on the underwear on the right side which was assumed to have been caused by electrical shock from the fan.
>   Therefore the cause of the death of Reverend Thomas Merton was as mentioned. There were no witnesses who might be suspected of causing the death. There is no reason to suspect criminal causes.[463]

By the end of this investigation rigor mortis had already begun to set in. The body was released by the police to Abbot Weakland, then washed and taken to the chapel at the conference center, where vigil was kept. At ten the next morning a Requiem Mass was concelebrated.

Whereas nobody claimed to have witnessed Merton's death, there were some twenty people who gave evidence of one kind or another about the discovery and the aftermath. Some of the discrepancies are natural enough, and are not very important. Others can be explained by the same respect for the dead which moved Abbot Weakland to forbid more photographs of the corpse.

The immediate question at the conference was confined to the cause of death, where there appeared to be two causes, electrocution and heart failure. The police investigation had not inspired much confidence. Many felt electrocution was deliberately played down to protect the reputation of the conference center. It may have been so. One thing argues for electrocution, especially since Merton had no history of heart condition.

A massive electric shock to the body produces an involuntary release of urine. The police report speaks of a pool of urine around Merton's body. Some of the witnesses mention it. Others do not. One mentions a pool of liquid without identifying it. Again, this was clearly a case of respect.[464] What is more important is that there had undoubtedly been some cleaning up very early after the discovery, out of the same respect for the dead. This would account for the confusion when two different pairs of drawers are described, and when it is said that the burn extended under the drawers, while the material was not singed.

There were other disturbances. The standard fan had been moved a number of times — once when Odo Haas tried to lift it, probably again before Dr. Weist drew a sketch to accompany her report to the police. A good many people seem to have been in the small room at certain times. Later that evening, as soon as Merton's body was removed, the other occupants of Cottage Number 2 were moved to accommodations elsewhere. Then the Thai servants not only stripped the room completely, but even took away the bushes outside the window and removed the topsoil of the flower beds. This was done, it was explained, because of their superstitions about death. Altogether, then, any number of things make it difficult to be confident of the scene at the time of Merton's discovery, or to unravel so many puzzles for a brief and sure account.

What seems the most likely reconstruction is that Merton came out of the shower either wearing a pair of drawers or naked. His feet may have been wet still from the shower. The standing fan had been on day and night during that hot week.[465] Merton may have slipped and drawn the fan sharply toward him for support, or he may have simply tried to change its position. The wiring was faulty, giving him a shock which was sufficient in itself to kill him as he cried out. It is quite possible the shock also gave him a massive heart attack, though this was a secondary cause of death.

There are still numbers of questions with this hypothesis. Why wasn't Merton thrown much more convulsively by the shock? Why were his hands at his sides, apparently unburned on the palms? One would expect them to have been burned, still adhering to the shaft of the fan until the current was disconnected.

Little attention seems to have been given to a wound on the back of Merton's head that had bled considerably. The obvious solution appears to be that it was caused when his head struck the floor.

However confused it is, the evidence still speaks overwhelmingly for an accident. There were rumors at once, and one has to remember that the year was 1968, that "brute of a year" Thomas Merton had prophesied, a season of well-earned paranoia. However briefly, even simplistically, the rumors are dealt with here, they have to be faced.

If Thomas Merton's death was not by accident, it was either a suicide or a murder. In December 1968, the motives for suicide can be dismissed out of hand on any evidence we have, while the circumstances in which Merton was found make such a supposition impossible to sustain. Murder cannot be so easily ruled out. There is no evidence whatsoever that Thomas Merton was murdered, only a situation in which he *could* have been murdered. The room was not secured from either the entrance, the window, or, as the Fathers discovered, from the door. No attempt was made to find if anyone had entered at three that afternoon, and all the evidence, if there had been any, would have been destroyed within hours of Merton's death. No convincing motive has come to light. Robbery can be dismissed: nothing was taken, though there was an expensive camera and a wallet in the room. In 1968, Merton's death would have furthered the political ends of no group. Those who felt some animosity toward the stands he had taken on various issues were not in Bangkok. Only the letters of 1967 in which he spoke of his desire to become an intermediary for peace remain to trouble an absolute certainty. By December 1968, at any rate, Merton was not an obvious target in Bangkok for either reasoning or unreasonable assassins.

While there are some grounds for the rumor he was murdered, they do not seem plausible. It is only a matter of real regret that his death was investigated in such a bungled and amateurish fashion and that there was no autopsy.

Merton's body was taken to the U.S. air base in Bangkok. In the bureaucratic red tape that developed, his Order waived an autopsy in Asia to speed his return to the United States.[466] In the end, it was five full days before his body was released for flight to America.

✳

Thomas Merton's death sent out an immediate shockwave. He had died sometime before 3 P.M., Bangkok time. A telegram was sent that night to Gethsemani. Crossing the International Date Line, it arrived some fourteen hours after his death, at 10 A.M. on December 10, at the monastery:

ABBOTT BURNS
TRAPIST POST OFC GETHSEMENI KY

DEPARTMENT REGRETS INFORM YOU FOLLOWING MESSAGE RECEIVED FOR YOU FROM AMERICAN EMBASSY BANGKOK THAILAND: "INFORMED BY ABBOTT WEAKLAND THAT THOMAS MERTON HAS DIED."
MR. HOBART LUPPI DIR. SPECIAL CONSULAR SERVICES
DEPT. OF STATE[467]

The tenth of December, 1968, was, to the day, the twenty-seventh anniversary of Thomas Merton's arrival at the Monastery of Our Lady of Gethsemani. It was also the birthday of Dom James Fox. When Dom James saw a party from the monastery approaching his hermitage, he assumed they had come to celebrate his birthday with him.[468] Later that same day, Dom James telephoned to share his grief with his friend Naomi Burton Stone.

Many were telephoned that day, and they started for Gethsemani from all over the United States, believing that the funeral would be held within a day or two. Father John Eudes Bamberger was almost killed when his car swerved during a blizzard in the mountains above Asheville, North Carolina, on the hurried return.

S. learned of Merton's death from a newspaper. Harold Jenkins heard it on the television news. Jinny Burton read it in a news magazine. Dan Berrigan heard at Cornell on bond awaiting a retrial. Gladys Marcus telephoned Robert Lax in the Greek islands. Ed Rice had had a crash on the freeway coming into New York. He abandoned his car and made it home to telephone a garage. A call came in from a friend to tell him of Merton's death. He returned to his abandoned car and sat in the bitter cold at 2 A.M., waiting for the wrecker and thinking about death. Naomi Burton Stone believed she was controlling her emotions until she came upon a large display for Rice-a-Roni in her local supermarket and remembered the "Care packages" for the hermit . . .[469]

❋

Merton had included the account of two dreams in *Conjectures of a Guilty Bystander*. The first was his own:

> I dreamt I was lost in a great city and was walking "toward the center" without quite knowing where I was going. Suddenly I came to a dead end, but on a height, looking at a great bay, an arm of the harbor. I saw a whole section of the city spread out before me on hills covered with light snow, and realized that, though I had far to go, I knew where I was: because in this city there are two arms of the harbor and they help you to find your way, as you are always encountering them.[470]

When John Howard Griffin's camera was returned to him from Gethsemani, after it had come back with Merton's effects from Bangkok, he found there was still film in it. When the film was developed, Griffin discovered the scene of the dream in almost all its details, except for the snow-covered hills: it was the photograph Merton had taken looking down from his penthouse room at the Oriental Hotel in Bangkok on December 6.[471]

The second dream was a dream Merton had taken from Karl Barth, a dream Barth had had about Mozart. What drew Merton to it was his own love of Mozart's music and a line of Barth's: "It is a child, even a 'divine' child, who speaks in Mozart's music to us."[472] In December

1968, Karl Barth's name appeared with that of Thomas Merton in the obituaries and the lives of both men were celebrated together at a Mass in Louisville where Mozart's music was played.

❊

After many delays, the body of Thomas Merton was at last flown from Bangkok to California, carried in the bay of a SAC bomber. Reaching the West Coast, it was transferred to a commercial carrier bound for Louisville. The closed casket was opened in New Haven, the hamlet close to Gethsemani. Dom Flavian Burns had difficulty identifying his friend. Father — and Doctor — John Eudes Bamberger made the positive identification.[473] The casket was resealed and taken to the monastery.

It was already afternoon on Tuesday, December 17. Father Chrysogonus had composed the Funeral Mass and Burial Service. This began with the words "I have always overshadowed Jonas with My mercy . . . Have you had sight of Me, Jonas My Child? Mercy within mercy within mercy."[474] Rain, turning to snow, fell on the crowd. Father Chrysogonus had asked that the words from the conclusion of *The Seven Storey Mountain*[475] be read to close the service:

> But you shall taste the true solitude of my anguish and my poverty and I shall lead you into the high places of my joy and you shall die in Me and find all things in My mercy which has created you for this end and brought you from Prades to Bermuda to St. Antonin to Oakham to London to Cambridge to Rome to New York to Columbia to Corpus Christi to St. Bonaventure to the Cistercian Abbey of the poor men who labor in Gethsemani:
>   That you may become the brother of God and learn to know the Christ of the burnt men.

That mercy had brought him, in a conversion and a journey which was at best half begun in 1946, to Christ in the Desert to the Redwoods to Alaska to Calcutta to New Delhi to Dharamsala to Kanchenjunga to Mahabalipuram to Polonnaruwa to Bangkok to Gethsemani.

There was disappointment as well as grief for many. For Merton's abbot there would be no realization now of his own hopes when he had sacrificed his solitude so that his friend could go deeper into solitude until it sang for many. For Father Matthew Kelty, Brother Maurice Flood, and others, there would now be no leader and partner in the experimental monasteries. For the Cistercian Order of the Strict Observance, others would have to carry the influence and ideas of Father Louis under different names . . . Meanwhile, there was solitude and there was contemplation without concept. The two friends Merton had been with that first summer at the cottage near Olean continued solitaries, one in a small house among fields in rural Long Island, the other on a Greek island . . . Meanwhile, there was Faith and the Absurd. Ernesto Cardenal wrote his *"Coplas a la Muerte de Merton,"*[476] an anti-poem asking Merton to enjoy the absurdities in all the circumstances of his death with a friend and fellow poet. The monastery where Merton had lived so long survived his direst predictions for its future, honored his accomplishments more than he would have believed, and missed his laughter. In the place named for a walled garden and a scene of anguish and resolution, his cross was one among many under cedars.

As for his friends, readers, critics:[477]

> The Master came at his right time
> Into the world. When his time was up,
> He left it again.
> He who waits his time, who submits
> When his work is done,
> In his life there is no room
> For sorrow or for rejoicing
> Here is how the ancients said all this
> In four words:
>   "God cuts the thread."
>
> We have seen a fire of sticks
> Burn out. The fire now
> Burns in some other place. Where?
> Who knows? These brands
> Are burnt out.

NOTES AND SOURCES
BIBLIOGRAPHY
INDEX

NOTES AND SOURCES

Published works by Thomas Merton are given here by title, except for the ten most frequently cited, for which initials are used. These are, with the edition from which the page numbers are given:

AJ	*The Asian Journal of Thomas Merton*, 1975, New Directions
CGB	*Conjectures of a Guilty Bystander*, 1968, Doubleday Image
CP	*The Collected Poems of Thomas Merton*, 1977, New Directions
LE	*The Literary Essays of Thomas Merton*, 1981, New Directions
MAG	*My Argument with the Gestapo*, 1969, Doubleday
ScJ	*The Secular Journal*, 1977, Farrar, Straus and Giroux, Noonday
SJ	*The Sign of Jonas*, 1953, Harcourt, Brace
SP	*Selected Poems of Thomas Merton*, 1967, enlarged, New Directions
SSM	*The Seven Storey Mountain*, 1948, Harcourt, Brace
WCT	*The Way of Chuang Tzu*, 1965, New Directions

In addition, initials have been used to identify ten of the most important unpublished sources in Merton's writings:

AN	Asian Notes, October–December 1968
FF	Drafts of reviews, travel notes, journals, etc., in the Fitzgerald File
LAB	"The Labyrinth," near-complete transcript of Merton's early novel
NJ	New Journal, 1952–53
PSJ	Perry Street Journal, 1939–40
RJ	Restricted Journals, 1956–68
SBJ	St. Bonaventure Journal, 1940–41
SN	Small Notebook, May–October 1968
SSMB	The typescript of "The Seven Storey Mountain" at Boston College
SSML	The typescript of "The Seven Storey Mountain" formerly in the collection of Sister Thérèse Lentfoehr, now at the Merton Center, Columbia University
VOW	"The Vow of Conversation"
CWL	Stands throughout for Merton's "Cold War Letters," 1962 collection. This was not printed, but it was widely circulated. The first figure is the number of the letter, the second is the page number in the mimeographed copy.

There are currently two bibliographies of Merton's writing. These are cited as follows:

Dell'Isola   *Thomas Merton: A Bibliography,* by Frank Dell'Isola, Kent State University Press, 1975. This is quoted first, as it covers the whole period from Merton's first publications to 1975. The first number given is that of the page. The letter and number following are Dell'Isola's index code.

Breit   *Thomas Merton: A Bibliography,* by Marquita Breit, Scarecrow Press, 1974. This begins in 1957 but includes more than 1800 items by and about Thomas Merton between 1957 and 1973. It is in process of being brought up-to-date. Again, the first number is that of the page, the second is Breit's item number or index code.

Works by other authors listed in the Bibliography are cited in abbreviated form. For easy reference, clue lines and their corresponding titles appear in boldface in the Bibliography. Works not in the Bibliography are cited here in full. Interviews conducted by the author are cited by the name of the person interviewed followed by the date of the interview. Tapes appear under their number, either in the catalogue of the archive or, in the case of the commercial tapes, after the name Electronic-Paperbacks, Chappaqua, N.Y.

The archives most frequently listed and given initials are:

AA   In the author's possession
BCSC   Boston College Special Collections, Chestnut Hill, Mass.
ESA   Elaine Sproat Archives, Williamsburg, Va.
FLSB   Friedsam Memorial Library, St. Bonaventure University, Olean, N.Y.
GRSU   The George Arents Research Library, Syracuse University, Syracuse, N.Y.
JLA   James Laughlin Archives, Norfolk, Conn.
MCC   The Merton Center at Columbia University, New York
MGA   Monastery of Our Lady of Gethsemani Archives, Trappist, Ky.
RBA   Richard Bassett Archives, Milton, Mass.
TMSC   The Thomas Merton Studies Center, Bellarmine College, Louisville, Ky.

Preface: Continuing Conversion, Continuing Autobiography

Title: Both phrases have been used often in reference to Merton's life and work. I was introduced to the first, "continuing conversion," in the writings of Elena Malits, C.S.C., and the second, "continuing autobiography," in the writings and lectures of Victor Kramer. I owe both these Merton scholars a debt.
    Epigraphs: "Keng's Disciple," WCT, 129. RJ, Oct. 2, 1967.

1. PSJ, Nov. 19, 1939, FLSB. Sections of *Finnegans Wake* had, of course, appeared earlier as "Work in Progress."
2. Merton largely appropriated the term *Macaronic* for his own use. The *American Heritage Dictionary* lists four definitions. See also O.E.D., Webster's International, etc.
3. In "A Poet's Journal," 13, Robert Lax says the resolution was to talk simply. He goes on to say Merton was determined to write simply. Interview with Lax, Sept. 29, 1980. The joint resolution covered both speaking and writing.
4. Some confusion has arisen between the title of Merton's unpublished novel and the book Merton's friend Ed Rice wrote and published about him in 1970, *The Good Times and Hard Life of Thomas Merton: The Man in the Sycamore Tree.*
5. SBJ, Oct. 27, 1940, FLSB.
6. Merton to James Laughlin, Aug. 17, 1946, JLA.
7. Interview with Ron Seitz, Aug. 2, 1980. This is given slightly differently by Seitz in "Thomas Merton, A Deathday Remembrance," 20.
8. Merton's draft to unnamed correspondent, Jan. 7, 1967, MGA.

Canigou

Among those I am especially indebted to in this section are John Stanley, who made available his work on the genealogy of the Mertons and the Jenkinses; Brother Patrick Hart, O.C.S.O., who provided all the notes on the family that had been sent to him for the Monastery Archives by Beatrice Katherine Merton; Richard Bassett, who provided the Tudor-Hart correspondence, as well as memories of Ruth and Owen Merton; Frank Seegraber, the librarian of Special Collections at Boston College Library; Dr. Robert Daggy and his staff — Debbie DiSalvo Heaverin, Lorrie Bennett, and David A. DiSalvo — at the Thomas Merton Studies Center, Bellarmine College; and Elaine Sproat, who is writing the biography of the New Zealand poet Lola Ridge and who made the Owen Merton–Evelyn Scott–Lola Ridge correspondence available. I am also indebted to Pat and Frank Priest (Pat Priest is the daughter of Elsie Hauck Holahan Jenkins), Roger MacLaughlin, and Betty Burroughs Woodhouse (Mrs. Thomas F. Woodhouse).

Epigraphs: Ruth Calvert Jenkins to Percyval Tudor-Hart, Dec. 20, 1911. "On the Anniversary of My Baptism," SP, 63; CP, 156.

1. Merton to Mary Childs Black, Jan. 27, 1962, TMSC, reproduced CWL, 24A, 46.
2. RJ, Nov. 4 and 5, 1961. The visit appears in an edited form in CGB, 200–201.
3. Merton to Brother M. Placid, Aug. 5, 1964, TMSC.
4. Preface to Argentine edition of "The Complete Works of Thomas Merton," Daggy, *Introductions*, 33.
5. If small, Prades had become the center of an international art dispute in the summer of 1913, when the American sculptor and collector George Grey Barnard was prevented from removing the remainder of the cloister at the ruined monastery of St. Michel de Cuxa to what was to become the Cloisters, at Fort Tryon, New York. Half the Cuxa cloister had already gone to New York, so that Merton is incorrect in saying the cloister "stone by stone, followed me across the Atlantic a score of years later," SSM, 6. Much of what remained of the cloister was incorporated into Mme. Baladud de Saint-Jean's bathhouse, and the whole story of the struggle between Barnard — backed by the people of Prades — and the Beaux-Arts Department in Paris — encouraged by international art lovers — is told in J. L. Schrader, "The Cloisters and the Abbaye," *The Metropolitan Museum of Art Bulletin* 37, no. 1 (Summer 1979): 3–52.
6. Owen Merton to Percyval Tudor-Hart, June 28, 1914, and notes written by Owen Merton on the back of a photograph, MGA.
7. Interview with Richard Bassett, May 12 and 15, 1980.
8. Owen Merton to Esmond Atkinson, June 1, 1912, TMSC.
9. Ruth Calvert Jenkins to Percyval Tudor-Hart, Dec. 20, 1911, RBA. Her apartment was in 9, Rue Scribe.
10. Ruth Calvert Jenkins to Percyval Tudor-Hart from Hotel St. Catherine, Amalfi, May 20, 1913, RBA. This interesting letter reveals that Ruth Merton had the same way of polarizing her feelings by contrasting places as "good" and "bad" that her son had, and that the party had taken the same route on foot that Merton was to take twenty years later.
11. Certified copy of An Entry of Marriage, General Registry Office, London, AA. Certificate number: MX 573414. St. Anne's, before the bombing in the 1940s, was the artists' church in London, as St. Paul's Covent Garden was the actors' church. St. Anne's was also the headquarters of a number of societies promoting social causes.
12. There is some difficulty in dating this. According to Richard Bassett, pacifism was "very much in the air" in Paris in 1912, and he believes Ruth became a pacifist there. John Stanley believes he has identified an Englishwoman, connected with the Bloodgood Nurseries, who became Ruth's friend, and converted her, both to pacifism and to Quakerism, during her visit to Douglaston just before her marriage.
13. Owen Merton to Esmond Atkinson, Jan. 10, 1916, TMSC.
14. Extrait d'Acte de Naissance, 1915 — original dated Feb. 2, 1915 — Mairie de Prades, Département des Pyrénées Orientales, République Française, AA. See also "Tom's Book," TMSC.

15. One New Zealand cousin, Charlie Merton, was killed in the First World War.
16. Quoted in Walter de la Mare's foreword to Edward Thomas, *Collected Poems*, 5.
17. Owen Merton to Esmond Atkinson, Jan. 10, 1916, TMSC.
18. The photograph, with the date on the back, is in the Monastery Archives.
19. SSM, 6.
20. The editing was done by Robert Giroux. What is almost certainly the setting copy, or copy marked by the editor for the printers, is in the Special Collections, Boston College.
21. LAB, 79 (89), FLSB.
22. Owen Merton to Percyval Tudor-Hart, June 28, 1914, RBA.
23. SSM, 21.
24. Tom took a hand-painted set of her china to England for the Bennetts in 1934. LAB, 1.
25. My information here is based in part on the experience of another American art student in Paris right after the First World War — my mother. Richard Bassett says that things were freer at the Tudor-Hart *atelier*, though there was a division of the sexes. Tudor-Hart had a tendency to run his students' lives and practiced a number of fads and interests. One of these was nudism.
26. Interview with the Priests, July 27, 1980. Notes, John Stanley.
27. "Tom's Book," TMSC.
28. Interview with Robert Lax, Sept. 12, 1980.
29. The Maryland episode is very conjectural and is based upon a comment quoted in the introduction by Mark Van Doren to SP, xi, and a fictionalized version of the Mertons' experiences in America, novel in manuscript, *The Grey Riddle*, by Evelyn Scott (Library, Humanities Research Center, University of Texas, Austin).
30. Photographs of 57 Hillside Avenue, Flushing, MGA.
31. Owen Merton to Percyval Tudor-Hart, Jan. 22, 1921, RBA.
32. Roger MacLaughlin to the author, Feb. 16, 1981, AA.
33. Owen Merton to Percyval Tudor-Hart, July 10, 1925, RBA.
34. Ruth's plans for a Browning Room are mentioned ten years earlier in her letter of Dec. 20, 1911, to Tudor-Hart: "For instance take the bedroom I intend to decorate for myself someday. The theme of it is that line from Browning, 'In the core of one pearl all the shade and the shine of the sea.' " RBA.
35. Owen Merton to Percyval Tudor-Hart, Jan. 22, 1921, RBA.
36. Betty Burroughs Woodhouse (Mrs. Thomas F. Woodhouse) to the author, Sept. 11, 1980, AA.
37. SSM, 8, 9.
38. Merton to Rosemary Ruether, Mar. 24, 1967, TMSC.
39. Ibid., Mar. 25, 1967, TMSC.
40. SSM, 10, 11. SSMB, 17, is even more emphatic: "My favorite reading was a large Geography book with maps and pictures of all the different countries. I do not pretend that I could understand all the maps, or figure out all the text. But I could read a few names of places, and remember what had been pointed out to me, so that I knew about Bombay and Calcutta in India, and all about France and New Zealand and Africa." BCSC.
41. Interview with Robert Lax, Sept. 29, 1980. Also Lax to the author, Dec. 23, 1983.
42. SSMB, 17. References, SSM, 9; CGB, 200.
43. See illustration 4.
44. Owen Merton to Percyval Tudor-Hart, Jan. 22, 1921, RBA.
45. There were many artists and children who became artists in those three houses on Hillside Avenue. At number 57 lived Owen, Ruth — a cruelly frustrated artist, even a cruelly frustrated designer by this time — Tom, who became a graphic artist and photographer, and John Paul, who made a beginning as a photographer. At the Burroughs house, there was Bryston, a painter, his wife, Edith, a sculptor, Betty, today a sculptor, and Alan, later a painter and expert restorer. Roger MacLaughlin at number 45 later won recognition for his designs on silver.
46. Interview with the Priests, July 27, 1980. Will of John Paul Merton, MGA.
47. SSM, 14–16. Other details from SSMB, 30, and from the records of Zion Church,

Douglaston. Merton makes a point in SSM of the car being hired on both occasions. Others believe Sam Jenkins already owned a Buick — interview with the Priests, July 27, 1980; John Stanley, etc.

48. SSM, 16.
49. SSM, 17.
50. Interview with Robert Lax, Sept. 12, 1980.
51. SSMB, 36.
52. SSMB, 37.
53. SSMB, 38.
54. Evelyn Scott to Lola Ridge, undated but late 1921. Letter 155, ESA.
55. Owen Merton to Lola Ridge, Cedar Cottage, Somerset, Bermuda, Oct. 23, 1922, ESA.
56. SSMB, 38. This is pared down to a sentence in SSM, 20.
57. Letter from Evelyn Scott to Lola Ridge, undated. Letter 48, ESA.
58. Ibid. Letter 170, ESA.
59. Ibid. Letter 87, ESA.
60. Arthur Callard of Hebden Bridge, Yorkshire, and I were exploring much the same material in 1979 regarding the Owen Merton-Evelyn Scott affair. See Callard, "Pretty Good for a Woman." Also correspondence between Callard and the author, 1982–83. I am grateful for a number of helpful points.
61. Evelyn Scott to Lola Ridge, undated. Letter 73, ESA.
62. SSMB, 40–42.
63. RJ, Jan. 24, 1966.
64. Owen Merton to James Wood, quoted by Richard Bassett in "Personal Memoires of Owen Merton," the catalogue of the exhibition "A Rediscovery: The Paintings of Owen Merton, 1887–1931" (The William A. Farnsworth Library and Art Museum, Rockland, Maine, Oct. 4–Nov. 29, 1978).
65. Evelyn Scott to Lola Ridge, Jan. 15, 1926, ESA. There is a suggestion that the real break came in London when Owen and his son were on their way to France. On August 24, 1926, Owen Merton writes to Lola Ridge that he has heard from Evelyn for the first time in eleven months. He goes on to say, "Tom's jealousy and irreconcilableness are perfectly enormous. There was no choice except to have the children together — and then every night for the rest of my life would have [been made] hideous with repentance" (ESA).
66. It is notable that Merton gives the date of leaving as August 25, 1925, in the autobiography, and notes this was the Feast of St. Louis (which would have meant little to him at the time). In his letter to Percyval Tudor-Hart of August 15, 1925 (RBA), Owen says they would leave on August 22, 1925. The important date for Tom was probably the sailing date from New York. The important date for Owen may have been leaving Ashuelot and the Jenkins family.

The Calvaire

Many of those already named assisted with material for this section, especially Richard Bassett. I am also indebted to Father Chrysogonus Waddell, O.C.S.O., to M. Gouyon, the owner of the Villa Diane in 1979, to M. G. Julian, archiviste, St. Antonin Noble Val, and to M. P. Perez of the Lycée Ingres, Montauban. As in "Canigou," Merton's account in SSM has been supplemented here, and sometimes corrected, in many cases from other records he left of his time in St. Antonin and Montauban. It would be impossible to record every deviation from SSM, or every reference to the autobiography. Some of the most important Merton sources used here other than SSM are: RJ, Sept. 2, 1956 (Merton edited this for CGB, 144–45); RJ, Sept. 25, 1965; SBJ, Mar. 23, 1941; PSJ, Oct. 23, 1939; as well as a number of passages in MAG.

Epigraphs: Owen Merton to Percyval Tudor-Hart, Sept. 18, 1925, RBA. SBJ, Mar. 23, 1941.

1. SSM, 3–4.
2. SSM, 4.
3. On the morning of July 16, 1979, Prisoner's Base or *barres* was being played in the Square du General Picquard across from the entrance to the Musée Ingres in Montauban. Tom would have passed this square on his way to the railroad station each Sunday morning in termtime, September 1926 to June 1928.
4. Owen Merton to Percyval Tudor-Hart, Dec. 17, 1926. Owen goes on to explain that the reason he cannot leave St. Antonin often on painting expeditions is that Tom is homesick: "I like to see him every weekend if I can" (RBA).
5. Merton explains elsewhere that there was no modern sixth in his time at Oakham, but that the best students were tutored by the headmaster for scholarships at the universities. LAB, 27.
6. LAB, 27–29.
7. Commenting on the time when he found Merton concentrating so hard in the room at St. Bonaventure in 1940 (see 18), Robert Lax says: "Maybe the time and place doesn't matter as much as the fact (what was it?) that just once I found him actually at work and looking as though he was working" (Lax to the author, Dec. 23, 1983).
8. *Exile Ends in Glory*, 73.
9. MAG, 182, etc. The Hôtel Rocamadour provides a link with the image of Rocamadour and the legend of Zacchaeus, "the man who climbed the sycamore tree to see Christ" (SSM, 44).
10. SP, 5–6; CP, 30–31.
11. SBJ, 59, Jan. 15, 1941.
12. SSM, 32.
13. Father Chrysogonus Waddell to Merton, Oct. 1, 1964, TMSC.
14. RJ, Sept. 25, 1965.
15. MAG, 241. The public laundry shed in the Place de la Condamine is still in use. Again, the description of Mother Berchmans working in the hand laundry during the early years of her religious exile in Japan in *Exile Ends in Glory* (242–43) contrasts what Merton had actually observed with much reworking of someone else's pious text.
16. SBJ, Nov. 13, 1940.
17. SBJ, Mar. 23, 1941.
18. SSM, 54. See also CP, 46, 82.
19. MAG, 238–39.
20. For M. Lanne, one of the supervisors, MAG, 202. For the censeur, MAG, 204. The censeur's name was probably Petrolacci, SBJ, May 18, 1941, where Merton names "the little Corsican" who "was very unpopular."
21. "On Remembering Monsieur Delmas," in Ernst, 47–53. Interview with M. P. Perez, July 19, 1979.
22. SBJ, Mar. 23, 1941. Also MAG, 183, SSM, 55, and Merton to Sister Thérèse Lentfoehr, Dec. 20, 1954, MCC.
23. RJ, Sept. 25, 1965. Interview with Father Chrysogonus Waddell, June 29, 1981.
24. SSM, 49, 56. MAG, 194.
25. Owen Merton to Percyval Tudor-Hart, Sept. 23, 1927, RBA.
26. Ibid., Aug. 19, 1927, RBA. This letter also contains information about the purchase and aid from Owen's mother.
27. SBJ, Mar. 23, 1941.
28. SSM, 39. The pine that grows by the well now also blocks much of the view of St. Antonin from the window of what used to be Tom's room.
29. There are several references to Merton's first visit to Marseilles: PSJ, Oct. 31, 1939, LAB, 39 (149), and Merton to Sister Thérèse Lentfoehr, Dec. 20, 1954, MCC. In SSM he says only that his father went there in the winter of 1927–28.
30. The catalogues of Owen Merton's shows in London, and in New Zealand, can be found in the library of the Victoria and Albert Museum, South Kensington, London, together with reviews, etc.
31. Owen Merton to Percyval Tudor-Hart, June 14, 1925, RBA. This letter quotes the whole of Fry's letter to Owen.

32. Ibid., June 30, 1924, RBA. The actual sum is impossible to read. The painting is listed as being in Sadler's collection in the catalogue of the 1925 show at the Leicester Gallery.
33. Owen Merton to Percyval Tudor-Hart, with copy of prospectus, June 4, 1928; Tudor-Hart to Owen Merton, saying the show was one of the five best that season in London and making offer, June 6, 1928; Owen Merton to Tudor-Hart, two undated letters but obviously written later in June 1928, the first, accepting the contract and saying he is off to collect Tom, the second, telling of the cancellation of the painting class, and of preparations so that Tom can enter an English school, all RBA.
34. Owen Merton to Percyval Tudor-Hart, second undated letter of June 1928, RBA.
35. SSM, 60.
36. MAG, 165. Merton gives the date as spring 1926. As there is no record he went with his father to England in that year, the much more likely date is June 1928. Merton is sometimes vague about years, fairly reliable about months and days.
37. Merton mentions "a screen he did for Bennett," SBJ, Mar. 23, 1941. This may have been destroyed with the Bennetts' flat in the blitz. Three screens, including the "Le Havre," are mentioned by subject in Owen Merton's letter to Tudor-Hart, July 23, 1929, RBA. Three screens, including the "Le Havre," survived a fire in Tudor-Hart's studio in Montreal and are now in the collection of Richard Bassett.
38. Owen Merton to Percyval Tudor-Hart, June 14, 1929, RBA.
39. Ibid., July 23, 1929, RBA.
40. Interview with Richard Bassett, May 15, 1980. Also much material about the house and its history, interview with M. Gouyon, July 18, 1979. The flood of 1930: interview with M. G. Julian, July 18, 1979, and *Guide illustré de Saint-Antonin-Noble-Val*, 52ff.

Brooke Hill

Apart from those already mentioned, I am especially indebted in this section to J. L. Barber, secretary of the Old Oakhamian Society, Father Irenaeus Herscher, O.F.M., formerly librarian emeritus of the Friedsam Memorial Library, St. Bonaventure University; to Naomi Burton Stone; and, at Clare College, Cambridge, to the Rev. Peter Judd, Chaplain, Dr. A. R. Peacock, Dean, Dr. R. C. O. Matthews, master, and Belinda Powell, secretary to the master. I have made judicious use of Merton's published novel and the fragments of the unpublished novels. As I explain elsewhere, it is fortunate that there is a useful guide to the factual and fictitious elements in "The Labyrinth." In collating the unpublished novels, the first number after the reference is my own page number, and this is followed by any number on the page, given in brackets here. I have limited any imaginative reconstruction of my own to one brief scene. Here, too, I build on sources, but so that the dramatic flow will not be interrupted these are documented at the end of the scene.

Epigraphs: "And did those feet in ancient time," preface, "Milton," *The Poetry and Prose of William Blake*, ed. David V. Erdman (Garden City, N.Y.: Doubleday, Anchor, 1965), 94–95. "Religio Medici," *Works of Sir Thomas Browne*, vol. 1, 80.

1. There are two full descriptions of Aunt Maud: FF, "Straits of Dover," 3 (145); SSM, 62.
2. LAB, 78–79 (88), FLSB. SSM, 62–63.
3. Merton mentions writing in his diary in 1929, PSJ, Dec. 14, 1939. He speaks of taking more than one journal with him when he left Oakham in December 1932: PSJ, Dec. 8, 1939.
4. PSJ, Sept. 26, 1939. See also PSJ, Dec. 14, 1939, for memories of Ripley Court. This follows the original, except that two spellings have been changed, Merton's "Julien" to Julian, and "Crystal" to Chrystal. Merton adds the name of the car in pencil, "Trojan."
5. Mrs. Trier to John Howard Griffin, July 30, 1971, AA. PSJ, Dec. 14, 1939.
6. PSJ, Oct. 31, 1939.

7. SSM, 69.
8. SSM, 71.
9. MAG, 42. In the novel the house is Danecape Hall. There is a good deal of detail about life at the Haughtons' that does not appear in SSM. I know of only one reference to the name of Merton's Scottish hosts, SBJ, May 18, 1941. Merton corrects the spelling, which was probably Horton at first.
10. MAG, 64.
11. MAG, 60; SSM, 70. In PSJ, Merton uses learning how to ride a horse as a wholly unexpected analogy to continuing conversion, PSJ, Jan. 5, 1940.
12. Tom had already been introduced to the work of Conan Doyle at Ripley Court, where one of the masters, Mr. Oslow, read out loud, SSM, 64. John Buchan's *The Thirty-Nine Steps* is mentioned in a very interesting context in ScJ, 215.
13. Interview with Father Augustine Wulff, July 10, 1981.
14. Merton's Audenesque lines in the poem "St. John Baptist," II, CP, 124, and throughout the Portsmouth Road section, MAG, 97–112.
15. MAG, 64 (where Tom is catechized on *The Jungle Book*) and elsewhere. Mr. Haughton had read aloud from *The Water Babies*, MAG, 68.
16. The Rev. F. H. Jerwood. SSM, 73–74. Interview with J. L. Barber, Aug. 6, 1979: Jerwood was "sincere but shallow." I recall an exactly similar sermon from the chaplain of my own school.
17. FF, 1.
18. SBJ, Jan. 15, 1941.
19. Interview with J. L. Barber, Aug. 6, 1979. *Public School Yearbook*, 1976.
20. SSM, 78.
21. John Paul Merton's will, dated Aug. 4, 1942, MGA. However, Merton does say there was some shuffling of investments in the trust after 1930, SSM, 77.
22. Ruth Iris Weiss Bennett was the daughter of N. Weiss of the Société de l'Histoire du Protestantisme Français. She had been at the wedding of Owen and Ruth Merton in the company of Tom Bennett, who was probably best man (though there is no evidence for this). Tom Bennett had told Owen and Ruth of his engagement to Iris when he was in Prades in 1915. She treasured the letters the Mertons wrote to her at this time and saved these from the blitz, which demolished the Bennetts' London flat. See her letter to Merton, Aug. 24, 1966, TMSC.
23. MAG, 132ff. SSM, 78–80.
24. SBJ, May 13, 1941. MAG, 133.
25. RJ, Dec. 4, 1964. Merton says he was confused as a child and thought this was the Whistler "who painted his mother."
26. Merton to Rosemary Ruether, Mar. 25, 1967. TMSC.
27. FF, 18, FLSB.
28. SBJ, Mar. 23, 1941. SSM, 83.
29. Interview with Richard Bassett, May 12, 1980.
30. SSM, 84. MAG, 141–42. Merton heard again from Professor Hering, RJ, Jan. 4, 1964.
31. "Strasbourg Cathedral," *The Oakhamian* 47 (Easter Term 1932): 18. He recalled both trips, RJ, Sept. 16, 1960. See also CGB, 187.
32. Thomas Merton to Percyval Tudor-Hart, Jan. 20, 1931, RBA.
33. Evelyn Scott to Lola Ridge, Oct. 4, 1931, 121, ESA.
34. FF, 11.
35. Interview with J. L. Barber, Aug. 6, 1979. Merton was sad to hear of Doherty's death: RJ, Dec. 2, 1959. Some details here from *The Oakhamian*.
36. Tom was in the fifth form three months after he arrived at Oakham. The Modern Sixth was officially recognized during Tom's last term, *The Oakhamian* 48 (Christmas Term 1932): editorial.
37. There is a description of the room, LAB, 26, though his study mate in this account is the fictional Jato Gordon. His true study mate, W. O. C. Hemmings, appears on FF, 16. See also SSM, 93.
38. FF, 5.
39. FF, 4–5, D. H. Highton.

40. LAB, 51. Also LAB, 48.
41. FF, 7. Indians, FF, 5.
42. FF, 9.
43. There are many accounts of Brooke Hill, among them: SSM, 86; SJ, 49–50, May 26, 1947; CGB, 259–60; FF, 14–16.
44. FF, 15.
45. FF, 16. Crossed through in original.
46. Interview with J. L. Barber, Aug. 6, 1979.
47. FF, 17.
48. This has to be pieced together from a number of sources. The incident is reported, SSM, 89–90. The woman's name appears, FF, 8. Her first name is repeated; it is said that she is going to Australia; and the fact that Tom is returning to England on the ship that brought him to America, all appear, LAB, 2ff. The name of that ship, SBJ, May 14, 1941. The fact that she was married, PSB, Oct. 1, 1939.
49. SSM, 90.
50. LAB, 1–7.
51. "A Tribute to Gandhi," *Seeds of Destruction,* 222; *The Nonviolent Alternative,* 178–79.
52. *The Oakhamian* 47 (Christmas Term 1931).
53. Ibid., 23–24. Censorship, interview with Father Irenaeus Herscher, Sept. 12, 1980. See 400.
54. *The Oakhamian,* 47 (Easter Term 1932): 21–22.
55. PSJ, Oct. 31, 1939.
56. MAG, Author's Preface.
57. Merton, "Wählt Hitler," *The Oakhamian* 47 (Summer Term 1932): 30.
58. FF, 22–23.
59. Dos Passos: SBJ, May 14, 1941. SSM, 99. "What Is a Historian?" PSJ, Oct. 1, 1939.
60. SSM, 52. SSM, 100. "I tossed them in a packet into the flames with a grand gesture."
61. FF, Notes on Miami, April 1940. SSM, 101.
62. "Iphigenia: Politics," CP, 37.
63. Naomi Burton Stone, "Notes on Thomas Merton," p. 11. AA.
64. MAG, 87.
65. RJ, June 26, 1965. VOW, 187.
66. MAG, 105.
67. RJ, June 26, 1965. VOW, 187.
68. *The Oakhamian* 48 (Christmas Term 1932): 13. "T. F. Merton (forward): A first class forward who improved every match: very keen and always fit: very fair hooker with a good turn of speed: defence excellent."
69. LAB, 27. SSM, 102.
70. Andrew (C. A. P.) Winser, *The Old Oakhamian* 31 (1969): 42.
71. G. Griffith to the Bishop of Nottingham, Mar. 3, 1942, MGA. We have "J. T. Merton" here — yet another name!
72. Interview with the Rev. Peter Judd, Aug. 10, 1979. LAB, 31.
73. LAB, 34. See also SSM, 102.
74. Eliot: PSJ, 161. "Mene": PSJ, 162. Oct. 31, 1939.
75. MAG, 143. The wallet is frequently mentioned in later journals on Merton's travels, and was with him all the way to Bangkok.
76. SSM, 103. That the letter was typed by Bennett's secretary seems likely from what Merton says on another occasion, LAB, 70.
77. LAB, 41.
78. SSMB, 120.
79. LAB, 56.
80. Ibid. This sentence has been struck out in the original.
81. LAB, 56–57. There is a full account here of his difficulties in praying. Among other things, he is afraid he is giving himself away by crossing himself wrongly.
82. Untitled poem, CP, 1012.
83. LAB, 46.
84. SBJ, May 13, 1941.

85. LAB, 53. Merton mentions the mosaics over and over again in published and un-published writing. There are several passages in SSM, 108–11. See also LAB, 49, 52, 53; SBJ, Aug. 4, 1941, and Sept. 27, 1941, where Merton tries to define, once and for all, what the mosaics in Rome have meant in his life.

86. LAB, 54, where Merton makes much of a sudden feeling of disgust with Lawrence. He may have reacted against too much veneration (as he did on a number of oc-casions in other circumstances). He records that friends of his father's, with whom he had stayed in St. Tropez, had talked only of Lawrence. LAB, 42.

87. I have risked holding back references here, so that the scene will not be inter-rupted. Merton bought *Ulysses* in Rome, LAB, 42. He records that he had begun to read this. He had also bought a copy of the Vulgate, SSM, 110. Again, I have mixed a number of accounts of this particular evening and the scene in his room in Rome. The only invention is the short stream of consciousness. I felt this jus-tified on the following grounds: he had just been reading *Ulysses;* he says, record-ing a not very different crisis eight years later, that his head was "full of a big doubletalk mixture of Te Deums and goodbye to everything I don't want." SBJ, Nov. 28, 1941.

    Merton gives an account of praying at Santa Sabina, SSM, 112. He links this to the morning following his crisis in the room, LAB, 55. His purchase of the ties and socks, PSJ, Oct. 1, 1939.

88. LAB, 55. From "wondering," this passage has been crossed through.

89. LAB, 50.

90. SSM, 94.

91. SSM, 113–14. LAB, 53.

92. SSM, 101.

93. LAB, 58.

94. Merton does this in a very similar way himself, MAG, 112.

95. SBJ, May 14, 1941.

96. This anchor presents a difficulty. Merton mentions it and gives it considerable im-portance, SSM, 13. He talks about it (RJ, Oct. 30, 1961), saying, "This is the ear-liest symbol of which I remember being conscious." It is not in Zion Church today, and photographs taken before the fire of 1924 do not show it in the only stained-glass windows. The anchor as a symbol of stability would have been a constant reminder at Gethsemani. There is an anchor raised in relief on each of the four sides of the plinth supporting the statue of St. Joseph with the Christ Child on St. Joseph's Hill, one of Merton's favorite walks in the 1960s.

97. LAB, 58–59.

98. SSM, 116.

99. SSM, 117. MacLeish and pacifism: PSJ, Nov. 21, 1939; SBJ, Sept. 5, 1941.

100. LAB, 63 (41); FF 32 (51); SSM, 119.

101. FF, 32 (51); SSM, 119.

102. LAB, 67 (78).

103. *Faith and Violence,* 228.

104. Merton to Nora Chadwick, May 26, 1964, TMSC. Merton mentions Telfer, MAG, 103.

105. *Faith and Violence,* 228.

106. Ibid., 232.

107. Ibid., 232.

108. Interview with Father Paul Bourne, Aug. 2, 1980.

109. SSMB, 162.

110. PSJ, Sept. 13, 1939.

111. PSJ, Oct. 1, 1939.

112. We know this is almost complete because in SBJ, on November 26 (?), 1940, after a visit to Boston, Merton reports Chester Kerr's reaction to the book, listing what Kerr liked and what he did not like. Together, these make up the contents of the present book, with only two items mentioned in Kerr's reaction but missing in the typescript. From the same report we have it confirmed that Jato Gordon is a fic-titious character. Like Terence Park, he obviously had an original. He is always

returning "home" to Bucharest, and it seems clear that something at least of Jato Gordon's character is modeled on Merton's schoolmate at Oakham, Tabacovici, "the Rumanian who had a study across the hall," PSJ, Jan. 14, 1940.

113. MAG, 104. Thomas admits to entering an amateur competition at the Rendezvous in playing the drums. It looks as if this is included in the crossed-out page of "The Labyrinth," 65 (76), though the Memphis is also mentioned.

114. Interview with Naomi Burton Stone, May 22, 1979. NBS, "Notes on Thomas Merton," 3, AA. Naomi Burton Stone to the author, Nov. 10, 1983.

115. Certificate of Naturalization, June 26, 1951, MGA. The scar is also mentioned in Merton's Declaration of Intention, 1938, MGA.

116. Interviews with Naomi Burton Stone, May 22, 1979, and May 11, 1980. Naomi Burton Stone to the author, Nov. 10, 1983. The visit was before 1965 (August) and Merton was novice master. He asked his agent to accompany him and the driver to the hospital in Bardstown to visit one of the novices. During their wait at the hospital, the conversation turned to the popularity at the time of palmistry, and to pass the time Naomi Burton Stone agreed to give a reading: "So I took his right hand and gazed at it and said automatically 'What's that scar?' and he removed his hand rather rapidly and said 'That's my stigmata' and the subject got changed."

117. Though the narrator, or someone unnamed, says "Ha, his luck. See? No scar." This comes right after the breaking of the window. LAB, 66 (77).

118. MAG, 138.

119. SP, 45; CP, 104.

120. SSM, 121. For further autobiographical details on Merton at Cambridge, see "Sports Without Blood: A Letter to Dylan Thomas 1948," CP, 232–36.

121. SSM, 121. For Aunt Maud's England see also FF, 91; LAB, 81.

122. SSMB, 167.

123. MAG, 30, 32.

124. For details about Merton's professors at Cambridge, FF, 24 (43) through 30 (50). He also discusses the eclectic range of his reading.

125. There are interesting details about Bullough on FF, 27 (46), where we learn he was a Catholic and that he died "the following summer."

126. PSJ, Oct. 31, 1939.

127. When this is first mentioned in the full account Merton gives of the January interview with his godfather, LAB, 80, the tone is almost joking. However, Merton refers to the matter again, LAB, 105, and he speaks of a decision to serve in the navy if war breaks out, LAB, 89. The interview was at Bennett's office, 21 Harley Street. See also SSM, 124–25, where an interview comes later in the year.

128. LAB, 76.

129. Difficulties with his landlady and pawning possessions, LAB, 71, 72, 76. Troubles with Iris Bennett, Merton to Mrs. Trier, Dec. 20, 1966, TMSC. Staying at hotels, PSJ, Dec. 11, 1939. Merton recalled the Regent Palace Hotel in MAG, 29–32.

130. RJ, Jan. 30, 1965. See also VOW, 132–33.

131. Furlong, 59.

132. See 448.

133. Columbia: interview with Robert Lax, Sept. 24, 1980. Lax says he had heard the rumors from Merton's fraternity brothers before he met Merton himself. Also interview with Edward Rice, July 19, 1980. G. Griffith to Bishop of Nottingham, Mar. 3, 1942, MGA. See also 96.

134. LAB, 71.

135. Thomas Merton's will, Feb. 17, 1944, MGA.

136. LAB, 90 (109). Crossed out in original.

137. SSM, 126.

138. See note 26 above.

139. Interview with Pat and Frank Priest, July 27, 1980.

140. LAB, 94.

141. MAG 144–48. SBJ Oct. 27, 1940. Sailing date, *The Times* (London), notice of White Star-Cunard Sailing to New York from Southhampton, Friday, November 30, 1934, 2.

142. MAG, 148.
143. LAB, 85 (98) to 86 (99). Crossed through in original.
144. Merton to Ruth Iris Weiss Bennett, Aug. 24, 1966, TMSC.
145. Interview with Robert Lax, Sept. 12, 1980. Letter from Lax to the author, Feb. 26, 1981. *A Catch of Anti-Letters*, 44, etc.
146. FF, 33 (60) through 35 (62). Merton mentions the riot in passing, SSM, 119. Page, Leitch, Knightley, 50, 51.
147. MAG, 104.
148. Page, Leitch, Knightley, 63 ff.
149. LAB, 99.
150. Rice, 22–23. Furlong, 60. Padavano, 9.
151. Merton's handwritten will on taking Simple Vows, Feb. 17, 1944, MGA.
152. MAG, title page. *The Complete Poetry of John Donne*, ed. John T. Shawcross (Garden City, N.Y.: Doubleday Anchor, 1967), 190. "A Hymne to Christ, at the Authors last going into Germany," 387. Slight differences in punctuation, but not spelling.

The Pasture, "Merton's Heart"

In this section the chief debts are to those who knew Thomas Merton at Columbia University, in Douglaston, and in western New York State: to Robert Lax and his sister, Gladys Marcus, to Edward Rice and Virginia Burton, to Pat and Frank Priest, to Robert Giroux, and, once more, to Naomi Burton Stone. There were many others who provided something of the story. At St. Bonaventure (a college when Merton was there, now a university), my chief debt is to Father Irenaeus Herscher, O.F.M., formerly librarian emeritus of the Friedsam Library, who was as generous to me just before his death as he was to Merton forty years ago. I am grateful to Dr. Louis Reith, manuscript librarian, and to the staff, and to Mrs. Finnbar Conroy, who provided a map just when it was needed, and much else. At Corpus Christi, I was made welcome by Monsignor Miles Bourke and his staff. At the Merton Center at Columbia University I received help from Father Paul Dinter and from Dorothy Lambert. The records of Zion Episcopal Church were opened to me by the Rev. Rex L. Burrell and Norma Sobeck. I am grateful to all the staff at the Columbia University Libraries, and especially to Kenneth A. Lohf, head librarian, to Paul R. Palmer of the Columbiana, and to Bernard R. Crystal, assistant librarian for manuscripts.

Epigraphs: i. preface to the Japanese edition of *Thoughts in Solitude*, March 1966. Daggy, *Introductions*, 96. ii. West, *Miss Lonelyhearts*, 26. Merton quotes this passage, AJ, 238–39. iii. RJ, July 20, 1956. Julien Green, French novelist of American parentage, the author of *The Closed Garden, Avarice House*, etc. Merton felt an affinity with Green and was fascinated by connections he discovered while reading Green's *Journals* in the mid-fifties.

1. Interview with Robert Lax, Sept. 12, 1980.
2. Breton, *Nadja* (trans.), 13–14; the earlier anecdote about Baudelaire is found in Palache, *Gautier and the Romantics*, and elsewhere. Merton's ambitions for the all-inclusive book are expressed a number of times in different ways. For example, on July 17, 1956, he began a new journal by saying (RJ): "And I have always wanted to write about everything. That does not mean to write a book that *covers* everything — which would be impossible and would cover nothing. But a book in which everything can go, a book with a little of everything. That creates itself out of everything. That has its own life — a faithful book. I no longer even look at it as 'a book.'"
3. PSJ, 20–22 (May 30). The passage is quoted in full, except for the short break indicated in the text.
4. SSM, 92.
5. Interview with Robert Lax, Sept. 11, 1980.
6. LAB, 95. Also SSM, 137.
7. *Columbian* (1937): 25, Columbia University Libraries.
8. LAB, 95. After reading Lyford's *The Airtight Cage* in 1967, Merton writes of the

changes in what was "a somewhat comfy middle class Jewish-Irish area when I was at college," RJ, Jan. 4, 1967.

9. "My own Studs Lonigan period." PSJ, Nov. 20, 1939.
10. RJ, June 16, 1961.
11. Columbia *Jester*, Virgin Issue (Sept. 1935): 12, 28, Columbia University Libraries.
12. Interview with Robert Lax, Sept. 12, 1980.
13. Mark Van Doren, *Autobiography* (New York: Harcourt, Brace, 1958), 211ff. Also RJ, Sept. 29, 1957, Merton talks of Van Doren's visit: "I was happy to have had him stand in these rooms, so wise a person, and lean against the bookshelf in the Scriptorium and talk about some things that had come up when he was at Hampton Institute the day before. The English Professor there complained that his students had no preparation to face Shakespeare and Mark said everyone is prepared to read Shakespeare by the time they are 18. They have been born, they have had Fathers, Mothers; they have loved, feared, hated, been jealous, etc."
14. Ibid., 211–12.
15. Interview with Robert Giroux, May 6, 1980. Giroux is somewhat puzzled by the important place Merton gives him in this section of SSM (154ff.). Robert Giroux remembered Merton and the story later, but he had graduated before he and Merton had much contact, other than this, at Columbia.
16. SSM, 141.
17. LAB, 97.
18. Interview with John Stanley, July 21, 1980. Apparently those who have been on the staff at the Casa Italiana since the mid-thirties recall no picket lines. But Merton says himself that it was a brief and informal demonstration in which few took part, SSM, 142–43.
19. SSM, 147.
20. Ibid.
21. PSJ, Oct. 31, 1939.
22. "The Straits of Dover," FF, FLSB, 1 (143).
23. *The Geography of Lograire*, 46.
24. *Columbian* (1937): 24, op. cit. But see "Learning to Live," *Love and Living*, 11.
25. Letter from Robert Lax to the author, Oct. 15, 1981. Lax's ellipsis.
26. Interview with Robert Lax, Sept. 27, 1980.
27. Ibid., Sept. 14, 1980.
28. Columbia *Jester*, Freshman's Guide (1936). 18, op. cit.: "The Onyx Club, best place on 52nd Street. There are no frills but it is always jammed. In the small hours it becomes the haven of musicians from all the classy places over on the Park. The only reason for going is Stuff Smith's swing band. Stuff, with little encouragement, will jam all night long. His immense enthusiastic following includes your correspondent. In addition to the rhythm Stuff is one of the funniest people in town. Hear him do 'Baby, Won't You Please Come Home?' " Stuff was much given to other novelty numbers like "I'se a Muggin' " and "Knock, Knock." The Onyx Club Orchestra at the time consisted of: Jonah Jones, trumpet; Hezekiah Leroy Gordon "Stuff" Smith, violin and vocals; James Sherman, piano; Bobby Bennett, guitar; Mack Walker, string bass; and Cozy Cole, drums. Of the Columbia journalists and jazz lovers, Barry Ulanov, on the *Review*, was the most expert. For 52nd Street, see SSM, 157.
29. Lax, "A Poet's Journal," 12–13. For another vivid description of Merton's walk at a later date see Kelty, "The Man," 19.
30. "The Straits of Dover," FF, FLSB, 2–3 (144–45). Much of this has been crossed out in original.
31. Interview with Pat and Frank Priest, July 27, 1980. Also interview with Virginia Burton, Nov. 14, 1981.
32. SBJ, Nov. 10, 1940. Merton talks of his visits to Nancy Hauck Boettcher, Sept. 1964, TMSC. See also Merton to Mrs. H. B. Jenkins (Elsie), June 16, 1965, TMSC.
33. "Geologists Take to the Road," *Columbian* (1937): 109, op. cit.
34. SSM, 158. He was cremated on Friday the 30th. Records of United States Cremation Co., Ltd., Fresh Pond Crematory, 61–40 Mount Olivet Crescent (another coin-

cidence of names!), Middle Village, Long Island, New York, N.Y. (TMSC). Cause of death: chronic myocarditis.
35. Interview with Robert Lax, Sept. 14, 1980.
36. Harold Jenkins to John Howard Griffin, Dec. 9, 1970, AA.
37. *Columbian* (1937): preface.
38. SSM, 156.
39. Tape A–164, Apr. 22, 1964, TMSC. Also SSM, 156.
40. *Columbian* (1937): 214.
41. Ibid., 218. See also *Seasons of Celebration*, 237–38.
42. Ibid., 217. Merton may have remembered the advertisement, however, recalling that the copy claimed that in World War I it had cost $25,000 to kill one combatant on either side. By the time of the Vietnam War, Merton noted that the price had risen to an estimated $1 million.
43. SSM, 3. This passage has a strongly cinematic effect.
44. SSM, 145.
45. "I Can't Get Started," written in 1935, lyrics by Ira Gershwin with music by Vernon Duke for the 1936 Ziegfeld Follies, this became the theme song of Bunny Berigan, whose recordings featured vocal and trumpet solo by Berigan.
46. SSM, 161.
47. The *Geography of Lograire*, 44ff. Also, during the description of the blitz in the novel, "The walls of all the buildings roar down at me like waterfalls," MAG, 18.
48. SSM, 159: "I had returned to the old idea of becoming a newspaper man."
49. SSM, 150.
50. Merton explains that this was something of an accident, SSM, 179–80.
51. Undergraduate transcript, Office of the Registrar, Columbia University, copy, Oct. 2, 1939, MGA.
52. Interview with Robert Lax, Sept. 27, 1980. Many of the details about the room at the boarding house are provided by Robert Lax. Some are confirmed by Merton in SBJ.
53. SSM, 160.
54. LAB, 97. SSM, 186. It is interesting that Merton's criticism of Huxley's eclecticism in using Christian sources parallels the criticism others were to make of Merton himself in the 1950s and 1960s. For Merton on Huxley's *Ends and Means*, see "Huxley and the Ethics of Peace."
55. SSM, 171.
56. Columbia Notebooks, Faddish-Siracuse File, "English Art of Poetry," 127556, Box 7, FLSB. PSJ, May 2, 1939: "Berryman is right about Wordsworth being a good poet." Merton continued to have trouble deciding about Wordsworth's poetry, however; see SBJ, Dec. 4 and 18, 1940; ScJ, 140.
57. SBJ, May 18, 1941.
58. Columbia *Spectator* (1937), Columbia University Libraries.
59. *Columbian* (1937): 218.
60. Interview with Edward Rice, July 19, 1980.
61. SSM, 145.
62. In SSM Merton misspells Tindall's name, which is interesting. The comment here is confirmed from a number of sources. Prof. Jack Willis of the English Department of the College of William and Mary, who was a student at Columbia of both Mark Van Doren and William York Tindall, reports that Tindall would speak of "the Merton myth." Interview, Oct. 12, 1979.
63. SSM, 199–200.
64. SSM, 189.
65. PSJ, Jan. 5, 1940. Cf. SSM, 182.
66. According to Merton, the novel received a B- and everyone was satisfied (SSM, 199). Robert Lax remembers that he got an A- and that some people were incensed because they thought that was too low. Interview with Lax, Sept. 14, 1980.
67. SSM, 191. The picture is reproduced in Rice, 30. Interview with Rice, July 19, 1980. For further stories and ironic comment on Bramachari, see the two stories Seymour Freedgood published in *Harpers*. In "The Holy Man in Blue Sneakers" (vol. 196

[February 1948]: 163–70), the Hindu monk is called Dasgupta, and in a not-too-fictional account calls unexpectedly on Freedgood while he is a soldier in India during World War II. "Grandma and the Hindu Monk" (vol. 202 [January 1951]: 45–51) gives an account of the monk's arrival at the Freedgood house at Wreck Lead, Long Island, and, probably in a somewhat disguised form, the reasons why Bramachari was moved to Columbia.

68. SBJ, Jan. 2, 1941.
69. PSJ, Sept. 13, 1939. Interview with Robert Lax, Sept. 12, 1980. Lax feels that it was hardly an argument. His chief objection was the word "to mortify." The conversation was clearly important to Merton, as he goes back to it a number of times, among other things regretting a rare argument with Lax. Merton quotes Lax as saying, "Nothing should be hard," PSJ, 149, Oct. 29, 1939.
70. Interview with Robert Lax, Sept. 13, 1980.
71. Ibid., Sept. 14, 1980.
72. PSJ, May 12, 1939.
73. SJ, Nov. 16, 1947, 81–82, "Nine years ago this fall my happiest days were in those cloisters . . ." See also "Canigou," note 5 above.
74. Merton's Columbia Blake Notebooks 1 and 2. Faddish-Siracuse File, FLSB. (N.B. Lightly edited, Merton's *Nature and Art in William Blake: An Essay in Interpretation* can be found as Appendix I, LE, 385–453. There are earlier drafts at TMSC and FLSB.)
75. Ibid., 1.
76. Columbia Blake Notebooks, 2, 127552, FLSB. Merton gives only part of the paragraph quotation. For the whole, see Wilson, *Life of Blake*, 346. Merton quotes or misquotes this passage over and over in published and unpublished work. For examples: SSM, 87, 190. And see here 142.
77. Columbia Blake Notebooks, 2, 127551, FLSB. Wilson, *Life of Blake*, 372.
78. LE, 448. A. K. Coomaraswamy, *Transformations of Nature in Art*, 145.
79. These are both interesting choices: "The true Sage keeps his knowledge within him while men in general set forth theirs in argument in order to convince each other," Chuang Tzu, chap. 2, and "Those who dream of the banquet wake to lamentation and sorrow. Those who dream of lamentation and sorrow wake to join the hunt." Both are opposite Merton's notes on the diary of H. Crabb Robinson on unnumbered pages in Columbia Blake Notebooks, 1, 127551, FLSB.
80. PSB, May 12, 1939.
81. SBJ, May 14, 1941.
82. *The Geography of Lograire*, 46.
83. SSM, 210.
84. SSM, 205.
85. "Religio Medici," *Works of Sir Thomas Browne*, vol. 1, 80. Merton was a renouncer, Lax a reconciler. For Merton renouncing renouncers, see CGB, 194.
86. Transcript of Graduate Study for A.M., Columbia University Registrar's Office. Copy, Oct. 2, 1939, MGA.
87. SSM, 214.
88. Interview with Edward Rice, July 19, 1980. Rice, 32.
89. SSM, 216–17.
90. Interview with Robert Lax, Sept. 14, 1980, details confirmed in letters to the author, Feb. 26 and Oct. 15, 1981.
91. SBJ, May 14, 1941: "The big argument at Jacobson's party and afterward, when I first told everybody I was going to become a Catholic. It was a big absurd argument, I forget about what: probably again about how much could be proved by reason, in religion."
92. Baptism Register. Corpus Christi. Entry 108, Nov. 16, 1938, 44. Conditional Baptism, Sponsors, Edward Rice. Priest, J. P. Moore. Copy, AA. It was St. Gertrude's Day, the name day of his New Zealand grandmother. He was confirmed on May 29, 1939.
93. Interview with Naomi Burton Stone, May 22, 1979.
94. Description, SBJ, Feb. 11, 1941.
95. PSJ, Oct. 16, 1939.

96. Ibid.
97. PSJ, Sept. 26, 1939.
98. SBJ, May 14, 1941. Merton records two such arguments — one against the Church with Bill Fineran in 1936; the second, with Robert Krapp, defending the Church. Both took place in the Gold Rail Tavern, a favorite meeting place for graduate students, 2850 Broadway, between 110th and 111th Streets. See also SSM, 231.
99. PSJ, Oct. 16, 1939.
100. SBJ, Feb. 11, 1941. Interview with Robert Lax, Sept. 14, 1980. SSM, 234–35.
101. For the reviews Merton published at this time, see LE, 462–89, and *A Thomas Merton Reader*, 71–76. "John Crowe Ransom — Standards for Critics," review of Ransom's *The World's Body, New York Herald Tribune*, May 8, 1938. "Vladimir Nabokov — Realism and Adventure," review of Nabokov's *Laughter in the Dark, New York Herald Tribune*, May 15, 1938. "John Cowper Powys — In Praise of Books," review of Powys's *Enjoyment of Literature, New York Herald Tribune*, Nov. 20, 1938. "Christine Herter — In Defense of Art," review of Herter's *Defense of Art, New York Herald Tribune*, Dec. 25, 1938. "Agnes Addison — Love of Change for Its Own Sake," review of Addison's (Richard B. Smith)'s *Romanticism and the Gothic Revival, New York Times*, Jan. 29, 1939. "R. H. S. Crossman — Restaging the *Republic*," review of Crossman's *Plato Today, New York Herald Tribune*, Mar. 19, 1939. "William Nelson — John Skelton, Scholar, Poet and Satirist," review of Nelson's *John Skelton, Laureate, New York Times*, May 28, 1939. "E. M. W. Tillyard and C. S. Lewis — A Spirited Debate on Poetry," review of Tillyard and Lewis's *Personal Heresy, New York Times*, July 9, 1939. "Hoxie Neale Fairchild — Background of Romanticism," review of Fairchild's *Religious Trends in English Poetry, New York Herald Tribune*, July 23, 1939. "G. Wilson Knight — That Old Dilemma of Good and Evil," review of Knight's *Burning Oracle, New York Times*, Sept. 24, 1939. "William York Tindall — D. H. Lawrence: Who Saw Himself as a Messiah," review of Tindall's *D. H. Lawrence and Susan His Cow, New York Times*, Jan. 14, 1940. Dell'Isola, 69–70. C1–C11.
102. SSM, 236.
103. Robert Lax to the author, Jan. 18, 1982: "Don't remember well, but think of it as being highly charged, intellectual, full of city images and ready at birth for the Gotham Book Mart." Lax goes on, interestingly, to suggest that "The Pastoral" was a forerunner to "Journal of My Escape from the Nazis" (MAG), just as *Cables to the Ace* was a forerunner to *The Geography of Lograire*. Merton mentions he is working on "The Pastoral," PSJ, Oct. 29, 1939. All that appears to remain of the project now is "Song (From Crossportion's Pastoral)," SP, 20–21; CP, 61.
104. PSJ, May 3, 1939.
105. PSJ, May 4, May 30, 1939. Also SBJ, May 14, 1941.
106. Interview with Robert Lax, Sept. 14, 1980. SBJ, Feb. 11, 1941. Also SBJ, May 14, 1941; SSM, 234–35.
107. PSJ, May 30, 1939.
108. Interview with Edward Rice, July 19, 1980. Picture appears in Rice, 8.
109. Robert Giroux, *Columbia College Today*, Spring 1969, 69.
110. See note 112, *Brooke Hill*, above for original of Terence Park. Merton had first called the character Terence Metrotone, but changed this when Harold Jenkins took this as "a kind of an acrostic for myself" (SSM, 241). The model for Jato Gordon is very likely to have been Tabacovici, a Rumanian who was in School House with Merton and had a study across the hall. See PSJ, Jan. 14, 1940. Jato Gordon is always returning to Bucharest, his home. Tabacovici went out as Merton's guest when Tom and Iris Bennett visited Oakham.
111. There is a possibility Merton had the near-complete copy of "The Labyrinth" with him, and there is some mystery about this. The copy was in a folder with the erroneous title "Journal of My Escape from the Nazis" in pencil on the cover.
112. SSM, 368.
113. The Fitzgerald File, given to Father Richard F. Fitzgerald, arrived at the Friedsam Library on June 11, 1974. The Faddish-Siracuse File, given to Fathers John F. Faddish and Aloysius Siracuse, arrived at the Friedsam Library, July 21, 1955.
114. PSJ, Jan. 30, 1940. He is trying the Michelet translation of Vico, after the Croce.

115. SSM, 239.
116. Rice, 54.
117. SSM, 246.
118. *New York Times,* June 18, 1939. (Copy, Columbia University Libraries.) The poem appears as "Fable For A War," CP, 712–13.
119. SSM, 241.
120. SSM, 239–40.
121. Most of the details are taken from SSM, 243, and from an interview with Robert Lax, Sept. 10, 1980. Cf. Rice, 36.
122. "remember how we hailed the opportunity of reading our words to the court in bradford?" *A Catch of Anti-Letters,* 38. For a similar way of publishing, and probably a memory of the discussion, see MAG, 220, 252. Also SBJ, July 16, 1941.
123. Isolated pages in FF, FLSB. Also SSM, 246.
124. Interview with Robert Lax, Sept. 11, 1980.
125. Rice, 36. Interview with Robert Lax, Sept. 11, 1980.
126. According to Lax, Joe Roberts joined the other three at the end of the stay that first summer. Lax remained at the cottage when Rice, Merton, and Roberts went on to New York City, staying there until the cold weather: "I lived on alone at the cottage — starving, practically, because everyone who knew how to cook had gone, and one day Gladys drove up to the cottage to tell me that Boyd Fitzpatrick, publisher of the newspaper, and brother of our neighbor, Mary Davis, wanted me to come and write copy for ads at the radio station" (Lax to the author, Apr. 30, 1982.) Robert Lax started working for the local station, WHDL, Olean, New York, in late October or early November 1939.
127. Rice, 43–53.
128. "The Man in the Sycamore Tree," 11–12, FF, FLSB.
129. Ibid., 28.
130. SBJ, Aug. 4, 1941. ScJ, 148, Jan. 2, 1941.
131. "The Man in the Sycamore Tree," 40.
132. Ibid., 41.
133. SSM, 248. See, too, Robert Lax to Merton, Oct. 12, 1963, *A Catch of Anti-Letters,* 27: "you were always saying you started the hitler war, but i knew no." Lax said a feeling of guilt at having started the war (or at least having made a contribution to the war's inevitability) was commonly expressed in the group of friends in 1940–41 (interview, Sept. 27, 1980).
134. The details here are combined from SSM, 249 and PSJ, Sept. 5, 1939 (37), confirmed in an interview with Virginia Burton, Nov. 14, 1981.
135. Most of the detail here, PSJ, Sept. 5, 1939 (37). (As the date is not altogether certain for the entry, the number on page is given also.)
136. PSJ, Oct. 31, 1939. Interview with Virginia Burton, Nov. 14, 1981. Merton mentions he found it difficult to keep up in drinking with the Virginians. Robert Lax's comment on this was, "We *all* found it difficult to keep up with the Virginians!" (Interview, Sept. 29, 1980. Lax visited Virginia later.)
137. Interview with Virginia Burton, Nov. 14, 1981.
138. ". . . swimming in the creek 3 A.M. Everybody furiously drunk." PSJ, Sept. 5, 1939.
139. This is a frequent theme in Merton's early writing; see PSJ, Dec. 14, 1939. "The propaganda *for* this war was all laid down firmly before by the *anti-war* people; they pointed out exactly how hateful nazis and fascists were. Those on the other side did a good job of making Russia hateful."
140. MAG, 28.
141. CWL, 24A, 46. Merton to Mary Childs Black, Jan. 27, 1962, TMSC.
142. Marco Pallis to Merton, Jan. 23, 1965, TMSC.
143. Interview with Virginia Burton, Nov. 14, 1981. Merton describes feeling faint at dinner. He had heard Chamberlain's voice from London announcing that the British and French ultimatum had expired, earlier, at the dock: "I remember for some inexplicable reason, the Sunday the war started, the Sunday of Labor Day weekend in 1939. I was on the dock at Southside, Urbanna, Virginia. Inside the musty

storeroom, next to the red cooler full of bottled Coca Cola and Dr. Pepper, a radio spoke — with the voice of a man from London, saying how quiet it was there. And I had a terrible toothache, and was full of despair about the war, but the sun was blazing hot and it was the finest day on the river you'd ever hope to see!'' SBJ, May 18, 1941. Cf. SSM, 250.

144. Interview with Virginia Burton, Nov. 14, 1981.
145. SBJ, Nov. 10, 1940.
146. PSJ, Sept. 8, 1939. Also SSM, 251.
147. "The Man in the Sycamore Tree," 55. For *Hell's Angels* and Merton's early memories of films of World War I, see 54.
148. PSJ, Oct. 15, 1939.
149. Ibid.
150. PSJ, Oct. 14, 1939.
151. "I can't invent a character fast enough . . ." PSJ, Dec. 20, 1939. Writing novels: SBJ, May 9, 1941.
152. SBJ, Sept. 27, 1941. See also SBJ, Jan. 25, 1941; ScJ, 154–57; PSJ, Dec. 18, 19, 1939.
153. PSJ, Oct. 1, 1939.
154. Quoted by E. W. F. Tomlin, in *R. G. Collingwood, Writers and Their Work,* no. 42 (published for the British Council and the National Book League, London 1953, 1961), 5. See also 177 and note 293 below.
155. Interview with Virginia Burton, Nov. 14, 1981. Ms. Burton remembered this at Nick's. From 1938, Meade Lux Lewis (1905–69), Albert Ammons (1907–49), and Pete Johnson (1904–67) were playing three-piano boogie woogie and solo regularly at Barry Josephson's Café Society, and they may have been taking part in jam sessions in other spots in Greenwich Village.
156. SSM, 252–53. Understandably, this was a favorite scene with journalists, see "Transition," *Newsweek*, Dec. 23, 1968, 91: "He had been a Trappist since 1941, after deciding to become a priest in 1939 — renouncing his Bohemian life one morning when he found himself sitting on the floor of his Greenwich Village apartment, listening to jazz records and eating breakfast straight out of the cereal cartons while still 'half stupefied' from a night on the town."
157. Interview with Father Raymond Flanagan, Sept. 28, 1980.
158. SSM, 268. PSJ, Jan. 13, 1940.
159. SSM, 260–65.
160. PSJ, Jan. 5, 1940. According to Robert Lax, this was Sy Freedgood's idea.
161. Interview with Robert Lax, Sept. 14, 1980.
162. SBJ, May 14, 1941.
163. SSM, 238.
164. Robert Lax recalls his arrival in Olean on a perfect December day. Merton was flourishing a "bull roarer" and in high spirits.
165. Connections with English schools, PSB, Jan. 25, 1940. Connections with the French lycée, SSM, 260.
166. PSJ, Oct. 6, 1939.
167. PSJ, Oct. 19, 1939.
168. Interview with Virginia Burton, Nov. 14, 1981.
169. Interview with Robert Lax, Sept. 12, 1980.
170. Interview with Virginia Burton, Nov. 14, 1981.
171. RJ, June 26, 1965. VOW, 187. See 423–24.
172. Interviews with Robert Lax, Sept. 14 and 27, 1980.
173. PSJ, Oct. 16, 1939.
174. Ibid.
175. PSJ, Dec. 11, 1939.
176. Ibid. SSM, 265–66.
177. FF, FLSB, 12.
178. SSMB, 79.
179. PSJ, Oct. 9, 1939.
180. PSJ, Dec. 21, 1939.
181. PSJ, Nov. 20, 1939.

182. Ibid.
183. PSJ, Oct. 6, 1939.
184. CP, 4.
185. Interview with Robert Lax, Sept. 12, 1980.
186. Terry, *Terry's Guide to Cuba,* 202. Pages on Miami and Cuba, Cuba 31, author's number on Merton's unnumbered pages, FF, FLSB. For Merton's view of *Terry's Guide,* ScJ, 42–47, Mar. 29, 1940.
187. PSJ, Oct. 1, 1939.
188. PSJ, Sept. 14, 1939.
189. PSJ, Jan. 5, 1940.
190. Interview with Naomi Burton Stone, May 11, 1980, and her unpublished notes, 11.
191. Pages on Miami and Cuba, Miami 4, FF, FLSB.
192. Ibid., 10–11.
193. Ibid., 14.
194. Ibid., 15. Merton's ellipsis.
195. This is found only in ScJ, 53–56. It was one of Merton's favorite passages in his own work.
196. Pages on Miami and Cuba. Unnumbered, author's collation, Cuba 34–35, FF, FLSB.
197. SSM, 279.
198. "Song for Our Lady of Cobre," SSM, 283; SP, 4–5; CP, 29–30.
199. SSM, 280.
200. Pages on Miami and Cuba. Cuba 10, FF, FLSB. Many years later, Merton was reminded of Sancti Spiritus: "A Cuban exile who does not speak English is here to be a family brother but I do not think he will be able to settle down. He comes from Santi Spiritus [sic], a lovely plain little town which I remember." RJ, July 18, 1964. Unfortunately, Merton's misgivings were justified. A few weeks later he had to restrain the Cuban from breaking up the kitchen. Ultimately the postulant left Gethsemani for another exiled Cuban family, much to Merton's regret.
201. ScJ, 75–77.
202. SSM, 282.
203. RJ, July 17, 1956.
204. Rotterdam: ScJ, 224, May 23, 1941; SBJ, Oct. 27, 1940. Perry Street: ScJ, 97–98, May 21, 1940; SBJ, May 14, 1941 (155).
205. PSJ, Feb. 13, 1940. Other details about John Paul, SSM, 287; John Paul's will, Aug. 4, 1942, copy, MGA. Interview with Robert Lax, Sept. 10, 1980. Interview with Edward Rice, July 19, 1980.
206. SBJ, June 11, 1941. ". . . he worries in the wrong way . . ."
207. ScJ, June 16, 1940, 109–10.
208. SBJ, May 14, 1941; SSM, 293. Details of the second summer at the Olean cottage are from such published sources as SSM, ScJ, Rice; from unpublished journals and some isolated pages in FF, FLSB; and, finally, from interviews in September 1980 with Robert Lax and his sister, Gladys Marcus. On Sept. 10, 1980, Robert Lax and the author made a visit to the Olean cottage.
209. SBJ, Nov. 10, 1940.
210. Interview with Robert Lax, Sept. 10, 1980.
211. Isolated pages, FF, FLSB.
212. Ibid. Also SSM, 288.
213. Isolated pages, FF, FLSB.
214. SSM, 290.
215. SSM, 292.
216. SSM, 297.
217. SBJ, Nov. 28, 1941.
218. SBJ, Nov. 29, 1941.
219. SSM, 298.
220. Interview with Virginia Burton, Nov. 18, 1981. The nail holes in the bathroom wall remain.
221. SBJ, Mar. 2, 1941.
222. SBJ, Dec. 2, 1940.

223. ScJ, preface, vii.
224. SBJ, Feb. 4, 1941.
225. SSM, 304.
226. SSM, 296.
227. SSM, 299.
228. Interview with Pat and Frank Priest, July 27, 1980.
229. SBJ, Feb. 22, 1941. The plan was to visit relatives of Robert Gerdy in Cleveland. Gerdy and Rice made up a separate party and the friends met in Shaker Heights. Rice, 41, 54.
230. SP, 9–10; CP, 35. *The New Yorker*, August 1, 1942, 27.
231. ScJ, Oct. 15, 1939, 14–21; PSJ, Oct. 15, 1939.
232. PSJ, Oct. 31, 1939.
233. See note 3, introduction.
234. SBJ, Nov. 2, 1940. Author's walk, Sept. 13, 1980.
235. SBJ, Jan. 2 and May 9, 1941.
236. SBJ, June 11, 1941. One of those mentioned was FLSB, 127560.
237. SBJ, Nov. 29, 1941.
238. SBJ, Nov. 28, 1941.
239. SSM, 301.
240. SBJ, Mar. 2, 1941.
241. RJ, Jan. 30, 1965.
242. O'Brien, "Thomas Merton at St. Bona's."
243. SBJ, Dec. 9, 1940.
244. SBJ, Nov. 27, 1940.
245. Drawings: Many of Merton's from this time are in the Friedsam. Rembrandt: SBJ, Mar. 4, 1941: "That was in November. The day I remembered the phrase 'O for the pencils of a Rembrandt' as used by Curzon in his Monasteries of the Levant."
246. SBJ, Nov. 10, 1940.
247. PSJ, Nov. 19, 1939.
248. ScJ, 20–21, Oct. 15, 1939. PSJ, May 12, 1939.
249. SSM, 305.
250. SBJ, Oct. 27, 1940.
251. SSM, 308.
252. Ibid.
253. The word "chastisement" reminds one of the first sermon given by the Jesuit, Père Paneloux, in *The Plague (La Peste)*, by Albert Camus, one of Merton's favorite writers in the early 1960s. *La Peste*, 109–14.
254. Betjeman, "Slough," *Collected Poems*, 22.
255. SBJ, Oct. 27, 1940.
256. Ibid.
257. Ibid.
258. SSM, 308.
259. PSJ, Oct. 31, 1939.
260. SBJ, Nov. 27, 1940.
261. SBJ, Dec. 18, 1940.
262. SBJ, Nov. 12, 1940.
263. SBJ, Jan. 2, 1941. Cf. ScJ, 148.
264. SBJ, Mar. 2, 1941.
265. Some interesting details on popular superstitions about the Trappists are recorded in a humorous way by Father Amadeus on the backs of pages of *The Seven Storey Mountain* stitched together to make a booklet. This was written in Louisville in about 1952 and is now at TMSC, see 228. For the article on the Trappists Merton would have consulted, see *The Catholic Encyclopedia*, 1912, vol. 15, 24–26. This attempts to dispel the rumors: "It may be well here to deny a few customs that have been attributed, by ignorance, to the order. The monks do not salute one another by the 'memento mori,' nor do they dig a part of their grave each day; in meeting each other they salute by an inclination of the head, and graves are dug only after a brother is ready to be placed in it." Interestingly enough, the article is signed

by Edmond M. Obrecht. Dom Edmond was the Abbot of Gethsemani, see *The Waters of Siloe*.

266. Merton is much more positive in his account in SSM (310). SBJ makes it clear he had not decided between Mexico and Gethsemani as late as March 23, 1941. He was probably thinking of joining John Paul in Mexico.
267. SBJ, Mar. 4, 1941.
268. ScJ, 128, Sept. 5, 1940.
269. Reported SBJ, Mar. 18, 1941. He says "Wednesday night," and I have followed this in giving the date. But Merton appears to be quite wrong in giving dates and days in SSM, 314ff.
270. SBJ, Mar. 18, 1941. Interview with Robert Lax, Sept. 12, 1980.
271. *Time*, Mar. 17, 1941, 12, correspondence, "Kicks in the Head." Merton says this issue had come out on Thursday, March 13. He was responding to "Silence, Exile & Death," an article that had appeared in the "Books" section of *Time* on February 10, 1941. His enthusiasm had obviously got Merton into arguments at St. Bonaventure's: on a number of occasions he says he wishes he had not called Joyce a Catholic. See note 247 above.
272. "April," SP, 26–27; CP, 72–73. SBJ, Mar. 18, 1941, SSM, 314–15.
273. "The Philosophers," CP, 3. SBJ, Mar. 18, 1941.
274. SBJ, Mar. 19, 1941; also SBJ, Mar. 23, 1940. The two accounts contradict SSM, 315–16.
275. Ironically enough, there is a photograph of Tom brushing his teeth in the bathroom at 57 Hillside Avenue. Ruth, who probably took it, wrote on the back for the New Zealand Mertons "America 'wash-a-teef!,' January 1917."
276. SBJ, Mar. 23, 1941.
277. SBJ, Apr. 5, 1941. Slightly altered, ScJ, 176.
278. SBJ, Apr. 18, 1941. "In the Public Library I didn't even feel like reading any of Evelyn Waugh's fine travel book 'They Were Still Dancing,' which I had read between trains there before."
279. SBJ, Apr. 5, 1941. Slightly altered, ScJ, 177.
280. SBJ, Apr. 7, 1941. Cf. ScJ, 183. Paraphrased SSM, 325.
281. Ibid.
282. The schedule of the day at the Monastery of Our Lady of Gethsemani in the winter, during the 1940s, has been somewhat summarized here. More precisely:

2	A.M.	Rise (Sunday rose at 1:30). Little Office of the Blessed Virgin Mary, lasting until about 2:30.
2:30		Mental Prayer for half an hour.
3:00		Canonical Office *(Matins* and *Lauds)*, Angelus, Private Masses, Interval.
5:30		*Prime* (Matutinal Mass), Chapter, Arranging of Couches, Frustulum (breakfast), Interval.
7:45		*Tierce*, High Mass, *Sext*, Work.
10:45		End of Work.
11:07		*None*, Particular Examen. Angelus.
11:30		Dinner, Grace, Interval.
1:30	P.M.	Work.
3:30		End of Work. Interval.
4:30		(about) *Vespers*, Mental Prayer.
5:30		Collation (supper). Interval.
6:10		Lecture (public reading). *Compline*, Salve Regina, Angelus, Examen.
7:00		Retire to Dormitory for sleep.

Merton talks of the High Mass as the heart of the day, SBJ, Apr. 9, 1941.
283. SSM, 320.
284. Campbell, *García Lorca*, 28.
285. SSM, 321.
286. SSM, 327.
287. SBJ, Apr. 10, 1941.

288. SBJ, Good Friday, Apr. 11, 1941.
289. SBJ, Sept. 4, 1941.
290. SSM, 331, where Merton mentions the walk outside the enclosure and that "the pressure was too heavy for me." SBJ, Sept. 4, 1941, Merton makes it much clearer that this was an act of rebellion. Also, "A Life Free from Care," tape and transcript of Merton's talk, Aug. 20, 1965, TMSC. *Cistercian Studies* 5, no. 3 (1970): 217–26.
291. "The Vine," CP, 42–43. Draft of poem, FF, FLSB.
292. SBJ, May 14, 1941. Merton spells *arguing* as "argueing" throughout.
293. Léautaud, *Journal of a Man of Letters*, 12 ff. Merton makes much the same point himself much later: "Yes, we have to learn to write disciplined prose. We have to write poems that are 'Poems.' But that is a relatively unprofitable and secondary concern compared with the duty of first writing nonsense. We have to learn the knack of free association, to let loose what is hidden in our depths, to expand rather than to condense prematurely. Rather than making an intellectual point and then devising a form to express it, we need rather to release the face that is sweating under the mask and let it sweat out in the open for a change, even though nobody else gives it a prize for special beauty or significance." "Why Alienation Is for Everybody," LE, 382. See also note 154.
294. Interview with Robert Giroux, May 6, 1980.
295. Interview with Robert Lax, Sept. 10, 1980. Lax says he introduced Merton to Cap Pierce, poetry editor of *The New Yorker*, and the idea of an article on the Trappists came up. Over lunch later, with Merton, Lax, Pierce, and the fiction editor, Gus Lobrano, all present, the subject came up again, and Merton went on repeating "No, no, no!" Merton and Lobrano got on very well, talking about Europe, and Lax heard for the first time of some of Merton's European experiences. Lobrano understood his reluctance about the Trappist article, but one thing puzzled him. He asked Merton, "If they're thinking about God all day, how do they drive their tractors?"
296. SBJ, Apr. 18, 1941.
297. SBJ, Nov. 12, 1940. Cf. ScJ, 132.
298. SBJ, Nov. 28, 1940.
299. SBJ, Sept. 28, 1941. See also CP, 391, "A Letter to Pablo Antonio Cuadra Concerning Giants."
300. SBJ, Aug. 4, 1941.
301. SBJ, Dec. 18, 1940.
302. SBJ, July 6, 1941. He spells *ocarina* "ocharina."
303. Hopkins, "The Habit of Perfection," line 1. *A Hopkins Reader*, 3.
304. Pritchett, Review of *Elected Silence*, Aug. 13, 1949, 174. The review started a considerable exchange, chiefly about the validity of writing about one's religious conversion. Letters appeared in *The New Statesman* on August 20, 27, September 3, 10, 17 and October 1, 1949. Noise: there may have been some physical basis in Merton's sensitivity to noise. In January 1967 he was having difficulty sleeping at the hermitage, where insomnia had never been a problem before. He resorted to earplugs, then had his ears examined by Dr. Francis J. Peisel in Louisville. Dr. Peisel reported to the monastery doctor, Father John Eudes Bamberger, on January 3, 1967, that "Father has tinnitus aurium due to degeneration of the acoustic nerve. He was started on Pavabid and we will recheck him in 3 months" (MGA).
305. SBJ, May 9, 1941. Merton puts the mention of the wild cherry trees earlier in SSM, see 333.
306. Interview with Edward Rice, July 19, 1980.
307. SBJ, May 5, 1941.
308. Ibid.
309. SBJ, June 11, 1941. SSM, 336.
310. MAG, Author's Preface.
311. Interview with Naomi Burton Stone, May 11, 1980. Also typed notes by Burton Stone. The book was *Straight Thinking in War Time*, by Robert H. Thouless.
312. Chester Kerr, editor of *The Atlantic Monthly* and of the Atlantic Monthly Publishing Company, returned the book simply as "uncommercial," see SBJ, July 27, 1941.

313. Isolated pages, FF, FLSB.
314. SSM, 337.
315. First published in 1878, the autobiography had been considerably tampered with and rewritten. In 1956, a text was discovered whose claim to be the original has been supported. There is an English translation by R. A. Knox (London, 1958).
316. Merton is critical of the taste and the writing style, SSM, 353–54.
317. Merton reports in SSM, 354, that his interest began with the Ghéon biography in October, but the journals have earlier references. Cf. Ghéon, *Sainte Thérèse de Lisieux.*
318. "Draupadi and the Five Pandavas," a dramatic interpretation of the *Mahabhárata,* by Lionel Haweis, typescript, copy 3 (Vancouver, B.C., 1941), 337, AA. For brevity, I have paraphrased. This is a scene in which the compassion of one of the Pandava brothers is tested. What Yudhishthira actually says in this translation is: "If this man is in Swarga, where are my kindred? It may be they need me more than I need Swarga." Indra replies, "Perhaps." Yudhishthira says, "Then grant that I add my suffering to theirs." The next scene is not unlike a Harrowing of Hell. Thus the compact Yudhishthira attempts to make is not unlike those attempted by St. Thérèse and Simone Weil. But see Merton's criticism of this kind of love as madness, *No Man Is an Island,* prologue, xiv.
319. Merton uses this quotation from Bloy often.
320. Merton to Dom Frederic Dunne, May 1, 1941, MGA. On the same theme, see also ScJ, 266–67; SBJ, Nov. 25, 1941.
321. SBJ, Nov. 29, 1940; ScJ, 132.
322. SBJ, Oct. 8, 1941. Merton returns to the subject that had interested him the November before in light of his new interest in St. Thérèse of Lisieux. For Kierkegaard, see ScJ, 132. Merton mentions reading *Fear and Trembling.*
323. There are many pages of notes in ink on *The Divine Comedy,* FF, FLSB. Many readers will have noticed that *My Argument with the Gestapo* begins with a descent into the Inferno (in this case the London Underground). Both MAG and SSM use Dante as a model, while SSM was originally more closely connected with Dante than it is now, see 9.
324. See 144. ScJ, 232. SBJ, Aug. 4, 1941.
325. SBJ, Aug. 4, 1941. Greatly edited, ScJ, 232.
326. SBJ, Aug. 4, 1941 only.
327. Ibid. Edited ScJ, 233.
328. Into this scene in SSM (340–44) Merton manages to feed a great deal of information about Catherine de Hueck's life and her work in Harlem, much of which Merton was to learn much later. This is done with great skill in the autobiography, so that it does not distract from the initial response.
329. SSM, 344.
330. Among SBJ, SSM, and ScJ, there appears to be a thorough mixup of dates on this occasion. I have followed SBJ, which gives "Sat. Aug. 15, 1941," though the Saturday was the 16th. (ScJ has Aug. 13, 1941, see 234.) Both agree that the first visit had been made the day before. SSM (344ff.) confuses things by saying he returned the evening of his first visit for the play. I have set the play on the Saturday evening, after which Merton went down to meet his friends at Godfrey's on East 18th Street. SBJ tells us he was staying again at 548 West 114th Street.
331. Jerdo Keating, "Tom Merton — As I Remember Him," 13. This article is most interesting, but should be used with a certain caution. There are many errors. Also SSM, 345.
332. SBJ, Aug. 15 (16), 1941; ScJ, 234.
333. Jerdo Keating, "Tom Merton," 13.
334. SSM, 348.
335. Yet Robert Lax has said, "We all saw Harlem through some kind of reading" (interview, Sept. 12, 1980). Merton was completely under the spell of García Lorca for some time: see the poem, "Aubade — Harlem," SP, 32–33; CP, 82–83, for one example out of many.
336. Cleaver, *Soul on Ice,* 34. Cited Twomey, "The Struggle for Racial Justice," 92.
337. SBJ, Oct. 18, 1941.

338. SBJ, Aug. 21, 1941.
339. SBJ, Aug. 31, 1941. SSM, 350–51.
340. SBJ, Aug. 31, 1941.
341. Merton appears to be in favor of laws that help the poor, only to conclude that such laws will still further divide the rich and the poor. His pages on war are even more confusing. In 1941 the Depression in America had been replaced by a certain degree of prosperity as the country moved to a wartime economy without a war. What Merton took to be Roosevelt's policy of providing others with arms to do the actual fighting disgusted him.
342. Merton reports both the incident of the man who came to Perry Street to ask for his fare back to New Jersey and the incident of the drunk in the turnstile as if they were scenes in comic films. See SSM, 272, 275. There is an equally unheroic pan-handling scene that appears in Merton's early fiction, in "Napoleon or Something," Columbia *Jester* 26, no. 9 (May 1936): 11–12, and in "The Man in the Sycamore Tree," 49–53, FF, FLSB. In each case the panhandler seems more intent on giving a lecture on religion than in getting a handout.
343. SBJ, July 27, 1941. See also SBJ, July 16, 1941.
344. SBJ, Sept. 6, 1941.
345. Our Lady of the Valley subsequently burned to the ground on the night of March 21–22, 1950. Merton heard of this at Gethsemani, SJ, 293.
346. SBJ, Sept. 27, 1941.
347. SBJ, Nov. 4, 1941.
348. Draft for "Huxley's Pantheon," 1, FF, FLSB. LE, 490–94.
349. Draft, 8. Put somewhat differently, LE, 493.
350. Draft, 9. Toned down considerably, LE, 494.
351. SBJ, Nov. 25, 1941. Edited, ScJ, 266.
352. Carbon copy of a letter from Merton to Catherine de Hueck, Oct. 6, 1941, FF, FLSB. Merton spells "inveigled" as here in text. He also starts the sentence "I think . . ." with a parenthesis. As he does not close this, I have taken the first parenthesis out.
353. Notes in ink on Huxley's *Grey Eminence*, FF, FLSB.
354. Blake's angels are often invoked in Merton's writing at this time. For one example, see ScJ, 5. Here, carbon copy of the letter from Merton to Catherine de Hueck, Oct. 6, 1941, FF, FLSB.
355. SBJ, Nov. 1, 1941.
356. Typed draft in FF, FLSB. SBJ, Oct. 29, 1941. ScJ, 256. The typed draft of "Vocation to the Lay Apostolate" is also at the Friedsam. In his letter to Catherine de Hueck of October 6, 1941, Merton writes: "I promised Mary Jerdo to send some articles and stuff I had lying around."
357. Typed draft of untitled essay, dated Oct. 23, 1941, FF, FLSB.
358. Ibid. Merton has "because of all kinds of rights . . ." I have deleted the "of" to make sense of the sentence.
359. Ibid.
360. SBJ, Nov. 1, 1941. The account is somewhat different in ScJ, 260–63, and in SSM, 358–59.
361. This is given only in SBJ, Nov. 1, 1941.
362. Ibid.
363. SBJ, May 9, 1941; Dec. 2, 1941.
364. SBJ, Nov. 4, 1941.
365. Ibid. SSM, 334, gives the incident when it took place, about a month after Merton had returned from the retreat at Gethsemani: "I looked, and the answer practically floored me. The words were: '*Ecce eris tacens.*' 'Behold, thou shalt be silent.' " He goes on to explain that this was the twentieth verse of the first chapter of St. Luke's Gospel, in which the angel addresses Zachary, the father of John the Baptist. But he was probably bending the text a little to say, "*Tacens:* there could not have been a closer word to 'Trappist' in the whole Bible . . ." He does not say, either, that this was his second attempt, "the first having been something I couldn't make out — but good — from the Bk of the Macchabees . . ." (SBJ, Nov. 29, 1941).

366. SBJ, Nov. 4, 1941.
367. Ibid.
368. Jerdo Keating, "Tom Merton," 14. Merton's account of hitchhiking to New York, SSM, 360–61.
369. SBJ, Nov. 24, 1941. Elements in this scene are taken from other sections of this journal. Cf. ScJ, 264; SSM, 363.
370. SBJ, Nov. 24, 1941, "The sense of exile bleeds inside me like a hemorrhage."
371. ScJ, 270. The retreat is described ScJ, 265. Betty Schneider's name is supplied in the original account, SBJ, Nov. 24, 1941.
372. SBJ, Nov. 30, 1941.
373. Jerdo Keating, "Tom Merton," 14.
374. SSM, 333, 337.
375. SBJ, Nov. 28, 1941, reporting the evening before.
376. The two accounts differ on a minor point. In SBJ Merton is reminded of the bell ringing for Matins at Gethsemani, in SSM (365), "as I afterwards calculated, it was just about that time that the bell is rung every night for the *Salve Regina*, towards the end of Compline." He says in this account also that he realized it was only in his imagination that he heard the bells of Gethsemani.
377. SBJ, Nov. 28, 1941.
378. Ibid.
379. Ibid.
380. SBJ, Dec. 2, 1941.
381. On November 29, 1941, Merton makes it clear he thinks he is still "out of the draft for a long while, and then only in limited service and even if I am not, I am ready to do whatever I am told: so going to the Trappists has nothing to do with the war." On December 2, 1941, he reports the letter from the draft board had come the previous afternoon, "But at least I had made up my mind and written to the Trappists, saying I wanted to come there Dec. 18" (SBJ). He goes on, "What God's will is, depends on what happens — if the Draft Board refuses my plea for a de-lay — if the Abbot accepts me, etc. If the army takes me and the Abbot refuses me — the worst thing that could possibly happen — I have a feeling it is still only the beginning of a long struggle leading to the cloister."
382. SBJ, Dec. 5, 1941.
383. Catherine de Hueck to Merton, Dec. 13, 1941, TMSC.
384. Father Thomas Plassmann, president of St. Bonaventure College and Seminary, to the Rt. Rev. Frederic M. Dunne, recommending Thomas J. Merton, Dec. 9, 1941: "Let me briefly state that Mr. Merton's scholarship is of a high order. His morality is above reproach. His ideals are the highest and noblest. His whole life bespeaks the firm convictions of a thorough Christian gentleman" (MGA).
385. Copy of bank account with the First National Bank, Olean, N.Y., showing a final balance on Dec. 5, 1941, of $167.43, together with a copy of the check for this amount, withdrawn on Dec. 9, 1941. MGA.
386. SSM, 368.
387. "Three Postcards from the Monastery," III, SP, 62–63; CP, 155. SP has a period at the end of the second line quoted here, rather than a comma.
388. "The City after Noon," CP, 213.
389. de Hueck, *Friendship House.* Also *Where Love Is, God Is.*
390. Naomi Burton Stone, *Sentinels,* 239.

Mount Purgatory

Much of the material on life at the monastery in the forties and fifties is taken from in-terviews and from a series of notes prepared by Father Tarcisius (Father James Conner). I am most grateful to all who provided information, where this has been individually cited and where it has not. I should like to express my gratitude in particular to: Dom John Eudes Bamberger, Brother Cassian Bigne, Father Paul Bourne, Father Flavian Burns, Brother Michael Casagram, Brother Caspar of 1954–55, Brother Frederic Collins, Father

James Conner, Brother Martin Deloach, Father Anastasius Fettig, Father Raymond Flanagan, Brother Maurice Flood, Dom James Fox, Brother Pascal Galligan, Brother Patrick Hart, Brother Alban Herberger, Dom Timothy Kelly, Father Matthew Kelty, Brother Norbert Meier, Brother Nivard Stanton, Father Chrysogonus Waddell, Father Augustine Wulff. Also acknowledged with gratitude here is material on the publishing of Merton's early work, provided by James Laughlin, Naomi Burton Stone, Robert Giroux; as well as George A. McCauliff and others cited.

Epigraph: Thomas à Kempis, *The Imitation of Christ*, 148.

1. Horace, Ep. 1. 14. 10/11.
2. Cited, André Chastel, *The Age of Humanism* (London: Thames and Hudson, 1962), 17.
3. Interview with Dom John Eudes Bamberger, Mar. 21, 1981. Interview with Dom Flavian Burns, Mar. 29, 1981. On the vow of stability, see SJ, 9–10.
4. Perhaps one ought to say two conflicts — the conflict over the two vocations, and the conflict over denying love, especially to women, which is submerged until the mid-sixties. See 411. In talking of such conflicts in others, RJ, Aug. 24, 1964: "A mature person can handle the situation fairly well. It seems to damage the young ones — sometimes quite badly. Perhaps it would not do so if they all came from a stable and secure Catholic environment. But their background is always too ambiguous. As for the supposed security the Rule seems to promise — the promise cannot be kept if certain basic problems are left unresolved, the human and usual problems of the insecure American teen-ager."
5. Merton uses the phrase "Edenic period" a number of times. For one example, see Merton to Czeslaw Milosz, May 6, 1960, TMSC.
6. "Easter Letter, 1968," TMSC.
7. Among the many references, see SP, 13, 16, 68. In CP, 31, 38, 46 (also on CP, 46, "The Blessed Virgin Mary Compared to a Window" from *Thirty Poems*), 109, 174, etc. Important references in Merton's prose, some later, include: WCT 53; *Seasons of Celebration*, 164, *Life and Holiness*, 26; Daggy, *Introductions*, 94.
8. PSJ, Oct. 16, 1939: "But now, on top of this, the argument in St. Thomas [Aquinas]: that the man who has repented of great sins should forsake even lawful things and give up even more than those who have always obeyed God, and sacrifice *everything*."
9. *Disputed Questions*, 74.
10. Interview with Father Paul Bourne, Aug. 3, 1980.
11. Interview with Dom John Eudes Bamberger, Mar. 22, 1981.
12. Interview with Father Paul Bourne, Aug. 3, 1980.
13. SJ, 152 (Jan. 31, 1949), "Evening Zero Weather," SP, 67–68; CP, 174–75; also interviews. On Feb. 4, 1958, Merton writes to Naomi Burton about "No Man Is an Iceberg (Not a Freudian slip, it is very cold here)" (Curtis Brown correspondence files, Columbia University Libraries).
14. SSM, 379.
15. Interview with Father Matthew Kelty, Apr. 6, 1980. Interview with Father Anastasius Fettig, Sept. 28, 1980.
16. SJ, 154 (Feb. 2, 1949).
17. AJ, appendix VII, 334.
18. SSM, 377–78.
19. SBJ, Nov. 29, 1941.
20. SSM, 412.
21. Thomas à Kempis, *The Imitation of Christ*, 134.
22. Hart, "A Witness to Life," 173. Raymond, *The Less Travelled Road. Zanesville* (Ohio) *Times Recorder*, Jan. 25, 1976. Notes, John Stanley.
23. SSM, 377. Lentfoehr, *Words*, 10. Groves, "The Gregarious Hermit," 89. Interviews. "A Letter to My Friends," CP, 90–92.
24. Brother Louis was told he could not write poems in the interval after the night office, SSM, 389–90.
25. SSM, 374.

26. SSM, 414.
27. SSM, 327.
28. Interview with Brother Caspar (1954–55), May 18, 1980, and interviews at Gethsemani, 1980, provided the details here.
29. Interview with Father Anastasius Fettig, Sept. 28, 1980.
30. Father Anthony Chassagne to John Howard Griffin, June 4, 1979, with notes enclosed dated Dec. 12, 1968. AA.
31. PSJ, Jan. 25, 1940.
32. Many of those interviewed have mentioned Merton's rapid grasp of the sense of a passage or a page. In part, this accounts for the extraordinary amount of reading he was able to do between 1941 and 1968. However, it should be said that the process was slowed down by the full notes Merton usually took and kept. At a rough estimate from the reading notes that survive, Merton must have spent an hour a day writing notes from his reading. There are two large ledgers at TMSC, numbers 1 and 2, that contain only "Notes on the Contemplative Life," written in the early monastery years. To my knowledge, no comprehensive list of all the surviving reading notebooks has been made to date.
33. This is the first line of Merton's poem, "Duns Scotus," SP, 65–67; CP, 164–65. In the poem, the line refers, of course, to the writings of Duns Scotus. I have referred it back to Merton's own writing at its best.
34. See 90. Handwritten will of Thomas James Merton, "in religion frater M. Louis," dated Feb. 17, 1944, and witnessed, MGA.
35. *The Waters of Siloe*, 120–22.
36. The facing was apparently done in 1907–8. I am grateful to Brother Patrick Hart for this detail, and for helping to check many of the points in this section.
37. During his novitiate, Brother Louis asked for a Lenten penance. The novice master knew he was taking a weekly shower and thought this unusual: for Lent Brother Louis would take only cold showers.
38. *Exile Ends in Glory*, 13. See also WCT, 28, *The New Man*, 24–25; *The Silent Life*, 8; Cf. Luke 18. 29/30.
39. *Exile Ends in Glory*, 31. According to Father Anthony Chassagne in the letter of June 4, 1970, to John Howard Griffin (above), Father Louis in the novitiate years was "witty and somewhat mischievous." Little of this gets into either the surviving journals or the other writing of the period. AA.
40. *Exile Ends in Glory*, 217.
41. SSM, 394.
42. Dom James Fox, "To the Gethsemani Diaspora," Feb. 1, 1969. MGA, AA.
43. SSM, 398–99. John Paul received provisional baptism at St. Catherine's, New Haven, July 26, 1942.
44. Last will and testament of John Paul Merton, Aug. 4, 1942, MGA.
45. Sgt. Observer Merton J. P. to Walter Hauck (Elsie's brother), Dec. 1, 1942. MGA.
46. SSM, 399.
47. SSM, 402.
48. Ibid.
49. Walter Hauck to Sgt. John Paul Merton, Mar. 11, 1943, returned, "Reported Killed," "Died of Injuries," dated May 22, 1943, MAG.
50. John Stanley has researched the details of John Paul's death, and the crash of Wellington bomber HE862L on the night of April 16–17, 1943. I am grateful to him for making the facts available. This information was not available to Merton and corrects the account, SSM, 402–3, and CGB, 175. "For My Brother: Reported Missing in Action, 1943," SSM, 404; SP, 12–13; CP, 35–36.
51. SSM, 408–9. Interview with Robert Lax, Sept. 10, 1980.
52. Dell'Isola, 142–43, F4–F14.
53. Madeleva, *My First Seventy Years*, 45.
54. Merton to James Laughlin, Aug. 19, 1950, JLA.
55. Interview with James Laughlin, Oct. 25, 1979. Interview with James Laughlin, Feb. 2, 1982.
56. Dell'Isola, 1, A1.

57. *Life*, 22, 20 (May 19, 1947), 91–94. For Merton on Lowell, see SJ, 81, Dec. 16, 1947.
58. Lowell, "The Verses of Thomas Merton," 240–42: ". . . a mannerism is made to bear the burden of inspiration . . ." etc.
59. For example, in the last lines of the poem to John Paul, Merton means that bell notes, not bells, will fall upon the "alien tomb." At least this is what he seems to mean. "For My Brother: Reported Missing in Action, 1943," SP, 12–13; CP, 35–36; SSM, 404.
60. Dell'Isola, 2, A2.
61. George McCauliff to the author, Jan. 16, 1981, AA.
62. Merton to James Laughlin, Sept. 28, 1945, JLA.
63. SJ, 27, Mar. 8, 1947.
64. Merton to James Laughlin, Nov. 2, 1945, JLA.
65. Ibid., Mar. 1, 1946, JLA.
66. SJ, 14. There is, however, an autobiographical sketch in three handwritten and tightly packed pages, dated Jan. 2, 1942, which Merton had written for Dom Frederic, "at the suggestion of my Father Master" (MGA).
67. SJ, 50, May 29, 1947: Merton says here that he had written SSM "three years ago." *What Are These Wounds?* x: Merton says here that *What Are These Wounds?* was "written before *The Seven Storey Mountain*. It was undertaken as an anonymous pamphlet in 1945 . . ." In the first account SSM was written in 1944; in the second, after 1945, or, at the earliest, late in 1945.
68. Merton to James Laughlin, Aug. 17, 1946, JLA.
69. Ibid., Jan. 6, 1946, JLA.
70. Father Anthony Chassagne to John Howard Griffin, June 4, 1970, AA. SJ, 15.
71. There is at the TMSC a notebook that belonged to Father Amadeus with, on one side, Father Amadeus's notes in ink on the Trappist life (see "The Pasture," note 265, above), on the other side carbon copies of typed pages of SSM, pages in the 600s with few corrections. These pages are stitched together.
72. Merton to James Laughlin, Apr. 8, 1948, JLA.
73. Traditionally, this was where the monks were buried, but at Gethsemani the monks' graveyard was on the west side of the abbey church. The court of the cloister was usually called the *préau* after French usage. Merton tended to call it the garth, after the English monastic tradition.
74. SJ, 14. For Merton's view of Chesterton, CWL, 18, 34; RJ, Jan. 11, 1959: "With Chesterton everything is 'of course,' 'quite obviously,' etc., etc. And everything turns out to be 'just plain common sense after all.' And people have the stomach to listen, and even to *like* it! How can we be so mad? Of course, Chesterton is badly dated: his voice comes out of the fog between the last two wars. But to think there are still people — Catholics — who can talk like that and imagine they know the answers."
75. SSM, 4. But sometimes "king" appears with a capital, sometimes not, while the passage does not appear at all in SSMB.
76. Interview with John Stanley, July 21, 1980.
77. SJ, 89.
78. RJ, Aug. 18, 1956.
79. SJ, 139, Dec. 6, 1948.
80. SJ, 274, Feb. 10, 1950.
81. Merton to Naomi Burton, Oct. 21, 1946, FLSB.
82. Naomi Burton, *Sentinels*, 243–44. Grace, *Life and Holiness*, 29–30.
83. Naomi Burton to Merton, Dec. 9, 1946, FLSB.
84. Ibid., Dec. 17, 1946, FLSB.
85. Naomi Burton, *Sentinels*, 245. Interview with Robert Giroux, May 6, 1980. Interview with Naomi Burton Stone, May 11, 1980.
86. SJ, 20–21, Dec. 29, 1946. It was the Feast of St. Thomas à Becket of Canterbury, and before reading the telegram, Merton had struggled with himself, deciding to take whatever it was as a gift from St. Thomas.
87. SJ, 21, Jan. 5, 1947. Also SJ, 25, Feb. 8, 1947.
88. Merton to Naomi Burton, Jan. 2, 1947, FLSB.

89. Naomi Burton to Mark Van Doren, Jan. 9, 1947, FLSB.
90. SJ, 24, Feb. 1, 1947.
91. See 333.
92. SJ, 25, Feb. 17, 1947, reporting on the previous day.
93. SJ, 23–24, Jan. 27, 1947.
94. Yet Merton says specifically on page 10 of *The Sign of Jonas* that "By making a vow of stability the monk renounces the vain hope of wandering off to find a 'perfect monastery.' " For the ideal city, see PSJ, Dec. 18, 1939. For the ideal monastery, see *The Silent Life*, etc.
95. SJ, 34–35, Mar. 30, 1947.
96. Merton to James Laughlin, Easter (Apr. 6), 1947, JLA.
97. Ibid., Jan. 2, 1947, JLA.
98. Naomi Burton to Merton, Feb. 21, 1947, FLSB.
99. Merton to Naomi Burton, Apr. 17, 1947, FLSB.
100. SJ, 40, Apr. 16, 1947.
101. Merton to Naomi Burton, Apr. 14, 1947, FLSB.
102. Naomi Burton to Merton, undated, FLSB.
103. SJ, 160, Feb. 15, 1949.
104. RJ, Aug. 11, 1961.
105. SJ, 109, July 2, 1948. See also Father M. Raymond, *Forty Years Behind the Wall* (Huntington, Ind.: Our Sunday Visitor, Inc., 1980), 8.
106. SJ, 45, May 1, 1947.
107. SJ, 46, May 1, 1947.
108. SJ, 6.
109. SJ, 46–47, May 1, 1947.
110. SJ, 52–53, June 13, 1947. Merton is writing about the previous day.
111. Interview with James Laughlin, Oct. 25, 1979.
112. The idea of a parallel translation and text (of which Merton talks in a letter to Naomi Burton, Aug. 1, 1947, FLSB) had to be set aside because of an earlier translation of the works of St. John of the Cross. The first title of *The Ascent to Truth* was "The Cloud and the Fire." There are frequent references to it under this name, both in the original journals and in SJ.
113. For Merton on the Apophatic tradition, see also *The New Man*, 15; *Zen and the Birds of Appetite*, 35, 62–63; *What Are These Wounds?*, 12–13, as well as *The Ascent to Truth*, esp. 16–17. See also Shannon, *Thomas Merton's Dark Path*.
114. SJ, 20, Dec. 29, 1946.
115. SJ, 139, Dec. 6, 1948.
116. Merton to James Laughlin, Feb. 8, 1948, JLA.
117. The initial idea may well have come from the "little books of *Meditations*," which Merton mentions having received from Parkminster, SJ, 54, June 21, 1947 (also SJ, 49, May 23, 1947). See Merton to James Laughlin, Nov. 26, 1947, JLA.
118. *The Ascent to Truth*, 168–69.
119. SJ, 15, 65, Sept. 15, 1947, etc.
120. Interview with Brother Patrick Hart and others at the monastery.
121. SJ, July 9, 1947. There is also a moving letter from Merton to James Laughlin, July 9, 1947, in which he speaks of "the big wound in the community" (JLA).
122. Interview with Pat and Frank Priest, July 27, 1980.
123. "A Letter to America," CP, 152. This is a major example of the "American Eden" theme in Merton's writing, and was written, as he would have said, in the "Edenic period."
124. SJ, 58, Aug. 8, 1947.
125. SJ, 41, Apr. 20, 1947.
126. SJ, 59, Aug. 14, 1947. Merton had been an early reader and admirer of Dylan Thomas's poetry. SBJ, Feb. 9, 1941, includes two full pages of notes on the poems and this comment on the prose: "Good writing, but too much incest and witchcraft." For Merton's strong dislike of anything to do with magic, see LE, 367 and 373, two examples taken from many. Merton had told James Laughlin of his early interest in Dylan Thomas (see letter of Nov. 2, 1945, quoted 226). It was an acci-

dent that the book got through from New Directions. The editor had sent it to Merton as an example of type that could be used for *Cistercian Contemplatives*. This is mentioned SJ, 59. Also interview with James Laughlin, Oct. 25, 1979.

127. SJ, 69–70, Oct. 12, 1947.
128. SJ, 58, July 20, 1947.
129. SSM, 393–94.
130. Baraket, *Cistercian Sign Language*, "to water," 127, illus.
131. "In the Rain and the Sun," *The Tears of the Blind Lions*, 24; CP, 215.
132. Interview with Robert Giroux, May 6, 1980.
133. Dell'Isola, 4, 5A. Published March 1948, although copyright 1947.
134. James Laughlin to Merton, Mar. 22, 1949, JLA.
135. Merton to James Laughlin, undated but clearly between Mar. 22 and Apr. 6, 1949, JLA.
136. James Laughlin to Merton, Apr. 6, 1949, JLA.
137. Dell'Isola, 14, A12.
138. Ibid., 3, A3.
139. Ibid., 3, A4.
140. *Figures for an Apocalypse*, Dell'Isola, 4, A5.
141. Dell'Isola, 5, A6.
142. Ibid., 6, A7.
143. Ibid., 8, A8.
144. Robert Giroux, unpublished script, talk at the Newman Club, August 1949. Letter to author, Feb. 15, 1984. Also interview with Giroux, May 6, 1980.
145. Robert Giroux, talk.
146. Naomi Burton, *Sentinels*, 245. Interview with Naomi Burton Stone, May 11, 1980. SJ, 110, July 11, 1948.
147. SJ, 110, July 11, 1948, talking about July 7.
148. SJ, 106–7, June 20, 1948.
149. Merton to Naomi Burton, Aug. 4, 1948, FLSB.
150. SJ, 114, Aug. 13, 1948, reporting on the day before.
151. Oury, *Dom Marie Gabriel Sortais*. See also *The Waters of Siloe*, 22.
152. SJ, 116, Aug. 20, 1948.
153. SJ, 117, Aug. 25, 1948.
154. SJ, 118, Aug. 25, 1948.
155. SJ, 118, Sept. 7, 1948, "The place sounds and smells like New York."
156. Interview with Brother Patrick Hart, Apr. 2, 1980. Also Hart, "A Witness to Life," 174. SJ, 146, Jan. 7, 1949.
157. Naomi Burton, *Sentinels*, 246. Interview with Naomi Burton Stone, May 11, 1980.
158. Robert Giroux, unpublished script, talk at the Newman Club, Aug. 1949. Letter to the author, Feb. 15, 1984.
159. Interview with Naomi Burton Stone, May 11, 1980. Stone, unpublished notes.
160. Giroux, *Editor*, 29.
161. Interview with Robert Giroux, May 6, 1980. Interview with Naomi Burton Stone, May 11, 1980. Stone, unpublished notes.
162. Cited, Cecil, *The Stricken Deer*, 223–24. The poem was "John Gilpin."
163. Twomey, "Thomas Merton: An Appreciation," 4, fn. 14, 12.
164. Evelyn Waugh to Harcourt, Brace ("Dear Sirs"), July 20, 1948. Copy, MGA. AA.
165. For an interesting discussion of Waugh as editor, see Davis, "How Waugh Cut Merton." *The Seven Storey Mountain* was published in England by Sheldon Press, London, 1973.
166. SJ, 135, Nov. 30, 1948.
167. Interview with Robert Giroux, May 6, 1980.
168. SJ, 50, May 26, 1947.
169. Graves and Hodges, *The Reader over Your Shoulder*, 38. Holographic journals and notebooks, 2, TMSC. (See letter from Thomas Merton to James Laughlin, Aug. 27, 1948, JLA). This is itself a quotation from Arnold Bennett's *Literary Taste*.
170. Ibid., 21. (I have corrected the quotation here.)
171. Dell'Isola, 8, A9.
172. SJ, 165, Mar. 6, 1949, reporting on the day before.

173. Ibid.
174. SJ, 177, Apr. 22, 1949 ("How much I need to go out of myself!"). SJ, 218–19, Aug. 17, 1949. SJ, 222–23, Aug. 25, 1949, etc.
175. Dell'Isola, 10, A10. SJ, 187, May 8, 1949.
176. SJ, 196–97, June 4, 1949, reporting events on June 1.
177. Interview with Naomi Burton Stone, May 11, 1980. Interviews at monastery.
178. "So I think very much of Our Lady of Cobre and of the question I once asked her," SJ, 178, Apr. 22, 1949. SSM, 282 (where the promise is made). SJ, 194, May 29, 1949 (where the promise is fulfilled).
179. "When we reached 100,000, I had a copy specially bound in morocco and took it to the monastery for Merton's ordination." Giroux, *Editor*, 30. This is often reported as copy 200,000, an error that is entirely understandable and only shows the general confusion as the numbers climbed to 275,000 by Labor Day, 1949.
180. The description of events during the period of Merton's ordination is drawn from a number of sources, including: SJ, 193–95, May 29, 1949; interview with James Laughlin, Oct. 10, 1979; interview with Robert Giroux, May 6, 1980; interview with Edward Rice, July 19, 1980; interview with Robert Lax, Sept. 25, 1980; correspondence between George A. McCauliff and the author, Nov. 1980, including letter to the author of Nov. 3, 1980, enclosing notes made at Gethsemani on May 23, 1949; Rice, 90–100.
181. McCauliff, notes (see note 180 above).
182. Ibid.
183. SBJ, Mar. 4, 1941.
184. Rice, 97. Rice also took a series of photographs, two of which face the description.
185. SJ, 110, July 11, 1948.
186. Rice, 97, etc.
187. RJ, May 3, 1959.
188. McCauliff, notes, op. cit.
189. Clare Boothe Luce to Merton, June 10, 1948, TMSC.
190. See correspondence, Clare Booth Luce to Merton, TMSC. Also, interview with Dom James Fox, July 11, 1981. Interestingly, Dom James did not know about the background of the gift.
191. SJ, 205, July 11, 1949.
192. SJ, 205–6, July 17, 1949. Merton points out that the Feast of Our Lady of Mount Carmel is kept on that day in the Order, "although to the world it was yesterday." Interview with Dom James Fox, Apr. 6, 1980.
193. See 151–52.
194. SJ, 224, Aug. 26, 1949. This is a short quotation from a longer passage.
195. This information came from a number of interviews at the monastery, cross-checked and collated. I am especially grateful to Father Anastasius Fettig, interviewed on Sept. 28, 1980, and to Brother Patrick Hart, interviewed many times over many years. See SJ, 133, Oct. 31, 1948; Merton receives permission to walk with James Laughlin outside the enclosure. SJ, 209–10, July 31, 1949. Title: Merton retained "The Whale and the Ivy," using this for part 5. The whale symbolized restlessness or adventurousness, while the ivy stood for stability and firmness of purpose. In autobiographical terms, this may be Merton's most charged title, especially when one recalls that he had once thought of the anchor as the symbol of adventurousness, then found it was the symbol for firmness in faith.
196. This was only at the end of the period covered by *The Sign of Jonas*. Merton reports that he is reading *Walden*, SJ, 316, Dec. 6, 1950, etc.
197. Dell'Isola, 11, A11. Published Sept. 5, 1949.
198. SJ, 158, Feb. 13, 1949. SJ, 204–5, July 10, 1949.
199. *The Waters of Siloe*, 210ff.
200. SJ, 259, Dec. 30, 1949.
201. SJ, 258, Dec. 27, 1949, reporting on the incident of the day before.
202. SJ, 283–84, Mar. 5, 1950.
203. Merton to James Laughlin describing his joy in reading Rilke, Dec. 10, 1949, JLA. Merton to Laughlin saying that the abbot has said no to publishing his own journals, May 1, 1950, JLA.

204. Dell'Isola, 15, A13.
205. A letter from the Bruce Publishing Company to Merton (first page only), June 23, 1949, MGA, gives the information that the suggested title "The Tiger Lily" was Merton's, and it contains the publisher's comment, ". . . this is an attractive life of a saint who has a very attractive personality despite the fact that she is a contemplative and a mystic . . ." One has to wonder how Merton reacted to the "despite"!
206. *What Are These Wounds?*, preface, x.
207. The chart has frequently been reproduced. See Forest, *Pictorial*, 65; Daggy, *Introductions*, 125–26. Merton made the chart on February 6, 1967 (RJ).
208. *What Are These Wounds?*, 164.
209. SJ, 110, July 11, 1948.
210. *What Are These Wounds?*, 39. For some reason the Albigensians or Cathari always brought out the worst in Merton prior to 1963, as if there were a lasting stigma to having been born on the fringes of the Albigensian lands seven hundred years after the heresy had been violently stamped out. There are references to the Cathari in a number of poems, 1947–49, notably in "St. John's Night," CP, 171. In 1963, Merton makes a complete turnabout. He learned on October 8, 1963 (RJ), that a man living in a village near Cordes "in my country," not far from St. Antonin, had discovered a series of caves where Albigensian *perfect* fasted to death in the *indura*. Fascinated, he read Zöe Oldenberg's *Massacre at Monségur*, finishing it on October 17, and her novel, *Destiny of Fire*, finishing it on October 22. The latter left him *"bouleversé."* Among the possibilities he explored were the following: "Is there any getting away from the fact that the Dominicans invented the methods of the modern police state?" and "The clear fact that some very sincere, courageous and holy people went to their death *convinced* that the Church was acting as an instrument of Satan. Did they have, subjectively, really serious reasons to think otherwise? Is it not true that this has affected the attitude of whole generations and whole regions toward the Church?" At the same time (RJ, Oct. 9, 1963), Merton was reading *One Million Dead*, a novel about the Spanish Civil War. See also CGB, 334–35. Cf. CGB, 142.
211. "The Christian in World Crisis," *Seeds of Destruction,* 117. Merton quotes this twice on the same page. St. Augustine, Letter 138.
212. Interview with Dom John Eudes Bamberger, Mar. 22, 1981.
213. Interview with Father Anastasius Fettig, Sept. 28, 1980, and other interviews at Gethsemani. Letter from Ken Stuart to John Howard Griffin, Jan. 28, 1971, AA. See also SJ, 346.
214. See note 200.
215. PSJ, Jan. 25, 1940.
216. Interviews at monastery.
217. Naomi Burton Stone, unpublished pages deleted from *Sentinels,* dated Sept. 28, 1956, from diary.
218. Ibid., pages dated late May 1963.
219. Merton to Rachel Carson, Jan. 12, 1963, TMSC.
220. Merton to Agnes Gertrude Merton, Apr. 20, 1965, TMSC. "Everything is fine, except that they have been spraying the alfalfa fields with an aeroplane and the stuff they use is very potent. It may kill some of the birds and even poison the deer if the creature eats some of it. In the end the insects suffer least, because they develop a resistant strain and the birds prey on them and die off. This is another of our follies."
221. Interview with Father Anastasius Fettig, Sept. 28, 1980.
222. Merton ran into exactly the same handicap in debate, both in his opposition to nuclear stockpiling, and, as a member of the building committee at Gethsemani, in his desire to have the new Chapter room left simple and with exposed brickwork. RJ, Nov. 20, 1960.
223. Interview with Father Anastasius Fettig, Sept. 28, 1980. Interview with Brother Alban Herberger, July 11, 1981.
224. Interview with Brother Frederic Collins, July 12, 1981. Much of the information on

these pages originated in, or was confirmed by, this interview with Brother Frederic.

225. Interview with Dom John Eudes Bamberger, Mar. 23, 1981, and interviews at Gethsemani, 1980–81.
226. Ken Stuart to John Howard Griffin, Jan. 28, 1971, AA.
227. Interview with Father Chrysogonus Waddell, June 29, 1981.
228. Interview with Father Augustine Wulff, July 10, 1981.
229. Interview with Dom Flavian Burns, Mar. 29, 1981. Much of the material on these pages was collated and confirmed in interviews with Dom John Eudes, Dom James Fox, Dom Flavian Burns, Dom Timothy Kelly, and others.
230. Interview with Father Matthew Kelty, Apr. 6, 1980. The Beguines, an order founded in Belgium in 1400, were the first women religious without enclosure.
231. Interview with Dom Flavian Burns, Mar. 29, 1981.
232. RJ, June–August 1960. He did, however, make the "Father Louis" bookstamp out of an eraser. Merton used this for years.
233. Interview with Dom John Eudes Bamberger, Mar. 21, 1981.
234. The three incidents were related in an interview with a monk at Gethsemani who has asked to keep his anonymity.
235. Merton to James Laughlin, May 20, 1950, JLA.
236. Ibid., June 6, 1950, JLA. Perhaps equally important to his publisher's interest in Oriental studies was the talk given in Chapter by a "chemist who has been helping us with some paint jobs" who turned out "to have been a postulant in a Zen Buddhist monastery in Hawaii" (SJ, 243, Nov. 24, 1949) This is the first mention of Zen in the published writing at the monastery and an interesting early example of the community's openness to hearing about another religious tradition.
237. SJ, 317, Dec. 13, 1950.
238. *The Ascent to Truth*, Author's Note, ix.
239. *The Ascent to Truth*, Dell'Isola, 16, A15. Published Sept. 20, 1951.
240. SJ, 261, Dec. 30, 1949 (. . ."sent off a lot of old galley proofs to Sister Thérèse and Father Connolly to save myself the trouble of burning them.")
241. The correspondence and the collection of Sister Thérèse Lentfoehr form part of the collections at MCC. For the beginning of the correspondence between Merton and Sister Thérèse, see "Sister Thérèse Lentfoehr, S.D.S.," etc., Daggy, *The Merton Seasonal*, 6, 3. Autumn 1981, 2–5, TMSC.
242. Merton to James Laughlin, May 20, 1950, JLA.
243. There is much correspondence on this, both at TMSC and in the Curtis Brown Files, Columbia University Libraries.
244. Gertrude S. Weiner to Merton, Nov. 5, 1951, Curtis Brown Files, Columbia University Libraries.
245. Pencil note by Naomi Burton on a letter from Merton to Mrs. Rosenthal, Jan. 18, 1955, Curtis Brown Files, Columbia University Libraries.
246. Naomi Burton, *Sentinels*, 250–53.
247. Interview with Naomi Burton Stone, May 11, 1980.
248. Naomi Burton Stone, unpublished notes, AA.
249. SJ, 320, Feb. 28, 1951.
250. Merton to W. H. Ferry, May 27, 1964, TMSC. CWL, 95, 157.
251. SJ, 321, Feb. 28, 1951. SJ, 323, Mar. 3, 1951.
252. SJ, 330–32, June 23, 1951, reporting on the events of the day before. A family brother, or familiar, was a layman who lived in the guest house, wore secular clothes, and gave his services free in return for a share in the spiritual and communal life of the monastery. They took no vows. There are now no family brothers at Gethsemani.
253. SJ, 330–32. Merton's certificate of naturalization, MGA. Interview with Brother Pascal Galligan, Mar. 24, 1981. Brother Pascal well remembers the flourishes.
254. Naomi Burton Stone, "The Merton I Knew," tape of talk given in Vancouver in 1978.
255. Interview with Father Chrysogonus Waddell, June 29, 1981.
256. A number of monks in interviews spoke of the enormous energy and enthusiasm

Father Louis put into fighting fires. This was underlined by Brother Patrick Hart.

257. Interview with Father Chrysogonus Waddell, June 29, 1981. Interview with Dom James Fox, July 11, 1981.

258. Many of these books on forestry containing notes in his hand are still in Merton's hermitage.

259. Interview with Father Chrysogonus Waddell, June 29, 1981. Interview with Dom James Fox, July 11, 1981.

260. This can be traced in correspondence between James Laughlin and Merton, 1950–52, JLA.

261. Interview with Robert Giroux, May 6, 1980. Interview with Naomi Burton Stone, May 11, 1980, and subsequent letters and telephone conversations. Giroux, *Editor*, 30. Interview with Dom James Fox, July 11, 1981. NJ, Oct. 30, 1952.

262. Interview with Father Chrysogonus Waddell, June 29, 1981.

263. NJ, July 25, 1952.

264. Ibid.

265. Ibid.

266. RJ, April 3, 1965.

267. NJ, July 25, 1952.

268. NJ, Oct. 10, 1952.

269. Ibid.

270. Naomi Burton Stone, tape of talk given in Vancouver, 1978, AA. Interview with Naomi Burton Stone, May 11, 1980.

271. NJ, Aug. 23, 1952.

272. NJ, Oct. 22, 1952.

273. Interview with Father Paul Bourne, Aug. 3, 1980. Father Paul provided many of the details on censorship and Trappist writing throughout. See also *Statut de la censure des publications dans l'Ordre, sixième séance, dimanche 14 septembre, après None,* 1952. Passed by the General Chapter of the Order, 1952. MGA.

274. NJ, Aug. 18, 1952. In sections, Merton may be paraphrasing the original comments of "the Georgia censor."

275. Interview with Brother Alban Herberger, July 11, 1981.

276. NJ, Oct. 10, 1952.

277. Ibid.

278. Father Barnabas Ahern to Merton, Jan. 14, 1953, TMSC. Father Barnabas is quoting a line from the previous letter of Merton's, which does not appear to be on file.

279. Letter from Merton to Father Barnabas Ahern, Jan. 22, 1953, TMSC.

280. Father Barnabas Ahern to Merton, Jan. 29, 1953, TMSC. Over and over, even Merton's most sympathetic advisers in the Church were to point out that he was by now so clearly identified with Gethsemani in the public mind that he could not leave without undermining everything he had already achieved. The article in *The Atlantic Monthly:* Graham, "Thomas Merton, A Modern Man in Reverse." Ahern had introduced Merton to Father Charbel, see SJ, 325, Apr. 11, 1951.

281. The Petrified Forest was so called because the religious statues that had been rejected for one reason or another from the monastery were left there among the wildflowers.

282. Interview with Father Anastasius Fettig, Sept. 28, 1980: "The monastery cooks used it for religious reading and meditation."

283. NJ, Jan. 28, 1953. It is extraordinary how closely this scene seems connected to the draft for a short story about a hermit in the Perry Street Journal (Dec. 19, 1939). That sketch itself seems linked to the painting of St. Francis receiving the stigmata by Giovanni Bellini in the Frick Collection. Perhaps the scene at St. Anne's has also a slightly surrealist touch in the watch without a crystal. The shed-hermitage still existed in 1981, though it was something of a wreck.

284. NJ, Sept. 1, 1952.

285. NJ, Sept. 13, 1952.

286. Merton to Dom Gabriel Sortais, Oct. 10, 1952, TMSC. NJ, Oct. 30, 1952.

287. Merton reports on October 30, 1952 (NJ), that the letter, with its somewhat acid

comments about monks and publishers, had arrived the day before. See also Dom Gabriel Sortais to Merton, Nov. 16, 1952, TMSC.

288. Merton to Naomi Burton Stone, May 3, 1954, Curtis Brown Files, Columbia University Libraries.

289. See note 273.

290. Merton to Mrs. Rosenthal, June 26, 1955, Curtis Brown Files, Columbia University Libraries. "The French translator of *Sign of Jonas* got a nice letter about the book from General de Gaulle, in which he said: 'I was really struck by the many inspired thoughts in these pages, thoughts at once lofty and deep, and always so simple! Another proof of the efficacy of God's grace . . .' "

291. Dell'Isola, 17, A17. Publishing date Feb. 5, 1953.

292. "In Defense of Thomas Merton," Father Dascian Dee, *Brown Studies* (Summer 1954): 99.

293. SJ, 328, June 13, 1951.

294. NJ, Oct. 22, 1952.

295. NJ, Oct. 22, 1952.

296. NJ, Dec. 29, 1952.

297. SJ, prologue, 10.

298. NJ, Feb. 14, 1953.

299. RJ, Aug. 15, 1959. Merton says that Terrell Dickey has lent him the book. RJ, Aug. 22, 1959, Merton talks of "The Years with James." Of *The Years with Ross* he says, "It is remarkable the mixture of objective criticism, legitimate impatience, admiration, resentment and love with which Thurber looks at Ross. Very edifying in its subtle way, and yet also there is something weird about it. Maybe neurotic. Which I guess Ross was and Thurber probably is."

300. Interview with Dom John Eudes Bamberger, Mar. 21, 1981.

301. Lord Acton to Mandell Creighton, Apr. 5, 1887, cited in Acton, *Essays on Freedom and Power*, 335. "Power tends to corrupt and absolute power corrupts absolutely."

302. Interview with Brother Caspar, May 18, 1980.

303. Merton to Dom James Fox, undated, but probably June 1949, renewing vows and promising obedience, MGA.

304. Merton to Dom James Fox, Oct. 20, 1968, MGA. Reproduced, letter from Dom James Fox "To the Gethsemani Diaspora," Feb. 1, 1969, 4, TMSC. MGA. AA.

305. There was, apparently, some question of making Merton the abbot at the Genesee foundation. He, at any rate, felt there had been a threat he would be elected. However, he was to prove unrealistic about a second such threat later on, see 503–4.

306. Interview with Dom James Fox, Apr. 6, 1980. See also Dom James Fox, "To the Gethsemani Diaspora," Feb. 1, 1969, 4, TMSC. MGA. AA.

307. The vow reads in full: "Private Vow Jesus-Mary. In honor of the simplicity and humility of the Most Blessed Virgin Mother of God, and the glory of her divine Son, Jesus Christ Our Lord, I, Frater Mary Louis Merton, O.C.S.O., vow that as long as I live I will never accept any election to the office of Abbot or Titular Prior either in this monastery or any other monastery of the Cistercian Order. Made and signed in his presence and with the full approval of my Reverend Father Abbot the Right Rev. Dom Mary James Fox, O.C.S.O." The vow is signed by Merton and by Dom James and dated October 8, 1952 (MGA).

308. Interview with Father Matthew Kelty, Apr. 6, 1980. See also Kelty, *Flute Solo*, 30: "Beyond that, there is a certain character to the art of weaving that makes it especially suited to a life of prayer."

309. CGB, 26–28. Tape 4-4-64, 16A, TMSC, etc.

310. SSM, 374, see 213–14.

311. RJ, Aug. 19, 1956.

312. Dell'Isola, 22, A21, Mar. 1, 1956.

313. *Bread in the Wilderness*, 38. *Fulfillment* is given as "Fulfilment" in the original.

314. Dell'Isola, 18, A18, Dec. 23, 1953.

315. This was mentioned by a number of those interviewed. Typical of the comments were those of Brother Pascal Galligan, interview, Mar. 21, 1981, Our Lady of the

Genesee, who said that with the bafflement had come real inspiration for his religious life. The statement given in the text should be balanced by this.

316. Dell'Isola, 20, A19, June 3, 1954. The title is somewhat confusing, but this is how it is listed. The Encyclical Letter is entitled "Doctor Mellifluus."
317. *The Last of the Fathers*, etc., preface, 9.
318. Especially Tape 4–4–64, B165, TMSC. But there are many references on other conference tapes. Interviews: Father Matthew Kelty, Apr. 6, 1980, and Brother Alban Herberger, who also spoke of Merton's spirited defense of King David as a man of passion "whom God loved," rather than King Solomon, who was simply wise — this interview, July 11, 1981. Also RJ, Aug. 10, 1962, where Merton speaks of a greater liking for Abelard than St. Bernard.
319. Dell'Isola, 21, A20. Mar. 24, 1955.
320. *No Man Is An Island*, 7 (in the paperback edition this is 22).
321. Cited SP, introduction by Mark Van Doren, xi. Also cited in the preface to *The Strange Islands*: ". . . the poem arrived about the same time as the fire truck from the nearest town."
322. Interview with Brother Patrick Hart, Apr. 3, 1980.
323. "Elegy for a Monastery Barn," SP, 87–88; CP, 288–89.
324. RJ, Sept. 29, 1957. The visit is mentioned in CGB, 12–13, but not the walk or conversation. Although Dorothy Van Doren visited, the walk can only have been made by the two men, as the site was inside the enclosure. Merton's journal entry is ambiguous, and I am grateful to Brother Patrick Hart for pointing this out in correspondence.
325. Interview with Father Anastasius Fettig, Sept. 28, 1980.
326. Interviews with Dom James Fox, Apr. 6, 1980, and July 11, 1981.
327. I am especially grateful to Brother Alban Herberger for the graphic description of Merton's second attempt to master the jeep. The details are confirmed in the reports of others, but Brother Alban was an eyewitness. Interview, July 11, 1981.
328. Interviews with Dom James Fox, Apr. 6, 1980, and July 11, 1981.
329. The letter from Dom Jean Leclercq to Merton, June 2, 1959, is in the confidential files of the Legacy Trust.
330. RJ, July 28, 1959.
331. Interview with Dom John Eudes Bamberger, Mar. 22, 1981.
332. Interview with Father Matthew Kelty, Apr. 6, 1980, confirmed by many others interviewed.
333. Interview with Father Anastasius Fettig, Sept. 28, 1980. Interview with Dom John Eudes Bamberger, Mar. 22, 1981.
334. Interview with Dom John Eudes Bamberger, Mar. 22, 1981.
335. Merton to James Laughlin, June 16, 1956, JLA.
336. RJ, Aug. 19, 1956.
337. Interview with Naomi Burton Stone, May 11, 1980.
338. Notebook number 9, "Ad Usum. "Fr." M. Louis. Psych Readings" dated 1955, TMSC. This contains a list of books on Oriental subjects Merton was reading at the end. The selections from Gandhi are taken from the two-volume edition of *Non-Violence in Peace and War*. Karen Horney, *New Ways in Psychoanalysis*. Gemelli, *Psychoanalysis Today*.
339. Merton to Naomi Burton Stone, May 2 and 22, 1956, FLSB.
340. Interview with Robert Giroux, May 6, 1980. Interview with Naomi Burton Stone, May 11, 1980, and subsequent correspondence.
341. Ibid., and interview with Dom James Fox, July 11, 1981.
342. Interview with Robert Giroux, May 6, 1980.
343. Dr. Gregory Zilboorg to Merton, June 6, 1956, TMSC. It is difficult to read this letter without feeling there is a strong current of sarcasm at Merton's expense. Among other things, Merton is advised to read Abraham, rather than Freud.
344. RJ, July 22, 1956.
345. RJ, July 20, 1956. For the full quotation, see title page of "The Pasture, Merton's Heart," 91.
346. RJ, July 20, 1956.
347. RJ, July 23, 1956.

348. Ibid. Interview with Dom John Eudes Bamberger, Mar. 23, 1981.
349. Diadochos of Photike, *Centuries*, Outlines, Chap. 22, 13, 5. RJ, July 29, 1956.
350. Woodcock, *Thomas Merton, Monk and Poet*, 141ff.
351. "In Silence" is printed here with the line breaks given in CP, 280. Merton obviously revised the poem. The original in the draft of RJ, July 27, 1956, begins: "Be still / Listen to the stones of the / Wall. Be silent. Then try / To speak your // Name . . . Listen to the Living / Wall. Who are you?/ Who / Are you? Whose / Silence are you?"
352. Interview with Father Augustine Wulff, July 10, 1981.
353. RJ, July 23, 1956.
354. RJ, July 25, 1956. "Penitents" sounds odd where one might expect "patients." Merton's italics.
355. Ibid. Merton's italics.
356. RJ, July 25, 1956. Difficult to read — "other" may be "minor." Merton had grounds for being astonished. In his letter to Merton of June 6, 1956 (TMSC), Zilboorg had discouraged him from reading Freud and suggested Abraham! (See note 343.)
357. RJ, July 29, 1956. The description given is of the previous Friday, July 27. Dom John Eudes Bamberger provided his memories of this evening in interviews, Mar. 21 and 23, 1981.
358. "J. F. Powers — *Morte D'Urban:* Two Celebrations," LE, 149.
359. RJ, July 29, 1956.
360. Interviews with Dom John Eudes Bamberger, Mar. 21 and 23, 1981.
361. Merton to Naomi Burton Stone, July 30, 1956, FLSB.
362. RJ, July 28, 1959. See 288.
363. Dom James Fox to Cardinal Archbishop Giovanni Montini, May 16, 1955, TMSC. The letter is given in Furlong, 206–7. By early 1956, Merton knew that the letter of Father Barnabas Mary Ahern of January 29, 1953, to *him,* had been quoted extensively in the letter to Montini. He also knew of his abbot's comments.
364. Interviews with Dom James Fox, Apr. 6, 1980, and July 11, 1981. It became clear that there were two conferences at Collegeville, and that Dom James was present at the second but not the first. Dom James recalled the outburst and the discussion about "the Hermit of Times Square." He also recalled that Merton had claimed Zilboorg looked like Stalin. (Merton may have been thinking of Cardinal Mindszenty as a person to associate himself with in the situation — "Cardinal Mindszenty's face with huge eyes popping out of his head is posted by the Scriptorium door, next to a polite comfortable picture of what he looked like before the Reds got at him with the needle." SJ, 158, Feb. 13, 1949. See also Merton to Naomi Burton Stone, Dec. 29, 1956, FLSB, about the book Robert Giroux had sent on Mindszenty, which had been read out in the Refectory.) The Gethsemani party left St. John's on August 4, 1956 — RJ, Aug. 3, 1956. The second conference, then, was between July 30 and August 4, 1956.
365. Merton to Naomi Burton Stone, Dec. 29, 1956, FLSB. The "I don't really need analysis" of the December letter may cover the change of plan. Merton had been hinting somewhat dramatically in his letters to Naomi Burton that autumn that he might not be at Gethsemani if she came unannounced to see him.
366. RJ, Mar. 10, 1963. It is of some interest that Zilboorg told others after the conferences at St. John's that Merton was obsessed with his father. Interview with Robert Giroux, May 6, 1980. Interview with Naomi Burton Stone, May 11, 1980.
367. Interview with Dom John Eudes Bamberger, Mar. 21, 1981.
368. Interview with Brother Alban Herberger, July 11, 1981. Interview with Dom John Eudes Bamberger, Mar. 21, 1981. Interview with Father Matthew Kelty, Apr. 6, 1980.
369. RJ, July 17, 1956.
370. NJ, Oct. 22, 1952.
371. Interview with Brother Michael Casagram, July 13, 1981.
372. RJ, Aug. 21, 1981.
373. "Readings from Ibn Abbad," part 7: "To a Novice," CP, 750. *Raids on the Unspeakable*, 148.
374. Structures: but in a letter of January 7, 1950, Merton wrote to James Laughlin, "I

am appalled by the structures we build between ourselves and Him — half the time in His honor" (JLA).

375. Dell'Isola, 24, A24. Jan. 3, 1957.
376. *The Silent Life*, 92.
377. RJ, Aug. 14, 1960; CGB, 166.
378. RJ, Oct. 5, 1957.
379. RJ, Aug. 8, 1957.
380. Dell'Isola, 25, A25. Mar. 27, 1957.
381. CP, 231.
382. CP, 245.
383. CP, 286–87.
384. PSJ, Oct. 1, 1939, "Merton's political memoirs — 5."
385. CP, 275.
386. CP, 247–73. Dell'Isola, 26, A26.
387. RJ, Sept. 2, 1956. Edited, CGB, 144–45.
388. RJ, Aug. 3, 1957. *Revista Mexicana de Literatura*. Merton also heard about the racial violence in Little Rock, Arkansas, from the Van Dorens during their visit on September 29. He comments how out of touch he feels.
389. Merton was reading Shirer's book in March 1960. References, RJ.
390. Anti-poem, see Merton's essay, "War and the Crisis of Language," reprinted in *The Non-Violent Alternative*, 237, "This is beyond parody." See also xx, 460.
391. Wittgenstein, *Tractatus Logico-Philosophicus*, 150–51, 7.
392. Rilke, *Archaïscher Torso Apollos, Neue Gedichte*, II. *Ausgewählte Werke*, II (Insel-Verlag, 1948), 155. Trans. M. D. Herter Norton, *Translations from the Poetry of Rainer Maria Rilke*, 181.
393. *The Waters of Siloe*, "Note on Contemplative Order," xxxii.
394. RJ, Apr. 28, 1957.
395. CGB, 21.
396. RJ, Nov. 12, 1957.
397. RJ, Nov. 11, 1957.
398. Merton mentions reading Suzuki at St. John's, see 293. However, he may have forgotten the Columbia reference: he had to ask James Laughlin how Suzuki's name was spelt. Merton to James Laughlin, Feb. 16, 1955, JLA. "I'm getting more and more interested in Japan."
399. Russia had entered the Space Age with the first experiment on October 4, 1957. On November 11, 1957, Merton records in RJ that Eisenhower's speech on space and defense had been read in the refectory on the 10th and the 11th.
400. RJ, May 1, 1957.
401. Merton was reading Bulgakof and Soloviev in the spring of 1957.
402. RJ, Apr. 25, 1957.
403. RJ, Mar. 30, 1958.
404. RJ, Mar. 6, 1958.
405. RJ, Sept. 1, 1956.
406. RJ, Oct. 25, 1957. Merton to Naomi Burton Stone, Aug. 24, 1957, FLSB. In the letter he says, "As for myself I am getting to be deeply ashamed of my own 'spiritual writings' . . . I am beginning to feel awful funny about those Thirty Seven Meditations. Wouldn't it be better just to forget about them? . . ." "Thirty-Seven Meditations" had been drafted three years before at St. Anne's. A revised and edited version was going through press in 1957, see notes 413 and 433 below.
407. RJ, Nov. 24, 1957. The operation in November 1957 was for piles. Fourteen months earlier, Merton wrote, "Impatience is not so much a vice as a full blown disease — hereditary. I have Pop's piles and his colitis . . ." RJ, Sept. 2, 1956.
408. RJ, Dec. 14, 1957.
409. RJ, Dec. 24, 1957. Also Merton to Naomi Burton Stone, Dec. 30, 1957, FLSB and Curtis Brown Files, Columbia University Libraries. In this letter, Merton explains the situation with the censors: "As I think I have told you before, the censors of our Order fulfill the function of quasi-editors and I am at the mercy not only of their theology but of their literary tastes . . ." Father Paul Bourne had com-

plained that there were far too many passages in languages other than English. Merton goes on to say that he feels left out of negotiations: "Did you think I was somehow too truculent about the whole affair? The fact that you thought I had to be influenced through the Abbot rather than approached directly seems to indicate some such attitude . . ." See 266.

410. Catherine de Hueck Doherty to Merton, Jan. 1, 1958, TMSC; Jan. 18, 1958, Curtis Brown Files, Columbia University Libraries. See also letters between Merton and Dom Gabriel Sortais, TMSC.

411. Merton to Naomi Burton Stone, Apr. 19, 1958, Curtis Brown Files, Columbia University Libraries.

412. *The Secular Journal of Thomas Merton*, Dell'Isola, 29, A31. Feb. 2, 1959.

413. Merton to Naomi Burton Stone, Jan. 3, 1959, Curtis Brown Files, Columbia University Libraries.

414. RJ, Sept. 16, 1958.

415. RJ, Oct. 26, 1957. This started something of a struggle, because Merton wanted to have the earlier version published, while both Robert Giroux and Naomi Burton Stone pointed out that the copy of the revised version was set and passed for printing. This is discussed in Merton's letter to Naomi Burton Stone, Dec. 30, 1957, FLSB and Curtis Brown Files, Columbia University Libraries. See other publishing correspondence at this time.

416. RJ, Jan. 31, 1958.

417. RJ, Feb. 15 and 19, 1958. Cf. CGB, 148.

418. See 270.

419. RJ, Mar. 19, 1958.

420. Ibid.

421. Ibid.

422. CGB, 156–58.

423. CGB, 157. See Traherne, *Centuries, Poems and Thanksgivings*, "The Third Century," 111, 3: "The Corn was Orient and Immortal Wheat . . ." Donald Allchin had sent Merton Traherne's *Centuries* on October 15, 1963. See correspondence, TMSC.

424. CGB, 9.

425. RJ, Sept. 20, 1965.

426. RJ, Feb. 28, 1958.

427. RJ, Mar. 4, 1958.

428. Proverbs 8: 30–31. The connection with Herakleitos playing at knucklebones with the children is one Merton enjoyed too: see "Herakleitos: A Study," *The Behavior of Titans*: "Time is a child playing draughts."

429. RJ, Sept. 10, 1966. Ironically, that person was S. Merton calculated that she had been born a few months before he passed through Cincinnati on his way to Gethsemani in December 1941. He goes on, "Strange connection in my deepest heart between [S] and the 'Wisdom' figure and Mary and the Feminine in the Bible — Eve etc. Paradise-wisdom . . ."

430. RJ, Mar. 19, 1958.

431. RJ, Apr. 11, 1958: "It is more or less definite that I am to get to work on a book about Soviet Russia — from the religious viewpoint."

432. RJ, June 12, 1958, etc.

433. Merton to Naomi Burton Stone, Apr. 12, 1958, Curtis Brown Files, Columbia University Libraries. In the same letter Merton says he is reconciled to the publishing of the revised version of *Thoughts in Solitude*.

434. Merton to Naomi Burton Stone, Apr. 19, 1958, Curtis Brown Files, Columbia University Libraries. Hürlimann, *Asia*.

435. Breit, 7, 92. *Silence in Heaven: A Book of the Monastic Life*. See also *"In Silentio": A Note on Monastic Prayer*, in *Seasons of Celebration*, 204–15.

436. Merton to Naomi Burton Stone, May 20, 1958, Curtis Brown Files, Columbia University Libraries. Hürlimann's *Asia* shows Mahabalipuram (pl. 43) and Polonnaruwa (pl. 152).

437. Thoreau, *Walden*, "Economy," 2.

438. Daggy, *Introductions*, 34.

439. Ibid., 35–36.
440. RJ, Sept. 22, 1957.
441. Dell'Isola, 27, A28. Apr. 8, 1958. Breit, 9, 108.
442. Respectively: *Thoughts in Solitude*, 78, 53, 33, 41, 65, 65.
443. *Thoughts in Solitude*, 66.
444. *Thoughts in Solitude*, 44, Merton's italics.
445. RJ, Mar. 30, 1958. Merton has "ones friends."
446. SSM, 57.
447. RJ, Feb. 19, 1958.
448. The connection went back to 1955. Brother Giles had been anxious to consult the artist about the placing of some new Stations of the Cross. While they were talking, Brother Giles said that Father Louis wanted to meet Victor Hammer. Merton and Hammer soon found they had much in common.
449. Dell'Isola, 28, A29. Spring 1958. 150 copies. Breit, 6, 78.
450. The press was named after a house in Settignano, outside Florence, close to Bernard Berenson's "I Tatti," where Victor Hammer and his first wife had lived. Much of the detail in these pages (and much that has had to be excluded) was provided by the correspondence between Merton and the Hammers (TMSC) and from an interview with Carolyn Hammer, Apr. 3, 1980.
451. Dell'Isola, 138, E17.
452. Merton to James Laughlin, Mar. 18, 1960, JLA.
453. Kelty, *Flute Solo*, 23.
454. RJ, July 25, 1958.
455. Interview with Father Matthew Kelty, Apr. 6, 1980. Interview with Brother Maurice Flood, Mar. 29, 1981.
456. RJ, Oct. 26, 1957. CGB, 140–41. Also RJ, Mar. 25, 1958.
457. Interview with Father Matthew Kelty, Apr. 6, 1980. Interview with Dom John Eudes Bamberger, Mar. 24, 1981. Interview with Dom Flavian Burns, Mar. 29, 1981.
458. Yet Merton was against the abolishing of the Chapter of Faults — Tape 4–4–64, B165, TMSC.
459. The material on the Chapter of Faults was crosschecked in a number of interviews; among the most helpful on this subject were Brother Alban Herberger (July 11, 1981) and Father Anastasius Fettig (Sept. 28, 1980).
460. Tape 4–4–64, 165A ("Seven Hail Marys for the group"), TMSC.
461. Interview with monk who wishes to remain anonymous, July 12, 1981.
462. Interview with Brother Alban Herberger, July 11, 1981. Also, interview with Father Raymond Flanagan, Sept. 28, 1980, on the subject of Merton's lack of interest in moral theology.
463. RJ, Dec. 30, 1958.
464. It was Hanekamp's radio that provided Father John of the Cross and Father Louis with much of the information during the Pasternak affair.
465. RJ, Jan. 2, 1959.
466. *New York Times*, Sept. 22, 1958, 29.
467. Correspondence between Merton and Pasternak can be found in *Boris Pasternak/Thomas Merton/Six Letters* (451), TMSC, etc.
468. A copy of Merton's letter to Aleksei Surkov of Oct. 29, 1958, can be found in the revised edition of *A Thomas Merton Reader*, 272–75.
469. *Tribute to Greatness* appeared in the *New York Times*, Feb. 1, 1959. *Boris Pasternak and the People with Watch Chains*, *Jubilee*, July 1959. (The "people with watch chains" was taken from a line in Pasternak's early poem, "My Sister Life." Merton had probably forgotten about the young man with a watch chain and no watch at Columbia.) In revised form, all three articles appeared in *Disputed Questions*, 1960, 7–67, and in LE, 37–84.
470. RJ, Jan. 25, 1959.
471. "The Pasternak Affair": *Disputed Questions*, 4; LE, 38. This essay, "In Memoriam," contains a criticism of those who rushed in to claim Pasternak for Christianity — a criticism that might fairly be made against Merton himself. The situation was not unlike his defense of Joyce as a "Catholic" in debates with Catholic and non-Catholic friends at St. Bonaventure's. SBJ, Nov. 10, 1940.

472. John Harris to Merton, Nov. 18, 1958, TMSC.
473. Ibid. Enclosure, letter from Boris Pasternak to John Harris. There is further evidence of what Merton's letters had meant. Writing in German to the publisher of Pantheon Books (which had brought out *Doctor Zhivago* in the United States), Pasternak says that Merton's correspondence with him had brought him great encouragement and that he valued Merton's insight into the novel.
474. Boris Pasternak to Merton, unsigned, Nov. 7, 1958, TMSC, *Six Letters.*
475. *Disputed Questions,* 22–23. LE, 50.
476. Boris Pasternak to Merton, Oct. 3, 1958, TMSC, *Six Letters,* 8. Pasternak's translations are thought to be excellent.
477. RJ, Mar. 3, 1959. He had to give up trying to learn Russian, as he had reluctantly to abandon learning Chinese a few years later. See 372.
478. Ibid.
479. RJ, Dec. 2, 1958. RJ, Mar. 25, 1959.
480. Boris Pasternak to Merton, Feb. 7, 1960, TMSC, *Six Letters,* 2.
481. RJ, Oct. 18, 1959. Merton records the news of Pasternak's death in his journal on June 1, 1960: "Pasternak died Monday. His story is finished. It now remains to be understood."
482. Merton to Naomi Burton Stone, Apr. 12, 1958, Curtis Brown Files, op. cit.
483. Dell'Isola, 30. A32. Breit, 7, 89. *Selected Poems of Thomas Merton,* with an introduction by Mark Van Doren and a photograph on the cover taken at Gethsemani by Shirley Burden.
484. RJ, Apr. 19, 1959.
485. Interview with Father Paul Bourne, Aug. 3, 1980. RJ, Apr. 1959.
486. RJ, Apr. 23, 1959. Merton reports that he and Dom Colomban shared the same stomach complaints, which Dom Colomban had had since he had been in a prison camp.
487. RJ, Apr. 23, 1959. Interview with Carolyn Hammer, Apr. 3, 1980.
488. Merton to Victor Hammer, May 14, 1959, TMSC.
489. Victor Hammer to Merton, June 2, 1959, TMSC.
490. Merton to Boris Pasternak, Oct. 23, 1958, TMSC, *Six Letters,* 11–12.
491. Rosen, "Chaos and Dostoyevsky's Women."
492. RJ, May 3, 1959.
493. RJ, May 7, 1959.
494. *Disputed Questions,* 74. "Mount Athos," 8–16. Dell'Isola, 81, C124. Breit, 36, 421.
495. RJ, Apr. 19, 1959.
496. Bishop James P. Davis to Merton, June 18, 1959, restricted correspondence. Merton appears to have met Bishop Davis earlier. He mentions that when "Bishop Davis of San Juan, Puerto Rico" visited Gethsemani, "Reverend Father brought him into the vault to look at some old books and I was speaking to him and began to ask him about *La Soledad.* I remembered her church in Camaguey, Cuba . . ." SJ, 64, Sept. 14, 1947.
497. Bishop Dwyer to Merton, July 24, 1959, restricted correspondence.
498. RJ, June 13, 1959.
499. Bishop Niedhammer to Merton, June 29, 1959, restricted correspondence. The plan to go to the Great Corn Islands was complicated by an abortive anti-Somoza rebellion. Merton read of this in the newspaper in Lebanon, Kentucky, while he was breakfasting on the way to Lexington with James Laughlin. Later that day, he said Mass for those who had been taken prisoner (RJ, June 16, 1959). He subsequently wrote to Somoza with a plea that the prisoners not be subjected to torture and received a reply of "Injured innocence," denying that prisoners were ever tortured in Nicaragua. He learned that Pablo Antonio Cuadra had escaped to Puerto Rico.
500. When he spoke to the abbot without giving anything away, he found Dom James sympathetic to the idea of more solitude at Gethsemani, but when Merton began talking of another kind of solitude "among Indians" or "on a small island," his attitude changed completely. RJ, July 12, 1959.
501. Interview with Brother Alban Herberger, July 11, 1981. The remark of Merton's about Trappist working parties is in the entry for April 23, 1947, SJ, 41.
502. RJ, July 2, 1959, talking about the day before.

503. RJ, June 11, 1959.
504. RJ, July 16, 1959.
505. RJ, June 13, 1959.
506. RJ, June 30, 1959.
507. Ibid. Merton says elsewhere that ill health was only one of the reasons, and that Cardenal felt Gethsemani had given all it could give him.
508. RJ, Aug. 17, 1959.
509. Dom Jean Leclercq to Merton, June 2, 1959, from Vichy, restricted correspondence. Leclercq felt too much publicity had already been given and that this would damage any chance of a transfer being permitted.
510. Merton to Bishop Dwyer, Sept. 1, 1959, restricted correspondence.
511. RJ, Sept. 6, 1959, reporting on the visit of the previous day.
512. RJ, Sept. 9, 1959.
513. Merton to James Laughlin, Oct. 19, 1959, JLA.
514. RJ, Oct. 6, 1959. Merton quotes from Dom Gregorio's letter about the "French monk."
515. RJ, Nov. 15, 1960.
516. Dell'Isola, 31, A34. Breit, 2, 23. Sept. 26, 1960.
517. RJ, Nov. 23, 1959.
518. RJ, Nov. 25, 1959. Mother Angela Collins had been advising Merton and he says she was enthusiastic for the Cuernavaca plan.
519. RJ, Nov. 28, 1959, reporting on Thursday, Nov. 26.
520. RJ, Nov. 3, 1959. Merton mentions being asked to write advertising on (RJ) June 2, 1958: "Brother Clement came in with a cheese ad. again, and I worked on it, God forgive me."
521. CP, 799–800, "CHEE$E, Joyce Killer-Diller." Merton was amused to hear through the cellarer that Ezra Pound had been enthusiastic about a gift of Gethsemani Monks' Cheese from the publisher when he was incarcerated in St. Elizabeth's. Merton to James Laughlin, Sept. 11, 1950, JLA.
522. RJ, Dec. 12, 1959.
523. RJ, Dec. 17, 1959.

Mount Olivet

The continuing help of many already mentioned is acknowledged here. I am especially grateful to those who have allowed me to cite letters, in particular Carolyn Hammer, Czeslaw Milosz, and W. H. Ferry. My colleague and friend, Dr. Janis L. Pallister, professor of Romance languages, read over my translations and made helpful suggestions. I should also thank Carolyn A. Davis, manuscript librarian of the George Arents Research Library of Syracuse University, and her staff.

Epigraphs: "A Midsummer Diary," 14. Merton has been talking of Camus, the Absurd, and *The Myth of Sisyphus*. Rilke, *Sonnette an Orpheus*, 1, 5, *Ausgewählte Werke*; trans. Leishman, *Selected Works*, 255.

1. RJ, Dec. 26, 1960. *Haec regina mea in saeculum seaculi*, "This queen of mine to the end of the ages."
2. Merton to Catherine de Hueck Doherty, Nov. 21, 1964, TMSC.
3. Merton to Beatrice Katherine Merton (Aunt Ka), Sept. 23, 1964, TMSC.
4. RJ, Dec. 10, 1960.
5. Dell'Isola, 34, A37, Jan. 1962. Breit, 5, 64.
6. Valerio Cardinal Prefect Valeri and Arcadio Cardinal Larraona to Merton, Dec. 7, 1959, in French, two pages, restricted correspondence.
7. *No Man Is an Island*, 138.
8. Ibid., Merton's italics.
9. Merton to Dom Gregorio Lemercier, Dec. 17, 1959, restricted correspondence. Translation: "Father Eudes believes that Father Abbot must have told them that one

day the psychiatrist Zilboorg had casually remarked that my desire for solitude was 'pathological.' Father Eudes does not support this opinion himself, and he told me yesterday that Zilboorg was a high-spirited person who changed his opinions about things in the twinkling of an eye. Actually, later on, he seemed to think about me in quite a different manner. But Father Abbot must have fastened upon this word and onto a few others — that Zilboorg supposedly said I might well try to get out of the Church and run off with a woman. Obviously, we're all human . . . But Father Abbot must have advanced these arguments very strongly. So that's what's happened . . ." (Merton's ellipsis).

10. Ibid. Translation: "an emotional, unstable sort of person who was trying to avoid living a normal, regular life."

11. Ibid. Translation: "Now at that moment I noticed the expression on Dom James's face: he thought he'd won. To say that I had an 'intimate friend' was as good as confessing to a particular friendship . . . It was all perfectly clear in his mind — I was a homosexual! — You see how he comes to his conclusions. And because of the pleas of a superior like this, the Sacred Congregation chucked my application out."

12. Document 1, dated Dec. 17, 1959, restricted correspondence.

13. Ibid.

14. Document 2, undated, but probably Dec. 17, 1959, "Concerning the rights of conscience," restricted correspondence.

15. Ibid.

16. Ibid.

17. Interview with Dom James Fox, July 11, 1981.

18. In his letter to Father Daniélou of Dec. 5, 1959 (restricted correspondence), Merton speaks of "an acute problem as regards liberty of conscience." There are a number of statements in the journals. The most important is on freedom and obedience, RJ, Mar. 18, 1960: "Perhaps I have been struggling with an illusionary idea of freedom — as if I were not to a great extent bound by my own history, the history of this community, of the country where I have become a citizen, etc. There are only certain very limited and special avenues of freedom open to me now, and it is useless to fight my way along where no issue is possible. This is true not only exteriorly but even interiorily and spiritually. To say that God can open up new ways is perhaps, among other things, to admit only that He has provided ways for me, of which I cannot yet be aware since I am too intent upon imaginary or experimental ones."

19. Conference Tape 164B, May 2, 1964, TMSC.

20. Malits, "Conjectures of a Guilty Participant," lecture given during the conference on Thomas Merton at Georgia State University, Atlanta, Feb. 27, 1980.

21. RJ, Dec. 18, 1959.

22. Ibid.

23. RJ, Dec. 20, 1959.

24. RJ, Dec. 26, 1959, describing the trip on the 22nd. Merton writes of the Founder of the Shakers, "Mother Ann Lee thought she was Sophia." He had visited Shaker-town briefly with James Laughlin on June 7, 1959.

25. Dell'Isola 60, B36. Breit, 150. Merton wrote the introduction only.

26. Shirley Burden to Merton, Dec. 16, 1959, Jan. 19, 1960, Mar. 21, 1960 (this letter mentions the Lourdes project and also introduces "Mr. and Mrs. Edward Deming Andrews," who were to be Merton's best contact with the Shakers, and friends. Shirley Burden's letter of January 11, 1961, gives a generous four pages of information on the Shakers, and ends, "Well, now you know all I know at present about the Shakers" (TMSC. AA).

27. PSJ, Oct. 22, 1939.

28. CGB, 148–49.

29. For his use of black and white in painting and drawing, see 163. Merton had shown a strong prejudice against color photographs of fall coloring in *The National Geographic* at St. Bonaventure (SBJ). Later, on October 10, 1961 (RJ), after taking a roll of color photographs of the hermitage, he writes: "It is 'enriched' with all kinds of

synthetic colors. It is full of spiritual plastics. It is . . . kodacolor." (Merton's ellipsis). He did take several rolls of color in New Mexico in May 1968.

30. CGB, 149.
31. Ibid.
32. RJ, Apr. 24, 1960.
33. For Merton as photographer see Griffin, *Wholeness*, Patnaik, *Geography of Holiness*. See also *Zen and the Birds of Appetite*, 5.
34. RJ, Dec. 31, 1959: "Got permission today for a few sessions with Dr. Wygal in Louisville — since I am sure Rev. Father's argument before the Congregation was based on a couple of wild remarks by Zilboorg that I was likely to take off with a woman and leave the Church, etc. So it would do no harm to find out if I am just suffering from neurotic instability or what I do not think I am."
35. Interview with Dom John Eudes Bamberger, Mar. 21, 1981.
36. RJ, July 4, 1960.
37. Interview with James Laughlin, Oct. 25, 1979. This is also covered in correspondence between James Laughlin and Ernesto Cardenal, and between Laughlin and the Hammers, JLA.
38. James Laughlin to Robert MacGregor, in pencil, Jan. 13, 1960, JLA.
39. Ibid.
40. See 192–93.
41. RJ, Jan. 14, 1960, talking about previous day.
42. Dell'Isola, 127. D4. Much delayed, it was published Apr. 26, 1961. Breit, 9, 117.
43. RJ, Feb. 14, 1960. Merton to James Laughlin, Jan. 29, 1960, JLA.
44. Business correspondence of Feb. 6, 1960, New Directions Archives, JLA.
45. First published in *New Directions* 17, 1961, the exchange between Merton and Suzuki appeared in *Zen and the Birds of Appetite*, 99–141, 1968.
46. Dell'Isola, 31, A34, Sept. 26, 1960. Breit, 2, 23. For the letter from Dom Gabriel Sortais see the correspondence file, TMSC. Merton refers to the letter, RJ, Feb. 14, 1960.
47. RJ, Feb. 27, 1960. Interview with Robert Giroux, May 6, 1980.
48. For example, RJ, July 12, 1959 — Merton had been reading Henri Troyat's *La Case de l'oncle Sam*. After expressing his admiration for French journalism, Merton says, "The faults of Gethsemani are American faults — puerility, rationalizations, idiot belief in gadgets, fetish worship of machines and efficiency, love of a big showey facade (and nothing behind it), phoney optimism, sentimentalism, etc."
49. See 315.
50. This was especially true in light of Merton's friendships through correspondence with those who were leading the non-violent opposition to France's war in Algeria, above all Louis Massignon. From 1959 until Merton learned of his death (RJ, Nov. 20, 1962), Massignon provided much information on the practical application of non-violence. He also established contacts between Merton and Moslem religious figures.
51. RJ, Apr. 24, 1960. Dom Gabriel had consulted with Father Paul Philippe. On January 31, 1960 (RJ), Merton celebrated the news that Father Philippe had taken Larraona's place as secretary to the Congregation of Religious — "certainly the best friend I have in Rome! What a birthday present!" Merton may or may not have known that Father Paul Philippe was also Dom James Fox's friend. A later collaboration with James Baldwin was also judged "inappropriate." Merton to Father Paul Bourne, May 1, 1963, TMSC.
52. RJ, Mar. 8, 1960, reporting on the night before.
53. Interview with Dom James Fox, July 11, 1981. Interview with Father Anastasius Fettig, Sept. 28, 1980. Dom James would also have had in mind the disastrous fire at Our Lady of the Valley; see note 345, "The Pasture."
54. Interview with Father Anastasius Fettig, Sept. 28, 1980. Much of the material here was provided or confirmed by Brother Patrick Hart.
55. RJ, Mar. 31, 1960.
56. RJ, July 12, 1960.
57. RJ, Mar. 29, 1960.
58. RJ, Mar. 24, 1960.

59. RJ, Jan. 17, 1960.
60. RJ, Feb. 3, 1960.
61. RJ, Mar. 16, 1960.
62. On January 14, 1960, Merton wrote (RJ): "Trevor-Roper's book, which solicits my agreement, and makes me wonder if I am being tempted to treachery. Too much of the instinct to be unfaithful to those with whom, after all, my lot has been cast. One has to remain identified to them in and with their faults. This running everywhere in search of rightness and purity ends nowhere. Still, his evaluation of Erasmus, More, the Recusants, and incidentally Newman, is moving and right. I will not be a propagandist — or is that a decision I have made too late? Silly question. I will try to no longer be one."
63. RJ, Mar. 8, 1960. The letter had arrived the day before.
64. RJ, Jan. 1, 1960.
65. RJ, Mar. 16 and 18, 1960.
66. RJ, Merton received news of the arrest of Louis Massignon and Father Régamey and the demonstration outside the Vincennes Prison on May 8, 1960.
67. RJ, Apr. 14 and 24, 1960.
68. Julian of Norwich (Lady Julian), *Revelations of Divine Love.* I have taken lines from chaps. 29 and 27, reversing these from their original order, and the translation into modern English is my own. In Clifton Wolters's translation into modern English, the relevant sections read: ". . . This our blessed Lord answered most humbly and cheerfully, showing me that the greatest wrong ever done was Adam's sin. This, moreover, is clearly recognized throughout Holy Church on earth. Furthermore he taught me that I should see the glorious reparation, for this making amends is incomparably more pleasing and honouring to God than ever was the sin of Adam harmful . . ." (29) ". . . But Jesus, who in this vision informed me of all I needed, answered, 'Sin was necessary — but it is all going to be all right; it is all going to be all right; everything is going to be all right . . .'" (27). Dorothy Day quotes Julian of Norwich in her letter to Merton on the Feast of the Assumption, 1961, TMSC.
69. RJ, Apr. 13, 1960.
70. RJ, Apr. 29, 1960.
71. RJ, Apr. 24, 1960.
72. RJ, Apr. 29, 1960. A skete is a collection of small cottages for hermits around a parent monastery — Eastern Orthodox Church, from Skete, the area in northern Egypt of the Desert Fathers.
73. RJ, May 8, 1960.
74. Ibid.
75. RJ, May 25, 1960.
76. Interview with Monsignor Raymond Treece, Aug. 8, 1980.
77. RJ, May 18, 1960.
78. RJ, Oct. 3, 1960.
79. RJ, Oct. 9, 1960.
80. RJ, Oct. 28, 1960, reporting on Oct. 25. Furniture: RJ, Oct. 29, 1960: "The other day we returned from Cincinnati through Lexington and had supper at Victor Hammer's. A pleasant evening. Rain on the shining streets, under the thick trees by the library. The warm lights of the house, and after supper, brandy in front of an open fire. Spoke of getting some furniture for the hermitage. He [Victor Hammer] knows someone who will copy the table he made for himself in his print shop . . ." RJ, Dec. 23, 1960: "Very cold. Zero this morning. Snow two nights ago, after the rainy day when David Rowland came from Lexington with the redwood table for Saint Mary of Carmel and got stuck in the mud behind the sheep barn." The redwood table Rowland made from Hammer's drawings was modeled on a Shaker schoolboy's desk. It is still in the hermitage.
81. RJ, Oct. 29, 1960.
82. RJ, Dec. 13, 1960.
83. But see note 51 above.
84. Interview with James Laughlin, Oct. 25, 1979, and correspondence. According to Laughlin, they were very worldly priests who offered to entertain him well in Spain,

and who were afraid Dom James might not let them see Father Louis, so they worked out an elaborate secret code and a number of plans worthy of a seventeenth-century Spanish drama. Merton obviously got mixed up, and in his account on July 30, 1960 (RJ), the pair are Mexican priests. Whatever their plans, they did not get into the monastery.

85. CWL, 69, 121.
86. RJ, Jan. 1, 1960. Merton made two important statements in a memorandum dated September 19, 1960, among the restricted correspondence: "The question of obedience is delicate . . . In point of fact there has to be some protection against my self-will."
87. T. F. Burns to Merton, Mar. 22, 1963, AA.
88. Merton to T. F. Burns, July 10, 1963, TMSC.
89. RJ, May 21, 1960.
90. Merton to Edward Deming Andrews, Aug. 22, 1961, postscript, TMSC.
91. RJ, Sept. 23, 1962. Cf. CGB, 259; CWL, 104, 171.
92. RJ, June 29, 1961. Somewhat altered, CGB, 49.
93. RJ, July 23, 1961. It should be St. Edmund Hall, Oxford, not St. Edmund's.
94. Merton to Czeslaw Milosz, Dec. 6, 1958, AA.
95. Czeslaw Milosz to Merton, Oct. 5, 1961, TMSC.
96. Milosz visited Merton at Gethsemani on September 10, 1964. They met briefly later on in California in 1968, see 541.
97. RJ, Feb. 24, 1959: "Fine letter from Czeslaw Milosz in Paris. I had written about *The Captive Mind*. He replied at length about Alpha, Beta, etc., gave information about books, said he had translated some poems of mine into Polish. Sense of dealing, for once, with a real person, with one who has awakened out of sleep." Czeslaw Milosz to Merton, undated, from Paris: "You are for me important, I feel in you a friend with whom I can be completely frank" (TMSC).
98. Merton to Czeslaw Milosz, Mar. 15, 1968, TMSC.
99. Czeslaw Milosz to Merton, July 16, 1959, TMSC.
100. Merton to Czeslaw Milosz, May 21, 1959, TMSC. AA.
101. Czeslaw Milosz to Merton, Jan. 11, 1959, TMSC.
102. CWL, 31, 58.
103. Victor Stier to W. H. Ferry, Dec. 15, 1968, AA.
104. Czeslaw Milosz to Merton, Jan. 17, 1959, TMSC.
105. Ibid., Feb. 28, 1960, TMSC.
106. Ibid.
107. Merton to Czeslaw Milosz, May 6, 1963, TMSC.
108. Czeslaw Milosz to Merton, May 19, 1963, TMSC.
109. RJ, Sept. 9, 1968.
110. Merton to Czeslaw Milosz, Feb. 28, 1959, TMSC.
111. Ibid.
112. Czeslaw Milosz to Merton, July 16, 1959, TMSC.
113. Ibid., undated, from California, Fall 1960 (?), TMSC.
114. Merton to Czeslaw Milosz, May 23, 1961, TMSC.
115. Czeslaw Milosz to Merton, June 15, 1961, TMSC.
116. Ibid.
117. Ibid., July 8, 1960, TMSC.
118. Ibid., Feb. 28, 1960, TMSC. Milosz had already opened this question in an undated letter from Paris, TMSC. AA.
119. CGB, 138–39. RJ, May 8, 1960.
120. Merton to Czeslaw Milosz, May 6, 1960, TMSC.
121. Czeslaw Milosz to Merton, Feb. 28, 1960, TMSC.
122. Ibid., Mar. 14, 1962, TMSC.
123. Merton to Czeslaw Milosz, May 21, 1959, TMSC.
124. RJ, Mar. 3, 1960.
125. Father Paul Bourne to Merton, Jan. 23, 1965, TMSC.
126. Ibid., Feb. 12, 1965, TMSC.
127. RJ, Sept. 2, 1962.
128. Merton to John Beecher, poet, printer, activist, July 9, 1963, TMSC.

129. Dell'Isola, 91, C209, *Blackfriars* 44, no. 521 (November 1963): 464–77. C210, *Blackfriars* 44, no. 522 (December 1963): 503–16. Breit, 32, 378. These appeared ultimately in *Seeds of Destruction*, 1964, part 1, 3–71.
130. Dell'Isola, 167, G40. Breit, 67, 780.
131. Dell'Isola, 28, A29. Breit, 6, 78.
132. RJ, Apr. 13, 1960. Dell'Isola, 138, E14. Breit, 8, 99.
133. RJ, May 16, 1960.
134. Dell'Isola, 138, E15. Breit, 15, 167. CP, 970–71. Also published in *Mystics and Zen Masters*, 66–68. The translation was made from the literal translation from the Chinese of I. A. Richards, at the back of his book on *Mencius on the Mind*, appendix. *The Ox Mountain*, 9–12. The "night-spirit" appears in I. A. Richards's text.
135. Dell'Isola, 138, E16. Breit, 3, 36. Included in *Emblems of Fury*, 149ff. CP, 363–71.
136. RJ, July 2, 1960.
137. Merton to Victor Hammer, May 14, 1959, TMSC.
138. RJ, Jan. 26, 1961. On September 18, 1959 (RJ), Merton wrote: "Have been reading a marvellous book of Theology by the Orthodox Father Paul Evdokimov who teaches at Saint Serge in Paris . . ." Merton spent much of the January retreat in 1960 reading and rereading Evdokimov before reading Quasimodo's poem on Auschwitz (see note 150 below), the "night face" here. (Corrected to Evdokimov.) See CGB, 337–39. See bibliography, 670.
139. RJ, Mar. 11, 1961.
140. CWL, 51, 92. Merton is trying to explain to Sister Madeleva at St. Mary's College, Notre Dame, why he left Julian of Norwich out of the notes on English mystics ultimately included in *Mystics and Zen Masters*. The letter is included in *Seeds of Destruction*, 274–75.
141. CP, 367.
142. CP, 370.
143. CP, 371.
144. SJ, 262, Jan. 3, 1950.
145. RJ, Oct. 29, 1960.
146. RJ, July 4, 1960.
147. RJ, July 18, 1961.
148. "An Elegy for Ernest Hemingway," last line, CP, 315–16.
149. CP, 345–49.
150. See also the pages on Shirer's book CGB, 241–43. The poem also has connections to Quasimodo's poem (see note 138 above). RJ, Jan. 26, 1961: "Quasimodo's wonderful poem on Auschwitz" . . . "I am deeply impressed by Quasimodo, richness, firmness of his imagery, sober, spiritual. He is no Marxist poet, even though his political sympathies may be that way. He is of my country" (CGB, 57–58).
151. See 178.
152. *The Geography of Lograire*, North, Queens Tunnel, see esp. 44, "Most holy incense burners of Elmhurst save us." See 398.
153. RJ, July 18, 1961.
154. Ibid. CGB, 55.
155. Dell'Isola, 86, C173. 87, C177a. *Carta a Pablo Antonio Cuadra con Respecto a los Gigantes* first appeared in *Sur*, 275 (March–April 1962): 1–13. In English, in *Emblems of a Season of Fury*, and CP, 372–91.
156. CWL, 3, 4.
157. RJ, Sept. 19, 1961.
158. RJ, Sept. 24, 1961.
159. Ibid.
160. RJ, Sept. 23, 1961.
161. RJ, June 6, 1961.
162. Interview with Naomi Burton Stone, May 11, 1980, and unpublished notes.
163. RJ, June 15, 1961.
164. RJ, Oct. 15, 1961. Merton announces the last bloom, on the Feast of St. Teresa.
165. CGB, 131, 151 (where he talks of Louis Massignon's idea of the *point vierge* of the spirit), 158.
166. CWL, 94, 154.

167. SP, 110–11 (This is the last line of "Grace's House"). CP, 330–31.
168. Dell'Isola, 170, G66. Breit, 69, 793. See Lentfoehr, *Words*, 86–87.
169. CWL, 94, 154.
170. Ibid.
171. RJ, Nov. 9, 1960.
172. CGB, 58.
173. "The Machine in the Fallout Shelter," *The Nonviolent Alternative*, 103–6. See also correspondence between Merton and Edward Rice, TMSC.
174. CWL, 1, 1.
175. RJ, June 6, 1960. CGB, 107, 175.
176. RJ, Oct. 23, 1961, "The General himself is more understanding [than his secretary] and Dom James too sees the point somewhat (they surprisingly released *Original Child Bomb* after the censors had definitely blocked it)."
177. Dell'Isola, 33, A36. Jan. 4, 1962. Breit, 5, 61.
178. Dell'Isola, 34, A37. Jan. 30, 1962. Breit, 5, 64.
179. Dell'Isola, 35, A38. Mar. 21, 1962, though copyright Dec. 1961. Breit, 6, 70.
180. RJ, Oct. 27, 1961.
181. Merton to T. F. Burns, Burns and Oates, July 10, 1963, TMSC.
182. Robert Lax to Merton, Mar. 13, 1964. *A Catch of Anti-Letters*, 38.
183. Dell'Isola, 37, A40. Spring 1963. Breit, 4, 38.
184. Dell'Isola, 36, A39. Oct. 24, 1962. Breit, 9, 106.
185. Merton to W. H. Ferry, May 8, 1962, and July 1, 1964, TMSC.
186. RJ, Oct. 7, 1962.
187. Shannon, *Thomas Merton's Dark Path*.
188. Dell'Isola, 85, C162. *Jubilee* 9, no. 8 (December 1961): 8–11. *New Seeds of Contemplation*, 290–97. *A Thomas Merton Reader*, 500–505. Breit, 29, 334.
189. *New Seeds of Contemplation*, 297.
190. RJ, Sept. 24, 1961.
191. Merton to Edward Deming Andrews, Aug. 22, 1961, TMSC.
192. Merton often mentions walking barefoot in the journals, and see *Seasons of Celebration*, 117: "Going barefoot is a joyous thing." His father, too, liked to kick off his boots working, even outside in winter: see 8.
193. CWL, 8, 14; 12, 23.
194. RJ, Mar. 12, 1962. Merton mentions the visit of Paul Sih, and that Sih had tried to teach him how to use the dictionary. See also the correspondence with Dr. John Wu, TMSC. On December 20, 1962, Dr. Wu writes to Merton, "We shall know it in Heaven why you are so Chinese in your ways of thinking . . ."
195. RJ, Mar. 12, 1962.
196. Merton speaks of the "dark way" in Sufism, CGB, 211. Among many other references, see CWL, 67, 114–16.
197. RJ, Jan. 19, 1962. James Laughlin had been there on the 16th and 17th.
198. RJ, Jan. 12, 1962. CGB, 220.
199. Conference Tapes 4–4–64, 165A. Cf. RJ, Jan. 3, 1962. Also, Merton to Edward Deming Andrews, Aug. 22, 1962, TMSC, reproduced CWL, 19, 25.
200. RJ, Mar. 24, 1962.
201. Merton to Father Paul Bourne, Apr. 28, 1962, TMSC.
202. Merton to W. H. Ferry, Dec. 21, 1961, TMSC.
203. Merton to James Laughlin, Dec. 31, 1961, JLA.
204. Dell'Isola, 62. B42. Sept. 1962. Breit, 15, 168.
205. RJ, Oct. 23, 1961.
206. RJ, Mar. 17, 1962. Merton to W. H. Ferry, Mar. 16, 1962, CWL, 55, 99–100.
207. Merton to W. H. Ferry, Mar. 6, 1962, TMSC. (It was Erasmus who numbered Socrates among the saints, though it is possible he was quoting from one of the Fathers of the Church.)
208. RJ, June 24, 1960.
209. Merton to W. H. Ferry, Jan. 18, 1962, TMSC.
210. Ibid. Also CWL: 13, 24; 58, 104–5; 59, 105–7; 105, 171–74.
211. "A Martyr for Peace and Unity: Father Max Josef Metzger (1887–1944)," *The Non-*

violent Alternative, 139–43. This article gives details of the founding of Una Sancta, Metzger's interest in ecumenicalism before World War II, his opposition to Hitler, and extracts from his prison letters. For Merton's interest, and reaction to the article, see CWL: 13, 24; 33, 61–62; 38, 69; 59, 107.

212. "Danish Nonviolent Resistance to Hitler," *The Nonviolent Alternative,* 165–67.
213. CWL: 38, 70; 55, 100; 90, 144, etc.
214. CWL: 25, 50; 72, 125; 90, 144–49. *The Nonviolent Alternative,* 16–17, 77, etc.
215. "Open Letter to the American Bishops," 1, TMSC. *Life and Holiness,* 80, "Faith is therefore a gratuitous gift of God, given according to God's good pleasure, refused by him to those who are obstinate in clinging to human prejudice and to the mythology of racial, national, or class pride . . .''
216. Merton to W. H. Ferry, June 4, 1962, TMSC. Edited in CWL, 77, 129–30. Also, "Saint Maximus the Confessor on Nonviolence," *The Nonviolent Alternative,* 172–77. RJ, May 1, 12, 1962, etc.
217. CWL, 90, 149. Szilard, "Are We On the Road to War?" 23–30. Also CWL: 84, 138; 90, 146.
218. CWL, 1961, 1962, preface, 4–5, TMSC.
219. CWL, 14, 27.
220. CWL: 19, 36; 53, 95–97; 103, 169 ("That Council! Such hopes and such fears!"); 105, 174.
221. "Letter from Thomas Merton — February, 1962," in *A Penny a Copy: Readings from the 'Catholic Worker,'* ed. Thomas C. Cornell and James H. Forest (New York: Macmillan, 1968), 207–9. Merton to Father Paul Bourne, Apr. 28, 1962, TMSC.
222. Dorothy Day to Merton, Oct. 10, 1961 (?), TMSC.
223. Nov. 7, 1958. RJ, Nov. 18, 1958: "Aldous Huxley's article on drugs that produce visions and ecstasies has reached me with the protests of various Catholic women (sensible ones). I wrote to him about it yesterday and the article is on the notice-board in the Novitiate Conference Rooms." Merton to Huxley, Nov. 27, 1958; Huxley to Merton, Jan. 10, 1959, TMSC. Both letters are published in *Letters of Aldous Huxley.* See also Sussmann, 140–42. Merton offered to write an article for the *Saturday Evening Post* in reply to Huxley, but this was turned down.
224. *Zen and the Birds of Appetite,* 28, "Meanwhile drugs appeared as a *deus ex machina* to enable the self-aware Cartesian consciousness to extend its awareness of itself while seemingly getting out of itself . . .''
225. Naomi Burton Stone to Merton, Aug. 12, 1964, FLSB.
226. RJ, Apr. 27, 1962.
227. "Prayer for Peace," *The Nonviolent Alternative,* 268–70.
228. Dom Gabriel Sortais to Merton, May 12, 1962, TMSC. Translation: "I am perfectly aware, dear Son, that you do not claim to be the only one to speak on the problem of atomic warfare and to be the person who inspired the Cardinal Archbishop of Chicago. I only want to emphasize quite clearly the differences between the two orders: (1) The one that teaches, that is linked to the hierarchy and also linked to those that the hierarchy chooses to delegate for that purpose; and (2) the one that prays, the one that belongs (among others) to the monk, or rather, to which the monk belongs.
   "Please understand that I am not asking you to remain indifferent to the fate of the world. But I believe you have the power to influence the world by your prayers and by your life withdrawn into God far more than by your writings. That is why I am not thinking about hurting the cause you are defending when I ask that you give up your intention of publishing the book you have finished, and abstain from now on from writing on the subject of atomic warfare, preparation for it, etc.''
229. Merton to W. H. Ferry, June 4, 1962, TMSC.
230. For just one example, see Merton to Leslie Dewart, Apr. 27, 1963, TMSC.
231. CWL, 61, 109.
232. *Seasons of Celebration,* 18.
233. Ibid.
234. *The New Man,* 72.
235. *Seasons of Celebration,* 7.

236. *The Nonviolent Alternative*, 234–47. "War and the Crisis of Language," Dell'Isola, 67, B72. Breit, 18, 197.
237. See 3. RJ, Nov. 4, 1961. Edited, CGB, 200–201.
238. Forest, "Thomas Merton's Struggle with Peacemaking," 23.
239. RJ, Apr. 14, 1962.
240. Merton to John Wu, Mar. 14, 1961, TMSC.
241. RJ, June 26, 1962. Merton records this as St. John the Baptist's Day.
242. Merton to John Wu, June 7, 1962, TMSC. The letter to Wu appears in CWL, 82, 136.
243. Undated, this is in the W. H. Ferry File, TMSC. Undoubtedly Ferry sent the cutting to Merton, who received it before May 19, 1962, when he records receiving a "heartbreaking picture of Chinese refugee girl in Hong Kong" (RJ).
244. "From the Second Chapter of a Verse History of the World," CP, 15.
245. "A Picture of Lee Ying," SP, 107–9; CP, 322–24.
246. Henry Fielding, *Tom Jones* (Harmondsworth: Penguin Classics, 1963), 109.
247. RJ, Mar. 2, 1962.
248. RJ, Aug. 21, 1962. Cf. CGB, 251.
249. Merton to Father Daniel Berrigan, Nov. 27, 1962, TMSC.
250. Merton to Ernesto Cardenal, Nov. 17, 1962; Feb. 25, 1963, TMSC.
251. RJ, Feb. 22, 1961.
252. Dell'Isola, 37, A41, Dec. 20, 1963. Breit, 3, 26.
253. RJ, Aug. 7, 1961. CGB, 188.
254. CGB, 187.
255. "On Remembering Monsieur Delmas," Ernst, 47–53.
256. Merton to John Wu, June 23, 1963, TMSC.
257. RJ, Dec. 17, 1962. "Today, I sent off three envelopes full of articles to the Goss-Mayrs in Vienna. They have seen the Abbot General and have his permission now to collect a "dossier" of my material and present it for consideration by the Council Fathers and Theologians who are perhaps to prepare a schema on nuclear war for the Council. In any case I am grateful to have some paper to offer, even though it may not be very clear theologically."
258. Merton tries to answer this accusation of Father John Ford, see CWL, 23, 41–43/44.
259. RJ, May 10, 1963.
260. RJ, June 4, 1963, reporting news of day before.
261. RJ, Nov. 14, 1963.
262. Forest, "Thomas Merton's Struggle with Peacemaking," 24.
263. Henry Miller to Merton, July 4, 1964, TMSC. This letter, with others of the Merton-Miller correspondence, was published in *Louisville Today*, May 1981, 33.
264. Interview with Monsignor Raymond Treece, Aug. 6, 1980.
265. RJ, Apr. 29, 1961. Interview with Brother Michael Casagram, July 13, 1981.
266. Rabbi Lou H. Silberman to the author, Oct. 31, 1980.
267. CGB, 245.
268. RJ, Oct. 2, 1963.
269. Ibid. Also CGB, 257.
270. RJ, Sept. 6, 1962. CGB, 197, 258. See also Groves, "The Gregarious Hermit," 89.
271. RJ, Apr. 15, 1967, etc.
272. Merton to Edward Deming Andrews, Dec. 28, 1962, TMSC: "I was touched at your thoughtfulness in sending me the music for the song 'Decisive Work.' It is what I would have expected, and I have learned it now, so that I can sing it to myself from time to time when I am alone . . ."
273. RJ, Sept. 15, 1962.
274. RJ, Jan. 4, 1963.
275. Ibid.
276. RJ, Jan. 25, 1963.
277. Dell'Isola, 157, F99. *Saturday Review*, August 10, 1963, 32. Breit, 50, 592. SP, 116–17. CP, 335–37.
278. The bombing took place on September 15, 1963. See "The Birmingham Bombing: Twenty Years Later, the Case that Won't Close," a strong, sensitive piece of investigative reporting by Howell Raines, *New York Times Magazine*, July 24, 1983.

279. RJ, Sept. 19, 1963.
280. CP, 626.
281. The photograph was by Chris McNair. Merton kept the tear-out in the front of his typescript of "The Vow of Conversation," but I have not been able to trace the source.
282. *Seeds of Destruction*, 63–64.
283. RJ, Jan. 18, 1967. (Inconsistent capitalization of "Negro" in original.)
284. Merton to W. H. Ferry, June 12, 1963, TMSC.
285. RJ, Mar. 24, 1962: "Yesterday finished the Griffin book 'Black Like Me,' moved and disturbed. As someone said — what there is in the South is not a negro problem but a white problem. The trouble is pathological." He had forgotten that on March 9, 1962, he wrote in his journal, "As Richard Wright said: 'There is no negro problem in the U.S., there is only a white problem.' " Merton not a Southerner: RJ, Feb. 10, 1966: "Today I finished a first draft of an article for Katallagete which was difficult to write. They insist on my writing something and I do not really know the South. So it is general! . . ."
286. "From Non-Violence to Black Power," *Faith and Violence*, 121–29. "Ethnocentric," 125. This is one of the few instances one can think of where Merton is practicing "doublethink" by Orwellian terms.
287. "In Acceptance of the Pax Medal, 1963," *The Nonviolent Alternative*, 258.
288. Merton to James Laughlin, Apr. 21, 1963, JLA.
289. Merton to Father John Loftus, Apr. 17, 1963, TMSC.
290. RJ, June 5, 1963.
291. The Thomas Merton Collection had been initiated at Bellarmine College Library in September, 1963, by a committee under the chairmanship of Father John T. Loftus. The abbot gave a reluctant approval, and the collection was formally opened on November 10, 1963. Merton's statement was read by Daniel C. Walsh. With gifts from Dr. and Mrs. Irvin Abell, Jr., and from Mr. and Mrs. Cornelius Hubbuch, the Merton Room came into being and was dedicated and opened on November 8, 1964. See *Merton Studies Center*, Merton, Horrigan, Griffin.
292. Interview with Dom Flavian Burns, Sept. 29, 1980.
293. Merton to Father Chrysogonus Waddell, Jan. 26, 1963, TMSC.
294. Ibid., Nov. 23, 1964.
295. RJ, Nov. 12, 1963.
296. RJ, Mar. 21, 1963.
297. RJ, Nov. 25, 1963.
298. RJ, Nov. 20, 1963, reporting on events of the day before.
299. RJ, Jan. 1, 1964. VOW, 1.
300. Interview with Brother Patrick Hart, Apr. 5, 1980.
301. RJ, Jan. 1, 1964. CGB, 346. *Faith and Violence*, 300.
302. RJ, May 8, 1960.
303. CWL, 68, 118.
304. CWL, 32, 60.
305. RJ, Apr. 17, 1964, reporting on the day before. VOW, 39.
306. *Gandhi on Non-Violence*, 8. Italicized in the original.
307. Ibid., 3.
308. RJ, May 14, 1960. He refers to *The Human Condition* in his introduction to *Gandhi on Non-Violence*, 7. RJ, Mar. 27, 1963, he reports he is reading Hannah Arendt's articles and is devastated by them.
309. *Raids on the Unspeakable*, 45–49. *The Nonviolent Alternative*, 160–62. Merton's italics.
310. RJ, Oct. 24, 1957, also Oct. 25, 1957. CGB, 14. There are many references to Merton's "devout meditation" on the massacre of European Jewry in *Conjectures of a Guilty Bystander*, most notably the passages on Christian anti-Semitism, 170–71 (see also note 314 below). Merton's contacts with Jewish scholars were of particular importance in the early 1960s.
311. CWL, 5, 7. Again, there are many references in the *Cold War Letters*, both to the Jewish religion, and to Merton's feeling of identity with the Jews.
312. CWL, 37, 67. On Feb. 6, 1962 (RJ), Merton mentions finishing *The Last of the Just*.
313. RJ, July 14, 1964. Merton reports on Heschel's visit the day before, and his trip

with Father Flavian to the Louisville airport to meet Heschel. He was obviously excited. On May 11, 1959 (RJ), Merton reported that Robert Lax had brought him a set of proofs of Heschel's *Between God and Man* to read. On the drive to the monastery, Heschel said he had little hope the Jewish Chapter would be accepted in the Council. See also VOW, 61.

314. RJ, Sept. 10, 1964, etc. Reading notebooks (#73, etc.) on Rolf Hochhuth's *Der Stellvertreter* (which Merton translates as "The Representative," possibly because the play had first appeared in English with this title in London). The critique, retitled "The Trial of Pope Pius XII: Rolf Hochhuth's *The Deputy*," written in 1963, was not published until 1981, see LE, 162–67. Merton sent an early draft of the critique to Justus George Lawler, the editor of *Continuum*. Lawler wanted to use it, but Merton was obviously nervous (RJ, Apr. 28, 1964; VOW, 44). On this subject Merton got really angry, ". . . Reflect that the Church in this rather imperfect sense (of Bishops, etc., speaking more or less humanely and politically) delivered the Jews over to Hitler without a murmur (here and there helping a few individuals to escape, to make it less intolerable to conscience)" (RJ, Sept. 10, 1964). In VOW, 74, this is edited, but only a little softened.

315. Merton to Abraham J. Heschel, Sept. 9, 1964, TMSC. VOW, 73–74.

316. Abraham J. Heschel to Merton, Oct. 30, 1964, TMSC. Part of Heschel's earlier bulletin on the Jewish Chapter and its revision read: "Jews throughout the world will be dismayed by a call from the Vatican to abandon their faith in a generation which witnessed the massacre of six million Jews and the destruction of thousands of synagogues on a continent where the dominant religion was not Islam, Buddhism, or Shintoism" (TMSC).

317. RJ, Aug. 24, 1964.

318. RJ, June 2, 1964. VOW, 43.

319. RJ, July 24, 1962. CGB, 246.

320. RJ, July 12, 1965 (the invitation had arrived on Wednesday, the 19th). VOW, 52.

321. RJ, June 12, 1964. James Laughlin was somewhat outraged by how little Merton was given for expenses (interview with James Laughlin, Oct. 25, 1979), especially in the light of the royalties paid on his books. In his interview of July 11, 1981, Dom James Fox stressed that Father Louis had taken a vow of poverty.

322. There are two main accounts of Merton's time in New York, June 15 to early June 18, 1964. These are RJ, June 20, 1964 (VOW, 53–56), and RJ, July 10, 1964 (VOW, 58–60). The two accounts are combined here. It is very hard to read Merton's room number at Butler Hall in the original journal. VOW gives it as 13Q on the thirteenth floor. The overview of New York is reported in RJ, June 20, 1964.

323. RJ, June 15, 1964. VOW, 53.

324. RJ, July 10, 1964. VOW, 58.

325. RJ, June 20, 1964. VOW, 54.

326. RJ, June 20, 1964. VOW, 56.

327. RJ, June 20, 1964. VOW, 54.

328. *Zen and the Birds of Appetite*, 62. *Mystics and Zen Masters*, 41.

329. RJ, July 10, 1964. VOW, 59: "Anything but soul-less," Merton was remembering the title "City Without a Soul," which was forced on him by the Moderator at Oakham. See 61.

330. RJ, Sept. 26, 1964. This was a Kodak Instamatic, lent to Merton by Brother Ephraim on September 22, when he photographed a cedar root on the porch of the hermitage. On September 24, Merton talks of "Zen photography" in his journal; the back came open and would not close (unlike his earlier Number 2 Brownie). On November 22, 1964, he was using the repaired camera to take photographs of an old root in the Gethsemani woods. RJ.

331. Merton first mentions "abstract drawings," RJ, Oct. 28, 1960, and again, Nov. 8, 1960. On September 8, 1963, Ulfert Wilke showed Merton a book of his own calligraphies (RJ). Merton sent his first submission of "calligraphic abstractions" to the journal *El Corno Esplumado* on September 18, 1963 (RJ). On January 10, 1964, Ad Reinhardt sent him some "almost transparent Japanese paper" on which he did some calligraphies (RJ). On August 27, 1964, Merton was at Ulfert Wilke's stu-

dio in Pee Wee Valley near Louisville, looking at Wilke's work and talking about framing his own calligraphies (RJ). Wilke helped him to frame and hang his show that November.

332. RJ, Jan. 16, 1964. VOW, 11, "I have an obligation to Paul Klee which goes deeper, even into the order of theology . . ." He mentions borrowing books on Klee (including Klee's diaries) from the University of Kentucky library, Sept. 10, 1966 (RJ).

333. See Masheck, ed., "Five Unpublished Letters from Ad Reinhardt to Thomas Merton and Two in Return."

334. RJ, Nov. 4, 1964.

335. RJ, Mar. 3, 1964. VOW, 25. The comment made was, according to Merton, "That is not the job of a monk, it is for the Bishops."

336. RJ, July 14, 1964. VOW, 61–62. The abbot's secretary was Brother Patrick Hart, then called Brother Simon.

337. Dell'Isola, 39, A42. Breit, 7, 88.

338. Merton to W. H. Ferry, June 8, 1964, TMSC. Someone at the Center has penciled in on the margin, "How does he stand it?"

339. RJ, July 23, 1964. VOW, 64.

340. RJ, Aug. 5, 1964. VOW, 68.

341. Reported, RJ, July 18, 1964. Edward Deming Andrews to Merton, Feb. 13, 1961, TMSC: "Another person who was sensitive to the spirit of Shaker craftsmanship was our, and your, friend, Mark Van Doren. His review of our book [*Shaker Furniture*], in *The Nation*, was entitled *Religion in Wood*."

342. *Religion in Wood*, introduction, 11. See also "Pleasant Hill, A Shaker Village in Kentucky," *Mystics and Zen Masters*, 193–220. His article "The Shakers" brought more mail than any other to that time, Merton says in RJ. Some of the letters to *Jubilee* were published in subsequent numbers.

343. Merton to Mary Childs Black (director of the Abby Aldrich Rockefeller Folk Art Collection, Williamsburg, Va.), Jan. 27, 1962, TMSC. This letter has been quoted from before, and it appears as letter 24 (a) in CWL, 44–46. There are two letters numbered 24, while there is a combined page 43/44 in this draft.

344. CWL, 8, 13. Professor Bruno P. Schlesinger of St. Mary's College, Notre Dame, Indiana, had written asking Merton's help and advice, as the college was starting a Program for Christian Culture. For a more positive response in the same letter, see 422. Cf. *Seeds of Destruction*, 245–46.

345. RJ, Jan. 13, 1964. VOW, 9. Cardinal Spellman wrote on May 18, 1964.

346. Merton to Francis Cardinal Spellman, July 1, 1964, TMSC.

347. RJ, Oct. 8, 1964. VOW, 81–82.

348. RJ, Oct. 12, 1964. Dom James had given him permission to sleep in the hermitage, "not necessarily all the time." Brother Colman moved a bed in on October 10. Merton spent his first night in the hermitage October 12/13, 1964. VOW, 82–83.

349. RJ, Sept. 25, 1964. VOW, 79–80.

350. RJ, Nov. 30, 1964.

351. RJ, Feb. 11 and Sept. 12, 1964.

352. CWL, 24, 46 (again, there are two letters numbered 24. This is the second, 24[b]).

353. To be enslaved by the concept of freedom was also, of course, a Kantian paradox. See also *Seasons of Celebration*, 30.

354. Zen training authoritarian, see *The Way of Chuang Tzu*, 16.

355. Conference Tape on Obedience, 4–22–64, A–164, TMSC.

356. SSM, 389.

357. Merton to Leslie Dewart, Aug. 11, 1964, TMSC.

358. RJ, Oct. 25, 1964. Marco Pallis, touring with the English Consort of Viols, had visited the day before. Arrangements had been made for the Consort to play at Gethsemani. These broke down because only the male musicians could enter the enclosure. VOW, 86.

359. RJ, Nov. 16, 1964. The visit had been on November 14–15. "Brother Antoninus, tall, bowed, gentle, benevolent, given to quiet laughter, was here . . ." VOW, 95–96.

360. "Rain and the Rhinoceros," *Raids on the Unspeakable*, 9–23. This was one of Mer-

ton's favorite essays. He records finishing it on December 20, 1964 (RJ). (VOW, 111), and sending it to *Holiday*, where it appeared in May 1965 (37, no. 5, 8–16). Dell'Isola, 96, C254. Breit, 40, 474.

361. Ibid., 14.
362. Ibid., 21. Merton's italics. Merton is quoting Ionesco (*Notes et contre notes*, 129).
363. Ibid., 23.
364. RJ, Nov. 17, 1964. VOW, 97–98. The opening address is given in *The Nonviolent Alternative*, 259–60. See also Forest, "Thomas Merton's Struggle with Peacemaking," 40–42.
365. Tape of talk given by Father Daniel Berrigan at St. John the Divine, Jan. 28, 1973, JLA. Also interview with Berrigan, Sept. 25, 1980.
366. RJ, Nov. 19, 1964. VOW, 98.
367. "An Enemy of the State," *The Nonviolent Alternative*, 134–38. This is in large part a review of Gordon Zahn's book about Franz Jägerstätter, *In Solitary Witness*.
368. RJ, Nov. 19, 1964. VOW, 98.
369. RJ, Nov. 10, 1964. VOW, 94.
370. "Signatures: Notes on the Author's Drawings," *Raids on the Unspeakable*, 179–82.
371. Merton to John Howard Griffin, Mar. 30, 1965, TMSC. Interview with Dom James Fox, July 11, 1981. Merton to John Pick, Mar. 30, 1965, TMSC.
372. Merton to Victor Hammer, Aug. 12, 1964, TMSC.
373. CP, 1005. Translation:

O Thou Father of splendor, Giver of light
To Thee I pray in joy, with light restored
Grant I beg to me Thy servant everlasting
Day in which no night makes sad the heart, and no shadow.

This is Merton's own translation. Written Nov. 4, 1964 (RJ).
374. RJ, Oct. 21, 1964. VOW, 86. This was before he purchased the Coleman light and stove at Sears in Louisville on November 6.
375. RJ, Jan. 17, 1965. VOW, 127.
376. RJ, Dec. 4, 1964. VOW, 104.
377. Merton to Lawrence Ferlinghetti, CWL, 7, 10–11.
378. RJ, Nov. 22, 1964. VOW, 99.
379. Everett Edelen had offered the land to the monastery, and Merton reports that he and Brother Nicholas went over to look at it on September 24, 1964 (RJ). (VOW, 78). Merton was surprised when Dom James proved interested in the idea of using the gift for establishing individual hermitages (Merton had been hoping for a collective *laura*). Merton reports the meeting, September 25, 1964 (RJ). (VOW, 78–79). The next time Father Louis saw Dom James (a day later), Father Louis was equally enthusiastic about the invitation to go to visit Zen monasteries in Japan, so that perhaps the abbot can be forgiven for feeling a little confused.
380. RJ, Jan. 6, 1965. VOW, 119–22. Merton spends pages describing his day bushwacking, and camping on the site of some cabins for freed slaves. It was obviously an exciting adventure, marred only by gazing up into the bomb bay of a passing SAC bomber.
381. Merton reports on his visit. He talks of Mother Luke Tobin's position on December 10, 1964 (RJ). (VOW, 108). Dan Walsh taught philosophy at the Convent for a considerable period.
382. Merton to Mother Mary Luke Tobin, Nov. 1, 1964, TMSC.
383. RJ, Jan. 25, 1965. VOW, 132–33.
384. See 83–84.
385. Merton to Mother Mary Luke Tobin, July 7, 1965. Stern, *The Flight from Woman*. Apart from the intriguing title, this is a rich grab bag of themes and ideas. Many of them Merton had already explored. Hence, perhaps, the attraction. Gregory Zilboorg and Paul Evdokimov make appearances, so does Sophia, and there is a long criticism of Cartesian thought. If some of this work is dated now, it is still stimulating reading.
386. RJ, Jan. 30, 1965. VOW, 132–33.
387. CGB, 190.

388. RJ, Jan. 31, 1965. VOW, 135.
389. RJ, Feb. 2, 1965. VOW, 136.
390. RJ, Jan. 30, 1965. VOW, 133.
391. Merton to John Wu, Feb. 4, 1965, TMSC.
392. RJ, Feb. 14, 1965. VOW, 139.
393. RJ, Feb. 16, 1965. VOW, 141.
394. RJ, Feb. 24, 1965. Merton gives only a very small account of this in VOW, 145. John Howard Griffin makes much of the incident in "The Controversial Merton," 80–81, believing it was a serious threat on Merton's life. It may be so, and Merton found threatening, or at least hostile, mail in his mailbox that same morning. I have preferred to follow the report of a number of monks at the monastery, that this was a joke in bad taste on Father Louis.
395. RJ, Feb. 9, 1965. VOW, 138.
396. Merton's first mention, RJ, Sept. 1, 1964 (VOW, 71). There was an interruption, but several other mentions follow early in 1965, with an important one on Newman and obedience on July 9, 1965 (RJ). (VOW, 193). Trevor, *Newman.*
397. "Gandhi and the One-Eyed Giant," *Gandhi on Non-Violence*, 3.
398. Ibid., 5.
399. RJ, May 10, 1965. VOW, 174.
400. The first, "A Note to the Reader," gives Merton's personal approach and explains the method of translating. "A Study of Chuang Tzu" sets Chuang Tzu in the historical and philosophical context.
401. Dell'Isola, 39, A43. Nov. 10, 1965. Breit, 9, 113
402. RJ, July 19, 1965. VOW, 195.
403. RJ, Apr. 15, 1965. VOW, 166.
404. RJ, Mar. 21, 1965. VOW, 156. It had happened on March 19.
405. RJ, Mar. 19, 1965, reporting on the day before. VOW, 155–56. Also, Merton to W. H. Ferry, Mar. 19, 1965, TMSC.
406. RJ, June 3, 1965. VOW, 179. Talking of Monday of that week.
407. RJ, June 6, 1965. VOW, 180. Reporting on Monday.
408. Weil, *The Iliad, or The Poem of Force.* Merton first refers to this in CGB, 138.
409. Carbaud, *Simone Weil: A Fellowship in Love.*
410. RJ, Mar. 5, 1965. VOW, 152.
411. "The Answer of Minerva: Pacifism and Resistance in Simone Weil." First published as "Pacifism and Resistance" in *Peace News*, April 2, 1965, then as "Pacifism and Resistance in Simone Weil," *Faith and Violence*, 76–84. It appears as "The Answer of Minerva: Pacifism and Resistance in Simone Weil" in *The Nonviolent Alternative*, 144–49, and in LE, 134–39. There are a number of small differences in the texts throughout.
412. "The Answer of Minerva." I have followed the text in *The Nonviolent Alternative*, 146.
413. See Pétrement, *Simone Weil: A Life*, chap. 10, "The Spanish Civil War, the Popular Front, and the First Trip to Italy (1936–1937)."
414. *The Nonviolent Alternative*, 148.
415. Ibid., 145.
416. CWL, 4, 6.
417. CWL, 41, 75. Merton's ellipsis.
418. Merton to Ernesto Cardenal, May 8, 1964, TMSC.
419. Ibid.
420. Dell'Isola, 39, A43. Nov. 10, 1965. Breit, 9, 113.
421. Dell'Isola, 64, B53. Oct. 1965. Breit, 3, 30.
422. Dell'Isola, 40, A44. Dec. 3, 1965. Breit, 7, 85.
423. *Seasons of Celebration*, 2.
424. Dell'Isola, 41, A45. Aug. 9, 1966. Breit, 7, 80.
425. Dell'Isola, 43, A49. May 5, 1967. Breit, 5, 54.
426. "Open Letter to the American Bishops," also "Schema XIII: An Open Letter to the American Hierarchy," see Breit, 41–42. This appeared in *Unity* (Montreal), *Vox Regis* (published by Christ the King Seminary, St. Bonaventure, New York), *Worldwide*.

427. Merton to W. H. Ferry, July 20, 1965, TMSC. This letter also gives details of the books Merton had finished writing and that were waiting in line to appear!
428. RJ, July 5, 1965. VOW, 191.
429. *Seasons of Celebration*, 153.
430. Ibid., 175.
431. SJ, 362.
432. *Seasons of Celebration*, 187.
433. Merton to Naomi Burton Stone, Aug. 9, 1965, FLSB.
434. Merton to Mother Mary Luke Tobin, July 18, 1965, TMSC.
435. Interview with Father Augustine Wulff, July 11, 1981.
436. Merton to Mother Mary Luke Tobin, July 18, 1965, TMSC. Apparently the hermitage had no lightning rods. These were installed only after John Howard Griffin, using an electric typewriter, was almost electrocuted at the hermitage in 1970. Griffin, *Hermitage*, 119–25.
437. RJ, July 18, 1965. VOW, 194. Merton had been exchanging early drafts of the open letter with Mother Mary Luke Tobin (see correspondence).
438. RJ, July 9, 1965. VOW, 193.
439. RJ, July 19, 1965. VOW, 195.
440. RJ, Aug. 17, 1965. VOW, 199, gives a much shorter version.
441. RJ, Aug. 17, 1965. This should be corrected to three women. Merton also wrote to Sister Thérèse Lentfoehr for support on Aug. 17, 1965, MCC. TMSC.
442. RJ, Aug. 17, 1965.
443. CWL, 8, 14. The letter is published, with some changes, in *Seeds of Destruction*, 245–50. The "Professor of Humanities" was Bruno P. Schlesinger, at St. Mary's College, Notre Dame, Indiana.
444. RJ, June 11, 1965.
445. Merton to Robert Lax, Nov. 10, 1965, *A Catch of Anti-Letters*, 63.
446. "The Garden," verse 8, *Poems of Andrew Marvell*, 53.
447. *The New Man*, 91. Merton's italics.
448. RJ, June 26, 1965. A somewhat edited version, VOW, 187.
449. RJ, Aug. 18, 1965, reporting on the day before. VOW, 199.
450. "A Life Free from Care," transcription of the tape made from the conference Merton gave at the novitiate, Aug. 20, 1965.
451. Merton to Robert Lax, Oct. 16, 1965, TMSC. *A Catch of Anti-Letters*, 62.
452. SSM, 156.
453. *Gethsemani: A Life of Praise.* Dell'Isola, 42, A47. Breit, 3, 31.
454. RJ, Aug. 28, 1965. This is not in VOW, which closes with the entry of September 6, 1965 (201–2), giving an impression that Merton had completely adjusted to his life as a full-time hermit and that it was, indeed, a "life free from care."
455. RJ, Sept. 25, 1965. Father Chrysogonus Waddell, who had just come back from Rome, and Father Flavian Burns were given permission to visit Merton at the hermitage. Father Chrysogonus gave Merton a fuller account than he had done in letters of his trip to Montauban and St. Antonin, and left photographs he had taken and the town guide to St. Antonin. See 35, 37–38, 41.
456. Merton to Ernesto Cardenal, Oct. 22, 1965, TMSC. Merton to His Excellency, the Most. Rev. Archbishop Paul Philippe, Secretary of the S. Congregation of Religious, undated, but asking to "be loaned by my community to his community, either with leave of absence, or, if your Excellency thought necessary, an exclaustration. The idea would be for me to continue my monastic life in his community while remaining a member of my own Order canonically." (This arrangement, which Merton admits would be viewed as "novel," is more and more his ideal solution to the situation posed by the vow of stability: he wants to serve elsewhere, or to be a hermit elsewhere, while remaining a member of the Gethsemani community, at least "canonically.") TMSC. Merton to His Holiness Pope Paul VI, undated, but on the same subject, pointing out that, to date, there had been little support for such foundations in Latin America from the United States, and that Gethsemani "could at least spare *one priest* in this very special case" (TMSC).
457. Merton to Ernesto Cardenal, Mar. 15, 1968, TMSC. Solentiname is an archipelago

of islands on Lake Nicaragua with a population of about a thousand, chiefly fishermen and their families. Here, with Merton's advice and encouragement, Ernesto Cardenal founded a church and commune, Nuestra Señora de Solentiname. As a reprisal for revolutionary activity, Solentiname's religious commune was bombed, occupied, and destroyed by Samoza's troops after the unsuccessful revolt of the FSLN in October 1977. Cardenal escaped, as he was abroad, raising funds for and representing the FSLN abroad. The commune has since been restored. Ernesto Cardenal is the Minister of Culture of the Frente Sandinista de Liberacíon Nacional. He remains a priest. For further details, see the notes in Cardenal, *Zero Hour and Other Documentary Poems*.

458. Merton to Ernesto Cardenal, Oct. 22, 1965, TMSC.
459. Merton to Father Daniel Berrigan, June 25, 1963.
460. RJ, Nov. 7, 1965. This had happened on All Saints Day, November 2, as a protest against the Vietnam War.
461. RJ, Nov. 11, 1965. The special-delivery letter was a day late, Merton reports. This had happened on the November 8, "a kid from the Catholic Worker burned himself alive in front of the U.N. Building. This is fantastic and horrible. He was an ex seminarian evidently. I cannot understand the shape of things in the Peace Movement or the shape of things at all in this country. What is happening? Is everybody nuts?"
462. Telegram from Merton to James Forest, Nov. 11, 1965, MGA. The telegram to Dorothy Day, on the same date, reads: JUST HEARD OF THE TRAGIC DEATH OF ROGER LAPORTE. AM DEEPLY SHOCKED AND CONCERNED ABOUT DEVELOPMENTS IN PEACE MOVEMENT. WILL THESE DO GREAT HARM TO CAUSE OF PEACE. DO THEY REPRESENT A RIGHT UNDERSTANDING OF NON-VIOLENCE. I THINK NOT. THOMAS MERTON.
463. Forest, "Thomas Merton's Struggle with Peacemaking," 43. Forest also gives the text of the telegram to him.
464. Ibid., 43–44, citing a letter from Merton to Forest.
465. RJ, Nov. 21, 1965. The deer, RJ, Nov. 13, 1965.
466. Ibid.
467. Merton to Father Daniel Berrigan, Nov. 19, 1965, TMSC.
468. RJ, Nov. 20, 1965.
469. On the taped talk by Father Daniel Berrigan at the Foundation of the Merton Center at Columbia, January 28, 1973 (JLA), Berrigan says that he felt Merton's distance from events was a real hindrance to him, and that it made distance between Merton and Berrigan. When Berrigan felt this was happening in 1965, he told Merton, who responded, "Come on down and we'll talk about it." At the Merton-Maritain Symposium in Louisville, September 25–26, 1980, Berrigan said that he thought Merton had been largely right — right at least for him.
470. Merton sketched out a number of titles on a page of Holographic Journal #11, Working Notebook, 1963- , TMSC. Among these were titles that became section titles, or that were used elsewhere, including "Barth's Dream" — the title for the whole book, until November 20, 1965 (RJ) — "To Each His Darkness," and "Interesting Era." *Conjectures of a Guilty Bystander*, Dell'Isola, 42, A48. Nov. 4, 1966. Breit, 2, 19. In November 1965, and in the middle of so many other things, the monk who was transcribing the book had a spiritual breakdown. At least in his journal, Merton responds with exasperation for the inconvenience, rather than sympathy for the sufferer.
471. RJ, Nov. 22, 1965.
472. RJ, Nov. 27, 1965, "There is a regular fury of drug-mysticism in this country. I am in a way appalled. Mysticism has finally arrived in a characteristic American mode."
473. RJ, Dec. 3, 1965. Merton was *bouleversé* by the arrival of the ikon from Pallis. Supposedly from Salonika, c. 1700, this represented the Holy Mother and Child, and, on panels that open out, St. Nicholas and St. George, St. Demetrius and St. Chorlandros ("whoever that is"). This ikon is still in the hermitage chapel.
474. RJ, Dec. 21, 1965.
475. RJ, Dec. 18, 1965.
476. RJ, Dec. 7, 1965.

477. RJ, Jan. 2 and 12, 1966. See "Nishida: A Zen Philosopher," Kitaro Nishida (1870–1945), eminent Japanese philosopher, *Zen and the Birds of Appetite*, 67–70. This is in large part a review of Nishida's *A Study of Good*.
478. RJ, Jan. 5, 1966.
479. RJ, Jan. 12, 1966.
480. RJ, Jan. 15, 1966.
481. Ibid.
482. Morrissey, "Talks with and about Thomas Merton." Breit, 101, 1150.
483. RJ, Jan. 22, 1966.
484. Merton to Aziz Ch. Abdul, Jan. 2, 1966, TMSC. The letter is given as Merton wrote it, except for an editorial ellipsis in the first paragraph quoted. Here Merton repeated a number of details about breakfast (eighteen words left out). Louis Massignon had introduced Merton to Aziz Ch. Abdul in 1960.
485. RJ, Feb. 7, 1966.
486. Merton to Aziz Ch. Abdul, Jan. 2, 1966, TMSC.
487. Ibid., Jan. 16, 1966, TMSC. This correspondence was a warm and detailed one.
488. RJ, Feb. 23, 1966. Back operation was unavoidable, RJ, Mar. 3, 1966.
489. RJ, Mar. 15, 1966. "How It Is: Apologies to an Unbeliever," *Harper's* 233, no. 1398 (November 1966): 36–39. As "Apologies to an Unbeliever," *Faith and Violence*, 205–14. Dell'Isola, 101. C290. Breit, 101. C290. Breit, 30, 351.
490. Daggy, *Introductions*, 87–98. Daggy provides an interesting introduction of his own on page 89 to this preface, which "is itself an essay on solitude." The second version is published with revisions made in April from the original draft written in March and taken to hospital. A third, revised and enlarged version, "Love and Solitude," was published in *The Critic* 25 (October–November 1966): 30–37. A careful comparison of the three drafts reveals much. S. advised Merton to make changes between draft one and two. Merton's experiences of the summer are reflected in the changes from version two to version three. See 456–57. Indeed, the whole struggle of the summer can be seen in Merton's desire to reconcile love *and* solitude. See, too, Merton's "Author's Note," which is reprinted with "Love and Solitude" in *Love and Living*.
491. RJ, Mar. 23, 1966. The Norway foundation from Gethsemani came to nothing, and here Merton felt Dom James had been unfairly treated by others in the Order.
492. Gethsemani Spire: Without seeing symbolism everywhere, one can only remark that it was a strange summer in which Merton saw the spire of Gethsemani taken down on the day he received his first letter from S. and at the beginning of his obsession with the new song by Joan Baez, "Silver Dagger." By August, the steeple, or spire, had become part of a dream. "I like the Abbey much better without the steeple. It is a much simpler, more modest, less forbidding place — it even has a strange charm, nestling in the trees instead of trying to dominate everything with a big false spire. But last night I dreamt they were putting the spire up again — temporarily — for a festival of some sort. The frame rose up with the ease of the works of an umbrella, but the spire was top heavy and I saw it was going to fall. There were many workmen up in it, and I cried out to God to prevent it from falling. Still it fell and all the workmen with it. Hundreds of workmen were lying on the ground injured. I went to the nearest of them — three negroes — and wanted to help them. I wanted to get a car to stop to pick them up but no car would do so — even one driven by a negro woman. I thought — 'What a stupid thing it was to try to put that old spire up again! Typical of Dom James!' I woke without knowing any more" (RJ, Aug. 15, 1966).
493. RJ, Mar. 23, 1966. Also Apr. 10, 1966.
494. "To Whom It May Concern," Thomas M. Marshall, M.D., July 21, 1971, AA.
495. RJ, Apr. 10, 1966.
496. The source for almost all the details in this paragraph is the second of the separate accounts Merton kept of the summer in addition to his journal. This is called "Retrospect." There is some confusion about the date; Merton says "Wednesday in Passion Week." But he keeps the anniversary of their first meeting on March 31, 1967 (RJ). The 31st was a Thursday in 1966.
497. Rilke, *Duino Elegies*, "First Elegy," 11, 31–33. I have used the J. B. Leishman and

Stephen Spender translation (London: Hogarth Press, 1957), 27. In the German of *Die Erste Elegie, Duineser Elegien:*

> . . . Warst du nicht immer
> noch von Erwartung zerstreut, als kündigte alles
> eine Geliebte dir an? . . .

498. "Retrospect," 5. "You had licked Eckhart completely."
499. Ibid. S. and a friend (also a student nurse) had read the preface and neither liked the draft.
500. Ibid., 6.
501. Ibid.
502. RJ, Apr. 12, 1966.
503. RJ, Sept. 4, 1966. "Retrospect," 8.
504. RJ, Apr. 24, 1966. He writes of his original intention. "Retrospect," 9, 11.
505. RJ, Apr. 19, 1966. To read the entries in the journal for Apr. 19, 21, and 22, is to sense the same quickening as in the famous scene from Pasternak's *Doctor Zhivago* in which Zhivago becomes aware he is in love with Lara. April 22: "More shouting on the steeple. Slowly the plates of lead come off, and the old brown lumber appears. Warm afternoon. For a while I sat in the sun surrounded by lovemaking bumblebees. The other day I saw the feathers of a cardinal which a hawk had killed, and was sad, thinking a pair had been broken up. Today I saw the male sitting beautifully on a fencepost singing joyfully — but at first no female. Then I saw her flying in and out of a big rose bush in the hedge, where the new nest is, and was happy."
506. "Retrospect," 10. S. had written four pages. She had quoted from *The Sign of Jonas,* talking of her own fear of hurting others with her love, and her sense that she shared his sense of loneliness in the passage of September 14, 1949 (SJ, 238).
507. "Retrospect," 11.
508. *Seasons of Celebration,* 181.
509. Merton quotes this line of St. Augustine often. See also *Mystics and Zen Masters,* 164. In his essay "Gertrude More and Augustine Baker," Merton quotes from *The Inner Life and Writings of Dame Gertrude More,* 152: "[They say] . . . that it is perilous to walk in the way of love and that (as some would seem to prove) *no soul in any other course or state is in such peril as is a soul that giveth herself to this pursuit"* (Merton's italics).
510. "A Midsummer Diary," "Retrospect."
511. RJ, Sept. 4, 1966.
512. RJ, Mar. 23, 31, 1967. The quotation is taken from the entry of March 23, when Merton speaks of their first parting in Holy Week, not their meeting in Passion Week.
513. RJ, Apr. 27, 1966.
514. "Retrospect," 9, 11.
515. RJ, Sept. 6, 1966.
516. Ibid.
517. RJ, Sept. 4, 1966. "Retrospect," 10, 11.
518. RJ, Apr. 27, 1966, but reporting on the day before. "Retrospect," 12. RJ, Apr. 28, 1966.
519. RJ, Apr. 27, 1966.
520. "Retrospect," 11, 12.
521. RJ, Apr. 27, 1966.
522. RJ, May 4, 1966.
523. "Retrospect," 17–19. A few of the details are taken from RJ, May 7, 1966, reporting on events two days earlier. Also, Merton to Nicanor Parra, Apr. 28, 1967, TMSC.
524. Photographs taken that day, May 5, 1966. Other details from "Retrospect," 18.
525. Nicanor Parra's comment, RJ, May 7, 1966, reporting on events two days earlier.
526. Interview with James Laughlin, Oct. 25, 1979.
527. "Retrospect," 19. She writes that night from the hospital, "Tom, I want to be with

you." He writes in his journal again about "a chaste marriage" and about the Maritains — then admits this is unrealistic.

528. Interview with John and Gladys Ford, Apr. 10, 1980.
529. "Retrospect," 20. RJ, May 9, 1966, reporting on events two days earlier.
530. "Purity," the fourth word in "Seven Words for Ned O'Gorman," *Love and Living*, 105.
531. RJ, May 20, 1966: "Instead of feeling impure I feel purified (which is in fact what I myself wrote the other day in the 'Seven Words' for Ned O'Gorman)." "Retrospect," 16, etc.
532. RJ, May 16, 1966, reporting on events two days earlier. "Retrospect," 21.
533. "Retrospect," 21. RJ, May 20, 1966.
534. "Retrospect," 21.
535. RJ, May 21, 1966 (the plan is made). RJ, May 23, 1966 (the plan is cancelled). He had also telephoned her on Sunday, May 22, 1966. "Retrospect," 21.
536. "Retrospect," 22. RJ, June 4 and 5, 1966.
537. "Retrospect," 21.
538. RJ, June 12, 1966. Also "Retrospect," 17. RJ, Sept. 4, 1966.
539. RJ, June 14, 1966. Wygal had called on June 12, the Sunday.
540. Ibid.
541. Ibid.
542. Interview with Dom Flavian Burns, Mar. 29, 1981.
543. RJ, May 17, 1966, etc.
544. Interview with Dom James Fox, July 11, 1981. This is confirmed by many of Merton's comments in the journal.
545. RJ, June 14, 1966.
546. RJ, June 15, 1966. He had admitted only the telephone calls to Dom James.
547. RJ, June 22, 1966.
548. RJ, June 25, 1966.
549. RJ, June 26, 1966, reporting on the day before.
550. RJ, July 10, 1966.
551. Interview with W. H. Ferry, Mar. 26, 1981.
552. RJ, July 12, 1966.
553. RJ, June 30, 1966, Merton simply writes that they had had "a good long talk" the day before. RJ, July 8, 1966, he talks of "Last week and its excesses . . ." RJ, July 29, 1966, he admits he was drunk. RJ, Sept. 4, 1966, he admits he was "really acting crazy!"
554. RJ, July 14, 1966, reporting on the day before. This is a very full entry.
555. RJ, July 16, 1966. The poem is called "Cherokee Park."
556. RJ, July 21, 1966.
557. RJ, July 29, 1966. The conference was the day before. The information about the job at Santa Barbara was not given at the conference and Merton learned of it later from W. H. Ferry — also of the strong feelings of the abbot. Interview with Dom James, July 11, 1981. Interview with W. H. Ferry, Mar. 26, 1981. There are also references in the Merton-Ferry correspondence at TMSC, e.g., Merton to Ferry, Aug. 25, 1966, TMSC, etc.
558. RJ, July 29, 1966.
559. RJ, Aug. 5, 1966, reporting on the day before.
560. RJ, July 29, 1966.
561. "A Midsummer Diary," 5.
562. Ibid., 1.
563. RJ, June 19, 1966. Also "A Midsummer Diary," 8.
564. There had been some strains in the friendship before. On February 29, 1964, Wygal had come out to the hermitage unexpectedly. It was Wygal's conviction "They were having a wonderful time." Merton says, "What actually happened was meaningless in the shape of an 'Event' " (RJ, Mar. 3, 1964). However, on July 9, 1965, the tone is different, and Merton admits he had been intolerant and impatient.
565. RJ, Sept. 4, 1966.

566. RJ, Apr. 25, 1966.
567. RJ, May 27, 1966.
568. RJ, May 24, 1966.
569. RJ, June 12, 1966.
570. "A Midsummer Diary," 1.
571. Ibid., 8.
572. In a sequence as strange as one from the novels of Thomas Hardy (not Merton's favorite novelist), Merton records a dream in which he is prevented from reaching S., who is swimming in one of the Gethsemani lakes. After this he describes a recent walk in which he had come upon the jacket of a monk's work outfit lying in the grass by the main road. The monk had gone A.W.O.L., "secretly Friday before dawn, with no money apparently, dressed in work pants and sweat shirt . . ." Finally, Merton describes the predawn fog around the hermitage and the smell of percolating coffee. RJ, Sept. 21, 1966. Apart from the extraordinary and evocative shifts these entries give, they prove that the idea of simply leaving Gethsemani "in work pants and a sweat shirt" had occurred to Merton more than once that summer.
573. "A Midsummer Diary," 2.
574. Ibid.
575. Merton to Robert Lax, June 7, 1966, *A Catch of Anti-Letters*, 86.
576. "A Midsummer Diary," 15.
577. Merton to Edward Rice, July 20, 1966, TMSC. "Nostradamus" appears as "The Prospects of Nostradamus," 68, of *Cables to the Ace*, CP, 437–40. There is a draft of this poem in Merton's reading notebook, "1966, March-April-May-June-July." GRSU. The poem was begun on April 13–14, 1966, just after Merton's return from St. Joseph's Hospital.
578. RJ, May 9, 1966.
579. "A Midsummer Diary," 9.
580. Ibid.
581. Ibid., 12.
582. RJ, June 4, 1966.
583. Isolated pages, Merton, 1966. JLA.
584. Ibid.
585. Although only a few of these will be noticed here, there are a great many references to S. in the 1967 journal, as well as in the poetry, including *The Geography of Lograire*.
586. Restricted poems. "Evening: Long Distance Call."
587. "A Christian Looks at Zen," first published as the preface of John C. H. Wu's *The Golden Age of Zen*, published by the National War College in cooperation with the Committee on the Compilation of the Chinese Library, 1967 (no month given), 1–27. Dell'Isola, 65, B60. Breit, 10, 124. *Zen and the Birds of Appetite*, 33–58.
588. Thich Nhat Hanh's visit almost gets squeezed out of the journal because of Merton's preoccupation with S. No mention of it is made until RJ, May 31, 1966. Merton was again friends with John Heidbrink of FOR, who sponsored Thich Nhat Hanh's speaking tour in the United States. On June 2, 1966 (RJ), Merton announces, "The visit of J. Heidbrink, A. Gould, and Thich Nhat Hanh last Saturday-Sunday was very impressive." Merton gained a good deal of information about Zen monasteries in Vietnam, before Thich Nhat Hanh fell ill on Sunday morning. (After they had all made a tape for Daniel Berrigan, Merton slipped away to try to telephone S., who had left Louisville and gone home when Merton told her not to try to come out to the monastery that weekend.) See also Forest, "Thomas Merton's Struggle with Peacemaking," 47–50.
589. RJ, June 2, 1966.
590. "Nhat Hanh Is My Brother," *The Nonviolent Alternative*, 264.
591. Merton to Robert Lax (Reverend Postum), July 15, 1966, *A Catch of Anti-Letters*, 90.
592. RJ, June 9, 1966.
593. RJ, June 2, 1966.
594. "A Midsummer Diary," 12.

595. Restricted poems. "Gethsemani, May, 1966."
596. *"Conjectures of a Guilty Bystander:* From a New Book by Thomas Merton," *Life,* Aug. 5, 1966, 60–73. One caption read, "Thomas Merton stands beside hand-hewn cross at the abbey where he lives and writes about his deep concern for the individual in today's angry world." This is above a full-color ad: "Us Tareyton smokers would rather fight than switch!"
597. See 87.
598. "The Tower of the Spirit," *The Way of Chuang Tzu,* 134.
599. RJ, Aug. 27, 1966.
600. "A Midsummer Diary," 4.
601. RJ, Aug. 27, 1966. Merton made a number of translations from the poetry of René Char, see CP, 856–59. He continued to be enthusiastic about the work of Edwin Muir, see the favorable comment on Muir in *Zen and the Birds of Appetite,* 64, and "The True Legendary Sound: The Poetry and Criticism of Edwin Muir," written in September 1966, first published in *The Sewanee Review* 75 (Spring 1967). LE, 29–36.
602. See note 490. Merton made the corrections to the first draft on April 14, 1966, taking into account the criticisms of S., and perhaps her friend, the other nurse to whom she had shown the typescript. On December 2, 1967 (RJ), he records that he had received a letter from a man and a woman teaching at Keele University, England, thanking him for what he had said about love. He was writing to the woman, but "the situation is somewhat artificial and strained because evidently she thinks I should leave here and can't understand why I don't. As if my staying here were somehow a betrayal. But that is no longer reasonable!"
603. RJ, May 11, 1967.
604. Document of Commitment, Sept. 8, 1966, MGA.
605. RJ, Sept. 10, 1966.
606. Merton had come to expect charges of being a "dual personality," half recluse, half publicist. He suspected his abbot of a double standard — that Dom James expected him to make money for the abbey, then criticized him when he did so. Moreover, Dom James could certainly be "careful" with money on occasion — in the name of the vow of poverty. But when Merton wrote that he had been released from hospital too early in April 1966, and when he told friends in letters he would not be allowed to go back into hospital because it cost too much, he was exaggerating. He *was* allowed to go into hospital that October, but to St. Anthony's, not to St. Joseph's — and for fairly obvious reasons.
607. Interview with Brother Martin Deloach, Nov. 7, 1980.
608. Visit to the cloister and garth, Apr. 4, 1980. See *Liturgical Arts* 36, no. 4 (August 1968), containing: William Schickel, "Unifying the Old and the New," 99–100; Merton, "Note on the New Church at Gethsemani," 100–101; Rev. Matthew Kelty, "Gethsemani: Impressions on a Renovation, 101, 106–7. This issue gives full photographic "before and after" coverage, including a full-page photograph of the renovated cloister garden, and floor plans before and after renovation.
609. Interview with Brother Frederic Collins, July 12, 1981.
610. RJ, Sept. 10, 1966, reporting on events two days before.
611. Dell'Isola, 44, A51. Mar. 31, 1968. Breit, 2, 10.
612. A selection of letters from the Merton-Lax correspondence was published as "A Catch of Anti-Letters," in *Voyages* 11, no. 1 and 2 (Winter-Spring 1968): 44–56. Breit, 22, 241.
613. Merton to W. H. Ferry, Oct. 4, 1966, TMSC.
614. RJ, Nov. 14, 1960.
615. *Bread in the Wilderness,* 54: ". . . And that is why some of the best poets of our time are running wild among the tombs in the moonlit cemeteries of surrealism . . ."
616. CWL, 46, 82.
617. "Why Alienation Is for Everybody," written in early 1968 for a "Prospectus of Writings" in Louisville's West End, LE, 382.
618. RJ, Oct. 13, 1966.
619. Interview with James Laughlin, Oct. 25, 1979.

620. Griffin, *Wholeness;* Griffin and Simon, *Maritain.*
621. Ibid. There are small variations in Griffin's various accounts of the visit. RJ, Oct. 13, 1966. The poem "Les Cinq Vierges, pour Jacques," CP, 819. Translation, "The Five Virgins," CP, 826–27.
622. RJ, Oct. 27, 1966.
623. RJ, Oct. 31, 1966. Sidi Abdeslam's name is spelled Abdesalam in Merton's account. I have taken the spelling from Sidi Abdeslam's signature on his letter to Merton, Feb. 14, 1967, TMSC. I gather the transfer of names from Arabic to English is open to any number of variant rules.
624. Merton's study of Faulkner is a subject in itself. For an introduction, see LE, "Baptism in the Forest: Wisdom and Initiation in William Faulkner," 92–116; "Faulkner and His Critics," 117–23; and appendix 3, "Two Transcriptions of Merton's Talks on William Faulkner (1967)," 497–536. See also *Opening the Bible,* 42–49.
625. See note 80 above.
626. Merton to W. H. Ferry, Jan. 26, 1966, TMSC. There are many references to Du Bay in the correspondence during the year. See also *Faith and Violence,* 139.
627. Merton to W. H. Ferry, Aug. 18, 1966, TMSC.
628. Ibid., Aug. 25, 1966, TMSC.
629. Merton's new enthusiasm marks an interesting change. He had not been interested earlier. RJ, Oct. 8, 1962, "Letter from Rabbi Gendler at Princeton wanting to interest me in 'Hostages for Peace' . . . About 'Hostage for Peace,' in itself it is a good idea. But like all such ideas it is more of a prank than an idea. It goes nowhere. Yet it might mean something, nevertheless. I would certainly sign up for it if I thought there were the remotest chance of getting an intelligent hearing from Dom James." See also CWL, 111, 180, for his reply to Rabbi Gendler. This, of course, was before the Vietnam War. The issue was to become very important in 1967.
630. S.C.L.C. Direction, Dec. 1, 1966, TMSC. Merton-Ferry Correspondence File.
631. Interview with Brother Martin Deloach, Nov. 7, 1980.
632. Merton records the visit in his journal, RJ, Dec. 10, 1966. Most of the details here are from his account. Father Chrysogonus Waddell was present at the debate over violence and non-violence in protest songs and I am grateful to him for information given in an interview, June 29, 1981. This is doubly interesting, as it had been Father Chrysogonus who had provided Merton earlier in the year with the phonograph and records, including the Baez recording of "Silver Dagger." Contrary to some accounts, Brother Richard Schmidlin was not present: he was sick at the time.
633. Merton to W. H. Ferry, Dec. 9, 1966, TMSC.
634. Ibid., Feb. 15, 1967, TMSC.
635. RJ, Jan. 29, 1967.
636. The title was decided on Nov. 2, 1967 (RJ).
637. Merton reports that this had been accepted, Dec. 10, 1966 (RJ).
638. *The Hudson Review* 20, no. 2 (Summer 1967): 211–18. Dell'Isola, 106, C318. Breit, 25, 290.
639. Ibid., 211.
640. Ibid., 216.
641. *Raids on the Unspeakable,* prologue, 6.
642. *The Hudson Review,* op. cit., 212.
643. "Learning to Live," *Love and Living,* 7.
644. Ibid., 12.
645. "Septuagesima Letter" 1967, MGA, TMSC.
646. RJ, Feb. 7, 1967.
647. RJ, Mar. 5, 1967.
648. Merton to Rosemary Ruether, Dec. 31, 1967, TMSC.
649. Ibid., Mar. 19, 1967, TMSC.
650. Ibid., Mar. 24, 1967, TMSC.
651. Ibid., Mar. 25, 1967, TMSC.

652. RJ, Mar. 20, 1967.
653. Interview with Dom James Fox, July 11, 1981.
654. RJ, Feb. 19, 1967. The letter from Sidi Abdeslam, dated February 14, 1967, can be found in the correspondence, TMSC. It is particularly interesting how much Merton *reads into* this letter, perhaps from the "what is not said" of the earlier interview.
655. RJ, Mar. 20, 1967.

Mount Kanchenjunga

Apart from those already mentioned, who again provided help and material for this section, I should like to thank the O'Callaghan family collectively and Thompson and Virginia Willett. I am equally grateful to those who allowed me to use letters they had written or in their possession, Brother Patrick Hart for the monastery, W. H. Ferry, Suzanne Butorovich, Victor Stier, Carolyn Hammer, John Yungblut (June Yungblut died in September, 1982, and John Yungblut is now remarried.), Jonathan Williams, John Balfour, John Moffitt, Dr. Soedjatmoko, and others.

Epigraphs: Rilke, *Sonnette an Orpheus*, 2, 13, *Ausgewählte Werke*; trans. M. D. Herter Norton, *Sonnets to Orpheus*, 2, 13, 94–95. Merton, AJ, 156–57, AN.

1. Marco Pallis to Merton, Jan. 23, 1965, TMSC. And see 314.
2. Father M. Bernard to Merton, Jan. 24, 1967, MGA.
3. Father M. Bernard to Dom James Fox, Jan. 24, 1967, MGA.
4. Note from Merton to Dom James Fox, undated but probably Jan. 30, 1967, written on Father M. Bernard's letter to him of Jan. 24, 1967, MGA.
5. Dom James Fox to Merton, Jan. 31, 1967, MGA.
6. Dom James Fox to Dom Colomban Bissey, Feb. 1, 1967, MGA.
7. Dom James Fox to Father M. Bernard, Feb. 1, 1967, MGA.
8. RJ, Jan. 29 and 30, 1967. "Shep.," for Shepherdsville, Kentucky.
9. Tommie O'Callaghan, "From Lamb Chops to Peanut Butter," in Wintz, "Thomas Merton — His Friends Remember Him." Interviews with O'Callaghan, April 1980.
10. RJ, Feb. 4, 1967. Interviews with Tommie O'Callaghan, April 1980, etc.
11. RJ, Dec. 2, 1966.
12. Interview with Thompson and Virginia Willett, Sept. 29, 1980.
13. RJ, Jan. 7, 1967.
14. Kroeber, *Ishi in Two Worlds*.
15. Cora DuBois, "The 1870 Ghost Dance." For further information on his sources, see *The Geography of Lograire*, 152–53. RJ, Nov. 7, 1967: "I have been working on the Ghost Dance Canto of Lograire. Goes like a charm! Everything there in Cora DuBois mimeograph report from Berkeley. Beautiful, haunting, sad stuff. All you have to do is quote the Indians' own words!"
16. Dorn, *The Shoshoneans*. This book points out that both "American Indians" and "Native Americans" are misnomers and only tribal names are the true ones. See also Dorn, *The Poet, the People, the Spirit*; and Merton's "The Shoshoneans," 42–43, 512.
17. Nabokov, *Two Leggings: The Making of a Crow Warrior*. Merton's review essay, "War and Vision," contains interesting information about his own practices and views of fasting. He had a chance to meet and talk with Nabokov in New Mexico, see 523.
18. "Ishi: A Meditation," review of Kroeber's book (see note 14), Breit, 31, 362–63. Dell'Isola 105–6, C312.
19. *Ishi Means Man: Essays on Native Americans*.
20. Merton to Brother Antoninus, Jan. 30, 1967, TMSC.
21. Romano Guardini, *Pascal for Our Time*. RJ, Jan. 10, 1967.
22. RJ, Jan. 18, 1967. The visit had been about a week before. It was from Will Campbell that Merton got his stories about the Ku Klux Klan, which he delighted in passing on to other visitors (RJ, May 30, 1967).
23. See 60.
24. RJ, Jan. 18, 1967.

25. Merton to Robert Lax, Jan. 18, 1967, *A Catch of Anti-Letters,* 107. Also RJ, Jan. 18, 1967.
26. RJ, Jan. 18, 1967.
27. This photograph appears on the cover of Lentfoehr, *Words.*
28. "A Christian Looks at Zen." Dell'Isola, 65, B60. Breit, 10, 124. *Zen and the Birds of Appetite,* 33–58.
29. Dell'Isola, 106, C314a. Breit, 42, 506. This very interesting essay might almost have been entitled "Against Descartes." Under the title "The New Consciousness," it also appears in *Zen and the Birds of Appetite,* 15–32.
30. Dell'Isola, 46, A53. Breit, 10, 118.
31. Merton to Naomi Burton Stone, Feb. 27, 1968, FLSB:

> Cargo movements properly so called originated in New Guinea and Melanesia around the end of the 19th century and developed there especially after World War II. But analogous movements have been cropping up everywhere in formerly colonial countries, and starting from Cargo as such I tend to find analogies all over the place, not only in Black Power but even to some extent in Catholic renewal as practised by some types . . .
>
> A Cargo movement is a messianic or apocalyptic cult movement which confronts a crisis of cultural change by certain magic and religious ways of acting out what seems to be the situation and trying to get with it, controlling the course of change in one's own favor (group) or in the line of some interpretation of how things ought to be. In some sense Marxism is a kind of Cargo cult. But strictly speaking, Cargo cults are means by which primitive and underprivileged people believe they can obtain manufactured goods by an appeal to supernatural powers (ancestors, spirits, etc.) and by following a certain constant type of pattern which involves: a) complete rejection and destruction of the old culture with its goods and values b) adoption of a new attitude and hope of immediate cargo, as a result of and a reward for the rejection of the old. This always centers around some prophetic personage who brings the word, tells what is to be done, and organizes the movement.

Merton goes on to show how all this is brought out in his recent work, the essays in what he is calling "Prophets and Primitives" — most of which came out together only after his death, in *Ishi Means Man.* But in the same letter to Naomi Burton Stone, he brings it from an anthropological study into the present with:

> Though all this may seem naive and absurd to western "civilized" people, I, in common with some of the anthropologists, try to spell out a deeper meaning. Cargo is relevant to everyone in a way. It is a way in which primitive people not only attempt by magic to obtain the goods they feel to be unjustly denied them, but also and more importantly a way of spelling out their conception of the injustice, their sense that basic human relationships are being ignored, and their hope of restoring the right order of things. If they want cargo it is not only because they need material things but because Cargo will establish them as equal to the white man and give them an identity as respectable as his. But if they believe in Cargo it is because they believe in their own fundamental human worth and believe it can be shown in this way.

> For further information see *The Geography of Lograire:* notes, 147–51, "Cargo Songs," 91–95, "Cargo Catechism," 102–4, "John the Volcano," 105–12, "Dialog with Mister Clapcott," 113–14, "And a Few More Cargo Songs," 115–16, etc. See also "Cargo Cults of the South Pacific," *Love and Living,* 70–82, the shorter, edited version of Merton's essay, or rather transcript from a conference tape on "Cargo Theology." Tape and transcript, TMSC. Merton first mentions Cargo Cults, RJ, Aug. 30, 1967. After this date, there are many mentions in letters to W. H. Ferry and others.
32. Much of the information given here is from an interview with Father Matthew Kelty, Apr. 6, 1980. See also Kelty, *Flute Solo.*
33. Merton to W. H. Ferry, July 23, 1966, TMSC. Merton asks about Edwin Muir, then mentions the fragment of a play by Jean Charlot about Cook in the Pacific, which

had been published in the same issue of *Mele* (Carta International de Poesia), Honolulu, which had contained Merton's poem "Night of Destiny."

34. See "The Ladies of Tlatilco," *The Geography of Lograire*, 27–30, which uses copy from *New Yorker* advertisements. But the ladies of Tlatilco had been on Merton's mind for some time.

35. RJ, Aug. 29, 1964, "Today for the first time in years seriously imagined a project for a novel. But I doubt if it is sound. And it would interfere with more important things."

36. RJ, Mar. 2, 1967, talks of the week before. "Camus: Journals of the Plague Years," LE, 181. (All seven of Merton's essays on Camus are included in part 2 of *The Literary Essays of Thomas Merton.*) Dell'Isola, 110, C344. Breit, 21, 236.

37. RJ, May 6, 1967.

38. Merton to Jonathan Williams, Nov. 29, 1966, TMSC.

39. Breit, 38, 453. The beginning of Merton's interest in Zukofsky (and his frustration in looking for the poet's work) — RJ, July 20, 1966. Cid Corman suggests reading all his work. "But how to get it!"

40. LE, 128. Review of Zukofsky's *All: The Collected Short Poems, 1956–64.*

41. "Message to Poets," *Raids on the Unspeakable*, 156.

42. Merton was certainly aware of this himself. RJ, Oct. 2, 1967: ". . . Writing this [*The Geography of Lograire*] is most fun for me now, because in it, I think I have finally got away from self-consciousness and introversion. It may be my final liberation from all diaries. Maybe that is my one remaining task."

43. William Carlos Williams to Merton, Apr. 6, 1961, TMSC. Merton replied on July 11, 1961, TMSC. RJ, Jan. 18, 1966, Merton said he liked Ginsberg's poetry better than that of Theodore Roethke. RJ, July 11, 1965, after reading the anthology, *A Controversy of Poets* (in which he had work himself), Merton wrote, "one must take Allen Ginsberg on his own terms."

44. RJ, Jan. 29, 1966 — one of the "boomerangs." The article: "Few Questions and Fewer Answers: Extracts from a Monastic Notebook." The passage Eshleman found offensive is on page 79.

45. Merton first mentions Basil Bunting: RJ, Oct. 16, 1966. The previous day he had found Bunting's work at the University of Louisville Library, "very fine, tough, Northumbrian, Newcastle stuff of the Kingdom of Caedmon." Merton to W. H. Ferry, Mar. 22, 1967, TMSC, praises Bunting.

46. Merton to W. H. Ferry, Sept. 14, 1967, TMSC: "The David Jones *Agenda* is a real event and a revelation. As I told you, I did not know him at all. This has me felled. It is just what I have looked for for so long: better than Bunting. With Jones, Bunting and Zukofsky we have the real poets and I wonder where they have been hidden. Of course it is no problem to keep a poet hidden from me as I don't see most of the mags (a subscription to Poetry was given but the Boss would never let it through)." The "David Jones *Agenda*" is the special issue of *Agenda* published Spring-Summer 1967.

47. Interview with the Rev. A. M. Allchin, Aug. 3, 1979. Merton reports he is "glad to be a Roman" after reading Allchin's *Silent Rebellion*, RJ, July 20, 1963. Allchin's first visit was on August 4, 1963, and Merton wondered "what it would be like to go to Oxford?" For insight into both Merton and David Jones, see Allchin, *Wedding*, esp. 146, 157–67. RJ, Sept. 14, 1967: "But the real discovery of these last days has been David Jones. Rich, exciting, resonant, witty Catholic poetry . . ."

48. The correspondence between Merton and Louis Zukofsky is almost as rich as that between Merton and Czeslaw Milosz. TMSC, Mar. 29, 1967, Zukofsky writes: "As we read you we see that we've obviously been talking to each other for years — all it needed was the 'accident.' " RJ, Mar. 11, 1967: Merton reviews what the correspondence had meant to *him*.

49. Merton lost one of his last secretaries in a somewhat dramatic fashion. He found a note from the monk in his table napkin, "said the Raphael Alberti poem on Rome which I gave him last week was too much, beyond his 'limit,' scandalous, would 'cause ill feeling' — he was very upset by it — and obviously didn't understand too well. Evidently thought Alberti was in a rage because the whore houses weren't

open or something. And Alberti wasn't even mad or mean — just pleasantly jok-ing about Rome. So now I suppose this is my signal that there is to be no more secretarial help here in the monastery for me — saw it coming last week" (RJ, Mar. 10, 1967).

50. RJ, Mar. 31, 1967.
51. Merton had seen an article by Slate about being in hospital: "Lay Lobotomy — Go Slow," John H. Slate, *The Atlantic Monthly*, Nov. 1965, 166–67. He had written to Slate in the summer of 1966. (RJ, Sept. 22, 1967.)
52. Merton to Robert Lax, Oct. 31, 1967, *A Catch of Anti-Letters*, 125. Merton mentions Slate is coming, RJ, Apr. 1, 1967. RJ, Apr. 6, 1967, Slate has arrived drinking and driving fast. The argument about "God and the Vietnam War" is mentioned. In a letter to John Slate (Mar. 24, 1967, TMSC), Merton warns Slate not to follow Sy Freedgood's example, then talks of the Trust: "Question of protecting material from misuse by well meaning idiots."
53. RJ, Apr. 16, 1967.
54. RJ, Apr. 21, 1967. The main picnic was on the 20th.
55. The photograph was taken up by the Gethsemani farm buildings and is shown in Forest, *Pictorial*, 89. Merton also referred to the photograph as "the only known photograph of God."
56. RJ, Apr. 22, 1967.
57. RJ, Apr. 24, 1967.
58. RJ, Apr. 22, 1967.
59. RJ, Apr. 21, 1967.
60. RJ, Apr. 19, 1967.
61. RJ, Apr. 21, 1967.
62. RJ, Mar. 31, 1967.
63. This is no exaggeration statement. Some of Merton's warmest letters from the East on his 1968 journey were written to Dr. Tom Jerry Smith. TMSC.
64. Merton to Dom John Eudes Bamberger (both were at Gethsemani), May 4, 1967, MGA.
65. RJ, May 21, 1967.
66. RJ, May 4, 1967.
67. *Albert Camus' "The Plague."* Dell'Isola, 44, A50. Breit, 1, 2. This is a 43-page pamphlet. Merton had also planned a full-scale book on Camus (RJ, July 5, 1967).
68. Dell'Isola, 45, A52. July 10, 1968. Breit, 3, 28.
69. RJ, May 10, 1967, reporting on the day before.
70. "He [Daniel Berrigan] wants to go to Hanoi, but may get thrown out of the Jesuits for doing it." (RJ, May 10, 1967). On April 15, 1967 (RJ), Merton had written, "Big Peace Demonstration today: but demonstrations do no good. Dan Berrigan is in a kind of crisis with his Superiors again — over the question of aid to war victims in both North and South Viet Nam. It is to be sent on a symbolic visit to V. N. and his Superiors won't allow it. He will probably go anyway." (Inconsistencies and ambiguities in original.)
71. RJ, May 10, reporting on the day before. It made it worse that he had just been reading about separations in Camus. "The incorrigible sorrow of all prisoners and exiles, which is to live in company with a memory that serves no purpose." And, incidentally, how far this is from his words about "the love of creatures" in SSM and even in *No Man Is an Island!*
72. RJ, May 13, 1967.
73. Ibid.
74. RJ, May 14, 1967.
75. On November 13, 1962 (RJ), reading William of Conches (c. 1100–1154) made Mer-ton think of his own role as a teacher, especially, perhaps, as he was then giving conferences with Dan Walsh on the School of Chartres. "Beautiful little chapter on the Teachers [in *Philosophia Mundi*]. I was very moved by it. I usually ignore this element in my own vocation, but obviously I am a writer, a student and a teacher as well as a contemplative of sorts, and my solitude etc., is that of a writer and teacher, not of a pure hermit. And the great thing in my life is, or should be, love

of truth. I know there is nothing more precious than the bond of charity created by communicating and sharing the truth. This is really my whole life."

76. RJ, May 17, 1967.
77. Family movie of the reception after Dan Walsh's ordination, O'Callaghan family.
78. Interviews with Tommie and Frank O'Callaghan, Apr. 1980, etc. These two incidents have now appeared elsewhere in print.
79. See, e.g., the letter from Merton to Jonathan Williams, May 19, 1967, which contains the line, "I went in and got stoned on champagne, which must have surprised the cult public" (TMSC).
80. RJ, June 1, 1967.
81. Ibid.
82. RJ, June 9, 1967, reporting on events three days earlier.
83. Suzanne Butorovich to Merton, June 15, 1967, TMSC.
84. Merton to Suzanne Butorovich, June 22, 1967, TMSC. He suggests she send her letters marked *"conscience matter* and make it look like you are just entering the convent or leaving it or something . . ." "Dear Disaster . . ." Merton to Suzanne Butorovich, July 18, 1967, TMSC.
85. Suzanne Butorovich to Merton, July 8, 1967, TMSC.
86. Merton to Suzanne Butorovich, July 18, 1967, TMSC.
87. Ibid., Sept. 5, 1967, TMSC. RJ, Jan. 25, 1965: "He [Father Illtud Evans] says the manager of the Beatles said on a TV program that he had read *Elected Silence* five times, that it was one of his favorite books. He described it as 'a novel about Roman Catholicism'!"
88. Suzanne Butorovich to Merton, Sept. 5, 1967, TMSC.
89. Ibid., Sept. 6, 1967, TMSC.
90. Ibid., Aug. 31, 1967, TMSC.
91. Merton to John and June Yungblut, Feb. 11, 1967, TMSC.
92. RJ, May 1, 1967: "Talked in the afternoon with Jack Yungblut from Atlanta and Dr. Young from Anderson, S.C. Jack Y. a Quaker — friend of M. Luther King, from whom he brought messages — exceedingly deferent, but very nice. We discussed his ms. on mysticism, which has good things in it. Will have to try to write him something on the Christological problems he raises but that is a subject I am shy of (as with Rosemary in her letters)." RJ, May 3, 1967: "Yesterday had to go (late afternoon) to see the allergist in St. Matthews. Spoke for a few minutes again with J. Yungblut and now also with his wife June Yungblut who is staying in Bardstown while he is here. She is doing a dissertation on Beckett, working under Cleanth Brooks, and I found her very interesting and likeable."
93. June Yungblut to Merton, May 7, 1967, TMSC.
94. Ibid., July 8, 1967, TMSC.
95. Merton to June Yungblut, Nov. 19, 1967, TMSC. RJ, Nov. 18, 1967:

> Today a letter came from AFSC (The Friends) in Philadelphia asking me to form part of an unofficial peace team that is to meet and talk with representatives of the NLF (Viet Cong) and try to get up some concrete proposals for Washington. A most unusual invitation, so unusual that if I were left to myself I'd have no alternative but to accept — and in my case I could not take it upon myself to refuse. I can't, in conscience, refuse. So I decided to turn it over to the Abbot. Was not able to talk to him, he was busy. Gave him the letter and I know very well what he will do! I don't think there is a chance in a million of his seeing the importance and significance of it and he won't think for 10 seconds of letting me go. And I'll probably have to put up with one of his more unreasonable sermons. All of which poses a problem. It really raises the question of my staying here . . .

On the same day, Merton talked at the hermitage to Father Methodius Telnack, of the Monastery of the Holy Spirit, Conyers, who knew the Yungbluts, and who was attending a meeting of cantors at Gethsemani. On November 21, 1967 (RJ), Merton was in Lexington. Dom James was having an operation . . . "Obviously no chance of my going to Cambodia! (A long note about that was in my mail when I got home.)"

96. Father Paul Bourne to Merton, Aug. 31, 1968. On June 28, 1967, Father Paul wrote, "Don't fret about censorship. I've about reached the point where I consider it 'inappropriate' . . ."
97. Dell'Isola, 43, A49. May 5, 1967. Breit, 5, 54.
98. Merton to Robert Lax, Oct. 8, 1966, *A Catch of Anti-Letters*, 96.
99. RJ, Sept. 10, 1967. But see Edward Rice to Merton, June 5, 1966, TMSC.
100. Merton to Father Basil De Pinto, O.S.B., Apr. 13, 1967, TMSC.
101. RJ, Jan. 18, 1964 — *The Moviegoer*, "What the hero is *not*." Merton especially liked the scenes in the fishing camp and with the crippled child. Merton to Walker Percy, end of Jan. 1964, TMSC.
102. Walker Percy to Merton, July 13, 1967. The novel is, of course, *Love in the Ruins*.
103. See 189.
104. Merton to Walker Percy, Aug. 24, 1967, TMSC.
105. Sundkler, *Bantu Prophets in South Africa*. Walker Percy to Merton, Aug. 27, 1967, TMSC.
106. Merton to Walker Percy, July 20, 1967, TMSC.
107. Walker Percy to Merton, Oct. 17, 1967, TMSC.
108. Robert Lax to Merton, Oct. 12, 1963, *A Catch of Anti-Letters*, 18.
109. CWL, 36, 67.
110. Merton to June Yungblut, Mar. 6, 1968, TMSC: "As a Catholic Buddhist of long standing and also in fact Quaker I naturally feel happy about the new Church . . .'"
111. Merton's feelings for his birthplace had been stirred as the result of a publishing tangle. When J. M. Cruzet of Editorial Selecta of Barcelona applied for the rights to translate *The Seven Storey Mountain* into Catalan, only to be told that all Spanish translation rights belonged to Editorial Sudamericana, Merton stepped in to help. Writing in fine Castilian Spanish, if not Catalan, to Sr. Cruzet on January 22, 1958, Merton told him that he was proud to have been asked and considered himself "in a sense, a Catalan since I was born in France in the area still known as 'Catalane' (trans. Debbie DiSalvo, TMSC). The Catalan edition, *La Muntanya dels Set Cercles* (alas, listed under *Spanish* in Breit, 78, 899, and not listed at all in Dell'Isola), translated by Guillem Colom, arrived at Gethsemani, April 7, 1963 (RJ). This copy, given to Sister Thérèse Lentfoehr, and now in the Merton Center at Columbia University, has the inscription, "This is Catalan — in a way my 'native' language." Merton was able to read Catalan: see letter from Merton to Louis Zukofsky, July 18, 1967, in which he talks about reading books in Spanish and "even lately, Catalan (article on the Catalan hermit movement and things like that!)" (TMSC.)
112. "Curriculum vitae Merton May 1967," typed, enclosure with letter from Merton to Jonathan Williams, May 19, 1967: "I am bad at writing these things, 'born on a chimney top in Strasbourg in 1999,' etc., but you can select what you want from this one, there is plenty of choice" (TMSC).
113. RJ, July 5, 1967, reporting on the day before.
114. RJ, July 13, 1967, reporting on events three days earlier.
115. RJ, July 16, 1967.
116. Victor Hammer to Merton, Feb. 3, 1965, TMSC.
117. Ibid., Feb. 22, 1960, TMSC.
118. Ibid., undated, in ink, almost certainly 1960, TMSC.
119. Merton to Carolyn Hammer, July 11, 1967, TMSC.
120. Merton to Suzanne Butorovich, Feb. 11, 1968, TMSC.
121. RJ, Aug. 1, 1967.
122. Interview with Brother Alban Herberger, July 11, 1961.
123. RJ, Aug. 4, 1967.
124. W. H. Ferry to Merton, Apr. 13, 1967, TMSC.
125. Merton to W. H. Ferry, Aug. 22, 1967, TMSC: "Maybe the Abbot considers me a prominent atheist, which is what Koenig is apparently here to see."
126. Dom James Fox to Cardinal Koenig, Aug. 7, 1967, MGA.
127. RJ, Aug. 4, 1967.

128. It made it worse to be present as translator in Chapter on August 4, 1967, when Dom Ignace showed the monks the slides of his travels in the Far East (RJ). At the same time, Merton was reading letters from Dom Jean Leclercq about *his* travels! (RJ, July 18, 1967.)
129. RJ, Aug. 2, 1967.
130. RJ, Aug. 28, 1967.
131. Bramachari (Dr. Mahanambrata B. Bhogavata-Gangottai) to Merton, May 28, 1965, TMSC.
132. RJ, Aug. 30, 1967.
133. Ibid.
134. Merton to Robert Lax, Jan. 26, 1967. *A Catch of Anti-Letters*, 110.
135. RJ, Aug. 30, 1967. Joost A. M. Meerloo's *Homo Militans: De psychologie van oorlog en vrende de mens* had been published in The Hague in 1964. Merton was reading the typescript of a translation on which Meerloo had asked him to collaborate. This set him to thinking about language in debate. RJ, Aug. 2, 1967.
136. RJ, Sept. 2, 1967.
137. RJ, Aug. 9, 1967.
138. RJ, Nov. 12, 1967, reporting on Nov. 11.
139. RJ, Sept. 7, 1967.
140. RJ, June 1, 1967. The abbot had first talked of retiring on May 30. On July 14 (RJ), Merton talks about "his elaborate little game of pretending he wants to retire (as a dream it is sincere . . .)."
141. RJ, July 20, 1967.
142. Discussion began at the General Chapter of 1967. Future Chapters would make it a more common practice to be elected for a term than for life.
143. RJ, Sept. 7, 1967.
144. RJ, Sept. 11, 1967.
145. RJ, Jan. 9, 1964.
146. RJ, Sept. 30, 1967.
147. RJ, Sept. 10, 1967.
148. Ibid., reporting on September 9.
149. RJ, Sept. 22, 1967.
150. Merton to Robert Lax, Sept. 5, 1967. *A Catch of Anti-Letters*, 118.
151. Robert Lax to Merton, Sept. 13, 1967. *A Catch of Anti-Letters*, 121.
152. Ibid., Oct. 15, 1967, 124.
153. RJ, Sept. 10, 1967.
154. RJ, Sept. 30, 1967. Merton used a line of Bachelard's on the cover page of "The Newsnatch Invention," the working notebook for, and perhaps the first draft of, *The Geography of Lograire* (#33 TMSC): *"Rendre imprévisible la parole n'est-il pas un apprentissage de la liberté?"* ("To render language unpredictable, isn't this an apprenticeship of liberty?") Bachelard (1884–1962), *La Poétique de l'espace*. See Lentfoehr, *Words*, 117 and note 152. See also the beginning of Sister Thérèse's essay "Social Concern in the Poetry of Thomas Merton."
155. RJ, Oct. 2, 1967.
156. MAG, 188.
157. RJ, Oct. 7, 1967. "The Street is for Celebration," written as an introduction for a book of photographs of Spanish Harlem by Monsignor Robert J. Fox, was not published at the time, but appears in *Love and Living*, 41–47.
158. RJ, Oct. 23, 1967.
159. RJ, Oct. 29, 1967, reporting on the day before.
160. Interviews with Tommie and Frank O'Callaghan, Apr. 1980, etc. Lentfoehr, "A Model of Delicate Compassion," in Wintz, "Thomas Merton — His Friends Remember Him," 38. This gives November 7, 1967, as the date, confirming Merton's account in the journal. However, this is given as the 5th in Robert Daggy's interesting account, "Sister Thérèse Lentfoehr, S.D.S."
161. See Lentfoehr, "Notes on Sources," *The Geography of Lograire*, 139–41.
162. Merton to Robert Lax, June 7, 1967, *A Catch of Anti-Letters*, 105. This speaks of "the poet Lothaire," rather than the kings.
163. RJ, July 18, 1964. VOW, 62. RJ, July 21, 1964. VOW, 64.

164. James Laughlin to the author, Nov. 15, 1983, saying Merton was very anxious to write his own long poem, like Pound's *Cantos* and Williams's *Paterson*. Laughlin had sent the New Directions editions of both to Merton, SJ, 140, Dec. 6, 1948. *Anáthémata* is by David Jones, see 479–80. Merton would soon become interested also in the long poems of Robinson Jeffers.

165. Merton to W. H. Ferry, Sept. 26, 1967, TMSC. "It is sheer joy to get back into *Finnegans Wake* again after all these years."

166. RJ, Nov. 12, 1967.

167. RJ, Dec. 9, 1967.

168. Merton to Jonathan Williams, Oct. 31, 1967, TMSC: ". . . Here is a concrete poem I am working on . . ." He encloses "Concrete racegram of Pluto king of hell as he meets white foe in Goal while one or both is/are set free into the fair." Consciously or unconsciously, Merton was illustrating yet another move in Prisoners' Base. It is signed "Thomas Merton, October 31, 1967." See 538.

169. Ibid., Dec. 13, 1967, TMSC.

170. RJ, Dec. 10, 1967.

171. W. H. Ferry to Merton, undated, but clearly July 1968, sent from Ghost Ranch, New Mexico, TMSC.

172. RJ, Dec. 18, 1967, reporting on the day before. Interview with Dom Flavian Burns, Mar. 29, 1981.

173. "MY CAMPAIGN PLATFORM for non-Abbot and permanent keeper of the present doghouse." Many copies of this exist. TMSC, etc.

174. This was confirmed in a number of interviews with those who were at Gethsemani in 1968.

175. Interview with Dom Flavian Burns, Mar. 29, 1968.

176. *The Odyssey*, trans. Fitzgerald, 4, 11. 561–64, 569. Quoted, RJ, Jan. 4, 1968.

177. RJ, Jan. 4, 1968.

178. RJ, Jan. 6, 1968, reporting on the events of the day before.

179. Ibid.

180. RJ, Jan. 8, 1968.

181. RJ, Jan. 11, 1968.

182. Ibid.

183. RJ, Jan. 13, 1968. Written on the day of, and before, the election.

184. RJ, Jan. 15, 1968, reporting earlier: "Two momentous days, heavy with snow and heavier with happenings . . ."

185. Ibid.

186. One example from many, letter to Father Basil Pennington, Institute of Cistercian Studies at West Michigan University, Kalamazoo (chairman of the board of directors of Cistercian Publications), Jan. 22, 1968, TMSC: "You know perhaps that our new Abbot is Fr. Flavian. A fellow hermit. I am very happy to have him. I am sure it will mean real newness of life. Why don't you all invite him up there and ask that he bring me along?"

187. RJ, Jan. 19, 1968.

188. *Mystics and Zen Masters*, 16. Whenever Merton uses a translation, he cites *Meister Eckhart*, trans. Blakney. This translation has a number of good points, but it is not very helpful on the vital question of rendering the word *Grunde*.

189. *Zen and the Birds of Appetite*, 63. See 238.

190. *Mystics and Zen Masters*, 25.

191. See 433. For Merton, the question was summed up in a line from the journals, "Idolatry is the basic sin" (RJ, Nov. 7, 1964), repeated often in one way or another in published work, unpublished, and in letters.

192. *Mystics and Zen Masters*, 14.

193. Goethe, *Italian Journey*, 335.

194. *Mystics and Zen Masters*, 26.

195. Ibid., 25.

196. Willey, *The Seventeenth-Century Background*, 12.

197. RJ, Jan. 21, 1968.

198. True even much earlier — "Use of torture in Viet Nam (by our side) is admitted without apology as something quite reasonable." (RJ, Jan. 4, 1965.) Merton was

right that something radical had happened at just this point: it was not simply a matter of degree.

199. RJ, Jan. 26, 1968.
200. Interview with Brother Alban Herberger, July 11, 1981.
201. This was probably on Friday, February 9, 1968, but there are some confusions in dates on the journal at this point.
202. RJ, Feb. 10 (?), 1968. Ironically, he writes, "Once was enough, and it was exhausting." His thought about driving a car is interesting.
203. RJ, Feb. 20, 1968. He had been in Louisville the day before, the 19th.
204. Ibid. He had talked to Mulloy the day before.
205. RJ, Mar. 7, 1968.
206. Merton to June Yungblut, Jan. 20, 1968, TMSC.
207. Merton to John and June Yungblut, Jan. 16, 1968, TMSC.
208. June Yungblut to Merton, Jan. 25, 1968, TMSC.
209. Ibid., Jan. 10, 1968, TMSC. It looks as if there is a typo here. June Yungblut actually wrote, "You are really a lot of fun, of fun to be with and a great companion."
210. Ibid.
211. Merton to June Yungblut, Mar. 6, 1968, TMSC.
212. MAG, 127.
213. RJ, Oct. 2, 1967.
214. RJ, Feb. 8, 1968.
215. RJ, Feb. 24, 1968, reporting on the day before.
216. Merton to Thomas McDonough, Archbishop of Louisville, Jan. 3, 1968, TMSC.
217. CWL, 75, 127. *Indiscrete* has been replaced here by "indiscreet." One should recall, too, the clear statement Merton made on his own need in the memorandum of September 19, 1960: "In point of fact there has to be some protection against my self-will." (See note 86, "Mount Olivet," above.)
218. Merton to Thomas McDonough, Jan. 3, 1968, TMSC.
219. Thomas McDonough to Merton, Jan. 8, 1968, TMSC.
220. Merton to Thomas McDonough, Feb. 10, 1968, TMSC.
221. Merton refers to this advantage a number of times. He wonders how Dom James will be elected abbot general when he does not speak French well. RJ, May 8, 1958, "Rev. Father secretly learns Spanish and this makes me angry because it means that he has no intention of taking me to South America if and when the time comes — if he can help it. And I have no doubt he will be able to help it." Some of the correspondence with Cardenal a year later is in Spanish. The correspondence with Daniélou, Lemercier, and others during the Cuernavaca crisis is in French.
222. RJ, Feb. 29, 1968. *Zen and the Birds of Appetite* finished.
223. RJ, Feb. 20, 1968. Foundations dug for addition.
224. RJ, Mar. 22, 1968.
225. RJ, Mar. 4, 1968, reported.
226. RJ, Feb. 29, 1968.
227. See also "Peace Council Joins Joseph Mulloy Draft Plea," *Louisville Courier-Journal*, Feb. 22, 1968, 10A. RJ, Mar. 11 and 15, 1968.
228. Merton to John Howard Griffin, Mar. 27, 1968, TMSC.
229. RJ, Mar. 30, 1968. See 307.
230. RJ, Jan. 15, 1968.
231. Interview with Dom Flavian Burns, Mar. 29, 1981. He pointed out to Merton that the Woman in Revelation was pregnant. Merton roared with laughter. A few days later he was much more somber about it.
232. RJ, Mar. 28, 1968.
233. RJ, Apr. 6, 1968.
234. RJ, Oct. 23, 1967. The combination was the date of the foundation of the Cistercian Order.
235. RJ, June 13, 1968.
236. RJ, July 23, 1968.

237. RJ, Mar. 21, 1968 — the Abbatial Blessing. Interview with Dom Edward Mc-Corkell, Mar. 29, 1981. It does seem as if Merton was being snubbed at the Blessing of Dom Flavian, even if he says, "I got out fast so as not to get involved with them."

238. Interview with Dom Edward McCorkell, Mar. 29, 1981.

239. Ibid.

240. Ibid.

241. Barbara Braveman to Merton, Oct. 11, 1967, TMSC.

242. Ibid., Mar. 21, 1968, TMSC.

243. RJ, Apr. 6, 1968.

244. Ibid. The owner of the restaurant, Louis Rogers, had been made an honorary Kentucky colonel, and he was named Colonel Hawk because he was a great hunter of birds. It is Colonel Hawk's Restaurant in the Bardstown telephone directory.

245. Ibid. But Susan Smith wrote to him on April 23, 1968, thanking him for the weekend and saying he had convinced her that President Johnson was a human being with a conscience. TMSC.

246. Ibid., Merton's ellipsis.

247. June Yungblut to Merton, Mar. 12, 1968, TMSC.

248. This letter is not in the correspondence files at TMSC. I have given the extract as it is quoted in RJ, Apr. 6, 1968, with the ellipses Merton gives in the journal.

249. RJ, Apr. 6, 1968, reporting on two days before.

250. Ibid.

251. Ibid.

252. On March 30, 1968, a second invitation had arrived from Asia, this time from Father M. Cyprien van den Bogaard, the superior of the monastery of Trappists at Rawa Seneng, Indonesia. Merton's note on the letter, passed to Dom Flavian, reads: "If you'd like to know what I personally would prefer — 'my own will' — it would be to go to Rawa Seneng and maybe to Japan (to some Zen places) and then to sneak home entirely avoiding Europe and the inevitability of going to various houses there. To me, the Trappists in Europe are of no interest whatever and there is no point in my getting involved with them . . ." He goes on, "About Bangkok, as I said, I am in the dark. I don't know what I think about it. I think the meeting might be a waste of time, but I just don't know" (MAG).

253. RJ, May 4, 1968.

254. Typescript, TMSC. AA. Now published. *Woods, Shore, Desert,* with photographs by Merton.

255. *Woods, Shore, Desert,* May 6, 6.

256. *The Geography of Lograire,* 119.

257. *Woods, Shore, Desert,* May 6, 6. Poulet, *Studies in Human Time.*

258. *The Geography of Lograire,* 127–30.

259. *Woods, Shore, Desert,* May 6, 7.

260. Ibid.

261. Ibid., May 7, 11.

262. Ibid., May 14, 17.

263. Ibid., May 17, 28.

264. Ibid., May 14, 20. He had heard about Aunt Kit's death from a nun in New Zealand, but the full details did not reach him until he received a letter from Aunt Ka, RJ, June 5, 1968. This, with the newspaper accounts she had enclosed of the disaster and the obituary, can be found at TMSC. The disaster took place on April 10, 1968. The obituary in the *Christchurch Press* has Merton, "well-known religious writer," and author of *Elected Silence,* as the *brother* of Agnes Gertrude Merton (79), rather than the great-nephew!

265. *Woods, Shore, Desert,* May 22, 1968, 40; May 30, 1968, 46.

266. Ibid., May 14, 18–20.

267. Ibid., May 22, 41–42.

268. Ibid., May 30, 46.

269. Ibid., 46–48.

270. Ibid., May 16, 22, 24.

271. Ibid., May 17, 30.
272. Ibid., 31.
273. Ibid., May 22, 38.
274. RJ, May 28, 1968.
275. Interview with Dom John Eudes Bamberger, Mar. 22, 1981. Dom John Eudes said he was somewhat overcome by this.
276. RJ, June 4, 1968.
277. RJ, June 6, 1968, reporting on the day before.
278. RJ, June 23, 1968. (See note 252 above.)
279. Many of these are preserved at TMSC. Copies, AA.
280. *Woods, Shore, Desert,* May 14, 16.
281. RJ, June 13, 1968. He also reports on the picnic on this day. Cf. Merton to John Slate, June 7, 1967, TMSC.
282. RJ, June 13, 1968.
283. Merton to James Baker, June 11, 1968, TMSC.
284. Martin E. Marty's review of *Seeds of Destruction,* "Sowing Thorns in the Flesh," had been critical of Merton. Merton defended his "pessimistic prophesy" in "Negro Violence and White Non-Violence." Marty retracted in "To: Thomas Merton. Re: Your Prophecy." RJ, Aug. 30, 1967.
285. RJ, June 26, 1968.
286. RJ, June 24, 1968.
287. RJ, June 23, 1968.
288. RJ, July 3, 1968.
289. Dell'Isola, 120, C414. *Sewanee Review* 77, no. 3 (Summer 1969): 543–54. Breit, 36, 431.
290. RJ, July 5, 1968.
291. RJ, July 17, 1956.
292. *Woods, Shore, Desert,* May 6, 9–10.
293. RJ, July 5, 1968. Dom Flavian says he found a very different picture than Father Louis had reported when he went to the Vina election and took a look at the coast. There were thick fogs and snakes everywhere. Interview with Dom Flavian Burns, Sept. 29, 1980.
294. RJ, July 19, 1968.
295. Snow, *Journey to the Beginning.* Merton quotes this at the back of the notebook full of Gandhi quotations, which became *Gandhi on Non-Violence.* Notebook 9, TMSC, dated 1955.
296. RJ, July 12, 1968.
297. RJ, July 21, 1968.
298. RJ, July 19, 1968.
299. RJ, July 22, 1968.
300. RJ, July 23, 1968. Merton's ellipsis.
301. Merton to June Yungblut, July 13, 1968, TMSC. Earlier in the letter, Merton writes of talking with Anselm Atkins, from the Monastery of the Holy Spirit, Conyers. In his journey, he describes the visit, "We had a short talk on the library balcony" (RJ, June 26, 1968, recording the day before).
302. RJ, July 21, 1968.
303. RJ, Aug. 1, 1968.
304. RJ, Jan. 7, 1967. RJ, Dec. 18, 1967.
305. Interview with Dom John Eudes Bamberger, Mar. 21, 1981. The interviews lasted three days, March 21, 22, 23. Some details are from different days.
306. Ibid.
307. Ibid.
308. RJ, July 27, 1968.
309. Ibid.
310. RJ, Aug. 5, 1968.
311. RJ, July 29, 1968.
312. Ibid. Merton's italics.
313. RJ, Aug. 10, 1968.
314. RJ, Aug. 13, 1968.

315. See note 252 above. There was even a plan (in his own head at least) of visiting his remaining relatives in New Zealand "on the way home." He discusses this in the journal and in a letter to John J. Merton, June 17, 1968, TMSC.
316. RJ, Aug. 13, 1968.
317. Interview with Dom Flavian Burns, Sept. 29, 1980. Dom Jean Leclercq was there on September 7, 1968, and his visit coincided with that of Edward Rice. There are photographs of Merton and Leclercq talking, Rice, 165, 169.
318. RJ, Aug. 20, 1968. This has the same melodramatic quality as quote in "Brooke Hill," note 60 above.
319. Rice, 164.
320. Interview with Edward Rice, July 19, 1980.
321. RJ, Sept. 7, 1968. Merton's "sic."
322. RJ, June 17, 1968.
323. RJ, Aug. 26, 1968. There are also some details of the trip in SN.
324. Dr. Soedjatmoko to John Howard Griffin, Aug. 7, 1970, three pages, AA. Merton learned the Indonesian word for such an exchange of good feelings and repeats this in the journal account on August 26, 1968, *Tjoztjoz* (SN, Aug. 26, 1968).
325. Dr. Soedjatmoko to John Howard Griffin, Aug. 7, 1970, AA.
326. RJ, Aug. 26, 1968.
327. Ibid.
328. RJ, Aug. 27 and Sept. 1, 1968, for Merton's account of the shopping expeditions. Also, interviews with Tommie and Frank O'Callaghan, Apr. 1980, etc.
329. Merton to Dom Flavian Burns, Oct. 9, 1968.
330. RJ, Sept. 3, 1968.
331. RJ, Sept. 9, 1968, for Merton's account. Brother Patrick Hart has provided a number of published accounts, for example, AJ, foreword, xxi–xxii, and, a very vivid account, Hart, *Monk*, prologue, 15–17.
332. RJ, Sept. 9, 1968. This entry in the journal called "The Hawk's Dream" provides the title from Jeffers:

> We have climbed at length to a height . . .
> The inhuman road, the wounded attempt, the remote lodestar . . .
> And the old symbols forgotten in the glory of that your hawk's dream.

Under this, Merton writes, "Sent *Geography* today." Antoninus, *Robinson Jeffers.*
333. "Sensation Time at Home," group of poems first published in Appendix 1, CP, 611–66.
334. RJ, Sept. 9, 1968.
335. Interviews with Dom Flavian Burns, Sept. 29, 1980, and Mar. 29, 1981. Merton did his best to keep the promise. Dom Flavian believes this accounts for Merton's nervousness about the cameras, and his attempt to hide his face from the camera during a final closeup in the television film of December 10, 1968, at the Bangkok conference. TMSC.
336. These relics were precious to Merton, and demonstrate (if any demonstration is needed at this point) that there was a strongly traditional side to Merton. The relics were returned with his body, spilling out of his spongebag when it was opened. They are now at the monastery.
337. Seitz, "Thomas Merton: A Deathday Remembrance." Supplemented by an interview with Seitz, Aug. 10, 1980. This is certainly the tone of Merton's journals.
338. Seitz provides some of the details. Also interviews with Tommie and Frank O'Callaghan, Apr. 1980, etc. Merton himself provides (or confirms) much here, SN, Sept. 11, 1968. Also RJ, Sept. 16 and 19 (Merton wrote up descriptions of the last two days in Louisville, and the time at Christ in the Desert and on the Reservation.)
339. SN, Sept. 11, 1968.
340. Part of Bellarmine College, Louisville. Today the Merton Room and the offices of the Thomas Merton Center occupy a section of this building.
341. RJ, Sept. 19, 1968. Also SN, Sept. 11, 1968.
342. Merton's concrete poem, "Pluto king of hell," enclosed with a letter to Jonathan Williams, Oct. 31, 1967, TMSC.
343. SN, Sept. 12, 1968.

344. SN, Sept. 16, 1968. In his letter to W. H. Ferry of September 4, 1968, Merton makes it clear the addition of the trip to New Mexico came about because he was determined to be present at the Indian festival on September 14–15. TMSC.
345. RJ, Sept. 19, 1968.
346. SN, Sept. 22, 1968.
347. RJ, Sept. 27, 1968.
348. Merton to Naomi Burton Stone (on *Monks Pond* stationery), Sept. 6, 1968. FLSB. The letter was mailed from the Redwoods.
349. Merton to W. H. Ferry, Sept. 26, 1968, TMSC.
350. RJ, Oct. 8, 1968. Also SN, Oct. 3, 1968.
351. Merton may have been especially susceptible to the students simply because they were French. On July 9, 1965 (RJ), he records meeting a group of French students by chance in the bookstore of the University of Louisville: ". . . We went and had coffee and talked. It was very enjoyable, interesting, intelligent talk, people from *home!!*" He invited them all (and their nineteen friends he didn't meet, also French) out to Gethsemani.
352. Merton to Dom Flavian Burns, Oct. 8, 1968, MGA.
353. RJ, Oct. 8, 1968. Interview with W. H. Ferry, Mar. 26, 1981.
354. Merton to Dom Flavian Burns, Oct. 9, 1968, MGA. In this letter he says he has telephoned the monastery because someone told him he would need a habit "to deal with the Buddhists." It would have cost eleven dollars to mail him the cowl also, and it was decided simply to send the habit.
355. Merton to Dom Flavian Burns, Oct. 9, 1968, MGA.
356. Steindl-Rast, "Man of Prayer."
357. RJ, Oct. 13, 1968.
358. Ibid.
359. AJ, Oct. 15, 1968, 4–5. AN, Oct. 15, 4.
360. SJ, Dec. 13, 1950, 317.
361. The September 1968 Circular Letter to Friends is reproduced as Appendix 1, AJ, 295–96. Copies of original: TMSC, MAG, AA, etc.
362. Much additional help in the preparation was given by Marco Pallis, Father Augustine Wulff, and others. The notes are especially helpful. There is some editing, and the editorial policy is explained on page xiv of the Editors' Notes. Here, all quotations are taken from "Asian Notes" and the journal, and are given unedited, except that the spelling conforms to *The Asian Journal*. "Asian Notes" (#40 TMSC, Bellarmine, C1–107 "A") takes over on October 15, 1968, from the small notebook of May–October 1968 (#36 TMSC, Bellarmine C1–106). "Asian Notes" was clearly intended for publication (one of the "two books" Merton mentions in his letter to Naomi Burton Stone of September 6, 1968), and it gives "If lost — please return to Thomas Merton c/o New Directions 333 6th. Av., New York, N.Y. 10014" on the title page of a Rutgers University spiral notebook. The "Asian Notes" continued to December 7, 1968. There is a gap in the journal (#8 TMSC, Bellarmine, C1–101 "B") between October 13 and October 24, after which the entries in the journal continue to December 8. The "Asian Notes" and the journal parallel one another fairly closely, with the proviso that the journal was not intended for publication. "Asian Notes" falls behind about two days. It is the journal, not "Asian Notes," that provides one of Merton's most celebrated passages, see 560–61. The pocket notebook (#39 TMSC, Bellarmine, C1–108 "C") is difficult to read. Most of the notes are addresses and plane timetables, though the poem "Kandy Express" was very skillfully transcribed from this by James Laughlin, who had been in Sri Lanka, and Naomi Burton Stone, who knew Merton's handwriting well. This appears in AJ, 222–28.
363. AN, Oct. 17, 1968, 9. AJ, Oct. 17, 1968, 10.
364. It is interesting to recall an earlier entry, "Calendar in the infirm refectory shows us now the Temple of the Emerald Buddha in Bangkok — a 'top tourist attraction.' Buddha too is in the tourist business in spite of himself, along with St. Peter, and The Christ of Conovado, and Niagara Falls and Islands in the Sun and Old Vienna and the Alps . . . etc." RJ, Mar. 15, 1964. Merton's ellipsis.

365. Notes "On Mindfulness" are provided by Bhikkhu Khantipalo as Appendix 2, AJ, 297–304.
366. AN, Oct. 19, 1968, 14–15. AJ, Oct. 19, 1968, 24–25.
367. AN, Oct. 19, 1968, 16. AJ, Oct. 19, 1968, 27.
368. Merton tells Marco Pallis that he was charged seventy dollars for overweight luggage. "We are the Dives and they are Lazarus," he says of Calcutta. Merton to Pallis, Oct. 20, 1968, MGA.
369. AN, Oct. 19, 1968, 17. AJ, Oct. 19, 1968, 28.
370. AN, Oct. 22, 1968, 21. AJ, Oct. 22, 1968, 32.
371. AJ, 307. "Thomas Merton's View of Monasticism" (informal talk delivered at Calcutta, Oct. 1968), Appendix 3.
372. AJ, 308. Ibid. Compare with AJ, 315–17, "Monastic Experience and East-West Dialogue," (notes for a paper to have been delivered at Calcutta, Oct. 1968), Appendix 4.
373. AJ, 316.
374. AJ, 318–19. "Special Closing Prayer," offered at the First Spiritual Summit Conference in Calcutta.
375. *The Asian Journal* is somewhat more enthusiastic than the journal on this point, and Merton's letters give a varied report. AJ, 34. Included is sketch of swami with saffron Kleenex, AJ, 40. RJ, Oct. 24, 1968: "On the whole the performance was depressing. Good people, efforts to communicate, but a sense of tired repetition of old formulas — a sense that little was really being said except words."
376. Amiya Chakravarty had advised Merton on Asian matters for some years. Merton dedicated *Zen and the Birds of Appetite* to him.
377. AN, Oct. 20, 1968, 20. AJ, Oct. 20, 30–31. See also note 12, AJ, 45. See also "November Circular Letter to Friends," AJ, Appendix 6, 323–24.
378. AJ, 129. This represents a major change of plan. He had wanted to avoid Europe in March. See note 252 above.
379. "November Circular Letter to Friends," AJ, Appendix 6, 320.
380. AN, Oct. 20, 1968, 21. AJ, Oct. 20, 1968, 31.
381. AN, Oct. 24, 1968, 24. AJ, Oct. 24, 1968, 35.
382. RJ, Oct. 28, 1968. AN, Oct. 29, 1968, 34. AJ, Oct. 28, 1968, 54; Notes, 71.
383. AN, Oct. 30, 1968, 35. AJ, Oct. 30, 1968, 65.
384. AN, Oct. 31, 1968, 38. AJ, Oct. 31, 1968, 69.
385. AN, Nov. 1, 1968, 39. AJ, Nov. 1, 1968, 78.
386. AN, Nov. 1, 1968, 39–40. AJ, Nov. 1, 1968, 79.
387. AN, Nov. 5, 1968, 59. AJ, Nov. 5, 1968, 107.
388. AN, Nov. 2, 1968, 40. AJ, Nov. 1, 1968, 79.
389. AN, Nov. 2, 1968, 41. AJ, Nov. 2, 1968, 84.
390. AN, Nov. 2, 1968, 41. AJ, Nov. 2, 1968, 82.
391. AN, Nov. 2, 1968, 43. AJ, Nov. 2, 1968, 86.
392. AN, Nov. 4, 1968, 55. AJ, Nov. 4, 1968, 102.
393. AN, Nov. 8, 1968, 72. AJ, Nov. 8, 1968, 125.
394. AN, Nov. 8, 1968, 75. AJ, Nov. 8, 1968, 125.
395. AN, Nov. 5, 1968, 58–59. AJ, Nov. 5, 1968, 105–6.
396. AN, Nov. 3, 1968, 50. AJ, Nov. 3, 1968, 96–97.
397. RJ, Nov. 4, 1968. AJ, Nov. 4, 1968, 103.
398. Ibid.
399. AN, Nov. 6, 1968, 64. AJ, Nov. 6, 1968, 112–13.
400. Brother David Steindl-Rast quotes the Merton line "We are sharecroppers of time" in his "Man of Prayer," 81.
401. AN, Nov. 7, 1968, 68–69. AJ, Nov. 7, 1968, 117. "One's own time . . ." At a period when Merton was examining contemplative life in the terms of his talk in Bangkok of December 10, 1968, an earlier quotation from the journal is relevant. RJ, Aug. 25, 1958: "Mother Benedict at Regina Landis talks to the nuns about Marx and that is what started me going. That is the way it *should* be. Our contemplative life must be rooted in our time. I see it more and more clearly. It involves at least an interior dialogue with what has been said and what is most challenging and

seminal. *Not* an apologetic. Real consideration, understanding, grasp. A contemplative life that takes cognizance of all that is articulate and is able to see, understand, judge — Not a contemplative life that "decides" blindly, hesitantly, in fear — and decides nothing. *Spiritualis judicat omnia."*

402. SBJ, Aug. 31, 1941.
403. AN, Nov. 11, 1968, 73. AJ, Nov. 12, 1968, 131. (AJ has "crumby" and a different date.) The change in Merton's view of Calcutta can be well seen in the difference between his description in a postcard to W. H. Ferry, October 28, 1968, and the letter to Ferry of November 11, 1968. TMSC.
404. "The Windamere is too cenobitic." AN, Nov. 13, 1968, 78. AJ, Nov. 13, 1968, 134.
405. AN, Nov. 16, 1968, 87. AJ, Nov. 16, 1968, 143.
406. AN, Nov. 16, 1968, 88. AJ, Nov. 16, 1968, 143.
407. AN, Nov. 18, 1968, 91. AJ, Nov. 18, 1968, 148.
408. RJ, Nov. 18, 1968. Not in AN. AJ, Nov. 18, 1968, 149.
409. AN, Nov. 19, 1968, 94. AJ, Nov. 19, 1968, 153.
410. AN, Nov. 19, 1968, 94–95. AJ, Nov. 19, 1968, 153.
411. AN, Nov. 19, 1968, 98. AJ, Nov. 19, 1968, 156–57.
412. AN, Nov. 19, 1968, 98. AJ, Nov. 19, 1968, 157. This also forms the conclusion to the parallel discussion of the doors in both AN and AJ. It would have been confusing to include this here: ". . . the door of emptiness. Of no-where. Of no place for a self. Which cannot be entered by a self. And therefore is of no use to someone who is going somewhere. Is it a door at all? The door of no-door . . ." See also Finley, *Merton's Palace of Nowhere.* This interesting study has the subtitle "A Search for God through Awareness of the True Self." While I have not found this always convincing, neither have I found Merton altogether convincing on the subject of the "true self."
413. Loreto College (spelled this way, unlike the Loretto in Kentucky) was next door to the Windamere Hotel (spelled that way and not like the lake in England, the favorite of the Romantic poets — as Merton explains, AJ, 134). The convent was a little way away. See entry for Nov. 13, 1968, AJ, 135.
414. "Toward a Theology of Prayer," introductory remarks. Edited transcript made by Brother Patrick Hart, 192. The original tape is at TMSC.
415. AN, Nov. 25, 1968, 109. AJ, Nov. 25, 1968, 170.
416. John Balfour to Brother Patrick Hart, Feb. 11, 1976, MGA.
417. Ibid.
418. AN, Nov. 25, 1968, 109. AJ, Nov. 25, 1968, 170.
419. AN, Nov. 26, 1968, 110. AJ, Nov. 25, 1968, 171.
420. RJ, Nov. 30, 1968. Not in AN. AJ, Nov. 25, 1968, 172.
421. AN, Nov. 28, 1968, 117. AJ, Nov. 28, 1968, 199.
422. AN, Nov. 27, 1968, 114. AJ, Nov. 27, 1968, 196.
423. AN, Nov. 28, 1968, 117. AJ, Nov. 28, 1968, 198. RJ, Nov. 30, 1968.
424. AN, Nov. 28, 1968, 118. AJ, Nov. 28, 1968, 202.
425. AN, Nov. 28, 1968, 119. AJ, Nov. 28, 1968, 204. Some differences.
426. AN, Nov. 29, 1968, 122. AJ, Nov. 29, 1968, 213.
427. Victor Stier to W. H. Ferry, Dec. 15, 1968. Copy sent to the author and cited with the kind permission of Mr. Stier.
428. Ibid.
429. AN, Nov. 29, 1968, 124. AJ, Nov. 29, 1968, 215. Merton found a Sunday newspaper and brought himself completely up-to-date — "Buz Sawyer (A whole new scene in The Paris *Herald-Tribune* of December 2)," AN, Dec. 4, 1968, 130. AJ, Dec. 4, 1968, 229.
430. AN, Nov. 30, 1968, 124. AJ, Nov. 30, 1968, 216.
431. Notebook C, TMSC. Much of this was deciphered by Naomi Burton Stone. A few lines are still conjectural. AJ, Dec. 3, 1968, 222–28. Merton says, "That which grew slowly toward me Friday/Flies rapidly away from me Tuesday." He is probably a little confused. It was Saturday he went to Kandy by train.
432. AN, Nov. 30 and Dec. 2, 1968, 124–27. AJ, Nov. 30 and Dec. 1 and 2, 1968, 216–20. Merton had met Bishop Nanayakkara at Gethsemani, see CGB, 137.
433. Victor Stier to W. H. Ferry, Dec. 15, 1968, AA.

434. AN, Dec. 3, 1968. AJ, Dec. 3, 1968, 222.
435. Victor Stier to W. H. Ferry, Dec. 15, 1968, AA.
436. RJ, Dec. 3, 1968: "The most impressive thing I have seen in Asia." See 560–61.
437. Victor Stier to W. H. Ferry, Dec. 15, 1968, AA.
438. Franklin J. Crawford to the author, Oct. 7, 1980, AA.
439. AN, Dec. 4, 1968, 129. AJ, Dec. 4, 1968, 228–29.
440. AN, Dec. 5, 1968 (Singapore), 131. AJ, Dec. 4, 1968 (Colombo), 230. But Merton says "I visited Polonnaruwa on Monday. Today is Thursday . . ." (AJ, 231). Thursday was December 5, 1968.
441. AN, Dec. 5, 1968 (Singapore), 131. AJ, Dec. 4 (but see note 440), 1968 (Colombo), 230.
442. See 120–21 and 363–64.
443. The second paragraph reads, "*Kammathana:* 'bases of action,' practical application and experimental knowledge, dharma teaching. Controls 'heart with outgoing exuberance.' 'The heart which does not have Dharma as its guardian.' Such a heart, when it finds happiness as a result of 'outgoing exuberance,' is a happiness which plays a part, increases the 'outgoing exuberance,' and makes the heart 'go increasingly in the wrong direction.' *Samadhi* = calm, tranquility of heart. 'Outgoing exuberance is the enemy of all things.' " AN, Oct. 17, 1968, 12. AJ, Oct. 17, 1968, 15.
444. AN, Dec. 5, 1968 (Singapore), 133. AJ, Dec. 4 (but see note 440), 1968 (Colombo), 231.
445. RJ, Dec. 3, 1968 (135), written in Ceylon. Not in AN. AJ, 233, 235–36. The passage from the journal appears on a date which would not be correct, either on December 4, or December 5, and there are some changes.
446. AN, Dec. 6, 1968 (entries begin in Singapore, then Merton marks Bangkok). Much of this material is given in AJ, to Dec. 8. The entries for December 6, 7, and 8 are thus somewhat confused in AJ. The walk recorded on p. 253, as "This evening" on December 8, was, in fact, a walk on the evening of December 6, soon after he had arrived from Singapore. On the evening of December 8, Merton was already at "the Red Cross place" at Samutprakarn. AN finishes on December 7, with "Hanuman turns and slays the Yaks (sic-sic) instead." The last entry in the journal, that of December 8, is included here.
447. AN, Dec. 7, 1968, 138. AJ, Dec. 7, 1968, 248. John Howard Griffin was able to recover the film and to process the film in Merton's camera. See Griffin, *Wholeness*. (See also note 252 above.)
448. See note 264 above. AJ, 250, he remembered the calendar.
449. RJ, Dec. 8, 1968.
450. Material checked and collated on the Bangkok conference and Merton's death would require a separate bibliography of some pages. I have tried to incorporate the majority of sources in the main bibliography. Here, a source is only cited when it is the *only* source of this particular information. Through the kindness of John Moffitt, I have not only had access to the several accounts he published, but to further comments and queries and to the correspondence between Moffitt and several of the key witnesses: Father Celestine Say, Archabbot Egbert H. Donovan, Father Francis de Grunne, and Dom Odo Haas, letters written, for the most part, in 1969. The police report, statements of witnesses, and material from the United States Embassy in Bangkok were made available to me from the Monastery of Gethsemani files.
451. Florendo, "The Final Ascent on the Seven Storey Mountain," 11, reported by Dom Bernando Perez.
452. Illustrated in *Bulletin de l'A.I.M.* 9, no. 9 (1968), the English edition.
453. Florendo, "The Final Ascent on the Seven Storey Mountain." Here Florendo quotes Father Celestine Say. Father Celestine presents the kind of problem that drives editors to despair. On his stationery, he has "From the desk of Fr. P. Celestino Say, O.S.B." (printed), and signs, "Regards, Celestine." I have not been able to fathom this mystery. Florendo refers to him as Father Celestino. I have referred to him throughout as Father Celestine.

454. "Marxism and Monastic Perspectives" (talk delivered at Bangkok on Dec. 10, 1968), AJ, Appendix 7, 334.
455. Merton to Father Daniel Berrigan, June 30, 1964, TMSC.
456. This account appears on the police report. Some further details were provided by Father de Grunne's correspondence with John Moffitt in 1969. AA. De Grunne states it was 3 P.M. Say thinks it was between 2:15 P.M. and 2:30 P.M.
457. Father Celestine Say to Dom Flavian Burns, Mar. 18, 1969, MGA.
458. Rt. Rev. Egbert H. Donovan to John Moffitt, Dec. 5, 1969. AA.
459. Father Celestine Say to Dom Flavian Burns, Mar. 18, 1969, MGA.
460. Deposition of Mother Edeltrud Weist, included with the Bangkok police report. Dated Dec. 11, 1968, Bangkok, MGA. This is printed in full for some reason in Griffin, *Hermitage*, 10–11.
461. Father Celestine Say to Dom Flavian Burns, Mar. 18, 1969, MGA.
462. "Police investigation report on the death of Reverend Thomas Merton, an American . . ." 2, MGA. This quotes the report from the examiner, Pol. Maj. Amnuay Tunprasert, Chief, Chemical and Physical Section, Scientific Crime Detection Laboratory, Police Department.
463. "Police investigation report . . ." 2–3. MGA.
464. Several people mention that Merton's face when he was found was "deep blue," or "deep bluish-red," that his features were contorted and that his mouth was half open. Mother Weist mentions that there were spots of the same deep "bluish-red" on Merton's lower arms and hands. She also mentions that his feet were contorted. She had a flashlight, an important fact in that dim room. She concludes, "I was convinced that it was due to an electric shock by the face." "Report on the first impressions after Rev. F. Thomas Merton's tragic death given by an eye witness, Sr. M. Edeltrud Weist O.S.B., Dr. med. Specialist of internal medicine, Prioress of the Missionary Benedictine Sisters in Taegu/South-Korea," MGA. (See note 460 above.)
465. This important detail is given in the letter from Father Celestine Say to Dom Flavian Burns, Mar. 18, 1969, MGA.
466. On the vexed question of why no autopsy was performed, there have been a number of answers. Abbot Weakland has said he was satisfied the cause of death seemed clear, the facilities in Bangkok for an autopsy were few, and he lacked the authority to order one. Dom Flavian Burns understood that if an autopsy was performed in Thailand, either the body would be greatly delayed in getting to the United States or Merton might have to be buried in Thailand.
467. Telegram (with errors) from the State Department in Bangkok to Dom Flavian Burns, MGA. Reproduced in Griffin, *Hermitage*, 30.
468. Dom James Fox, "To the Gethsemani Diaspora," Feb. 1, 1969, AA.
469. Interviews and letters. Rice, 184–85. Naomi Burton Stone, "Reflections on Thomas Merton," tape of talk given at St. Bonaventure University, Oct. 3, 1977.
470. *Conjectures of a Guilty Bystander*, 188–89.
471. Griffin, *Wholeness*, 144.
472. CGB, 11, quoting Barth.
473. Interview with Dom John Eudes Bamberger, Mar. 22, 1981, also identification tag, MGA. This reads: typed, "CIV THOMAS J. MERTON NEW HAVEN, KENTUCKY"; in ink, "Removed from the coffin by myself. I was the only one who saw and recognized the corpse on arrival so as to identify it. It was easy for me to make this identification in spite of the greatly swollen features but Fr. Flavian, the only other observer said he could not recognize him tho he [illegible] Fr. John Eudes MD." AA.
474. "Funeral Mass and Burial Service for Our Brother among Those Who Sleep in Christ FATHER LOUIS," MGA. Mozart's Sonata in D Major (K. 311), second movement (Andante), was included in this service also. SJ, Epilogue, 362. Ellipsis, service sheet.
475. SSM, 422–23.
476. Cardenal, *Apocalypse and Other Poems*, 45–58.
477. *The Way of Chuang Tzu*, 57.

BIBLIOGRAPHY

I Merton Books

Albert Camus' "The Plague." Introduction and commentary. Religious Dimensions in Literature Series. New York: Seabury Press, 1968.
The Ascent to Truth. New York: Harcourt, Brace and Company, 1951. New York: Harcourt Brace Jovanovich, Harvest paperback, 1981.
AJ
The Asian Journal of Thomas Merton. Edited from the original notebooks by Naomi Burton Stone, Brother Patrick Hart, and James Laughlin. Consulting editor: Amiya Chakravarty. New York: New Directions, 1973. Paperback edition, 1975.
A Balanced Life of Prayer. Trappist, Ky.: Abbey of Our Lady of Gethsemani, 1951.
Basic Principles of Monastic Spirituality. Trappist, Ky.: Abbey of Our Lady of Gethsemani, 1957.
The Behavior of Titans. New York: New Directions, 1961.
Boris Pasternak, Thomas Merton, Six Letters. Foreword by Naomi Burton Stone. Introduction by Pasternak's sister, Lydia Pasternak Slater. Lexington, Ky.: King Library Press, University of Kentucky, 1973.
Bread in the Wilderness. New York: New Directions, 1953.
Breakthrough to Peace: Twelve Views on the Threat of Thermonuclear Extermination. Edited with an introduction by Thomas Merton. Essays by: Lewis Mumford, Tom Stonier, Norman Cousins, Erich Fromm and Michael Maccoby, Howard E. Gruber, Gordon C. Zahn, Walter Stein, Herbert Butterfield, Allen Forbes, Jr., Joost A. M. Meerloo, Jerome D. Frank. New York: New Directions, 1962. (Also includes Merton's essay "Peace: A Religious Responsibility," 88–116.)
Cables to the Ace, or Familiar Liturgies of Misunderstanding. New York: New Directions, 1968.
Cassian and the Fathers. Notes for a Conference Given in the Choir Novitiate. Trappist, Ky.: Abbey of Our Lady of Gethsemani, about 1960.
A Catch of Anti-Letters. With Robert Lax. Foreword by Brother Patrick Hart. Mission, Kans.: Sheed, Andrews and McMeel, 1978.
Cistercian Contemplatives: Monks of the Strict Observance at Our Lady of Gethsemani, Kentucky, Our Lady of the Holy Ghost, Georgia, Our Lady of the Holy Trinity, Utah. A Guide to Trappist Life. Trappist, Ky.: Abbey of Our Lady of Gethsemani, 1948.
Cistercian Life. Spencer, Mass.: Cistercian Book Service, 1974.
The Climate of Monastic Prayer. Foreword by Douglas V. Steere. Cistercian Studies Series, no. 1. Kalamazoo, Mich.: Cistercian Publications, 1981.

CP
The Collected Poems of Thomas Merton. New York: New Directions, 1977.
CGB
Conjectures of a Guilty Bystander. Garden City, N.Y.: Doubleday, 1966. Doubleday Image paperback, 1968.
Contemplation in a World of Action. Introduction by Jean Leclercq, O.S.B. Garden City, N.Y.: Doubleday, 1971. Doubleday Image paperback, 1973.
Contemplative Prayer. New York: Herder and Herder, 1969.
Disputed Questions. New York: Farrar, Straus and Cudahy, 1960. Farrar, Straus and Giroux, Noonday paperback, 1977.
Early Poems 1940–42. Anvil Press Publications, no. 9, Lexington, Ky.: Anvil Press, 1971.
Elected Silence. Introduction by Evelyn Waugh (*The Seven Storey Mountain* edited by Evelyn Waugh, see 248.). London: Hollis and Carter, 1949.
Emblems of a Season of Fury. New York: New Directions, 1963.
Exile Ends in Glory. The life of a Trappistine, Mother M. Berchmans, O.C.S.O. Milwaukee: Bruce Publishing Company, 1948.
Faith and Violence. South Bend, Ind.: University of Notre Dame Press, 1968.
Figures for an Apocalypse. New York: New Directions, 1948.
Gandhi on Non-Violence. Selections and long introductory essay, "Gandhi and the One-Eyed Giant." New York: New Directions, 1965.
The Geography of Lograire. New York: New Directions, 1969.
Gethsemani: A Life of Praise. Trappist, Ky.: Abbey of Our Lady of Gethsemani, 1966.
Gethsemani Magnificat. Centenary of Gethsemani Abbey. Trappist, Ky.: Abbey of Our Lady of Gethsemani, 1949.
Guide to Cistercian Life. Trappist, Ky.: Abbey of Our Lady of Gethsemani, 1948.
Hagia Sophia. Lexington, Ky.: Stamperia del Santuccio, 1962.
He Is Risen: Selections from Thomas Merton. Niles, Ill.: Argus Communications, 1975.
Introductions East and West. See Daggy, editor, section III.
Ishi Means Man. Essays on Native Americans. Foreword by Dorothy Day. Woodblock by Rita Corbin. Greensboro, N.C.: Unicorn Press, 1976.
The Last of the Fathers: Saint Bernard of Clairvaux and the Encyclical Letter "Doctor Mellifluus." New York: Harcourt, Brace and Company, 1954. Harcourt Brace Jovanovich, Harvest paperback, 1981.
Life and Holiness. New York: Herder and Herder, 1963. Doubleday Image paperback, 1964.
Life at Gethsemani. Photographs by Shirley Burden, Terrell Dickey, and a monk of Gethsemani. Trappist, Ky.: Abbey of Our Lady of Gethsemani, 1958.
LE
The Literary Essays of Thomas Merton. Edited with an introduction by Brother Patrick Hart. New York: New Directions, 1981.
The Living Bread. New York: Farrar, Straus and Cudahy, 1956.
Love and Living. Edited by Naomi Burton Stone and Brother Patrick Hart. Essays: "Learning to Live," "Love and Solitude," "Love and Need," "Creative Silence," "The Street Is for Celebration," "Symbolism: Communication or Communion?" "Cargo Cults of the South Pacific," "Seven Words for Ned O'Gorman," "Christian Humanism," "Christian Humanism in the Nuclear Era," "The Universe as Epiphany," "Teilhard's Gamble," "Rebirth and the New Man in Christianity," "The Climate of Mercy," "The Good News in the Nativity." New York: Farrar, Straus and Giroux, 1979. New York: Bantam, 1980.
A Man in the Divided Sea. New York: New Directions, 1946.
Meditations on Liturgy. Oxford: A. R. Mowbray, 1976. See *Seasons of Celebration*, below.
The Monastic Journey. Edited by Brother Patrick Hart. Mission, Kans.: Sheed, Andrews and McMeel, 1977. New York: Doubleday Image paperback, 1978.
Monastic Peace. Photographs by Shirley Burden. Trappist, Ky.: Abbey of Our Lady of Gethsemani, 1958.
Monks Pond. Four issues of the quarterly (Spring–Winter 1968) edited by Merton. Trappist, Ky.: Abbey of Our Lady of Gethsemani.

MAG

My Argument with the Gestapo. A Macaronic Journal (Working title, "Journal of My Escape from the Nazis.") Garden City, N.Y.: Doubleday, 1969. New York: New Directions paperback, 1975.

Mystics and Zen Masters. New York: Farrar, Straus and Giroux, 1967. New York: Dell, Delta paperback, 1969.

Nativity Kerygma. Trappist, Ky.: Abbey of Our Lady of Gethsemani, 1958.

The New Man. New York: Farrar, Straus and Cudahy, 1961. Farrar, Straus and Giroux, Noonday paperback, 1979.

New Seeds of Contemplation. New York: New Directions, 1962.

No Man Is an Island. New York: Harcourt, Brace and Company, 1955. New York: Doubleday Image paperback, 1967.

The Nonviolent Alternative. A revised edition of *Thomas Merton on Peace.* Introductory appreciation by Gordon C. Zahn. New York: Farrar, Straus and Giroux, 1980.

Opening the Bible. Collegeville, Minn.: Liturgical Press, 1970. Revised edition, 1983. London: George Allen and Unwin, 1972. (Originally written as an introductory essay for the Time-Life Bible, which was never published, this fine short study contains pages on the concept of time in Faulkner's *The Sound and the Fury,* a review of Pasolini's film *The Gospel According to St. Matthew* — which Merton had seen in Louisville with Jack Ford [RJ, October 28, 1966, reporting "When I was in hospital last Friday"] — and pages on Bonhoeffer's prison letters.)

Original Child Bomb: Points for Meditation to be Scratched on the Walls of a Cave. New York: New Directions, 1962. Greensboro, N.C.: Unicorn Press, 1982.

A Prayer of Cassiodorus. From the treatise 'De Anima.' Preface and translation by Merton. Worcester, England: Stanbrook Abbey Press, 1956.

Praying the Psalms. Collegeville, Minn.: Liturgical Press, 1956.

Prometheus: A Meditation. Lexington, Ky.: King Library Press, University of Kentucky, 1958.

The Psalms Are Our Prayer. Paternoster Series, no. 15. London: Burns, Oates and Washbourne, 1957.

Raids on the Unspeakable. New York: New Directions, 1966.

Redeeming the Time. London: Burns and Oates, 1966.

Seasons of Celebration. New York: Farrar, Straus and Giroux, 1965. Farrar, Straus and Giroux, Noonday paperback, 1977.

ScJ

The Secular Journal of Thomas Merton. New York: Farrar, Straus and Cudahy, 1959. Farrar, Straus and Giroux, Noonday paperback, 1977.

Seeds of Contemplation. New York: New Directions, 1949.

Seeds of Destruction. New York: Farrar, Straus and Cudahy, 1964. Farrar, Straus and Giroux, Noonday paperback, 1980.

SP

Selected Poems of Thomas Merton. Introduction by Mark Van Doren. New York: New Directions, 1959. Enlarged edition, 1967.

SSM

The Seven Storey Mountain. New York: Harcourt, Brace and Company, 1948. Many editions, including Doubleday Image paperback, 1970.

The Seven Storey Mountain. London: Sheldon Press, 1975. (Complete and unedited, and in that way different from *Elected Silence,* see above.)

SJ

The Sign of Jonas. New York: Harcourt, Brace and Company, 1953. New York: Doubleday Image paperback, 1956.

Silence in Heaven: A Book of Monastic Life. London: Thames and Hudson, 1956.

Silence in Heaven: A Book of Monastic Life. New York: Studio Publications and Thomas Y. Crowell, 1956.

The Silent Life. New York: Farrar, Straus and Cudahy, 1957. Farrar, Straus and Giroux, Noonday paperback, 1978.

The Solitary Life. Lexington, Ky.: Stamperia del Santuccio, 1960.

Spiritual Direction and Meditation. Collegeville, Minn.: Liturgical Press, 1960.

The Strange Islands. New York: New Directions, 1957.
The Tears of the Blind Lions. New York: New Directions, 1949.
Thirty Poems. New York: New Directions, 1944.
Thomas Merton on Peace. Introduction by Gordon C. Zahn. New York: McCall Publishing Company, 1971. See *The Nonviolent Alternative.*
Thomas Merton on St. Bernard. Cistercian Studies Series, no. 9. Kalamazoo, Mich.: Cistercian Publications, 1980.
Thomas Merton on the Psalms. London: Sheldon Press, 1977.
A Thomas Merton Reader. Edited by Thomas P. McDonnell. New York: Harcourt, Brace and World, 1962. Revised and enlarged edition, New York: Doubleday Image paperback, 1974.
Thoughts in Solitude. New York: Farrar, Straus and Cudahy, 1958. Farrar, Straus and Giroux, Noonday paperback, 1978.
The Tower of Babel. New York: New Directions, 1957.
The True Solitude. Selections from the Writings of Thomas Merton. Selected by Dean Walley. Kansas City, Mo.: Hallmark Editions, 1969.
The Waters of Siloe. New York: Harcourt, Brace and Company, 1949. New York: Doubleday Image paperback, 1962.
The Way of Chuang Tzu. New York: New Directions, 1965.
What Are These Wounds? The life of a Cistercian Mystic, Saint Lutgarde of Aywières. Milwaukee: Bruce Publishing Company, 1950.
What Is Contemplation? Holy Cross, Ind.: St. Mary's College Press, 1948. Springfield, Ill.: Templegate, 1981.
What Ought I to Do? Sayings from the Desert Fathers of the Fourth Century (Verba Seniorum). Translated by Merton. Lexington, Ky.: Stamperia del Santuccio, 1959.
The Wisdom of the Desert. New York: New Directions, 1960.
Woods, Shore, Desert. A notebook, May 1960. Photographs by Merton. Foreword by Brother Patrick Hart. Introduction and notes by Joel Weishaus. Santa Fe: Museum of New Mexico Press, 1982.
Zen and the Birds of Appetite. New York: New Directions, 1968.

Translations into European languages of Merton's work referred to in the text:

Catalan
La Muntanya dels Sets Cercles. 2 vols. Translated by Guillem Colom. Biblioteca selecta. Barcelona: Editorial Selecta, 1963. See "Kanchenjunga," note 111.
French
La Nuit privée d'étoiles. Paris: Editions Albin Michel, 1951. (Unfortunately, this translation by Marie Tadie of *The Seven Storey Mountain* has been edited and excludes, among other things, passages about St. Antonin.)
La Révolution noire. Paris: Castermann, 1964. (The translation is by Marie Tadie. Some of the material in *Seeds of Destruction* appeared here for the first time. French censors of the Order were more lenient on racial questions.)
La Signe de Jonas. Paris: Editions Albin Michel, 1951. (This translation of *The Sign of Jonas* by Marie Tadie appeared after a considerable struggle over censorship questions, and was read with pleasure by General de Gaulle, see 275.)
German
Grazias Haus. Einsiedeln, Switzerland: Johannes Verlag, 1966. (A translation, by Marta Gisi and Lili Sertorius, of *Selected Poems of Thomas Merton* and *Emblems of a Season of Fury.* See 367.)
Spanish
Obras Completas. Buenos Aires: Editorial Sudamericana, 1958. (With Merton's extensive introduction, see Daggy, *Introductions,* below, and see 314–15.)

II Merton Articles, Introductions, Essays

Merton published well over three hundred individual essays, articles, and excerpts from forthcoming books in his lifetime. An equal number has been reissued or published for the first time since his death in 1968. There are still unpublished articles. No attempt could be made here to give even a representative list. Readers should check Dell'Isola and Breit, though even together these are not complete to 1975. Considerable bibliographical help is provided in the pages of *The Merton Seasonal* of Bellarmine College, published quarterly, TMSC, edited by Dr. Robert E. Daggy.

Listed here are the seventy articles, or short pieces published first independently, which I felt to be most closely connected with the text of this biography. As the sixteenth-century topographer John Norden wrote when introducing his mileage tables in *Description of Cornwall*, "Beare with defectes, the use is necessarie."

"Art and Worship." *Sponsa Regis* 31, no. 4 (December 1959): 114–17.
" 'Baptism in the Forest': Wisdom and Initiation in William Faulkner." *The Catholic World* 207, no. 1239 (June 1968): 124–30. Also introduction to *Mansions of the Spirit*, edited by George A. Panichas, 19–42. New York: Hawthorn Books, 1967. See also LE, 92–116.
"The Black Revolution." *Ramparts* 2, no. 3 (December 1963): 4–23. For other citations, see Dell'Isola and Breit. See also *Seeds of Destruction*.
"Boris Pasternak and the People with Watch Chains." *Jubilee* 7, no. 3 (July 1959): 19–31. See also *Disputed Questions*, 7–24.
"Camus: Journals of the Plague Years." *Sewanee Review* 75, no. 4 (1967–68): 717–30. See also LE, 218–31.
"Carta a Pablo Antonio Cuadra con Respecto a los Gigantes." *Sur* 275 (March–April 1962): 1–13. (Many publications of this in English, see Dell'Isola and Breit.)
"A Christian Looks at Zen." Introduction to *The Golden Age of Zen*, by J. C. Wu. National War College in cooperation with the Committee on the Compilation of the Chinese Library, 1967. See also *Zen and the Birds of Appetite*, 33–58.
"The Cross Fighters: Notes on a Race War." *The Unicorn Journal* (1968): 26–40. See also *Ishi Means Man*, 35–52.
"Day of a Stranger." *Hudson Review* 20, no. 2 (Summer 1967): 211–18. See also *A Thomas Merton Reader*, 431–38. Now issued under the same title as a book, with photographs by Merton, introduction by Robert E. Daggy, foreword by Brother Patrick Hart. Layton, Utah: Peregrine Smith, 1982.
"A Devout Meditation in Memory of Adolf Eichmann." In *New Directions 18*, edited by James Laughlin. New York: New Directions, 1964. (This may have appeared more frequently than any other piece by Merton: see Dell'Isola and Breit. It was published in *Ramparts* 5, no. 4 (October 1966): 8–10. See also *Raids on the Unspeakable*, 45–52, and *The Nonviolent Alternative*, 160–62.)
"Easter: The New Life." *Worship* 33, no. 5 (April 1959): 276–84. See also *Seasons of Celebration*, 144–57.
"Few Questions and Fewer Answers. Extracts from a Monastic Notebook." *Harpers* 231, no. 1386 (November 1965): 79–81.
"Hagia Sophia." *Ramparts* 1, no. 5 (March 1963): 65–71. (For the many other publications, see Dell'Isola and Breit. For publication as a book, see section I.)
"Herakleitos the Obscure." *Jubilee* 8, no. 5 (September 1960): 24–31. See also *The Behavior of Titans*, 75–106, and *A Thomas Merton Reader*, 258–71.
"The Hot Summer of Sixty-Seven." *Katallagete* (Winter 1967–68): 28–34. See also *Faith and Violence*, 165–81.
"Huxley and the Ethics of Peace." *The Columbia Review* 19, no. 2 (March 1938): 13–18.
"Huxley's Pantheon." *The Catholic World* 152, no. 908 (November 1940): 206–9. A review of Aldous Huxley's *After Many a Summer Dies the Swan*. See also LE, 490–94.
Introduction to *Breakthrough to Peace: Twelve Views on the Threat of Thermonuclear Extermination* (see section I).
Introduction to *The City of God*, by Saint Augustine. Translated by Marcus Dods, D.D., ix–xv. New York: Random House, 1950.
Introduction to *God Is My Life: The Story of Our Lady of Gethsemani*, by Shirley Burden, 7–9. New York: Reynal, 1960.
Introduction to *Religion in Wood, A Book of Shaker Furniture*, by Edward Deming Andrews and Faith Andrews, vii–xv. Bloomington, Ind.: Indiana University Press, 1966. Excerpts reprinted by kind permission.
"Ishi: A Meditation." *The Catholic Worker* 33 (March 1967): 5–6. See also *The Nonviolent*

Alternative, 248–53, and *Ishi Means Man,* 25–32.

"Learning to Live." In *University on the Heights,* edited by Wesley First, 187–99. Garden City, N.Y.: Doubleday, 1969. See also *Love and Living,* 3–13.

"Letters to a White Liberal," pt. 1. *Blackfriars* 44, no. 521 (November 1963): 464–77. See also *Seeds of Destruction,* 3–71.

"Letters to a White Liberal," pt. 2. *Blackfriars* 44, no. 522 (December 1963): 503–16. See also *Seeds of Destruction,* 3–71.

"A Life Free from Care." *Cistercian Studies* 5, no. 3 (1970): 217–26.

"Message to Poets." *El corno emplumado* 10 (April 1964): 127–29. Also published in *Americas* 16 (May 1964): 29ff., and in *Eco contemporaneo* 8/9 (Winter 1965): 60–62. See also *Raids on the Unspeakable,* 155–61.

"The Monk As Marginal Man." *The Center Magazine* 2 (January 1969): 33.

"Mount Athos." *Jubilee* 7, no. 4 (August 1959): 8–16. See also *Disputed Questions,* 68–82.

"The Negro Revolt." *Jubilee* 11, no. 5 (September 1963): 39–43. A review of William Kelley's *A Different Drummer.* See also *Seeds of Destruction,* 72–90, and LE, 168–77.

"Negro Violence and White Non-Violence." *The National Catholic Reporter* 3, no. 44 (September 6, 1967): 8:1. A letter in reply to Dr. Martin E. Marty responding to Marty's "Thomas Merton. Re: Your Prophecy" (see section III).

"News of the Joyce Industry." *Sewanee Review* 77, no. 3 (Fall 1969): 543–54. See also LE, 12–22.

"Nhat Hanh Is My Brother." *Jubilee* 14, no. 4 (August 1966): 11. See also *Faith and Violence,* 106–8, and *The Nonviolent Alternative,* 263–64.

"Nonviolence Does Not, Cannot Mean Passivity." *Ave Maria* 108, no. 8 (September 7, 1968): 9–10.

"Note on the New Church at Gethsemani." *Liturgical Arts* 36, no. 4 (August 1968): 100–101.

"Nuclear War and the Christian Responsibility." *The Commonweal* 75 (February 9, 1962): 509–13.

Ernst
"On Remembering Monsieur Delmas." In *The Teacher,* edited by Morris L. Ernst, 47–53. Englewood Cliffs, N.J.: Prentice-Hall, 1967.

"An Open Letter to the American Hierarchy: Schema Thirteen and the Modern Church." *Worldview* 8, no. 9 (September 1965): 4–6.

"The Ox Mountain Parable of Meng Tzu." *The Commonweal* 74 (May 12, 1961): 174. See also *Mystics and Zen Masters,* 66–68, and CP, 970–71.

"Pacifism and Resistance." *Peace News* (April 2, 1965) 5:1, 8:1. A review of Jacques Cabaud's *Simone Weil, A Fellowship in Love.* See also *Faith and Violence* ("Pacifism and Resistance in Simone Weil"), 76–84, and *The Nonviolent Alternative* ("The Answer of Minerva"), 144–49.

"Paradise Bugged." *The Critic* 25, no. 4 (February–March 1967): 69–71. A review of *All: The Collected Short Poems (1956–1964),* by Louis Zukofsky. See also LE ("The Paradise Ear"), 128–33.

"The Pasternak Affair in Perspective." *Thought* 34, no. 135 (Winter 1959–60): 485–517. See also *Disputed Questions,* 3–67.

"Poetry and Contemplation: A Reappraisal." *The Commonweal* 69 (October 24, 1958): 87–92. See also *A Thomas Merton Reader,* 399–415.

"Poetry and the Contemplative Life." *The Commonweal* 46 (July 4, 1947): 280–86.

Preface to *Alone with God,* by Dom Jean Leclercq, xiii–xxvii. New York: Farrar, Straus and Cudahy, 1961.

"The Primacy of Contemplation." *Cross and Crown* 2, no. 1 (March 1950): 3–16.

"Rain and the Rhinoceros." *Holiday* 37, no. 5 (May 1965): 8–16. See also *Raids on the Unspeakable,* 9–23.

"Reflections on the Character and Genius of Fénelon." Introduction to *Fénelon Letters,* by François de Salignac de la Mothe-Fénelon, 9–30. Selected and translated by John McEwen. London: Harville Press, 1964. American edition: *Letters of Love and Counsel.* New York: Harcourt, Brace and World, 1964.

"Rites for the Extrusion of a Leper." *The Kentucky Review* 2 (February 1968): 26–30. (Appeared elsewhere, see Dell'Isola and Breit.)

"The Self of Modern Man and the New Christian Consciousness." The R. M. Bucke Memorial Society Newsletter Review (Montreal) 2, no. 1 (April 1967). See also as "New Consciousness," in *Zen and the Birds of Appetite*, 15–32.

"The Shakers." *Jubilee* 11, no. 9 (January 1964): 37–41. See also "Pleasant Hill, A Shaker Village in Kentucky" in *Mystics and Zen Masters*, 193–202.

"The Shelter Ethic." *The Catholic Worker* 28, no. 4 (November 1961): 1:1, 5:1. See also "The Machine Gun in the Fallout Shelter," *The Nonviolent Alternative*, 103–6.

"The Shoshoneans." *The Catholic Worker* 33, no. 6 (June 1967): 5–6. See also *Ishi Means Man*, 5–16.

"A Signed Confession of Crimes against the State." *The Carleton Miscellany* 1, no. 4 (Fall 1960): 21–23. See also *The Behavior of Titans*, 65–71, and *A Thomas Merton Reader*, 116–19.

"The Street Is for Celebration." *The Mediator* 20 (Summer 1969): 2–4. See also *Love and Living*, 41–47.

"Symbolism: Communication or Communion?" In *New Directions 20*, edited by James Laughlin. New York: New Directions, 1968. (The essay has appeared a number of times, see Dell'Isola and Breit. See also *Love and Living*, 48–69.)

"Teilhard's Gamble: Betting on the Whole Human Species." *The Commonweal* 87 (October 27, 1967): 109–11. See also *Love and Living*, 166–72.

"Terror and the Absurd: Violence and Non-Violence in Albert Camus." *Motive* 29 (February 1969): 5–15. See also LE, 232–51.

"Thomas Merton Notes on Sacred and Profane Art." *Jubilee* 4, no. 7 (November 1956): 25–32.

"Thomas Merton on the Strike." (On the Strike for Peace) *The Catholic Worker* 28, no. 7 (February 1962): 7.

"The Time of the End Is the Time of No Room." *Motive* 26, no. 3 (December 1965): 4–9. See also *Raids on the Unspeakable*, 65–75.

"Toward a Theology of Prayer." Talk given to the Jesuit Scholastics at St. Mary's College, Kurseong, near Darjeeling, November 25, 1968. *Cistercian Studies* 3 (1978): 191–99.

"Tribute to Greatness." A comment on *Doctor Zhivago*. *New York Times Book Review*, February 1, 1959, 14:1.

"The Vietnam War: An Overwhelming Atrocity." *The Catholic Worker* 34, no. 3 (March 1968): 1:2, 6:1, 7:3. See also *Faith and Violence*, 87–95.

"War and the Crisis of Language." In *The Critique of War* (Contemporary Philosophical Explorations), edited by Robert Ginsberg, 99–119. Chicago: Henry Regnery, 1969. See also *The Nonviolent Alternative*, 234–47.

"War and Vision: The Autobiography of a Crow Indian." *The Catholic Worker* 33, no. 12 (December 1967): 4ff. A review of Peter Nabokov's *Two Leggings: The Making of a Crow Warrior*. See also *Ishi Means Man*, 17–24.

"Wisdom and Emptiness: A Dialogue by Daisetz T. Suzuki and Thomas Merton." In *New Directions 17*, edited by James Laughlin (where it appears with a large group of Merton's translations and introductory notes to the poets he is translating). New York: New Directions, 1961. See also *Zen and the Birds of Appetite*, 99–138.

"The Wisdom of the Desert." *Harper's Bazaar* 2989 (December 1960): 82–85. Excerpts from *The Wisdom of the Desert*.

"Writing as Temperature." *Sewanee Review* 77, no. 2 (Summer 1969): 535–42. A review of Roland Barthes's *Writing Degree Zero*. See also LE, 140–46.

"The Zen Revival." *Continuum* 1 (Winter 1964): 523–38.

"Zen: Sense and Sensibility." *America* 108, no. 21 (May 25, 1963): 752–54. A review of Dom Aelred Graham's *Zen Catholicism*.

III Books and Articles about Merton, or with Extensive References to Merton. A Selective List

Again, the number of books and articles about Thomas Merton is enormous. *The Merton Seasonal* of Bellarmine College, published quarterly, TMSC, edited by Dr. Robert E. Daggy, usually lists from fifty to a hundred new titles in each issue. The number of theses is approaching two hundred. Titles here have been selected, on the whole, with regard to the text. A few have been chosen for general interest, or because they bring a fresh approach to a subject that has not been treated extensively elsewhere. A selection of early reviews of Merton's work is included, with important critical and biographical studies, to the summer of 1983. Few theses are listed, and I have chosen against all but one or two studies that appeared in a language other than English. I have also decided, with few exceptions, against articles simply giving personal reminiscences of meeting Thomas Merton.

Allchin, Arthur Macdonald. "A Liberator, a Reconciler." *Continuum* 7 (Summer 1969): 363–65.
———. "Remembering Tom: My Most Unforgettable Character, Thomas Merton." *Anglican Digest* 23, no. 1 (Lent 1981): 35–37.
———. *The World Is a Wedding, Explorations in Christian Spirituality.* London: Darton, Longman and Todd, 1978.
Bailey, Raymond. *Thomas Merton on Mysticism.* Garden City, N.Y.: Doubleday Image paperback, 1976.
Baker, James Thomas. *Thomas Merton, Social Critic: A Study.* Lexington, Ky.: University Press of Kentucky, 1971.
———. *Under the Sign of the Water-Bearer: A Life of Thomas Merton.* Drama. Louisville, Ky.: Love Street Books, 1977.
Bamberger, Dom John Eudes, O.C.S.O. "The Cistercian." *Continuum* 7 (Summer 1969): 227–41.
———. "The Monk." See Hart, *Monk* (1983), 37–58.
———. "Thomas Merton: Monk and Author." See Twomey, *Paradox*, 138–47.
Berrigan, Daniel, S.J. "The Peacemaker." See Hart, *Monk* (1983), 219–27.
———. "The Trappist Cemetery — Gethsemani Revisited." Poem. *Continuum* 7 (Summer 1969): 313–18.
Breit
Breit, Marquita. *Thomas Merton: A Bibliography.* Metuchen, N.J.: Scarecrow Press (with the American Theological Library Association), 1974. (Covers works from 1957 to 1973.)
Bucks, René, O.C.D. "The Contemplative Critic." See Hart, *Monk* (1983), 229–35.
Burns, Dom Flavian, O.C.S.O. "Epilogue: A Homily." See Hart, *Monk* (1983), 265–66.
Burton, Naomi. "A Note on the Author and This Book." Foreword to *My Argument with the Gestapo: A Macaronic Journal*, by Merton, 11–15. New York: New Directions, 1975.
Burton *Sentinels*
———. *More Than Sentinels.* Autobiography. Garden City, N.Y.: Doubleday, 1965.
———. "I Shall Miss Thomas Merton." *Cistercian Studies* 4, no. 3 (1969): 218–25.
———. "The Merton I Knew," tape of talk given in Vancouver, 1978.
———. "Reflections on Thomas Merton," tape of talk given at St. Bonaventure University, Oct. 3, 1977.
Cameron-Brown, Aldhelm, O.S.B. "Zen Master." See Hart, *Monk* (1983), 161–71.
Cardenal, Ernesto. "Death of Thomas Merton." Poem. In *Apocalypse and Other Poems,* edited by Robert Pring-Mill and Donald D. Walsh, 45–58. New York: New Directions, 1977.
———. "Desde la trapa." *Abside* (Mexico) 22 (July–September 1958): 314–24.
Chakravarty, Amiya. "Epilogue." See Grayston-Higgins, *Pilgrim in Process,* 171–73.
———. Preface to *The Asian Journal of Thomas Merton,* vii–ix. New York: New Directions, 1973.
Conner, Tarcisius, O.C.S.O. "Monk of Renewal." See Hart, *Monk* (1983), 173–93.
Daggy, Robert E. "Sister Thérèse Lentfoehr, S.D.S.: Custodian of 'Grace's House' and Other Mertoniana. A Memoir." *The Merton Seasonal* (Bellarmine College) 6, no. 3 (Autumn 1981): 2–6.
Daggy *Introductions*
———, editor. *Introductions East and West: The Foreign Prefaces of Thomas Merton.* Foreword by Harry James Cargas. Greensboro, N.C.: Unicorn Press, 1981. Excerpts reprinted by kind permission of Unicorn Press, P.O. Box 3307, Greensboro, N.C. 27402.

Davis, Robert Murray. "How Waugh Cut Merton." Reprint of article in *The Month* (April 1973). See Grayston-Higgins, *Pilgrim in Process*, 175–83.

Day, Dorothy. "Thomas Merton, Trappist." *The Catholic Worker* 34, no. 12 (December 1968): 1:6.

de Hueck, Catherine. *Friendship House*. New York: Sheed and Ward, 1946.

Dell'Isola

Dell'Isola, Frank. *Thomas Merton: A Bibliography.* Kent, Ohio: Kent State University Press, 1975.

De Pinto, Basil, O.S.B. "In Memoriam: Thomas Merton, 1915–1968." In *The Cistercian Spirit: A Symposium in Memory of Thomas Merton*, edited by M. Basil Pennington, O.C.S.O., vii–x. Spencer, Mass.: Cistercian Publications, 1969.

———. *Where Love Is, God Is.* Milwaukee: Bruce Publishing Company, 1953.

Dubbel, Earl S. "In Defense of Thomas Merton." Letter, *Atlantic Monthly* 191 (March 1953): 20.

Dumont, Charles, O.C.S.O. "The Contemplative." See Hart, *Monk* (1983), 125–39.

———. "A Contemplative at the Heart of the World — Thomas Merton." And "Un contemplatif au coeur du monde: Thomas Merton." *Lumen Vitae* 24 (December 1969): English edition, 633–46, French edition, 466–78.

Ernst

Ernst, Morris L., editor. *The Teacher.* Anthology containing Merton's "On Remembering Monsieur Delmas" and other interesting material. Englewood Cliffs, N.J.: Prentice-Hall, 1967.

Evans, Illtud, O.P. "Elected Speech: Thomas Merton and the American Conscience." Review of *Seeds of Destruction. Tablet* 220 (November 12, 1966): 1269–70.

———. "Merton at Prayer." Review of *Climate of Monastic Prayer. Tablet* 226 (April 15, 1972): 351.

———. "Thomas Merton." *Tablet* 223 (January 4, 1969): 22–23.

Ferry, W. H. "The Difference He Made." *Continuum* 7 (Summer 1969): 320–22.

Finley, James. *Merton's Palace of Nowhere: A Search for God through Awareness of the True Self.* Foreword by Henri Nouwen. Notre Dame, Ind.: Ave Maria Press, 1978.

Flint, R. W. "Ten Poets." Including a review of *The Tears of the Blind Lions. The Kenyon Review* 12, no. 4 (Autumn 1950): 705–8.

Florendo, Abraham C. "The Final Ascent on the Seven Storey Mountain." *Mirror* (January 18, 1969): 10–11.

Forest, James H. "Merton's Peacemaking." *Sojourners* (December 1978): 13–18.

———. "Thomas Merton, A Friend Remembered." *Fellowship* 44, no. 11 (December 1978): 6–7.

———. *Thomas Merton: A Pictorial Biography.* New York: Paulist Press, 1980.

———. *Thomas Merton's Struggle with Peacemaking.* Erie, Pa.: Benet Press, 1983.

———. "Thomas Merton's Struggle with Peacemaking." See Twomey, *Paradox*, 15–54.

Fox, Dom James, O.C.S.O. "The Spiritual Son." See Hart, *Monk* (1983), 141–59.

Furlong

Furlong, Monica. *Merton, A Biography.* San Francisco: Harper and Row, 1980. New York: Bantam, 1981.

Gianni, Robert Edward. "Return: Thomas Merton's Ethics." *Cistercian Studies* 16, no. 3 (1981): 221–33.

Giroux *Editor*

Giroux, Robert. **"The Education of an Editor."** Bowker Memorial Lecture, 1981. *Publisher's Weekly* 221, no. 2 (January 8, 1982).

———. "Thomas Merton, 1915–1968." *Columbia College Today* (Spring 1969): 69–71.

Graham, Aelred, O.S.B. "The Mysticism of Thomas Merton." *The Commonweal* 63 (1955): 155–59.

———. "Thomas Merton, A Modern Man in Reverse." *Atlantic Monthly* 191, no. 1 (January 1953): 70–74.

Grayston, Donald. "Autobiography and Theology: The Once and Future Merton." See Grayston-Higgins, *Pilgrim in Process*, 71–84.

Grayston-Higgins *Pilgrim in Process*

———, and Michael W. Higgins, editors. *Thomas Merton: Pilgrim in Process.* Introduction by Grayston and Higgins. Foreword by Brother Patrick Hart. Toronto: Griffin House, 1983. A collection of essays. For contents, see under Chakravarty, Davis, Grayston, Griffin (Ernest), Higgins (Michael W.), Kaplan, Kent, Labrie, Lentfoehr, Nicholls, O'Driscoll, Russell, Thompson, Weaver, Zahn.

Gregory, Horace. "Life and Poems of a Trappist Monk." *New York Times Book Review,* October 3, 1948, 4, 33.

Griffin, Ernest. "Wallace Stevens and Thomas Merton: A Study of the Religious Imagination." See Grayston-Higgins, *Pilgrim in Process,* 55–68.

Griffin, John Howard. "The Controversial Merton." See Twomey, *Paradox,* 80–91.

———. "Les Grandes Amitiés." *Continuum* 7 (Summer 1969): 286–94.

Griffin *Hermitage*

———. *The Hermitage Journals. A Diary Kept While Working on the Biography of Thomas Merton.* Edited by Conger Beasley, Jr. Kansas City; Kans.: Andrews and McMeel, 1981.

Griffin *Wholeness*

———. *A Hidden Wholeness: The Visual World of Thomas Merton.* Photographs by Merton and John Howard Griffin. Dunwoody, Ga.: Norman S. Berg ("Sellanraa") and Boston: Houghton Mifflin, 1977.

———. With Yves R. Simon. *Jacques Maritain, Homage in Words and Pictures.* Foreword by Anthony Simon. Albany, N.Y.: Magi Books, 1974.

———. "In Search of Thomas Merton." In *The Thomas Merton Studies Center.* Essays by Merton, John Howard Griffin, and Monsignor Alfred Horrigan. Santa Barbara, Calif.: Unicorn Press, 1971.

Groves, Gerald. "Fourteen Years with Thomas Merton." *Critic* 21 (April-May 1963): 29–32.

———. "The Gregarious Hermit." *The American Scholar* 49 (Winter 1979-80): 89–93.

Hart, Brother Patrick, O.C.S.O. "The Ecumenical Monk." See Hart, *Monk* (1983), 209–17.

———. Introduction to *The Literary Essays of Thomas Merton,* edited by Hart, xi–xvi. New York: New Directions, 1981.

———. "Last Mass in the Hermitage." *Continuum* 7 (Winter-Spring 1969): 213–15.

———, editor. *The Message of Thomas Merton.* Cistercian Studies Series, no. 42. Kalamazoo, Mich.: Cistercian Publications, 1981. Contributors: Archbishop Jean Jadot, Hart, Flavian Burns, Victor A. Kramer, Elena Malits, E. Glenn Hinson, Deba P. Patnaik, John F. Teahan, Chalmers MacCormick, George Kilcourse. Lawrence S. Cunningham, Dennis Q. McInerny, William H. Shannon, James W. Douglass. Kalamazoo, Mich.: Cistercian Publications, 1981.

Hart *Monk*

———, editor. *Thomas Merton, Monk. A Monastic Tribute.* New York: Sheed and Ward, 1974.

———, editor. *Thomas Merton/Monk: A Monastic Tribute.* Enlarged edition. Kalamazoo, Mich.: Cistercian Publications, 1983. See contributors and essays under: Bamberger, Burns, Cameron-Brown, Conner, Dumont, Fox, Hart, Kelty, Leclercq, Lentfoehr (3), Ryan, Saword, Steindl-Rast, Berrigan, Bucks, Haughton, Lima, Souza e Silva, Veilleux.

———. "A Witness to Life: Thomas Merton on Monastic Renewal." See Twomey, *Paradox,* 173–93.

Haughton, Rosemary Luling. "Afterward, Then and Now." See Hart, *Monk* (1983), 267–70.

———. "Bridge between Two Cultures." *Catholic World* 209 (May 1969): 53–54.

Hauser, Richard J., S.J. *In His Spirit: A Guide to Today's Spirituality.* New York: Paulist Press, 1982.

Higgins, John J., S.J. *Thomas Merton on Prayer.* Garden City, N.Y.: Doubleday Image paperback, 1975. Originally published as Merton's *Theology of Prayer,* Cistercian Studies Series, no. 18. Spencer, Mass.: Cistercian Publications, 1971.

Higgins, Michael W. "Window, Tower and Circle: The Wandering Monk and the Quest for Integration." See Grayston-Higgins, *Pilgrim in Process,* 3–16.

Jerdo Keating, Mary. "Tom Merton—As I Remember Him." *Community* 33, no. 2 (Winter 1973): 13–14.

Kaplan, Edward K. "Contemplative Inwardness and Prophetic Action: Thomas Merton's Dialogue with Judaism." See Grayston-Higgins, *Pilgrim in Process,* 85–105. This essay has an appendix with the correspondence between Abraham Joshua Heschel and Merton at TMSC.

Kelly, F. J., S.J. *Man before God: Thomas Merton on Social Responsibilities.* Garden City, N.Y.: Doubleday, 1974.

Kelly, Richard. "Thomas Merton and Poetic Vitality." *Renascence* 12 (Spring 1960): 139–42, 148.

Kelty, Matthew, O.C.S.O. *Flute Solo, Reflections of a Trappist Hermit.* Mission, Kans.: Andrews and McMeel, 1979.

———. "Gethsemani: Impressions on a Renovation." *Liturgical Arts* 36, no. 4 (August 1968): 101, 106–7.

———. "The Man." See Hart, *Monk* (1983), 19–35.

Kent, Ian, with William Nicholls. "Merton and Identity." See Grayston-Higgins, *Pilgrim in Process*, 106–20.

Knitter, Paul F. "Thomas Merton's Eastern Remedy for Christianity's 'Anonymous Dualism.' " *Cross Currents* 31, no. 3 (Fall 1981): 285–95.

Kramer, Victor A. "The Autobiographical Impulse of Merton's Early Prose." *American Benedictine Review* 34, no. 1 (March 1983): 1–20.

———. "Merton's Affirmation of Merton: Writing about Silence." *Review* (University of Virginia, Charlottesville) 4 (1982): 295–333.

———. "Thomas Merton's Concern about Institutionalization, Bureaucracy, and the Abuse of Language." In SEASA, 79, 52–58. Proceedings, Southeastern American Studies Association. Edited by Don Harkness. Tampa: American Studies Press, 1979.

Labrie, Ross. *The Art of Thomas Merton.* Fort Worth, Tex.: Texas Christian University Press, 1979.

———. "Thomas Merton: The Role of the Artist." See Grayston-Higgins, *Pilgrim in Process*, 41–54.

Landy, Joseph. "The Meaning of Thomas Merton." *America* 138 (February 21, 1953): 569–70.

Lax, Robert, with Merton. *A Catch of Anti-Letters* (see section I).

———. "Harpo's Progress: Notes toward an Understanding of His Ways." Paper prepared for the Maritain-Merton Symposium, *Spirituality in Secularized Society*, Louisville, Ky., September 25–26, 1980.

———. "A Poet's Journal." *Columbia Forum* 12, no. 4 (Winter 1969): 9–15.

Leclercq, Dom Jean, O.S.B. "The Bangkok Conference: Last Memories." Bulletin de l'A.I.M., no. 9, 17–21. English edition. Paris: Secrétariat de l'aide à l'implémentation monastique, 1969.

———. "The Evolving Monk." See Hart, *Monk* (1983), 93–104.

———. Introduction to *Contemplation in a World of Action*, ix–xx. Garden City, N.Y.: Doubleday, 1971.

———. "Merton and History." See Twomey, *Paradox*, 313–23.

Lentfoehr, Sister Thérèse, S.D.S., "Social Concerns in the Poetry of Thomas Merton." See Twomey, *Paradox*, 111–37.

———. "The Solitary." See Hart, *Monk* (1983), 59–77.

———. "The Spiritual Writer." See Hart, *Monk* (1983), 105–23.

———. "Two Poems." See Hart, *Monk* (1983), 205–7.

Lentfoehr *Words*

———. ***Words and Silence, On the Poetry of Thomas Merton.*** New York: New Directions paperback, 1979.

———. "The Zen-Mystical Poetry of Thomas Merton." See Grayston-Higgins, *Pilgrim in Process*, 17–26.

Lima, Paulo Alceu Amoroso. "A Man for His Time." See Hart, *Monk* (1983), 253–59.

Logan, John. "Babel Theory." Review of *The Strange Islands*. *The Commonweal* 66 (July 5, 1957): 357–58.

Lowell, Robert. "The Verses of Thomas Merton." *The Commonweal* 42 (June 22, 1945): 240–42.

McInerny, Dennis Q. *Thomas Merton: The Man and His Work.* Cistercian Studies Series, no. 27. Washington, D.C.: Cistercian Publications, 1974.

Malits, Elena, C.S.C. "Conjectures of a Guilty Participant: Reflections on Reading Thomas Merton." *Sisters Today* 50, no. 4 (December 1978): 231–39.

———. "Merton's Metaphors: A Monk's Signs and Sources of Spiritual Growth." Paper delivered at the Eighth Cistercian Conference on Medieval Studies at Western Michigan University, Kalamazoo, May 6, 1978. Copy, TMSC, AA.

———. *The Solitary Explorer, Thomas Merton's Transforming Journey.* San Francisco: Harper and Row, 1980.

———. "Thomas Merton and the Possibilities of Religious Imagination." Paper delivered at the Merton Commemoration at Columbia University, November 28, 1978.

———. "Thomas Merton: Symbol and Synthesis of Contemporary Catholicism." *The Critic* 35, no. 3 (Spring 1977): 26–33.

———. " 'To Be What I Am': Thomas Merton As a Spiritual Writer." See Twomey, *Paradox*, 194–212.

Margaret, Helene. "Exciting Autobiography Condemns Modernism." Review of *The Seven Storey Mountain. Books on Trial* 7 (1948): 133 and 144.

Marty, Martin E. "Sowing Thorns in the Flesh." Review of *Seeds of Destruction. Book Week* 2 (January 17, 1965): 4.

———. "To: Thomas Merton. Re: Your Prophecy." *National Catholic Reporter* 3 (August 30, 1967): 6.

Masheck, Joseph, editor. "Five Unpublished Letters from Ad Reinhardt to Thomas Merton and Two in Return." Illustrated, paintings and calligraphies. *Art Forum* (December 1978): 23–27.

Mayhew, Leonard F. X. "Mystic and Poet." Review of *The New Man. The Commonweal* 75 (March 16, 1962): 650.

The Merton Studies Center. Essays by Merton, John Howard Griffin, and Monsignor Alfred Horrigan. Santa Barbara, Cal.: Unicorn Press, 1971.

Michelfelder, William. "A Search beyond the Self." Review of *Disputed Questions. Saturday Review of Literature* 43 (September 24, 1960): 24.

Moffitt, John. "The Bangkok Meeting: Chronicle." Bulletin de l'A.I.M., no. 9, 7–16. English edition. Paris: Secrétariat de l'aide à l'implémentation monastique, 1969.

———. "By His Death." See Twomey, *Paradox*, 233–34.

———. "Thomas Merton: The Last Three Days." *The Catholic World* 209 (July 1969): 160–63.

Morrissey, James. "Talks with and about Thomas Merton: Monk, Man and Myth." *Courier-Journal Magazine* (Louisville, Ky.), January 23, 1966, 15–16, 20, 25.

Nicholls, William, with Ian Kent. "Merton and Identity." See Grayston-Higgins, *Pilgrim in Process*, 106–20.

Nouwen, Henri J. M. *The Genesee Diary: Report from a Trappist Monastery.* Garden City, N.Y.: Doubleday Image paperback, 1981.

———. Foreword to *Merton's Palace of Nowhere*, by James Finley, 7–9. Notre Dame, Ind.: Ave Maria Press, 1978.

———. *Thomas Merton, Contemplative Critic* (originally entitled *Pray to Live*). San Francisco: Harper and Row, 1981.

The Oakhamian. The School Magazine of Oakham School, Oakham, Leicestershire, England. Vol. 47 (Christmas Term, 1931; Easter Term, 1932; Summer Term, 1932), 48 (Christmas Term, 1932 . . .), etc. From Merton's own set, bound. FLSB.

O'Brien, Tess. "Thomas Merton at St. Bona's." Merriwood College, *The Bay Leaf* (October 1958): 34–39.

O'Driscoll, Herbert. "Prologue: Hermitage of a Thousand Windows." See Grayston-Higgins, *Pilgrim in Process*, xv–xxxviii.

Padovano

Padovano, Anthony T. *The Human Journey — Thomas Merton: Symbol of a Century.* Garden City, N.Y.: Doubleday, 1982.

Pallis, Marco. "Thomas Merton, 1915–1968: An Appreciation of His Life and Work by One Who Knew Him." *Studies in Comparative Religion* 3 (1969): 138–46.

Patnaik, Deba Prasad, editor. *Geography of Holiness. The Photography of Thomas Merton.* New York: Pilgrim Press, 1980.

Peloquin, Charles Alexander. "To Remember." *Liturgical Arts* 37 (February 1969): 52–53.

Pennington, M. Basil, O.C.S.O., editor. *The Cistercian Spirit: A Symposium in Memory of*

Thomas Merton. Cistercian Studies Series, no. 3. Spencer, Mass.: Cistercian Publications, 1970.

———. "The Climate of Monastic Prayer." Review. *Theological Studies* 31 (1970): 207–8.

Pritchett, V. S. Review of *Elected Silence. The New Statesman and Nation* (August 13, 1949): 174–75.

Rago, Henry. "From the Belly of the Whale." Review of *The Sign of Jonas. The Commonweal* 57 (1952–53): 526–29.

Redman, Ben Ray. "In the Belly of a Paradox." Review of *The Sign of Jonas. The Saturday Review of Literature* 36 (February 21, 1953): 45–46.

Rice

Rice, Edward. *The Good Times and Hard Life of Thomas Merton, The Man in the Sycamore Tree.* An Entertainment by Edward Rice. (A title that manages to combine early Merton with both James Thurber and Graham Greene!) Garden City, N.Y.: Doubleday Image paperback, 1970. Richly illustrated.

———. "Thomas Merton, 1915–1968." *Columbia College Today* (Spring 1969): 66–69.

Russell, Kenneth C. "Merton on the Lay Contemplative: Explicit Statements and Reflected Light." See Grayston-Higgins, *Pilgrim in Process,* 121–31.

Ryan, Patrick, O.C.S.O. "Two Poems." See Hart, *Monk* (1983), 91–92.

Saword, Sister Anne, O.C.S.O. "A Nun's Tribute." See Hart, *Monk* (1983), 195–204.

———. "Tribute to Thomas Merton." *Cistercian Studies* 3, no. 4 (1968): 265–78.

Seitz, Ron. "Thomas Merton: A Deathday Remembrance." *U.S. Catholic* (December 1968): 16–22.

———. "Thomas Merton: A Remembrance." *Courier-Journal Magazine* (Louisville, Ky.), December 4, 1983, 22–29.

Shannon *Path*

Shannon, William H. *Thomas Merton's Dark Path: The Inner Experience of a Contemplative.* New York: Farrar, Straus and Giroux, 1981.

Shenker, Israel. "Thomas Merton Is Dead at 53; Monk Wrote in Search of God." *New York Times,* December 11, 1968, 1, 42.

Souza e Silva, Sister Emmanuel de, O.S.B. "The Friend of Latin America." See Hart, *Monk* (1983), 237–51.

Stark, Philip M., S.J. "A Summer at Gethsemani." *Continuum* 7 (Summer 1969): 306–12.

Steindl-Rast, David, O.S.B. "Destination: East; Destiny: Fire–Thomas Merton's Real Journey." See Twomey, *Paradox,* 148–72.

———. "Man of Prayer." See Hart, *Monk* (1983), 79–89.

———. "Recollections of Thomas Merton's Last Days in the West." *Monastic Studies* 7 (1969): 1–10.

Stone, Naomi Burton; see Burton, Naomi.

Süssman

Süssman, Cornelia and Irving. *Thomas Merton.* Garden City, N.Y.: Doubleday Image paperback, 1980. A reprint of *Thomas Merton: The Daring Young Man on the Flying Belltower.* New York: Macmillan, 1976.

Sutton, Walter. "Thomas Merton and the American Epic Tradition: The Last Poems." *Contemporary Literature* 14, no. 1 (Winter 1973): 49–57.

Teahan, John F. "A Dark and Empty Way: Thomas Merton and the Apophatic Tradition." *The Journal of Religion* 58, no. 3 (June 1978): 276.

Thompson, William M. "Merton's Contribution to a Transcultural Consciousness." See Grayston-Higgins, *Pilgrim in Process,* 147–69.

Thurston, Bonnie Bowman. "Self and the Word: Two Directions of the Spiritual Life." *Cistercian Studies* 18, no. 2 (Summer 1983): 149–55.

Twomey, Gerald, C.S.P. "The Struggle for Racial Justice." See Twomey, *Paradox* (below), 92–110.

———. "Thomas Merton: An Appreciation." In *Thomas Merton: Prophet in the Belly of a Paradox* (see below), 1–14.

Twomey *Paradox*

———, editor. *Thomas Merton: Prophet in the Belly of a Paradox.* New York: Paulist Press, 1978. A collection of essays. For individual essays, see under: Bamberger, Forest, Griffin (John Howard), Hart, Leclercq, Lentfoehr, Malits, Moffitt, Steindl-Rast, Twomey (2), Zahn.

Van Doren, Mark. *Autobiography.* New York: Harcourt, Brace and Company, 1958.

————. "Thomas Merton." *America* 120 (January 4, 1969): 21–22.

————. "Thomas Merton, 1915–1968." *Columbia College Today* (Spring 1969): 65–66.

Veillieux, Armand, O.C.S.O. "Monk on a Journey." See Hart, *Monk* (1983), 261–63.

Voigt, Robert J. *Thomas Merton: A Different Drummer.* Liguori, Mo.: Liguori Publications, 1972.

Waddell, Father Chrysogonus, O.C.S.O. "A Letter to Mother Laetitia about the Funeral of Father Louis." *Liturgy* 4, no. 1 (March 1970): 37–43.

Waugh, Evelyn. Foreword to *Elected Silence*, v–vi. London: Hollis and Carter, 1949.

Weaver, Mary Jo. "Thomas Merton and Flannery O'Connor: The Urgency of Vision." See Grayston-Higgins, *Pilgrim in Process*, 27–40.

Wintz, Jack, O.F.M. "Thomas Merton–His Friends Remember Him." Essay and interviews with Father Irenaeus Herscher, Brother Patrick Hart, Tommie O'Callaghan, Sister Thérèse Lentfoehr, John Howard Griffin. *St. Anthony Messenger* 86, no. 7 (December 1978): 32–41.

Woodcock

Woodcock, George. ***Thomas Merton, Monk and Poet: A Critical Study.*** Vancouver: Douglas and McIntyre, 1978.

Zahn, Gordon C. "Maritain, Merton, and Non-Violence." *Cross Currents* 31, no. 3 (Fall 1981): 296–306, 319.

————. "Merton on Peace." See Grayston-Higgins, *Pilgrim in Process*, 135–46.

————. "Original Child Monk: An Appreciation." Introduction to both *Thomas Merton on Peace* and *The Nonviolent Alternative*, ix–xli. New York: Farrar, Straus and Giroux, 1980.

————. "Thomas Merton: Reluctant Pacifist." See Twomey, *Paradox*, 55–79.

IV   General
A Selected List of Articles and Books Mentioned in the Text or Closely Connected to the Text.

Acton, Lord, John Emerich Edward Dalberg. *Essays on Freedom and Power.* Selected with a new introduction by Gertrude Himmelfarb. Cleveland: World Publishing Company, Meridian Books, 1955.

Altizer, Thomas. *The New Apocalypse: The Radical Christian Vision of William Blake.* East Lansing: Michigan State University Press, 1967.

————, with William Hamilton. *Radical Theology and the Death of God.* Indianapolis: Bobbs-Merrill, 1966.

————, editor. *Toward a New Christianity: Readings in the Death of God Theology.* New York: Harcourt, Brace and World, 1967.

Anselm, Saint. *Saint Anselm.* Translated from the Latin by Sidney Norton Deane. Basic Writings: "Proslogium," "Monologium," "Gaunilon's: On Behalf of the Fool," "Cur Deus Homo." Introduction by Charles Hartshorne. La Salle, Ill.: Open Court Publishing Company, 1968.

Antoninus, Brother [William Everson]. *Robinson Jeffers: Fragments of an Older Fury.* Berkeley: Oyez, 1968.

Arberry, A. J. *Sufism: An Account of the Mystics of Islam.* New York: Harper and Row, Harper Torchbooks, 1970. (First published London: George Allen and Unwin, 1950.)

Arendt, Hannah. *Eichmann in Jerusalem. A Report on the Banality of Evil.* New York: Viking Press, 1963. Collected and edited essays reporting the Eichmann trial. (First published in *The New Yorker*, February 16 to March 16, 1963).

————. *The Human Condition.* Garden City, N.Y.: Doubleday, 1959.

Augustine, Saint. *The Confessions.* Translated by E. B. Pusey, D.D., with a foreword by A. H. Armstrong. London: Dent, Everyman's Library, 1970 (first edition, 1907).

Bachelard, Gaston. *La Poétique de l'espace.* Paris: Press Universitaires de France (B.P.C.), 1953.

Barakat, Robert. *Cistercian Sign Language.* Cistercian Studies Series, no. 11. Kalamazoo, Mich.: Cistercian Publications, 1975.

Barth, Karl. *Call for God.* Translated by A. T. Mackay. New York: Harper and Row, 1967.

————. *Christ and Adam: Man and Humanity in Romans 5.* Translated by T. A. Smail. New York: Harper and Row, 1957.

————. *God Here and Now.* Translated by Paul M. Van Buren. New York: Harper and Row, 1964.

————. *The Word of God and the Word of Man.* Translated with a new foreword by Douglas Horton. New York: Harper and Row, Harper Torchbooks, 1957.

Benedict, Saint. *The Rule of Saint Benedict.* Translated with an introduction and notes by Anthony C. Meisel and M. L. del Mastro. Garden City, N.Y.: Doubleday Image paperback, 1975.

Berdyaev, Nikolai Aleksandrovich. *The Realm of the Spirit and the Realm of Caesar.* Translated by Donald A. Lowrie. New York: Harper and Row, 1953.

————. *Slavery and Freedom.* New York: Scribners, 1944.

————. *Solitude and Society.* New York: Scribners, 1938.

Betjeman, Sir John. *Collected Poems.* Compiled with an introduction by the Earl of Birkenhead. London: John Murray, 1958.

Blake, William. *The Poetry and Prose of William Blake.* Edited by David V. Erdman. Garden City, N.Y.: Doubleday, Anchor, 1970.

Bonhoeffer, Dietrich. *Letters and Papers from Prison.* Edited by Eberhard Bethge. Translated by Reginald Fuller. New York: Macmillan paperback, 1962 (originally entitled *Prisoner for God*).

————. *Prayers from Prison.* Translated by Johann Christoph Hampe. Philadelphia: Fortress Press, 1978.

————. *True Patriotism. Letters, Lectures, and Notes, 1939–45, from the Collected Works, Vol. 3.* Edited with an introduction by Edwin H. Robertson. Translated by Edwin H. Robertson and John Bowden. New York: Harper and Row, 1973.

Breton, André. *Nadja.* Revised edition. Paris: Editions Gallimard, 1964.

————. *Nadja.* Translated by Richard Howard. New York: Grove Press, 1960.

Browne, Sir Thomas. *Religio Medici: The Works of Sir Thomas Browne*, vol. 1. Edited by Geoffrey Keynes. London: Faber and Faber, 1964.

Buber, Martin. *Eclipse of God: Studies in the Relationship between Religion and Philosophy.* New York: Harper and Row, Harper Torchbooks, 1952, 1957.

————. *Hasidism and Modern Man.* Edited and translated by Maurice Friedman. New York: Horizon Press, 1958.

————. *I and Thou.* Translated by Ronald Gregor Smith. New York: Scribners, 1958.

Bulgakof, Sergei Nikolaevich. *Du Verbe incarné* [Agnus Dei]. Translated from the Russian by Constantin Andronikof. Paris: Aubier, Editions Montaigne, 1943.

Bunting, Basil. *Collected Poems.* London: Fulcrum Press, 1968, 1970.

Callard, Arthur. " 'Pretty Good for a Woman': A Quest for Evelyn Scott." *London Magazine* 21, no. 7 (October 1981): 30–39.

Campbell, Roy. *Lorca: An Appreciation of His Poetry.* Studies in Modern European Literature and Thought. Cambridge: Bowes and Bowes, 1952.

Camus, Albert. *Le Mythe de Sisyphe.* Paris: Editions Gallimard, 1942.

————. *The Myth of Sisyphus and Other Essays.* Translated by Justin O'Brien. New York: Alfred A. Knopf, 1955.

————. *La Peste.* Paris: Editions Gallimard, 1947.

————. *The Plague.* Translated by Stuart Gilbert. New York: Alfred A. Knopf, 1948.

Carbaud, Jacques. *Simone Weil: A Fellowship in Love.* New York: Channel Press, 1964.

Cardenal, Ernesto. *Apocalypse and Other Poems.* Translated and edited by Robert Pring-Mill and Donald D. Walsh. New York: New Directions, 1977. (This contains "The Death of Thomas Merton," 45–58, which had first appeared in the New Directions annual as "Coplas on the Death of Merton.")

————. *The Gospel in Solentiname*, 4 vols. Translated by Donald D. Walsh. Maryknoll, N.Y.: Orbis Books, 1976–80.

————. *In Cuba.* Translated by Donald D. Walsh. New York: New Directions, 1974.

————. *Zero Hour and Other Documentary Poems.* Selected and edited by Donald D. Walsh.

Introduction by Robert Pring-Mill. Translations by Paul W. Borgeson, Jr., Jonathan Cohen, Robert Pring-Mill, and Donald D. Walsh. New York: New Directions, 1980.

The Catholic Encyclopedia, 15 vols. Vol. 15 contains the article "Trappists" by Dom Edmond Obrecht. New York: Robert Appleton, 1912.

Cecil, Lord David. *The Stricken Deer, or The Life of Cowper.* London: Constable, 1929.

Cleaver, Eldridge. *Soul on Ice.* New York: McGraw-Hill, 1968.

Coomaraswamy, A. K. *Transformation of Nature in Art.* Cambridge, Mass.: Harvard University Press, 1934. New York: Dover Publications, 1956.

The Documents of Vatican II. Walter M. Abbott, S.J., general editor, and the Very Rev. Msgr. Joseph Gallagher, translation editor. New York: America Press, 1966.

Donne, John. *The Complete Poetry of John Donne.* Edited by John T. Shawcross. Garden City, N.Y.: Doubleday, Anchor, 1967.

Dorn, Edward. *The Poet, the People, the Spirit.* Vancouver: Talonbooks, 1976.

―――. *The Shoshoneans.* Photographs by Leroy Lucas. New York: William Morrow, 1967.

DuBois, Cora. "The 1870 Ghost Dance." University of California Publications in Anthropological Records, vol. 2, no. 1. Berkeley: University of California Press, 1939.

Eckhart, Meister. *Meister Eckhart: A Modern Translation.* Translated with an introduction by Raymond B. Blakney. New York: Harper and Row, Harper Torchbooks, 1941. (This is the edition from which Merton quotes.)

Evdokimoff, Pavel (also Evdokimov, Paul). *La Femme et le salut du monde. Etude d'anthropologie chrétienne sur les charismes de la femme.* Paris: Editions Casterman, 1958.

―――. *Le Mariage, sacrement de l'amour.* Paris: Editions du Livre français, 1945.

―――. *L'Orthodoxie.* Neuchatel and Paris: Delachaus et Niestlé, 1959.

Gandhi, Mohandas. *Non-Violence in Peace and War.* 2 vols. 3d edition. Ahmedabad: Navajivan Publishing House, 1948 (this is the edition Merton used).

Gemelli, Agostino. *Psychoanalysis Today.* Translated by John S. Chapin and Salvator Attansis. New York: P. J. Kenedy, 1955.

Ghéon, Henri. *Sainte Thérèse de Lisieux.* Paris: Flammarion, 1934.

Goethe, Johanne Wolfgang von. *Italian Journey.* Translated by W. H. Auden and Elizabeth Mayer. New York: Pantheon, 1962. San Francisco: North Point Press, 1982. Original American publisher, Pantheon Books, a division of Random House, 1962. Excerpts reprinted by permission of Pantheon Books and North Point Press.

Graves, Robert, with Alan Hodges. *The Reader over Your Shoulder: A Handbook for Writers of English Prose.* New York: Macmillan, 1944.

Griffin, John Howard. *Black Like Me.* Boston: Houghton Mifflin, 1961.

―――. *The John Howard Griffin Reader.* Selected and edited by Bradford Daniel. Boston: Houghton Mifflin, 1968.

Guardini, Romano. *Pascal for Our Time.* Translated by Brian Thompson. New York: Herder and Herder, 1966.

Guide illustré de Saint-Antonin-Noble-Val. Montauban: Société des Amis du Vieux Saint-Antonin, 1975.

Heschel, Abraham Joshua. *Between God and Man: An Interpretation of Judaism from the Writings of Abraham J. Heschel.* Selected and edited with an introduction by Fritz A. Rothschild. New York: Free Press, 1965.

―――. *God in Search of Man: A Philosophy of Judaism.* New York: Harper and Row, Harper Torchbooks, 1966.

―――. *Man's Quest for God: Studies in Prayer and Symbolism.* New York: Scribners, 1954, 1966.

―――. *Who Is Man?* Palo Alto, Calif.: Stanford University Press, 1965.

Hochhuth, Rolf. *The Deputy.* Drama. Translated by Richard Winston and Clara Winston. Preface by Albert Schweitzer. New York: Grove Press, 1964. (A translation of *Der Stellvertreter.*)

Homer. *The Odyssey.* Translated by Robert Fitzgerald. Garden City, N.Y.: Doubleday, 1963.

Hopkins, Gerard Manley [G. F. Lahey, S.J.]. *Gerard Manley Hopkins.* London: Oxford University Press, 1930.

―――. *A Hopkins Reader.* Selected by John Pick. London: Oxford University Press, 1953. Garden City, N.Y.: Doubleday Image paperback, 1966.

Horney, Karen. *New Ways in Psychoanalysis*. New York: W. W. Norton, 1939.

Hürlimann, Martin. *Asia*. London: Thames and Hudson, 1957.

Huxley, Aldous. *After Many a Summer Dies the Swan*. New York: Harper and Brothers, 1939.

――――. "Drugs That Shape the Mind." *The Saturday Evening Post* (November 7, 1958).

――――. *Ends and Means*. New York: Harper and Brothers, 1937.

――――. *Grey Eminence: A Study in Religion and Politics*. London: Chatto and Windus, 1941. New York: Harper and Row, 1941.

――――. *The Letters of Aldous Huxley*. Edited by Grover Smith. New York: Harper and Row, 1969.

Ionesco, Eugène. *Notes et contre notes*. Paris: Editions Gallimard, 1962.

――――. *The Rhinoceros and Other Plays*. Translated by Derek Prouse. New York: Grove Press, 1960.

Jeffers, Robinson. *The Selected Poetry of Robinson Jeffers*. New York: Random House, 1937.

John of the Cross, Saint. *Ascent of Mount Carmel*. Translated and edited by E. Allison Peers. Garden City, N.Y.: Doubleday Image paperback, 1958.

Jones, David. *Anathémata*. London: Faber and Faber, 1952, 1972.

――――. Special issue, *Agenda* 5, no. 1–3 (Spring–Summer 1967).

――――. *In Parenthesis*. Introduction by T. S. Eliot. London: Faber and Faber, 1937; also 1963, 1969, 1975.

Joyce, James. *Finnegans Wake*. New York: Viking Press, 1939.

――――. *Ulysses*. New York: Random House, 1934.

Julian of Norwich. *Revelations of Divine Love*. Translated into modern English with an introduction by Clifton Wolters. Harmondsworth: Penguin Classics, 1966.

Kempis, Thomas à. *The Imitation of Christ*. Included in *The Consolation of Philosophy*. Introduction by Irwin Edman. New York: Random House, Modern Library, 1943.

Kroeber, Theodora. *Ishi in Two Worlds: A Biography of the Last Wild Indian in North America*. Berkeley: University of California Press, 1964.

Lahey, G. F., S.J. See Gerard Manley Hopkins.

Lax, Robert. *The Circus of the Sun*. New York: Journeyman Books, 1959. Reprinted as *circus zirkus cirque circo*, Zürich: Pendo, 1981.

Leahy, Maurice, editor. *Conversions to the Catholic Church: A Symposium*. New York and Cincinnati: Benzinger Brothers, 1933.

Léautaud, Paul. *Journal littéraire*. Paris: Mercure de France, 1956.

――――. *Journal of a Man of Letters*, 1898–1907. Translated by Geoffrey Sainsbury. London: Chatto and Windus, 1960.

Legge, James. *The Chinese Classics*. 5 vols. Shanghai: Oxford University Press, 1935. (Merton's set from Chung Hwa Book Company, Taipei, is at TMSC.)

――――. *The Texts of Taoism*. New York: Julian Press, 1959.

Lekai, Louis J. *The Cistercians, Ideals and Reality*. Kent, Ohio: Kent State University Press, 1977.

Lorca, García. *Lorca*. See Campbell, Roy.

Lyford, Joseph P. *The Airtight Cage: A Study of New York's West Side*. New York: Harper and Row, 1966.

Madeleva, Sister M., C.S.C. *My First Seventy Years*. New York: Macmillan, 1959.

Marcel, Gabriel. *Journal métaphysique*. Paris: Editions Gallimard, 1927.

――――. *Metaphysical Journal*. Chicago: Henry Regnery, 1952.

――――. *Le Mystère de l'être*. Vol. 1: *Réflexion et mystère*. Vol. 2: *Foi et réalité*. Paris: Aubier, 1951.

――――. *The Mystery of Being*. Vol. 1: *Reflection and Mystery*. Vol. 2: *Faith and Reality*. Chicago: Henry Regnery, 1951.

Maritain, Jacques. *Art et scolastique*. Paris: Louis Rouart et Fils, 1927.

――――. *Frontières de la poésie et autres essais*. Revised edition. Paris: Louis Rouart et Fils, 1935.

――――. *Art and Scholasticism* and *The Frontiers of Poetry*. Translated by Joseph W. Evans. South Bend, Ind.: University of Notre Dame Press, 1974. (First published New York: Scribners, 1962.)

――――. *Creative Intuition in Art and Poetry*. New York: Pantheon, 1953.

Marvell, Andrew. *The Poems of Andrew Marvell.* Edited by Hugh Macdonald. London: Routledge and Kegan Paul, Muses Library, 1952.
Meerloo, Joost Abraham Maurits. *Homo Militans: De psychologie van oorlog en vrende de mens.* The Hague: Servire, 1964.
Milosz, Czeslaw. *The Captive Mind.* New York: Alfred A. Knopf, 1953. New York: Random House, Vintage paperback, 1981 (with a new introduction by the author).
———. *Postwar Polish Poetry.* Translated and edited by Czeslaw Milosz. Garden City, N.Y.: Doubleday, 1965. (According to Milosz, Merton introduced him to Doubleday.)
More, Dame Gertrude. *The Inner Life and Writings of Dame Gertrude More.* Revised and edited by Dom Benedict Weld-Blundell, O.S.B. 2 vols. London, 1910. London: R. T. Washbourne, 1937.
Mounier, Emmanuel. *Le Personnalisme.* Paris: Presses Universitaires de France, Que sais-je? Series, 1955.
Nabokov, Peter. *Two Leggings: The Making of a Crow Warrior.* New York: Thomas Y. Crowell, 1967.
Nishida, Kitaro. *Intelligibility and the Philosophy of Nothingness.* Translated and introduced by Robert Schinzinger. Tokyo: Maruzen Company, 1958.
———. *A Study of Good.* Translated by V. H. Viglielmo. Tokyo: Japanese National Commission for UNESCO. Ministry of Education, 1960.
Oury, Dom Guy-Marie. *Dom Marie-Gabriel Sortais (1902–1963), Abbé Général des Cisterciens réformés.* Solesmes, France: 1975.
Page, Leitch, Knightley
Page, Bruce, David Leitch, and Phillip Knightley. **Philby: The Spy Who Betrayed a Generation.** Introduction by John le Carré. London: André Deutsch, 1968.
Palache, John Garber. *Gautier and the Romantics.* New York: Viking Press, 1926.
Pallis, Marco. *Peaks and Lamas.* New York: Alfred A. Knopf, 1949.
———. *The Way and the Mountain.* London: Peter Owen, 1960.
Pasternak, Boris. *Doctor Zhivago.* Translated by Max Hayward and Manya Harari. New York: Pantheon, 1958.
———. *Selected Poems.* Translated by Jon Stallworthy and Peter France. Harmondsworth: Penguin, 1984.
Percy, Walker. *Love in the Ruins: The Adventures of a Bad Catholic at a Time near the End of the World.* New York: Farrar, Straus and Giroux, 1971.
———. *The Moviegoer.* New York: Alfred A. Knopf, 1961. New York: Farrar, Straus and Giroux, Noonday paperback, 1967, 1971.
Pétrement, Simone. *Simone Weil: A Life.* Translated by Raymond Rosenthal. New York: Pantheon, 1976.
Poulet, Georges. *Studies in Human Time.* Baltimore: Johns Hopkins University Press, 1956.
Pound, Ezra. *The Cantos.* New York: New Directions, 1975.
Quillet, Pierre. *Bachelard: Présentation, choix de textes, bibliographie.* Paris: Editions Seghers, Philosophes de tous les temps, 1964.
Raymond, Father M. (Flanagan). *The Less Travelled Road, or Memoirs of Dom Mary Frederic Dunne, First American Trappist Abbot.* Milwaukee: Bruce Publishing Company, 1953.
Richards, I. A. (Ivor Armstrong). *Mencius on the Mind: Experiments in Multiple Definition.* New York: Harcourt, Brace and Company, 1932. (Appendix: passages of psychology from Mencius in Chinese, transliterated, and English, 44 pages at end.)
Rilke, Rainer Maria. *Selected Works,* Vol. 2, *Poetry.* Translated by J. B. Leishman. London: Hogarth Press, 1980.
———. *Sonnets to Orpheus.* Translation by M. D. Herter Norton. With parallel German text (*Sonnette an Orpheus. Ausgewählte Werke,* Insel-Verlag). New York: W. W. Norton, 1962.
———. *Translations from the Poetry of Rainer Maria Rilke.* Translated by M. D. Herter Norton. New York: W. W. Norton, 1962.
Robinson, John Arthur Thomas, Bishop of Woolwich. *Honest to God.* London: SCM Press, 1963.
Rosen, Nathan. "Chaos and Dostoyevsky's Women." *The Kenyon Review* 20, no. 2 (Spring 1958): 257–77.
Schwartz-Bart, André. *The Last of the Just.* Translated by Stephen Becker from *Le Dernier des justes.* New York: Bantam, 1961.

Scott, Evelyn.
———. *Escapade.* New York: Thomas Seltzer, 1923.
———. *The Golden Door.* New York: Thomas Seltzer, 1925.
———. *Migrations: An Arabesque in Histories.* New York: Albert and Charles Boni, 1927.
———. " 'Pretty Good for a Woman': A Quest for Evelyn Scott." Arthur Callard. *London Magazine* 21, no. 7 (October 1981): 30–39.
Shirer, William L. *The Rise and Fall of the Third Reich: A History of Nazi Germany.* New York: Simon and Schuster, 1960.
Snow, Edgar. *Journey to the Beginning.* New York: Random House, 1958.
Solovyov, Vladimir Sergeyevich (also Solov'ev). *God, Man and the Church: The Spiritual Foundation of Life.* Translated by Donald Attwater. Milwaukee: Bruce Publishing Company, 1938.
———. *The Justification of the Good: An Essay on Moral Philosophy.* Translated by Natalie A. Duddington, with a note by Stephen Graham. New York: Macmillan, 1918.
———. *The Meaning of Love.* Translated by Jane Marshall. New York: International Universities Press, 1948.
Sortais, Dom Gabriel. See Oury, Dom Guy-Marie.
Stern, Karl. *The Flight from Woman.* New York: Farrar, Straus and Giroux, 1965.
Strachey, Lytton. *Eminent Victorians.* New York: G. P. Putnam's Sons, 1925.
Sundkler, Bengt Gustaf Malcolm. *Bantu Prophets in South Africa.* London: Lullworth Press, 1948.
Suzuki, Daisetz Teitaro. *Living by Zen.* Edited by Christmas Humphreys. London: Rider and Company, 1972.
———. *Outlines of Mahayana Buddhism.* Introduction by Alan Watts. New York: Schocken, 1963. (First published London: Luzac and Company, 1907.)
Szilard, Leo. "Are We on the Road to War?" *Bulletin of the Atomic Scientists* (April 1962). The text of a speech Szilard had given at nine American colleges. Readers were asked to respond to the author in writing before May 31, 1962.
Terry, T. Philip. *Terry's Guide to Cuba, Including the Isle of Pines.* Boston: Houghton Mifflin, 1927.
Therrien, Vincent. *La Révolution de Gaston Bachelard en critique littéraire.* Paris: Editions Klincksieck, 1970.
Thomas, Edward. *Collected Poems.* London: Faber and Faber, 1936.
Thoreau, Henry David. *Walden and Civil Disobedience.* Edited by Sherman Paul. Boston: Houghton Mifflin, Riverside Editions, 1960.
Thouless, Robert H. *Straight Thinking in War Time.* London: Hodder and Stoughton, 1942.
Torlesse, Charles Martin. *Some Account of Stoke by Nayland, Suffolk.* London: Harrison and Sons, 1877.
Torlesse, Frances H. *Bygone Days: A History of the Family of Torlesse,* 1914. London: Harrison and Sons, 1914.
Traherne, Thomas. *Centuries: Poems, and Thanksgivings.* 2 vols. Edited by H. M. Margoliouth. London: Oxford University Press, 1958.
Trevor, Meriol. *Newman.* 2 vols. Garden City, N.Y.: Doubleday, 1962.
Trevor-Roper, Hugh Redwald. *The Last Days of Hitler.* New York: Macmillan, 1947.
———. *Men and Events. Historical Essays.* New York: Harper and Row, 1957.
Troyat, Henri. *La Case de l'Oncle Sam.* Paris: Table Ronde, 1948.
Van der Post, Laurens. *The Heart of the Hunter.* New York: William Morrow, 1961.
———. *The Lost World of the Kalahari.* New York: William Morrow, 1958.
———. *Venture to the Interior.* New York: William Morrow, 1951.
Weil, Simone. *The Iliad; or The Poem of Force.* Translated by Mary McCarthy. Pendle Hill Pamphlet, no. 91. Wallingford, Pa., 1956. This had appeared earlier in the November 1945 issue of *Politics.*
West, Nathanael. *Miss Lonelyhearts and The Day of the Locust.* New York: New Directions paperback, 1959.
Willey, Basil. *The Seventeenth-Century Background: Studies in the Thought of the Age in Relation to Poetry and Religion.* (New York: Columbia University Press, 1942). Published in Great Britain by Penguin, Peregrine, in association with Chatto and Windus, 1962. British paperback edition cited. Excerpt reprinted by kind permission of the author's Literary Estate and Chatto and Windus.

Williams, William Carlos. *Paterson*. New York: New Directions, 1951 (with first four books).

Wilson, Mona. *The Life of William Blake*. New York: Jonathan Cape and Robert Bellou, 1932. London: Oxford University Press, 1971.

Wittgenstein, Ludwig. *Tractatus Logico-Philosophicus*. German text, *Logisch-Philosophische, Abhandlung*, with a new translation by D. F. Pears and B. F. McGuinness. London: Routledge and Kegan Paul, 1961. Published in the United States by Humanities Press, Atlantic Highlands, N.J., 1963.

Zahn, Gordon. *German Catholics and Hitler's Wars: A Study in Social Control*. New York: Sheed and Ward, 1962.

———. *In Solitary Witness: The Life and Death of Franz Jägerstätter*. New York: Holt, Rinehart and Winston, 1964.

Zukofsky, Louis. *All: The Collected Poems, 1956–64*. New York: W. W. Norton, 1966.

INDEX